China in Revolution

China in Revolution

History Lessons

Joseph W. Esherick

ROWMAN & LITTLEFIELD
Lanham • Boulder • New York • London

Published by Rowman & Littlefield
An imprint of The Rowman & Littlefield Publishing Group, Inc.
4501 Forbes Boulevard, Suite 200, Lanham, Maryland 20706
www.rowman.com

86-90 Paul Street, London EC2A 4NE

Copyright © 2022 by The Rowman & Littlefield Publishing Group, Inc.

All rights reserved. No part of this book may be reproduced in any form or by any electronic or mechanical means, including information storage and retrieval systems, without written permission from the publisher, except by a reviewer who may quote passages in a review.

British Library Cataloguing in Publication Information Available

Library of Congress Cataloging-in-Publication Data

Includes bibliographic references and index.
ISBN: 978-1-5381-6276-7 (cloth)
ISBN: 978-1-5381-6277-4 (paperback)
ISBN: 978-1-5381-6278-1 (electronic)

∞™ The paper used in this publication meets the minimum requirements of American National Standard for Information Sciences—Permanence of Paper for Printed Library Materials, ANSI/NISO Z39.48-1992.

For Lisl and Jenny

Contents

Author's Preface ... ix

Foreword: Reflecting on *China in Revolution* ... xiii
by Elizabeth J. Perry

PART I: ON IMPERIALISM

1 The Apologetics of Imperialism ... 3

2 From Anti-Imperialism to Postcolonial Theory ... 25

PART II: A DIVERSE AND CHANGING CHINA

3 Local Elites: Resources and Strategies ... 51

PART III: FROM EMPIRE TO REPUBLIC

4 From Qing to China ... 111

5 Sun Yat-sen: Father of the Nation ... 145

6 Reconsidering 1911 ... 171

PART IV: REVOLUTION

7 War and Revolution ... 193

8 Rethinking the Communist Revolution ... 229

9 Deconstructing the Party-State ... 259

PART V: CONTEMPORARY CHINA

10	On "The Restoration of Capitalism"	295
11	Political Theater in Modern China	327

Afterword: History Lessons	369
Series Page	383
Selected Bibliography	389
Index	411
About the Author	425

Author's Preface

The rise of China compels us to consider how China's past helps to understand its present. Journalists, pundits and academics fill the media with explanation of the rise of this new superpower. This volume may not satisfy those seeking simple answers to the new Chinese challenge. It does, however, address the issues that historians have engaged to shed light on the Chinese Revolution and the evolution of modern China. It also represents something of an intellectual autobiography, revealing my principal concerns in a career spanning over a half-century in the field of modern Chinese history.

The Chinese state media talk endlessly of the "century of humiliation" in which a weakened China was preyed upon by Western and Japanese imperialism, and this volume opens with a consideration of the role of imperialism and its impact on the rise of Chinese nationalism. Scholars in both China and the West have stressed the stability and unity of China's imperial authoritarian tradition, but Part II of this volume stresses the diversity and change that characterized Chinese social and economic life. Overcoming images of a static and changeless China helps us to understand the rapid changes of China today. In the transition from empire to nation, China alone successfully maintained its imperial borders. This anomaly of history is discussed in Part III, which continues to examine the roots of the 1911 Revolution that toppled the empire and ushered in the Republic of China. In Part IV, we turn to the massive social and political revolution that brought the Chinese Communist Party to power in 1949. We first consider the eight-year (1937–1945) War of Resistance to Japan and its fundamental transformation of Chinese politics and society, detailing the many ways in which Chiang Kai-shek's wartime Nationalist Party paved the way for the

Communist Revolution. We then turn to the Communist Revolution itself, with "Ten Theses" suggesting a general approach to the revolution, and a detailed study of the revolution in one county of Northwest China. In Part V, we turn to contemporary China, with an old polemical essay on Mao Zedong's battle against "capitalist restoration" in the Cultural Revolution, and an historical anthropology of ritual and political theater in the protests of 1989. A final essay draws some limited lessons that we might learn from this history. Each chapter opens with a brief explanation of the context in which the original essay was written. Through these introductions, the reader may appreciate both my own intellectual evolution, and the shifting concerns of modern Chinese social history. As such, this volume is an introduction both to key issues of modern Chinese history, and to my own changing views on this subject.

The original versions of most essays are reproduced with only minor editorial changes: typographical errors and mistakes in grammar and spelling have been corrected, romanization has been altered to a consistent use of *pinyin* (including within direct quotations), references have been modified to a uniform endnote format, usage and editorial conventions have been adjusted to conform to the press's requirements, some dissertations and unpublished works have been updated to their current published form, and footnotes have been added to identify individuals or institutions that may not be well known to a general audience. I would like to express my gratitude to the journals and presses that have authorized the republication of these essays. Their original titles and place of publication are indicated in the chapter introductions. A select bibliography includes the major cited works on modern China and the most important comparative literature. Two essays have been substantially reworked for this collection. Chapter 3, in Part II, on "Local Elites" has been abbreviated from the "Introduction" and "Concluding Remarks" co-authored with the late Mary B. Rankin in *Chinese Local Elites and Patterns of Dominance*. Chapter 7 on "War and Revolution" has been revised to focus more precisely on the impact of the War of Resistance against Japan and to assess the war's impact on the fate of the Chinese Revolution. Finally, an afterword on "History Lessons" has been written for this volume, addressing the question of what history can add to help us understand China today.

I am particularly grateful that Professor Elizabeth J. Perry has agreed to write the generous Foreword to this volume, placing the chapters here in the context of the books I have authored and edited. Liz is not only one of my oldest friends in the field, she has been particularly helpful in providing advice and criticism over the years. Timothy Cheek, Mark Selden, and many of my former graduate students—Jeremy Brown, Michael Chang, Madeleine

Dong, and Zheng Xiaowei, in particular—have offered useful suggestions to make this publication possible. Finally, and most essentially, my wife Ye Wa has assisted in ways both personal and professional to enhance the research included here.

Joseph W. Esherick
Berkeley, California
May 2022

Foreword

Reflecting on China in Revolution

Elizabeth J. Perry

I first met Joe Esherick forty-five years ago when I was a graduate student in the University of Michigan Political Science Department, spending winter break back home in Eugene, Oregon, where Joe was then teaching in the University of Oregon History Department. I had happened to see his newly published book, *Reform and Revolution in China: The 1911 Revolution in Hunan and Hubei* (1976), on display at the campus bookstore. Attracted by the title, I purchased the book, read it with great interest and admiration, and resolved to overcome my usual diffidence to approach the author in person to express appreciation for his scholarship and seek his advice on my own in-progress dissertation on the Chinese Revolution. As a budding political scientist with a fascination for Chinese history, I was struck by the way in which *Reform and Revolution* reinterpreted a familiar historical event so as to provide a more persuasive explanation of larger political processes. Joe was clearly a bit taken aback by an office visit from an unannounced and effusive fan of his work, but he kindly answered my questions about the approach and sources that underlay his impressive social history.

Previous studies of 1911 had focused on the machinations of Sun Yat-sen, Yuan Shikai, and other elites in reaction to the imperial court's last-ditch reform efforts, paying little attention to their consequences for ordinary Chinese. Esherick's account offers a starkly different perspective, firmly grounded in local history, that reveals the deeply unsettling impact of the late Qing reforms. Rather than assume, as the prevailing paradigm of Modernization Theory would have it, that China, like Meiji Japan, might have been spared the costs of violent revolution had the Manchus only risen to the challenge of properly managing their reform effort, Esherick depicts reform and revolution not as alternative and equally available policy choices but as interconnected and interdependent processes. Reform begat revolution because of its profoundly destabilizing effects on society. China's peasantry and urban poor, while denied the benefits of the New Policies, suffered nevertheless under the financial burden that the reforms imposed. The 1911 Revolution, then, was not simply a product of exiled revolutionaries, politicized students or ambitious militarists; it was "a popular uprising which was really responding to an internal dynamic of its own" (59). With "class contradictions" having reached a "crisis" (63), Esherick acknowledges "the difficulty—perhaps even the impossibility—of changing China through reform" (161). To be sure, 1911 was a far cry from the tumultuous and transformative upheavals that would follow in its wake, yet the alienation that it generated between the rural masses and the increasingly Westernized "urban reformist elite" served, in Esherick's formulation, as a "precondition" for Mao Zedong's peasant revolution (257).

A few years later, I got to know Joe Esherick better. In the summers of 1978 and 1979, we both attended conferences at Harvard on rebellion and revolution in China. The China field was quite contentious in those days, the divisive Vietnam War having drawn to a close only a few years earlier. The political fault lines that divided scholars of China were apparent at both conferences and seemed, to my discomfort, to separate largely along disciplinary lines—with historians criticizing social scientists for an attachment to Modernization Theory and social scientists attacking historians for Marxist or quasi-Marxist inclinations. As a freshly minted political scientist more sympathetic to Marxism than to Modernization Theory, I gravitated toward the historians. Among the historians, Joe's interventions at the conferences were especially memorable, combining a firm commitment to getting the facts straight with a progressive, yet undoctrinaire, approach toward explaining them.

My respect for Joe's mode of scholarship grew in the years that followed when I had an opportunity to observe it firsthand and we became good friends and collaborators. In 1979–1980, thanks to fellowships from the Committee on Scholarly Communication with the People's Republic of China, we were both fortunate to spend a research year in China as part of the first academic exchange between the US and the PRC—Joe based at Shandong University and I at Nanjing University. Then in the early 1980s, we conducted field work together on a multi-year NEH-sponsored Sino-American research project. Those were the years when Joe researched and wrote his masterful book, *The Origins of the Boxer Uprising* (1987).

As with his book on the 1911 Revolution, Esherick's study of the Boxers offered a radical retelling of a well-known incident in modern Chinese history based on a careful and comprehensive investigation of untapped local sources. But, thanks to the new opening with China, the availability of archival and oral history sources was in this case far richer, allowing for a much deeper exploration of Shandong society than had been possible a decade earlier in his study of Hunan and Hubei. Comparisons could now be made at the level of counties, rather than provinces. The result was a fine-grained examination of popular culture and its contributions to the rise of a momentous social movement. In contrast to Esherick's first book, which foregrounded the role of institutions (provincial assemblies, secret societies, the Tongmenghui), *The Boxer Uprising* focuses on folk beliefs and practices. After demonstrating (by a stepwise multiple regression analysis) an inverse correlation between the geographic concentration of gentry and bandits, Esherick proceeds to show how the diverse natural and social ecology of Shandong shaped marked differences in ritual repertoires. He traces the wellsprings of the Boxer Uprising to the impoverished villages of the province's northwest, where freewheeling practices of spirit possession emboldened ordinary peasants to combat the growing number of Christians in their midst. The disruptive effects of imperialism are depicted less in economic than in cultural terms—with the aggressive actions of foreign missionaries, especially the Catholic Society of the Divine Word (SVD), shown to have played a catalytic role in sparking the conflagration.

Esherick ends his second monograph, like his first, with an eye toward the implications of the study for the Communist Revolution that would unfold in subsequent decades. The Boxers, along with the New Policies and the Revolution of 1911 that they helped to trigger, contributed to a growing chasm between elites and masses that set the stage for an earth-shattering revolution yet to come. Repelled by the rampages of the Boxers, reformers of the late imperial and early republican periods eschewed mass participation in favor of elite privilege. By contrast, Esherick concludes, Mao Zedong would see in the struggling and seething peasantry "the potential for a great storm sweeping over China" that emboldened him "to light the spark and start another prairie fire" (313).

The Origins of the Boxer Uprising is recognized as a classic in the study of modern Chinese history, having garnered both the John King Fairbank Prize of the American Historical Association (for the best book in East Asian History) and the Joseph R. Levenson Prize of the Association for Asian Studies (for the best book on modern China). As an exemplar of Esherick's mode of scholarship, the book is noteworthy not only for its authoritative revision of our understanding of the roots of the Boxer Uprising, but also for an epilogue in which Esherick places the case of the Boxers in comparative context, drawing apposite parallels to the Ghost Dance of the Sioux Indians as well as to the Taiping Rebellion.

Entitled "Beyond the Idol of Origins," the epilogue reveals Esherick's affinity for the social science method. He characterizes the mission of the historian not as a search for hoary ancestry but as an effort to *explain* the case under consideration. For that purpose, a "detailed analysis of the contemporary environment" is deemed essential (316). Variables such as "agricultural productivity, commercialization, natural disasters, social formations, degrees and forms of stratification, strength of the orthodox elite, and the extent of banditry" are "not simply examined as *background* for the social movements under examination, but as *preconditions* for the specific form that these movements took" (318). While different configurations of such preconditions do not predict the emergence of specific types of social movements in some reductionist fashion, "the social environment will *constrain* the possible forms that a social movement might take in any given area" (319). Certain kinds of preconditions (such as a weak local elite and a mobile peasantry) allow for the possibility of massive popular uprisings like the Boxers, yet these structural variables, Esherick stresses, are insufficient to account for the outbreak of any particular movement. Instead, the analyst must assign due weight to the critical intervening variable of folk culture: "the heart of my argument has been that it was the popular culture of the west Shandong peasants which provided the link between structure and event" (321). Beliefs and practices of spirit possession and invulnerability, popularized through operas performed at local temple fairs, were the animating elements of the Boxer Uprising.

Having produced pathbreaking studies of two dramatic way stations on the road toward the Communist Revolution, Joe was ready to focus on the main event. In the late 1980s he embarked on what would turn out to be a more than thirty-year journey to investigate the social origins of Mao's hallowed revolutionary capital, culminating just this year in the publication of *Accidental Holy Land: The Communist Revolution in Northwest China* (2022).

The long gestation of his book on the founding of Mao's wartime base area, delayed by an ultimately unsuccessful effort to gain access to archival party documents, did not mean that Joe was taking a break from scholarship. In the intervening decades, he published *Ancestral Leaves: A Family Journey through Chinese History* (2011), a wonderfully engaging and humanizing narrative that follows an elite Chinese family (that of his wife, Ye Wa) through centuries of tumultuous history. He also co-edited a series of landmark volumes on critical issues in Chinese history: *Chinese Local Elites and Patterns of Dominance* (1993), *Remaking the Chinese City: Modernity and National Identity* (2001), *The Chinese Cultural Revolution as History* (2006), *Empire to Nation: Historical Perspectives on the Making of the Modern World* (2006), and *China: How the Empire Fell* (2013). And, consistent with his longstanding interest in identifying and introducing underutilized primary sources, he coauthored *Chinese Archives: An Introductory Guide* (1996).

Foreword: Reflecting on China in Revolution xvii

The period between the publications of *Boxer Uprising* and *Accidental Holy Land* was also the time when Joe composed the original versions of all but two of the eleven chapters that comprise this collection of his essays. The essays serve not only to update and elaborate the claims in his earlier books, but to anticipate the evolving arguments of his monograph on the Communist Revolution. The first three parts of *China in Revolution: History Lessons* consider questions of imperialism, elites and 1911; the last two parts are concerned with the Communist Revolution and its implications for the PRC party-state. Joe provides informative introductions for each chapter, situating each in the context of the political circumstances and intellectual debates that prevailed at the time it was first written. The essays open an illuminating window onto Esherick's own development as a scholar and on the maturation of the modern China field more broadly.

China in Revolution reveals a creative and committed yet circumspect historian-cum-social scientist at work, determined to establish the facts of the case and only then, on the basis of careful induction, to hazard an explanation and an attempt at wider generalization. Even at his most polemical, Esherick's biting critiques (of Fairbank on imperialism and Hevia on the Macartney mission) are driven by a devotion to empirical accuracy; theory, whether of the modernization or postmodern variety, must not be allowed to trump reality. Even in his most doctrinaire phase, represented by the chapter on Marxist ideology, Esherick cites, with approval, Mao's primary criticism of the Soviet textbook on political economy: "the text proceeds from general principles instead of investigating history and proceeding inductively."

The chapters in this volume suggest intriguing historical continuities (in elite strategies of domination, theatrical modes of popular protest, and the territorial boundaries of the state) across the watershed divides of imperial, republican, and Communist China. Esherick emphasizes, however, that persisting patterns must be persuasively demonstrated and explained, not simply assumed. Skepticism toward the aura of inevitability that surrounds so much of the historiography on the Chinese Revolution stands out as the most prominent theme of the volume. Unexpected contingencies, Esherick stresses, can dramatically alter what may appear in retrospect as fixed historical trajectories. Neither the swift collapse of the Qing in the "sudden revolution" of 1911 nor the eventual victory of Mao's "protracted revolution" in 1949 was a foregone conclusion.

While a healthy dose of empiricism and skepticism are evident across the full range of Joe's diverse scholarly *oeuvre*, that is not to say that his views of the Chinese Revolution remained unchanged. Over time, he grew decidedly less sympathetic to Mao's revolution. Esherick puts it bluntly in his 1995 article, "Ten Theses on the Chinese Revolution": "the revolution was not so much a process of liberation as a process wherein a new structure of domination was created to do battle with, to defeat, and to replace another structure of domination" (xxx). The harsh reassessment reflected both his own observations and research and the accumulation of new scholarship that highlighted the profound influence of an oppressive Stalinist model on Mao Zedong and the Chinese Communist Party. Esherick's growing disenchantment with Mao's revolution dovetailed with his suspicion toward reductionist models of historical change. Although an explanation for the causes of the revolution would need to begin with a serious investigation of structural preconditions, "the revolution itself was an extended historical process in which a series of contingent events interacted over time and space to constrain and ultimately determine the revolutionary outcome."

It should come as no surprise then that Joe's new monograph on the Communist Revolution in Northwest China is full of surprises! *Accidental Holy Land* (2022) is certainly not the epic story of a Communist Party's predestined march toward political victory, borne on the wings of massive popular support. It is instead a richly detailed account of the many coincidences and conjunctures that in combination led to an unexpected and outsized outcome. In my endorsement of the book, I wrote: "Shattering the myth of historical inevitability, this meticulously researched and beautifully crafted study is a refreshing corrective to previous interpretations of the Chinese Revolution. Esherick's gripping tale of battling bandits and Bolsheviks in the making of Mao's wartime sanctuary lays bare the indeterminate and contingent course of one of the most momentous events of the twentieth century. Scholars and general readers alike will learn much from this authoritative work by America's premier historian of the Chinese Revolution."

Esherick's emphasis on the role of contingency in the unfolding of Mao's revolution does not imply a retreat from explanation, however. As he puts it, "What happened was not inevitable, but it is explicable" (viii). Like his studies of 1911 and the Boxers, Esherick begins his search for the origins of the Shaan-Gan-Ning base area with a deep dive into local history—in this case extending all the way down to the village level. He has much to say about the dire socioeconomic circumstances of the northern Shaanxi countryside and its enduring patterns of peasant rebellion. But in the end, the main explanatory weight rests neither on local institutions (as in 1911) nor on local culture (as with the Boxers) but on a series of historical happenstances—from Mao's chance reading of a newspaper story to Chiang Kai-shek's kidnapping in Xi'an—that in combination decided the course of the Chinese Revolution.

Ultimately, it seems, the chief lesson that Esherick would have us take away from his study of the Chinese Revolution is an appreciation for its extraordinary complexity, shaped by multiple actors operating on many different levels: "Local context matters. National affairs matter. Global developments matter. Organization and discipline matter. The political choices of key leaders matter a great deal; and so does the personal agency of ordinary individuals—even the 'backward' and 'ignorant' peasants of Shaanbei" (210).

At first glance, it may appear as though the steady gain in granular historical detail visible across the corpus of Esherick's monographic work has taken a toll on the social science quest for generalizability. But, while *Accidental Holy Land* does not seek to advance a general theory of revolution, its concluding roster of key variables—from local to global, structural to agentic—points to the author's continued appreciation of the social science method. The goal is not one of thick description but, rather, of inductive identification allowing for comparative analysis. Esherick summarizes his approach in the concluding afterword of *China in Revolution*: "China is different to be sure, but it is also part of a human drama that is open to comparative study. The task of the historian is to identify and analyze what is distinctive about China. We must study both the global trends of which China is a part, and the things that are particular to China" (371). In other words, the historian's search for singularity and the social scientist's concern for comparability go hand in hand.

Over the past half century, the modern China field, humanists and social scientists alike, have benefited enormously—in terms of both scholarship and friendship—from a shared commitment to interdisciplinarity. Joe observed in his provocative "Ten Theses" in 1995: "Fortunately, the time is past when historians worked on China before 1949 and political scientists and sociologists worked on the period since, neither attending the other's conferences or reading enough of the others' books. But we need to go further" (233). Accurate as that encouraging assessment was at the time, the growing ascendance of disciplinary hegemony across the American academy in recent years threatens such productive intellectual cross-fertilization. Reflecting on the outstanding scholarship of my esteemed colleague and dear friend, Joe Esherick is an opportune reminder of the imperative to escape the narrow confines of disciplinary siloes in a common effort to meet the most pressing challenge of our time—making sense of China.

Part I

ON IMPERIALISM

Chapter One

The Apologetics of Imperialism

The Chinese Revolution was waged against imperialism and feudalism. The meaning of "feudalism" was vague and contested, including everything from the entire Confucian order of patriarchal society and autocratic governance to landlordism and warlord rule. There was much greater agreement on the nature of imperialism. It began with the Opium War of 1839 to 1841 and extended through the "century of humiliation" under the "unequal treaties" that opened foreign-dominated treaty ports in Shanghai and other cities, imposed low and fixed tariffs, and protected foreigners from Chinese jurisdiction through extra-territorial privileges. When the "unequal treaties" were finally abolished in 1943, Chiang Kai-shek proclaimed that "the unequal treaties were the main cause of our failure to build a nation."* Mao identified imperialism and feudalism as "the main factors that suppressed and obstructed the progressive development of Chinese society," and termed imperialism "the first and most fiendish enemy of the Chinese people."†

While Chinese blamed China's delayed modernization on imperialism, American academics, led by John K. Fairbank at Harvard, saw the Western impact as a stimulus that failed to produce a modernizing response comparable to Japan (and capable of resisting Japanese aggression) because of certain deficiencies in Chinese society and culture. There is no question that the arrival of Western merchants, diplomats, missionaries, and the motley assortment of scoundrels who flourished in the treaty ports fundamentally altered the trajectory of Chinese history. Modern China was very much the product of this new confrontation with Western and Japanese imperialism.

---

* Chiang Kai-shek, *China's Destiny and Chinese Economic Theory*, trans. Philip Jaffe (New York: Roy Publishers, 1947), 105.
† Mao Zedong, "Zhongguo geming yu Zhongguo gongchandang" [The Chinese Revolution and the Chinese Communist Party], *Mao Zedong xuanji* (Beijing: Renmin chubanshe, 1962), 2: 627–28.

Nonetheless, there is significant debate about the nature and extent of the impact of imperialism.

In the United States, this debate was fueled in the 1960s by the controversy surrounding American involvement in the Vietnam War. A Committee of Concerned Asian Scholars was formed to oppose that war as another example of American imperialist opposition to revolutionary movements in Asia. Chinese history entered the debate with an article by Jim Peck attacking John Fairbank and the Harvard school, proposing a "revolutionary Marxist" analysis as an alternative to Fairbank's supposed modernization theory that denied the pervasive and negative effects of imperialism in China.[*]

The overtly polemical piece republished here was my contribution to that debate. Peck's eloquent piece had exposed the "professional ideology" that elided the issue of imperialism by focusing on domestic factors that determined "China's response to the West," a signature formulation of the Harvard school of Chinese Studies. Peck's "revolutionary Marxist" approach envisioned capitalism and imperialism creating institutional structures that subjugated, impoverished, and disempowered the people of the Third World. Despite the passion and power of Peck's critique, he had not addressed the empirical question of imperialism's actual impact on China. My essay sought to show that the economic and political impact of imperialism, including a century of foreign invasion, was real, significant, and negative. The point, in other words, was to replace the Harvard paradigm's focus on China's failed response with an analysis that explained how the economic and political structures of imperialism limited China's options for autonomous development.

Several aspects of this debate are notable. John K. Fairbank wrote lengthy responses to both Peck's essay and mine.[†] While vigorously defending his own views, he treated our essays as a "welcome note of criticism." While protesting against "whopping generalities—like capitalism, imperialism, communism," he studiously avoided *ad hominem* attacks, and in later years he never bore a grudge for my youthful transgressions of teacher-student norms and generously supported my appointment at the University of California, San Diego. Most importantly, Fairbank rightly held that "Joe Esherick's picture of imperialism in China is unrealistic in leaving the Chinese too passive." If the "response to the West" paradigm could be faulted for ignoring the ways

---

[*] James Peck, "The Roots of Rhetoric: The Professional Ideology of America's China Watchers," *Bulletin of Concerned Asian Scholars* 2, no. 1 (October 1969): 59–69. Republished in Edward Friedman and Mark Selden, eds., *America's Asia: Dissenting Essays on Asian-American Relations* (New York: Pantheon Books, 1971)

[†] John K. Fairbank and James Peck, "An Exchange," *Bulletin of Concerned Asian Scholars* 2, no. 3 (April–July 1970): 51–70, and John K. Fairbank, "Letter to the Editor," *BCAS* 5, no. 2 (September 1973), 32–33. Paul A. Cohen eloquently expands on this point in *Discovering History in China: American Historical Writing on the Recent Past* (New York: Columbia University Press, 1984), 97–154.

in which imperialism constrained economic and political options in China, my focus on the role of imperialism gave too little agency to the Chinese people. One of the challenges of modern Chinese history is to recognize the domestic sources of change in China, both before and after the Opium War, a topic addressed in chapter 3. But it is also necessary to acknowledge that with the arrival of Western and, later, Japanese economic, political, and military intervention in China, a new world with a new set of challenges emerged.

Today, I would admit that Western technology, economic structures, and legal systems in the treaty ports opened new opportunities for many Chinese, from entrepreneurs to factory workers; but it is equally true that those same structures limited their options in other ways. The task before us remains to acknowledge that Western and Japanese imperialism fundamentally changed the dynamics of modern Chinese history, and to assess with precision the diverse and complex aspects of the imperialist impact on China. In doing so, we will surely discover that the impact varied over time and place, that it was different in the treaty ports and in the interior, different on diverse segments of the population, and that any assessment of positive and negative aspects—any attempt at what the Chinese call *pingjia* (评价)—is bound to oversimplify the many ways in which social, economic, and political opportunity structures were fundamentally altered by Western and Japanese imperialism.

HARVARD ON CHINA: THE APOLOGETICS OF IMPERIALISM*

The classic works on modern China—by Harold Isaacs, Edgar Snow, Jack Belden, even Mao Zedong himself—have all led us to believe that the revolutionary ferment that surged through China in the twentieth century was the result of rural impoverishment, economic stagnation, and governmental weakness and decay. All of them stressed the crucial role of Western and Japanese imperialism that had reduced China to such a sorry state in the first half of the twentieth century.

Recently, however, a growing number of American scholars—a remarkable percentage of whom have been trained at Harvard and had their works published by Harvard's East Asian Research Center—have put forth a radical new version of China's modern history. Imperialism, it seems, was largely beneficial to China. On the economic side, Chi-ming Hou assures us that "foreign capital was largely responsible for the development of whatever economic modernization took place in China before 1937."[1] Furthermore, "the often-held assumption that the traditional or indigenous sector of the Chinese

---

* This chapter was originally published as "Harvard on China: The Apologetics of Imperialism," *Bulletin of Concerned Asian Scholars* 4, no. 4 (1972): 9–16. Reprinted with permission.

economy (handicrafts, small mines, junks, etc.) suffered severe decline as a result of foreign economic intrusion lacks factual basis."[2]

John Schrecker's study of Germany in Shandong fully endorses these conclusions:

> The direction of the German impact was positive. Qingdao, a tiny, isolated fishing village in 1897, had become a major port by the time the Germans left. It had an efficient administration and modern public services and schools. It also had up-to-date facilities for transportation, communication and banking. As a result, commercial activities flowered, and there was even some industrial growth. It was German capital, skills, personnel and international contracts which laid the foundation for this development.[3]

For Schrecker, an even more important contribution of Western imperialism was its encouragement of the spread of nationalism, which became "the most significant development of the last decades of the Qing." Nationalism became possible only when the West taught China to perceive its problems "not in traditional terms but rather within the framework of new ideas and categories derived from the West."[4]

Foreigners were similarly responsible for China's institutional "modernization." John K. Fairbank, the founding father of the Harvard school, has noted that the Imperial Maritime Customs Service "assisted China's effort at modernization within the framework of the treaty system,"[5] and that the employment of foreigners to administer China's customs was in fact "one of the most constructive features of the treaty system."[6] Similarly, in 1913, when Yuan Shikai was forced to turn the administration of China's salt gabelle over to foreigners in order to secure foreign financial support for his effort to eradicate Sun Yat-sen's Guomindang (Kuomintang or KMT), the result was "the modernization of the Chinese salt administration."[7] Finally, for any who might have feared that the foreigners were modernizing urban society and political institutions while the peasantry was suffering in increasing poverty, Ramon Myers has assured us that "There is not any evidence that peasant living standards before 1937 declined."[8]

In short, imperialism fostered economic development, progressive Western-style nationalism, and institutional modernization. The Chinese may have suffered wounded pride and cultural shock at having modernization so abruptly forced down their throats, but basically what the West did was both necessary and good. The anti-imperialism of both the Guomindang and the Chinese Communist Party (CCP) was thus short-sighted—the result of a failure to understand the beneficent inevitability of Western-type modernization.[9]

While the conclusions of these Harvard studies need not be accepted as definitive, they cannot be dismissed out of hand. An extensive monographic literature, backed by thorough research and patient scholarship, has made the Harvard school the source of today's "normative science" in the China field. Scholars interested in developing alternatives to the Harvard paradigm will have to produce works of similar scholarly quality in a variety of key areas—the handicraft industry, the treaty port economy—before a viable alternative to the Harvard paradigm can be presented. This chapter has a more modest aim: to identify some of the pitfalls of the Harvard approach and to advance some tentative suggestions for an alternative paradigm.

Throughout, the focus of discussion will be the role of imperialism in nineteenth- and twentieth-century China. Surely no exercise is more difficult than the effort to factor out and measure in isolation the role of one particular force in the organic development of a nation's history. One cannot expect to get back to imperialism as the "first cause" or "prime mover" of some particular historical development. One can, however, attempt to assess the role of imperialism in interaction with the complex of forces shaping the development of modern Chinese history, and demonstrate that imperialism was something more than the misunderstood, maligned scapegoat of Chinese nationalism.

The term "imperialism" should be understood to refer to the total historical process wherein foreigners intervened to restructure the economy, society, polity, and culture of Third World nations in ways that serve the economic and political interests of the metropolitan powers. In apologetic scholarship, such restructuring is generally regarded as part of the process of "modernization." The hypothesis of this chapter is that imperialism produced economic, social, and political disruptions, distortions, and instability of such a nature as to make successful modernization of any bourgeois-democratic variety impossible. Revolution became the logical alternative.

It is convenient to begin a discussion of imperialism in China with the Opium War. Back in 1841, John Quincy Adams expressed an authoritative Harvard view of that Anglo-Chinese conflict:

> The justice of the cause between the two parties—which has the righteous cause? You have perhaps been surprised to hear me answer, Britain. Britain has the righteous cause. But to prove it, I have been obliged to show that the opium question is not the cause of the war. . . . The cause of the war is the kowtow! the arrogant and insupportable pretension of China that she will hold commercial intercourse with the rest of mankind, not on terms of reciprocity, but upon the insulting and degrading forms of lord and vassal.[10]

Subsequent Harvard men have stuck loyally to Adams's view that China's reluctance to trade with the West was "insupportable" and that opium was not really the cause of the war. To quote Fairbank himself:

> By the nineteenth century, the Chinese position on foreign relations, like the contemporary seclusion policy of Japan, was out of date and no longer supportable. . . . In demanding diplomatic equality and commercial opportunity, Britain represented all the Western states, which would sooner or later have demanded the same things if Britain had not. It was an accident of history that the dynamic British commercial interest in the China trade was centered not only on tea but also on opium.[11]

In fact, the central role of opium was far from "an accident of history." There were demonstrable economic causes for the opium trade: not only was the sale of Bengal opium an important source of revenue for the British administration in India, but opium was the only commodity marketable in China in sufficient quantity to balance the triangular trade between China, Britain, and India. This paramount position of opium among China's imports did not result from an ignorant xenophobic Chinese resistance to Western manufactures but from a well-informed conviction that China could get along very well without them. Thus, even if other Western states "sooner or later" had made the same demands as Britain, opium would have been a major issue. As late as 1870, well after the opening of China by the "armed opium propaganda"[12] of the West, opium constituted 43 percent of China's imports, and it remained the largest single Chinese import until 1890.[13] Opium, then, was the West's only feasible entree into the China market and its role was hardly "accidental." Furthermore, the fact that opium-pushing remained the West's most important economic activity through all but the last decade of the nineteenth century clearly influenced China's "response to the West." It might be argued, for example, that the puritanical Taiping opposition to opium was a major barrier to trade between the rebel areas and Shanghai, and that the Taiping threat to the opium trade moved the foreign community to aid in the suppression of the rebellion. In any case, in assessing the *impact* of imperialism in China, we must be constantly aware of its unique and narcotic *content*.

The importance of opium in China's foreign trade was of course due to the inability of other foreign products to compete in China's already well-developed indigenous producing and marketing system. It is often noted by those who stress the limited or benign effects of imperialism that China's per-capita foreign trade was the lowest of all eighty-three countries listed by the League of Nations.[14] This is undeniable. China was relatively successful in resisting the impulse of the Western bourgeoisie to "nestle everywhere, settle everywhere, establish connections everywhere."[15] China was never reduced to the status of an Egypt, an India, or an Argentina. Furthermore, after 1949, revolutionary China, "aided" by the US economic blockade, was cut off from the West and from the possibility of falling into a state of permanent economic dependence. This happened precisely at the time when the United

States acquired the ability and the will to make far greater economic inroads into the economies of the Third World than had ever before been possible. In effect, Mao's revolution—itself in part a response to and product of imperialism—prevented imperialism from running its full course.

Despite this abbreviation of imperialism's impact, China's involvement in the international market economy had long since become sufficiently intense to induce severe distortions in its own economy. In 1842, 92 percent of China's exports were silk and tea; in 1868, their percentage was 93.5; by 1890, the percentage figure had fallen to 64.5 though, in absolute terms, the trade continued to grow. Throughout the nineteenth century, tea and silk constituted at least one-half of China's annual exports.[16] In response to this strong export demand, many peasants shifted their meagre resources to the production of tea and silk, and a substantial proportion of the production of these commodities was exclusively for the export market: at least 40 percent of the tea in the late nineteenth century,[17] and 50 to 70 percent of the silk as late as the 1920s.[18] By World War II, foreign markets for Chinese tea and silk had virtually disappeared, and countless thousands of Chinese peasants found themselves deprived of their livelihood.[19] While the conventional Western wisdom sees the moral of this tale of tea and silk to be the inability of an incompetent Chinese government and an inefficient Chinese business establishment to enforce quality control and compete effectively with Japanese silk and Japanese and Ceylonese tea,[20] the inescapable facts remain that (1) foreigners had created, controlled, and then closed a market for Chinese goods, and to that extent China had been a victim of a world market in which it was essentially a passive participant; and (2) for China to have competed effectively, it would have had to allow foreign tea plantations on the South Asian model (which would have meant an intensification of imperialist influence in China), or to have established efficient governmental supervision of these industries as was the case in Japan. The latter would have required a far stronger Chinese government than—as we shall presently see—was possible before the final expulsion of the imperialists in 1949.

With the decline of the tea and silk trade, China's exports became considerably more diversified, escaping the sort of restrictive dependence on the export of two or three primary products that still plagues most Latin American and African nations. This diversification of exports, however, was not accomplished by a shift from the export of extractive commodities to the export of manufactures. In fact, between 1913 and 1936, beverages, foodstuffs, and raw materials increased from 46.5 to 60.5 percent of China's exports, while manufactures and semi-manufactures declined from 50.9 to 39.5 percent.[21] In effect, China's foreign trade was increasingly conforming to that pattern so common to underdeveloped nations: it was exporting products the demand for which is relatively inelastic and likely to fall as manufactured substitutes are developed. Thus, in the postwar years, an unblockaded China would have found its hog bristles replaced by plastics, its silk overwhelmed by synthetic fabrics, its tong and linseed oil replaced by government-subsidized production in the United States, and its tin and tungsten replaced by lower grade South American ores that the US learned to refine efficiently in the course of war production.[22]

Well before the 1950s, the terms of trade had turned against China. The net barter terms of trade (= price of imports over price of exports, 1913 here taken as 100) stood at 76.5 in 1870 and had risen to 122.9 by 1935.[23] What this meant, in effect, is that in 1935 China would have had to export 160 percent as much in real goods to buy the same imports it got in 1870. Needless to say, the pattern of international trade prices that has prevailed since World War II would have produced a far greater deterioration in the Chinese terms of trade had China remained within the "Free World" trading system in the 1950s and 1960s.[24]

If we turn from China's exports to its imports, we are immediately faced with the enormous question of their effect on handicraft production. Albert Feuerwerker's meticulous study of the cotton textile industry indicates that handicraft spinning of cotton yarn was severely crippled by foreign imports as early as 1910, suffering a 50 percent reduction from an estimated 4,883,381 *dan* (石) average annual production for 1871 to 1880 to 2,449,715 *dan* for 1901 to 1910. Handicraft *weaving* (with foreign and domestic factory yarn) managed to hold its own but weaving could only absorb one-tenth of the two-million-person-years of labor released by the decline in spinning.[25] Furthermore, there was a tendency for weaving to concentrate in urban weaving shops, which made it an unlikely alternative source of income for peasants who used to spin at home in the winter months to supplement their meagre earnings. Cotton spinning is the classic case of the crippled handicraft, but it is not the only one: Feuerwerker elsewhere notes that "native iron and steel production in Hunan and Jiangxi nearly disappeared by the end of the nineteenth century,"[26] and of course Standard Oil's kerosene replaced vegetable oil for lighting purposes. Obviously, in the absence of tariff autonomy, China was powerless to shield any of these handicraft industries from the immediate and drastic impact of the imports, or, for that matter, to reshape in any way the pattern of its foreign trade.

Despite all this, it is undoubtedly true, as Feuerwerker contends, that

> The simplistic indictment of "foreign capitalism" by some contemporary Chinese historians for having progressively "crushed" and "exploited" domestic handicraft industry from the mid-nineteenth century onward is belied by the actual state of the Chinese economy as late as the 1930s. . . . Anyone who would

claim that the Hunan or Sichuan peasant in the 1930s dressed in Naigawata cottons, smoked BAT cigarettes, and used Meiji sugar has a big case to prove.[27]

Is it, however, necessary to prove these propositions? Feuerwerker's own research has demonstrated the decline in handicraft spinning. In addition, he has acknowledged that when handicraft weaving relies on yarn from foreign mills, handicraft production becomes "ancillary to the mechanized factories" and "subservient to foreign capitalism."[28] Handicraft workshops thus prove incapable of contributing to the development of an independent, self-sufficient national economy. Furthermore, as we attempt to assess the impact of foreign trade on socio-political developments in China, we should note the conclusions of Frederic Wakeman on Guangdong at the time of the Opium Wars: "The rural areas in which the decline of cottage industry seemed most marked were precisely those areas which were most antiforeign. It was almost as if the peasantry rationally blamed their plight on foreign imports."[29] The inescapable fact remains that imperialism transformed a remarkably stable, albeit "underdeveloped" Chinese economy into an increasingly unstable and dependent economy in which millions of peasants would experience displacement and deprivation traceable to the vagaries of the international market. To such peasants—for whom one bad year could mean perpetual debt and poverty—there was little solace in the thought that the textile industry was being mechanized, GNP was rising, and "modernization" was taking place.

***

The effects of foreign investments in China were somewhat different from the effects of foreign trade. Foreign trade produced instability, while the very permanence of capital investment produced a lasting impact on the structure of the Chinese economy. Both, however, made the Chinese economy more dependent on foreigners. Here it is perhaps appropriate to reexamine the claim in the first-cited apologist's work on economic imperialism in China: "Foreign capital was largely responsible for the development of whatever economic modernization took place in China before 1937."[30] Quite obviously, this same proposition could be stated somewhat differently: the modern sector of the Chinese economy was under the domination of foreign capital. To be sure, this was not true of all segments of the industrial sector: smaller, labor-intensive, consumer goods industries were generally left for Chinese capital to develop. In the areas where foreigners concentrated, however, they overwhelmed all native competition. The key sectors of mining and transportation were almost an exclusive foreign preserve. In 1920, 99 percent of the pig iron, 99 percent of the iron ore, and 76 percent of the coal mined by modern methods was extracted from foreign mines. In the same year, 83 percent of the steamer tonnage cleared through Maritime Customs, and 78 percent of that on China's main internal waterway, the Yangzi River, was in foreign bottoms. Foreign control of railways resulted largely from loans rather than direct investment, but according to one set of figures, foreign capital controled 93 percent of China's railways in 1911, 98 percent in 1927, and 91 percent in 1936.[31]

The degree of foreign control of a given industry was determined above all by the relationship of the industry to foreign trade. A mercantile mentality dominated the treaty ports of China, so that foreigners invested in areas that served to increase the trade of China with their home country. Thus in 1936, 16.8 percent of all foreign investment was directly in the import-export trade, 20.5 percent in the banking and finance institutions which served that trade, 25.0 percent in transport, 9.0 percent in treaty port real estate, 5.1 percent in communications (telephone and telegraph) and public utilities, all largely for the benefit of the treaty port population, and only 19.6 percent in manufacturing.[32] Even within that manufacturing total, some of the most important enterprises were closely linked to foreign trade. Cigarette production, for example, was 63.3 percent foreign, and led to substantial imports of American tobacco. As one American commercial attaché boasted: "With American salesmanship and American initiative it became possible to convert a tobacco producing and exporting nation into one of the leading importers and consumers of American tobacco products."[33]

Foreign investment's ancillary role to foreign trade led to a degree of geographic concentration that was clearly inimical to the best interests of China's balanced economic development. In 1931, 76.6 percent of all foreign capital in China was invested in either Shanghai or Manchuria.[34] Chinese industries then concentrated where foreigners had developed public utilities and transport facilities, so that in 1930, 61.5 percent, in 1931, 53.7 percent, and in 1932, 61.0 percent of all newly registered Chinese firms were located in the one province of Jiangsu (which then included Shanghai).[35] Similarly, the foreign-built Chinese railway network was notorious for its service to the political and commercial interests of the foreign powers, and its irrationality from the standpoint of China's own development.[36] Perhaps the most striking illustration of this was the Russia-built Chinese-Eastern Railway and its connecting branch to Port Arthur, which were built on the Russian gauge to link with the Trans-Siberian Railway, and conversely to prevent convenient linkage with the rest of China's railways.[37]

Banking and finance absorbed more direct foreign investment than any other sector of the economy (investment in transport being largely indirect, in the form of loans), and foreign banks were notably disinterested in the economic development of China. Early in the twentieth century, the American minister to China, Paul S. Reinsch, complained that

> The only American bank in China, the International Banking Corporation, then confined itself strictly to exchange business and to dealing in commercial paper; it had developed no policy of responding to local industrial needs and helping in the inner development of China. All the foreign banks had wholly the treaty-port point of view. They thought not at all of developing interior regions upon which the commerce of the treaty ports after all depends. They were satisfied with scooping off the cream of international commercial transactions and exchange operations.[38]

The foreign banks in Shanghai demonstrated the accuracy of Reinsch's analysis by their behavior after the US Silver Purchase Act of 1934, which greatly inflated the gold value of China's silver currency. Between December 1933 and September 1935 (while the silver stocks of Chinese banks rose slightly from Ch.$271.8 million to $293.4 million), holdings of foreign banks fell from Ch.$275.7 million to $42.7 million—less than one-sixth their original level. As one author put it, "Financiers and speculators in China found it more profitable to export silver as a commodity than to use it in China as capital."[39] In the credit contraction that resulted, twenty-four of ninety-two Chinese textile mills suspended operations,[40] and many firms were forced to sell out to Japanese business interests.[41]

In general, foreign financial interests loaned substantial sums to Chinese business enterprises only when their object was to gain control of the enterprise. Such was the case with Japanese loans to the Hanyeping Coal and Iron Company in the early twentieth century. By 1915 and the Twenty-One Demands, Japan was in a sufficiently strong position to demand control of the company, which ultimately produced exclusively for the use of Japan's domestic steel industry.[42] The experience of the Kaiping coal mines was not so very different, except that even after substantial foreign loans in the 1890s, Herbert Hoover and his British employers were still obliged to engage in a great deal of legal finagling to capture control of the Chinese company during the Boxer disturbance.[43]

Though much evidence has recently been marshalled in support of the proposition that foreign capitalism never "oppressed" native Chinese enterprises, and that it in fact fostered the "coexistence" of the two forms of enterprise and a rational division of the market,[44] there is considerable room left for doubt. Certainly, it would be difficult to persuade the Chinese stockholders of either the Hanyeping or Kaiping mines that imperialism had aided their native industries. In the 1911 period, British diplomatic pressure was crucial in realizing the victory of the British Green Island Cement Company over a local Chinese rival for the South China market.[45] But diplomatic intervention was usually not necessary for foreign firms to crush their Chinese competitors. In most cases, their larger size, greater capitalization, longer experience, better access to raw materials, and the ever-present protection of extraterritoriality were sufficient to allow foreign firms to overwhelm Chinese competitors. Thus by 1905, two of three Chinese steamship companies organized in 1899–1900 to run between Hankou and Changsha had folded after British and Japanese firms put ships on the route.[46] Perhaps foreign financiers demonstrated their power most convincingly in their struggle during the last years of the Qing to persuade the imperial government to take railway contracts away from the provincial Chinese companies and give them to a foreign consortium. The comparative "surplus" of capital in the industrialized nations allowed them to offer loans at far lower rates than those prevailing in China. Therefore, from the Manchu government's point of view, it was "cheaper" to have foreigners build the railways than Chinese. As a result, the provincial railway companies were quashed and the foreigners built China's railways.

The crucial proof of the depressing effects of foreign capitalism on native Chinese industrial growth is unquestionably to be found in China's experience during and immediately following World War I, when foreign competitors diverted their attention from China to the war and then to the reconstruction of Europe. Native Chinese industry and handicrafts experienced their greatest growth in precisely this period, when China was spared the impact of Western economic intervention and suffered its steepest decline in 1920 to 1922 when the foreigners returned.[47]

Another argument often advanced by the apologists is that foreign businesses induced a positive "imitation effect" in the native economy: they taught by example and trained the cadre for economic development.[48] Unfortunately, the foreigners—whose enterprises and attitudes were largely mercantile and often speculative—provided a very poor model for a national bourgeoisie interested in development.[49] Franz Fanon has commented with characteristic perceptiveness on the weakness of a national bourgeoisie that imitates the Westerners with whom it comes in contact: "It follows the Western bourgeoisie along its path of negation and decadence without even having emulated it in its first stages of exploration and invention. . . . In its beginning, the national bourgeoisie of the colonial countries identifies with the decadence of the bourgeoisie of the West."[50]

Finally, if one is to weigh the net effect of foreign investments in China, it is essential to note that the net capital flow was not *to* but *from* China. Far more was repatriated in profits than was ever invested or reinvested in China. The average annual outpayment in the years 1902 to 1913 was US$31.8 million, and in 1914 to 1930, US$72.3 million.[51] In the entire period between

1902 and 1930, the inflow/outflow ratio was 0.57.[52] This, of course, does not include the staggering cost of the Boxer and Japanese indemnities that China was forced to pay in the early years of the twentieth century. Feuerwerker has calculated that the cost, between 1895 and 1911, of 476,982,000 taels for the Boxer indemnity and the loans to pay the Japanese indemnity amounted to "more than twice the size of the total initial capitalization of all foreign, Sino-foreign and Chinese owned manufacturing enterprises established between 1895 and 1913."[53]

***

To this point, I have concentrated almost exclusively on economics. It is necessary, however, to realize that imperialism was a total system—economic, political, social, and cultural—and that its component parts were intimately interrelated. A key example is the institution of extraterritoriality, which in its basic sense was a political or juridical limitation of China's sovereignty—a removal of foreigners from the jurisdiction of the Chinese system of justice. Obviously, though, it had key economic consequences. By exempting treaty port industries from most Chinese taxation, it gave them a considerable advantage. One calculation of the cost per bale of cotton yarn for Chinese and Japanese factories in China shows that taxes represented 13.2 percent of the cost of production in the Japanese mill, and 34.3 percent in the Chinese.[54] Beyond these tax advantages of foreign industries was the considerable advantage of exemption from arbitrary exactions by the Chinese government. It was these factors as much as any others that attracted a substantial amount of Chinese capital into foreign enterprises. Thus extraterritoriality and treaty ports created the conditions for an indirect attack on native Chinese industries by channelling elsewhere the developmental capital needed by those Chinese enterprises. It has been estimated that in the 1890s, 400 million *taels* in Chinese capital were invested in foreign enterprises.[55] The search for security under extraterritoriality also attracted substantial funds from Chinese depositors in foreign banks. Since, as we have noted, these banks were not involved in promoting local industry, this capital was removed from the local economy to finance international trade or foreign exchange speculation.[56] The resources of these banks were further enhanced by their "right" to issue currency for domestic circulation in China—a right claimed on the basis of extraterritoriality. Since these notes were issued with less than 100 percent reserves, "they were the equivalent to an interest-free loan from the Chinese public to the foreign banks."[57]

The gunboat-backed protection that extraterritoriality provided for foreign enterprises often gave them a decisive advantage over Chinese competitors.

Foreign insurance companies, recognizing this fact, became an integral part of the system that virtually guaranteed foreign domination of China's internal steamship navigation. As one study put it:

> It was the unwillingness of the foreign [insurance] companies to insure junks which frequently persuaded the Chinese to ship their goods by foreign vessels. Thus the advance of foreign shipping in China waters and foreign insurance companies went hand in hand. In 1863 the British consul in Tianjin remarked that the "principle of marine insurance annihilates the native craft. 'Can you insure?' is a question which the Chinese merchants invariably put."[58]

At this point, the apologetic school will reply: this is only one side of the coin, and the wrong side at that. The critical issue is not the security that extraterritoriality provided for foreign enterprises, but the failure of the Chinese government to provide similar security for Chinese enterprises. The advantages enjoyed by the foreign banks were not as important as China's failure to develop a banking system that would support its own economic development. The tax advantages of foreign companies protected by exterritoriality are thus less worthy of attention than the excessive burden that the Chinese government placed on the modern sector of its own economy. In short, "the idea that the unequal treaties prevented China's industrialization . . . is oversimple and inadequate to explain what happened. Decision lay first with the Chinese government; only the government's default gave the treaty port its later dominant role."[59]

This is a serious, though fatally flawed argument, and it must be answered with some logical precision. In the first place, concepts of economic security, economic advantage, or even tax advantage are clearly relative, and China's deficiency in these regards was significant only in comparison to Western enterprises protected by extraterritoriality—that is, China was deficient only given the fact of imperialism.[60] In the absence of the network of foreign banks, insurance companies, steamship companies, and treaty port enterprises, Chinese capital, trade, and entrepreneurial personnel would not have been absorbed by the treaty port economy that imperialism had created. The "opportunity cost"—the cost in lost opportunities for healthy indigenous economic growth in China—was real and was directly attributable to the foreign presence.[61]

Second, while it might be argued that the political and military weakness of China allowed the foreign powers to make their initial inroads in China during the nineteenth century, once the foreigners were established, their very presence guaranteed the perpetuation of political weakness. A strong China, capable of providing a political and economic "environment conducive to domestic capital formation"[62] was inconceivable given the fact of imperialism in China. The foreign presence, far from providing a solution, lay at the root of the problem. While the coexistence, claimed by the apologists, of domestic and foreign industry in China was at least theoretically possible, the coexistence of a strong sovereign China and a foreign presence over which it had no jurisdiction or control was a logical impossibility.

This conclusion proceeds from the very nature of sovereignty. To the extent that the foreign powers limited China's sovereignty, they inevitably weakened China politically. Every concession that the foreigners wrung from the reluctant Qing—from the rights of missionaries to spheres of influence—reduced the legitimacy of the dynasty in the eyes of the Chinese population. By the first decade of the twentieth century, the Qing was reduced to little more than a despised tax-collecting agency for the foreign powers. Nearly one-half of the imperial government's revenue was devoted to loan service and indemnity payments.[63] Now if China had been able to increase its import tariff, it might have been able to meet these obligations while assisting indigenous economic development. (In the years between China's tariff autonomy in 1929 and the onset of the Sino-Japanese War, China's tariff receipts increased roughly five-fold in spite of the effects of world depression on foreign trade.)[64] But in the nineteenth and early twentieth centuries, the West set China's tariffs, and China suffered accordingly, both politically and financially.

To turn from the macroscopic to the microscopic, one final example might illustrate how imperialism helped to make China ungovernable. The Sino-British Mackay Treaty of 1902 provided that foreign firms be given three weeks' notice of any prohibition of rice exports from one locality to another. The terms of this treaty were cited by the British in 1906 to prevent a prohibition of exports from Hunan, which Qing officials had desired during a flood-induced famine. Later, when a major popular uprising occurred, the British Consul explained that "much as I sympathize with any measure tending to alleviate the distress of the famine-stricken people, it was nevertheless my duty to see that Treaty stipulations were complied with."[65] Four years later, the same situation arose again: the British insisted that three weeks of exports be allowed, the price of rice soared, and the famous Changsha rice riot of 1910 resulted, taking both foreign missions and businesses and Chinese government offices and schools as its targets. Foreign restrictions on China's sovereignty were such that the government was often totally powerless to prevent such outbreaks of popular discontent.

Just as the unequal treaties sometimes tied the hands of the Chinese government, so the knowledge and fear of the foreign threat often severely limited the options open to the Chinese government. In the nineteenth century, such officials as Li Hongzhang, a man fully committed to economic and military self-strengthening, objected to the construction of railways not on the superstitious grounds that they would disturb *fengshui*, but on the very realistic grounds that they would provide the means for foreign military invasion.[66] Turning to politics in the twentieth century, there can be no doubt that the leaders of the 1911 Revolution felt compelled to make their revolution acceptable to the foreign powers in order to prevent intervention or even partition by the imperialists. Inevitably this meant tempering whatever radical nationalism was present in the revolutionary movement.

If the imperialists closed options for some, they opened up options for others. If Yuan Shikai had not had the imperialists to turn to for his Reorganization Loan in 1913, he would have had to come to terms with the Guomindang and the reformist gentry leaders who had led the fight against foreign railway loans in the spring of 1911, and had guided the revolution that brought down the Qing in the fall. Foreign financial support allowed Yuan to bypass and ultimately overwhelm this province-based gentry nationalism.

The imperialists' role during the warlord era was scarcely more progressive. To be sure, the powers regretted the disruption of trade that warlordism produced. One must also admit that other than Japanese aid to Zhang Zuolin and Duan Qirui,* the extent of imperialist support for particular warlords is still an open question. Nonetheless, by bestowing the legitimacy of diplomatic recognition and the revenues of the customs administration on anyone who succeeded in capturing Beijing, the powers encouraged the game of musical chairs that the warlord governments played in Beijing. The economics of imperialism made it more profitable for a warlord to capture Beijing than to straighten out the finances and develop the economy of the area that he controlled. When he did concern himself with his local base, the warlord demonstrated one of the clearest lessons learned from the West: there is money in opium. The cultivation of "foreign mud," as it was called, was encouraged as a key source of many warlords' tax revenues. Imperialism, then, was an integral part of the process that led to China's political disintegration in the first half of the twentieth century. To the extent that political collapse intensified the effects of flood, drought, and famine in the 1920s, 1930s, and 1940s, imperialism contributed to the impoverishment of the Chinese peasantry.

* * *

This chapter has mentioned a series of distinct economic, social, and political effects of imperialism in China. For analytical purposes, it has been necessary to isolate the various effects of the foreign presence. Now, however, it is

---

* Zhang Zuolin (张作霖, 1875–1928) in the Northeast (Manchuria) and Duan Qirui (段祺瑞, 1865–1936) in Beijing were two notoriously pro-Japanese warlords in the early republic.

necessary to tie the separate pieces together and to assess the total impact of imperialism on China. Imperialism came to China as an unwelcome intruder: pushing opium, Christianity, and cotton yarn. The opium enhanced political corruption and moral decay; the Christianity threatened the values and the status of the gentry; and the yarn deprived handicraft spinners of their livelihood. Many suffered, a few were helped, and the people blamed the government for its failure to adequately deal with the intruders. The government, unable to rid the country of the imperialists, ultimately found itself relying on them to collect Customs revenues, help suppress the Taiping and lesser rebellions, and provide financial assistance in the form of loans. The imperialist powers, for their part, were willing to offer sufficient support to conservative governments to maintain the status quo with a modicum of political stability, but were quite unwilling (and unable) to aid in the creation of a political regime capable of restoring full sovereignty to China. In the realm of economics, the energies of imperialism were directed toward the profitable development of China's foreign trade and such ancillary industries as seemed to serve that general end. While they were hardly successful in fundamentally restructuring China's massive agrarian economy in the direction of foreign trade, they skewed the modern sector of the economy in that direction and in so doing produced a type of "false modernization" that had little or no hope of producing sustained economic growth.[67]

If one were to try to restate this argument in terms of the Harvard school's "response to the West" paradigm, one would say that the West presented China with a problem: how to preserve its sovereignty against the economic, political, and military incursions of imperialism; and even suggested a model solution: economic and political modernization along the lines of Western bourgeois democracy. The only difficulty was that the solution was bound to fail precisely because of the very imperialism that presented the problem in the first place. This is not to say that internal factors did not also contribute to the failure of that solution. They did indeed play a role. *Theoretically*, however, they were less significant, for the proposition "In the absence of imperialism, internal factors would have guaranteed an unsuccessful response to the West," is meaningless: in the absence of imperialism, the problem of the response to the West would not exist.[68]

Finally, it is not necessary or proper to suggest that China's response to the West was a "failure"—even if imperialism is held to be the cause of "failure." That proposition is true only if Japan's imitation of Western finance capitalism and economic and military imperialism is to be the model of "success." What the Chinese case implies is that any victim nation's attempt to collaborate or coexist with imperialism is destined to fail. Imperialism, in effect, eliminates for its victims the possibility of a bourgeois-democratic road to development. However, in China the very struggle to eliminate the economic, political, social, and psychological vestiges of imperialism produced the basis of sustained, self-reliant economic and political growth. Maoism, it is safe to say, is inconceivable in the absence of imperialism, and China's decision to follow a Maoist path to development can hardly be judged a "failure."

NOTES

1. Chi-ming Hou, *Foreign Investment and Economic Development in China: 1840–1937* (Cambridge, MA: Harvard University Press, 1965), 130.

2. Ibid., 218.

3. John E. Schrecker, *Imperialism and Chinese Nationalism: Germany in Shantung* (Cambridge, MA: Harvard University Press 1971), 258.

4. Ibid., 256, 258.

5. John K. Fairbank, Edwin O. Reischauer and Albert M. Craig, *East Asia: The Modern Transformation* (Boston: Houghton Mifflin, 1965), 318.

6. John K. Fairbank, *The United States and China*, third edition (Cambridge, MA: Harvard University Press, 1971), 146.

7. S. A. M. Adshead, *The Modernization of the Chinese Salt Administration* (Cambridge, MA: Harvard University Press, 1970).

8. Ramon Myers, *The Chinese Peasant Economy, Agricultural Development in Hopei and Shantung, 1890–1949* (Cambridge, MA: Harvard University Press, 1970), 124.

9. James Peck's perceptive article, "The Roots of Rhetoric: The Professional Ideology of America's China Watchers," in Edward Friedman and Mark Selden, *America's Asia: Dissenting Essays on Asian-American Relations* (New York: Vintage, 1971), 40–66, presents a brilliant analysis of the basic assumptions and hidden purposes behind such theories. The present essay is a more mundane attempt to demonstrate that these theories are wrong.

10. John Q. Adams in *Boston Evening Transcript,* November 24, 1841, quoted in T. W. Overlach, *Foreign Financial Control in China* (New York: Macmillan, 1919), 8.

11. Fairbank, Reischauer, and Craig, *East Asia: Modern Transformation*, 136. For the Harvard monograph that is either the basis for Fairbank's statement, or perhaps the detailed working out of Fairbank's views, see Hsin-pao Chang, *Commissioner Lin and the Opium War* (Cambridge, MA: Harvard University Press, 1964), esp. 15.

12. The phrase belongs to Karl Marx, from *New York Daily Tribune*, September 20, 1858, in Shlomo Avineri, ed., *Karl Marx on Colonialism and Modernization* (Garden City, NY: Doubleday-Anchor, 1969), 340.

13. Albert Feuerwerker, *The Chinese Economy, ca. 1870–1911* (Ann Arbor, MI: Center for Chinese Studies, 1969), 51–52. (This publication later appeared as "Economic Trends in the Late Ch'ing Empire, 1870–1911" in John K. Fairbank and Kwang-ching Liu, eds., *The Cambridge History of China*, vol. 11: *The Late Ch'ing, 1800–1911*, Part II [Cambridge: Cambridge University Press, 1980]).

14. Ibid., 56

15. Karl Marx, *The Communist Manifesto* (Chicago: Gateway Edition, 1954), 20.

16. George C. Allen and Audrey G. Donnithorne, *Western Enterprise in Far Eastern Economic Development: China and Japan* (New York: Macmillan, 1954), 259; Yu-kwei Cheng, *Foreign Trade and Industrial Development of China: An Historical and Integrated Analysis through 1948* (Washington, DC: University Press of Washington, 1956), 34.

17. Boris P. Togasheff, *China as a Tea Producer* (Shanghai: Commercial Press, 1926), 167, gives export figures of more than 2 million piculs per year for the 1880s. Liu Ta-chung and Yeh Kung-chia, *The Economy of the Chinese Mainland: National Income and Economic Development, 1933–1959* (Princeton, NJ: Princeton University Press, 1965), 135, 257, gives three million piculs as the total production of processed tea in 1933 when Chinese exports had virtually ceased altogether (Chi-ming Hou, *Foreign Investment*, 194). Even if we assume that domestic consumption was constant between the 1880s and the 1930s (unlikely given China's rising population) total annual production in the 1880s would have been five million piculs, of which exports would be 40 percent.

18. Hou, *Foreign Investment*, 194.

19. Ibid., 190–94; D. K. Lieu, *The Silk Industry of China* (Shanghai: Kelly and Walsh, 1941), 254–57; Chen Han-seng, *Industrial Capital and Chinese Peasants* (Shanghai: Kelly and Walsh, 1939), 24.

20. Allen and Donnithorne, *Western Enterprise*, 52–68.

21. Cheng, *Foreign Trade*, 35.

22. Ibid., 230–31.

23. Hou, *Foreign Investment*, 198; see also C. F. Remer, *Foreign Investments in China* (New York: Macmillan, 1933), 218.

24. See, for example, some of the statistics cited in Harry Magdoff, *The Age of Imperialism: The Economics of US Foreign Policy* (New York: Monthly Review Press, 1969), 154–58.

25. Albert Feuerwerker, "Handicraft and Manufactured Cotton Textiles in China, 1871–1910," *Journal of Economic History* 30, no. 2 (June 1970), esp. 371–75; one *dan* = 133 1/3 lbs.

26. Feuerwerker, *Chinese Economy, 1870–1911*, 29.

27. Feuerwerker, "Handicraft Textiles," 377.

28. Feuerwerker, *Chinese Economy, 1870–1911*, 29.

29. Frederic Wakeman, *Strangers at the Gate: Social Disorder in South China, 1839–1861* (Berkeley: University of California Press, 1966), 187–88.

30. Hou, *Foreign Investment*, 130.

31. Ibid., 127–28.

32. Ibid., 16.

33. Julean Arnold, *China: A Commercial and Industrial Handbook* (Washington: Government Printing Office, 1926), 206. The 63.3 percent figure derives from Yu-kwei Cheng, 40.

34. Remer, *Foreign Investments*, 73. I have excluded the "undistributed" portion of Remer's figures (largely loans for government administration) and recalculated the percentages.

35. Albert Feuerwerker, *The Chinese Economy, 1912–1949* (Ann Arbor, MI: Center for Chinese Studies, 1968), 13. (A revised version of this publication appeared as "Economic Trends, 1912–1949" in John K. Fairbank ed., *The Cambridge History of China*, vol. 12: *Republican China 1912–1949*, Part 1 [Cambridge: Cambridge University Press, 1983]).

36. Hou, *Foreign Investment*, 64; Allen and Donnithorne, *Western Enterprise*, 140.

37. Overlach, *Foreign Financial Control in China*, 87.

38. Paul S. Reinsch, *An American Diplomat in China* (Garden City, NY: Doubleday, Page, 1922), 102.

39. Cheng, *Foreign Trade*, 77, figures are from 79.

40. Feuerwerker, *Chinese Economy, 1912–1949*, 22.

41. Cheng, *Foreign Trade*, 39.

42. See Albert Feuerwerker, "China's Nineteenth Century Industrialization: The Case of the Hanyehping Coal and Iron Company, Ltd." in C. D. Cowan, ed., *The Economic Development of China and Japan* (London: G. Allen and Unwin, 1964).

43. See Ellsworth C. Carlson, *The Kaiping Mines (1877–1912)*, second edition (Cambridge, MA: Harvard University Press, 1971), 58–83. Hoover, then an engineer in the employ of the British promoter C. A. Moreing, obtained control of the Kaiping Mining Company when the Chinese director and his German advisor Gustave Detring sought foreign ownership as protection against possible Russian seizure during the latter's anti-Boxer activities. Hoover then helped Moreing convert what the Chinese had viewed as a temporary arrangement into permanent foreign control.

44. See especially Hou, *Foreign Investment*, 125–264.

45. Edward Friedman, *The Center Cannot Hold: The Failure of Parliamentary Democracy in China from the Chinese Revolution to the World War of 1914* (PhD diss., Harvard University, 1968), 265 ff.

46. Shiraiwa Ryūhei and Yasui Shōtarō, *Konan* [Hunan] (Tokyo: 1905), 130–36.

47. See, for example, the indexes of industrial production in John K. Chang, "Industrial Development in China, 1912–1949," *Journal of Economic History* 27 (March 1967): 65–68.

48. Hou, *Foreign Investment*, 134–36.

49. See also Allen and Donnithorne, *Western Enterprise*, 31; Rhoads Murphey, *The Treaty Ports and China's Modernization: What Went Wrong?* (Ann Arbor, MI: Center for Chinese Studies, 1970), 48.

50. Franz Fanon, *The Wretched of the Earth* (New York: Grove Press, 1968), 153.

51. Remer, *Foreign Investments*, 167.

52. Hou, *Foreign Investment*, 100.

53. Feuerwerker, *Chinese Economy, 1870–1911*, 71–72.

54. Hou, *Foreign Investment*, 143.

55. Wang Jingyu, in *Lishi Yanjiu*, 1965: 4, 69–70.

56. Allen and Donnithorne, *Western Enterprise*, 113–14. For a discussion of the same effect in other economies, see Thomas Balogh, *The Economics of Poverty* (New York: Macmillan, 1966), 12, 30–32.

57. Hou, *Foreign Investment*, 57.

58. Allen and Donnithorne, *Western Enterprise*, 120.

59. Fairbank, Reischauer, and Craig, *East Asia: Modern Transformation*, 349.

60. Obviously, China was also deficient in comparison to the home economies of the West and Japan, but since Chinese capital was not realistically free to invest in those economies, this deficiency is not significant for the present argument.

61. On the subject of opportunity costs; see H. W. Singer, "The Distribution of Gains between Investing and Borrowing Countries," *American Economic Review* 40 (May 1950), esp. 476.

62. This felicitous phrase is provided by Chi-ming Hou (*Foreign Investment*, 91) to describe the presumed (but nonexistent) effect of foreign investment's "catalytic role."

63. Feuerwerker, *Chinese Economy, 1870–1911*, 63–70.

64. Cheng, *Foreign Trade*, 57.

65. Bertram Giles dispatch from Changsha, July 23, 1906, Foreign Office file 228/1628.

66. Ssu-yu Teng and John K. Fairbank, *China's Response to the West: A Documentary Survey, 1839–1923* (New York: Atheneum, 1971), 110.

67. For one of the most provocative recent articles on this theme, see Bergère, "De la Chine classique à la Chine actuelle: Fluctuations économiques et revolution, pour une histoire économique de la Chine moderne," *Annales: Economies, Sociétés, Civilizations* 25, no. 4 (July–August 1969): 860–75.

68. Albert Memmi has made a very similar point, argued somewhat differently: "The question of whether the colonized, if let alone, would have advanced at the same pace as other people has no great significance. To be perfectly truthful, we have no way of knowing. It is possible that he might have not. The colonial factor is certainly not the only one which explains the backwardness of a people. . . . However . . . can one justify the historical misfortune of one people by the difficulties of another? The colonized peoples are not the only victims of history, but the historical misfortune peculiar to the colonized was colonization" (Albert Memmi, *The Colonizer and the Colonized* [Boston: Beacon Press, 1967], 112).

Chapter Two

From Anti-Imperialism to Postcolonial Theory

Some thirty years after my critique of the Harvard School, the China field was much changed. While Fairbank had critiqued "imperialism" as a "whopping generalization," the term was now conventionally used to characterize the Western and Japanese intervention in China. The critique of imperialism had also expanded as postcolonial and postmodern theory spread from the field of literature to history in the effort to give voice to native and subaltern peoples, the description of whose world had often been dominated by the colonial record. In the Middle Eastern and South Asian world from which these ideas spread, the result was often beneficial. But the results were more mixed when it came to China, a country that was never colonized, and for which there existed a rich Chinese record to correct the colonial accounts.

In the history of early Western encounters with China, few events are more notorious than Lord Macartney's mission to China in 1793. Macartney traveled to China laden with elaborate chronological and astronomical devices to impress the Manchu emperor in an effort to open the empire to trade and diplomatic relations. After his famous meeting with the Qianlong Emperor, the latter wrote to King George that "we have never valued ingenious articles, nor do we have the slightest need of your country's manufactures," a rejection that has long been interpreted (or misinterpreted) as a disinterest in European scientific advances. In his book, *Cherishing Men from Afar*, James Hevia launched a vigorous defense of the Chinese response, and a postmodern critique of Macartney's Enlightenment-informed imperialist intent.

My critique of Hevia's book generated more controversy, both pro and con, than any piece I have written. A Chinese version, together with a sharp dissent from UCLA professors Ben Elman and Ted Huters, was published in the Hong Kong magazine *Ershiyi shiji* (二十一世紀, twenty-first century), which then provoked further contributions, generally supportive of my position, from

Zhang Longxi (張隆溪), Luo Zhitian (羅志田), and Ge Jianxiong (葛劍雄).* Hevia himself responded in a later issue of *Modern China*, which I rebutted with a brief "Tradutore, Traditore" in the same issue.† Despite the sharp differences evident in these exchanges, at least one Chinese historian took the incident as a model of scholarly debate from which Chinese academics had much to learn.‡ It is also important to recognize the substantial agreement on certain methodological points that are reflected elsewhere in this volume. I share with Hevia a fundamental concern for the role of ritual in Chinese politics and culture, and the need for a more anthropological understanding of ritual as a contested cultural practice rather than a fixed set of behavioral rules. Further discussion of the role of ritual will be found on chapter 5 on the election of Sun Yat-sen as China's first president and especially in the final chapter on political theater in modern China.

Though my critique begins with issues of translation, it was fueled by distress over the growing influence of post-modern theory in historical studies, as represented in Hevia's stated intent "to destabilize the . . . relationship between sources (facts) and interpretations." The sources in this case were largely Qing court documents. In my view, the language used in these texts had relatively fixed meanings, so that the emperor could understand precisely what his officials were reporting and could in turn make his own will clear. It is the historian's task to grasp that meaning and (if writing in a foreign language) to translate it accurately. My criticism of post-modern theory was particularly distressing to Fabio Lanza, who concluded his book on the Committee of Concerned Asian Scholars with a critique of my "antitheory backlash." In Lanza's account, "Esherick's enthusiasm for 'modernity'" had the effect of "indirectly reasserting the old 'Harvard school' view of China" that I had once critiqued.§ Lanza failed to see that the heart of my critique in "Apologetics of Imperialism" was not a matter of political stance, but a question of getting the facts right: imperialism *did* have a real and negative impact on China's development.

The primary message here seems more relevant today than ever. Lanza (and Hevia's) view seemed to be that political consistency in opposing imperialism should trump the quest for historical accuracy. That is no doubt consistent with the post-modern position that, in the words of one trio of critics, "the writing of history . . . is not about truth-seeking, it's about the politics

---

* See *Ershiyi shiji* (二十一世紀), no. 44 (1997.12), 45 (1998.2), 46 (1998.4), 49 (1998.10).

† James Hevia, "Postpolemical Historiography: A Response to Joseph W. Esherick," *Modern China* 24, no. 3 (1998): 319–27; and Esherick "Tradutore, Traditore: A Reply to James Hevia," *Modern China* 24, no. 3 (1998): 328–32.

‡ Li Bozhong, "'Heweiya shijian' he "Yabalahan anjian'" [The Hevia incident' and the 'Abraham case'], *Zhonghua dushubao* 1998, no. 10: 5.

§ Fabio Lanza, *The End of Concern: Maoist China, Activism, and Asian Studies* (Durham: Duke University Press, 2017), 190–92.

of the historians."* Fortunately, in American universities, the postmodern ascendancy has ended in most history departments, its critical interventions having produced few substantive contributions to the discipline. In Europe, despite the continental origins of much postmodern theory, its influence on history was more constrained; and in China, the movement's New Left allies have been reduced to apologists for Xi Jinping's authoritarian regime.† Nonetheless, in an age of "fake news" and "alternative facts," it is more essential than ever to stress the merits of truth-seeking—even while recognizing that the quest may be a Sisyphean struggle, and the truths will inevitably be tentative and subject to revision and reinterpretation as new sources and methods are discovered. If the historian's honest quest for the truth about the past is sacrificed to politically correct positioning, then history is reduced to political propaganda and scholars are no more credible than the politicians promoting alternative facts.

CHERISHING SOURCES FROM AFAR‡

The 1997 Joseph R. Levenson Prize for the best book on pre-twentieth-century China was awarded to James L. Hevia for *Cherishing Men from Afar: Qing Guest Ritual and the Macartney Embassy of 1793*.[1] The selection committee, which included two eminent Qing historians, praised Hevia's skillful combination of "post-modern interpretation and new archival resources to present a revisionist account" of the Macartney mission. In a similar vein, William Rowe wrote on the book's dust jacket that "*Cherishing Men from Afar*, extremely impressive in its marshalling of basic Qing material, accomplishes something quite remarkable: the product of a postmodern critical sensibility, it will also satisfy the most traditional of scholars on sinological grounds."

In recent years, discussions of history and theory have often focused on the contributions of postmodern (or poststructural or postcolonial) theory to the study of the past. With the award of the Levenson Prize by a committee

---

* Joyce Appleby, Lynn Hunt, and Margaret Jacob, *Telling the Truth about History* (New York: Norton, 1994), 244.

† On the New Left in China, see the essay and translations of David Ownby in https://www.readingthechinadream.com/new-left.html (accessed August 21, 2021).

‡ Originally published as "Cherishing Sources from Afar," *Modern China* 24, no. 2 (April 1998): 135–61. Reprinted with permission. I would like to express my thanks to Perry Anderson, Michael Bernstein, Michael Chang, Chow Kai-wing, Benjamin Elman, Marta Hanson, Philip Huang, Richard Kraus, Elizabeth Perry (who deserves special thanks for the title), Ye Wa, Zhang Longxi, Zhu Yong, two anonymous readers for *Modern China*, and audiences in Los Angeles and Beijing for helpful comments on an earlier version of this article. Needless to say, none of these people is in any way responsible for the views expressed here, and some (especially Benjamin Elman) would surely dissociate themselves from my critique.

that explicitly notes the author's postmodern interpretation, Hevia's study is established as a model of what that body of theory has to contribute to our understanding of China's history. It is that contribution that I would like to assess in this critique.

The Macartney mission is one of the most extensively studied events in Sino-Western relations. The unsuccessful effort of the British plenipotentiary to expand trade with China and station a permanent embassy in Beijing left a substantial English-language record of journals and retrospective accounts. In 1936, Earl Pritchard initiated the modern scholarship on the mission with his volume on *The Crucial Years of Early Anglo-Chinese Relations, 1750–1800*, which exploited these records, Western archives, and recently published documentation from the Qing imperial archives.[2] He followed in 1943 with an article discussing the critical ritual issue of the kowtow (*koutou* 叩头) during Macartney's audience with the Qianlong emperor.[3] Meanwhile, John K. Fairbank and Teng Ssu-yu had written a seminal article "On the Ch'ing Tributary System," the institutional context within which the Qing sought to contain Macartney's mission.[4] In 1962, J. L. Cranmer-Byng published a scholarly edition of Macartney's journal.[5] Most directly comparable to Hevia's work is a study by the French scholar-diplomat Alain Peyrefitte, who gained access to previously unexplored memorials from the Qing archives in Beijing and published a long volume on the mission, which appeared in French in 1989 and in English in 1992 under the title *The Immobile Empire*.[6] Peyrefitte's book owed much to a detailed Chinese study by Zhu Yong, also published in 1989, *Buyuan dakai de Zhongguo damen* (The Chinese gate that was unwilling to open).[7]

Given all of this previous scholarship, the critical acclaim for Hevia's volume is a remarkable tribute. The contributions of the volume are not based on any new evidence. Indeed, there are a number of sources cited by Peyrefitte—including Zhu Yong's book, twenty-one volumes of Macartney's correspondence in the Wason Collection at Cornell, and a critical diary, held in the Duke University library, by the son of Macartney's secretary, to say nothing of the less accessible Jesuit archives—that Hevia has not consulted (or at least has not cited). What is new is the author's analytical perspective. According to the publisher's blurb, "The history of this encounter, like most colonial and imperial encounters, has traditionally been told from the Europeans' point of view. In this book, James L. Hevia consults Chinese sources—many previously untranslated—for a broader sense of what Qing court officials understood."[8]

Hevia himself states the case in terms of the sacred text of "postcolonial" scholarship: Edward Said's *Orientalism*. Said, says Hevia, has exposed the "pervasive practice among orientalists and their area studies successors—the tendency to apply 'objectivist' Western theory, particularly social science models, to non-Western data" (7).[9] The social science models that Hevia seeks to challenge are structural-functional systems theory, the "sociological treatment of ritual," and the notion of a sinocentric world order (xi–xii). These models manifest themselves in scholarly analyses of late imperial Chinese foreign relations in terms of a "tribute system," an analytical framework that Hevia proposes to replace with "Qing guest ritual."

Briefly stated, past scholarship, beginning with Fairbank and Teng, argued that the tribute system "functioned to legitimize the ruling house" (10). Although subsequent research has revealed considerable Qing flexibility in applying the tribute system, such scholars as John Wills have noted the Qing court's insistence on maintaining ceremonial supremacy and its consequent inability to adjust rationally to the demands of a new commercial age.[10] To Hevia, this reflects a Western "functional-instrumental interpretation of ritual" in which rituals are a "typical feature of archaic or premodern societies . . . [and] indicate an absence of fully conscious rationality" (19). What particularly offends Hevia is the idea that the Qing considered rituals to be fixed protocols, was confined by ritual tradition, and used ritual instrumentally to maintain its political supremacy. Following some recent anthropological theory, he argues that "ritual practices themselves produce power relations" (21)—though exactly how ritual produces power and why some people (such as emperors) are more successful at this trick than others is never fully explained.

More concretely, the new interpretation that Hevia offers of Qing policy toward the Macartney mission involves the following elements. First, the "Qing imagining of empire" (30) did not involve the sinocentric world order proposed by the tribute system model but a "multitude of lords" of which the Manchus were overlords. Foreign relations did not involve "crude distinctions between civilization and barbarism" but a process of incorporation "through centering, into the rulership of the Qing empire" (128). Second, the "guest ritual" that governed tributary missions is understood as "discourses about agency . . . rather than as the rote repetition of a fixed body of rules" (131). Thus, in the Macartney mission, the Qing was not insisting on a fixed ritual but was flexibly "channeling along a centering path" (chapter 6) in an effort to induce properly submissive behavior on Macartney's part. Indeed, by the end of the book, Hevia has managed to make the Chinese the flexible party, and the British attempt to establish diplomatic relations and the mutual recognition of sovereignty becomes a rigid commitment to a Eurocentric hierarchy: "In the case of the Qing imperium, superior and inferior were realized through complex dialogues continually working toward the inclusion of the powers of others in the emperor's rulership. In the naturalized and naturalizing discourse of the British, superiority and inferiority were intrinsic to agents, aspects of their nature" (212).

There is indeed much to be commended in this bold reinterpretation and in Hevia's rethinking of the Qing "foreign relations." His chapter on "A Multitude of Lords: The Qing Empire, Manchu Rulership, and Interdomainal Relations" draws ably on the fine scholarship of Joseph Fletcher, David Farquhar, Pamela Crossley, Mark Elliott, Ning Chia, and others to construct a nuanced picture of Qing rulers' complex and multidimensional relations with their Inner Asian neighbors.[11] The important role of Manchu identity and Tibetan Buddhism in managing this relationship is well described and provides a useful reminder that there is more than a purely Chinese sinocentric order involved in the Qing imperium. On the British side, his analysis and critique of Macartney's peculiarly late eighteenth-century "naturalist gaze" as the ambassador traveled through China is an interesting new take on the oft-described mission. In general, his effort to recast the encounter as one between "two expansive imperialisms" with "competing and ultimately incompatible views of the meaning of sovereignty" (xii, 28) is a worthy enterprise and well worth applauding.

But our concern here is the new light shed on the Chinese side of the Macartney encounter. When Hevia criticizes past scholarship's "functional-instrumental interpretations of ritual," he accuses its proponents of an "orientalist construction" in which "it matters little what Qing sources have to say on the subject; all such sources can easily be translated into the regularities of the observer's discourse, producing knowledge that quite clearly claims to be superior to that of historical Chinese subjects who are under the sway of appearances and illusions" (19–20). Previous scholars, in short, have imposed their interpretation (discourse) on the Qing sources. Hevia proposes to "reconstruct the particulars of [Qing imperial forms of interdomainal relations] in their own terms" and, in doing so, to offer "an alternative way of understanding imperial ritual" (28).

As I have noted above, none of this is being done with any new sources. Hevia is looking at exactly the same Chinese sources that Peyrefitte used, many of which were available and used by Pritchard long before. But he returns to these sources with a new postmodern sensibility, one that avoids privileging any particular reading of a text. In Hevia's own words, "one of my main purposes is to destabilize the taken-for-granted relationship between sources (facts) and interpretation" (225). This, of course, gives considerable liberty for a variety of theoretical imaginings. But has he indeed succeeded in rescuing the Chinese sources from the biases of orientalist construction to understand them "in their own terms"?

TRANSLATION AND INTERPRETIVE IMAGINATION

Unfortunately, a poor benighted victim of orientalist training such as myself has some habits that arouse a certain scepticism. My custom is to read a book beginning with the back matter. In this case, my attention was drawn to certain anomalies in the glossary.[12] In Hevia's glossary, we find *huangdi* (皇帝, emperor, or "supreme lord") written with the characters for Yellow Emperor (黃帝); *gongcha* (an error for *gongchai* 貢差, tribute emissary) written *yechai* (頁差, page emissary), with *gongdan* (貢單, tribute list) similarly rendered *yedan* (頁單). For *kenqiu wuyan* (懇求無厭, insatiable requests), we get *kenqiu wuya* (狠求無壓); for *maodu wuyan* (冒瀆無厭, unbearably annoying), we get *maomai wuyan* (冒賣無厭); and perhaps most startling, we see *yishi tongren* (一視同仁, "treating all with the same benevolence") rendered with the "man/human" character for *ren* (人) instead of "benevolence." This short list hardly exhausts the errors in the glossary, and the number of howlers such as these in a relatively brief glossary does not inspire confidence that the author is equipped to get us closer to the original meaning of Qing documents.

But let us turn to the text itself. There are several places where Hevia encounters frequently repeated terms or phrases that he finds significant enough to deserve explicit commentary. Let us first consider the concept of "centering" or "channeling along a centering path," as he titles chapter 6 on the reception of the Macartney mission up to the point of the audience with Qianlong. The phrase that he glosses as "centering" is *fengjian shizhong* (豐儉適中), which Peyrefitte (and his English translators) have no difficulty rendering as "the mean between prodigality and parsimony."[13] Hevia is quite aware of this meaning, which he renders "negotiating a mean between overabundance and scarcity," but he adds a postmodern sensitivity to bodily positioning and associates it with a textual coding that "channels action away from extremes and toward a contingent spatial center" (123). His argument then relates this phrase to imperial rituals in which the arrangement of participants emphasizes a "pivotal center and plural human agency" (124).

There are two problems here. First, there is nothing in the text that refers to either "channeling" or a "path," and the *zhong* in this phrase has nothing to do with physical centering. It simply means moderation or the mean. The association with physical centering is entirely a product of Hevia's postmodern imaginings. More important, the flexible moderation embodied in the phrase *fengjian shizhong* was not a constituent element of Qing ritual protocols (it does not appear in the ritual texts) but was an admonition from the emperor who was constantly intervening to adjust the treatment of Macartney to ensure that ceremonies met the political needs of the moment. By treating this "centering" as an essential part of Qing guest ritual, Hevia obscures the critical tension between officials seeking to handle the embassy properly according to ritual protocols and an arbitrary emperor chastising his subordinates whenever anything went wrong for their failure to apply the flexible moderation of *fengjian shizhong*.[14]

An even more interesting case is the common documentary phrase *fangwei tuoshan* (方爲妥善), where, of course, the *fang* is equivalent to the modern *baihua* preposition *cai* (才), and the phrase means "then and only then will it be appropriate." But Hevia's mind is fixed on physical positioning, and he renders it "squaring with proper circumstances." He even favors us with a full grammatical explanation: "This particular grammatical form recurs often in the court records. It seems to refer to action which accords with an existing classification category. In other words, the *fang wei* construction places recent or unfolding action into preexisting classification schemes, while the classification construction I have previously made reference to, the use of *shu* (屬), constitutes the class at the same time that actions under consideration are placed into it" (145n). This is utter nonsense or, as the Chinese would put it, *wangwen shengyi* (望文生義, looking at a text and inventing a meaning).

A final example in this regard concerns the term *tizhi* (體制), "fundamental rules," "institutions," or simply "system." Hevia discusses it in the context of an imperial edict admonishing provincial officials to "conform to [*fu* 符] the fundamental rules" governing relations with foreigners. But a crucial part of Hevia's argument is the notion that the Qing guest ritual did not involve conformity to a fixed body of ritual protocols, so he rejects the conventional understanding of the term. Eager to introduce agency at any possible point, he renders the phrase "Our imperial order" and argues that the term "included a notion of imperial will or, perhaps given the context, the emperor's intentions" (143n). This certainly smacks of wilful imagining. The term *tizhi* appears with great frequency in Qing documents, and it is always used to describe a set of institutions fixed long in the past that must not be changed. Indeed, the rhetorical reference to *tizhi* almost invariably signals a conservative appeal to adhere to established institutional forms. Only in the late nineteenth century (or again in the 1980s, with PRC efforts at *tizhi gaige* 體制改革) do we see appeals to change what is still regarded as a fixed, but now negatively valued, set of institutions.

BACK TO THE SOURCES

These repeated misreadings of the Qing texts are sufficient to belie William Rowe's assertion that this study will "satisfy the most traditional of scholars on sinological grounds." (Quite obviously, I am not satisfied, and I would hope that I am not in a category beyond "the most traditional.") But is the sum of these and many similar errors sufficient to undercut Hevia's main argument? If we went back to the original Qing sources and compared them to Hevia's narrative summaries and translations, would we come up with a markedly different picture of the Macartney mission? As a first test of this proposition, we could certainly say that both Zhu Yong's 1989 study and Peyrefitte's day-by-day summary of the embassy's reception based on the British, Jesuit, and Chinese published and archival sources produce a strikingly different narrative. Indeed, it is precisely the narrative that Hevia's book challenges: a tale of trade-driven British expansion colliding with a proud and sinocentric Qing state stubbornly insisting that Macartney conform to the forms of a tribute mission. Peyrefitte's book has been justly criticized for its essentialist view of Chinese culture and its ill-informed notion of an "Immobile Empire." But there have been few complaints over the accuracy of Peyrefitte's account of the embassy itself. Indeed, Frederic Wakeman has praised his "splendid recreation of Lord Macartney's mission to China" and noted Peyrefitte's reliance on "a five-person team of Chinese specialists, headed by the brilliant Qing historian Pierre-Henri Durand, to translate the Qing documents into French."[15] Is the difference between these two accounts simply a matter of interpretation? Or are there cases where Hevia's readings of the Qing texts are so skewed that we could call them simply wrong, and wrong in ways that affect important issues of interpretation?

Fortunately, the Chinese archival sources on the Macartney mission are now readily available. In 1928 to 1930, the Palace Museum in Beijing (then Beiping) published many of the key documents in the series *Zhanggu congbian* (掌故叢編, 1928–1930). And now, thanks to financing from a French multinational corporation arranged by Peyrefitte, facsimile reproductions of 783 documents on the embassy have been published by the First Historical Archives in Beijing (*Yingshi Majia'erni fanghua dang'an shiliao huibian*; hereafter cited as YSSL).[16] In effect, all the Chinese documentation available to Hevia and Peyrefitte is now open to scrutiny.

It seems appropriate to begin with the title of Hevia's book. "Cherishing men from afar" translates the Chinese phrase *huairou yuanren* (懷柔遠人).[17] Hevia explains the phrase in the first lines of his book:

> The title of this book is taken from a phrase that recurs often in Qing court records. Cherishing men from afar is both a description and an injunction.... The sage ruler showed compassion and benevolence to those who were outside of his immediate dominion; he cherished those who traveled great distances to come to his court. These notions were at the heart of the rituals that organized relations between Qing emperors and other powerful rulers. (xi)

Quite clearly, Hevia here is intent on countering the notion that the Qing excluded foreigners prior to its "opening" in the Opium War, replacing it with a benevolent and compassionate incorporation of foreigners into the Qing realm.

But does *huairou* mean "cherish"? Most Chinese dictionaries give a definition of "pacify" (*anfu* 安撫) or "cause to submit."[18] The key classical referent is clear: the Doctrine of the Mean (Zhongyong 中庸) section of the *Book of Rites* (*Liji* 禮記) includes the phrase *rou yuanren, ze sifang guizhi; huai zhuhou, ze Tianxia weizhi* (柔遠人，則四方歸之，懷諸侯，則天下 畏之): "Treat men from afar flexibly, and they will resort to you from the four quarters; embrace the feudal lords and all under Heaven will submit to you." Although Legge does misleadingly translate the *huai* in this passage as "cherish,"[19] commentators and dictionaries from the Tang dynasty on have all glossed both *huai* and *rou* and the compound *huairou* as "pacify" (*anfu*) and associated this passage with the proper treatment of tributary missions. Since the passage makes clear that the purpose of *huai* and *rou* is to cause other lords to resort to (or return in) allegiance to (*gui*) the ruler, and to submit to or stand in awe and dread of him (*weizhi*), it is difficult to imagine the terms or their compound meaning "cherish"—especially in the late imperial understanding of this passage.

This being said, it must be acknowledged that *huairou* does refer to the "soft" side of pacifying foreigners. The *huairou* policy is one of treating foreign guests graciously, so long as they are properly submissive. It is, indeed, not too far from an obsolete Shakespearian usage of cherish, meaning "to entertain kindly (a guest)."[20] What is missing from the term cherish, however, is the element of manipulating, subjecting, and controlling that is included in the term *huairou*. More important, *huairou* was only one side of the Qing policy toward foreigners. As Qianlong makes clear, the flexibility embodied in the *huairou* policy must be balanced by the firmness of the Chinese rules and regulations:

> This is my policy on outer barbarians (*waiyi* 外夷) coming for audiences. If they are sincere, reverent and submissive, we will add to our gracious treatment in order to demonstrate a compassionate flexibility (*huairou*). If they evince signs of arrogance, however, then they will not receive the blessings of our gracious ceremonies, and we will reduce the ritual forms for their reception in order to show our fundamental institutions (*tizhi*). This is the proper way to subject foreign principalities (*jiayu waifan* 駕馭外藩).[21]

There are a number of other occasions where Hevia's translations have problems. Most of these are quite minor and need not concern us. But the cumulative effect of these little errors is an account of the Macartney mission that seriously distorts the documentary record. Let us consider one particularly important document, a Grand Council court letter of September 23, 1793, as a test of Hevia's reading. It was issued just as the embassy was departing Beijing and represents the court's summary of the entire unhappy episode.

Hevia recognizes this as an important ("fascinating") document and devotes three pages to analyzing it. (184–86).[22] Qianlong reviews the letter from George III with its request for a permanent ambassador in Beijing and explains why this must be rejected. Here is Hevia's summary of Qianlong's (Hongli's) reasoning:

> Explaining that West Ocean people (missionaries) who asked to enter imperial service wore court dress, lived in official residences, and were not allowed to return to their native land, Hongli reasoned that a British ambassador presumably would not be willing to do the same. His speech and clothing would be different and he would simply be wandering about Peking. Moreover, since they lacked an understanding of appropriate ritual relationships, their requests could be classed as nonsense (*wuyan*). (185)

The first part of this is unobjectionable, but the sentence beginning "Moreover . . ." is hopelessly muddled. Unable to think of any compound pronounced *wuyan* and meaning "nonsense," one goes to the glossary to find, under *wuyan*, *wuya* (無壓, "not-press"), which does not make any sense at all. But if one checks the original source,[23] there is no *wuyan* anyway but instead *wuwei* in the passage *ji fei Tianchao tizhi; yu gaiguo yi shushu wuwei* (既非天朝體制；於該國亦殊屬無謂). Thus, the meaning of the entire passage becomes the following: an ambassador confined to the capital, in strange clothes and speaking a strange language, "would not only be contrary to the institutions of the Celestial Court, but would also be quite useless (*wuwei*) to that country [England]."[24] No one is failing to understand appropriate ritual relationships or having requests classified as nonsense. Instead, we have the Qianlong emperor insisting that the British proposal failed to conform to the Chinese *tizhi* and thus could not be of any benefit to England. (Qianlong, it seems, was less allergic to structural-functional analysis than Hevia.)

Hevia continues,

> In addition, it had become clear that the pronouncements in the English king's communication were different from requests made by his ambassador. While the latter had had his errors pointed out in clear instructions, there was still a discontinuity between the feelings expressed by the English king and the troublesome and annoying entreaties made by his ambassador. Accordingly, these foreigners had been classified as ignorant (*wuzhi* 無知). At present it was uncertain what the English reaction would be to the emperor's refusal to grant their requests, but they might try to stir up trouble in Canton. (185)

This is an extremely important point, for Hevia's argument about Qing guest ritual rests on the proposition that Qianlong perceived no fundamental conflict with the British king. The conventional history treats this encounter as a fated conflict between a rigid Qing insistence on the tribute system and an expansive West demanding a diplomacy based on multiple sovereignty to support its ambitions for more trade. But Hevia insists that Qing guest ritual was an "open-ended" "discourse about agency" (131–32). The failure of the Macartney encounter, therefore, did not have to do with the incompatibility of British and Qing diplomatic protocols but derived instead from the failure of Qianlong's officials to properly handle Macartney by "channeling along the centering path." The failure of the embassy was then "not a question of cross-cultural misunderstanding, but the failure on the part of the imperial officials to properly organize [the ritual process]" (186).

In earlier edicts, we do see the Qianlong emperor presuming that King George, by sending a tribute mission, was proceeding from a position of sincerity, and the problem was only in the handling of his ambassador.[25] But now Qianlong has read the letter that Macartney brought from George III. Hevia to the contrary notwithstanding, the "discontinuity" between king and ambassador has accordingly disappeared, and Qianlong now realizes that the British king himself could pose a threat to a peaceful order. Here is a literal translation of the passage in question:

> When that country's king prepares a memorial laying out his earnest requests, it is different from the ambassador himself submitting a petition. The ambassador can be reprimanded face to face. [To the king], we have issued an imperial letter ordering and rebutting him clearly. When these people sailed here from far across the oceans, we thought they were still reverently submissive and thus treated them generously. But since the ambassador arrived, he has made repeated demands and been quite troublesome. It seems that these barbarians are truly ignorant. Now we have refused their request to leave someone in the capital. After their king receives the imperial command, perhaps, because he has not achieved his desires, he will be disappointed and, relying on his far-off location, seek excuses to make trouble.[26]

The only "discontinuity" between the king and Macartney is that it is impossible to reprimand the king in person; it is necessary to send an imperial letter. As we shall see presently, Qianlong was convinced that the successful conclusion of the negotiations over the rituals for Macartney's audience resulted from Heshen and the Grand Council chastising the ambassador face-to-face. That the English king could not be similarly instructed was thus a major concern. Consequently, Qianlong was not simply worried about the embassy stirring up trouble in Canton but about trouble beginning with the far-off English king. Once he has received George's letter, Qianlong is well aware of the fact that there is more involved here than the improper handling of the embassy.

If we were simply dealing with a young scholar whose command of classical Chinese was uncertain, one might be more forgiving of errors such as these. But Professor Hevia is an associate editor of the journal *Positions* and, as I have noted, is purposefully seeking to "destabilize the taken-for-granted relationship between sources (facts) and interpretation." This stance is justified by a body of theory derived from literary studies that rejects any fixed meaning of a text and objects to "privileging" any particular reading or understanding of a text. Such theory provides marvellous freedom for those of great imagination but seems particularly inappropriate when applied to official documentary sources.[27]

The texts in question are edicts and memorials of the Qing bureaucracy. Like any large organization, the Qing bureaucracy required that its internal communications be as clear and unambiguous as possible. It was necessary that the emperor and his ministers have a common understanding of the documents. It is this requirement that produced the conventional phrases with well-established meanings and well-known classical allusions that we are discussing here—phrases that were clear and unambiguous to all contemporary readers and should be equally clear to modern scholars of the period. If we are to understand properly the nature of Qing rule, we need to stick to these conventional meanings and be a good deal more restrained in our imaginings. It would be a tremendous disservice to our field if strengths in cultural theory and imagination were recognized as acceptable substitutes for a basic command of the Chinese language.

GUEST RITUAL IN EIGHTEENTH-CENTURY CHINA

At this point, I would like to turn to the question of ritual. It goes without saying that the ritual texts that Hevia analyzes in his chapter on "Guest Ritual and Interdomainal Relations" are similar to bureaucratic communications in the effort be as unambiguous as possible. Indeed, the great bulk of the chapter on "guest ritual" (*binli* 賓禮) in the *Da-Qing tongli* (大清通禮) consists of the careful delineation of the ritual protocol for tributary missions. It is difficult to read in these texts much room for the sort of agency that Hevia wishes to find in the ritual process. It is, therefore, unsurprising that he translates only from the preface to the section. Unfortunately, even here he has problems, and I must beg the reader's indulgence for one last foray into the sources and their translation. Hevia breaks up the brief preface into three parts, indicated by the ellipses below:

> In the *Rites of Zhou* the Grand Conductors of Affairs (*Daxingren* 大行人) handled (*zhang* 掌) the rites and ceremonies of the guest. Kingdoms external to the nine provinces were called foreign kingdoms (*fanguo* 蕃國). Each of these kingdoms took its most precious things (*guibao* 貴寶) to be the offering (*zhi* 摯).... In our time the enunciated teachings of the imperial family (*guojia shengjiao* 國家聲教) have reached the various peoples of the four directions who come as guests. The various kingdoms from beyond the mountains and seas have recorded this. For over a hundred years, the Board of Rites, by Imperial Order, has feasted and rewarded them.... Various ceremonial canonical writings have been examined, combined, and thus compiled to make Guest Ritual. (118)

The problems here are largely of punctuation, so in the interest of space, let me simply give a more accurate translation, with a few endnotes to guide the reader:

> In the *Rites of Zhou*, the Senior Messenger[28] handles the rites and ceremonies of guests. Outside the nine provinces are [places] called the barbarian domains. Each of these takes its valuable and precious things as offerings. Our state's prestige and civilizing influence[29] reach to the four barbarians (*siyi* 四姨) and guests come from the various domains in the mountains and seas beyond the frontier. [These visits] have been recorded in the Ministry of Rites for over one hundred years. There are detailed and complete documents on rituals involving imperial patents and enfeoffments, banquets, and gifts. Therefore, we compile these into [a protocol] on guest ritual.[30]

The key point here is that it is not the foreign domains that have been recording these visits. That would be of little concern to the Qing court. It is the Board of Rites that, since the founding of the dynasty, has been collecting complete records of tribute missions and other rituals involving foreign lands, and now it is time to compile these into a definitive text on "guest ritual."

Properly translated, it is easy to see in this preface the application to foreign relations of a process of searching for ritual origins, studying past practices, and compiling the results in an authoritative ritual text—a process of ritual codification that affected many spheres of life in eighteenth-century China.[31] It should be possible to study this eighteenth-century attention to ritual without recourse to pejorative connotations that dichotomize ritual and rationality as symbolic of traditional and modern forms of social intercourse—connotations to which Hevia quite properly objects. The recent anthropological treatment of ritual as a "'strategic mode of practice'" is both useful and apt.[32] Similarly, interpreting ritual as a process—and often a contested process—and more than simply the "rote repetition of a body of fixed rules" (131) aids our understanding of any ritual encounter. On all of these counts, Hevia has introduced a useful conceptual vocabulary to enrich our understanding of Qing court ritual.

At the same time, we must not allow a modern (or postmodern) anthropological approach to ritual practice to obscure the significance of the eighteenth-century Chinese commitment to ritual codification. The very purpose of compilations such as the *Da-Qing tongli* was to establish and promote proper ritual to restore order to a world perceived as increasingly guided by vulgar and heterodox customs.[33] These rituals were generally regarded as fixed in heaven. In the words of the great eighteenth-century scholar Dai Zhen, "Rituals are the organizing principles of heaven and earth; they are the perfect rules, only those who understand heaven will know them."[34] This, indeed, was what distinguished the Qing imperium from "barbarians" such as the British, who, in their ignorance, did not understand ritual. Thus, the above-cited court letter of September 23 explicitly contrasts "the rituals and laws of the Celestial Court" (*Tianchao lifa* 天朝禮法) with the categorically different "customs" (*fengsu* 風俗) of the British.[35]

Rituals anywhere are always represented as fixed by nature, the gods, or tradition, and the Qing institutional commitment to ritual codification added to the rigidity of ritual protocol. This does not in any way preclude the strategic use of ritual, the contesting of these protocols in practice, or their strategic alteration in extraordinary circumstances. But it adds to the symbolic approach to ritual a recognition of the fact that ritual also played a regulating and legitimating function. It should be possible to recognize that particular rituals legitimate particular political and social formations. (In this case, tribute mission ritual both symbolized and legitimated a sinocentric [or at least a Qing-centric] political order.) In such instances, a rigid adherence to ritual may well reflect an unrealistic effort to preserve a doomed institutional form. Hevia rejects such functionalism because it represents a claim to "knowledge . . . superior to that of historical Chinese subjects" (20). I would argue that the Qing state was quite aware of the legitimating function of ritual, so no superior claim is necessary on the question of ritual function. As for the unrealistic nature of Qing ritual rigidity, I have no difficulty in claiming that the combination of historical hindsight and the accumulated knowledge gained from modern historical and social science does allow us to see that the expansive force of European (and especially British) capitalism made the Qing tribute system unsustainable, and that insight does allow us to claim knowledge superior to the Chinese court of the eighteenth century.

I would revise Hevia's account to give the following interpretation of the role of ritual in the Macartney mission to Qianlong's court. We must begin by recognizing that both sides regarded ritual as extremely important. It was precisely because of his own understanding of the symbolic impact of ritual that

Macartney refused to kowtow. When he proposed a compromise—he would kowtow to the emperor if one of the emperor's officials of similar rank would kowtow to a portrait of King George—it was one that explicitly signified an equivalence of the two sovereigns.

For his part, the Qianlong emperor was initially quite favorably disposed to the embassy, which was reported to him as a tribute-bearing mission from a king with sincere intentions, whose ambassador was behaving in a reverent and submissive (*gongshun* 恭順) manner.[36] Soon after hearing of the embassy's impending arrival, Qianlong proposed following the precedent of the Portuguese embassy of 1753,[37] an important point since that embassy involved several departures from the protocols detailed in the *Da-Qing tongli* for imperial audiences (most important, the Portuguese ambassador kneeled on one knee and was permitted to present his king's letter directly to the emperor).[38] Later, Qianlong indicated his willingness to adjust ritual forms to make things go smoothly and severely chastised the embassy's Manchu escort for insisting on the fine points of ceremony.[39] On the other hand, he was very anxious that the imperial audience be performed according to the established protocol, and his officials (understandably) were even more concerned that their sovereign be properly honored—and that they not be held personally responsible for any ritual breech in the audience ceremony. In all of this process, it was necessary that court rituals be represented as fixed and inflexible. No one would dare suggest otherwise, certainly not to Macartney, not even to other members of the bureaucracy.[40] As problems with the embassy continued, the court's attitude hardened, and on the day of Macartney's arrival in Rehe, a draft proposal for the imperial audience was presented involving strict adherence to the protocols for "guest ritual" in the *Da-Qing tongli*.[41]

When Macartney arrived in Rehe and his proposal for the ritual equivalence of Qianlong and King George was presented, a crisis loomed, which was only resolved by several days of delicate negotiations. Peyrefitte's sinologist-assistant, Pierre-Henri Durand, has provided a brilliant analysis of these negotiations and the resolution of the ritual issue.[42] He does so by painstakingly comparing the Chinese and English record, an exercise that Hevia deliberately avoids in his effort to emphasize "the different conceptual frameworks that Qing and British actors brought to the encounter" (xii). In this, Hevia certainly reflects a tendency in much postmodern scholarship to focus on the representation of an event rather than the event itself. The problem is that in this case, the two are inseparable, even for Hevia. Central to his mission is demonstrating Qing flexibility on ritual issues. To demonstrate that flexibility, it is necessary to understand what actually happened in Macartney's audience with the emperor. This has always been a point of contention in the history of the mission, for as Pritchard noted long ago, and Durand reiterates, the Chinese sources deny any departure from Chinese ritual protocol, while the English sources insist that Macartney followed the Western practice of kneeling on one knee before the emperor.[43] Hevia's solution to this dilemma is both simple and remarkable: he accepts the accounts of Macartney and Staunton (168–69). So much for understanding ritual encounters in the Qing's own terms!

Durand's analysis of the documentary record is far more thorough, careful, subtle, and illuminating. He argues that in the negotiations over the audience ritual, both sides needed to compromise, but both also needed to save face and to be able to report its own version of events for the historical record. He also notes that the English and Chinese contemporary records agree on the tension of the initial standoff following the presentation of Macartney's proposal, which provoked angry edicts from the emperor on September 9 and 10. Resolution was reached by the 11th, when the emperor reported that following stern admonitions from the grand councillor and imperial favorite Heshen, the English had shown remorse and dread (*huiju* 悔懼), become "sincerely submissive," and shown that they "respect the laws and regulations of our heavenly dynasty."[44] As Peyrefitte had suggested before, and Durand argues with even more convincing detail, the compromise was almost certainly that the British should follow the precedent of the Portuguese embassy and perform a modified kowtow in which they would kneel on one knee three times and bow three times with each kneeling. Macartney could then claim that he only kneeled, and the Chinese could claim that the three kneelings and nine prostrations had been performed.[45]

In all of this, several additional points must be clearly recognized. The Qianlong emperor and his court were intensely interested in the progress of the embassy, but that interest was almost exclusively focused on the ritual behavior and manifest attitudes (respectfully submissive or wilfully arrogant) of its leaders, the size and portability of its tribute, and the expense of provisioning the large English retinue. Macartney's efforts to show off the scientific advances of the West failed utterly: neither the emperor nor his ministers showed any interest in astronomical instruments or experimental demonstrations. Macartney's efforts to secure diplomatic representation in Beijing were dismissed out of hand, and no interest was shown in increasing trade. Indeed, by focusing on the ritual of the embassy, Hevia has missed one of the ironies of this history: on ritual matters, Qianlong's court was willing to make tactical adjustments, but on the substantive issues of diplomatic representation and increased trade, there was no compromise at all. Ritual thus proved more flexible than the institutional arrangements of the Chinese *tizhi*. There is no getting around the decisive import of Qianlong's letter to King George: "we have never valued ingenious articles, nor do we have the slightest need of your country's manufactures."[46]

Given all of this, it is rather difficult to accept Hevia's argument that the encounter was "not a question of cross-cultural misunderstanding." It was precisely that (in addition to being the collision of two conflicting imperialisms). One element of that misunderstanding was the Qing court's complete focus on the ritual manipulation of this "tribute mission," to the exclusion of any serious consideration of Macartney's efforts to increase trade, open diplomatic representation, and educate (or, more accurately, impress) the Qing with a clearer apprehension of recent advances in Western science and technology.

METHODOLOGY AND THE POLITICS OF POSTCOLONIAL SCHOLARSHIP

Finally, let us turn to the methodological and political positions taken in this work. Hevia states his postmodern position forthrightly:

> Reconstructing the past is not simply about bringing new evidence to light, applying new methodologies, or exposing previous biases. It is also about engaging in the politics of the production and distribution of knowledge with which all scholarship is involved. At issue, then, is not how to make accounts *less* interested or *less* ideological, but how to locate our own historiography in relation to multiple interpretative positions and the structures of power that we deal with daily. (226)

I have no difficulty in agreeing to the first two sentences in this passage: all good scholarship has political implications. When we engage in scholarly debate and controversy, political positions are revealed and tested. But I cannot accept the notion that what matters is only how we "locate our historiography in relation to . . . the structures of power," or that we are under no obligation to be "less interested or less ideological." Especially given Hevia's previously stated intent "to destabilize the taken-for-granted relationship between sources (facts) and interpretation" (225), the historian is here released from any obligation to see that his or her interpretation squares with the sources. Nor is he or she required to minimize personal biases or ideological positions in reading such sources in an effort to produce an accurate reconstruction of the past. This strikes me as both methodologically indefensible and politically suicidal. How can we expect our scholarship to be persuasive beyond a community of committed true believers if it places greater value on a correct political position than an accurate representation of the past? Politically effective scholarship must be founded on some credible claims to truth value that can be recognized even by those holding different political views.

Hevia's approach is quite different, but he is honest enough to show how his political position drives his interpretation of the Macartney mission. George Macartney—together with Adam Smith, Edward Gibbon, James Boswell, and others—was a member of the Literary Club in London. There they engaged in debate and "manly conversation" (Gibbon's phrase) as part of a broader public sphere in eighteenth-century England. When he got to China, Macartney and his colleagues used "the valorized attributes of public sphere culture" (including its objectionable gendering of the idea of open debate) to structure their writings on China (64–65). They engaged in "observation, measurement, calculation, and comparison" and wrote from the position of the "'disinterested' observer" (95). In the complex negotiations over ritual for the audience, Macartney saw the Chinese appealing to "immutable laws . . . as a general shield against reason and argument" (102).[47] After the failure of the embassy, the British came to the position that the Chinese would abandon their unreasonable practices only if confronted with firmness and force—which is what happened in the Opium War and subsequent imperialist wars against China (230).

When modern scholars from Fairbank to Pritchard to Wills returned to the study of this mission, they held that the Qing insisted on the forms of the tribute system because it functioned to legitimate its rule (Fairbank) or because the Chinese rulers focused excessively on ceremonial appearances (Wills). In either case, "they are very much entrenched in the pervasive Euro-American intellectual practices that Said and others have identified as Orientalism; they are also part of more general cultural projects that have served to constitute the 'West' as a privileged area of intellectual, political, and economic activity since at least the middle of the last century" (17–18). Not only do interpretations that "apply 'objectivist' Western theory, particularly social science models, to non-Western data" serve to privilege the West (7), but they also suggest that "the Qing government must bear the responsibility not only for its own collapse, but for Western gunboat diplomacy as well" (19). Therefore, all such scholarship serves to apologize for imperialism, and since we evaluate scholarship by the standards of political correctness, all of this must be rejected.

While it is clear what Hevia is against, it is less clear what he is arguing for. Like most postmodern scholarship, political critique eclipses any discussion of the political alternative to an Enlightenment public sphere. But the problems and the political naïveté of Hevia's position are revealed when he briefly treats recent Chinese scholarship on the Macartney mission. He is clearly disappointed to see Chinese scholars who "appear (wittingly or not) to reproduce Euro-American interpretations of Sino-Western conflict" (243). His only explanation is that they are simply "appropriating the intellectual framework of the colonizers" (246)—victims, it would seem, of auto-Orientalizing. He seems blind to the fact that his dismissal of Chinese scholarship on Macartney and the Qing reproduces perfectly the Eurocentric colonial position: these poor backward Chinese are unable to understand the latest advances in Western theory—in this case, postmodern and postcolonial discourse.[48]

A moment's reflection suggests that our Chinese colleagues are not necessarily so mindlessly gullible as Hevia suggests. To Chinese scholars, the open debate of "public sphere culture" and the emerging scientific spirit of "observation, measurement, calculation, and comparison"—indeed, the whole complex of Enlightenment values that Macartney represented—do not appear particularly threatening. American scholars can enjoy all the material comforts of modern life while criticizing the discourse of modernity, but Chinese scholars recognize that scientific-technological advances are required for comparable improvements in the lives of the Chinese people. Accordingly, they have no difficulty in criticizing Qianlong's arrogance and illusions of self-sufficiency and chastising him for a lack of interest in Western technical achievements.[49] The self-righteous critique of modernity is much more difficult for those still struggling to help their country modernize.

As one who has also been a critic of imperialism in China and an advocate for an anti-imperialist scholarship,[50] I would have to say that this is one of the most troubling aspects of the new postcolonial scholarship represented by Hevia and his colleagues in *Positions*. Postcolonial scholarship expands the earlier generation's anti-imperialist critique of Western and Japanese military, political, and economic exploitation of China and other countries in Asia to include a critique of the "colonial" culture of modernity, rationality, science, and technology. Any Asian who advocates these things is "appropriating the intellectual framework of the colonizers." There is a disturbing arrogance in critiquing Chinese scholars for being "thoroughly modernist, and hostile or dismissive toward the concerns and beliefs of the Qing leaders" (246). The postcolonial critics seem to be suggesting that the Chinese should keep their minds and their aspirations back in the Qing (and safely exotic) rather than aspire to the modernity of the West. I would submit that the effect of this critique is to deny to Asians and other Third World peoples the necessary intellectual and political tools to modernize and strengthen their countries to defend themselves against imperialism.

Finally, we should not be surprised that Chinese scholars are wary of an academic regime that judges scholarship by its political position. They have lived in a world where there is no obligation to maintain a connection between source and interpretation or to be less ideological, and where the critical standard is the correctness of one's political position. In such a regime, political correctness will inevitably be determined by those with power. It is little wonder that Chinese historians are more comfortable with the slogan "seek truth from facts" than with the postmodern position of scholars such as Hevia.

We may find such contemporary Chinese scholars excessively positivist, with too much faith in a knowable objective truth. But we need not believe in an absolute truth to insist that the meaning of historical sources is not infinitely elastic. We must recognize, as our Chinese colleagues do, what Appleby, Hunt, and Jacob have called "the benefits of a shared commitment to objective knowledge." Appleby et al. have redefined historical objectivity as an "interactive relationship between an inquiring subject and an external object." A commitment to this social and processual definition of objectivity "forces people to examine rigorously the relationship between what they bring to their subject and what they find; it undergirds methodological rules that facilitate debate; it encourages people to perform the arduous task of knowledge-seeking."[51] This sort of commitment provides, for our Chinese colleagues, the only protection they have from the political dictates of the state. I would submit that a similar commitment on our part might provide some protection from the imaginative excesses of scholars such as James L. Hevia.

NOTES

1. James L. Hevia, *Cherishing Men from Afar: Qing Guest Ritual and the Macartney Embassy of 1793* (Durham, NC: Duke University Press, 1995).

2. Earl F. Pritchard, *The Crucial Years of Early Anglo-Chinese Relations, 1750–1800* (New York: Octagon, 1970 [original: 1936]).

3. Earl F. Pritchard, "The kowtow in the Macartney embassy to China in 1793," *Far Eastern Quarterly* 2, no. 2 (February 1943): 163–203.

4. J. K. Fairbank and S. Y. Teng, "On the Ch'ing tributary system," *Harvard Journal of Asiatic Studies* 6 (1941): 135–246.

5. J. L. Cranmer-Byng, *An Embassy to China, Being a Journal Kept by Lord Macartney during His Embassy to the Emperor Ch'ien-lung, 1793–1794* (London: Longmans, 1962).

6. Alain Peyrefitte, *The Immobile Empire*. Jon Rothschild, trans. (New York: Knopf, 1992 [French original: 1989]).

7. Zhu Yong, *Buyuan dakai de Zhongguo damen: 18 shiji de waijiao yu Zhongguo mingyun* [The Chinese door that was unwilling to open: Eighteenth century foreign relations and China's fate] (Nanchang: Jiangxi Remnin chubanshe, 1989).

8. Hevia, *Cherishing Men*, back cover.

9. Rather than burdening this text with excessive footnotes, all references to Hevia's book will be noted by page numbers within parentheses.

10. John E. Wills Jr., *Embassies and Illusions: Dutch and Portuguese Envoys to K'ang-hsi, 1666–1687* (Cambridge, MA: Council on East Asian Studies, Harvard University, 1984.)

11. Joseph Fletcher, "Ch'ing Inner Asia, c. 1800" and "The Heyday of the Ch'ing Order in Mongolia, Sinkiang and Tibet," in Denis Twitchett and John King Fairbank, eds., *The Cambridge History of China*, vol. 10, Part I (London: Cambridge University Press, 1978), 35–106, 351–406; David Farquhar, "Emperor as Bodhisattva in the Governance of the Ch'ing Empire," *Harvard Journal of Asiatic Studies* 38 (1978): 5–34; Pamela Crossley, "The Rulerships of China," *American Historical Review* 97, no. 5 (1992): 1468–83; Mark C. Elliott, "Resident aliens: the Manchu experience in China, 1644–1760" (PhD diss., University of California, Berkeley, 1993) [Later published as *The Manchu Way: The Eight Banners and Ethnic Identity in Late Imperial China* (Stanford, CA: Stanford University Press, 2001)]; Ning Chia, "The Lifanyuan and the Inner Asian Rituals of the Early Qing (1644–1795)," *Late Imperial China* 14, no. 1 (1993): 61–92.

12. For the reader's convenience, I have included the characters here in the text, which was not possible in the original article.

13. Peyrefitte, *Immobile Empire*, 68.

14. See Kai-Wing Chow, review of *Cherishing Men from Afar, American Historical Review* 102, no. 3 (June 1997): 867–68.

15. Frederic Wakeman, "The English Lord and the Chinese Emperor," *Washington Post Book World* 23, no. 13 (28 March 1993): 11.

16. First Historical Archives, ed., *Yingshi Majia'erni fanghua dang'an shiliao huibian* [Collection of archival materials on the Macartney Embassy to China], hereafter cited as YSSL (Beijing: Guoji wenhua chubanshe, 1996). I am indebted to Perry Anderson for calling my attention to this publication and to Zhu Yong for helping me find a copy in Beijing.

17. I would like to acknowledge the assistance of Benjamin Elman, Philip Huang, and Zhang Longxi in elucidating the meaning and classical origins of this phrase.

18. *Ciyuan* (Beijing: Commercial Press, 1988), 636; Morohashi Tetsuji, (1950) *Dai Kan-Wa jiten* [Great Chinese-Japanese dictionary] (Tokyo, 1950; Taipei reprint), vol. 4: 4622.

19. James Legge, *The Chinese Classics*, second edition, revised vol. 1: *Confucian Analects, The Great Learning, and the Doctrine of the Mean* (Taipei reprint: n.d.), 409–10.

20. *Compact Edition of the Oxford English Dictionary* (New York: Oxford University Press, 1971), vol. 1, 391.

21. *Zhanggu congbian* [Collected texts for grasping antiquity] (Beijing: Palace Museum, 1928–1930): 7/54a.

22. For a contrasting interpretation, see Peyrefitte, *Immobile Empire*, 266.

23. *Zhanggu congbian*, 8/64b.

24. Qianlong repeats very similar language at least twice in explaining his rejection of an English ambassador in Beijing. In both cases, instead of the compound

wuwei, which might be rendered as "senseless" (that is "pointless," but not "nonsense"), he uses the compound *wuyi* (無益, "without benefit") (Zhu Yong, *Buyuan dakai*, 238, 257). I have thus rendered *wuwei* as "useless," a translation also suggested by Mathews' *Chinese English Dictionary*, 1069.

25. *Zhanggu congbian*, 4/32b, 7/41a.

26. Ibid., 8/64b.

27. Hevia's discussion of the court's rejection of one of Macartney's requests regarding trade illustrates the extent of the liberties he feels entitled to take with his sources. He reports that the grand councillors "could only conclude that he [Macartney] was still ignorant (*wuzhi*) of court protocols." A footnote explains that "the record actually says that the emperor's servants have concluded that the ambassador *did* understand the relations (*shang zhi tizhi* 尚知體制) [*Zhanggu congbian*, 8/60a]. "Based on what preceded this observation and what follows . . . I believe this to be a misprint in the collection being considered here." (Hevia, 182) The original memorial survives in the Shangyudang and has been reproduced in the YSSL (153–54). Had Hevia taken the trouble to consult it in the archives, he would have discovered that there is no misprint in the *Zhanggu congbian* collection. His reading is purely the product of his own imaginings.

28. Charles Hucker, *A Dictionary of Official Titles in Imperial China* (Stanford, CA: Stanford University Press, 1985), 466. Hucker notes that this official was responsible for the receptions of feudal lords (*zhuhou* 諸侯) at the royal court during the Zhou and that the term continued as an unofficial reference to the Chief Minister of the Court of State Ceremonial (Honglusi 鴻臚寺).

29. A reference to *Ciyuan* (1377) would have saved Hevia from reading *shengjiao* as "enunciated teachings" and also provided a critical classical allusion: the phrase comes from the "Tribute of Yu" section of the Book of Documents (*Shangshu*).

30. *Da-Qing tongli*, 1756 (vol. 655 of Taiwan Commercial Press reprint) 43/1a.

31. Kai-wing Chow, *The Rise of Confucian Ritualism in Late Imperial China: Ethics, Classics, and Lineage Discourse* (Stanford, CA: Stanford University Press, 1994); Angela Zito, "Grand Sacrifice as Text/Performance: Ritual and Writing in Eighteenth Century China" (PhD diss., University of Chicago, 1989), chap. 4.

32. Hevia, *Cherishing*, 21, quoting Catherine Bell, *Ritual Theory, Ritual Practice* (New York: Oxford University Press, 1992).

33. *Da-Qing tongli*, imperial preface.

34. Cited in Chow, *Confucian Ritual*, 189. I have slightly altered Chow's translation, based on a suggestion from Benjamin Elman (who generously supplied the original text) and reference to Morohashi Tetsuji's *Dai Kan-Wa jiten*.

35. *Zhanggu congbian*, 8/64b; cf. 5/31b.

36. *Zhanggu congbian*, 1/2b, 6/32b.

37. *Da-Qing Gaozong chao (Qianlong) huangdi shilu* (Taipei reprint, n.d.: 1421/6a), hereafter cited as *QSL*; YSSL, 92.

38. Hevia believes that the Portuguese precedent was first suggested by the Shandong governor Jiqing and cites his memorial of Qianlong 58/1/21 (3/3/1793) as evidence that "local officials were not passive recipients of orders from the court" (139). In fact, had he read the memorial correctly, he would have realized that Jiqing

in this instance was precisely a passive recipient of court orders, for the passage in question is clearly indicated (by the terminal *qinci* 欽此) as a direct quote from the edict published in the *Shilu*.

39. *Zhanggu congbian*, 5/25; Hevia, 156–57.
40. *Zhanggu congbian*, 3/18b, 20b; Hevia, 187.
41. YSSL, 146–47.
42. P. D. Durand (Dai Tingjie) "Jianting ze ming—Majia'erni shihua zaitan" [Listening to it, it becomes clear: A new look at the Macartney mission], YSSL, preface, 114–29.
43. Pritchard, "The kowtow;" Durand, "Jianting," 114.
44. YSSL, 51, 149.
45. Peyrefitte, *Immobile Empire*, 224–25; Durand, "Jianting," 117–29.
46. Peyrefitte, *Immobile Empire*, 291. I have corrected "manufacturers," an apparent typo, to "manufactures" in this passage. The original is in the YSSL, 165–66. Although Chinese scholars have quite uniformly criticized Qianlong's disinterest in Western science (Dai Yi, *Qianlong di ji qi shidai* [The Qianlong emperor and his times]. [Beijing: Renmin daxue chubanshe, 1992]; Zhu Yong, *Buyuan dakai*), some American scholars have questioned his alleged lack of concern. Joanna Waley-Cohen opens her article on "China and Western Technology in the Late Eighteenth Century" with this quote from Qianlong's letter. But she reads it as a "piece of propaganda" by an emperor who "preferred not to admit publicly his interest in and awareness of the potential of foreign technology" (Joanna Waley-Cohen, "China and Western Technology in the Late Eighteenth Century," *American Historical Review* 98, [December 5, 1993]: 1525–44). Reading the statement as propaganda occasioned by Macartney's effort to open China to trade is somewhat problematic, given that edicts of 1759 and 1761 use almost exactly the same language in denying China's need for foreign goods (Zhu Yong, 78, 80). To demonstrate Qing interest in Western technology, Waley-Cohen concentrates on the example of artillery, but her argument is hardly compelling. She notes the contributions of the Jesuits Adam Schall and Ferdinand Verbiest in teaching the early Qing the science of gunnery, then notes that Schall's text of 1643 was reprinted in 1841 at the height of the Opium War, and Verbiest's 200-year-old cannon designs were also still in use at that time. She goes to great length to detail the contribution of the Jesuit Felix de Rocha to the Qing's southwestern campaigns in 1777, but his contribution seems to have been to point out the lessons of Schall's manual of 150 years earlier on the importance of calculating the angle of fire. When one compares this to the contemporaneous Japanese *Rangaku* scholars' study of Western technology, this continued use of centuries-old military technology is not terribly impressive.
47. Here Hevia is citing Cranmer-Byng, *An Embassy to China*, 153.
48. I am indebted to Zhang Longxi for pointing out the full implications of Hevia's position.
49. Dai Yi, *Qianlong*, 425–32; Zhu Yong, *Buyuan dakai*, 282–308.
50. See the first chapter in this collection.
51. Joyce Appleby, Lynn Hunt, and Margaret Jacob, *Telling the Truth about History* (New York: Norton, 1994), 261, 269.

Part II

A DIVERSE AND CHANGING CHINA

Chapter Three

Local Elites: Resources and Strategies

When the modern China field developed in the United States in the 1950s and 1960s, the focus was very much on what Fairbank had termed "China's Response to the West."* Much of the scholarship done in this period concerned such key events as the Opium War, missionary incidents, the foreign-administered Imperial Maritime Customs, intellectual responses to the Western impact, foreign sympathizers of Sun Yat-sen's revolutionary movement, and, as one moved into the republican era, the role of missionary-sponsored universities and hospitals, and the Western-inspired currents of thought in the New Culture and May Fourth Movement.† In chapter 1, we have seen one reaction to this scholarship: its underestimation of the negative effects of imperialism. A second issue was this scholarship's suggestion (and sometimes explicit assertion) that China had been uniformly static before the impact of the West. In reaction to this, there was a growing attention to domestically generated change in China.

In the conventional historiography and mass media representations, imperial China was a stable, unified empire ruled by a core of mandarins selected

---

* This was the title of an influential documentary collection widely used in courses on modern China: Teng Ssu-yu and John K. Fairbank, *China's Response to the West: A Documentary Survey, 1839–1923* (Cambridge, MA: Harvard University Press, 1979).

† Representative titles would include John King Fairbank, *Trade and Diplomacy on the China Coast: The Opening of the Treaty Ports, 1842–1854* (Cambridge, MA: Harvard University Press, 1953); Paul A. Cohen, *China and Christianity: The Missionary Movement and the Growth of Chinese Antiforeignism, 1860–1870* (Cambridge, MA: Harvard University Press, 1963); Joseph R. Levenson, *Liang Ch'i-ch'ao and the Mind of Modern China* (Cambridge, MA: Harvard University Press, 1959); Tse-tsung Chow, *The May Fourth Movement: Intellectual Revolution in Modern China* (Cambridge, MA: Harvard University Press, 1960); Harold Z. Schiffrin, *Sun Yat-sen and the Origins of the Chinese Revolution* (Berkeley: University of California Press, 1970); Philip West, *Yenching University and Sino-Western Relations* (Cambridge, MA: Harvard University Press, 1976). Much of this literature, or Fairbank's summary in his textbooks, dominated my undergraduate education at Harvard.

through examinations in the Confucian classics. Dynasties might rise and fall, but the bureaucratic system endured. Western scholars and modern Chinese nationalists agreed that the old regime was unified, conservative, and resistant to change. As historians of modern China in the United States, Europe and Japan joined disciplinary trends toward social history, both the diversity of China and its capacity for change became more apparent. By the 1980s, after the United States and China established diplomatic relations and opportunities opened for archival and field work, the local and regional diversity of China became both a matter of personal experience and an object of academic research. In addition, it became clear that the old image of an unchanging China with a strong state that dominated society was seriously flawed.

While many of my generation were researching the twentieth century, our mentors were overwhelmingly historians of the Qing. It was, accordingly, the transition from the late empire to the republican era that consumed our attention as we sought to understand both the decline of the Confucian order and the origins of China's modern revolutions. Work on modern China was already showing that at the local level, Chinese society was exceptionally diverse: the imperial state and the uniform written language masked great variation in local ecologies, village and kinship structures, communications, dialects, degrees of commercialization, and social organization. At the same time, it was clear that Chinese society was anything but static: population, marketing systems, tenancy relations, and cropping patterns were all changing. Older notions of a gentry society of examination-degree-holding elites needed adjustment. We needed to devise new conceptual categories to analyze these changes.

This chapter proposes a more flexible and dynamic approach to analyzing Chinese elites. It goes beyond old definitions of the gentry in terms of examination degrees by specifying the geographical or functional arenas that elites dominated, and then identifying the resources—material, social, personal, or symbolic—and the strategies that elites deployed to gain and maintain their status. This approach allows us to examine informal networks linking elites, patronage bonds, brokerage, cultural hegemony, and the way in which all of these changed over time. This chapter is adapted from the "Introduction" and "Conclusion" to a volume on *Local Elites and Patterns of Dominance*, co-authored with the late Mary B. Rankin. The original essays were so much a joint production that I find it impossible to identify my own contribution, though the abbreviated version included here is my own.

The *Local Elites* volume was the result of a workshop in Banff attended by a number of young scholars who later went on to distinguished careers in the field: Stephen Averill, Timothy Brook, Prasenjit Duara, William Rowe, Keith Schoppa, David Strand, Madeleine Zelin, and others. Their papers, cited in the notes, provided much of the substantive scholarship on which this chapter is based. As historians of modern China, we were all interested in the ways in which traditional degree-holding gentry families were able to use their status, connections, and symbolic capital to maintain elite status in the modern era as businessmen, intellectuals, military men, or technical experts. I would later explore this phenomenon in *Ancestral Leaves*, a history of one elite family from the Qing, through the Republic, and into the People's Republic of China.

The evidence for elite continuity that comes from a more dynamic conception of Chinese local elites has important implications of our understanding of contemporary China and the Chinese Revolution. Both the persistence of the old elite and the flexible strategies of networking, brokerage, and patronage that allowed it to maintain its dominance help to explain the Communists' resort to violence in land reform and the campaigns against "counter-revolutionaries" to exterminate and discredit the old ruling class. At the same time, culturally legitimated strategies of networking and patronage are certainly linked to the persistent reliance on connections (*guanxi* 關係) within the socialist system.

LOCAL ELITES AND PATTERNS OF DOMINANCE[*]

The revered Chinese philosopher Mencius wrote: "There are pursuits proper to great men and pursuits proper to lesser men. . . . Therefore it is said, 'Some labor with their hands, and some labor with their minds. Those who labor with their minds govern others. Those who labor with their hands are governed by others. Those who are governed provide food for others. Those who govern are provided with food by others.' This is universally regarded as just."[1] Until the nineteenth century, all complex civilizations accepted the notion that society was hierarchically ordered, that wealth and status would be unequally distributed, that certain people were properly qualified to rule, and that men and women owed deference to their social "betters." It was taken for granted that a society would have an elite. The only question was the type of elite it should be. Would a single elite monopolize wealth, status, and power? Or did merchants, for example, have more wealth, aristocrats more status, and state functionaries more power?

When Western scholars asked such questions about China, they readily associated elite status with office holding and the bureaucratic state. From a European perspective, the autocratic power of China's imperial bureaucracy

---

[*] Edited and abbreviated from the "Introduction" and "Concluding Remarks," co-authored with Mary B. Rankin, in Joseph W. Esherick and Mary B. Rankin, eds., *Chinese Local Elites and Patterns of Dominance* (Berkeley: University of California Press, 1990), 1–24, 305–45. Reprinted with permission.

was overwhelming: here was an enormous land of 400 million people ruled over by a bureaucracy of imperially appointed officials who qualified for office through state-sponsored examinations open to all, without regard to wealth or family pedigree.[2] This view of an all-powerful state readily associated elite status with state service. Thus Max Weber began his essay on Chinese society with the judgment that "for twelve centuries social rank in China has been determined more by qualifications for office than by wealth."[3] In a similar vein, the sinologist Etiènne Balazs wrote of "the uninterrupted continuity of the ruling class of scholar-officials."[4]

Weber focused on a unique, unified Chinese elite: the literati, and the Confucian culture they embodied. Both Weber and Balazs stressed the weakness of competing elites in China. The absence of a hereditary landed aristocracy or clerical hierarchy was one obvious contrast to Europe, but Weber and Balazs were particularly concerned with explaining the weakness of the bourgeoisie. Chinese cities, they argued, were administrative centers dominated by imperial bureaucrats and Confucian scholar-officials, not self-governing communities of self-confident, world-transforming capitalist entrepreneurs.[5] As a result, the Chinese scholar-official elite ruled uncontested and essentially unchanged for centuries.

Although scholars like Weber and Balazs assumed an essentially homogeneous Chinese elite, this was not simply a political elite of bureaucrats. It also included former officials and potential officials—all those who had passed the examinations and assimilated the ethics and assumptions, the manners and mores of Confucian culture. Out of office, in their native counties, these men were treated with deference due their learning, their potential influence with the bureaucracy, and their families' usually substantial wealth in land. They were the local elite. During the nineteenth century, English diplomatic and missionary writers on China introduced the term "the Chinese gentry" to describe this social group, which they considered similar to the nonaristocratic/noncommoner rural landowning class in England. Despite the English terminology, Europeans generally found the Chinese gentry stubbornly conservative, ignorant of the wider world, and fiercely proud.

When Western-trained Chinese social scientists looked at China's traditional elite, they used the same term and shared many of the negative views. To these Chinese nationalists, the gentry, with their commitment to humanistic Confucian education and their disdain for technical knowledge or professional training, were responsible for China's backwardness. In the words of the London-trained anthropologist Fei Hsiao-tung (Fei Xiaotong), the gentry

> monopolized authority based on the wisdom of the past, spent time on literature, and tried to express themselves through art. . . . The vested interests had no wish to improve production but thought only of consolidating privilege. Their

main task was the perpetuation of established norms in order to set up a guide for conventional behavior. A man who sees the world only through human relations is inclined to be conservative because in human relations the end is always mutual adjustment.[6]

Thus, before systematic study of Chinese society began in the mid-twentieth century, there was already a substantial consensus among sociologists and sinologists, Western China hands and Chinese nationalists: China had a single, culturally homogeneous elite called literati, scholar-officials, or gentry. This elite was closely tied to the imperial state, which conferred elite status through the examination system (status which, by the late imperial period, could be passed on to heirs only in limited ways and only by the highest officials) and specified the Confucian curriculum that socialized aspirants for examination degrees. This elite was remarkably enduring, so that one scholar even described the entire period from 206 BCE (the founding of the Han dynasty) to 1948 (the year before the founding of the People's Republic) as one of "gentry society."[7] The gentry's divorce from manual labor and technical knowledge, their conservative commitment to Confucian values, and their stubbornly successful defense of a privileged position in society made them a barrier to technical modernization and economic development.

Studies of the Local Elite

The lowest level of bureaucratic administration in China was the county (*xian* 縣), of which there were 1,436 at the end of the eighteenth century.[8] This meant that, on average, each county magistrate governed almost 300,000 people. By contrast, there were about 3,000 persons per administrator under the old regime in France.[9] Because the "law of avoidance" prevented Chinese officials from serving in their home province, the county magistrate was always an outsider, typically serving three years or less. China's thinly spread and weakly rooted state apparatus had limited ability to penetrate local society, and much of the governance fell to local elites operating outside the formal bureaucracy. Considerable scholarly attention was devoted to dissecting the anatomy of these local elites.

Gentry Studies

The earliest systematic studies of Chinese local elites were done by a generation of Chinese scholars working in American universities who defined Chinese elites as gentry and continued the Weberian tradition of distinguishing them from Western elites. Their concern was the late imperial period—the Ming (1368–1644) and Qing (1644–1911) dynasties—and they focused on the gentry's relationship to the state: their recruitment through the examinations and their service in local governance. Ch'ü T'ung-tsu (Qu Tongzu) stressed the gentry's role as intermediaries between the bureaucracy and the people, a role guaranteed by their legally protected access to local officials whose Confucian culture and training they shared. Ch'ü explicitly treated the gentry as "the local elite."[10] Chang Chung-li (Zhang Zhongli) described the social position of the gentry: their fiscal and legal privileges (favorable land tax rates and immunity from corporal punishment) and their functions in education, public works, local defense, tax collection, and cultural leadership. He also addressed the question of stratification within the gentry and provided a useful estimate of the size of the gentry in the mid-Qing period.

Chang divided the gentry into upper and lower strata. At the top were about 80,000 active and retired civil and military officials, including all who had passed the highest exam and earned the *jinshi* (進士) degree (about 2,500 for the prestigious civil degree). About 8,000 men (combining civil and military) held the provincial *juren* (舉人) degree, but failed to pass the *jinshi* or go on to official roles. The lowest level of the upper gentry was the *gongsheng* (貢生) degree holders, about 27,000 in number. The total size of the upper gentry, including all who qualified for regular appointment to office, was thus about 125,000 people at any given time. The lower gentry were not eligible for regular appointment. There were two main groups of lower gentry: 555,000 *shengyuan* (生員) who had passed the examinations at the county and prefectural level (of whom 460,000 were civil *shengyuan* and the rest military), and 310,000 *jiansheng* (監生), virtually all of whom had purchased the degree. The total size of the degree-holding gentry class was thus about one million individuals, who, with their immediate families, represented about 1.3 percent of the Chinese population.[11]

Ho Ping-ti (He Bingdi) noted the strongly hierarchical organization of Chinese society and focused on the question of social mobility. He hypothesized that substantial mobility into the elite mitigated the inherent injustice of the hierarchical order and thus helped explain the persistent dominance of the gentry class. By analyzing the backgrounds of *jinshi* degree holders, he concluded that the gentry were quite open to new blood, and he stressed "the overwhelming power of the bureaucracy and the ability of the state . . . to regulate the major channels of social mobility."[12] Robert Marsh reached a similar conclusion from a detailed study of 572 Qing officials.[13]

In all these works, the Chinese elite was perceived as equivalent to the gentry class, defined by the single criterion of examination degrees. Chang's second book, *The Income of the Chinese Gentry*, revealed significant occupational diversity within the gentry and underlined the importance of commercial wealth. Nonetheless, by defining elites as holders of state-conferred degrees, all these works stressed elite-state relations more than the role of elites in local society and suggested a uniformity of local elites across China. Little attention was paid to possible variations in elite types—and especially to the possibility that degree-holding gentry might be quite unimportant in some areas. Finally, the fundamentally sociological approach of these works lent a disturbingly static cast to their analysis. Defining eliteness by unchanging imperial degrees, titles, and offices suggested that, despite any mobility, the basic nature of Chinese society remained the same. We were trapped in Balazs's "uninterrupted continuity of a ruling class of scholar-officials."

The State and Local Society

Japanese scholars have been much less concerned with the gentry's links to the central state and more intent on elucidating the socioeconomic foundations of elite power, especially in studies of "gentry landholding." In the Ming dynasty, the gentry were exempt from onerous corvée labor requirements. As a result, many peasants commended land to gentry families to escape the corvée, substantially increasing gentry landholding and decreasing imperial tax revenues. Elite families' widespread use of bond servants gave them a coterie of personal dependents to bolster their domination of local society. According to a Ming document of 1479,

> When moving about [powerful magnates] ride in sedan chairs or on horses and take along a group of three to five bondservant companions (*puban* 僕伴) who follow them on their rounds. Relying on their power and wealth they conspire to occupy the landed property of small peasants (*xiaomin* 小民), forcefully drag away cows and horses and make the children of free people into bondservants (*nu* 奴).[14]

Under the Qing, the commutation of corvée labor duties to tax payments in silver and the elimination of most gentry tax privileges significantly reduced the structural conflict between state and gentry interests. In a widely influential formulation, Shigeta Atsushi saw this new Qing arrangement, not as "gentry landlordism" built on privileged status and personal dependency relations, but as "gentry rule." All scholars agreed that the disappearance of most forms of personal dependency in the seventeenth and eighteenth century made the landlord-tenant dyad much less important. Shigeta's notion of gentry rule was designed to encompass their much broader sociopolitical domination of small peasant landowners. Such freeholders might still rely on local gentry for access to the local magistrate or for paternalistic relief in times of emergency. Though no longer personally dependent on an individual gentry "master," they were socially dependent on a preeminent gentry elite.[15]

Japanese scholarship has been important in elucidating local sources of gentry power as opposed to state-conferred status. Landholding, control of irrigation networks, local relief efforts, and other community activities all tended to serve gentry domination of local society. Several scholars pointed to the appearance of the term *xiangshen* (鄉紳, rural gentry) in the sixteenth century and a growing gentry concern for their position in local society.[16] This scholarship suggested a secular trend toward the localization of elite power parallel to the "localist strategy" of lineage formation, militia organizing, and local marriage alliances that Robert Hymes saw emerging in the Southern Song (1127–1279).[17]

Some of these phenomena can be understood as a cyclical process of elite-state competition for local control. As nomadic pressure weakened the Southern Song state, members of the local elite had less incentive to orient themselves toward a failing central state. The strong state restored by the Ming severely restricted the prerogatives of the local gentry, but gradually the gentry expanded their landholdings and privileges until the state was so weakened that it fell to peasant rebellion and Manchu invasion. With the early Qing state, the pendulum again swung in the direction of strong central government until the mid-nineteenth-century rebellions threatened central bureaucratic control over local society, with rural elites filling the power vacuum. This elite ascendancy is particularly evident in Philip Kuhn's study of gentry militia fighting the Taiping and other rebellions. Local militarization led to "the supremacy of 'gentry managers'" as they assumed ever greater responsibility for local security, tax collection, and public works. The abolition of the examination system in 1905 and the collapse of the imperial system in 1911 did not end gentry rule in China: "China's rural elite survived into the twentieth century and indeed in some respects solidified its position in rural society."[18]

There is a strong tendency for this literature to view elite-state competition as a zero-sum game. The autocratic state seeks full fiscal and coercive power over rural society, while local elites check the state's institutions. Frederic Wakeman suggested a "dynamic oscillation" between integration into the imperial system and autonomy from it.[19] Studies of merchant brokerage and tax-farming proposed a similar process: the state assigned power over local taxes and markets to merchants in order to increase its own revenues, but these powers expanded in the nineteenth and twentieth centuries with the advance of commercialization and the devolution of state power.[20] Nonetheless, most of this literature saw order as the product of state control; elite organizing was a symptom of crisis, conflict, or the disintegration of established order.[21] This tendency provoked one a Middle Eastern specialist to ask:

Would China look different if it were studied as the outcome of individual choices and actions rather than from the perspective of a total system? What would China look like from an approach which emphasized the differences between localities and provinces. . . ? Could informal or illegal phenomena, which seem to "deviate" from the Confucian conception of society and from the systematic ordering of society, be considered substantial realities in their own right rather than variant aspects of the Chinese system? Instead of seeing Chinese institutions as given forms for the organization of Chinese society, could they be interpreted as the outcomes of the informal dynamics of Chinese social life?[22]

Approaches from Local History

By shifting focus from state certification of elite status to the activities of local elites, we see a more diverse elite than the scholar-gentry norm. Early twentieth-century field studies showed a consensus among local residents about who qualified as gentry, yet many of these "gentry" possessed none of the normal academic qualifications. One study from Yunnan in Southwest China found several so-called gentry who rose through corrupt dealings as military officers and one family whose members had killed an opium dealer for his cash, fled, and later returned to establish themselves as respectable merchants and landlords.[23] A similar diversity of late imperial types emerged from local history research of the 1960s and 1970s.

Hilary Beattie's study of Tongcheng, Anhui, directly challenged Chang Chung-li and Ho Ping-ti's focus on degree holders and stressed the importance of land and lineage. She explicitly sought to uncover the "long-term strategy" whereby families maintained elite status over long periods—a conclusion that clearly conflicted with Ho Ping-ti's stress on elite mobility. The strategy she identified was "a joint programme of systematic land investment coupled with education," in which lineage charitable estates protected land from partition and supported education in lineage schools.[24]

Because education for the examinations was still central to Beattie's elite strategy, her local elite remained close to the conventional mold. Johanna Meskill's *Chinese Pioneer Family* expanded the Chinese elite to include local strongmen. In the frontier society of eighteenth- and early-nineteenth-century Taiwan, the local elite perpetuated its local dominance through its military power and control of irrigation. Only at the end of the nineteenth century did families show signs of gentrification and a cultured, literati life-style.[25]

If Meskill's study and the earlier Yunnan field work taught us that frontiers might differ significantly from the "gentry society" norm and that elite society might change significantly over time, Keith Schoppa's study of twentieth-century Zhejiang showed that elites could vary significantly within a single province. Building on a modified version of G. William Skinner's core-periphery analysis, Schoppa found a more diverse, functionally specialized, commercialized, and politically organized elite in the prosperous lowland provincial core; a greater role of new military elites in the intermediate zones; and considerable continuity of entrenched oligarchies in the more isolated, hilly periphery.[26]

Schoppa's work is particularly important in treating the modern transformation of the local elite. Together with Mary Rankin's study of Zhejiang in the late Qing,[27] his book provides a comprehensive picture of elite organizing from the Taiping Rebellion to the accession of the nationalist government in 1927. Instead of disintegrating state power, Rankin and Schoppa see elite activism, social mobilization, and political development at the local level. In their work, local elite activity is much broader, less defensive, and more enduring than the militia organizing stressed by Kuhn. They note the diversity of the local elite and the fusion of merchant and gentry groups, especially in the commercialized core. Contrary to the image of a conservative gentry elite, both scholars demonstrate the elite's readiness to adopt new associational forms—chambers of commerce, educational associations, professional associations, and special interest organizations—following the removal of Qing prohibitions on private associations in the early twentieth century.

QUESTIONS AND CONCEPTS

The growing body of local history work revealed that Chinese local elites were much more diverse, flexible, and changeable than earlier notions of gentry society suggested. Nonetheless, Chinese society remained profoundly hierarchical, and elite families (and the state) paid careful attention to rank, the marks of status, and culturally embedded relations of superior and inferior. People clearly knew who was higher or lower on the social scale.[28] The question for analysts was how to identify, describe, and analyze the dominant individuals and families in local arenas.

This central question suggests several corollaries. What resources and strategies did local elites rely upon to *rise* to local prominence, and to *maintain* their status? How important was the state as either a source of wealth and status, or as a key actor in local political processes? What were the critical arenas of local elite activity, and how were these arenas related to each other? How much continuity was there in the local elite? How different were local elites in different areas of China? What aspects of the local environment explain regional variation in elite types? How did the nature of local elites, and the strategies and resources on which they relied, change over time?

What process effected these changes, and what were the crucial watersheds? In particular, how did twentieth-century elites differ from late imperial elites?

To answer these questions, we have supplemented the familiar Weberian and Marxist analytical categories with concepts used by anthropologists studying individual practices within specific social structures. *We define local elites as individuals or families that exercised dominance within a local arena*, thus deliberately avoiding a definition in terms of one or more of the Weberian categories of wealth, status, and power.[29] Useful as these categories are—and we will use them repeatedly—they often suggest an association of merchants or industrialists with wealth, aristocrats or gentry with status, and government officials with power. If used to *define* an elite, not just to characterize elite types, these categories tend to ossify social reality. One easily loses sight of changing determinants of elite status and the complex interactions of wealth, status, and power. Similarly, without denying the existence of classes in Chinese society, we avoid defining the elite in terms of class. If "class" means simply a shared relationship to the means of production, it becomes too narrow and static a category to encompass the economic diversity of Chinese elites; if it means the conscious articulation of that shared relationship, it refers to a historical stage that had not yet arrived in China.[30] *Patterns of dominance* call attention to an *underlying coerciveness* upholding the social position of Chinese elites, and the concept allows us to focus on the *dynamic and processual aspects of elite power* and the dialectical relationship of elites to subordinate actors in local society.

Local elites act within local arenas; and here we take local to mean county level or lower. To maintain their position, local elites often seek influence at higher levels of the administrative hierarchy or rely on external social connections and economic resources, but they focus their activity and purpose on the local arena. *An arena is the environment, the stage, the surrounding space, often the locale in which elites and other societal actors are involved.* Arenas may be either *geographical* (village, county, province) or *functional* (military, educational, political); and the concept of an arena includes the repertory of values, meanings, and resources of its constituent actors.[31]

Because the available resources and social environments of local arenas differ markedly across China, we would expect corresponding differences among local elites. Analyzing the characteristics of arenas helps explain the observed diversity of Chinese local elites and social environments, despite the bureaucratic uniformity of administrative divisions or examination degrees. When we recognize the higher level of commercialization in regional cores or the disturbed conditions producing local militarization in peripheries, we can better understand the different environments and resources available to elites in different areas of China and different periods in Chinese history, which naturally produce different types of elite. We should neither anticipate that all county elites will be similar, nor expect that all *shengyuan* will act in the same way because they have the same rank. Only careful attention to the social environment within which elites operate can reveal the diversity of Chinese local elites.

To maintain their dominance, elites must control certain **resources**: *material* (land, commercial wealth, military power); *social* (networks of influence, kin groups, associations); *personal* (technical expertise, leadership abilities, religious or magical powers); or *symbolic* (status, honor, particular lifestyles, and all the cultural exchanges that inform Pierre Bourdieu's concept of "symbolic capital").[32] Elites, or would-be elites, use their resources in **strategies** designed to enhance or maintain their positions. The focus on strategies calls attention to the *dynamic processes* of creating and maintaining elite power. Human agents, active creators of their own history, pursue practices and strategies that, through repetition over time, produce, maintain, and amend cultural structures. These structures in turn shape and constrain the social environment for subsequent activity in an arena.

This *dialectical interaction of strategy and structure* provides a more dynamic picture of elite action than can be derived from structural analysis alone. Elites pursued strategies of lineage formation to protect family resources from division through partible inheritance; and lineages in turn became structures shaping the arenas in which elites contended. In a more modern context, elites advanced their political objectives by forming associations, which then became resources in a new structure of political contention. The intersection of resource, strategy, and structure provides a conceptual map to chart the rise, persistence, transformation, or decline of local elites.

The choice of terms to describe elite actors is influenced by the complexity of resources and strategies. We use "elite" because it can encompass all people—gentry, merchants, militarists, community leaders—at the top of the local social structure, and because the diverse resources of elite families often place them in more than one functional category. Gentry were only one, although a particularly important type of elite in late imperial China. We have broadened the definition of gentry to include culture, lifestyles, networks, and local reputation, as well as degree holding. Gentry were the keepers of a particular set of cultural symbols that denoted refinement. These sociocultural attributes, associated with the literati image, conferred more distinctive status than the land and wealth possessed by a still wider variety of elites.

This broader definition is intended neither to divorce the gentry from examination degrees nor to make the term synonymous with "influential persons." A family that failed to produce a degree holder over long periods would not qualify as "gentry." Cultural expertise, symbolic display, patronage, and social alliances could, however, keep a family within the ranks of the *local* gentry during generations when it did not succeed in the examinations. Degrees also functioned as cultural symbols buttressing claims to cultural prominence. Cultural mastery thus overlapped with, but did not duplicate, the skills required for examination success. Cultural display and symbols also helped set lower limits to the gentry category by distinguishing gentry, with or without degrees, from others, such as village community leaders, who lacked the same cultural credentials. Although a cultural definition of gentry is less precise than characterizations in terms of degree holding, it reflected a social dynamic in which gentry, like other elites, were defined not only by the state but also in relation to their local arenas.

REGIONAL VARIATIONS IN CHINESE LOCAL ELITES

Geographical context is so important to understanding the diversity of local elites that it is important to introduce the major regions of China, beginning with the much-studied Lower Yangzi region, the southeastern coastal provinces where anthropologists have done much of the work on Chinese lineages, and the small-peasant dominated villages of the North China plain.[33]

The Lower Yangzi Region

In late imperial times, the Lower Yangzi and its Jiangnan core formed the wealthiest and most commercially developed region in China with the most degree-holding gentry.[34] Since the Ming, the Jiangnan elite had amassed substantial landholdings, and by Qing times, the substantially urbanized gentry lived the leisured life of absentee landlords in administrative centers or the small towns that lined the canals. Their scholarly and cultural activities set the standard for the empire, and our images of gentry society and literati culture are largely based on Jiangnan norms.[35]

The wealth and official status of the Lower Yangzi gentry gave them exceptional power, which was enhanced by social and cultural cohesiveness. Complex networks based on marriage alliances, philanthropic activities, academies, and poetry clubs connected the Jiangnan gentry and promoted their cultural hegemony. Lower Yangzi elite families organized lineages and established charitable estates; but lineages were less defensive and boundary-conscious than those of the southeast. Networks linking the gentry outweighed kinship units dividing them.[36]

As the most commercialized region in China, the Lower Yangzi provided ample mercantile resources for elites. Because there were more degree holders than government jobs, some supported themselves as teachers, scholars, and managers, but others turned to trade. As foreign trade and the rise of Shanghai expanded opportunities in the nineteenth and twentieth centuries, merchants and gentry were increasingly fused.[37] With multiple sources of support, Lower Yangzi elites were the least dependent on the central state. Their autonomy grew after the Taiping Rebellion when they dominated the bureaus and agencies that repaired the destruction of infrastructure and waterworks.[38] When treaty ports provided havens for political organizing, elites were well prepared to translate their autonomy into political activity.[39] By contrast, village elites were rare and weak. As Jiangnan landlords moved to towns and cities, there were less truly rural, community-oriented elites and few rural militia. Instead, absentee landlords acted in the villages through their agents and rent-collection bursaries supported by county governments.[40]

Local Elites in the Southeast

Strong lineage organization was the most distinctive characteristic of rural society in the southeastern provinces of Guangdong, Fujian, and Taiwan. As frontier areas in the Ming and early Qing, land had to be developed, and communities had to be defended, though the scale of predation was small enough for an armed community to defend itself. Complex lineages came later, influenced by Confucian norms and the officially sanctioned ancestral estate, but took unique strength from the defensive need for community solidarity.[41]

In many ways, southeastern elites behaved like those of the Lower Yangzi: turning to commercial ventures, pursuing examination degrees, and forming associations with other elites in the county seat or market towns. Before the mid-nineteenth century, foreign trade had more impact than in any other region; in Fujian it gave rise to absentee landlordism very similar to Jiangnan.[42] In other ways, rural elites in the southeast exploited commercial resources in markedly different ways. Many sought monopoly control and collected fees from local markets, ferries, or docks.[43] Such exclusive arrangements produced territorial competition among elites, and gentry associations became "alliances" of kinship groups, rather than expressions of shared culture and social interests.[44] Thus in the southeast, the vertical, kin-based structure of lineages seemed stronger than the horizontal gentry networks of Jiangnan.

North China Elites

The unirrigated fields of North China were much poorer and more vulnerable to natural disasters than the rice-growing areas of the Yangzi and the southeast. Landlords owned only about 10 percent of the land on the North China plain. In the vast regions without convenient water transport, and hence little commerce, local elites preserved more of the traditional Confucian disdain for mercantile activity.[45]

Scholars working on the North China plain have been impressed by the weakness of the degree-holding gentry in predominantly rural counties. North China degree holders were concentrated in a few major cities, especially Beijing and the provincial capitals, in contrast to the wide dispersal of gentry in towns of the Lower Yangzi.[46] With weak county-level gentry, village elites were likely to deal directly with the local magistrate's yamen. Some of the most important rural leaders in this area were either village brokers or sub-bureaucratic functionaries such as *lizhang* (里長) or *xiangbao* (鄉保).[47]

The power of the county government was greater than in Jiangnan or the southeast. North China elites had neither a strong economic base in land and commerce nor powerful networks to confront the imperial state. As a result, the state loomed larger in the north, and access to officials was, in itself, a mark of elite status. Thus one village informant described the "village gentry" as those "who know the county magistrate."[48] Finally, the weak degree-holding elite in poor areas prone to disorder removed a check on village strongmen, militia leaders, and bandits who emerged as state power declined in the late nineteenth and twentieth centuries.

Elites in the Middle and Upper Yangzi

We know less about Yangzi valley elites above the delta, and new studies by Madeleine Zelin and William Rowe represent some of the first English-language studies on the subject.[49] The Middle Yangzi differed from North China in its stronger gentry and more widespread and complex patterns of landlordism, but we do not find the southeastern pattern of large corporate lineages. With fewer degree holders than Jiangnan, local elites retained more contacts with rural communities, continuing their considerable involvement in agriculture and water control, and successfully rallying peasants into militia against the Taiping.[50] However, like the Lower Yangzi elite, the elite of both the Middle and Upper Yangzi relied increasingly on mercantile wealth as well as land.

Timing is the likely explanation for these patterns. The rebellions at the end of the Yuan and Ming dynasties had a particularly devastating impact on the Middle and Upper Yangzi, which reverted to frontier status at the end of the Ming. In the early Qing, immigrants resettled and reclaimed the land; by the late Qing, the core cities of the Middle Yangzi began to rival the commercial development of the Lower Yangzi. Considering the later timetable of development, these elites may represent an earlier stage of a single Yangzi valley prototype.

Elites in the Periphery

The regional elites that we have described are mostly the elites of regional cores. We must not, however, neglect the distinction between core and peripheral elites. Peripheries tended to be more violent and disorderly. Elites were more likely to command militia, and their coercive resources were generally greater than those in the cores. Government officials, important in the county seat, had less leverage in the countryside. Merchants, too, entered rural areas as unpopular outsiders controlling long-distance trade. The multiple waves of immigration and the transfer of mercantile capital into landholding could result in complicated, multilayered tenancy systems and large-scale defensive organizations like lineages.

The county seat and magistrate appear more important to the county elites of peripheral society. Both the hilly topography and the focus of trade on the export of hill products like tea and lumber discouraged the growth of multiple linked market centers; the county seat was usually the local economic center. Without the upper degrees and connections that gave access to higher bureaucratic arenas, peripheral elites could not circumvent the authority of the county magistrate, instead seeking lucrative fiscal posts in the local government.[51]

The evidence regarding elite continuity is contradictory. The instability of the Jiangxi periphery encouraged fluid elite structures with considerable downward mobility. By contrast, in the Zhejiang periphery some elite families remained locally prominent for centuries.[52] The key variable may be the degree of social strife in an area, with more settled peripheries like Zhejiang's able to support long-entrenched elites; but the question deserves further investigation.

Frontier Elites

On the edge of Han Chinese society, frontiers—even less socially and economically integrated with the cores—were largely beyond the reach of state power.[53] Frontier elites had to establish themselves as community leaders in rough, sparsely settled societies and lead their followers against indigenous non-Han natives and competing immigrant groups. Hence, military power was the most important resource of frontier elites—shared by strongmen on Taiwan, militia leaders in Guizhou, and Muslim and Han elites in the ethnically divided, strife-ridden northwest. In this respect, frontier elites were similar to those on the internal peripheries; but because the state was weaker, elites relied more on their own local resources.[54]

Frontiers developed through several stages in the Qing, starting with Han migration in the seventeenth and eighteenth centuries, followed by mounting conflict with the indigenous populace, and increasing governmental efforts to pacify and control these regions. Toward the end of the nineteenth century, the process of gentrification seems to have overtaken elites on widely separated frontiers. Despite its political and military weakness internationally, the Qing state in its final years was unusually effective on the frontier and served as a catalyst for cultural integration. It is ironic that just as the Confucian consensus was breaking down along China's coastal core, the frontier elites began to gentrify.

MEASURING ELITE CONTINUITY

One fundamental factor shaping the strategies of Chinese elites was their relative insecurity. Elites in China had few reliable long-term guarantees of status compared to old-regime elites in Europe or to elites in caste societies like India. The European nobility, especially on the continent, was a hereditary status group with legal guarantees, rights to landholding, and tax privileges that far exceeded those available to the Chinese gentry.[55] Although the long-accepted contrast between primogeniture in Europe and partible inheritance in China has been overdrawn,[56] there is little doubt that Chinese adherence to dividing property equally among sons made it more difficult to maintain the family patrimony then in societies with entail and "strict settlement."[57] An examination degree, with its attendant legal privileges, was the orthodox route to elite status in late imperial China. However, unlike caste or estate societies, status in China was not an effective substitute for wealth because in the long run it depended on wealth—to educate heirs, cultivate connections, and maintain the cultivated lifestyle that set the elite apart.

To assess mobility in Chinese society, we must distinguish between the continuity of elite personnel and the social continuity of elites. Continuity of personnel means that specific families maintained elite status over long periods of time even though the nature of the elite may have changed. Social continuity refers to the persistence of a particular elite type, although families belonging to that elite may change over time. Previous studies have argued that the Chinese gentry maintained its dominance through the examination system's openness to new talent and ambition.[58] More recent research on local elite families has demonstrated that dominance could be maintained for long periods of time without relying on degrees and office.[59] We will argue that the late imperial elite was changing in important ways, but the persistence of elite-identifying lifestyles through the nineteenth and into the twentieth century indicates that in comparative terms there was a remarkable social continuity of the Chinese elite. It is time to acknowledge both mobility in the scholar-official elite and continuity in the local elite.

How can we explain the combination of social continuity and continuity of personnel in China? The landholdings of the Chinese elite were too small to be the foundation for elite status. Twentieth-century surveys indicate that landlords, comprising 3 to 4 percent of the population, owned only about 39 percent of the cultivated land,[60] and given the enormous number of petty landlords, local-elite families probably owned less than half of that amount. In late-nineteenth-century England, by contrast, 3,500 to 4,500 great gentry families owned between 70 and 75 percent of the land.[61] In Russia, nobles and the crown essentially monopolized landholding; France was similar to China, but ecclesiastical, noble, and bourgeois landholders still owned roughly 60 percent of all land on the eve of the French Revolution.[62]

The Chinese elite could not maintain its status simply through officeholding and links to the state, for that entailed unbroken success in the examinations, which no family could guarantee. Rather than land or office, it was the flexible reliance on multiple resources and a broad repertoire of strategies that enabled local elites to preserve their positions. Chinese local elites became masters at dealing with ambiguous mixtures of security and insecurity; their multiple resources allowed options in dealing with new situations. This flexibility served them well. When the twentieth century brought marked and rapid social discontinuities, many elite families maintained their social standing in the face of unprecedented changes. To understand this flexible elite repertoire, we must look more closely at the nature of the late imperial elite and the resources and strategies it employed.

STATUS, CLASS, AND STRATIFICATION OF THE LATE IMPERIAL ELITE

Insecure status in late imperial China and the interdependence of status and wealth produced a different interaction between the principles of status and class than one finds in other parts of the world. Unlike continental Europe or India, in China, merchants were not kept apart by rigid status boundaries, and commercial wealth interacted with status throughout the Qing period. There was strong consciousness of social distinctions, with superiority demonstrated through lifestyles, honor, and cultural display, all of which required wealth, but also cultural mastery that could not simply be bought. Qing society was also distinguished by weak personal dependence between elites and nonelites. Legally dependent, serf-like bonded tenants began to disappear during the late Ming in the face of commercialization and peasant uprisings.

If neither legal privilege, nor relations of production, nor personal dependence were the basis for elite dominance, were relations to the state the key?

The state was the source of the degrees, honors, and titles held by the gentry, and past work on Chinese stratification has focused on the role of the state. Philip Kuhn has powerfully argued that Chinese views of hierarchy embodied in Confucian social norms were reinforced by the hierarchy of degrees and state office, and that the distinctions between rulers and ruled overwhelmed social divisions, dividing the state sector from all others.[63] State-certified status was certainly of great importance, but this still seems too much a view from the imperial center. Hierarchical perceptions were also nurtured within family and local social systems.

The other main approach to social stratification, analyzed in detail in the Japanese scholarship cited above, has focused on economic relations between landlords and tenants and the effects of the Ming-Qing commercial expansion in Central and South China. This literature suggests growing class distinctions between wealthy landowning gentry living in towns and cities, small landowners and wealthy cultivators in the villages, and poor peasants and wage laborers at the bottom of the social hierarchy. In his pursuit of rural revolution, Mao Zedong divided the local elite into three layers based essentially on the size of their landholdings.[64]

These two approaches—through state-conferred status and from economic position—have not been systematically related to each other, and neither alone offers a comprehensive model. The studies that resulted from the Banff conference suggest that it is most fruitful to look at the arenas dominated by local elites. Starting from Mao's economic classification of the elites in Xunwu, Stephen Averill examined the many factors that defined family position in the Jiangxi hill country. The result was a map of local power and status. At the top were a few great households, based in the county seat or biggest market centers, who had the highest reputations, broadest connections, greatest influence, and most resources. Below them were middle-elite families, often in smaller towns, who commanded smaller quantities or a smaller range of the same resources and whose influence did not extend so far. At the bottom of the elite were insecure families whose resources were barely adequate to warrant inclusion in the upper reaches of society. The factors determining elite status varied, yet local people had no difficulty identifying dominant families and ranking them within local arenas.[65]

LOCAL ELITE RESOURCES

We may think of local elites competing for limited resources, the relative importance of which varied among local arenas and geographical regions. These resources also served different functions in acquiring or maintaining elite status. The most basic resources were the familiar list of education and office, commercial wealth, military power, and land. Education was surely the most prized resource—as a means to earn examination degrees and professional expertise during the republic. A high examination degree under the imperial system not only allowed entrance to bureaucratic office and a chance to enter national circles of power, it also guaranteed access to the local magistrate simply on the presentation of one's calling card and insured that local officials would treat the holder with appropriate courtesy and respect. Education thus functioned as a steppingstone to broader arenas outside the locality. It put elites into official positions or gave them contacts they could use to act as patrons for kin and community. Within the local arena it increased community status, broadened social alliances and marriage prospects, and conferred the prestige that legitimized local dominance.

Although education was a crucial value in elite society, its importance as a local resource, and especially the importance of degree holding, varied markedly. Lower degrees were of little value in areas like Jiangnan with many *jinshi* and *juren*, but could be an important local resource on peripheries or the North China plain where higher degree holders were rare. Even there, however, lower degrees provided negligible access to higher arenas. The diligent scholar from a poor family who succeeded in the metropolitan examinations was a persistent, but seldom realized ideal in late imperial China. Some wealth was needed to support a boy through years of study, so a degree, especially an upper degree, was likely to be a return on previous generations' economic resources that had already moved the family to at least the lower local elite. Degree holding was, however, effective in maintaining elite status. Once examination success and office holding had established a family in the local elite, the family was well placed to garner resources to educate sons and win more degrees in future generations.

Wealth from trade was perhaps more important to the rise than the maintenance of elite families, although it was often vital to both. References to "raising one's family through trade" abound in local gazetteer elite biographies. Commercial wealth was such an important resource because of the growing opportunities in the Ming and Qing periods and also because this wealth was so easily converted to status—in the form of education, degrees, or lifestyles—or into landholding. Multiple strategies of family maintenance based on commerce, education, and landholding became well established in the Lower Yangzi during the Ming. Throughout China, commercialization made mercantile wealth a widespread resource for gentry and military men as well as traders during the Qing, and in a few places even earlier.[66]

In a society where soldiering was theoretically even more disparaged than trade, military degrees brought little status in core areas, although they had more weight in peripheral zones with few civil-degree holders. Military power was most important on frontiers and peripheries not firmly under government control. Elites in core zones were more likely to use their greater rapport and influence with officials to obtain protection from government forces. In other areas, like parts of Guangdong and Fujian, piracy, banditry, and lineage or village feuding were common over protracted periods, even after the areas had left their frontier origins behind.[67] On the North China plain, control of local forces became increasingly vital as banditry and warlordism spread during the late nineteenth and twentieth centuries.

In general, military force was more useful in acquiring than in preserving elite status. The founders of several Hanyang lineages studied by William Rowe rose as officers in the Ming armies during the Yuan-Ming transition, but they quickly used their military resources to acquire land and began the pursuit of education and civil degrees. Military power did not have the legitimacy to sustain elites over long periods. As a more practical matter, even the declining state proved in the northwest during the 1870s that it could smash local forces if its power was focused on a particular area. Thus even frontier strongmen needed more reputable resources to maintain their position in the long run.[68] In general, however, military power tended to be a temporary resource that assumed importance in troubled times of rebellion or dynastic transition, but diminished in importance once order was restored.[69]

Finally, land was the most commonly acquired resource of local elites and was the ideologically approved source of wealth in Confucian China. Land ownership demonstrated status and brought wealth through rents or direct management, more stable sources of income than trade. The image of the gentry landlord is particularly associated with the Lower Yangzi, but peripheral elites also bought land to establish their position. Merchants in Middle Yangzi lineages invested large amounts in land. They also reclaimed flooded land—a common way of acquiring land in the southeast and Yangzi valley.[70]

Landholding was probably more useful for maintaining status than entering the elite. It was possible for peasants gradually to improve their economic positions and build up their landholdings; however, a family needed money to buy land, and it was difficult to accumulate such wealth from agriculture alone. The wealthy merchant acquired more than the diligent peasant. Furthermore, land was a scarce resource in China, and growing population pressure made it difficult to accumulate. Large tracts could be acquired on frontiers or in areas depopulated by rebellions. In most times and places, land was accumulated only slowly, in small pieces and scattered plots. Nor was land always safe: records of ownership could be lost or destroyed in times of war or rebellion.

Unlike other elites in the world, Chinese elites were not defined by a few key resources—land, caste status, or inherited titles. In one sense they might be considered weaker than an elite with an unassailable claim over a basic social resource. However, they compensated for their lack of monopoly by a remarkable flexibility in using the resources available in their local arenas. Mercantile wealth, especially in commercialized regions like the Yangzi valley and the southeast, could also be significant in some peripheries and frontiers. Landed wealth was more common in the fertile south than the north; education was more useful in peaceful cores, and military power in troubled peripheries. But the resources of elites were not all internal to their arenas. In fact, a crucial aspect of elite power was access to external arenas.

THE SPAN OF ELITE ACTIVITY: LOCALITY AND OVERLAPPING ARENAS

Frequent reliance on both local and external resources was basic to local elite strategies. Anthropologists working on other parts of the world have found that external resources are essential if local elites are to maintain their dominance over time.[71] In a closed local system, leveling processes will gradually narrow elite-mass distinctions. Outside resources and outwardly directed strategies appear particularly significant to understanding late imperial and republican elites. Indeed, as Philip Kuhn provocatively asked at our conference: were there any genuinely local elites in China? Were they not all culturally bound to a China-wide system defined by the Confucian state, which offered every well-educated boy a hypothetical chance to pass the examinations? What other factors pulled elites away from home?

From their local arenas in village, district, town, county, and city, elites ventured into both wider (extending over larger geographical areas) and higher (focusing on higher levels of administrative or commercial hierarchies) arenas. Participation in these higher and wider arenas typically required more resources (higher degrees, greater wealth) and sometimes different resources (education rather than land) and brought greater opportunities for power. Some successful local elites moved permanently up and out of their original arenas, often migrating to other provinces, but during the late imperial period, they typically maintained contact with a home base. Many brought outside resources to their home localities and returned home during and at the end of sojourning careers that had increased their resources. For this reason, it is often difficult to draw clear lines between local, provincial, and national elites in China because the same person might appear in each stratum as he moved back and forth between arenas at different points in his career. Patterns of local dominance typically had an outside dimension.

The state-oriented pull of the examinations and bureaucracy is only part of the picture. G. William Skinner added the concept of marketing systems with ascending orders of central places grouped into economic macroregions.[72] The degree of economic integration varied markedly, but it increased during the late imperial period. Through this system, trade fostered external elite interests as much as did bureaucratic office. The form of urbanization in China, with small towns dispersed throughout the countryside in an interlocking hierarchy of central places, influenced local elites' external strategies.[73] As long-distance trade increased and manufacturing centers developed, traders established regional and interregional associations with others from their locality. The growing numbers of scholars from places like the Lower Yangzi also formed their own provincial or regional networks outside the bureaucracy.[74]

Skinner has called attention to the importance of sojourning in late imperial China, as a family strategy to bring resources into otherwise disadvantaged areas.[75] In places like Huizhou, Anhui, and certain Shanxi and Shaanxi counties, sojourning merchants brought back wealth to buttress their local position; and the clerks and private secretaries from Shaoxing county in Zhejiang did much the same thing, relying upon their bureaucratic connections.[76] Scholars and merchants, elite and poor, people from wealthy areas or from peripheries found employment away from home. Elite families' links to wider commercial, bureaucratic, or academic arenas brought resources to enhance dominance at home. The importance of relationships outside one's home arena helps explain why brokerage between arenas and patronage by elites with access to higher arenas were so essential to local elite activity. Above all, local elites' transactions, mediations, and gatekeeping roles between intersecting arenas required them to face two directions: in toward their local arenas and out toward nonlocal determinants of their local power; and they cultivated connections and developed strategies in this double context.

LOCAL ELITE STRATEGIES

All elites must plot and maneuver to preserve their status. Early modern European elites rigorously husbanded their economic resources, arranged advantageous marriages, and practiced strict family discipline including birth control.[77] In China, the insecurity of elite status required strategies devised in a context of intense competition for scarce resources. Elite competition was exacerbated by divisions based on kinship, ethnicity, locality, networks, and differential access to markets, productive resources, water, or political power. We see competition to win examination degrees or dominate markets, divisions between old and new money or local people and outsiders, fights among militia leaders and different religious groups. This competition could become violent, particularly in the peripheries and on frontiers but also sporadically in more settled regions.

If elite strategies often assumed social conflict, they were also tempered by expected patterns of behavior that fostered civility. Cultural ideals of harmony reinforced unities arising from community or kinship, resistance to outside threats, or common education, experiences, and associations.[78] Elite strategies were crucially divided between those that tended to enhance elite competition and those that tended to unite elites as a self-conscious dominant class.

A catalog of the strategies pursued by local elites would be long. They constructed marriage alliances, sent sons into different occupations to diversify resources, and carefully cultivated connections with their equals and superiors. Such strategies might be pursued by families seeking to rise within the elite or to maintain their positions. During the Ming and Qing, trade became the preeminent strategy for upward mobility. Men could also rise to prominence by commanding military forces, but strongmen had to broaden their strategies to retain power over time. Marriage was an avenue to enter the elite and to remain there and deserves further study. Education-based strategies to acquire upper degrees offered the possibility of moving into the highly prestigious national scholar-official elite.

Shaping Lineage Organization

Chinese lineage organization, a particular focus of anthropological study, was both a kinship system and a socioeconomic institution growing out of elite strategies to maintain local power. Lineages were defined by locality as much as by genealogy; they date their founding from the patriline's moving to the locality, and the coincidence of lineage and territorial community could result in a locally powerful social organization. Lineages were also closely associated with elites, particularly in South and Central China—their founding typically followed a family's rise to elite status.[79]

Lineages played an important role in the "localist strategy" emerging among Southern Song elites. Lineage formation came in waves, and peaks tended to coincide with periods of devolving state power, when elites were turning their attention to maintaining local dominance more than advancing in the national bureaucracy. This was not, however, the only factor governing the growth of lineage power. Several local studies note that the accumulation of lineage land took place in the wake of major social disruptions and depopulation: the Yuan-Ming transition in the Middle Yangzi, the 1660s relocation of coastal populations in Guangdong, and the rebellions of the Ming-Qing transition in southern Anhui. Some late-Qing growth of lineage landholding in Jiangnan may have resulted from the availability of land in the wake of the Taiping Rebellion, and it certainly reflected the increasing managerial initiatives taken by Lower Yangzi elites in this period.[80]

Lineage resources benefited the whole patriline, and the charitable estates of the Yangzi valley indicate genuine concern for the well-being of relatives. Rubie Watson clearly shows, however, that lineage structures also helped perpetuate the position of the elite managers. It is useful to distinguish between elites in a lineage and the more problematic concept of elite lineages—that is, those with unusual local power or many degree holders. Elite lineages included many nonelite members, but certain families or branches used the lineage as a resource to maintain their status. They might act as patrons for nonelites in the lineage, but they might also dominate nonelite members, whose interests might not coincide with their own.[81] Lineages both defended group interests and enhanced elite power within them.

Madeleine Zelin dramatically illustrates how lineage estates (*tang* 堂) could be adapted to function as a business corporation. William Rowe further suggested that in the nineteenth century, lineage, welfare, or commercial *tang* all acted like "trusts": legal entities with designated uses and limited liability.[82] Whatever the nature of these trusts, they clearly demonstrate the institutional flexibility of lineages. Lineages combined a measure of sanctified inviolability, by virtue of their association with an ancestral legacy, with a capacity for corporate action that was easily adapted to business requirements.

The lineages described by Brook and Rowe fall into the different pattern of the Middle and Lower Yangzi valley, where lineages were widespread and numerous but owned less land in their charitable estates (*yizhuang* 義莊) and did not go into business.[83] Even without huge assets they were corporate organizations for the primary lineage purpose of defending against the progressive fission of family wealth through the custom of partible inheritance. These lineage estates thus functioned much as did entail in Europe, producing an undivided and inalienable patrimony.[84] Lineages limited the claims of collateral kinsmen on elite family wealth while providing a "somewhat broader pool of elite resources and junior agnates" for the difficult, recurrent task of succeeding in the examinations.[85]

Scholars have found evidence of kinship solidarity, transmittal through patrilines, and even lineages, within North China,[86] but these lineages were usually much smaller and weaker with little or no corporate property or organization. If any organization existed, it usually focused on the ritual honoring of ancestors. Elites on the North China plain lacked the resources of land, wealth, and education to support the kind of lineages seen in the south. Northern elite families tried to preserve their wealth through the patriline and rose and fell more rapidly.

The Construction of Networks

Lineages, in general, protected existing resources and excluded outsiders from access to them. At the same time, elites also had to look outside their kin group to preserve their local positions, and for this purpose networks were important. Whereas lineages were constructed to exclude claimants who might drain resources, networks included selected useful outsiders; whereas lineages were especially useful in elite competition, networks enhanced elite cooperation and solidarity; whereas lineage protected existing resources, networks expanded resources; whereas lineage activity often focused on the local arena, networks reached beyond locality. Networks, pervading all societies, have been defined as "quasi-groups," unbounded social fields with no clear leaders or organization linking friends, neighbors, affinal relatives, and occupational associates.[87] Both horizontal networks between approximate social equals and vertical networks linking inferiors and superiors were essential components of Chinese social relations.

Certain characteristics of late imperial society encouraged Chinese local elites to form horizontal networks: the linkages between local and larger political, commercial, and social structures; the connections and support systems originating in the academies and examinations and continuing through government service; the lack of firm status guarantees, which put a premium on support from personal allies; the weak legal protection for real and mercantile wealth, which made powerful connections indispensable. Networks were an important vehicle for *guanxi* (關係, connections, relationships), a pervasive element in Chinese social interaction. In the absence of firm guarantees of elite status, bonds of *guanxi* were constantly created and recreated through elite social practice and extended through ongoing networks.

Timothy Brook's study gives the fullest picture of an elite subcommunity defining itself within the local arena of Yin County, Ningbo, where an aristogenic upper gentry provided its own social certification, creating a long-lived upper class bound by horizontal networks. If not completely impermeable, this status-conscious network maintained its identity against less prominent elites by a dense web of interconnections. Marriage alliances were particularly powerful, and the Chinese principle of *mendang hudui* (門當戶對, literally: "the gates are matched and the households paired") favored marriages between social equals. Affinal ties, poetry clubs, community schools, historically oriented scholarship on dead heroes of the anti-Manchu resistance, and the organization of local relief were among the many activities through which Ningbo elites defined exclusive membership and reaffirmed social solidarity.

In addition to forming networks to solidify their position within the local arena, local elites were linked outward by both vertical and horizontal networks. Gentry, especially upper gentry, cultivated friendships with upper-degree holders and scholars in other arenas or with officials in the bureaucracy. Outward-reaching literati networks were particularly visible in the Lower Yangzi where dense commercial networks and a large community of upper-degree holders fostered broad contacts among local elites and with their friends in government. Elsewhere, Kuhn has noted that militia networks formed in Hunan during the Taiping Rebellion sponsored the rise of a powerful group of provincial officials in the late nineteenth century.[88] Networks also linked sojourning merchants to one another and to their native arena. Common place of origin was a principle around which networks were frequently established, and when enough people from the same locality sojourned within a given town or city, they gave institutional expression to such ties by forming native-place associations (*huiguan* 會館).[89] Thus, the vehicles for networking varied with the resources available to the elites of a particular area at a particular time, but the propensity to form networks was widespread, encouraged both by culture and the overlapping arenas.

Vertical Networks and Patronage

Vertical networks linking men of unequal wealth and status were equally common. Some incorporated unequal patron-client relationships that provided one side with loyal supporters and the other with access to influence, employment, or reflected glory. Late imperial society was replete with such patronage ties, linking teachers and students, civil service examiners and successful candidates, officials at different levels of the administrative hierarchy, wealthy merchants and artists, military commanders and subordinate officers, lineage elites and ordinary members, shopkeepers and apprentices. Such ties continued into the republican period. In the Jiangxi hills, school ties with educators helped protégés enter middle schools. Vertical networks might also link elites to marginal figures like the bandit leaders who provided military muscle in return for protection and markets.

Patronage was pervasive in China. As in other partly commercialized agrarian societies, village-level patronage allowed peasants without power, knowledge, or contacts to affect decisions that impinged on their lives.[90] The role of patron ideally fell to a powerful member of the community—landlord, lineage head, or manager—who would be trustworthy in representing the community and effective in pressing the interests of its members. Thus the manager of a major lineage trust in Guangdong was chosen because his wealth, knowledge of the world, and connections made him an effective patron. In North China villages—with few landlords, less resources, and less developed kinship structures—skillful patrons might rise from humble circumstances and, in striking contrast to village elites in the southeast, from outside a village's dominant kin group.[91]

Above the village level, patronage was equally important. If imperfect market development made middlemen necessary for economic transactions, the imperfect political integration of the late empire made patrons necessary for bureaucratic access and official appointment. The best access to county officials was through men who shared their culture and lifestyle—the gentry. Because the powerful upper gentry of core areas had links to higher levels of officialdom, which could be utilized to overturn an unfavorable local decision, gentry were particularly desirable patrons.[92] A successful examination candidate was expected to act as patron for his home community by providing introductions, encouragement, and sometimes jobs, and by using his government connections to promote and defend local or kinship interests. The great surplus of Qing degree holders meant that official appointment depended on patronage networks, which inevitably worked to the advantage of core areas with prestigious and well-connected elite families. Non-gentry elites also used patronage to enhance their community interests. Frontier strongmen might patronize young scholars, thus building clientage networks that could later enhance their elite status. As commercialization fostered the practice of sojourning during the late imperial period, sojourning merchants became patrons providing jobs for relatives or associates from their home area.[93]

Patronage implies paternalism and reciprocity, but patron-client relations were asymmetrical, particularly when clients were from lower social strata. An act of patronage underlined the patron's superiority, conferred or confirmed authority, built a useful clientele, and conferred symbolic capital. Patronage also enhanced elites' reputations, made these reputations available to their clients, and increased the legitimacy of their claims to superiority by softening the dominance they exercised as landlords, usurers, or merchants.

Brokerage and Mediation

Brokerage was closely linked to patronage, for successful patrons often performed brokering roles; but patrons had particularistic ties of mutual obligation to their clients, ties brokers often lacked. Like patrons, brokers were most effective if they had wealth, status, and reputation, which tended to make brokerage an elite function. Conversely, however, because brokering was an empowering role, where elite brokers were weak or unwilling to serve, nonelites could perform brokerage roles and gain power over local arenas.

Prasenjit Duara's research on North China provides the fullest analysis of brokerage's impact on elite dominance.[94] Brokers acted in market systems where buyers had imperfect information. Negotiations through intermediaries, reflected in the customary practice of middlemen guaranteeing agreements, was culturally preferred. Brokers acted between two arenas, and the intersection of overlapping arenas made their role common. The ideal broker was a community patron with outside contacts and some wealth. Even if he lacked significant material resources, the ideal broker possessed "face" that inspired trust on both sides. In resource-poor northern villages with weak kin structures, this symbolic capital might be enough to bring a man into village elite circles.

It is striking that although brokerage, like patronage, might indicate imperfect market integration, both economic development and state-building efforts in the Qing and republic probably *increased* the need for brokers. Compradors rose as brokers between foreign traders and Chinese merchants or producers. Tax farmers became more visible in the nineteenth and twentieth centuries, inserting their own interests while brokering between a revenue-hungry state and reluctant taxpayers. Middlemen purchased handicraft products or raw materials from peasant households for factories or foreign markets. Third-party introductions were necessary in many social and political situations, and the breakdown of order during the republic created a need for patron-brokers who could defend their communities against coercive state power.

If brokerage connected different arenas, mediation was a community function that required a person of some local stature. Traditionally, dispute settlement fell to those with demonstrated authority derived from status and wealth. The cultural value placed on harmonious relationships, coupled with the hesitancy to submit to corrupt judicial processes, placed a premium on informal mediation of the frequent disputes within Chinese society. One apparent distinction between the powers of the old nobility of England and the Chinese gentry is that the former had local judicial authority denied to Chinese elites by the state. This difference narrows, however, if one considers the social authority possessed by a mediator: his powers were not legally secured; his aim was reconciliation, not judgment or punishment; and the sanctions at his disposal might include censure or fines but rarely any corporal punishment or confinement. Nonetheless, the social authority derived from mediation, like that from brokerage and patronage, enhanced the influence of elite leaders.

This discussion of networks, patronage, brokerage, and mediation indicates the extraordinary importance of interpersonal relations in defining and preserving elite status in China. The theoretically autocratic imperial state monopolized authority but possessed limited power. As a result, most local governance was worked out in the local arena through informal arrangements. Patrons and brokers were required to guarantee and maintain these arrangements with local officials, negotiate tax rates and remissions, guarantee loans and land sales, and mediate disputes between competing interests. Over time, performing these roles became an elite function, and the behavior patterns associated with patronage, brokerage, and mediation—serious demeanor, cultivated bearing, proper regard for ceremony, broad community concern, and apparent impartiality tempered by a respect for human feelings—became integral parts of elite culture. To the extent that these roles were necessary and the behavior associated with their performance was accepted as proper, the elite could use them to maintain its cultural hegemony.

CULTURAL HEGEMONY AND PATTERNS OF DOMINANCE

We began our discussion with the notion that elites are defined by their dominance in local arenas, and we have explored the resources and strategies that individuals and families employed to attain and maintain elite status. We must now focus on the strategies employed by elites to dominate local arenas. Ties of personal dependency—of bondservants and servile tenants—were rare after the Ming dynasty. In general, Qing and republican elites dominated free men and women. The coercive resources available to elites were designed for use against outsiders or in outside arenas, but militia could be used against peasants at home, and the knowledge that elites commanded such force deterred insubordination. Such military resources were important on frontiers, peripheries, and the southeast coast, but, except in times of rebellion, they were far less important than the economic resources of elites in core areas. Landlords demanded half the harvest in rents, merchants controlled markets and manipulated prices, and moneylenders extracted usurious interest payments. Elite-peasant relations were clearly unequal and the threat of coercion was real. The patterns of symbolic violence embedded in these relations were many-stranded and reinforcing.[95]

Economic domination by landlords and merchants was increasingly important as commercialization intensified and spread across China. The roles of middlemen or guarantors required by commercial transactions were often filled by well-connected elite patrons. The resulting patron-client ties subordinated more than just tenants: freeholding peasants might especially require such services, for they had to deal with local functionaries who collected their land tax and validated their land deeds. Acts of patronage demonstrated status and increased legitimacy. When a patron was successful as protector and broker, he added to his symbolic capital and created bonds of obligation and loyalty among his clients. Cultural hegemony could under many circumstances replace more overt, coercive, and illegitimate dominance while ensuring that elites retained their privileged positions.[96]

As patrons, elites garnered support by conveying a sense of reciprocity and mutuality in personal relations. The most essential relationships to cultivate were those with other elites in shared or higher arenas, for through those relationships local elites could make the deals requiring their patronage and brokering. Thus the very same strategies of resource accumulation and network building that brought men acceptance among their elite peers also earned them deference from the wider population. It follows that elites were anxious to display their elite status, for that very display validated their status and indicated that they might successfully perform elite roles. The theater of symbolic display allowed them to broadcast their claims to their social equals and superiors and to legitimize their power over inferiors.

The state examination system played an important role in encouraging respect for education and the educated and by spreading hierarchic Neo-Confucian values. The examinations, monthly Confucian lectures under the *xiangyue* (鄉約) system, handbooks of family instructions, and almanacs spread values like unity, harmony, hierarchy, and respect, which benefited both state and elites.[97] Another range of values—including reciprocity, magnanimity, and community—were less exclusively related to orthodox Confucianism, and were more closely intertwined with Buddhist concepts of charity and the communal orientations of agrarian society. These norms were ingrained more by social practices than by state policies. The diffusion of cultural norms thus flowed from several sources, and values were not shaped solely by one Confucian elite that controlled national institutions and the "media of indoctrination" and consciously integrated Chinese culture with a single ideology.[98]

When we move from the values themselves to the ways in which elites used them to inspire respect and create power, culture appears more an active process of expressing values rather than a code of predetermined meanings.[99] Confucian learning was important for late imperial elites, but so was local service and conspicuous consumption, especially in ritually important matters like weddings and funerals. Nondegree-holding lineages might use such cultural symbols even more effectively than families with many degree holders,[100] and the masses were familiar with these symbols. Lifestyles played a critical role in converting the basic resources of status into the stuff of social domination. Cultural hegemony could under many circumstances replace more overt, coercive, and illegitimate dominance while ensuring that elites retained their privileged positions.[101]

The most famous picture of the lifestyles of the top elite is the novel, *The Dream of the Red Chamber*, which describes the refined pleasures and sorrows of the Jia family in its opulent mansions and lovely gardens. We sense the many dimensions of display when scholar-friends show off their knowledge of poetry in suggesting names for features in the new garden; when thousands of townspeople line the streets to view an elaborate funeral procession; and when a woman in the household is told to hire a new maid to maintain the number of servants when parvenu families were adding to theirs.[102] Few could match the Jias' wealth, but the historical record is full of accounts of cultural display in the life-styles of the rich and famous. Even local elites were defined by education, refinement, opulence, and pedigree—not simply examination degrees. These cultured lifestyles spread from the economic cores to the frontiers, as Meskill shows for Taiwan.[103]

Lifestyles and high culture became part of the symbolic capital of elites, and the symbols of status required public display. Thus gentry wore scholars' robes and buttons on their caps. They rode in sedan chairs and built elaborate ancestral halls. Weddings cementing alliances between elite families and funerals demonstrating filial piety were carried out with lavish and expensive ceremony. Such individual acts of symbolic display formed a holistic, culturally infused image that elicited deference and respect. The expense of such display ensured that elite status would be available only to those of some wealth, but simpler behavioral patterns were equally important to the elite image. These patterns survived into the republican era, as seen in Lenore Barkan's portrait of Sha Yuanbing: a stern but just man, intolerant of moral laxity and ignorance, but concerned over the affairs of district, province, and nation; a learned scholar sitting in his library surrounded by books. This image, not just his prestigious *jinshi* degree, contributed to Sha's community prominence for two decades after the end of the imperial examinations.

Symbolic capital was also created through welfare activities benefiting the community. Such charity was always offered in a public manner: sponsorship of religious festivals, highly visible soup kitchens, donations to temples carefully recorded on specially carved stone stele. Such behavior created capital in the form of obligations of deference, respect, service, or favors through social intercourse. Cultural symbols opened the way to future material rewards through opportunities to gain wealth or amass a following of clients.[104] What F. G. Bailey calls the "small politics of reputation" pervaded social relations.[105] Higher and lower poles were held together by shared values, similar views of the proper social scheme of things, and a sense of limits beyond which it was improper for power to go.

Elites often lived side by side with the poor. This proximity made their cultured lifestyle more visible and, at the same time, inspired—or forced—them to assume responsibility for poor neighbors. They easily fell into the role of patrons to potential clients next door—a role that expanded into continuous involvement in local philanthropy during the Qing. It was also easier for the poor to evaluate the rich and to set forth terms for their continued deference.[106] Because the status of Chinese elites was not entirely secure, and because hierarchy was combined with expectations of magnanimity, the Chinese poor were periodically able to hold their superiors accountable. Rioting was one recourse when circumstances surpassed the tolerance of the poor.

The limited latitude for disorder in still basically ordered society reduced social tensions by providing an outlet for the energies and grievances of the lower classes that stopped short of full social conflict.[107] Chinese elites did not necessarily approve, but mainly tolerated, disorderly festivals, unorthodox sects, and minor riots that were more likely to target the state than themselves. Sometimes they also participated in unrest. A stock figure in Chinese history and literature is the disgruntled *shengyuan* who led or joined the masses in protest.

The centrality of the patron image in legitimizing power and exercising dominance is revealed in situations where it was inoperative or broke down. Much of the social conflict in China, as in premodern agrarian Europe, occurred between different localities. Such conflict not only directed we-they consciousness away from inequalities at home but also reinforced the patron-client nexus by increasing the need for elite leaders capable of defending the community. A more serious threat came from the portion of the masses with whom they could not form patron-client relationships. Sectarian bands and the geographically mobile underclass, including laborers along transport routes, peddlers, miners, seasonal workers, disbanded soldiers, beggars, and criminals—all of whom escaped the vertical networks of local dominance—presented a more fundamental problem. Traditional elites were not very successful in developing strategies—other than periodic philanthropy like the "winter defense" distributions of food and clothing—to meet this kind of challenge as it escalated after the mid-nineteenth century.

Esherick's study of the Boxer uprising illustrates just how destabilizing the unrooted poor might be in an area where community ties were eroded and local elites lacked material and symbolic resources to maintain control.[108] But the itinerant lower fringes of society did not often invade the structures through which elites maintained dominance. This kind of challenge only arose during the republic, when left-wing and revolutionary elites began to organize groups against the old vertical structures of authority. Class solidarities were revealed as Beijing shop owners cooperated to suppress a unionization movement of workers and clerks.[109] The more forceable reactions of landlords to the first Communist attempt to organize peasants in Haifeng County, Guangdong, during the early 1920s suggests a rural version of the same class conflict.[110] Elites did not want to pay higher wages, accept lower rents, or give up land. More importantly, organizations like peasant unions threatened the very structure of patronage and denied the symbolic capital upon which so much elite authority rested. At that point conflict, not paternalism, dominated elite-mass social relations, and the stakes escalated to matters of life and death.

CHANGES IN ELITES OVER TIME

The resources and strategies discussed in the previous section formed the heart of the elite repertoire. Actual practices varied as conditions changed, and during the entire period from Ming to the republic, Chinese elites changed as well. Periodic political crises of rebellion, war, and dynastic change destroyed old families and created conditions favoring social mobility. The Yuan-Ming transition in the fourteenth century was probably even more disruptive in this respect than the seventeenth-century transition from Ming to Qing.[111] In the nineteenth century, the Taiping and other rebellions loosened elite social structures across China. More fundamental was the larger process of economic, social, and political change: commercialization, increased foreign trade, militarization, functional specialization, growing and politicized voluntary associations, and the shifting political context of republican China. During the late imperial period, these processes changed the elite without fundamentally altering the elastic social structures. Toward the end of the nineteenth century, social structures changed as well, with consequences for elite relations to the state above and the populace below.

The Growing Importance of Commerce

Although some have traced China's commercial revolution to the Song,[112] the dramatic growth in local markets, handicraft production for the market (especially cotton textiles), interregional trade, and a vigorous money economy began during the Ming. Population growth, new crops (corn, sweet potatoes, tobacco), an extended reign of peace, and the influx of silver from the New World fueled this expansion. The new commercial activity provided an important new avenue to elite status. Some merchants like the Fan family of Shanxi and the salt merchants from Huizhou made enormous fortunes during the seventeenth and eighteenth century through government monopolies in salt, copper, and other commodities.[113] More fortunes were made in trade beyond strict government supervision: first in grain, then in handicraft products (especially cotton cloth and silk), and, in the southeastern coastal provinces, in foreign trade with Japan, Taiwan, and Southeast Asia.[114]

In the sixteenth and seventeenth centuries, references to parvenu merchants were often colored by classical Confucian disdain for profit making. Some literati certainly felt compelled to protect their status against the challenge of commercial wealth,[115] but literati disdain for mercantile activity eventually became more pro-forma than real. Sumptuary laws were breaking down, merchants were purchasing degrees and interacting with gentry, and gentry families were rising from merchant backgrounds.[116] By mid-Qing times, gentry families commonly engaged in usury and trade, and merchant families supported Confucian academies and gentry publication projects. The cultured sons of merchants were accepted into the gentry elite, and merchants eagerly assimilated the norms of the literati, bought land, and joined in philanthropy and other public works.[117] The social/cultural fusion of merchant and gentry elites was largely accomplished in the commercialized zones by the end of the eighteenth century, setting the stage for broader political collaboration in the nineteenth.

In the nineteenth century, trade with the West opened further commercial opportunities, which were effectively exploited by established trading families. With backgrounds in handicraft production and trade with Southeast Asia, the merchants of Foshan, west of Canton, were among the first licensed by the Qing to trade with the British. When treaty ports were established following China's 1842 defeat in the Opium War, such men had skills and connections to work as compradors for Western firms.[118] Ambitious men from Canton and other coastal entrepots followed opportunities for foreign trade in Shanghai. Although these treaty ports were peripheral to the Chinese economy as a whole, many successful Chinese business elites escaped marginality by acquiring official titles, purchasing land, and becoming patrons and philanthropists in their hometowns; some advised officials on intercourse with the West. Strategically located to insert themselves into a changing elite, these men added specialized expertise to the classical cultivation that traditionally qualified one to rule.[119]

The gradual erosion of literati exclusiveness was further illustrated by the massive sale of examination degrees in the late nineteenth century. With the Qing's desperate efforts to raise revenue, one-third of the gentry class purchased their degrees, and two-thirds of the official establishment had qualified by the "irregular" route of purchase.[120] As merchants purchased examination degrees and official titles, and venality of office undermined

Confucian assumptions about bureaucratic qualifications, merchants and gentry were drawn together in local arenas and routinely identified as *shenshang* (紳商), or "gentry-merchants." In the twentieth century, this new hybrid class became an integral part of an emerging business elite.

This changing relationship of Chinese merchant and gentry elites is particularly important for comparative history. There is no question that the Chinese gentry was more open to mercantile wealth than the nobility of continental Europe, but the parallel to England—where the purchase of a country house and the assumption of a proper lifestyle could qualify wealthy merchants for gentry status—is striking indeed. Because this allegedly "open" English elite is often credited with England's political stability and the country's economic modernization, it is fair to ask why a seemingly comparable Chinese elite had the former effect, but not the latter.[121] Three things seem to distinguish the Chinese and English cases.

First, the type of trade accorded proper status differed in the two countries. The 1700 edition of Edward Chamberlayn's *Angliae Notitia*, the standard reference of the day, dropped all disparaging comments on "shopkeeping" and proclaimed that "in England as well as Italy to become a merchant of foreign commerce, without serving any apprenticeship, hath been allowed as no disparagement for a gentleman born, especially to a younger brother." But domestic wholesale or retail trade remained beyond the pale.[122] By contrast, the Ming and Qing dynasties periodically restricted and prohibited foreign trade. The prohibitions were demonstrably ineffective and not seriously enforced for long periods by the Qing, but they still left those engaged in foreign trade open to disparagement as "criminal merchants and sly people . . . [who] secretly trade with foreigners in prohibited goods."[123] The Chinese in effect *reversed* the British evaluations of domestic and foreign trade, which certainly inhibited the sort of overseas trade that fueled so much of Europe's early modern expansion.

Second, the greater Chinese acceptance of domestic commerce may also be related to the reasonably firm separation of ownership and management.[124] Modern industrialists deliberately sought to end this separation as part of a new "bourgeois practice."[125] Because earlier Chinese merchants left most direct commercial dealings to their managers, they were less tainted by money grubbing and freer to pursue the cultivated lifestyle of the gentry.

Finally, the economic geography of merchant-gentry relations was different in England and China. The landed gentry who ruled England through the mid-nineteenth century were closely tied to London, where they maintained townhouses, rubbed shoulders with the great merchants, invested in banking and overseas ventures, and formed the connections which made England "a nation of aristocrats and squires ruling in the interest of bankers and overseas merchants."[126] In effect, the structure of elite power in England concentrated capital and influence in London, where it fueled the nation's economic modernization.

In China, the most powerful commercial interests were not concentrated in the nation's capital, nor did they derive from the Jiangnan economic heartland. The typical Chinese merchant was a sojourner: from Huizhou (in the hills of southern Anhui), Jiangxi, or the interior northern provinces of Shanxi and Shaanxi, soon joined by Fujianese and Cantonese from the southeast. During the nineteenth century, Ningbo merchants rose through foreign trade and banking. Thus, the Chinese merchant was always something of an outsider, who met the gentry on the latter's ground and, inevitably, on the latter's terms. As an outsider, the merchant was also dependent on bureaucratic favor, which left him vulnerable to potentially extravagant demands for "contributions." The wide range of sojourning also meant that investments were not concentrated in one or a few centers.[127] Sojourning merchants remitted a substantial portion of their profits back to widely separated, and in some cases peripheral, areas from which they had come.[128] In fact, the different merchant-gentry interaction in China deflected the London-style concentration of wealth by returning capital to the hinterland.

In this context, the new entrepreneurial elite in Wuxi, or epitomized by Zhang Jian in Nantong, is important. In the twentieth century, these local gentry-merchant elites began operating their own enterprises in the economic heartland. Not only were profits kept in areas of potential economic development, but money began flowing from land to commerce and industry in areas where new elites were not outsiders, but dominant players in the local political arena.

The Rise of Military Elites

In the mid-nineteenth century, the threat of rebellion generated militia to defend the established order. Philip Kuhn has studied the militarization in the Middle Yangzi valley, and Edward McCord has documented the phenomenon in Guizhou. In provinces like Hunan, the gentry under Zeng Guofan maintained firm control of militia networks, but the Guizhou militia networks were an avenue for new men to enter the elite. The same was probably true in Anhui and in North China—where the orthodox gentry were weaker than Hunan, and the state relied on new elements to combat the rebellions.[129]

The militarization of local society was not a continuous process. In Guizhou, the original militia leaders abandoned military roles to concentrate on patronage networks and promote education, while in Hunan, republican warlords were not an evolution from Qing militia.[130] Nevertheless, by the early twentieth century, the status of military men was rising significantly, as nationalist ideology preached the need both to train military professionals and to spread military training and values among the general population.[131] This late Qing rise of the military was the foundation for the ascent of the men who would dominate China during the warlord era and (to a lesser extent) under Chiang Kai-shek's Guomindang.

How did the militarization of national and provincial elites affect local elites? Here the record is mixed, with military power playing a fairly minor role among Lower Yangzi elites. On the peripheries and in North China, where gentry and commercial elites were weak, local elites became significantly militarized.[132] On the frontiers, where coercive resources were always important, they became even more so in the twentieth century. In an era when modern rifles were readily available from foreign suppliers and provided a weapon that was infinitely more threatening than the swords, spears, and flintlocks of earlier dissidents, local military elites became a serious force to be reckoned with. This greater power of military technology did not, however, increase the status of local militarists. The small-scale local commanders were too close to bandits and "local bullies"—and their use of coercive power was too destructive to the fabric of local societies—to be legitimate. The character of elites, new or old, was compromised as they substituted more direct forms of domination for cultural hegemony.

Functional Elites

The twentieth-century rise of business and military elites was the most visible example of a process whereby discrete functional elites arose alongside (or in place of) the old gentry elite. But the process was not simply the functional specialization of the elite creating a pluralist society; occupations were not that separate. Averill refers to the great households in Jiangxi as "small-scale conglomerates."[133] Wuxi elites were both industrialists and landlords, the scions of prominent gentry families, and members of the new nationalist regime. Functional categories may mask the extent to which old elites diversified to protect their interests and underplay the importance of established networks and associations.

Evidence of specialization begins before the twentieth century. Benjamin Elman has argued that the eighteenth-century complex of academies, libraries, and printing houses in the Lower Yangzi supported a prestigious group of professional academics.[134] The medical profession provided respectable employment for upwardly mobile men or sons of gentry families who would or could not follow the standard examination route—much as the younger sons of English gentry families became attorneys.[135] Merchants specialized in particular trades or in banking. Local management, another respectable career, might involve special skills in water control, famine relief, or philanthropic activity. Law and administration required more specialists during the Qing, including respectable occupations such as private secretaries in the bureaucracy, less respectable jobs such as clerks, and clearly disreputable callings such as the pettifoggers (*songgun* 訟棍) who serviced the everyday lawsuits of ordinary citizens.[136] Specialization was slowly redefining the acceptable range of elite occupations, but on the whole it elaborated established gentry and merchant roles. Skill in certain approved occupations did not markedly improve status unless combined with other factors—birth, education, social connections, personal rectitude—that were commonly accepted social markers.

Elites were certainly becoming more functionally specific in the twentieth century; professional elites were more prominent and more organized. Various "circles" (*jie* 界) of educators, merchants, industrialists, journalists, lawyers, and financiers emerged as publicly identified and frequently organized contenders for influence in republican China. The elite's functional repertoire broadened, and the required level of expertise increased with specialized training. More important, functional competence was gradually becoming an independent source of status. In the seventeenth and eighteenth centuries, elites may have engaged in commerce, but such involvement did not per se contribute to elite status. By the twentieth century, with the formation of chambers of commerce and the official encouragement of trade, commercial or industrial prominence was likely to earn one a position among the local elite. As this shift began during the late Qing New Policies, upper-degree holders with local standing and also business interests headed chambers of commerce, conferring status on these institutions while simultaneously gaining influence from them.

As the republic progressed and elite functions proliferated, more elites were defined by their competence in functional roles rather than their embodiment of gentry cultural ideals—by their jobs and occupations rather than by their backgrounds and behavior. We see this at the village level in the new "professional" brokers; these village elites were new men—upwardly mobile hucksters. We see it at the county level in the silk industrialists of Wuxi. Now more occupations conferred elite status and more routes provided upward mobility, particularly through the army. New men appeared, but elite, or near-elite, families were best positioned to acquire new skills. Long-established patterns of elite flexibility and adjustment to changing conditions meant that even as the nature and institutions of the elite changed, there was still continuity in personnel. Though the *social* continuity of the old elite was broken, the *biological* continuity of elite families was preserved. Averill describes a particularly interesting variation of this process: young Communists challenged the old order due to the respectability and status conferred by their family positions within it.¹³⁷

Finally, we should note that in many cases, the twentieth-century emergence of functional elites is often described as the rise of less legitimate, less prestigious elite types. This is certainly true, and the new men out to make their fortunes were often more openly exploitative than established elites. Even so, legitimacy is a normative judgment, and not all change represented social erosion. Normative standards are slow to change, but they do, in time, catch up with social realities. We should remember that it was late in the nineteenth century, one hundred years after the onset of the industrial revolution, before English industrialists were regarded as respectable.

The Emergence of a Local Elite Public Sphere

The imperial state had always been extremely suspicious of independent elite associations, though in the late Ming, the Jiangnan elite managed to transform scholarly and cultural networks into organizations for political activity. The Qing cracked down severely on associational activity that looked at all political, but they did not prohibit all organized local gentry activity. Philanthropic associations—including foundling homes, societies providing support for widows, and famine-relief bodies—were the most important types of local elite organization. The Qing reasserted state supervision in the eighteenth century, though the resulting united welfare agencies (*tongshan tang* 同善堂) were run by local elites.¹³⁸ Even during the eighteenth-century height of Qing state power, local elites were gradually outstripping bureaucratic authorities in such arenas as community-oriented water control projects of the Yangzi valley and South China.¹³⁹ State policy encouraged this tendency toward extrabureaucratic elite initiative. In the nineteenth century, the Qing delegated more tax collection powers to local gentry, merchants, brokers, and guilds.¹⁴⁰ Commercial taxes were collected outside the bureaucracy, enhancing the fiscal power of merchant and gentry groups.

The mid-nineteenth century represented a major watershed in the growth of autonomous local-elite power. Philip Kuhn has shown how elite autonomy was enhanced by militia building. Susan Mann's work on taxation, William Rowe's on Hankou guilds, and Mary Rankin's on elite initiatives during the post-rebellion reconstruction demonstrate the emergence of autonomous structures of local-elite power in the last half century of the Qing. Rowe and Rankin have analyzed this process in terms of a growing, community-focused "public sphere" of organized elite activity between the official bureaucracy and the private sphere of families, kin groups, and business enterprises.¹⁴¹

If the Qing discouraged an overt *political* role for local elites before the 1890s, the 1902 to1911 New Policies of the Qing government explicitly permitted elite political mobilization in local assemblies and councils and also gave elites larger powers in education, economic development, and public security. Elite mobilization built upon the "public sphere" activities and networks of the nineteenth century, but the new political context fundamentally altered the import of elite behavior. China's defeat in the Sino-Japanese War of 1894–1895, the threat of partition in the 1897–1898 Scramble for Concessions, and foreign occupation of the capital and Manchuria in the wake of the Boxer Uprising gave rise to an unprecedented wave of nationalist sentiment. The rise of the Chinese press fanned this sentiment; general politicization of elite activities followed—a politicization that soon promoted hostility to the Qing dynasty. Provincial assemblies, local chambers of commerce and educational associations, study societies, and political associations, really proto-parties, provided powerful institutional bases for political opposition and helped bring about the Republican Revolution in 1911.

Republican elites controlled even greater organizational resources in private associations and quasi-governmental professional associations (*fatuan* 法團). These resources could lead to the appearance of a "civil society," a more autonomous successor to the public sphere, in which independent groups might organize, explicitly pursuing the interests of their members. A new type of local politics emerged in this civil society, a constituency politics of associations as interest groups, which threatened to replace the old politics of networks and personal relations. This politics developed in the cities of core areas, but even the peripheries were ultimately affected by the new politics, with revolutionary consequences.[142]

A new mass politics emerged, capable of threatening elites from below but using the same organizational forms that elites had devised to press their interests against the state. Whereas the Qing had successfully prohibited open political activity for some 250 years, politics dominated the twentieth century; the genie was out of the bottle, and the forms, structures, and discourse of elite politics changed irrevocably. Once the public pursuit of private interest was legitimized, once elites began to function as representatives as well as patrons, once appeal was made to progress and change as well as harmonizing accommodation to cultural norms, the polity was transformed in ways that presented both new opportunities and new challenges to local elite dominance.

The Fragmentation of the Elite

The late imperial gentry elite was arguably the most unified (though not uniform) elite in the world. Examination degree holders set the behavioral norms and defined the lifestyles that set the elite apart. The examination system unified the gentry nationally, guaranteeing a comparable number of lower degrees to each county and providing preferential quotas of upper degrees for underdeveloped frontier provinces.[143] No clerical, aristocratic, or military elite challenged the gentry; and the commercial elite imitated, joined, and slowly transformed the gentry—but did not compete for power.

The late-nineteenth- and twentieth-century transformation of the elite placed unprecedented strains on elite unity. The emerging public sphere opened new arenas for elite activity. Elites came increasingly to focus on their separate local arenas as much as the national exams. But the environments, resources, and interests of these local arenas differed markedly, encouraging differences in elite behavior as well. The gap widened between economic cores and peripheral zones. The cores benefited from the commercial expansion of the nineteenth and twentieth century and recovered more quickly from the rebellions. When new schools were established to replace the examinations abolished in 1905, official funds favored the provincial capitals. Core elites had the will and resources to finance schools in their own communities, and the peripheries fell further behind. Core elites organized more quickly, extensively, and effectively and pressed their agendas in higher political and economic arenas.[144]

Although Rankin and Schoppa have stressed the gap between core and periphery, Esherick has emphasized the role of an "urban reformist elite" in the 1911 Revolution, and Kuhn has written of a modernizing "new urban elite that found it increasingly hard to identify itself with the problems of rural China."[145] There is substantial overlap between these urban-rural and core-periphery cleavages. The major urban centers were all in regional cores, and the elites of these cities diverged most markedly from those in peripheries. The urban elites were more commercialized, more functionally differentiated, more likely to be trained in modern schools and affected by Western culture, and more committed to models of economic modernization that favored the cities and the cores. These characteristics often put them at odds with the elites of rural hinterlands, who were more concerned with protecting their own security against a rising tide of banditry and communist insurgency than they were with the core elite's fancy blueprints for economic development and political reform. To the hinterland, the urban elites were "false foreign devils;" to the cities, the rural elites were "local bullies and evil gentry."[146]

Just as important as these broad social fissures in the elite were more particularistic splits that came with the politicization of functional differentiation. Warlord struggles could turn elite divisions into bloody affairs; and the ideological polarization of the 1920s colored a wide variety of local factional quarrels. With different functional groups represented by their own associational structures, and with political groups forming factions to compete for political advantage, it was inevitable that the old elite would lose some of its cohesion. Broad consensus still existed on who the elites were and what qualified them to rule; but the challenge to that consensus was growing, and the internal solidarity of the elite was fractured.

Local Elites and the State

All these changes in Chinese elites affected their relationship to the state. It makes sense to begin our discussion in the eighteenth century, the most effective era of imperial bureaucratic governance. Here we see a state capable of impressive initiatives in land reclamation, resettlement, water control, and famine relief, but its powers were increasingly circumscribed by local interests as the century progressed.[147] The process, however, involved more than the devolution of state power. We have reviewed a series of initiatives, dating back to the late sixteenth century, through which local elites gradually established a public sphere for their activities in philanthropy, education, local defense, water control, public works, fiscal affairs, and, in the twentieth century, in professional associations, journalism, political organization, economic development, and local self-government. Local elites were not just filling gaps left by a disintegrating state. They were developing new strategies and institutions to guide political developments in accord with their interests and ideals.

By 1911, provincial and local elites perceived their interests and ideals to be incompatible with the Qing state. The symbiosis of imperial state and gentry elites had come to an end, and the latter joined the republican revolution. But the revolution was not simply a triumph of local elites over the state; and the republican period was more than the political disintegration of the empire.[148] Most importantly, the modern competition between state and local elites was not a zero-sum game. As local elites were organizing in new ways and increasing their resources, the state was doing the same. Beginning with hesitant nineteenth-century reactions to foreign imperialism and internal rebellion, the state was enlarging and modernizing its armies, increasing its fiscal resources with new commercial taxes, and improving its communications with telegraphs, steamships, and (by the 1890s) railways. The late Qing state took an impressive range of economic initiatives through the new Ministry of Agriculture, Industry, and Commerce and the Ministry of Post and Telecommunications, plus the Bank of China and all their local appendages. The New Army and the police greatly strengthened the coercive forces of the state; and campaigns to eradicate opium demonstrated the Qing's will to use its new powers.

Under the republic, economic development projects expanded to include cooperative formation and sericulture improvement. Social reforms broadened into widespread attacks on footbinding and popular "superstition," which could be dramatically intrusive even when sporadic. Tax increases and the conscription of corvée labor brought the weight of the state much more directly to bear on the average peasant. Such changes had a major impact on village society as old elites with community status were replaced by more exploitative parvenus connected to the bottom rungs of the new state apparatus.[149] Even if it was not very effective, a process of state building was certainly going on, and local elites were involved and reacting to it.

Elite-state relations in the late Qing and the republic reflected a conjuncture of cyclical devolution of state power with secular trends of state building and elite mobilization. The competitive expansion of both state and elite power, in a context of increasing elite organization and politicization, resulted in a conflict between elites and the state that was uncharacteristic of the late empire. Authoritarian/bureaucratic/militarist governments failed to build a broad constituency for modernizing state building but kept elite associational politics from developing into a serious bourgeois democratic alternative. Expanding state resources were not effectively translated into control or legitimacy; and the most effective republican era government, the Guomindang's Nanjing regime, showed, in David Strand's words, "a remarkable capacity to . . . punish its natural allies" among the local elite.[150] As the Guomindang shifted from mobilization to a bureaucratic style of statebuilding, it found that it could neither replace local elites nor win their loyalties. Far from successfully establishing a corporatist state, the nationalist government vitiated locally run services without providing effective substitutes.[151]

The changing elite relationship to the state, and what it meant for local dominance, can be illustrated by looking at brokering roles. In areas like North China or regional peripheries, where elite material resources in land or commercial wealth were limited, the elite's privileged access to the magistrate and local bureaucracy was one of the most important foundations of influence. The literature on the late imperial gentry has stressed this role as intermediary between the state and rural society. Local elites were brokers: acting between the official world and the local community, participating in both and (in a sense) belonging totally to neither. F. G. Bailey has written insightfully about brokers in South Asia. The broker "must make the villagers believe that he can communicate with and manipulate clerks and officials in a way that the ordinary villager cannot." This entailed a "complex task of presenting himself to the world." He must wear "a normative mask of devotion to the public weal, which had, however, to be sufficiently transparent to allow clients to see his skill at maneuvers which were normatively condemned."[152]

This description does not fit the gentry or community-rooted brokers of the Qing, who had the symbolic capital, and sometimes the genuinely high status, to justify their credentials in both arenas. It certainly seems to apply to the new type of village brokers described by Prasenjit Duara. Duara's new middlemen are recognized as necessary but often, it seems, despised; and as Bailey notes, "the middleman is despised in proportion to the disparity of the two cultures" between which he must operate.[153] The process of state building increased not only the extractive demands of the state but also the cultural distance between it and rural society. Those who served as brokers to the new state were increasingly looked upon with contempt. Respectable members of the community drew back from such tasks; and a new brokering elite stepped in. Where the imperial state had served as a source of legitimacy for local gentry, the republican state both fostered and delegitimized a new brokering elite.

On the one hand the devolution of state power left locally entrenched oligarchies unchecked by the central state. Such unchecked power was likely to be used abusively, and the repeated complaints against "local bullies and evil gentry" indicate that this was indeed the case. At the same time, equally disreputable men rose to act as brokers for the expanding state. The appearance of such unchecked, illegitimate, and exploitative parvenu elites increased social tensions and created constituencies for the radical young intellectuals who returned home to promote revolution. Because governmental power was most important in North China, both the devolution of state power and the rise of state-brokerage roles should be most important there too. The revolution grew in the north and the peripheries, where local yamens were a more important focus of elite activity, and independent networks of elite cohesion were less developed. That revolution might have been crushed had the nationalists created a more effective coalition elsewhere, but in the core areas the stalemate between Guomindang state-making and local-elite organizing left both groups incapable of mounting an effective counterrevolutionary effort.

These changes in modern Chinese elites relate more to context and structure than to behavior and strategy. The behavioral continuities across fundamental changes in economic structures and technology are extremely important. They suggest that the most distinctive characteristics of Chinese elites are to be found in behavioral patterns rather than the static attributes associated with the degree-holding gentry. This interpretation suggests new ways to look at the interaction of structure, practice, and change in Chinese society.

Flexible reliance on multiple resources was one of the most important characteristics of late imperial elites, who were never guaranteed enough of any one resource in education, land, commerce, or military power to be defined by that single attribute. Because they had long since learned to exploit changes in the available resources, they readily adjusted to the new opportunities and challenges brought by the forces of "modernization" intruding from the West and Japan. As a result, many twentieth-century Chinese elites came from the same families that had dominated their localities for generations.

The social resources, constructed in shifting contexts by elites themselves, were the most resilient. Dense networks of human relationships (*guanxi*), cultural symbols, and behavioral norms held elites together. Aware of their social superiority, Chinese elites set out to construct webs of influence to protect their status. Such social relationships proved an enduring social resource during the process of China's modern transformation, as preexisting connections facilitated elite control of twentieth-century institutions. This same continuity insured that modern forms of association were regularly infused with the status- and display-conscious norms of older elites.

Networks were fostered by the larger context of Chinese society. Neither economic integration nor bureaucratic rationalization had progressed to the extent that patrons, brokers, and middlemen could be dispensed with. Such roles were particularly important for activities that crossed arena boundaries, and China was replete with intersecting arenas: between levels of the economic and administrative hierarchy, between state and society, between upper and lower classes. In the political realm, the combination of formal integration and informal delegation of state power left unusual room for elites to exercise their patronage and brokering roles. These roles existed in dialectical interdependence with the elite's cultural hegemony; hegemony supported their monopoly of these roles and was reinforced by successful performance.

The Chinese elite's exercise of dominance through cultural hegemony, while hardly unique, was certainly striking. Cultural symbols and behavioral norms identified these elites, gave them social cohesion, and advertised their superiority. Culture-given interpretation of elite daily life was basic to the ways in which elites defined themselves locally and legitimized their dominance. Elite culture meant literati activities, to be sure, but also included patronage, philanthropy, mediation of social conflicts, avoidance of physical labor, mastery of courteous social intercourse, and public and ceremonial display of affluence. These forms of behavior proved remarkably adaptable to the social requirements of modern life, and many were found in the practices of republican as well as late imperial elites.

These characteristics—elite flexibility, reliance on networks and other social resources, and cultural hegemony—can assist us to understand the interplay of unity and diversity among Chinese local elites and the *historical* processes of elite transformation in late imperial and republican China. Unlike static conceptions of gentry society, they help explain the flexible adaptations that sustained many elite families in the hybrid elite society of the twentieth century. They also allow us to focus on those structural changes that fragmented the modern elite, fundamentally altered its relation to the expanding state, and ultimately left it prey to the revolutionary forces that united a new stronger state above and mobilized the masses below. With that new combination, the cultural hegemony of the old Chinese elites was brought to an end, but it remains to be seen how many of their behavioral norms might still survive.

NOTES

1. Mencius, *Mencius*, trans. by W. A. C. H. Dobson (Toronto: University of Toronto Press, 1963), 117.

2. There were some exceptions to the principle of open access: certain base groups such as actors and entertainers, Guangdong boat people, Jiangnan beggar communities, and Anhui bond servants were disqualified from the examinations. Ping-ti Ho, *The Ladder of Success in Imperial China: Aspects of Social Mobility, 1368–1911* (New York: Columbia University Press, 1962), 18–19.

3. Max Weber, *The Religion of China: Confucianism and Taoism*, trans. Hans H. Gerth (Glencoe, IL: Free Press, 1951), 107–8.

4. Etiènne Balazs, *Chinese Civilization and Bureaucracy*, trans. H. M. Wright (New Haven, CT: Yale University Press, 1964), 6.

5. Weber, *Religion of China*, 13–20; Balazs, *Civilization and Bureaucracy*, 66–78.

6. Hsiao-tung Fei, *China's Gentry: Essays on Rural-Urban Relations*, edited by Robert Park Redfield (Chicago: University of Chicago Press, 1953), 74.

7. Wolfram Eberhard, *A History of China* (Berkeley: University of California Press, 1971), 71–75. Eberhard is unusual in seeing this much continuity in the Chinese elite. Most scholars see a shift from an aristocratic to an examination-based elite beginning in the mid-Tang dynasty (618–906); and the term "gentry" is usually reserved for the late imperial elite.

8. T'ung-tsu Ch'ü, *Local Government in China under the Ch'ing* (Stanford, CA: Stanford University Press, 1962), 2. This figure includes 1,280 counties and 154 departments (*zhou* 州). Because departments were virtually undistinguishable from counties in size and administrative level, we group the two. "County elites" means "county or department elites."

9. This figure was supplied by Robert Forster at the Banff conference. Cf. Roland E. Mousnier, *The Institutions of France under the Absolute Monarchy*, vol. 2: *The Organs of State and Society*, trans. Arthur Goldhammer (Chicago: University of Chicago Press, 1984).

10. T'ung-tsu Ch'ü, *Local Government*, 168.

11. Chung-li Chang, *The Chinese Gentry: Studies on their Role in Nineteenth-Century Chinese Society* (Seattle: University of Washington Press, 1955), 71–141. The distinctions between upper gentry, lower gentry, and commoners have been debated by Chang, Ho Ping-ti, and Ch'ü T'ung-tsu. For a summary of views on this issue and of Chinese terms translated as gentry, see Min Tu-ki, *National Polity and Local Power: The Transformation of Late Imperial China*, edited by Philip Kuhn and Timothy Brook (Cambridge, MA: Harvard Council on East Asian Studies, 1989).

12. Ping-ti Ho, *Ladder of Success*, 52.

13. Robert Marsh, *The Mandarins: The Circulation of Elites in China, 1600–1900* (Glencoe, IL: Free Press, 1961), 187–88.

14. *Huang Ming tiaofa shilei zuan* [Categorized substatutes and regulations of the Ming dynasty], cited in Oyama Masaaki, "Large Landownership in the Jiangnan Delta Region during the Late Ming-early Qing period" in Linda Grove and Christian Daniels, eds., *State and Society in China: Japanese Perspectives on Ming-Qing Social and Economic History* (Tokyo: University of Tokyo Press, 1984), 130–31. On gentry landownership, see the articles by Tanaka Masatoshi, Tsurumi Naohiro, and Shigeta Atsushi in the same volume. Mori Masao, "Nihon no Min-Shin jidai shi kenkyū ni okeru kyōshinron ni tsuite" [Theories on local gentry in Japanese studies of the Ming-Qing period], *Rekishi hyōron* 308, 312, 314 (1975–1976), provides a thorough introduction to this literature. For English summaries, see Mori Masao, "The Gentry in the Ming Period—An Outline of Relations between Shih-ta-fu and Local Society," *Acta Asiatica* 38 (1980): 31–53, and Linda Grove and Joseph W. Esherick, "From Feudalism to Capitalism: Japanese Scholarship on the Transformation of Chinese Rural Society," *Modern China* 6, no. 4 (1980): 397–438.

15. Shigeta Atsushi, "The Origins and Structure of Gentry Rule," in Grove and Daniels, *State and Society*, 335–85. Shigeta's concern is similar to that of English historians of the eighteenth century: how did the ruling gentry class maintain its dominance as the wage economy eroded personal dependency?; see E. P. Thompson, "Patrician Society, Plebian Culture," *Journal of Social History* 7, no. 4 (1974): 133–65.

16. Masao, "The Gentry," 35–37, 47; Shigeta Atsushi, "Origins," 337, 351.

17. Robert Hymes, *Statesmen and Gentlemen: The Elite of Fu-chou, Chiang-hsi, in Northern and Southern Sung* (Cambridge: Cambridge University Press, 1986).

18. Philip A. Kuhn, *Rebellion and its Enemies in Late Imperial China: Militarization and Social Structure, 1769–1864* (Cambridge, MA: Harvard University Press, 1970), quotes from 213, 223.

19. Frederic Wakeman Jr., "Introduction: The Evolution of Local Control in Late Imperial China," in Wakeman and Carolyn Grant, *Conflict and Control in Late Imperial China* (Berkeley: University of California Press, 1975), 4, 8.

20. Susan Mann (Susan Mann Jones), *Local Merchants and the Chinese Bureaucracy, 1750–1950* (Stanford, CA: Stanford University Press, 1987).

21. For a classic example, see Kung-ch'üan Hsiao, *Rural China: Imperial Control in the Nineteenth Century* (Seattle: University of Washington Press, 1960).

22. Ira M. Lapidus, "Hierarchies and Networks: A Comparison of Chinese and Islamic Societies," in Wakeman and Grant, *Conflict and Control*, 42.

23. Yung-teh Chow, *Social Mobility in China: Status Careers Among the Gentry in a Chinese Community* (New York: Atherton Press, 1966), 158–72, 220–25; cf. Hsiao-t'ung Fei, *China's Gentry*; Hsiao-t'ung Fei and Chang Chih-i, *Earthbound China: A Study of Rural Economy in Yunnan* (Chicago: University of Chicago Press, 1945).

24. Hilary Beattie, "The Alternative to Resistance: The Case of T'ung-ch'eng, Anhui," in Jonathan Spence and John E. Wills, eds., *From Ming to Ch'ing: Conquest, Region and Continuity in Seventeenth-Century China* (New Haven, CT: Yale University Press, 1979), 4.

25. Johanna Menzel Meskill, *A Chinese Pioneer Family: The Lins of Wu-feng, Taiwan, 1729–1895* (Princeton, NJ: Princeton University Press, 1979).

26. R. Keith Schoppa, *Chinese Elites and Political Change: Zhejiang Province in the Early Twentieth Century* (Cambridge, MA: Harvard University Press, 1982).

27. Mary Backus Rankin, *Elite Activism and Political Transformation in China, Zhejiang Province, 1865–1911* (Stanford, CA: Stanford University Press, 1986).

28. Hill Gates, "Social Class and Ethnicity," in Emily Ahern and Hill Gates, eds., *The Anthropology of Taiwanese Society* (Stanford, CA: Stanford University Press, 1981), 241–81.

29. See Max Weber, "Class, Status, Party," in H. H. Gerth and C. Wright Mills, eds., *From Max Weber: Essays in Sociology* (New York: Oxford University Press, 1958), 180–95.

30. E. P. Thompson's comments on England ("Eighteenth-Century English Society: Class Struggle without Class?" *Past and Present* 3, no. 2 [1978], 146–50) would seem to apply to China as well.

31. Marc J. Swartz, "Introduction," in Marc J. Swartz ed., *Local-Level Politics: Social and Cultural Perspectives* (Chicago: Aldine Publishing Co., 1968), 6, 8–10.

32. Pierre Bourdieu, *An Outline of a Theory of Practice*, trans. Richard Nice (Cambridge: Cambridge University Press, 1977), 171–83.

33. This discussion is based on G. William Skinner's macroregions as described in *The City in Late Imperial China* (Stanford, CA: Stanford University Press, 1977). Detailed accounts of eighteenth-century society in Skinner's macro-regions appear in Susan Naquin and Evelyn S. Rawski, *Chinese Society in the Eighteenth Century* (New Haven, CT: Yale University Press, 1987), 138–216. For core-periphery distinctions, see Schoppa, *Chinese Elites*, chap. 1.

34. For example, 23.6 percent of all *jinshi* came from the Lower Yangzi provinces of Zhejiang and Jiangsu during the Ming and Qing. Ping-ti Ho, *Ladder of Success*, 227–28, 246–47.

35. On the Jiangnan elite of the Ming, see Frederic Wakeman Jr., *The Great Enterprise: The Manchu Reconstruction of the Imperial Order in Seventeenth-Century China* (Berkeley: University of California Press, 1985), 92–126. For the Qing, see Naquin and Rawski, *Chinese Society in the Eighteenth*, 55–72, 147–58.

36. Wakeman, *Great Enterprise*, 99n; Naquin and Rawski, *Chinese Society in the Eighteenth*, 151; Patricia Buckley Ebrey, "Types of Lineages in Ch'ing China: A Reexamination of the Chang Lineage of T'ung-ch'eng," *Ch'ing-shih wen-t'i* 4, no.

9 (1983): 1–20; and (for an earlier period), Linda Walton, "Kinship, Marriage, and Status in Song China: A Study of the Lou Lineage of Ningbo, c. 1050–1250," *Journal of Asian History* 18, no. 1 (1984): 35–77.

37. Rankin, *Elite Activism*, 2–8, 45–6, 61–2.

38. Ibid., 202–309; Mann, *Local Merchants*, 94–120.

39. Rankin, *Elite Activism*, 202–309; Schoppa, *Chinese Elites*, 59–77.

40. The Japanese literature on this process is extensive. See especially Muramatsu Yūji, *Kindai Kōnan no sokan* [Rent bursaries in modern Jiangnan] (Tokyo: Kindai Chūgoku kenkyū iinkai, 1970); Suzuki Tomoo, *Kindai Chūgoku no jinushi sei* [The landlord system of modern China] (Tokyo: Kyūko shoin, 1977). Kathryn Bernhardt, *Rents, Taxes, and Peasant Resistance: The Lower Yangzi Region, 1840–1950* (Stanford: Stanford University Press, 1992) introduces this subject in English.

41. The classic works are Maurice Freedman, *Lineage Organization in Southeast China* (London: Anthone, 1958) and *Chinese Lineage and Society: Fukien and Kwangtung* (London: Anthone, 1966). On frontier conditions and lineage formation, see Freedman, *Chinese Lineage*, 162–66; Burton Pasternak, "The Role of the Frontier in Chinese Lineage Development," *Journal of Asian Studies* 28, no. 3 (1968): 551–61. On Confucian models, see David Faure, *The Structure of Chinese Rural Society: Lineage and Village in the Eastern New Territories, Hong Kong* (Oxford: Oxford University Press, 1986), 142–44, 149–65.

42. Lin Xiangrui "Qingdai qianqi Fujian dizhu jingji de ruogan tedian" [Some characteristics of the landlord economy in early Qing Fujian], *Lishi yanjiu* 1985, no. 1: 61–72.

43. Rubie Watson, *Inequality Among Brothers: Class and Kinship in South China* (Cambridge: Cambridge University Press, 1985), 90

44. Freedman, *Chinese Lineage*, 68–76, 82–5; Faure, *Structure of Rural Society*, 23–26, 111–13, 128–40.

45. For example, *Shan xianzhi* [Gazetteer of Shan County], 1759.2: 77a–77b.

46. For a discussion of the Shandong gentry, see Joseph W. Esherick, *The Origins of the Boxer Uprising* (Berkeley: University of California Press, 1987), 28–37. For the eighteenth century, see Susan Naquin, *Shantung Rebellion: The Wang Lun Uprising of 1774* (New Haven, CT: Yale University Press, 1987), 29–32.

47. Philip C. C. Huang, *The Peasant Economy and Social Change in North China* (Stanford, CA: Stanford University Press, 1985), 224–33; Esherick, *Boxer Uprising*, 238, 242.

48. Niida Noboru et al., eds, *Chūgoku nōson kanko chōsa* [Survey of village customs in China] (Tokyo: Iwanami Shoten, 1981), 4: 506. A communist organizer stressed the ties of local elites to county officials during the war against Japan. Wang Yu-chuan, "The Organization of a Typical Guerrilla Area in South Shantung," in Evans F. Carlson, ed., *The Chinese Army: Its Organization and Military Efficiency* (New York: Institute of Pacific Relations, 1940).

49. See the essays by Madeleine Zelin ("The Rise and Fall of the Fu-Rong Salt-Yard Elite: Merchant Dominance in Late Qing China") and William T. Rowe ("Success Stories: Lineage and Elite Status in Hanyang County, Hubei, c. 1368–1949") in Esherick and Rankin, *Local Elites and Patterns of Dominance*, 51–109.

50. Peter C. Perdue, *Exhausting the Earth: State and Peasant in Hunan, 1500–1850* (Cambridge, MA: Harvard Council on East Asian Studies, 1987), esp. 168–70, 226–27.

51. In twentieth-century Zhejiang local magistrates often pressed innovations in the periphery in contrast to elite leadership in the cores. Schoppa, *Chinese Elites*, 102, 132–34, 187.

52. Ibid., 130–31; *Yongkang xianzhi* (*Gazetteer of Yongkang County*) (1822), 2: 20b, 3: 8a–11a.

53. For a breakdown of types of frontiers and frontier cycles of development, see Richard Von Glahn, *The Country of Streams and Grottoes: Expansion, Settlement and Civilization of the Sichuan Frontier in Song Times* (Cambridge, MA: Harvard Council on East Asian Studies, 1987), 215–20. See also William Rowe, "Approaches to Chinese Social History," in Oliver Zunz, ed., *Reliving the Past: The Worlds of Social History* (Chapel Hill: University of North Carolina Press, 1985), 251–52; and for the eighteenth century, Naquin and Rawski, *Chinese Society in the Eighteenth*, 199–205, 226–27.

54. Jonathan N. Lipmann's conference paper was further developed in *Familiar Strangers: A History of Muslims in Northwest China* (Seattle: University of Washington Press, 1997).

55. Jerome Blum, *The End of the Old Order in Rural Europe* (Princeton, NJ: Princeton University Press, 1978), 11–12, 21–22, chap. 2.

56. Jack Goody, Joan Thirsk, and E. P. Thompson, eds., *Family and Inheritance: Rural Society in Western Europe, 1200–1800* (Cambridge: Cambridge University Press, 1976).

57. Lawrence Stone and Jeane Fawtier Stone, *An Open Elite? England, 1540–1880* (Oxford: Oxford University Press, 1986), 69–104.

58. Ping-ti Ho (*The Ladder of Success*, 258) makes this argument.

59. See especially Hymes, *Statesmen and Gentlemen*; Odoric Wou, "The Political Kin Unit and the Family Origin of Ch'ing Local Officials," in Joshua Fogel and William T. Rowe, eds., *Perspectives on a Changing China: Essays in Honor of C. Martin Wilbur* (Boulder, CO: Westview, 1979), 69–88; Hilary Beattie, *Land and Lineage in China: A Study of T'ung-ch'eng County, Anhwei, in the Ming and Ch'ing Dynasties* (Cambridge: Cambridge University Press, 1979), 129; Meskill, *Pioneer Family*; and essays by Rowe, Brook and Watson in *Local Elites*, 51–81, 27–50, 239–60.

60. Joseph W. Esherick, "Number Games: A Note on Land Distribution in Prerevolutionary China," *Modern China* 7, no. 4 (1981): 401.

61. G. E. Mingay, *The Gentry: The Rise and Fall of a Ruling Class* (London: Longman, 1976), 59; see also F. M. L. Thompson, *English Landed Society in the Nineteenth Century* (London: Routledge and Paul,1963), 32, 112–17. The English figures derive from the New Doomsday Survey of 1873 and suggest that 0.0016 percent of the population owned 80 percent of the land.

62. Blum, *End of the Old Order*, 19–20.

63. Philip Kuhn, "Chinese Views on Social Stratification," in James Watson, ed., *Class and Social Stratification in Post-revolutionary China* (Cambridge: Cambridge University Press, 1984), 17, 27.

64. Mao Zedong, *Report from Xunwu*, trans. Roger R. Thompson (Stanford: Stanford University Press, 1990), 122, 132–56. On social stratification in the Lower Yangzi, see Lynda Bell in *Local Elites*, 113–39; on Hunan, Perdue, *Exhausting the Earth*, 150–63, 179–80; on North China, Huang, *Peasant Economy*; on Taiwan, Stevan Harrel, "The Decline of Ethnicity and the Transformation of the North Taiwan Elite," paper presented at Banff conference.

65. Stephen C. Averill, "Local Elites and Communist Revolution in the Jiangxi Hill Country," in *Local Elites*, 282–304; see also Cao Xueqin, *The Story of the Stone*, trans. David Hawkes (Baltimore: Penguin, 1974), vol. 1: 111, for a reference to a "Magistrate's Life-Preserver," identifying the rich and powerful in a county.

66. R. Keith Schoppa, *Xiang Lake—Nine Centuries of Chinese Life* (New Haven, CT: Yale University Press, 1989); Von Glahn, *Streams and Grottoes*, 181–202; Stevan Harrell, "Decline of Ethnicity;" and the essays by Rowe and Zelin in *Local Elites*, 51–109.

67. Harry J. Lamley, "Hsieh-tou: The Pathology of Violence in Southeastern China," *Ch'ing-shih wen-t'i* 3, no. 7 (1977): 1–39; and Rubie Watson's essay in *Local Elites*, 239–60.

68. Meskill, *Pioneer Family*, chaps. 11–12; Harrel, "Decline of Ethnicity;" Rowe essay in *Local Elites*, 51–81.

69. Kuhn, *Rebellion and its Enemies*, chap. 3; Edward A. McCord, "Militia and Local Militarization in Late Qing and Early Republican China: The Case of Hunan," *Modern China* 14, no. 2 (1988): 156–97, and the McCord essay in *Local Elites*, 162–88.

70. Rowe's essay in *Local Elites,* 51–81; also Perdue, *Exhausting the Earth*, 205–18; Faure, *Structure of Rural Society*, 42–43. 173.

71. Joan Vincent, "Political Anthropology: Manipulative Strategies," *Annual Review of Anthropology* 7 (1978): 175–94.

72. G. William Skinner, "Marketing and Social Structure in Rural China," Parts 1, 2, *Journal of Asian Studies* 24, no. 1 (1964) and 24, no. 2 (1965); and *The City in Late Imperial China*. For examples of progressive marketing integration in the Lower Yangzi see essays by Yoshinobu Shiba and Mark Elvin, 391–474, in the latter volume.

73. Gilbert Rozman, *Urban Networks in Ch'ing China and Tokugawa Japan* (Princeton, NJ: Princeton University Press, 1973), 278–84.

74. Benjamin Elman, *From Philosophy to Philology: Intellectual and Social Aspects of Change in Late Imperial China* (Cambridge, MA: Harvard Council on East Asian Studies, 1984), 112–29.

75. Skinner, *The City in Late Imperial China*.

76. James Cole, "The Shaoxing Connection: A Vertical Administrative Clique in Late Qing China," *Modern China* 6, no. 3 (1980): 317–26.

77. Robert Forster comments at the Banff conference.

78. On the cultural tempering of conflict, see Stevan Harrell, *Ploughshare Village: Cultural and Context in Taiwan* (Seattle: University of Washington Press, 1986), 135–36.

79. For a survey of the literature on lineages, see James Watson, "Chinese Kinship Reconsidered: Anthropological Perspectives on Historical Research, *The China*

Quarterly 92 (1982): 589–622. Essays in Ebrey and Watson, *Kinship Organization*, contain much historical information on lineages. On Anhui, see Beattie, *Land and Lineage*; Ye Xian'en, *Ming-Qing Huizhou nongcun shehui yu dianpuzhi* [Servile tenancy in rural Huizhou] (Hefei: Anhui renmin chubanshe, 1983); and Harriet Zurndorfer, "The Hsin-an ta-tsu chi and the Development of Chinese Gentry Society, 800–1600," *T'oung-pao* 67 (1981): 154–215. On the New Territories, see Faure, *Structure of Rural Society*. Finally, see essays by William Rowe and Rubie Watson in *Local Elites*, 51–81, 239–60.

80. Jerry Dennerline, "The New Hua Charitable Estate and Local Level Leadership in Wuxi County at the End of the Qing," *Papers from the Center for Far Eastern Studies*, University of Chicago 4 (1979–1980): 19–70; Beattie, *Land and Lineage*; and essays by Rowe and Watson in *Local Elites*, 51–81, 239–60.

81. Watson essay in *Local Elites*, 239–60. Keith Schoppa underlined this point at the Banff conference.

82. See Zelin's essay in *Local Elites*. Faure (*Structure of Rural Society*, 56–60) also used the term "trust" to refer to these lineage corporations. On corporate aspects of Chinese social organization, see P. Steven Sangren, "Traditional Chinese Corporations: Beyond Kinship," *Journal of Asian Studies* 43, no. 3 (1984): 391–415.

83. In addition to Brook and Rowe's essays in *Local Elites* (27–81), see Ebrey, "Types of Lineages."

84. Dennerline ("The New Hua Charitable Estate," 42) also treats charitable estates as corporate and charitable entities.

85. Brook and Rowe in *Local Elites*, 34, 75.

86. Susan Naquin, "Two Descent Groups in North China: The Wangs of Yung-p'ing Prefecture;" and Evelyn S. Rawski, "The Ma Landlords of Yang-chia-kou in Late Ch'ing and Republican China," in Ebrey and Watson, *Kinship Organization*, 210–73; and Prasenjit Duara, *Culture, Power, and the State: Rural North China, 1900–1942* (Stanford, CA: Stanford University Press, 1988).

87. J. A. Barnes, "Class and Committees in a Norwegian Island Parish," *Human Relations* 7 (1954): 39–58.

88. Kuhn, *Rebellion and its Enemies*, 84; Kenneth E. Folsom, *Friends, Guests, and Colleagues: The "Mu-fu" System in the Late Ch'ing Period* (Berkeley: University of California Press, 1968).

89. He Bingdi, *Zhongguo huiguan shilun* [Historical survey of Landsmannshaften in China] (Taibei: Xuesheng shuju, 1966).

90. S. N. Eisenstadt and L. Roniger, *Patrons, Clients, and Friends: Interpersonal Relations and the Structure of Trust in Society* (Cambridge: Cambridge University Press, 1984), 66, 73. In such respects as lack of community cohesion and kin structure, North China fits Eisenstadt's model better than the Yangzi valley and South China.

91. See Duara's essay in *Local Elites*, and his *Culture, Power, and the State*.

92. See G. William Skinner, "Mobility Strategies in Late Imperial China," in Carol A. Smith, ed., *Regional Analysis*, vol. 1: *Economic Systems* (New York: Academic Press, 1976), 334, 342, 357, on the better political access of cores with many degree holders. The account in Meskill (*Pioneer Family*, chap. 10) of the Lin family's long

struggle to get a hearing at court is a wonderful example of the difficulties faced by poorly connected peripheral elites.

93. On patronage and its functions in China, see Eisenstadt and Roninger, *Patrons, Clients, and Friends*, esp. 48–50, 139–45, 203–219.

94. See Duara's essay in *Local Elites*, and his book: *Culture, Power, and the State*.

95. See Bourdieu, *Outline of a Theory of Practice* for a discussion of "symbolic violence."

96. The concept of cultural hegemony originated in Antonio Gramsci, *Selections from the Prison Notebooks*, ed. and trans. by Quintin Hoare and Geoffrey N. Smith (New York: International Publishers, 1971), 12; see also Raymond Williams, *Marxism and Literature* (Oxford: Oxford University Press, 1977), 108–9; E. P. Thompson, "Eighteen-Century English Society," 163; and T. J. Jackson Lears, "The Concept of Cultural Hegemony: Problems and Possibilities," *American Historical Review* 90, no. 3 (1985): 567–93.

97. See Johnson, Nathan, and Rawski, eds., *Popular Culture*, esp. the articles by Evelyn Rawski, James Hayes, and Victor Mair.

98. Johnson, "Communication, Class, and Consciousness," 47–48.

99. Sherry B. Ornter, "Theory in Anthropology since the Sixties," *Comparative Studies in Society and History* 26, no. 1 (1984): 153; Robert Weller, *Unities and Diversities in Chinese Religion* (Seattle: University of Washington Press, 1987).

100. We thank Keith Schoppa for this observation.

101. Frederic Wakeman Jr. (*The Fall of Imperial China* [New York: Free Press, 1975], 19–28) points to the significance of elite life-styles. Essays by William Rowe and Timothy Brook in *Local Elites and Patterns of Dominance*.

102. Cao Xueqin, *Story of the Stone*, 1: chap. 18; 2: 196–97; 3: 248.

103. Meskill, *Pioneer Family*, chaps. 11–12.

104. Bourdieu, *Outline of the Theory of Practice*, 171–83, where he describes the ostentatious reciprocal gift giving of North Africa.

105. F. G. Bailey, "Gifts of Poison," in Bailey ed., *Gifts and Poison: The Politics of Reputation* (New York: Shocken Books, 1969), 2.

106. Ibid., 163. Thompson hypothesizes that the poor imposed some of their own terms as a price for the hegemony of the nobility. He explores this same issue in "Patrician Society," 403.

107. See William T. Rowe, *Hankow: Conflict and Community in a Chinese City, 1796–1895* (Stanford, CA: Stanford University Press, 1989), chap. 5.

108. Joseph W. Esherick, *The Origins of the Boxer Uprising* (Berkeley: University of California Press, 1987), 235–40.

109. David Strand, *Rickshaw Beijing: City People and Politics in the 1920s* (Berkeley: University of California Press, 1989), 227–93.

110. A Haifeng landlord stated that the main order of business was to teach troublesome peasants a "lesson in the law" (Robert B. Marks, *Rural Revolution in South China: Peasants and the Making of History in Haifeng County, 1570–1930* [Madison: University of Wisconsin Press, 1984], 184). On the violence in Haifeng, see Fernando

Galbiati, *P'eng P'ai and the Hai-Lu-Feng Soviet* (Stanford, CA: Stanford University Press, 1985).

111. This view is shared by Ping-ti Ho (*Ladder of Success*, 55, 230–31) and Beattie, *Land and Lineage*, 268–69.

112. Mark Elvin, *The Pattern of the Chinese Past* (Stanford, CA: Stanford University Press, 1973), 164–78. For a general summary of the issues, see Ramon Myers, "Transformation and Continuity in Chinese Social and Economic History," *Journal of Asian Studies* 33, no. 2 (1974): 265–78.

113. On Shanxi merchants, see Wei Qingyuan and Wu Qiyan, "Qingdai zhuming huangshang Fan-shi de xingshuai" [The rise and fall of the famous Qing period imperial merchants, the Fans], *Lishi yanjiu* 1981, no. 3: 127–44; Li Hua, Shilun Qingdai qianqi de Shanxi bang shangren [On the early Qing Shanxi merchants], *Lishi yanjiu* 3 (1983): 304–32. On the Huizhou salt merchants, see Ping-ti Ho, "The Salt Merchants of Yangchou," *Harvard Journal of Asiatic Studies* 17 (1954): 130–68.

114. Huang Qichen and Deng Kaisong, "Ming Jiajing zhi Chongzhen nianjian Aomen duiwai maoyi de fazhan" [The development of Macao's foreign trade between the Ming Jiajing and Chongzhen periods], *Zhongshan daxue xuebao* 1984, no. 3: 88–97; Yu Siwei, "Qingdai qianqi Guangzhou yu Dongnanya de maoyi guanxi" [Trade between Canton and SE Asia in the early Qing], *Zhongshan daxue xuebao* 1983, no. 2: 73–83; Luo Yixing, "Ming-Qing shiqi de Foshan shangren" [Foshan merchants of the Ming and Qing], *Xueshu yanjiu* 1985, no. 6: 81–90.

115. Willard Peterson, *Bitter Guard: Fang I-chih and the Impetus for Intellectual Change* (New Haven, CT: Yale University Press, 1979), 67–80.

116. Angela Ning-Jy Sun Hsi, "Social and Economic Status of the Merchant Class of the Ming Dynasty, 1368–1644" (PhD diss., University of Illinois at Urbana-Champaign, 1972), 135–66, 138–42, 171–78.

117. The Huizhou salt merchants provide some of the best examples of this process. See Ping-ti Ho, "Salt Merchants," and Ye Xian'en, *Ming-Qing Huizhou*.

118. Luo Yixing, "Ming-Qing Foshan."

119. See also Yen-p'ing Hao, *The Comprador in Nineteenth-Century China: Bridge Between East and West* (Cambridge, MA: Harvard University Press, 1970).

120. Chung-li Chang, *Chinese Gentry*, 114–41. This process led Ho Ping-ti (*Ladder of Success*, 256) to conclude that "money, after 1850 at the latest, had overshadowed higher academic degrees as a determinant of higher status."

121. See Stone and Stone, *Open Elite?* on the English case. The Stones argue against a notion of an open English elite but present much evidence that seems to support it. They summarize (3–6) some effects attributed to England's "open" elite.

122. Cited in Stone and Stone, *Open Elite?* 23.

123. Wang Shizhen (mid-sixteenth century) cited in Elvin, *Patterns*, 172–75.

124. See Linda Grove, *A Chinese Economic Revolution: Rural Entrepreneurship in the Twentieth Century* (Lanham, MD: Rowman & Littlefield, 2006), chap. 2, for a full discussion; also Elvin, *Patterns*, 172–75.

125. See Linda Bell chapter in *Local Elites*, 113–39.

126. Stone and Stone, *Open Elite?* 420.

127. On the wide geographic range of the Shanxi merchants, see Li Hua, "Shilun Shanxi shangren." The investment of Shaanxi merchants in the Liliugong salt wells is an example of such scattering of investments; see Zelin essay in *Local Elites*, 82–109.

128. Ye Xian'an (*Ming-Qing Huizhou*, 123–43) provides compelling examples of this "feudalization" of merchant profits through "contributions to the state and the purchase of land."

129. Marianne Bastid-Bruguière, "Currents of Social Change," in John K. Fairbank and Kwang-ching Liu, eds., *The Cambridge History of China*, vol. 11, *The Late Ch'ing, 1800–1911*, Part II (Cambridge: Cambridge University Press, 1980), 539–40.

130. McCord essay in *Local Elites*, 162–88, and "Militia and Local Militarization."

131. Edmund Fung, *The Military Dimension of the Chinese Revolution: The New Army and its Role in the 1911 Revolution* (Vancouver: University of British Columbia Press, 1980), 62–113.

132. Guy S. Alitto, "Rural Elites in Transition: China's Cultural Crisis and the Problem of Legitimacy," *Select Papers from the Center for Chinese Studies*, University of Chicago, no. 3 (1978–1979), 220–21; also Elizabeth Perry, *Rebels and Revolutionaries in North China, 1845–1945* (Stanford, CA: Stanford University Press, 1980) on how militarized groups fitted into nineteenth- and twentieth-century North China society.

133. Averill, "Local Elites and Communist Revolution," in *Local Elites*, 285.

134. Elman, *From Philosophy to Philology*, 87–138,

135. Dennerline, *Chia-ting Loyalists*, 118–19; on the English case, Michael Miles, "'A Haven for the Privileged': Recruitment into the Profession of Attorney in England, 1709–1792," *Social History* 11, no. 2 (1986): 196–210.

136. On private secretaries, Cole, "The Shaoxing Connnection;" on pettifoggers, Melissa Macauley, *Social Power and Legal Culture: Litigation Masters in Late Imperial China* (Stanford, CA: Stanford University Press, 1998).

137. Averill in *Local Elites*, 282–304; Galbiatti, *P'eng P'ai*.

138. Liang Qizi (Angela Leung), "Mingmo, Qingchu minjian cishan huodong de xingqi—yi Jiang-Zhe diqu wei li" [The Rise of private philanthropy in the late Ming and early Qing—examples from Jiangsu and Zhejiang], *Shihuo yuekan* 15, nos. 7–8 (1986): 309–10, 313, 317, 322; cf. Joanna H. Smith, "Benevolent Societies: The Reshaping of Charity During the Late Ming and Early Ch'ing," *Journal of Asian Studies* 46, no. 2 (1987): 309–38; and more generally Naquin and Rawski, *Chinese Society in the Eighteenth Century*, 44–46, 58.

139. Perdue, *Exhausting the Earth*, 164–233.

140. Perdue, *Exhausting the Earth*, 75; Mann, *Local Merchants*; Rowe, *Hankow: Conflict*, chap. 4.

141. Kuhn, *Rebellion and Its Enemies*; Mann, *Local Merchants*; Rowe, *Hankow: Conflict*; Rankin, *Elite Activism*.

142. Averill in *Local Elites*.

143. Ping-ti Ho, *Ladder of Success*, 236.

144. Rankin, *Elite Activism*, 8, 62, 176, 217, 258; Schoppa, *Chinese Elites*, 67, 95–109, 121–24, 136, 140–41, 152, 186–90.

145. Joseph W. Esherick, *Reform and Revolution in China: The 1911 Revolution in Hunan and Hubei* (Berkeley: University of California Press, 1976), 66–69, 99–105, 243–52; Kuhn, *Rebellion and Its Enemies*, 224. Note that Rankin rejects this notion of a split between urban and rural elites in economically developed cores. See Rankin, *Elite Activism*, 232–33, 243; and "Rural-Urban Continuities: Leading Families of Two Chekiang Market Towns," *Ch'ing-shih wen-t'i* 3, no. 2 (1977): 67–104.

146. On the twentieth-century use of the term *tuhao lieshen* (土豪劣绅), see Philip Kuhn, "Local Self-Government under the Republic: Problems of Control, Autonomy, and Mobilization," in Wakeman and Grant, *Conflict and Control*, 287–95.

147. Perdue, *Exhausting the Earth*; Pierre-Etienne Will, *Bureacratie et Famine en China au 18e Siècle* (Paris: Mouton, 1980); Naquin and Rawski, *Chinese Society in the Eighteenth Century*; also R. Bin Wong, Pierre Etienne Will, James Lee, Peter Perdue, and Jean Oi, *Nourish the People: The State Civilian Granary System in China, 1650–1850* (Ann Arbor: University of Michigan Press, 1991).

148. One of the best textbooks on twentieth-century China is *China in Disintegration* by James E. Sheridan (New York, 1975). For an application of this idea to local elites, see Alitto, "Rural Elites."

149. In addition to his essay in *Local Elites*, see Duara, *Culture, Power, and the State*.

150. See Strand essay on "Mediation, Representation, and Repression," in *Local Elites*, 217.

151. Joseph Fewsmith, *Party, State, and Local Elite in Republican China: Merchant Organizations and Politics in Shanghai, 1870–1930* (Honolulu: University of Hawai'i Press, 1985) argues for a corporatist state; Barkan responds in her article in *Local Elites*, 191–215.

152. F. G. Bailey, *Stratagems and Spoils: A Social Anthropology of Politics* (New York: Schoken Books, 1969), 77.

153. Ibid., 171.

Part III

FROM EMPIRE TO REPUBLIC

Chapter Four

From Qing to China

When I began my training in modern Chinese history, the field was dominated by Qing historians: John K. Fairbank at Harvard, where I began my studies; Joseph R. Levenson, succeeded by Frederick Wakeman at Berkeley, where I did my PhD; Albert Feuerwerker at the University of Michigan, where I wrote my dissertation; Mary Wright at Yale, Hsiao Kung-ch'üan at the University of Washington, and Ho Ping-ti at the University of Chicago. All of these scholars taught that the Qing dynasty laid the foundation for modern China. The first chapter here deals with one of the most obvious yet important aspects of that legacy: the borders of modern China. Before the Qing, no Chinese dynasty extended its administration to the vast frontier regions of Tibet, the Mongolian steppe, or the far western territory now known as Xinjiang—regions that, to this day, remain contested frontiers of a Han-Chinese-dominated polity. The Manchus who ruled the Qing established these borders, and with the exception of Mongolia, the borders survived the Republican Revolution of 1911. Since the Manchus redefined the territory of China and 1911 Revolution was directed against Manchu rule, how did this happen?

The dissolution of the Soviet Union along ethnic lines and the ethnonationalist conflict that consumed the former Yugoslavia led to a wealth of new scholarship on the end of empires and the rise of nationalism. In the early 2000s, I had a number of conversations on this topic with my colleague Miles Kahler, a political scientist who then headed UCSD's Institute for International, Comparative, and Area Studies. From these conversations came a workshop, a research conference, and eventually a volume of comparative studies on *Empire to Nation.** My primary contribution to that volume was this chapter on the Chinese case.

In the nineteenth century, virtually the entire world, with the exception of the Americas, was ruled by empires: British, French, Russian, Chinese, Ottoman, Hapsburg, German, Belgian, Dutch, Spanish, and Portuguese. Those empires crumbled and fell as a result of the world wars of the twentieth century, creating the contemporary world of nation states. In most cases, the empires split up into their constituent ethno-nationalist units, though that did not happen in Russia until the dissolution of the Soviet Union. The notable exception to this rule was China, which alone survived with its imperial borders pretty much intact. In China, and in much of the world today, this is regarded as unproblematic, the natural product of centuries of unified empire. This chapter takes exception to that conclusion, looking specifically at the fall of the empire in 1911 and the fact that at the time, other options were seriously considered.

From the perspective of the present day, a further implication of this chapter is relevant. The resistance of Mongolia and Tibet to incorporation in the new Republic of China was fundamentally connected to the question of religion. The distinct Tibetan Buddhist faith of the two populations and the support of the religious hierarchy were instrumental to the national aspirations of Mongolia and Tibet. This fact is no doubt relevant to the current PRC regime's suppression of Islamic identity in Xinjiang—quite independent of the party-state's commitment to atheistic Marxism or any alleged connection to terrorism among the population.

HOW THE QING BECAME CHINA†

Of all the world's great empires, China alone kept its territory basically intact as the Qing Empire was transformed, in 1911, into the Republic of China and, in 1949, into the People's Republic. This was a remarkable achievement. At the turn of the twentieth century, China was regarded as the "sick man of Asia;" the European powers and Japan had repeatedly defeated China at war and claimed spheres of interest in its territory; global commentators were contemplating China's partition—a fate that the Chinese press

---

* Joseph W. Esherick, Hasan Kayali, and Eric Van Young, *Empire to Nation: Historical Perspectives on the Making of the Modern World* (Lanham, MD: Rowman & Littlefield, 2006).

† Originally published as "From Qing to China," in *Empire to Nation: Historical Perspectives on the Making of the Modern World*, 229–59 (Lanham, MD: Rowman & Littlefield, 2006), co-edited with Hasan Kayali and Eric Van Young. I would like to acknowledge the research assistance of Brent Haas, Jeremy Murray, Zhang Jun, and Zheng Xiaowei in the preparation of this essay, and Miles Kahler and the other participants in the "Empire to Nation" conference for helpful comments on earlier drafts. Reprinted with permission.

routinely described as the "carving up of the melon." The same historical process that saw the Ottoman and Habsburg empires crumble in the late nineteenth century and collapse after World War I seemed to be affecting China. Russia, the other great contiguous empire of this age, also fell during the Great War, but managed a reconfiguration as the Union of Soviet Socialist Republics, keeping its peripheral ethnicities together in what some have called an "affirmative action empire."[1] Seventy years later, that transitional form disappeared, and the old Russian Empire has now been divided into nation-states. Thus, in the twenty-first century, China alone survives within its old imperial borders, Outer Mongolia and Taiwan notably excepted—a 14 percent loss in territory (mostly Mongolian steppe) but a mere 2 percent loss in population. (See map 4.1.)

In nationalist historiography, China's achievement is unproblematic. To a point, the argument is persuasive. China has a long history of unified empire dating from the founding of the Qin dynasty in 221 BCE, and a common culture and traditions shared by many Chinese long before that time. Though Chinese spoke a variety of dialects, the literate classes had a common written language whose classical texts formed the basis for an examination system that was the dominant route to official position from medieval times. As success in the imperially administered exams became the mark of elite status, the educational system was increasingly oriented toward a fixed corpus of classical texts, histories, and commentaries, yielding a remarkably uniform process of cultural and political socialization throughout the empire. With a strong centralized state and an elite whose status derived from participation in state-sponsored culture, there were few autonomous sources of local power and authority. China's main religious traditions, Buddhism and Daoism, were institutionally weak, and the ordination of clergy was controlled by the state. By late imperial times, as the homogenizing effects of elite culture trickled down to the general population, Chinese worshipped the same gods, performed the same family and community rituals, and donned similar styles of clothing and adornment, thus participating in a shared culture that made them "Chinese." Recognizing the cultural core of Chinese identity, much of the literature on modern Chinese nationalism describes a natural progression from Chinese "culturalism" to a new more politicized identification with the nation in the twentieth century.[2] In the comparative literature, China's legacy of shared (written) language, culture, and customs together with its long history of centralized bureaucratic governance has led some to classify China with the "historic nations" of Western Europe (notably England and France) in contrast to the more consciously created modern nations of Eastern Europe, Africa, and Latin America.[3]

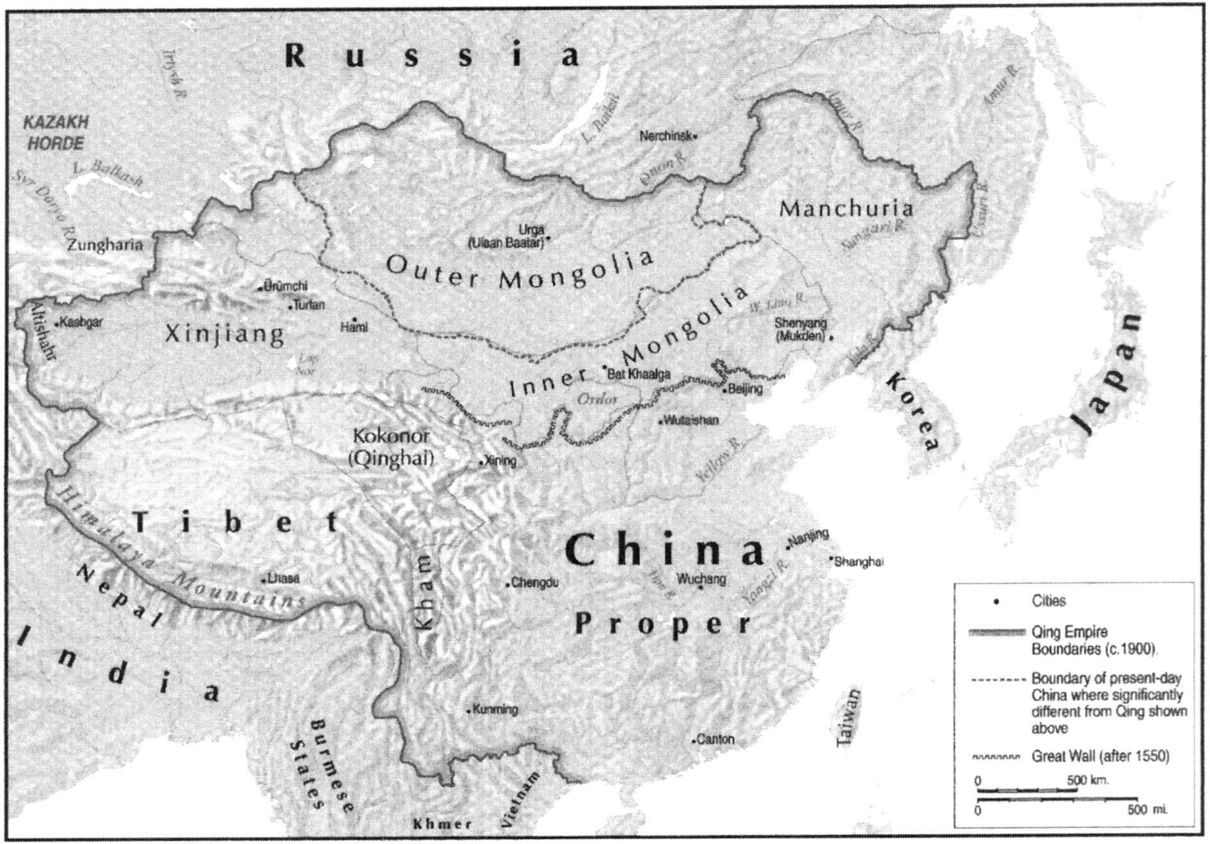
Russia
KAZAKH HORDE
Irtysh R.
L. Balkash
Syr Darya R.
Zungharia
L. Baikal
Nerchinsk
Onon R.
Amur R.
Manchuria
Sungari R.
Ussuri R.
Urga (Ulaan Baatar)
Outer Mongolia
Inner Mongolia
W. Liao R.
Shenyang (Mukden)
Yalu R.
Korea
Japan
Ürümchi
Turfan
Hami
Kashgar
Altishahr
Xinjiang
Bat Khaalga
Beijing
Ordos
Wutaishan
Kokonor (Qinghai)
Xining
Yellow R.
Tibet
Himalaya Mountains
Lhasa
Nepal
India
Kham
Chengdu
China Proper
Nanjing
Shanghai
Wuchang
Yangzi R.
Kunming
Canton
Taiwan
Burmese States
Khmer
Vietnam
Cities
Qing Empire Boundaries (c.1900)
Boundary of present-day China where significantly different from Qing shown above
Great Wall (after 1550)
0
500 km.
0
500 mi.

The problem with this line of reasoning is that modern China's borders do not correspond to the historic boundaries of shared culture of the ethnic Chinese (or Han) people, nor to the boundaries of the premodern Chinese state. Fully half of the territory of present-day China was acquired by conquest during the Qing dynasty, a dynasty in which the ruling house was not Han Chinese but Manchu intruders from beyond the Great Wall. Most of this expansion took place only in the eighteenth century. Before the Qing dynasty, the borders of China shifted substantially over the centuries, but they generally followed the Great Wall in the north and ended in the foothills of the Tibetan plateau in the west, an area conventionally referred to as "China proper."[4]

THE QING EMPIRE AND CHINA

It was only under the Manchus that Mongolia, Tibet, and the Muslim areas of Xinjiang (sometimes called Chinese Turkestan) were incorporated into the empire. The Manchus made allies of neighboring Mongol tribes even before their conquest of China in 1644. Mongols were incorporated into the Qing military apparatus; their princes were given imperial recognition and allocated specific domains in the Mongol homeland (essentially feudalizing a nomadic people); and the Manchu court routinely took Mongol princesses as imperial consorts. By the early eighteenth century, recalcitrant Mongol tribes in the west were conquered and all of Mongolia was brought under Qing rule. The Mongols followed the Tibetan brand of Buddhism, which was also adopted by the Qing court. This helped to ease the incorporation of Tibet, and the relationship between the Dalai Lama and the Qing emperor was conceived as between priest and patron, allowing Tibetans to claim the religious authority they most revered, while the Qing asserted political supremacy and backed it up with a resident Manchu commissioner and a small military garrison in Lhasa. Xinjiang was brought into the empire by a long series of military campaigns in the eighteenth century, though revived Muslim resistance required extensive military efforts in the nineteenth century as well.[5]

The Qing made a clear institutional distinction between its rule of China proper and the system of control in the frontier regions. Ninety-five percent of the empire's population was Han Chinese, and especially in its early years, the Manchus made every effort to confine them to China proper, forbidding emigration beyond the Great Wall and banning inter-marriage with the peoples of the frontier.[6] China within the Great Wall was ruled through the well-known system of centralized bureaucratic rule with metropolitan officials in Beijing carrying out the court's policies through a territorial administration of provinces, prefectures, and counties. Officials were centrally appointed from a pool generated mostly by the imperial examinations, and local administration was largely left to Han Chinese officials. Both the structure of governance and the content of the Qing legal code were based on the precedents of previous Chinese dynasties, especially those of the Ming court which the Manchus succeeded. In most respects, the Manchu court can be said to have ruled China proper in a Chinese manner.[7]

On the frontiers, the situation was quite different. Simply put, if rule of the Chinese center was centralized and bureaucratic, the prevailing pattern on the ethnic frontiers was indirect and feudal. In this respect, the Qing Empire looked a lot like most other large empires. The emperor related separately to each of the frontier peoples. Pamela Crossley has termed this "simultaneous" emperorship, stressing the distinct cultural modes of each inter-ethnic interaction, and noting the monuments on which imperial instructions were separately inscribed in Manchu, Chinese, Mongolian, Tibetan and Arabic scripts.[8] Institutionally, the Manchu homeland was administered by Manchu military governors. In Mongolia, the Qing ruled through Mongol princes, hereditary noblemen whose ranks were confirmed by the Qing court, in exchange for which they offered annual tribute. In Tibet, the Qing supported the secular and religious authority of the Dalai Lama and the Tibetan nobility from whom lay officials were chosen. In Xinjiang, the most important oasis cities were controlled by hereditary princes with titles conferred by the Qing court, with more distant regions under an indigenous officialdom of *begs*.[9] Distinct legal regimes prevailed on the frontier, with the Mongols governed by laws more appropriate to their nomadic lifestyle, and Islamic law applied in Chinese Turkestan.[10] All of this was coordinated in the capital by the Court for Frontier Dependencies (Lifanyuan 理藩院)—an office quite distinct from the Six Boards which governed China proper. Significantly, the Court for Frontier Dependencies was the exclusive preserve of Manchus and Mongols. Han Chinese were excluded from interference in frontier affairs.[11] The net result of this institutional arrangement was that the elites of the ethnic frontiers were tied politically and institutionally to the Manchu emperor rather than to the Chinese state. In the case of the Mongols and Tibetans, there was a religious dimension in this special relationship to the Qing, expressed in the Qing court's own strategic adherence to Tibetan Buddhism and the highly visible patronage that emperors provided for temples in their capital and summer hunting retreat. Given the enormous power and prestige of the clerical establishment in Tibet and Mongolia, this spiritual tie provided a bond that a modern secular nation would find difficult to replicate.[12]

Chinese statesmen of the Qing period were quite conscious of the distinct nature of the frontier regions. In modern Chinese, the term for China is *Zhongguo* (中國) often literally translated as "Middle Kingdom." The term is of ancient origins, its earliest usage referring to the "central states" of the pre-unification period. The connotation of *Zhongguo* was the primacy of a culturally distinct core area, centered in the Yellow River valley, as distinguished from the "barbarians" (*yi* 夷) of the periphery. As the meaning of the term evolved, *Zhongguo* always kept this central implication: it was a culturally defined concept, which welcomed the possibility that frontier "barbarians" could be assimilated (*ronghua* 融化) and become part of the Chinese culture area. After the Qin-Han unification of the empire more than 2,000 years ago, *Zhongguo* was often applied to the area directly administered by the imperial state.[13] In the Qing, the term became more flexible, with the empire sometimes referred to as the Great Qing (Da-Qingguo 大清国) and sometimes as *Zhongguo*. The early and mid-Qing emperors repeatedly sought to identify their expanded empire as *Zhongguo*, and the term was commonly used in communications and treaties with foreign states.[14] Domestically, however, not all Chinese accepted this equivalence, as evidenced by criticism of Qianlong's campaigns beyond the traditional borders in the west.[15] A common (and influential) early nineteenth-century conception of *Zhongguo* is provided in the magisterial work, *Shengwuji* (聖武記, Military history of the Qing dynasty), by the great statecraft scholar Wei Yuan. He began his discussion of the frontier regions in this way: "Mongolia is the general name for several nomadic polities (*guo* 國). The seventeen provinces [of China proper] and the three eastern provinces [of Manchuria] are *Zhongguo*. To the west of *Zhongguo* are the Muslim areas, to the south the Tibetans, to the east Korea, and to the north Russia."[16] Thus Wei Yuan included Manchuria within *Zhongguo*, but regarded the other frontier dependencies as something quite distinct.

The historical geography of late imperial China is thus relatively clear. On the frontiers of China proper there were Mongol, Tibetan, and Muslim regions where the languages, cultures, customs, and religions of the native populations were distinct from those of the Han Chinese. Prior to the Qing dynasty, and in most cases prior to the eighteenth century, none of these regions were incorporated into the Chinese empire, despite periodic military forays at the height of the Han and Tang dynasties. To the extent that frontier elites adhered to the Qing, their loyalty was to the Manchu court rather than to China itself. The question thus arises: How were these areas kept within the Chinese polity once the Manchu empire collapsed? How did the Qing become China?

In the popular imagination of the contemporary Western world, this problem is commonly envisioned in terms of the occupation of Tibet by the Chinese Communists' People's Liberation Army in 1950.* The flight of the Dalai

---

* Since this article was published, Xinjiang has joined Tibet as a focus of global attention, with PRC efforts to "reeducate" the Uyghur Muslim population. Needless to say, the analysis here applies to Xinjiang as well as Tibet.

Lama to India in 1959, the establishment of a Tibetan government in exile in Dharamsala, and international campaigns to "Free Tibet" have made Tibet the best-known portion of the former Chinese empire with aspirations to national independence. In the Western (and especially the Hollywood) imaginary, the issue is usually framed as an atheistic communist assault on Tibetan culture and religion.[17] While the central Chinese state only established effective direct control of the border regions under the Chinese Communists, the Republic of China from its founding in 1912 made the same claims to sovereignty over Tibet and the rest of the Qing Empire as did the People's Republic of China. Indeed, in one important respect, the republic went even farther—claiming Outer Mongolia as part of China, even after the Soviet-supported founding of the Mongolian People's Republic in 1924. If we are to understand how the new Chinese nation managed to inherit the territory of the Qing, we must focus on the moment of transition from empire to nation—the 1911 Revolution that established the Republic of China.

THE 1911 REVOLUTION AND CHINESE NATIONALISM

The revolution was sparked by an army mutiny in the central Chinese city of Wuchang on October 10, 1911. The mutiny was led by junior officers who were members of an alliance of revolutionary parties dedicated to the overthrow of the Manchus and the establishment of republican government. Within weeks, civil and military elites throughout China, but especially in the south, carried out province-level coups and declared their independence of the Qing. By the end of the year, representatives of the revolutionary provinces had selected Sun Yat-sen, long the leader of revolutionary groups in exile, to be president of the new republic, which was formally established on the first day of 1912. It took another six weeks for the Qing to abdicate and, with Sun's consent, pass power to the reformist premier and founder of the modern army in North China, Yuan Shikai.[18]

The 1911 Revolution was a relatively quick and painless transition. The ease with which political elites welcomed the establishment of the new republic revealed the extent of their disaffection from the Qing. This disaffection had deep and complex roots, but the most fundamental cause was the dynasty's ineffective defense against the assaults of Western and Japanese imperialism. Defeat in the Sino-French War of 1884–1885 led to French control of the former Chinese tributary state in Vietnam. Ten years later came the shock of military defeat at the hands of Japan, a smaller country long regarded as culturally and politically subordinate to China. This defeat was both humiliating and starkly threatening to the empire, for it not only resulted in another neighboring tributary state, Korea, falling under foreign domination (Japan would annex it as a full colony in 1910), but also produced the first major loss of Chinese territory as the province of Taiwan was ceded to Japan. China's defeat also convinced the European powers that the Qing regime might soon prove unviable, so the British, French, Germans, and Russians soon marked off spheres of influence in moves widely regarded as preparation for partition of the empire.

In 1900, ultra-conservative princes in the Manchu court gave their support to the anti-foreign Boxer Uprising, bringing on the occupation of the capital by an international expeditionary force of eight nations, who then forced humiliating terms on the court.[19] This brought to the surface, even among relatively moderate Han officials, widespread sentiment that the Manchus themselves were the source of China's weakness. When in 1904–1905 the Qing could only stand aside and watch as Japan and Russia fought a major war in Manchuria to settle which would be the dominant power in the Manchu homeland, even more Chinese were convinced of the feckless nature of Qing rule.[20]

Critics of the Qing fell into two broad camps: reformers and revolutionaries. The revolutionaries, with Sun Yat-sen as their most famous representative, held that overthrowing Manchu rule was the necessary first step to China's revival. The reformers advocated replacing Qing autocracy with constitutional monarchy. For both groups, the primary motivation was nationalism, and all agreed that only by transforming the subjects of the Qing Empire into citizens with rights to political participation and a stake in their country could one inspire the political, economic, and military commitment necessary to strengthen the country against foreign threats. The Qing court responded with a major New Policies (*xinzheng* 新政) reform program: training a New Army, replacing the exams in the ancient classics with a modern school system, encouraging economic development, building railroads and stringing telegraph lines, establishing a postal system, preparing for constitutional government, and permitting far more open discussion of political affairs in a vibrant newspaper and periodical press.[21]

To understand the nationalist thinking that guided political developments in the early twentieth century, it is instructive to look briefly at the writings of several key thinkers. The most influential public intellectual of the era was Liang Qichao (梁啓超), a prolific propagandist and editor of a variety of reformist publications after the Qing drove him into exile in 1898.[22] Liang was a passionate advocate for nationalism, which he called (following Japanese usage) *minzu zhuyi* (民族主義). The *zhuyi* in this term is simply "-ism," but *minzu* combines the characters for "people" (*min*) and "lineage" (*zu*) thus carrying the sense of a people with shared ancestry—often conceived as common descent from the Yellow Emperor.[23] In the usage of the time, it usually meant "nation," but it could also mean simply "people" (as in the Mongol people), nationality, or even "race."[24] Liang wrote in one essay, "Nationalism is the most brilliant, just, and fair of the world's ideologies (*zhuyi*). No other people (*zu*) shall infringe on our freedom, and we do not have the freedom to infringe on the freedom of other peoples."[25]

This was a perfectly sensible statement of the basic principle of nationalist thinking, but it begged the question of who exactly the "Chinese people" were—whose freedom was to be protected and what other people were protected from infringement. In one famous passage, Liang wrote, "Our greatest source of embarrassment is the fact our country has no name. In common parlance, we refer to the people of Xia, Han, or Tang which are all dynastic names. Such foreign terms as *Chendan* (晨旦) or *Shina* (支那) are not the names we call ourselves." He went on to argue that using dynastic names was an affront to the Chinese nation, while using foreign names denied mastery of one's own identity. In the end, he concluded that although "Middle Kingdom (*Zhongguo*) or *Zhonghua* (中華) cannot avoid the appearance of [excessive] pride or self-importance, causing others to ridicule us," still, these terms were the least offensive and the ones "people are used to saying."[26]

As to who was included in the Chinese (*Zhonghua*) nation, Liang was not entirely consistent, but his answer was generally that the Chinese people or nation (*Zhonghua minzu*) were those "conventionally called the Han people." He went on to argue that the Han people were a historically constructed ethnicity including many groups that had been culturally distinct in ancient times but gradually came to be absorbed and assimilated into one people.[27] After the fall of the Qing, Liang directly confronted the implications of this logic. He noted that common descent, language, and religion were all conducive to nation-formation, but the defining feature of a nation was "national consciousness." He observed that in ancient texts, the peoples of southern China had accepted their "barbarian" identity, asserting a cultural difference from *Zhongguo* in the North, but over time they had all come to share the same national consciousness. More recently, the Manchus had initially distinguished themselves from the Han, but during the course of the Qing dynasty they had adopted the Chinese language (and forgotten their own) and were now part of the "Chinese nation."[28] The Mongols, by contrast, had always distinguished themselves from the Han, "thus the Mongols, from beginning to end, have never been a part of the Chinese nation (*Zhonghua minzu* 中華民族)." Nonetheless, Liang argued that the Mongols, like the Muslims of Xinjiang and the Tibetans, lived within the borders of China, that China had historically gained strength from diversity (a sort of multiculturalism in Chinese garb), and that the absorptive power of Han culture throughout history would eventually prove capable of assimilating these people as well.[29]

If Liang Qichao tended to associate the Chinese nation with the Han people, the tendency was even clearer among the revolutionaries, much of whose rhetoric was based on an ethnic Han nationalism fed by anti-Manchu racism. This was, after all, an age in which Social Darwinist thinking was extremely influential, and discussions of a Chinese (or Yamato, English, or Aryan) "race" were thoroughly commonplace. Some commentators distinguished the terms *zhongzu* (種族 race) and *minzu* (nation or nationality), though in practice the two were often conflated.[30] Discussions of why the Manchus could not be entrusted to rule China often cited a line from the ancient *Zuozhuan* (左傳) text that used the common character (*zu*) in these two terms: "Those who are not our kind (*zu*) are certain to be of a different mind."[31] Whether the difference was conceived as racial, ethnic, or national, the revolutionaries consistently regarded the Manchus as Other—and inferior.

Anti-Manchu racism was a staple of revolutionary propaganda. One of the most influential revolutionary tracts was "The Revolutionary Army," by Zou Rong (鄒容). Zou excoriated the "lowly nomadic Manchu bandit tribe with its wolf-like ambitions." According to Zou, rule by the Manchus had deprived China of its national character (*guoxing* 國性), racial character (*zhongxing* 種性), and self-reliant character. When he gets around to discussing the Chinese race, Zou Rong's classification is quite remarkable. The Manchus are included as a subset of the Mongols, who are in turn included with the Turkic peoples in a Siberian race. These are clearly distinguished from the Chinese race (*Zhongguo renzhong* 中國人種), which includes first the Han people (who are equated to "the Chinese" [*Zhongguo ren*]) and also the Koreans, Thais, Japanese, Tibetans, and "other East Asian peoples." The publication of Zou's pamphlet in 1903 was an important moment in the activation of Han Chinese nationalism. He imagined a bright future for the Chinese who in ancient times had populated the neighboring countries of East Asia, then migrated to Southeast Asia and the Americas in the modern era, and soon promised to become "the masters of the twentieth-century world."[32]

Zhang Binglin (章炳麟), a noted classical scholar who became editor of the revolutionary paper *Minbao*, produced a steady stream of revolutionary propaganda from exile in Japan. Known for his virulent anti-Manchu rhetoric, Zhang combed Chinese history for references to the barbaric and subhuman character of the nomadic peoples on China's northern borders.[33] For our purposes, one of his most important essays is entitled "Explaining the Republic of China," in which he lays out the parameters of the republic that the revolutionaries wished to form. He begins by examining the meaning of *Zhongguo* and *Zhonghua*, arguing in familiar terms that they are really "names of an ethnic group (*wenhua zhi zu* 文化之族)." It is culture that defines what it means to be Chinese: "Ritual and education (*lijiao* 禮教) are the standard." Thus it is possible for barbarians, if they absorb Chinese culture and assimilate, to become Chinese.

He then turns to the critical question of China's borders. "The borders of *Zhongguo* are the counties and prefectures of the Han dynasty and the people are called the Hua [華, Chinese] people. If we only take the borders of the Han, then Mongolia, the Muslim areas, and Tibet are not on the map; managing them will have to wait." Returning to his cultural standard of what it means to be Chinese, Zhang then notes that Korea and Vietnam have similar customs and use the Chinese written language, so they should be included in the Republic of China—though he admits that their political independence of China (and control by the rival empires of Japan and France) make this impractical. By contrast, the Tibetans, Muslims, and Mongols have no customs in common with China, except the Tibetans' Buddhist religion. So to these, Zhang essentially offers self-determination: "we should let them stay or leave as they choose."

In principle then, Zhang's ethnic nationalism leads to the conclusion that the Qing dynasty's frontier dependencies were not part of China and should be allowed to determine their own fate. He then cites a number of practical considerations that suggest a quite different approach. In contrast to Vietnam and Korea (which should be part of China but have fallen under foreign colonial domination), Xinjiang, Mongolia and Tibet, though not originally part of China, at least do not belong to anyone else. They could accordingly be incorporated into the new Republic of China if properly assimilated. He explains how this might be done (though not in terms that the targets of assimilation would necessarily find attractive). The Muslims, Zhang says, are very clever so they can be educated—aided by the many Han colonists in Xinjiang. The Mongols are stupid, but the Han merchants who trade with them can help transform them. Sinicizing the Tibetans would have to begin with language, as they are the most isolated. So Han colonization, trade, and cultural assimilation are the mechanisms whereby the Republic of China might hold onto the frontier regions of the Qing.[34]

With such thinking dominating the revolutionary ranks, it is hardly surprising that the 1911 Revolution broke out under the banner of Han nationalism. The Chinese nation was generally conceived as coterminous with the Han people—and it was in order to revive the fortunes of the glorious Han nation that the Manchu yoke was thrown off. Proclamations of the revolutionary government in Wuchang repeatedly appealed to the aspirations for self-government by the people of the eighteen provinces of China proper, which were represented on the revolutionary flag by eighteen stars.[35] This Han Chinese nationalism was ritually celebrated in a ceremony attended by the revolutionary leaders in honor of the Yellow Emperor. A military anthem was played, with the following inspiring verses:

Raise the Han, Raise the Han,
Raise our great Han.
Destroy the Manchu, destroy the Manchu.
Destroy the thieving Manchu.
The spirit of the Yellow Emperor
Helps us to kill the thieves.[36]

In the first weeks of the uprising, the revolutionary press was full of talk of revenge against the Manchus and "racial revolution." Nor was this simply a matter of rhetoric: in Wuchang and several other cities (most notably Xi'an), there were pogroms of wholesale slaughter of Manchus in their garrisons.[37]

THE 1911 REVOLUTION AND THE FRONTIER

If this was the 1911 Revolution viewed from the Chinese center—rising Han Chinese nationalism resulting in a "racial revolution" to overthrow the Manchus because of their ineffective resistance to imperialist encroachment—what did the process look like from the frontiers? As we have seen, the fundamental Qing policy involved a systematic differentiation of the ethnic frontiers from the Han areas of China proper. Over time, however, this distinction was gradually attenuated. In Mongolia, more and more elements of the Qing code were introduced into the Mongol statutes, until by the nineteenth century the Mongol regions were basically governed by the same laws as China proper.[38] In Manchuria, the Qing initially prohibited Han settlement so as to "preserve the upright and ancient customs of the Manchus" and prevent their "tainting by Han customs." It set aside agricultural land as bannerland and proscribed its sale to Chinese. But over time, illegal Han migrants bought up most of this bannerland and established a customary legal regime for land transactions which mirrored that of the North China plain whence they had come.[39] By the late eighteenth century, Han migrants had become so numerous in parts of Manchuria and Inner Mongolia that counties on the model of those in China proper were established alongside the Manchu and Mongol banner institutions, to govern the Han population.[40] In Xinjiang, the Qing state found it necessary to promote trade to finance this eighteenth-century addition to the empire, and Han merchants soon brought their customs, culture, and families to the "New Dominions" of the west. Their settlements were initially called "Manchu cities" (*Mancheng* 滿城) after the Qing garrisons they served, but by the 1840s, they were known as

"Han cities" (*Hancheng* 漢城) in a process that has been characterized as the "Hanization" of the empire.[41]

In the first half of the Qing reign, commerce and colonization by the surplus population of North China were the main forces driving this gradual assimilation of the frontier regions. But even in this early period, the threat posed by the Russian expansion across Siberia impelled the court's closer attention to the periphery. As early as the seventeenth century, the Qing enlisted Jesuit missionaries to carry out a systematic mapping of its frontiers, an endeavor that paralleled other early modern states' efforts to mark their borders and control the populations within them.[42]

The nineteenth century brought a further mitigation of the distinction between the lands within and beyond the Great Wall. Han Chinese migration into Manchuria and Inner Mongolia accelerated, so that by the end of the century their numbers far exceeded those of the native populations. In Xinjiang, when the Muslim rebellions of mid-century were suppressed by Han Chinese armies, many soldiers stayed on as military colonists, thus enhancing the Han presence. By 1884, the growing Russian threat in the fertile Ili River region led to the reorganization of Xinjiang into a province, making it the first of the frontier regions to be fully incorporated into the administrative apparatus of China proper.[43]

By the end of the nineteenth century, the imperialist threat was a major complicating factor in center-periphery relations. The challenge to Qing supremacy in East Asia naturally began on the imperial frontiers—in a process parallel to that experienced by the Ottoman Empire in the Mediterranean region. On the outer edges of the Qing world order were the tributaries to the Qing court: states that acknowledged the Manchu emperor as Son of Heaven, offered regular tribute, and had their rulers' authority endorsed by the emperor in return.[44] These were the first to drift away or fall under the control of one of the great powers. Thus Vietnam was absorbed into French Indochina, and the Ryuku islands and Korea were dominated by and eventually incorporated into the Japanese empire. Then the inner periphery was threatened. In 1895, the offshore island of Taiwan was lost to Japan. In the aftermath of the Russo-Japanese War of 1904–1905, the two powers signed agreements to recognize Russia's preeminent interests in Mongolia and Northern Manchuria (where the Chinese-Eastern Railway linked the Trans-Siberian Railroad to Vladivostok), while Japan claimed southern Manchuria and adjacent portions of Inner Mongolia as its sphere. Fears that Russia would dominate Central Asia from the North led Britain to seek greater influence in Tibet, to protect its position in India. Thus in 1903–1904 the Younghusband expedition was dispatched to Lhasa, a serious military challenge to Qing sovereignty there.[45]

The Qing response was predictable: it sought to strengthen central control of the periphery, a move that fundamentally challenged the established distinction between direct control through provincial and county administrators in China proper, and indirect rule through ethnic elites on the frontier. As noted above, Xinjiang was made a province in 1884. In an attempt to check Russian and Japanese designs on Manchuria, a new governor-general's office was established there in 1907, governors were appointed to the three Northeastern provinces, and Han Chinese officials pressed an aggressive program of economic, political, and military modernization. Thus the Qing homeland ceased to be a special Manchu domain and was integrated into the administrative system of China proper.[46] There were proposals to transform Mongolia and Tibet into provinces as well, but the Qing was not prepared to move so quickly on that front. The court did, however, establish a number of new counties in the areas of Inner Mongolia in which Han Chinese farmers were settling in large numbers.[47]

By this time, Qing proscriptions against Han migration into the border regions had been completely reversed. Far from trying to keep Han away from the frontier regions, now the court actively encouraged settlement. Surveys were made of Mongol lands and resources, offices were established to promote colonization, and laws forbidding the intermarriage of Han and Mongols were abolished. Most of this migration was into Manchuria and Inner Mongolia, where Han greatly outnumbered Mongols and Manchus by the end of the dynasty, but there were extensive Han agricultural colonies in Outer Mongolia as well. The new arrivals were not particularly solicitous of the peoples whose lands they were occupying. In the words of an English traveler, "Very noticeable was the air of superiority assumed by the Chinese, as if they wished to impress on all that they were the ruling race. The Russians and Mongolians almost fraternized, but the Chinese traveler treated the Russian with almost the same scant courtesy as he dealt out to the unfortunate Mongol."[48]

In the final years of its rule, the Qing extended its New Policy reforms to the border regions. The most dramatic efforts were made in Ulan Batur in Outer Mongolia. There the Manchu commissioner established an Office of Military Training as the basis for a Mongol army on the frontier. Other bureaus were founded for police training, public hygiene, commerce, agriculture, economic development, and foreign relations. A school was established to educate a new Mongol elite in the modernizing ways of the reformed Qing Empire. All of this was quite costly, and the burden fell on a resentful local population. In addition, the conservative clerical establishment in Ulan Batur did not exactly welcome these intrusions, and conflicts between monks and Chinese merchants and administrators became a significant source of tension.[49]

In Tibet, conflict was even more pronounced. Major problems began with the British invasion of 1903–1904, which led to the occupation of Lhasa, the flight of the Dalai Lama to Mongolia, and his dismissal by the Qing court. The British incursion sparked a vigorous Qing response, the initial focus of which was to extend direct control to the Kham region—the largely Tibetan areas between Sichuan Province and central Tibet. The clerical establishment was particularly targeted: decrees limited the number of monks, resisting monasteries were destroyed, and tribute previously paid to monasteries was now demanded as taxes for the Qing state. Meanwhile a Chinese school and military college were established in Lhasa, and roads and telegraph lines were planned to link Tibet more closely to China. The Dalai Lama sought relief from any possible quarter, first appealing for Russian aid, then when this effort was rebuffed, seeking to make peace with the Qing, and finally returning to Lhasa in 1909. No sooner had he arrived in Lhasa than the Qing sent a large military force to control him, causing him to flee to India. From there, the Dalai Lama sought to enlist the British as intermediaries in an effort to negotiate a new relationship with the Qing.[50]

A similar dynamic ensued in Mongolia, as the intrusive New Policy reforms drove the Mongols to seek independence even before the 1911 Revolution. There too, the clerical leadership was critical, and it also sought help abroad to realize Mongol aspirations for autonomy. A diverse group of Inner and Outer Mongol leaders gathered around the religious leader of the Mongols, the "Living Buddha" Javzandamba Khutagt, and, in July 1911, sent a delegation to St. Petersburg seeking Russian support. Their petition to the tsar stressed the importance of Tibetan "yellow-sect" Buddhism among the Mongols and noted that they had "respectfully submitted to Manchu Khans earlier, because they [the Manchus] had worshipped in the Buddhist religion and spread the blessings." Common religion was the bond that united the Mongols and Manchus. "[B]ut in recent years," the petition continued, "high ranking Chinese [sic] officials have become powerful and begun to meddle in our national affairs. In particular, the worst thing is their violation, in the name of the 'New Policy,' of the old traditions by taking over land to use for farming." The Mongols' primary complaint was against the New Policy reforms and increased Han migration, and the perceived threat to their religion was a key motivating factor. Thus they appealed for Russian support: "As we know, from international precedents, any weak and small nation which can rely on a bigger and stronger nation can become independent."[51]

As the preceding narrative shows, when the 1911 Revolution broke out, both Tibet and Mongolia were already poised to assert their independence.

The other frontier areas were less threatened. The three Northeastern provinces of Manchuria were by that time largely populated by Han Chinese. In Xinjiang, the process of "Hanization" had been going on since the eighteenth century as Qing emperors encouraged trade and Han colonization to bolster the frontier economy. Perhaps even more significantly, these were also the areas that had been fully integrated into the Chinese administrative structure of provincial and local officials. But in Tibet and Mongolia, a hereditary aristocracy and a powerful yellow-hat Buddhist clerical establishment in well-funded and broadly supported monasteries provided independent sources of power and authority for peoples who sought to form new nation-states. In both regions, the preeminent religious figure became the leader and rallying point for the new regime: the Dalai Lama in Tibet and Javzandamba Khutagt in Mongolia.

In Tibet, the 1911 Revolution first sparked a mutiny of the Qing garrison against the Manchu commissioner (*amban*), and then a successful Tibetan effort to drive off the Chinese troops, who demonstrated little will to remain in this distant and unforgiving frontier post. The Dalai Lama returned from exile and declared that the patron-priest relationship which had tied his predecessors to the Manchu emperors was at an end and Tibet would henceforth be independent. Though skirmishes between Tibetans and Chinese in the Kham border region continued throughout the republican era, central Tibet established a de facto independent regime which would last until 1950.[52] In Mongolia, after news of the Wuchang Uprising reached Ulan Batur, the leaders of the independence movement declared the Bogd Javzandamba Khutagt Great Khan of the Mongol nation. Their position was quite clear: Mongolia's subordination was to the Qing, and now that the Chinese had risen against the Qing, Mongolia should resume its independent status. As one group of nobles put it: "Originally Mongolia was not part of China, but because it followed the Qing royal house from the first day, it owed that house a great debt. Mongolia has absolutely no connection at all with China. Consequently, today when the Qing court has been destroyed, Mongolia has no natural connection with China and should be independent."[53] Others spoke in terms closer to the modern rhetoric of national self-determination: "we Mongols have different traditions, language, and literature from those of the Chinese. Our Mongolian and Chinese cultures are as far apart as heaven and earth."[54] As news of anti-Manchu violence by Chinese revolutionary forces reached Mongolia, the Mongol leadership became even more convinced that there was no place for them within a Han-dominated Republic of China.[55] Their new parliament vowed to "protect our race, protect our religion, and protect our territorial integrity."[56]

DEFINING THE REPUBLIC OF CHINA

This was a critical turning point in modern Chinese history. How would the new Republic of China respond to Tibetan and Mongol attempts to establish independent nations of their own? It has been noted that adjustments in a nation's borders tend to be made early in its history, and once adjusted, borders remain remarkably stable.[57] We have already seen that prominent public intellectuals of this era, from Liang Qichao to Zhang Binglin, questioned whether Mongolia, Tibet, and the Muslim areas should be included within China. The critical question in the first years of the republic is what I would call the Ataturk counter-factual: why did the leaders of the Chinese nation that emerged from the Qing *not* make the same choice as the leaders of the Turkish nation that emerged from the Ottoman Empire? The foundational statement of Turkey's nationalist program, the National Pact, stated that "The territories inhabited by an Ottoman Muslim majority (united in religion, race, and aim) formed an indivisible whole, but the fate of the territories inhabited by an Arab majority, which were under foreign occupation, should be determined by plebiscite." A similar right to secession was offered to Ottoman provinces ceded to Russia in 1878 but later granted autonomy by the Bolsheviks, and to western Thrace.[58] The question thus becomes: why did the Han Chinese who led the 1911 Revolution not concentrate their nation-building efforts on the (relatively) culturally homogeneous Han areas of China proper, making the same offer of independence through plebiscite to the ethnically distinct peoples on the periphery of the former Qing Empire?

Recall that when the revolution broke out in Wuchang in October 1911, it was in the name of Han national self-determination, and the revolutionary flag of eighteen stars represented the eighteen provinces of China proper. Within a few weeks, however, as former constitutional monarchists and army officers joined the revolutionary camp, the vision of a new republic encompassing the five major nationalities—Han, Manchus, Mongols, Tibetans and Muslims—gained precedence.[59] Still, in the first months of the new republic, debate on this issue continued, phrased as a contest between the Greater China principle (*Da Zhongguo zhuyi* 大中國主義) and the China Proper (*Benbu Zhongguo* 本部中國) position.[60] The supporters of the latter view essentially advocated the Ataturk solution: preserving China proper but "placing the rest in a category that could be included or not." An article summarizing this debate in early 1912 (written, it must be noted, by a proponent of the Greater China position) stated the heart of the China Proper argument in the following terms: "Although China is divided among five peoples, actually only the Han have a national consciousness and political understanding. The Manchus and Muslims lag behind. The Mongols and Tibetans are like a herd of animals, primitive, simple and isolated. They have no idea what national politics are all about." The China Proper advocates admitted that the Great Powers coveted the frontier regions, but argued that it would be possible to insist on genuine independence for the frontier peoples, with a guarantee from the powers that they would not interfere. In this way, it was thought, China could avoid frontier conflicts which would weaken the young republic.[61]

It is clear, however, that the China Proper position was a minority viewpoint in public debate under the young republic. The uniformly nationalistic press provided, as one foreign paper put it, "safety valves which are allowing hotheaded patriots to vent their energies,"[62] and these patriots readily adopted an expansive conception of the Chinese nation. Often the Japanese, including an associate of Sun Yat-sen, were blamed for advocating the China Proper position as a means to advance their own designs on Manchuria.[63] Who in China might have supported this position is unclear. Presumably some of the committed Han nationalists who had rallied to the eighteen-star flag still supported a nation of China Proper. One foreign paper claimed that a "high Chinese official" allowed that the loss of Mongolia would mean only "one less incumbrance [sic]" and essentially supported the China Proper position.[64] In addition, the Chinese press often lamented the lack of public outcry against Mongolian independence—suggesting that many people did not regard this as a major loss.[65] It is likely that some merchants and businessmen would have preferred the government spend less of their tax dollars on distant frontiers and more on developing China proper. Nonetheless, articulate arguments for a republic limited to China proper are difficult to find. That, however, is less important than the fact that the debate did occur. For what we really need to understand are the arguments for the position that prevailed: the Greater China view.

On New Year's Day, 1912, in his inaugural speech as provisional president of the Republic of China, Sun Yat-sen enunciated the fundamental principle that the new regime would be a republic of five peoples that would include all of the territory of the Qing: "The people are the foundation of the state. Unifying the Han territories, Manchuria, Mongolia, the Muslim lands and Tibet means uniting the Han, Manchu, Mongol, Hui and Tibetan ethnicities (*zu*) as one people (*yiren*, 一人). This is called the unity of the nation (*minzu*)."[66] When the Qing abdicated six weeks later, the edict concluded with wishes for peace and "the continued territorial integrity of the lands of the five races, Manchu, Han, Mongol, Hui and Tibetans in one great Republic of China."[67] The conventional phrase to capture this new ideal was "the five races as one family" (*wuzu yijia* 五族一家), reflected in the new five-bar national flag of the republic, with one color for each of the major ethnic groups.[68] In the first year of the republic, prominent politicians, intellectuals and military leaders formed a number of new associations to promote ethnic harmony and national unity: the Republican Unity Society (*Gonghe tongyi hui* 共和統一會), the Republic of China Great Harmony Association (*Zhonghua minguo datong hui* 中華民國大同會), the Society for the Progress of Citizens of the Five Races (*Wuzu guomin hejin hui* 五族國民合進會) to name a few. The last of these even proposed a shared bloodline linking all to a common ancestor in ancient China—a seemingly desperate attempt to construct an ethnic-genealogical definition of the nation that included more than just the Han.[69]

This new rhetoric of ethnic unity had some difficulty in displacing the discourse of Han restoration and anti-Manchu "racial revolution" (*zhongzu geming* 種族革命). A front-page editorial in the leading revolutionary paper, *Minlibao*, stated in early November 1911, "Once we have wreaked our great revenge and the republic is established, then we must combine the Muslims, Tibetans, Mongols and Manchus into one state (*guo*) with equal rights."[70] Revenge against the Manchus was still endorsed as the first stage of the revolution—without acknowledging that acts of revenge would certainly complicate later efforts at unity. Another article explained that this was a racial revolution only because the government was Manchu-controlled and it was necessary to overthrow the Manchu minority. But a few lines later, the author proclaimed that "an inferior minority people (*minzu*) certainly cannot rule over a superior majority people."[71] The superiority of the Han was an unshakeable conviction in the revolutionary camp. Even in an article directly addressed to Manchu bannermen, which made the usual argument that "this is a political revolution, not a racial revolution," there appeared the boast that "Half of the empire is already held by the Great Han (*Da-Han* 大漢)." It promised that once the republic was formed the Han would "regard all with equal benevolence" (*yishi tongren* 一視同仁), using a conventional phrase that the Manchu emperors pledged to their subjects. Such talk left no doubt that in the new republic, the Han would be running the show.[72]

How this new republic was conceived, and how its leaders proposed to deal with the frontier peoples, is most easily examined in terms of relations with the Mongols, for the "Mongol Problem" was the most frequent focus of public discussion. To the Mongols (as to all others) the republic first promised freedom and equality of treatment. In 1912, a commissioner was sent to a Mongol area in the Northeast to explain the meaning of the republic and the president who headed it. His message, recorded in extremely simple colloquial Chinese (presumably the language deemed appropriate to "stupid Mongols"), was that a president was chosen by the people for his talent and virtue, and the principle of equality of the races meant that if an appropriately qualified Mongol were to arise, he too could be president.[73] The problem was that the most influential people in the Mongol lands were the princes. They were realistic enough to recognize that they were hardly likely to be elected president, and that equality threatened their privileged access to land and the stipends they had received from the imperial government. Thus a group of Mongol princes and lamas in Beijing formed a United Mongol Society (*Menggu lianhehui* 蒙古聯合會) which met with the new president Yuan Shikai in the spring of 1912, demanding that the princes' land rights be protected, and their stipends be unchanged from what they received under the Qing. In general, Yuan and his more conservative party favored preserving some privileges for the princes—in an obvious attempt to tie them to the new republic. But the more radical republicans were generally opposed. The right to grant stipends and patents of nobility to frontier elites was one clear advantage that an empire had over a republic of citizens equal under the law. The Chinese republic tried to get around this by recognizing the local political authority of the princes, offering them official titles, and treating them with ritual respect. This was one of the many ways in which the institutions of empire continued under the republic, but it was a constant source of tension for the new regime.[74]

To any Mongol who had access to the Chinese press, the promises of equal citizenship in the republic were unlikely to be very persuasive. In much of the public discussion of the Mongol question, references to "stupid Mongols" (*yu-Meng* 愚蒙) were so common as to become a conventional epithet.[75] The secular modernists of the new republic were overtly hostile to the powerful Lamaist clergy in Mongolia (and Tibet). The fact that these frontier regions chose religious leaders to head their governments only confirmed the revolutionaries' view that these lands were too steeped in superstition to be ready for national self-determination.[76]

In all the discussion about which peoples were to be included in the new Republic of China, there were few convincing arguments that the five "races" of China really constituted a single nation. The mantra of "five races as one family" was endlessly repeated, but nobody really tried to demonstrate why they constituted a single family; nobody was able to show—especially show to the satisfaction of the Tibetans and Mongols—why they constituted one nation. The arguments that dominated the public debate were far more pragmatic and instrumental. Two themes were prominent above all others: the loss of the frontiers would expose China proper to partition; and the Mongols and Tibetans were too weak and backward to protect themselves from foreign control, so they should be assimilated and modernized under Chinese leadership.

The first argument was made most succinctly in an article that appeared in the revolutionary paper *Minlibao* in the spring of 1911, even before the revolution broke out:

Mongolia, the Muslim lands, and Tibet have long been included in our territory. Together they form China's border screen (*pingfan* 屏藩). If Mongolia were lost, it would be impossible to protect the lands north of the Yellow River. If the Muslim frontier were lost, then the Guanzhong area [around Xi'an] could not rest in peace. If Tibet were lost, the southwestern provinces could not sleep easily. If we wish to defend China proper and the Northeast provinces, we must first defend Mongolia, the Muslim lands and Tibet. But in race, religion and customs, these lands are different from us. If we do not first promote the ideal of the nation-state (*guojia* 國家) and explain the relationship of the races, once the old regime is overthrown and the new state is established, the Mongols, Muslims and Tibetans may secede from our country and follow some foreign power.[77]

The notion of the frontier areas as a border screen (*pingfan* or *fanli* 藩篱) was a common theme and derived from a comparable Qing usage. In a sense, these areas were treated as a buffer zone to protect China proper from foreign threats.[78] The discourse reflected the fundamentally subordinate and instrumental role that frontier peoples were given in the new republic: their job was to protect the Chinese heartland.

Needless to say, this attitude denied the Mongols and Tibetans the capacity to form nation-states in their own right. The meta-narrative of modern world history takes the nation-state as the active agent, tells a story of nation-building and emerging national consciousness across the globe, and locates the subject of history in the nation.[79] Chinese intellectuals and politicians had no difficulty in locating their own history within this narrative, as they saw China struggling to cast off the Manchu yoke, acquiring a new sense of national consciousness and patriotism, and fending off imperialist threats in order to build a strong, prosperous, and independent nation. But they seemed quite incapable of imagining that Mongols and Tibetans could be engaged in the very same process in their own right.

When Mongolia declared its independence and announced to the Chinese that it had "elevated the Bogd as the Khaan and our nation is called 'Mongol,'"[80] the reply of Yuan Shikai, the new president of the Republic, was distinctly condescending in both tone and substance:

My honorable Lama, we know you are merciful to all creatures and are honest and loyal. Therefore, I would like to explain to you the matter of benefits and harm in order to avoid any misunderstanding. If any country in the world wants to be independent it must have enough people, finance, and military power, and effective political and judicial institutions, before it can exist and ultimately become an independent nation. Otherwise it will be annexed by other countries.

He went on to explain that Mongolia's population was small, less than that of one Chinese province; its economy was backward and unable to support a strong state; its soldiers still fought with bows and arrows and did not know how to use guns; and its governance was still based on a feudal system distinctly lacking in the elements of modern administration.[81]

Given this view of the backward and inherently subordinate circumstances of the frontier peoples, the Chinese solution was quite consistent: the Han migration and agricultural development of Mongolia and Xinjiang that had begun during the late Qing should be encouraged, accelerated, and organized. In the host of publications on "the Mongol problem" and frontier affairs that appeared in the early years of the republic, this was an unvarying theme.[82] The fact that Han migration had been a prime factor provoking Mongol aspirations for independence was rarely acknowledged in these writings. It was simply the best way to develop the region, to spread the Chinese culture and education that would tie the frontier more closely to China, and to provide the fiscal base for a frontier regime capable of warding off foreign intervention. When agents of these policies encountered local resistance, it was typically attributed to "stupid Mongols who lack understanding."[83]

IMPERIALISM ON THE FRONTIERS

Lurking behind this Chinese skepticism of Mongol and Tibetan capacity for national independence was the conviction that their aspirations for liberation were being manipulated by foreign powers. This was not altogether a figment of the Chinese imagination. After all, in the run-up to independence the Mongols had sent a delegation to St. Petersburg to plea for Russian support, and in 1911, the Dalai Lama was in India seeking aid from the British imperial authorities. In the negotiations with China following the 1911 Revolution, both Mongols and Tibetans demanded mediation by their foreign protectors.[84] As we have seen, in their initial approach to the tsar, the Mongols described themselves as a "weak and small nation" that required the assistance of the stronger Russians. We must also recognize that the feudal nature of Mongol and Tibetan governance, plus the fact that both new governments (and especially that of Tibet) had a fundamentally theocratic nature, meant that the administrative structures typically associated with successful nation-building were in fact lacking in these regions. For these reasons, Chinese suspicion that Mongolia and Tibet would be easy targets for imperialist manipulation were not entirely unfounded.

There was also good reason to be suspicious of the imperial ambitions of Britain and Russia. The British, after all, had earlier sent a military expedition to occupy Lhasa in Tibet. The Russians maintained a small military presence in Ulan Batur and, in 1911, Russian policy toward China was particularly aggressive. The Sino-Russian Treaty of 1881, which had solved an early crisis over the Ili region in Xinjiang, was up for renewal in 1911. In the spring, the Russians presented the Chinese with an ultimatum that was regarded as a threat of war unless commercial and other concessions were made along the Qing Empire's northern border and the Russian-controlled railway in northern Manchuria. In the words of the Qing minister of war, "all Russian measures have the object to tear Mongolia from us."[85] The Russian presence in Ulan Batur was so important that when the Chinese press received news from Mongolia, it typically came through Russian diplomats in Beijing, and there was understandable fear that Mongolia's independence movement was being manipulated from abroad.[86]

These fears reached their peak in November 1912, with the signing of the Russian-Mongol agreement guaranteeing Mongol autonomy. The agreement followed a secret but widely reported Russo-Japanese Entente of July, which established the two powers' respective spheres of influence in Manchuria and Mongolia.[87] The Russians recognized "self-rule" in Mongolia, and promised assistance to prevent Chinese military forces or migrants from entering Mongol territory, in return for which they gained substantial advantages of commercial access to the region.[88] The reaction in China was quick and furious. The press was full of calls for immediate military action from opinion leaders and army officers across the country. Nationalists from the former revolutionary parties soon to emerge victorious in parliamentary elections were particularly outspoken, and there was intense pressure on President Yuan Shikai to do something.[89]

Especially notable in the public outcry over the Russo-Mongol agreement was the utter eclipse of any discussion of Mongol aspirations or even of Mongolia's place within the new republic. The issue was now Russian interference in Chinese affairs. As one article put it, "this is not an internal matter, but an external one (*duiwai* 對外)"—a matter of confronting an imperialist threat to partition the nation.[90] The well-worn anti-imperialist discourse of protecting the nation from partition was mobilized in defense of the new republic, and it served to sublimate any discussion of who should properly be part of the nation. By acting in concert with Russia, the Mongols could not be recognized as independent political agents in their own right and were no longer a subject of debate in China. Now it was all about resisting Russia.

There was one further important complication. The Russo-Mongol agreement had supported Mongol self-rule, but it failed to specify the borders of an autonomous Mongolia. This was not entirely accidental, for the Mongols in Ulan Batur—who included several activists from Inner Mongolia—insisted on a Greater Mongolia that would include all lands occupied by the Mongols under the Qing. The Russians, however, were primarily interested in Outer

Mongolia, and had already conceded Japan's preeminent interest in the Inner Mongolian areas bordering on Manchuria. The compromise left the borders of Mongolia unspecified, and soon Greater Mongol nationalists began supporting raids on Chinese settlers in Inner Mongolia.[91] In most of the affected areas, the population was now overwhelmingly Han Chinese—as high as 95 percent in some parts.[92] As a result, these Mongol raids were widely portrayed as rebel attacks on Chinese territory. Since the Mongols were regarded as pawns of the Russians, such frontier incursions only enhanced fears that the loss of Mongolia would put all of North China in danger.[93]

Exactly the same dynamic was evident on the Tibetan frontier. One of the persistent difficulties in Chinese-Tibetan relations in the modern era has been the specification of the borders of Tibet. In particular, the Chinese have resisted claims of the Lhasa authorities (and now of the Tibetan exile regime in Dharamsala) to a Greater Tibet that includes the Kham region of eastern Sichuan and the Tibetan areas of Qinghai. Soon after the Tibetans declared independence, they sent troops to attack Chinese outposts in the disputed regions. When the Chinese, Tibetans, and British attempted to negotiate a new status for Tibet in 1914—negotiations in which the Chinese were willing to grant full autonomy to the Dalai Lama's government in Outer Tibet (or Central Tibet, depending on one's perspective)—the agreement ultimately broke down over the borders of the Tibetan territory.[94]

On the frontier between China proper and the ethnic periphery, and especially in Manchuria, Inner Mongolia, and Xinjiang, the demographic explosion that tripled the Han population during the Qing period propelled an inexorable tide of Han migrants into the ethnic borderlands. The result was the usual complex mosaic of interspersed ethnic enclaves that one sees on the ethnic frontiers of any former empire. As the process of imperial (and later post-socialist) collapse in Europe has demonstrated, these are the most difficult places to draw coherent new state boundaries. From the standpoint of the center, the best way to avoid conflict—whether domestic or international—is to draw the line at the imperial boundaries. The boundaries of the Qing had the advantage of being set by treaty, especially on the northern border with Russia. They were, consequently, a good deal clearer than the internal ethnic frontiers. When the educational reforms of the late Qing introduced geography into the curriculum, textbooks were written to publicize the international boundaries. As a result, the emerging Chinese citizenry may not have known what it meant to be Chinese (or in what way the Mongols and Tibetans were also Chinese), but it did know that Mongolia and Tibet were included within the territory of China.[95]

This brings us to the final irony in the story of how China maintained the borders of the empire. As we have seen, the Chinese of the early republican era presented few coherent arguments to explain the principles of inclusion in the new Chinese nation. Their most consistent and compelling argument was that the frontier regions must be kept as a protective screen to guard against the partition of China proper. The threat of imperialism—the fear that the Great Powers would carve up China like a melon—was the rationale that trumped all others. There is no question that this threat was real. Japan had already taken Taiwan and Korea and established a foothold in southern Manchuria; Russia was insisting on a special position in northern Manchuria and Mongolia; Great Britain demanded autonomy for Tibet as a condition for recognizing the new republic;[96] and the other powers were marking off "spheres of influence" as well. But it is equally true that some powers, most notably Great Britain, the United States, and Germany, were convinced that their economic interests were best served by preserving the territorial integrity of China. This was the case during the late Qing dynasty, when John Hay's "Open Door" notes sought to commit the powers to recognize the territorial integrity of the Qing Empire. It was equally true when the Republic of China presented itself as the successor state of the Qing, willing to honor the debts and treaty obligations of the former dynasty.[97] As the US secretary of state, Philander Knox, stated on the eve of the Manchu abdication, "It is therefore evident to this Government that all the powers have up to the present by common consent not only refrained from independent action and from interfering in China's internal affairs, but have acted in full accord with their mutual assurances that they would respect its integrity and sovereignty."[98]

This was not mere rhetoric, nor was it wishful thinking. Even the powers most involved in the independence movements on China's frontiers, the Russians in Mongolia and the British in Tibet, in the end, supported solutions that acknowledged China's sovereignty while endorsing some form of autonomy for the Tibetans and Mongols.[99] The consensus on respecting the territorial integrity of China within the borders of the Qing broke down in only one instance. After the Bolshevik Revolution, when the Soviet Union was confronted with White Russian armies operating from Mongolia, it sponsored a Mongolian Communist Revolution in Outer Mongolia, which was thenceforth permanently separated from Chinese territory. Otherwise, the Republic of China remained intact—its willingness to assume the financial and treaty obligations of the Qing earning international recognition of its sovereignty within the Qing borders.

In the end, then, the international environment may have been decisive in determining that China alone would keep its territory intact as it transitioned from empire to a nation. On the frontiers of the former Qing Empire, the Great Powers showed none of the commitment to national self-determination that the Versailles Conference endorsed in the Habsburg and Ottoman lands of Eastern Europe and the Balkans in the wake of World War I. At the same time, the imperialist actions of the Powers inspired in the Han Chinese a new sense of nationalism, a commitment to determine China's own destiny, and to develop the country economically, politically, and militarily so that it would no longer endure the humiliations inflicted on the Qing. If the new Republic of China was to overcome and reverse the weakness of the Qing, it could hardly accept borders that were less than those of the Manchu regime. So the threat of imperialism was real enough to inspire the Chinese nationalism that claimed the territory of the Qing, but not so real as to bring the actual breakup of empire.

NOTES

1. Terry Martin, *The Affirmative Action Empire: Nations and Nationalism in the Soviet Union, 1923–1939* (Ithaca, NY: Cornell University Press, 2001). Edward Walker's "The Long Road from Empire: Legacies of Nation Building in the Soviet Successor States" in Joseph W. Esherick, Hasan Kayali, and Eric Van Young, *Empire to Nation: Historical Perspectives on the Making of the Modern World* (Lanham, MD: Rowman & Littlefield, 2006), 299–339, argues powerfully that regarding the Soviet Union as an "empire" is a recent and questionable usage.

2. Joseph R. Levenson developed the notion of Chinese "culturalism" in his *Confucian China and its Modern Fate*, esp. vol. 1 (Berkeley: University of California Press, 1958). For more recent discussions of Chinese culturalism and nationalism, see Henrietta Harrison, *Inventing the Nation: China* (New York: Oxford, 2001), 1–3, 9–32; Michael Ng-Quinn, "National Identity in Premodern China: Formation and Role Enactment," in *China's Quest for National Identity*, eds. Lowell Dittmer and Samuel S. Kim (Ithaca, NY: Cornell University Press, 1993), 32–61; James Townsend, "Chinese Nationalism," 1–30, and Prasenjit Duara, "De-Constructing the Chinese Nation," 31–55, in *Chinese Nationalism*, ed. Jonathan Unger (Armonk, NY: M. E. Sharpe, 1996). For a Chinese perspective, see Li Guoqi, "Zhongguo jindai minzu sixiang" [Modern Chinese nationalist thought] in *Jindai Zhongguo sixiang renwu lun: Minzu zhuyi* [Essays on major figures in modern China and their thinking: Nationalism], ed. Li Guoqi (Taibei: Shibao wenhua chubanshe, 1982 [first edition: 1970]), 19–43.

3. E. J. Hobsbawm, *Nations and Nationalism since 1780: Programme, Myth, Reality* (Cambridge: Cambridge University Press, 1990), 137.

4. The main exception to this pattern came in the second and first centuries BCE when the aggressive Han dynasty emperor Wudi established military colonies in desert oases to the west, in what is now Xinjiang. Also, of course, during the Yuan dynasty (1264–1368), the Mongols ruled a much larger empire from a capital in present-day Beijing.

5. Joseph Fletcher, "Ch'ing Central Asia, c. 1800" and "The Heyday of the Ch'ing Order in Mongolia, Sinkiang and Tibet," in *The Cambridge History of China*, vol. 10:

Late Ch'ing, 1800–1911, Part I, ed. John K. Fairbank (Cambridge: Cambridge University Press, 1978), 35–106, 351–408. See also the special issue of the *International History Review* 20, no. 2 (June 1998) on Manchu colonialism; Owen Lattimore, *The Mongols of Manchuria* (New York: John Day, 1934), 37–87.

6. Robert H. G. Lee, *The Manchurian Frontier in Ch'ing History* (Cambridge, MA: Harvard University Press, 1970), 20–21.

7. I am aware that a substantial body of recent scholarship has stressed the distinctly Manchu nature of Qing rule. Most notably, one could cite Pamela Crossley, *Orphan Warriors: Three Manchu Generations and the End of the Qing World* (Princeton, NJ: Princeton University Press, 1990) and her even more impressive *A Translucent Mirror: History and Identity in Qing Imperial Ideology* (Berkeley: University of California Press, 1999); Mark C. Elliott, *The Manchu Way: The Eight Banners and Ethnic Identity in Late Imperial China* (Stanford, CA: Stanford University Press, 2001); and Evelyn C. Rawski, *The Last Emperors: A Social History of Qing Imperial Institutions* (Berkeley: University of California Press, 1998). The debate on just how Manchu or sinified the Qing dynasty became is well represented in Rawski's "Presidential address: Reenvisioning the Qing: The Significance of the Qing Period in Chinese History," *The Journal of Asian Studies* 55, no. 4 (November 1996): 829–50, and the response by Ho Ping-ti, "In Defense of Sinicization: A Rebuttal of Evelyn Rawski's 'Reenvisioning the Qing,'" *The Journal of Asian Studies* 57, no. 1 (February 1998): 123–55.

8. Crossley, *Translucent Mirror*, 10–11, 296–336.

9. Fletcher, "Ch'ing Central Asia"; Lee, *The Manchurian Frontier*, 59–66; Nicola Di Cosmo, "Qing Colonial Administration in Inner Asia," *International History Review* 20, no. 2 (June 1998): 287–309. "Beg" derives from a Turkic word, later pronounced "bey" meaning prince or governor. Under the Qing, *begs* were appointed officials divided into several ranks.

10. Dorothea Jeuschert, "Legal Pluralism in the Qing Empire: Manchu Legislation for the Mongols," *International History Review* 20, no. 2 (June 1998): 310–24; James A. Millward, *Beyond the Pass: Economy, Ethnicity, and Empire in Qing Central Asia, 1759–1864* (Stanford, CA: Stanford University Press, 1998), 122; Fletcher, "Ch'ing Central Asia," 77.

11. Ning Chia, "The Lifanyuan and the Inner Asian Rituals in the Early Qing (1644–1795)," *Late Imperial China* 14 (1993). The conventional translation of Lifanyuan is Court of Colonial Affairs, but the Chinese term "fan" does not imply "colonies" in the usual sense of people transplanted from the motherland, but rather frontier dependencies or subordinated polities in a feudal system.

12. David M. Farquhar, "Emperor as Boddhisattva in the Governance of the Ch'ing Empire," *Harvard Journal of Asiatic Studies* 37 (1978): 5–34; Joanna Waley-Cohen, "Religion, War, and Empire-Building in Eighteenth-Century China," *International History Review* 20, no. 1 (June 1998): 336–35; Rawski, *The Last Emperors*, 244–63.

13. Zhang Dengji, "'Zhongguo' gainian de neihan yu liubian xiaokao" [A short study of the meanings and evolution of the term "Zhongguo"], *Zhongguo dalu yanjiu jiaoxue tongxun* 53 (November 2002): 17–20; Wang Ermin, "Zhongguo mingcheng shuyuan jiqi jindai quanshi" [On the origins of the term "Zhongguo" and its modern

Chinese explication], in *Zhongguo jindai sixiang shilun* [Studies on modern Chinese thought], ed. Wang Ermin (Taibei: Huashi chubanshe, 1977): 441–80.

14. Gang Zhao, "Reinventing China: Imperial Qing Ideology and the Formation of Modern Chinese National Identity in the Early Twentieth Century," *Modern China* 32, no. 1 (2006): 3–30. This impressive article is more convincing in documenting Qing imperial attempts to redefine the meaning of "Zhongguo" than in demonstrating that Chinese scholars before the twentieth century accepted the application of the term to the entire Qing Empire.

15. Millward, *Beyond the Pass*, 38–43.

16. Wei Yuan, *Shengwuji* [Military history of the Qing dynasty] (Taibei reprint, n.d., original preface, 1842), vol. 3: 1a–2a, 185–87.

17. The best survey of contemporary Tibetan history is Tsering Shakya, *The Dragon in the Land of Snows: A History of Modern Tibet Since 1947* (New York: Columbia, 1999); for the American popular imaginary, see Orville Schell, *Virtual Tibet: Searching for Shangri-la from the Himalayas to Hollywood* (New York: Henry Holt, 2000).

18. Joseph W. Esherick, *Reform and Revolution in China: The 1911 Revolution in Hunan and Hubei* (Berkeley: University of California Press, 1976); Ernest P. Young, *The Presidency of Yuan Shih-k'ai: Liberalism and Dictatorship in Early Republican China* (Ann Arbor: University of Michigan Press, 1977).

19. Lanxin Xiang, *The Origins of the Boxer War: A Multinational Study* (London: RoutledgeCurzon, 2003).

20. Edward J. M. Rhoads, *Manchus & Han: Ethnic Relations and Political Power in Late Qing and Early Republican China, 1861–1928* (Seattle: University of Washington Press, 2000), 71–75; Kauko Laitinen, *Chinese Nationalism in the Late Qing Dynasty: Zhang Binglin as an anti-Manchu Propagandist* (Copenhagen: Nordic Institute of Asian Studies, 1990), 47.

21. Douglas R. Reynolds, *The Xinzheng Revolution and Japan* (Cambridge: Harvard University Council on East Asian Studies, 1993).

22. See Joseph R. Levenson, *Liang Ch'i-ch'ao and the Mind of Modern China* (Cambridge, MA: Harvard University Press, 1959); Chang Hao, *Liang Ch'i-ch'ao and Intellectual Transition in China, 1890–1907* (Cambridge, MA: Harvard University Press, 1971).

23. Harrison, *Inventing the Nation*, 102–4,

24. See Frank Dikötter, *The Discourse of Race in Modern China* (Stanford, CA: Stanford University Press, 1992), 107–25.

25. Liang Qichao, "Guojia sixiang bianqian yitong lun" [Distinctions in the change in thinking about the state], *Yinbingshi heji* (Shanghai: Zhonghua shuju, 1941), vol. 6: 20.

26. Liang Qichao, "Zhongguo shi xulun" [Outline of Chinese history], *Yinbingshi heji*, vol. 6: 3.

27. Liang Qichao, "Lishi shang Zhongguo minzu zhi guancha" [An examination of the Chinese nation in history] (1906), *Liang Qichao quanji*, vol. 6 (Beijing: Beijing chubanshe: 1999): 3419.

28. It is notable that progressive Manchus of the late Qing made exactly the same argument. See Wuzesheng [pseud.], "Man-Han wenti" [The Manchu-Han problem], in *Datong bao* (Tokyo), no. 1 (June 1907) (Taibei reprint ed.): 61–67.

29. Liang Qichao, "Lishi shang Zhongguo minzu zhi yanjiu" [A study of the Chinese nation in history] (1922), *Liang Qichao quanji*, vol. 6 (Beijing chubanshe: 1999): 3435–51, quotes from 3435.

30. Laitinen, *Chinese Nationalism in the Late Qing Dynasty*, 12–14, 94–95; James Reeve Pusey, *China and Charles Darwin* (Cambridge, MA: Harvard Council on East Asian Studies, 1983), chaps. 2–3.

31. Sun Zhongshan [Sun Yatsen], speech of June 25, 1911, *Sun Zhongshan quanji* (Beijing: Zhonghua shuju, 1981), vol. 1: 523; see also Wang Jingwei cited in Laitenen, *Chinese Nationalism in the Late Qing Dynasty*, 113.

32. Zou Rong, "The Revolutionary Army," *Xinhai geming* [1911 Revolution], ed. Zhongguo shixue hui (Chinese Historical Association) (Shanghai: Shanghai renmin chubanshe, 1957), vol. 1: 331–64 (quotes from 335, 336, 354–55). For an English translation of this work, see Tsou Jung, *The Revolutionary Army: A Chinese Nationalist Tract of 1903*, trans. John Lust (The Hague: Mouton, 1968).

33. The best English-language study of Zhang Binglin is Laitinen's *Chinese Nationalism in the Late Qing Dynasty*.

34. Zhang Binglin, "Zhonghua minguo jie" [Explaining the Republic of China], in *Zhang Taiyan quanji* (Shanghai: Shanghai renmin chubanshe, 1985), vol. 4: 252–62.

35. Zhang Yong, "Cong 'shiba xing qi' dao 'wuse qi'—Xinhai geming shiqi cong Hanzu guojia dao wuzu gonghe guojia de jianguo moshi zhuanbian" [From the eighteen-star flag to the five-color flag: The change from a Han national state to a republic of five races in the 1911 Revolution period], *Beijing daxue xuebao (zhexue shehui kexue ban)* 39, no. 2 (March 2000): 109; the revolutionary proclamations are in Zhongguo shixuehui, ed., *Xinhai geming* [1911 Revolution] (Shanghai: Shanghai renmin chubanshe, 1957), vol. 5, 136–52 (hereafter cited as XHGM).

36. *Minlibao* (hereafter *MLB*), October 25, 1911 (cited in Harrison, 133).

37. Rhoads, *Manchus and Han*, 187–204.

38. Jeuschert, "Legal Pluralism," 311–17.

39. Christopher M. Isett, "Village Regulation of Property and the Social Basis for the Transformation of Qing Manchuria," *Late Imperial China* 25, no. 1 (June 2004): 124–86.

40. Lattimore, *Mongols of Manchuria*, 290–91; Lee, *Manchurian Frontier*, 73.

41. Millward, *Beyond the Pass*, 124–52, 251.

42. Peter C. Perdue, "Boundaries, Maps, and Movement: Chinese, Russian and Mongolian Empires in Early Modern Eurasia," *International History Review* 20, no. 2 (June 1998): 263–86.

43. Kwang-ching Liu and Richard J. Smith, "The Military Challenge: The Northwest and the Coast," in *The Cambridge History of China*, vol. 11: *The Late Ch'ing*, Part II, eds. John K. Fairbank and Kwang-ching Liu (Cambridge: Cambridge University Press, 1980), 235–43.

44. J. K. Fairbank and S. Y. Teng, "On the Ch'ing Tributary System," *Harvard Journal of Asiatic Studies* 6 (1941): 135–246; John King Fairbank, ed., *The Chinese*

World Order: Traditional China's Foreign Relations (Cambridge, MA: Harvard University Press, 1968).

45. John Gilbert Reid, *The Manchu Abdication and the Powers, 1908–1912: An Episode in Pre-War Diplomacy* (Berkeley: University of California Press, 1935), 2–16, 124–33; Melvyn C. Goldstein, *A History of Modern Tibet, 1913–1951* (Berkeley: University of California Press, 1989), 45–46.

46. Reid, *Manchu Abdication*, 11; Lee, *Manchurian Frontier*, 138–79.

47. Nakami Tatsuo, "A Protest against the Concept of the 'Middle Kingdom': The Mongols and the 1911 Revolution," in *The 1911 Revolution in China: Interpretive Essays*, eds. Etô Shinkichi and Harold Z. Schiffrin (Tokyo: University of Tokyo Press, 1984), 131, 134–35; Wang Qinyu, *Menggu wenti* [The Mongol problem] (Shanghai: Commercial Press, 1931), 31–33.

48. H. G. C. Perry-Aysough and R. B. Otter-Barry, *With the Russians in Mongolia* (London: John Lane the Bodley Head, 1914).

49. Urgunge Onon and Derrick Pritchatt, *Asia's First Modern Revolution: Mongolia Proclaims its Independence in 1911* (Leiden: E. J. Brill, 1998), 4–5; Zhang Qixiong, *Wai-Meng zhuquan guishu jiaoshe, 1911–1916* [English title: Disputes and negotiations over Outer Mongolia's national identity, unification or independence and sovereignty, 1911–1916: An observation based on the principle of the Chinese world order] (Taibei: Academia Sinica, 1995), 22–23.

50. Goldstein, *A History of Modern Tibet*, 45–58; Dahpon Ho, "The Men Who Would Not Be Amban and the One Who Would: Four Frontline Statesmen and Qing Tibet Policy, 1905–1911," *Modern China* 34, no. 2 (2008): 210–46.

51. Petition of Javzandamba Khutagt and three others, July 29, 1911, cited in Onon and Pritchatt, *Asia's First Revolution*, 9–10. See also discussion in Nakami, "A Protest."

52. See Goldstein, *A History of Modern Tibet*; Dahpon Ho, "The Men Who Would Not Be Amban and the One Who Would." Given the completeness of Goldstein's and Ho's treatments, and the fact that in the early Republic most of the Chinese discussion was on Mongolia, the remainder of this chapter will follow the Chinese sources and focus on Mongolia.

53. Onon and Pritchatt, *Asia's First Revolution*, 40; see also Perry-Aysough and Otter-Barry, *With the Russians in Mongolia*, 42.

54. Onon and Pritchatt, *Asia's First Revolution*, 62.

55. "Mengren hebi huaiyi" [Why are the Mongols suspicious?], *MLB*, December 13, 1911, 4. Wu Tingfang, the revolutionaries' representative in negotiations with the Qing authorities, responded to a cable from several Mongol princes denying rumors that his party's program was a "narrow nationalism" (Guo Xiaocheng, "Menggu duli ji" [An account of Mongolia's independence], *XHGM*, vol. 7: 291).

56. Proclamation of Mongol parliament, January 17, 1912, *XHGM*, vol. 7: 306–7.

57. Rustow, *A World of Nations*, 22, cited in Lowell Dittmer and Samuel S. Kim, "In Search of a Theory of National Identity" in *China's Quest for National Identity*, 8.

58. Cited in Erik J. Zürcher, *Turkey: A Modern History* (London: I. B. Tauris, 1993), 144.

59. Zhang Yong, "Cong shiba xing qi," 110–11.

60. The author of the article (cited in the following note) also called the China Proper policy the "Lesser China principle" [Xiao Zhongguo zhuyi 小中国主义] but it is unlikely that the advocates of this view would have used such a term.

61. "Zhonghua minguo zhiding xin xianfa zhi xianjue wenti" [Problems that must be solved before deciding on a new constitution for the Republic of China], *MLB*, January 27, 1912, 1. This long essay is continued on February 4 and 7, 1912.

62. *The Celestial Empire* (Shanghai), November 23, 1912, 288.

63. *Shenbao*, editorials of October 2, 5, and 8, 1912. The Japanese advocate of this position was Fukumoto Sei.

64. *The Celestial Empire* (Shanghai), November 23, 1912, 288.

65. *MLB*, November 18, 1912; *Shenbao*, February 14, 1913; *Shibao*, September 14, 1912.

66. "Linshi Dazongtong xuanyan shu" [Proclamation of the provisional president], *Sun Zhongshan quanji* (Beijing: Zhonghua shuju, 1981), vol. 2: 2.

67. Abdication edict of February 12, 1912, in Zhongguo dier lishi dang'an guan, ed. *Zhonghua minguo shi dang'an ziliao huibian* (Nanjing: Jiangsu People's Press, 1979), 217–18.

68. Harrison, *Inventing China*, 133–35.

69. Founders of the Republican Unity Association included Wu Tingfang, Zhang Jian, Chen Qimei and Wang Jingwei (*MLB*, December 21 and 23, 1911); the Republic of China Great Harmony Association included a number of Manchus and Mongols along with the Hunan governor Tan Yankai (*MLB*, March 19, 1912, 12); the Society for the Progress of Citizens of the Five Races included the revolutionary leader Huang Xing, Vice-President Li Yuanhong and leading figures of the Beijing government: Liang Shiyi, Duan Qirui, Cai Yuanpei. On ethnic-geneological vs. civic-territorial definitions of nations, see Anthony D. Smith, *The Ethnic Origins of Nations* (Oxford: Blackwell, 1986).

70. "Minguo qingzhu wen" [In celebration of the republic], *MLB*, November 7, 1911, 1.

71. *MLB*, November 20, 1911, 3.

72. "Ning-Hang liangcheng zhi qiren kan" [Bannermen of Nanjing and Hangzhou: Look!], *MLB*, October 29, 1911, 1. The same "equal benevolence" phrase is used in *MLB*, November 8, 1911, 1.

73. Zhou Zhengchao, *Meng-shi jilue* [An account of Mongol affairs] (n.p.: 1913), 3a–b, 15–16.

74. On Mongol honors, titles and stipends under the republic, see Zhuo Hongmou, *Menggu jian* (Mongol reference) (Beijing: self-published, 1919), chap. 9: 44–80; Guo Xiaocheng, "Menggu duliji," 291; Onon and Pritchatt, *Asia's First Revolution*, 60–61; *XHGM*, vol. 7: 300–302; "Menggu weilai zhi xingzheng" [The future administration of Mongolia], *MLB*, April 7, 1912, 7; "Lun youdai Menggu tiaojian" [On the conditions for privileged treatment of the Mongols], *MLB*, June 20, 1912, 2; *Dongfang zazhi* 17, no. 17 (August 5, 1920): 134; and 17, no. 18 (August 31, 1920): 145; and also the essay by Uradyn Bulag in Esherick, Kayali, and Van Young, *Empire to Nation*, 260–95.

75. For examples, see "Menggu wenti" [The Mongol problem], *MLB* editorial, January 14, 1912, 1.

76. Telegram from Gu Baoheng in Ulan Batur, December 20, 1911, *XHGM*, vol. 7: 296–97; *MLB*, November 22, 1912, 6–7 on punishing the "demon monks."

77. "Lianhe Han-Man-Meng-Hui-Zang zuzhi mindang yijianshu" [Memorandum on uniting the Han, Manchus, Mongols, Muslims and Tibetans in a People's Party], *MLB*, March 21 and 22, 1911, 1 (quote from March 22 issue). For similar sentiments, see "Lun wai-Meng zhi weiji riji" [The Outer Mongolian crisis worsens day by day], *MLB*, April 14, 1912; "Gonghe tongyi hui yijianshu" [Memorandum on the Republican Unity Party], *MLB*, December 21 and 23, 1911; also, *MLB*, June 10, 1912, 2.

78. See "Menggu wenti," *MLB*, January 14, 1912, 1; and "Wuhu! Sanbainian xiongfan" [Alas! The brave fence of 300 years], *MLB*, November 6, 1910, 3. Officials of the new republic even spoke to the Mongols' independent regime in the same terms, affirming the established relationship in which the Tibetans and Mongols "follow their traditional life-style and shield the western and northern regions" (Telegram from the department of Mongolian Affairs, early 1912, cited in Onon and Pritchatt, 60). For Qing examples, see Zhang Yuxin, *Qingdai qianqi geminzu tongyi guannian de lishi tezheng* [The historical characteristics of early Qing concepts of unity of the various peoples], *Qingshi yanjiu* 1996, no. 2, 36.

79. This discussion is inspired by Prasenjit Duara, *Rescuing History from the Nation: Questioning Narratives of Modern China* (Chicago: University of Chicago Press, 1995), chap. 1.

80. Telegram of March 12, 1912, in Onon and Pritchatt, *Asia's First Revolution*, 61–62.

81. Telegram from Yuan Shikai to the Bogd, in Onon and Pritchatt, *Asia's First Revolution*, 62–63.

82. The magazine *Xibei zazhi* [The Northwest], founded in November 1912 to promote the development of the northern and western frontiers, is typical; see also *Choubian zouyan* [Proposals on border affairs] (n.p. [Beijing?], n.d. [early 1910s]); *Renzi bianshi guanjian* [My humble opinions on border affairs, 1913] (Beijing: 1913); Jin Nan, *Mengshi yiban* [A general account of Mongol affairs] (n.p. [Beijing?]. n.d. [1910s]).

83. Zhou Zhengchao, *Meng-shi jilue*, 12–13.

84. Onon and Pritchatt, *Asia's First Revolution*, 41–77; Goldstein, *Modern Tibet*, 53–88. The parallelism in the strategies of Mongolia and Tibet was hardly accidental. Not only were the two areas linked by a common religion, but the Dalai Lama had fled to Mongolia in 1904, and the two new regimes offered each other mutual recognition in 1912 (Onon and Pritchatt, *Asia's First Revolution*, 112–13).

85. Yinchang to German minister in Beijing, reported in dispatch of March 30, 1911, in Reid, 216. See also "Wei Gang," [pseud.] *E-Meng jiaoshe shimo* [Full account of the negotiations with Russia and Mongolia] [1912], in Zuo Shunsheng, *Zhongguo jinbainian shi ziliao* [Historical materials on the last one hundred years of Chinese history] (Taipei: Taiwan Zhonghua shuju, 1966), vol. 1, 583–90.

86. As one reads pro-Mongol accounts of the independence movement, one is struck by the close communication between Mongols and both official Russian

representatives and Russian Mongolists who served as advisors and intermediaries in Russian-Mongol affairs (Onon and Pritchatt, *Asia's First Revolution*, esp. 79–107).

87. Nakami, "A Protest," 141–42.
88. Onon and Pritchatt, *Asia's First Revolution*, 46–50.
89. Wei Gang, *E-Meng jiaoshe shimo*; *MLB*, November–December 1912.
90. *MLB*, November 22, 1912, 2.
91. Onon and Pritchatt, *Asia's First Revolution*, 19–21, 42–53; Nakami, "A Protest," 143.
92. Onon and Pritchatt, *Asia's First Revolution*, 22 (The figure is for the Jirim League).
93. *MLB*, December 1, 1912.
94. Goldstein, *Modern Tibet*, 65–75. For an overview of the borders of Tibet, as defined by the various parties over time, see Shakya, xiii–xv.
95. See the "Ministry of Education approved" *Man-Meng-Xin-Zang shulue* [Account of Manchuria, Mongolia, Xinjiang, and Tibet] by Jin Zhonglin (Kaifeng, Rugushan fang, 1909); Gang Zhao, "Reinventing China."
96. *The Celestial Empire*, September 7, 1912, 367; September 21, 1912, 446; September 28, 1912, Supplement, 58.
97. This was the consistent policy from the first days of the revolution. See Esherick, *Reform and Revolution*, 190.
98. Philander Knox, February 3, 1912, cited in Reid, *Manchu Abdication*, 290.
99. Onon and Pritchatt, *Asia's First Revolution*, 58, 68–71; Nakami, "A Protest," 144–46; Goldstein, *Modern Tibet*, 68–75.

Chapter Five

Sun Yat-sen: Father of the Nation

Sun Yat-sen is arguably the most widely respected Chinese political leader of the modern era, celebrated by both the Communist Party and its rivals in the Nationalist Party (Guomindang or Kuomintang). Sun devoted his life to the cause of revolution, first promoting the overthrow of the Qing dynasty, then allying his Nationalist Party with the Communists in a partnership that would unify the nation soon after his death in 1925. After they came to power, Sun's Nationalist Party successors built an enormous mausoleum in Nanjing, which remains a popular monument to this day. Nationalist officials held weekly memorial services in his honor and constructed a ruling ideology around his Three People's Principles (Sanmin zhuyi 三民主義). During the War of Resistance against Japan, the Communists and Nationalists again allied against the national enemy, both parties claiming to rule according to Sun's Three People's Principles, and Sun was officially proclaimed the Father of the Nation: Guofu (國父). This title derived from Sun's role in ending the imperial system, and specifically to his selection as "provisional president" for a few months in 1912, before being pushed aside by Yuan Shikai, the military leader and last premier of the Qing.

Sun Yat-sen was no George Washington; but he was frequently compared to the United States' first president, which underscores the importance of understanding how he was elected in 1911. My PhD dissertation and first monograph analyzed the 1911 Revolution. The book was a social history of the revolution that toppled China's last empire, an effort to go beyond the conventional narrative centered on Sun Yat-sen's overseas activities and his Revolutionary Alliance (Tongmenghui), and to examine developments internal to China. Yet in December 1911, Sun Yat-sen returned to China and was quickly elected as the provisional president of the new Republic of China. Given Sun's minimal role in the uprisings against the Qing, his sudden emergence as the Father of the Republic surprised me. This chapter, originally written for a conference commemorating the eightieth anniversary of 1911, is an effort to explain that selection.

The essay is important for two reasons. First, although Sun's selection as the first provisional president of the republic is an important moment in the narrative explaining his emergence as Father of the Nation, his election to this post was scarcely mentioned in the contemporary press. His inauguration as president, which took place late at night without any photographic record, was only briefly reported in the newspapers, which remained focused on events in Beijing, the Qing capital. Although, in retrospect, the selection of China's first republican president was a momentous break from China's imperial past; at the time, it was barely noticed. As the historian analyzes and interprets historical developments, it is necessary to remember that contemporary participants and observers may not recognize the significance of critical turning points in history. What is settled past to us was an unknown future at the time.

Second, and perhaps even more important, we learn from this example how myths are created that bear little resemblance to the view of the time. Sun Yat-sen was in Colorado when the 1911 Revolution broke out. The revolution was led by army officers and former constitutionalists who had lost faith in the monarchy's capacity to reform. Sun's own role was minimal, but he returned to China at a time when China needed a leader to rally around. Within a few months, he was sidelined again, and his entire career was marked more by failure than success. Indeed, it may be argued that his reputation was saved by his early death: he never had to make the hard choices required in actually ruling China. Nonetheless, the Nationalist Party needed a hero and quickly set about creating a revolutionary narrative around Sun and elevated his Three Principles of the People into a ruling ideology. The historian's role is to examine the facts behind these myths, to understand history as it happened, not as it is later reconstructed for current political purposes.

FOUNDING A REPUBLIC, ELECTING A PRESIDENT: HOW SUN YAT-SEN BECAME *GUOFU*[*]

When the Wuchang uprising broke out on October 10, 1911, Sun Yat-sen got the news from the morning paper in Denver, Colorado. For the next two and a half months, as the fate of the revolution was being decided by successive

---

[*] Originally published as "Founding a Republic, Electing a President: How Sun Yat-sen Became Guofu," in Harold Shiffrin and Eto Shinkichi, eds., *China's Republican Revolution* (Tokyo: University of Tokyo Press, 1994), 129–52. Reprinted with the publisher's permission.

provincial coups on behalf of the republic, Sun took a time-consuming return trip to China by way of New York, Washington, London, Paris, and then a long sea voyage through the Suez Canal to Singapore, Hong Kong, and finally Shanghai. His ostensible reason for choosing this course over the direct route across the Pacific was to mobilize foreign support (especially financial aid) for the revolution, and the Chinese press carried exaggerated reports of his success.[1] When he arrived in Shanghai on Christmas Day, 1911, Sun felt compelled to announce to his comrades: "I haven't a penny to my name. What I have brought back is a revolutionary spirit, nothing more."[2] Despite the minimal role he had played in the revolution, and his disappointing performance in garnering foreign support, four days after his arrival in Shanghai, Sun Yat-sen was elected president of the provisional government, and on January 1, 1912, he was inaugurated as the first president of the Republic of China.

In previous research on the 1911 Revolution, I argued that the fall of the Qing was the product of social and political forces internal to China. Exiled professional revolutionaries like Sun Yat-sen had little to do with the revolution, which was largely carried out by New Army officers and former constitutionalists—the military and civil arms of what I termed China's "urban reformist elite." The argument that Sun and his party, the Tongmenghui (同盟會, TMH),* led the revolution was, to me, an unconvincing conspiracy theory, designed to promote the political legitimacy of the Guomindang (successor party to the TMH) and of Sun Yat-sen himself.[3]

Although I continue to believe that domestic political actors were more important than revolutionary exiles like Sun Yat-sen, I have long been troubled by one nagging question. If the military governments in the revolutionary provinces were dominated by military officers and constitutionalist gentry, and if, even among revolutionaries in provinces like Hubei, the organizational presence of the Tongmenghui was minimal, why then did representatives of the new provincial military governments, when they met in Nanjing on December 29, 1911, select Sun Yat-sen as provisional president? Why not the leader of the Hubei military government, Li Yuanhong,† or a prominent

---

* The Tongmenghui, often translated as the Chinese Revolutionary Alliance, was founded in Tokyo in 1905. It united the main regionally-based revolutionary groups under one banner, with Sun Yat-sen as leader, and a membership largely composed of overseas Chinese and students studying in Japan. After the 1911 Revolution, it was reorganized as the Guomindang (國民黨, Kuomintang in the old [and Taiwan] romanization).

† Li Yuanhong (黎元洪, 1864–1928) of Hubei, was a brigade commander in the New Army in Wuchang when the 1911 Revolution broke out in that city. He was thrust into command of the Hubei Military Government and led it through the revolutionary process, then served as a relatively powerless vice president in the early republic.

and respected constitutionalist like Zhang Jian?* In the end, of course, the job would fall to a man who well represented civil and military reformers within the elite—Yuan Shikai.† But how did Sun win that first election to be provisional president?

This question seems to me significant for a number of reasons. First, there is the fundamental empirical puzzle outlined above. Sun was a long-exiled revolutionary with a curious mix of political views. On his return to China, he stressed two prescriptions for China's future: socialism and the need for foreign loans from the capitalist countries of the West.[4] The elite reformers and military men who carried out the revolution certainly did not share Sun's sympathy for socialism; and the revolutionary tide of 1911 had begun with an outburst of protest against the sort of foreign loans (in this case, for railways) that Sun was now proposing. How, in this context, did Sun emerge as the chief representative of the revolutionary camp?

Second, the question seems to me important because Sun's election as provisional president is a key part of the ideological edifice that proclaims Sun "Guofu" (國父)— Father of the Republic.[5] Sun's stature in the national historiography of modern China on both sides of the Taiwan Straits is comparable to that of George Washington in the United States. But we know much more about how George Washington became the first president of the United States two hundred years ago than we do about how Sun was selected in 1911. As an indication of the historiographic problem, I would note that the prominent Shanghai magazine *Dongfang zazhi* (*Eastern Miscellany*) devoted only two and a half lines, a total of fifty-five characters, to its report of the election.[6] Despite the importance of the election that qualified Sun to become *Guofu*, contemporary sources are remarkably sparse.

Third, anyone concerned with China's struggle for democracy must recognize that one part of the problem has been the difficulty of establishing legitimacy for democratic political institutions. In China, democracy has usually been viewed as a means to an end: a way of involving and mobilizing the populace for the task of expanding national wealth, power, and prestige. But since national wealth, power, and prestige are the real goals—frustration with democratic forms has frequently led China's modernizers to forsake democracy

---

* Zhang Jian (張謇, 1853–1926) earned first place in the imperial examination system, then forsook an official career to become an entrepreneur of industrial projects in his native Jiangsu. In the final years of the Qing, he was active in the movement for constitutional government, serving as president of the Jiangsu provincial assembly.

† Yuan Shikai (袁世凱, 1859–1916) rose through the military and commanded the New Army in North China. In the early twentieth century, he held a variety of civil positions, promoting military, police, and administrative reforms under the Qing before the new regent forced him into retirement in 1909. After the Wuchang Uprising, he was recalled to serve as the last premier of the Qing, then president of the republic from 1912 to 1915. He died in 1916 after a brief and abortive attempt to restore imperial rule.

for dictatorship. This tendency can be seen from Liang Qichao's[*] advocacy of "enlightened despotism," to Qian Duansheng's[†] 1934 call for an "able and idealistic dictator,"[7] to the current promotion of "new authoritarianism" by He Xin[‡] and his ilk. Democratic institutions have scarcely acquired legitimacy in their own right. To an outright functionalist, institutions are legitimated through a demonstration over time that they actually work. Additionally, however, in the early stages of any new political institution, validating rituals play an important role in promoting acceptance of the new institutions. Thus, my final area of interest is the political rituals involved in Sun Yat-sen's ascension to the presidency. How much of a break were they from prior imperial rituals? How successful were they in validating the inauguration of the new republic?

FORMING A PROVISIONAL GOVERNMENT

Following the outbreak of revolution in Wuchang, all of the southern provinces and Shaanxi and Shanxi in the north soon declared their independence from the Qing court in Beijing. Although these provinces established military governments and declared their adherence to republican principles, there was no central authority to coordinate the actions of the provincial revolutionary forces. Consequently, on November 7, Li Yuanhong, military governor of Hubei, sent a circular telegram urging provinces to form a common government. His primary rationale remained central to most subsequent efforts to organize a provisional revolutionary government: if the revolutionaries wished foreign recognition, even as a warring party toward which the foreign powers would preserve neutrality, they would have to unify under one government.[8] They also needed some central authority to negotiate a nationwide settlement with the opposing Qing forces.[9]

Several days later, the military governors of Jiangsu and Zhejiang (acting with the encouragement of such prominent constitutionalists as Zhang Jian) suggested to Chen Qimei,[§] the TMH military governor of Shanghai,

---

[*] Liang Qichao (梁啓超, 1973–1929) of Guangdong was a brilliant and prolific scholar, journalist, and promoter of constitutional government in the final years of the Qing. As a promoter of constitutional monarchy, he was an opponent of Sun Yat-sen's revolutionary movement, but defended and served under the republic after the revolution.

[†] Qian Duansheng (錢端升, 1900–1990), a political scientist with a doctorate from Harvard, was a prominent legal scholar under the Nationalist government and advocate for authoritarian rule.

[‡] He Xin (何新, 1949–) was a prominent promoter of "new authoritarianism" under president and CCP general secretary Jiang Zemin in the 1990s.

[§] Chen Qimei (陳其美, 1878–1916) of Zhejiang joined the Tongmenghui as a student in Japan, then introduced Chiang Kai-shek into the organization and became his patron. In 1911, Chen led the revolution in Shanghai and became the military governor. In the early republic, after fleeing abroad, he returned to organize military opposition to Yuan Shikai's imperial restoration but was assassinated, presumably at Yuan's order.

that provincial delegates gather in that city to organize a new government. Their interesting cable took the early American Continental Congress as the model for a central legislative body with very limited powers. Representatives of these three revolutionary governments sent cables urging all provinces to send delegates to Shanghai.[10] The military governor of Zhenjiang (in Jiangsu), Lin Shuqing (another TMH member), followed with the first explicit proposal for a provisional president (*linshi da zongtong* 臨時大總統); and on November 13, Chen Qimei called on all provinces to send delegates to Shanghai to organize a provisional government.[11] Three days later, representatives from the Lower Yangzi and Fujian, who had already gathered in Shanghai and named their group "The Assembly of Delegates from the Provincial Military Governments" (*Gesheng dudufu daibiao lianhehui* 各省都督府代表聯合會), cabled Li Yuanhong, urging him to accept Shanghai as the site for the assembly, given its favorable access to the outside world.[12]

This was clearly not the direction that Li Yuanhong expected his proposal to go. His was the first revolutionary province and now the prime focus of the imperial government's counterattack, and he expected to preside over the formation of a new central government. Now Shanghai had stolen his thunder.[13] Li quickly cabled Shanghai, urging the delegates there to proceed to Wuchang. On November 19, the Shanghai delegates agreed to recognize Wuchang as the central government and asked Li Yuanhong to appoint Wu Tingfang* as foreign minister.[14] Three days later, two representatives from Li Yuanhong, including the TMH member Ju Zheng,† persuaded the group in Shanghai to repair to Wuchang. On November 24, this decision was modified: one representative from each province would stay behind in Shanghai to handle such things as foreign affairs from that pivotal international city.[15] By the time the delegates arrived in Wuchang, Hankou and Hanyang across the river had been lost to the Qing forces, and Wuchang was under periodic artillery bombardment. The delegates met in the English concession in Hankou and, on December 2, adopted an Organizational Charter for the Provisional Government of the Republic of China. The charter's first clause provided for a provisional president to be elected by a two-thirds' majority of the representatives of the provincial military governments, with each province having one vote.[16]

---

* Wu Tingfang (伍廷芳, 1842–1922) was born in Malacca and educated in Hong Kong and London, where he was admitted to the bar. He served as a diplomat under the Qing, then supported the revolution and served as their chief negotiator in 1911–1912.

† Ju Zheng (居正, 1876–1951) joined the Tongmenghui as a student in Japan, then returned to his native Hubei shortly before the revolution. Later he would become a member of the right-wing Western Hills faction of the Nationalist Party.

SELECTING A PRESIDENT

The formation of a provisional government headed by a president was thus decided. But the identity of that president was anything but certain. Abroad, Sun Yat-sen was the best-known revolutionary, and such papers as the *New York Times* and the London *Times* predicted as early as mid-October that he was the revolutionaries' likely choice as president.[17] On October 31, Sun cabled his military adviser Homer Lea* (who would accompany him back to China) claiming, "The state of [our] organization in the provinces is very good. They all wish me to assume leadership."[18] Lea and others would later claim that Sun received a cable in London in which fourteen provincial delegates invited him back to China to assume the presidency.[19] But no direct evidence of these cables appears to exist, and none of the provincial delegates' accounts mentions such an invitation to Sun. Still, Sun probably expected to lead a revolutionary government on his return, though by the time he reached London, he seems to have abandoned these early illusions. On November 16, he cabled the newly organized assembly of provincial delegates: "For the presidency, Li Yuanhong should of course be proposed. I hear that Li has requested that Yuan Shikai be proposed. If found appropriate, this would also be fine."[20]

The situation within China was a good deal more complex. In a widely cited telegram, Cheng Dequan (程德全), the former Qing governor who had become military governor of Jiangsu, proposed, on November 14, that Sun Yat-sen be invited back to form a provisional government. "Mr. Sun Zhongshan was the first to advocate revolution," Cheng cabled to his fellow military governors. "Chinese and foreigners alike greatly trust and respect him. There is no one but him to organize a provisional government."[21] Cheng's suggestion may have reflected support for Sun in some Jiangsu revolutionary army units, which told the Shanghai press that "for the office of president, only Sun Yat-sen will do."[22] However, I have found no direct evidence of any enthusiastic response to Cheng's suggestion from the other military governors. On December 12, the TMH-affiliated military governors of Guangxi referred to Cheng's cable and asserted that "many provinces have already agreed."[23] This perhaps reflected a favorable view toward Sun in Guangxi and neighboring Guangdong (under Sun's close ally Hu Hanmin†), but it is unlikely to have

---

* Homer Lea (1976–1912) of Denver, Colorado, was an American adventurer with considerable oratorical skills, but physical disabilities that left him short and slight. Lea became fascinated by China and organized armies first for the defenders of the Guangxu emperor and later for Sun Yat-sen. He traveled to China with Sun in 1911, but soon suffered a stroke and died.

† Hu Hanmin (胡漢民, 1879–1936) of Guangdong joined the Tongmenghui as a student in Japan and edited the party paper (*Minbao* 民報). After the successful Guangdong revolution in 1911, he returned to head the new military government. In the 1920s and 1930s, he was a prominent leader of the Guomindang and rival of Chiang Kai-shek.

reflected the sentiment of the Yangzi Valley military governors. Their views are perhaps best indicated by Hunan governor Tan Yankai's apparent response to Cheng's demarche.* On November 24, Tan suggested that since Sun had been abroad for many years, he should stay there as plenipotentiary ambassador (*quanquan dashi* 全權大使) to negotiate with foreign governments on behalf of the new republic.[24]

Even within the Tongmenghui, Sun's leadership was not uncontested. The former editor of the TMH journal, *Minbao,* the independent-minded Zhang Binglin,[†] had long been critical of Sun Yat-sen within party circles. After he returned to Shanghai following the revolution, his home became a meeting place for revolutionary partisans.[25] There, and in the press, he argued, "If the president is to be selected on the basis of merit, then it should be Huang Xing;[‡] if on the basis of talent, then Song Jiaoren;[§] if on virtue, then Wang Jingwei."[26] In another declaration, on December 1, Zhang wrote that it was "childish" to await Sun's return to select a national leader. Those who favored Sun, Zhang argued, did not know him. But Zhang assured these people that from his own experience he could say that "Sun is strong at theorizing. This is the talent of an elder statesman, but he should not be forced into an official position."[27]

In its first long defense of Sun, on the eve of his return, the TMH's *Minlibao* acknowledged such opposition, complaining, "Those opposed to Sun are waving their flags and beating their drums, misleading our troops." But it focused on what was always one of Sun's major selling points, his alleged popularity in the West: "Mr. Sun has a sort of magical power which can cause Europeans and Americans of any position to fall over themselves in praise after a single meeting. Previously, Europeans knew only Li

---

* Tan Yankai (譚延闓, 1880–1930), son of a prominent Qing official and holder of the highest *jinshi* examination degree, was a leader of the constitutionalist movement and president of the Hunan Provincial Assembly at the end of the Qing. After the assassination of Hunan's first revolution leader in 1911, he succeeded to the position of military governor. After 1912, he joined the Guomindang and remained a figure in the Nationalist Party and government until his death.

† Zhang Binglin (章炳麟, 1869–1936), also known as Zhang Taiyan (章太炎), was a scholar of philology whose deep resentment of Manchu rule led him to the revolutionary movement, where he edited the Tongmenghui's *Minbao* in Japan. Long a critic of Sun Yat-sen, he became a proponent of preserving China's "national essence" under the republic.

‡ Huang Xing (黃興, 1874–1916), from Hunan, was the military leader of the Tongmenghui. Holder of the lowest examination degree, he was sent to Japan for further study where he developed an interest in military affairs and revolutionary politics. After a failed revolt in his home province, he fled to Japan, joined the Tongmenghui, and became the most important military leader of its several failed uprisings.

§ Song Jiaoren (宋教仁, 1882–1913), also from Hunan and a close friend of Huang Xing, studied politics and joined the revolutionary movement in Japan. The most prominent advocate of parliamentary government, he was assassinated at Yuan Shikai's orders after orchestrating the transformation of the Tongmenghui into the Guomindang to compete in national elections.

Hongzhang* in China. After Li's death, they knew Yuan Shikai. Now they know Sun Yat-sen, and Yuan is second to him." The *Minlibao* closed with an appeal that Chinese not concede to Europeans "the willingness to worship a hero."[28]

In the revolutionary provinces, Sun's clearest rival for the presidency was Li Yuanhong. As early as October 14, the *Minlibao* had referred to the Hubei military governor as "the revolutionary president" (*geming da zongtong* 革命大總統). In late October, Li Yuanhong told the foreign consuls in Hankou that he had been proclaimed "president of the Republic of China," and dismissed Sun Yat-sen as a candidate for the presidency, saying that Sun's methods were "too theatrical."[29] More concretely, in early December, after the Shanghai delegates recognized Li's Hubei regime as the central government, he began selecting a cabinet as a first step toward establishing a national regime. Several provinces, including the TMH-dominated Guangdong regime, quickly responded to Li's request for nominations of seven cabinet ministers.[30] Finally, among the provincial delegates who would eventually select the president, the TMH leader Tan Renfeng† reported that prior to Sun's return, 60 percent favored Li Yuanhong, 30 percent favored Huang Xing, and only 10 to 20 percent favored Sun.[31]

Just as threatening to Sun's chances was an emerging consensus that if Yuan Shikai could be persuaded to support the republic, he should be selected as its first president. No sooner had the revolution broken out in Wuchang than the Qing court realized that only Yuan's return to power gave it any hope of survival. But it was not until November 1, after he ignored a series of lesser appointments, that Yuan Shikai was named premier of the new Qing cabinet; and it was two more weeks before he left his Henan home to take up office in Beijing. On the same day (November 14) that he entered Beijing and met with the Qing princes, his son, Yuan Keding (袁克定), visited the British minister, Sir John Jordan, and claimed that the revolutionaries wished Yuan to become premier.[32] Given Sun Yat-sen's telegram from London two days later, reporting and agreeing to Li Yuanhong's suggestion that Yuan be president, Yuan Keding's report has considerable credibility.

Yuan Shikai kept a number of channels open for communication with the revolutionaries, not the least of whom was Zhu Fuhuang (朱芾皇), a TMH member from Yuan's native place, who had become close to Yuan Keding while a student in Japan. Zhu was financial and foreign affairs deputy of the

---

* Li Hongzhang (李鴻章, 1823–1901) of Anhui earned the highest *jinshi* examination degree as a young man, then became a leading commander in the Qing suppression of the Taiping Rebellion. In the late nineteenth century, he was the most powerful Qing statesman and diplomat, often charged with negotiating treaties after China's defeat in war.

† Tan Renfeng (譚仁鳳, 1860–1920) of Hunan was a senior member of the Tongmenghui and participant in many anti-Qing uprisings.

Beijing-Tianjin branch of the TMH, organized by Wang Jingwei after his release from prison. Yuan Keding was his father's link to Zhu and Wang, and these two were instrumental in relaying a peace proposal suggesting what would, in time, be the final resolution: a Qing abdication and selection of Yuan as president.[33]

Many in the revolutionary camp certainly favored this solution, and some reports claim that on December 2, the provincial delegates in Hankou agreed that if Yuan adhered to the republic, he should be elected president.[34] But once Yuan Shikai accepted the Qing premiership, revolutionary rhetoric against him heated up in Shanghai. On November 18, the *Minlihao* lead editorial called Yuan a "bandit, public enemy, and slave of the Manchus." On November 29, the paper called for the assassination of "Yuan the bandit" (Yuan *zei* 袁賊). Especially in the wake of the bloody and destructive Qing recapture of Hankou and Hanyang, there were urgent calls to increase pressure on Yuan and the Qing by establishing an alternative national regime.[35]

CONFLICT OVER A GENERALISSIMO

This was the context for an extraordinary move by the provincial delegates who had stayed behind in Shanghai. Meeting together with the military governors of Jiangsu and Zhejiang and several TMH leaders, the Shanghai delegates agreed to make Nanjing, which had just been taken by the revolutionary forces, the site of a provisional government headed by Huang Xing as generalissimo and Li Yuanhong as his deputy.[36] It was a precipitous act, proposed on the spontaneous suggestion of one delegate seeking a means to unify the military command. So little preparation had gone into this move that the election was carried out by the delegates scribbling names on folded scraps of paper.[37]

The underlying reasons for this sudden act are not entirely clear, but in addition to the genuine need to unify the revolution's military command, there appears to have been a coincidence of two sets of interests. One was the TMH. Huang Xing had just arrived in Shanghai from Wuhan. In Hubei, the troops he commanded had suffered a major defeat in Hanyang, and many were dissatisfied with the performance of Huang and the TMH staff he had brought with him. Huang, for his part, was discouraged by the defeat and had advocated abandoning Wuhan to concentrate the revolutionary forces in Nanjing. This suggestion further enraged the Hubei revolutionaries who had precipitated the Wuchang Uprising, and Huang left the province in some ill odor.[38] In Shanghai, Huang met with his TMH comrades, who were one group wishing to make him generalissimo. According to a *Minlibao* correspondent,

"It was entirely Song Jiaoren and Chen Qimei who, fearing that Wuchang would in fact become the central government and that this would be disadvantageous to the TMH, stirred up the Shanghai delegates to enact this silly farce. Their original intent was truly loyalty to the TMH, but as soon as this action was announced, the reputation of the TMH fell disastrously."[39]

The competition with Wuchang is notable. In mid-November, after both Shanghai and Wuchang had invited delegates to form a national government, the TMH party paper, *Minlibao*, strongly supported Wuchang, because party members (led by Huang Xing and Song Jiaoren) had concentrated their attentions on the revolution there.[40] By early December, however, Huang Xing and the other TMH stalwarts from the area had left for Shanghai, unable to challenge Li Yuanhong politically in Hubei, and Li Yuanhong was selecting nominations for cabinet ministers in his proposed central government. At this point, *Minlibao* argued for Nanjing as the capital, on grounds that Wuchang was insecure under Qing attack.[41]

But there were others behind this move besides the TMH leaders. The group that selected Huang included also the military governors of Jiangsu and Zhejiang, both representatives of the reformist camp and close to the constitutionalists around Zhang Jian. They (and others) supported this decision in part because it left the post of presidency vacant and available for Yuan Shikai, whenever he came around to supporting the republic.[42]

Li Yuanhong reacted angrily. On the one hand, the action was clearly irregular: the Shanghai delegates were supposed to serve only as a communications office (*tongxin jiguan* 通信機關) and had no decision-making authority. Voting by the three Jiangnan military governors and the participation of such TMH leaders as Zhang Binglin and Cai Yuanpei,* who had no credentials, further compromised the legitimacy of the assembly.[43] Secondly, the organizational charter adopted for the new provisional government carried no provision for a generalissimo, and the Hankou delegates who had drafted the charter urged Li to reject the demarche by the Shanghai group.[44] Finally (and perhaps most importantly), the decision undermined Li's own attempt to organize a central government, and made Li a subordinate to Huang Xing—reversing the chain of command that had existed in Hubei.[45]

Given the reaction of Li Yuanhong and the delegates in Hankou, Huang Xing proved reluctant to take up the post, though the *Minlibao* continually referred to "Generalissimo Huang" and praised him extravagantly as the "George Washington of New China."[46] Meanwhile, the Hankou assembly

---

* Cai Yuanpei (蔡元培, 1865–1940), from Zhejiang, held the highest *jinshi* degree, studied philosophy in Europe, was an early advocate of anarchism, and later joined the Tongmenghui. Under the republic, he promoted educational reform and served as president of Peking University in the critical May Fourth period.

of provincial delegates left on December 8 for Nanjing, which they also approved as the site for the provisional government. There they began formal deliberations on the 11th, meeting in the Jiangsu Provincial Assembly building.[47] On the 14th they scheduled the election of president for two days later, but on the 15th, the Zhejiang delegate (perhaps working in concert with the Jiangnan constitutionalists) arrived from Hubei to announce that he had heard that Yuan Shikai's representative to the peace negotiations, Tang Shaoyi,* had intimated to Li Yuanhong that Yuan's cabinet would favor a republic. Accordingly, the selection of a president was postponed (to leave the post available for Yuan), and the delegates affirmed the decision of the Shanghai group to make Huang Xing generalissimo. This now aroused the Jiangsu-Zhejiang officers, who had led the capture of Nanjing, to announce that they would not serve under the commander defeated in Hanyang. So the delegates reversed the positions of the two rivals, making Li Yuanhong generalissimo and Huang his deputy. When this failed to resolve the problem, they further urged that since Li could not leave Wuchang, the deputy-generalissimo should assume command in Nanjing. By this time both Li and Huang had been offended by the process, and both repeatedly declined to accept.

In the assembly, tempers began to flare, so that by December 21, TMH members were jumping about and screaming that the demotion of Huang Xing was an insult. They particularly blamed the delegates sent by the provincial assemblies of the northern provinces that had not yet joined the revolution, accusing them of being traitors and partisans of Yuan Shikai. Some drew pistols and threatened their adversaries. Since one representative had already suffered an attempted assassination for allegedly being a secret constitutionalist, such threats were not taken lightly.[48] The whole exercise of selecting a leader for the provisional government was endangering the unity of the revolutionary camp and inviting ridicule of the democratic process.[49]

As the stand-off between Li Yuanhong and Huang Xing continued, Sun Yat-sen arrived in Shanghai. There can be no doubt that one reason for the selection of Sun was to resolve the leadership crisis of the provisional government.[50]

SUN YAT-SEN RETURNS TO CHINA

Sun Yat-sen's ship arrived in Hong Kong on December 20. There he was met by his Cantonese TMH colleagues led by the military governor of

---

* Tang Shaoyi (唐紹儀, 1862–1938), from Guangdong, studied in the United States in the 1870s, then returned to serve the Qing in several diplomatic posts. In 1911, he was the Qing representative in negotiations with the new revolutionary authorities.

Guangdong, Hu Hanmin, and a group of long-time Japanese comrades in arms. Hu Hanmin tried to persuade Sun to remain in Guangdong to prepare a firm base for the party's struggle against the conservative forces in the North, but Sun would have none of it:

> Strategically speaking, Shanghai and Nanjing are the front line. Were I not to put my life on the line, and instead retreat to Guangdong to prepare for future battles, that would be taking the easy way out. When our comrades across the country are craning their necks, watching for my return, what would they say of me if I did this? I rely on the hearts and minds of the people. The enemy relies on military force. Why should I use my weak point instead of my strength? . . . If I do not go to Shanghai and Nanjing, there is no one else capable of deciding the great issues of domestic and international affairs.

The extraordinarily persuasive Sun not only convinced Hu Hanmin that he must go on to Shanghai, but also persuaded Hu to go with him, leaving the military governorship of Guangdong in the hands of a man who would later become a key rival, Chen Jiongming.*[51]

In terms of pure power politics and geopolitical strategy, Hu Hanmin's proposal that Sun consolidate a political base in Guangdong was a sound suggestion. After all, this was essentially the strategy that Sun was forced to follow ten years later. As the cited passage suggests, Sun's inflated estimation of his own indispensability was certainly a key factor in the decision to proceed to Shanghai. But there was also a keen recognition—significant as an indicator of the nature of politics in the new China—that appearances are both important and powerful. Here was Sun, in Li Yuanhong's terms, recognizing the need for the "theatrical."[52] Sun *had* to go to Shanghai, to place himself on the line—and in the limelight.

Hu Hanmin telegraphed Chen Qimei and Huang Xing in Shanghai, telling them of Sun's impending arrival, and on December 23, *Shenbao* published the news.[53] If Sun and Hu, with this telegram, hoped to inspire a dramatic welcome for Sun's homecoming, they were sadly disappointed. Their boat entered the harbor in a thin mist and dense fog, so the gunboat that Chen Qimei sent to meet them failed to make contact. The expected salute from the Wusong fort was not fired, the welcoming crowd was sparse, and the press reported mostly the large number of foreigners accompanying Sun, focusing on Homer Lea and the Japanese. Even the revolutionary *Minlibao* carried the story only on page five.[54]

---

* Chen Jiongming (陳炯明, 1878–1933), a lower gentry member from eastern Guangdong, led one revolutionary group to overthrow the Qing regime in the province. A progressive proponent of local reform, he first welcomed Sun Yat-sen in Guangzhou, then in the 1920s opposed Sun's attempts to use the province as a base for national revolution.

Welcoming telegrams came from many quarters, but most spoke in general terms and raised no hopes or expectations of a particular political role for Sun. Only Xu Shaozhen, commander of the Jiangsu-Zhejiang forces that had taken Nanjing (and contributed to the political confusion by rejecting Huang Xing as generalissimo) spoke of Sun as a leader. Xu compared Sun to George Washington, saying, "None but you can serve as a guiding light for the fatherland."[55]

On December 26, two critical events occurred: the assembly of provincial delegates met in Nanjing to hear a message relayed from Huang Xing: though he had recently agreed to serve as acting generalissimo, now that Sun Yat-sen had returned, he had changed his mind. He urged the assembly to proceed immediately with the election of president. The date was set for the morning of December 29. The decision was announced in the *Minlibao,* and all delegates were urged to return to Nanjing for the elections.[56] On the same day, Huang Xing and Chen Qimei hosted a banquet for Sun Yat-sen in Hardoon Garden. Most accounts suggest that at this banquet, Huang and Chen first proposed having Sun elected president, but obviously Huang already had this in mind when he urged Nanjing to proceed with the election. Chen and Huang invited the provincial representatives to the banquet, using the opportunity to press Sun's case with the men who would make the decision.[57] It seems likely that during informal meetings on December 25, the idea had already been broached, and the banquet was designed to sell the idea to the provincial delegates. Discussions continued in an evening gathering of TMH leaders at Sun's home. According to Hu Hanmin, since most of the provincial delegates (with the exception of Zhili and Fengtian) were TMH party members, the selection of a president "was naturally to be decided by the party. Thus, the highest cadres met to discuss this in Sun's home."[58]

There was a fortuitous coincidence of interests between the assembly in Nanjing and the TMH leaders in Shanghai. The assembly needed a resolution to its deadlock over a generalissimo, and Sun Yat-sen provided a convenient solution to the Huang Xing-Li Yuanhong standoff. Chen Qimei surely promoted the idea of a leadership position for Sun Yat-sen in the provisional government, since on December 24, he had invited the Nanjing assembly to send representatives to Shanghai to greet Sun.

According to one of the assembly's representatives, Wang Youlan, they proceeded to Shanghai on the 26th, to welcome Sun and offer him the position of generalissimo of the provisional government. Wang explicitly states that this decision was in order to resolve the dispute between Li Yuanhong and Huang Xing. Since the assembly had decided earlier on the 26th to select a provisional president, it seems curious that its representatives were to offer Sun the post of generalissimo.[59] In any case, Sun rejected the idea of a generalissimo. Always conscious of the international milieu, he pointed out that a generalissimo would not be recognized as a chief of state. Wang explained that they were using that designation in order to hold the presidency vacant for Yuan Shikai. But Sun countered with the assurance that once Yuan Shikai truly supported the republic, Sun would yield the presidency to him. Then, with his typical confident quest for the maximum, Sun added that his title should not be provisional president, but just president—to which the representatives demurred, saying that this would require amendment of the charter and would have to be discussed in Nanjing.[60]

For these delegates from the provinces, their three hours with Sun were memorable. Sun's long years abroad had clearly left him marked with a series of mannerisms that the representatives found extraordinarily refreshing:

> What surprised me at the time was Sun's manner of speaking: honest and direct, straight and to the point. Knowing he was right, he would not yield. He felt that only he could do the job. He was completely free of the mannerisms of the Chinese gentry: their false modesty and affected airs. Though these were small matters, in them one could sense his greatness.[61]

There can be little doubt that these representatives returned to Nanjing prepared to convey to their colleagues a favorable impression of Sun's leadership abilities.

Although the events of the 26th largely settled the issue of Sun's election, there were still significant internal differences in the TMH over the shape of the new government. In the evening meeting on December 26, Song Jiaoren raised strong objections to the presidential system, expressing his preference for a parliamentary system with a cabinet and premier. Sun Yat-sen strenuously objected, arguing that, in extraordinary times, the powers of the president must not be circumscribed. "We cannot set up legal restraints on the one person who has been entrusted and selected. I am not willing to follow the opinions of others and stand apart like some holy excrescence, while the great plans for the revolution are ruined."[62] Sun, "his face red and his ears flushed,"[63] was quite unhappy, but the discussion was inconclusive. Huang Xing, who had unsuccessfully attempted to dissuade Song from pressing his views, in the end proposed letting the Nanjing delegates decide the matter, and he and Song went to address them.[64]

In Nanjing, Song and Huang met with the provincial delegates, and Song argued at great length for the merits of a parliamentary system. In the end, he simply antagonized the delegates with his stubbornness, so that they not only refused to change the charter but also rejected Song when he was later proposed as Minister of Internal Affairs in Sun Yat-sen's first cabinet. For an advocate of a cabinet/parliamentary system, Song's first formal dealings with a parliament ended in dismal failure.[65]

THE ELECTION

The election for the post of provisional president took place on the morning of December 29. For such a momentous event—the election of a republican president after centuries of uninterrupted imperial rule—it was an exceedingly simple operation. There was no debate, no nominating speeches, and an absolute minimum of fanfare. For someone looking for ritual, this election was a great disappointment.

The delegates had nominated candidates the night before and sealed the ballot box. The election was to begin at 9:00 a.m., but Tan Renfeng had just arrived from Wuchang and the meeting began with his report from the revolutionary front with the Qing forces. Then, at 10:00 a.m., a representative of the Jiangsu military governor opened the box of nominations. Apparently, the governor himself and the Nanjing commander were supposed to preside over the election, but a bomb scare had caused them to flee to Shanghai.[66] Tang Erhe from Zhejiang presided, announcing that this election would open a new page in China's four thousand years of history. He then read the list of nominees: Li Yuanhong, Huang Xing, and Sun Yat-sen. After announcing the rules whereby each province was entitled to one vote, he called out the name of each province and one representative came forward to vote. When the votes were counted, revealing sixteen for Sun Yat-sen and one for Huang Xing, the crowd called out, "Long live the Republic of China," three times. Then a band burst forth with music, and the students and soldiers in the crowd celebrated happily. Its work done, the assembly sent a telegram to Sun announcing his election and dispatched representatives to escort him to Nanjing.[67]

In the next few days, the assembly several times revised the Charter of the Provisional Government—to provide for a vice-presidency, to which Li Yuanhong was elected, and to eliminate the specification of cabinet positions, so that the president would have more freedom to organize the government. This latter move was argued on the basis of the American constitutional model and the expressed wishes of Sun Yat-sen. But the revisions were undertaken hastily, and the wording was ambiguous and required reworking the next day. It was not a terribly auspicious beginning for China's republican government, and some delegates were embarrassed by the amateurish impression they were making.[68]

The most important act of the assembly had certainly been the election of a provisional president. We must still ask how Sun won such an easy victory. In part, the assembly had obviously been frustrated and exhausted by the conflict between Li Yuanhong and Huang Xing over the selection of a generalissimo. Since, in addition to Sun, Li and Huang were the only other nominees, there was no alternative to Sun that did not promise to reopen the earlier controversy. The only other conceivable candidate was Yuan Shikai, and everyone, including Sun, agreed that Yuan Shikai would be elected president as soon as he agreed to support the republic. In fact, as soon as Sun was informed of the vote, he telegraphed Yuan Shikai, saying that "a vacant seat awaits," and had the telegram published in the revolutionary paper in Shanghai.[69] In many ways, Sun Yat-sen was simply an opportunistic selection—a way of pasting over the rift between Li Yuanhong and the TMH, between Hubei and Shanghai—and a way of filling the position of provisional president so that a provisional government could be formed to pursue the negotiations with Yuan and the Qing court from a position of maximum strength.

Indeed, the TMH pressed forward with the election of a president in part to preempt the Qing decision to convene a constitutional convention to determine China's new form of government. All expected such a convention to opt for a republican form of government, and, at the time, news of the convention eclipsed Sun's election as president. Thus, the *New York Times* reported from Shanghai, "The action of the Nanking provincial delegates in electing Sun Yat Sen President is farcical, and probably was designed to prevent his lapse into the background."[70] In the end, much to the dismay of Yuan Shikai, Sun's election threw all plans for a constitutional convention into disarray.[71] Indeed, the opportunistic decision to press for the election of Sun Yat-sen may have deprived China of a more legitimate transition to democracy.

Another factor in Sun's favor was the composition of the assembly of provincial delegates that voted. Returned students from Japan and TMH members were disproportionately represented in the assembly. For example, twenty-two of the forty-five delegates are listed in Tahara Tennan's biographical dictionary of early republican figures. Of these, eighteen had studied abroad (sixteen in Japan and two in the United States). A known minimum of eight were TMH members, and this is certainly a significant underestimation. The key fact is that when the military governments selected delegates to this assembly, they sent men with experience abroad and some ability to work in national revolutionary politics. They did not necessarily select men who represented the forces that led the revolution in their own provinces.

This was surely the case in the provinces of Hunan and Hubei. When Hubei sent people like TMH members and Japan-returned students Ju Zheng and Hu Ying* as its representatives, it certainly was not sending men who shared the views of Li Yuanhong and the gentry-military officer group that dominated the Hubei military government. The Hubei leadership may, indeed, have thought it was getting TMH troublemakers out of the way—just as they were

---

* Hu Ying (胡瑛, 1884–1933) was a Hunanese revolutionary and associate of Huang Xing who was released from jail to participate in a radical Hankou military government that challenged Li Yuanhong's collaboration with constitutionalists in Hubei.

clearly thankful to see Huang Xing leave after the fall of Hanyang. But by sending such representatives, Li Yuanhong deprived himself of even a favorite son vote from the Hubei delegate. Similarly in Hunan, the veteran TMH revolutionary Tan Renfeng (who apparently cast the lone vote for Huang Xing) surely did not represent the interests of the constitutionalist gentry who dominated the Hunan government.[72]

The provincial military governments were primarily concerned with provincial affairs. They did not take this assembly, or the provisional national government it was to form, very seriously. I have seen no evidence that any province issued instructions to its delegates in the vote for the presidency. Having taken this attitude, they provided a small opportunity for the TMH and Sun Yat-sen to advance their own prominence on the national scene—and a much larger opportunity for Sun to make his mark on history.

THE INAUGURATION

Having been elected president at the end of the solar year, Sun Yat-sen seized the opportunity to switch China to the Western calendar. He announced his intentions when he met the assembly delegates in Shanghai: "We must learn from the West and follow the civilized nations of the world. Changing to the solar calendar is the first important reform of our successful revolution. It must be done."[73] When the delegates brought this suggestion back to the assembly, most opposed the idea. It was debated again after Sun's election, and, according to one report, he refused to come for the inauguration until the calendar was changed. The assembly agreed late on December 31 and cabled Sun to come the next day for the inauguration.[74]

Sun set out from Shanghai in a special train on the morning of January 1, 1912. A crowd of some ten thousand army men and members of civic organizations gathered to send him off. Cannons fired a twenty-one-gun salute. Crowds gathered at stations along the route, many crying out, "Long live the Republic." In Wuxi, several hundred female students lined the platform and cried out, "Long live," as the train stopped. Sun welcomed their representatives onto the train and shook hands. At Nanjing, the provincial delegates were among the welcoming party at the station. The five-colored flag of the republic was flown along the route into the city. There was another twenty-one-gun salute, a military band played, and the assembled foreign consuls removed their hats in greeting. Despite a cold drizzle, crowds lined the streets, shouting their welcome. Paper lanterns decorated with the colors of the flag hung outside. It was 6:15 p.m. before Sun reached the Presidential Palace. Surrounded by a heavy guard and wearing a tan Western-style suit that he had had made the night before, Sun Yat-sen proceeded on the final part of the route in a horse-drawn carriage while a band played a victory march. The Presidential Palace was brightly lit with electric lights. Huang Xing greeted him at the door.[75]

Given the late hour of Sun's arrival, the inaugural ceremony did not begin until ten o'clock at night. Held in the main hall of the Presidential Palace, which was the old viceroy's yamen, the ceremony began when Sun, Xu Shaozhen (the Nanjing military commander), Huang Xing, and Hu Hanmin entered from the rear. Civil and military officials were present in Western formal dress. Martial music initiated the ceremony, followed by the announcement of the assembly's election results. Sun uttered an oath of office that included the promise to resign as soon as order was restored and the foreign powers recognized the republic. The civil officials bowed three times to Sun, and the army fired a twenty-one-gun salute. Then Jing Yaoyue, a TMH member and Japan-returned student from Shanxi who represented the assembly of provincial delegates, conferred on Sun the seal of office, which was later used to produce white cloth souvenirs for the participants. Jing made a short speech that stressed the overthrow of Manchu autocracy, the French and American models of people's rights and equality, and the provisional president's obligation to obey the charter and the will of the people.

Sun's acceptance speech (or "declaration"—*xuanyan* 宣言) emphasized the need to construct a new unity of races and regions. He acknowledged provincial differences and promised that an end to Qing autocracy would mean a new relationship of mutual advantage between the center and the provinces. The content of his speech was interesting enough (center-provincial relations always seem to rise to the fore when China is in political crisis), but equally interesting was the fact that Hu Hanmin read the speech on Sun's behalf. Personal oratorical prowess was still not fully necessary for political leadership in China.* Sun's "declaration" was followed by brief words of praise from the military officers and more martial music to end the ceremony.[76]

Most notable about this ritual was its almost entirely Western inspiration. Costuming: the military wore Western uniforms, and Sun, first a suit and then formal wear, as did the civil officials. Music: military bands and victory marches. Greetings: hand-shaking, tipping of hats, and twenty-one-gun salutes. The speechmaking was a new addition to Chinese political ritual. Only the lanterns, the seal of office, and the bowing of officials preserved a certain Chinese flavor.

---

* For a contrasting view of the importance of oratory in republican China, see David Strand, *An Unfinished Republic: Leading by Word and Deed in Modern China* (Berkeley: University of California Press, 2011).

Sun's procession into Nanjing was also notable. In contrast to imperial processions, which were greeted by cleared streets or reverently silent crowds, these crowds were noisy, shouting out welcome and approval. The crowds even included women—a dramatically new addition to the political audience. This was a new, more public ritual for a Chinese ruler, but it also resembled the ritual progress of a popular Chinese official.[77]

With the inauguration of Sun and the new Chinese republic, China was most certainly introducing new ritual forms that represented a fairly radical break with the past. The very prominence of Western models indicated that this new generation of leaders felt that imitating the West was part of being "civilized," and that such behavior was necessary to gain recognition, approval, and (hopefully) aid from the Western powers, who had themselves become important participants in the ritual.

It is doubtful, however, that these foreign rituals were very effective in legitimating the new republic.[*] The fact is, the election of Sun Yat-sen resulted from a series of opportunistic political maneuvers. It was part of a larger political effort to resolve the conflicts among the revolutionaries and strengthen their hand for negotiations with Yuan Shikai. Everyone knew that the real political game was elsewhere: in the provinces, or in the political bargaining between the southern provinces and Yuan Shikai. Electing a president was a sideshow. That is how the position fell to Sun Yat-sen—but it is also part of the reason why democratic legitimacy has been so difficult to establish in China.

NOTES

1. See, for example, *Minlibao*, October 21 and 30, 1911.

2. *Sun Zhongshan xuanji* [Selected works of Sun Yat-sen] (Beijing, Renmin chubanshe, 1956), vol. 1: 185; Luo Gang, *Zhonghua minguo Guofu shilu* [The true record of the Father of the Republic of China] (Taibei, Zhongzheng shuju, 1988), vol. 2: 1606–7.

3. Joseph W. Esherick, *Reform and Revolution in China: The 1911 Revolution in Hunan and Hubei* (Berkeley: University of California Press, 1976). See also Winston Hsieh, *Chinese Historiography of the 1911 Revolution: A Critical Survey and Selected Bibliography* (Stanford, CA: Hoover Institution Press, 1975).

---

[*] Henrietta Harrison has provided a detailed study of political rituals in early republican China, noting their distinctly foreign flavor, but also arguing persuasively that on the ritual level, they were effective in creating a new republican citizen: *The Making of the Republican Citizen: Political Ceremonies and Symbols in China, 1911–1929* (Oxford: Oxford University Press, 2000).

4. Wang Gengxiong, *Sun Zhongshan shishi xianglu, 1911–1913* [A detailed record of Sun Yat-sen's activities, 1911–1913] (Tianjin: Tianjin renmin chubanshe, 1986), 54, 78, 80–81; Luo Gang, *Zhonghua minguo Guofu shilu*, 1622, 1625.

5. Sun was formally declared "Guofu" on April 1, 1940, by a government edict that proclaimed that he had "created the Republic of China with his own hands," Luo Jialun et al., *Guofu nianpu* [Chronological biography of the Father of the Republic], enlarged edition (Taibei, Zhongguo Guomindang zhongyang weiyuanhui, 1985), vol. 2: 1305.

6. *Dongfang zazhi* 8, no. 10 (April 1912).

7. Qian Duansheng, in *Dongfang zazhi* 31, no. 1 (1934), cited in K. S. Liew, *Struggle for Democracy: Sung Chiao-jen and the 1911 Chinese Revolution* (Berkeley: University of California Press, 1971), 201.

8. Li Yuanhong telegram, November 7, 1911 (Xinhai 9/17) in Luo Jialun, ed., *Geming wenxian* [Documents of the revolution] (Taibei, n.d.), 1: 1; Ping Yi, "Linshi zhengfu chengli ji" [An account of the founding of the provisional government], *Dongfang zazhi* 8, no. 11 (1912): 5.

9. Gu Zhongxiu, *Zhonghua minguo kaiguo shi* [The founding of the Republic of China] (Taibei: Wenxing shudian, 1962 [original: 1914]), 40; Liu Xingnan, "Xinhai gesheng daibiao huiyi rizhi" [A daily record of the assembly of provincial delegates in 1911–1912], in *Xinhai geming huiyilu* [Memoirs of the 1911 Revolution] (Beijing: Renmin chubanshe, 1961), vol. 6: 243. (Gu was a Zhili member of the Assembly of Provincial Delegates [see below], representing his province's provincial assembly; Liu was a correspondent covering the assembly for the *Minlibao*).

10. Liu Xingnan, "Xinhai gesheng daibiao," 241.

11. Luo Jialun, *Geming wenxian*, vol. 1: 2–3; see also Zhang Kaiyuan and Lin Zengping, *Xinhai geming shi* [A history of the 1911 Revolution] (Beijing, Zhonghua shuju, 1981), vol. 3: 288–91.

12. Liu Xingnan, "Xinhai gesheng daibiao," 241–42.

13. Apparently, cable traffic along the Yangzi had been interrupted, and Shanghai and the Lower Yangzi revolutionary regimes had never received Li's suggestion that the delegates gather in Wuchang—though other south and central China regimes had already agreed to Li's proposal. (Xu Shishen, *Guofu dangxuan linshi dazongtong shilu* [A true record of the Father of the Republic's election as provisional president] (Taibei: Guoshi zongbianshe, 1967), 8, 14–15.

14. Liu Xingnan, "Xinhai gesheng daibiao," 242.

15. See Li Yuanhong's undated cable in Luo Jialun, *Geming wenxian*, vol. 1: 3. In it he refers to a November 9 (Lunar 9/19) cable summoning provincial delegates to Hubei, but that cable is not included in his collected documents. On the Shanghai delegates' action, see Gu Zhongxiu, *Zhonghua minguo kaiguo*, 34–35; Liu Xingnan, "Xinhai gesheng daibiao," 242–43.

16. Liu Xingnan, "Xinhai gesheng daibiao," 244–46; Gu Zhongxiu (who gives December 3 as the date), *Zhonghua minguo kaiguo shi*, 35–39.

17. *New York Times*, October 13 and November 18, 1911; London *Times*, November 17, 1911. *Minlibao* reported these foreign predictions of a Sun Yat-sen presidency

on October 15 but specifically labeled them foreign speculations. On October 16, it similarly reported English press support for Huang Xing as president.

18. Luo Gang, *Zhonghua minguo Guofu shilu*, vol. 2: 1526. The identity of "they" is unclear, but it appears to mean the leaders of the TMH. The "leadership" that Sun was to assume may only have been leadership of the party. However, the cable begins with a negative comment on the "ambition" of Li Yuanhong. On October 28 (while Sun was in New York), the *New York Times* reported a Li Yuanhong meeting with the foreign consuls. Li spoke disparagingly of Sun and claimed to be "President of the Republic of China." Sun was presumably responding to Li's bid for national leadership that he coveted for himself.

19. Ibid., vol. 2: 1540–41; Wang Gengxiong, *Sun Zhongshan shishi xianglu*, 30.

20. *Minlibao*, November 17, 1911; cf. Zhang Kaiyuan and Lin Zengping, *Xinhai geming shi*, vol. 3: 297n; Luo Gang, *Zhonghua minguo Guofu shilu*, vol. 2: 1549–50.

21. Luo Jialun, ed., *Geming wenxian*, vol. 1: 4.

22. *Shenbao*, November 23, 1911, cited in Zhang Kaiyuan and Lin Zengping, *Xinhai geming shi*, vol. 3: 296. This report appears to have been inspired by a similarly worded cable from the commander of a "Dare-to-Die Corps" in Yangzhou. (See *Minlibao*, November 19, 1911.)

23. Yi Guoqian et al., eds., *Li Fuzongtong (Yuanhong) zhengshu* [The official writings of Vice-President Li Yuanhong] (Shanghai: Gujin tushuju, 1915), vol. 1: 22–23. Interestingly, the Guangxi leaders (there were two military governors) suggested a procedure that was contrary to that stipulated in the Organization Charter drawn up in Hankou, and which (if followed) probably would have denied Sun the presidency. They suggested that each military government cable its choice to Nanjing, with the provisional presidency going to whoever gained a majority. This would have put the decision with the military governors, where Sun certainly had less support than in the TMH-inclined Assembly of Delegates.

24. Ibid., vol. 1: 12.

25. Ju Zheng, "Xinhai zhaji" [Notes on 1911], in *Ju Juesheng xiansheng quanji* [Complete works of Mr. Ju Zheng] (Taibei: n.p., 1954), vol. 2: 527; Young-tsu Wong, *Search for Modern Nationalism: Zhang Binglin and Revolutionary China, 1869–1936* (Hong Kong: Oxford University Press, 1989), 84–95.

26. Hu Hanmin autobiography cited in Zhonghua minguo kaiguo wushinian wenxian [Documents on the fiftieth anniversary of the founding of the Republic of China] 2.2 Kaiguo guimo [The founding] (Taibei: Wenxian bianzuan weiyuanhui, 1961), 46.

27. Tang Zhijun, ed., *Zhang Taiyan zhenglun xuanji* [A selection of the political writings of Zhang Binglin] (Beijing: Zhonghua shuju, 1977), 527–28.

28. *Minlibao*, December 20, 1911. Prior to this article, the *Minlibao* had shown no special inclination toward Sun, and had in fact frequently referred to him as Sun Wen, using the Qing government's derogatory character (汶) for his given name. (See *Minlibao*, October 25, November 13 and 18, and December 17, 1911.)

29. *New York Times*, October 28, 1911; cf. *Minlibao*, October 29, 1911, citing Reuters. (See also note 17, above.)

30. *Minlibao*, December 2 and 4, 1911.

31. Tan Renfeng, "Shisou paici xulu," *Xinhai geming ziliao huiji* [Selected materials on the 1911 Revolution] (Hong Kong, Cuncui xueshe, 1980), vol. 4: 62.

32. Luo Gang, *Zhonghua minguo Guofu shilu*, vol. 2: 1546–47, 1528.

33. Ibid., 1564; Ju Zheng, "Xinhai zhaji," 526; Sui Xiheng et al., "Ji Jing-Jin Tongmenghui ersan shi" [A few things about the Beijing-Tianjin TMH], in *Xinhai geming huiyilu*, vol. 6: 57 58.

34. Zhang Nanxian, *Hubei geming zhizhi lu* [The known record of the revolution in Hubei], 388, cited in Luo Gang, *Zhonghua minguo Guofu shilu*, vol. 2: 1567. Zhang Kaiyuan and Lin Zengping, *Xinhai geming shi*, vol. 3: 293n, cites two other sources besides Zhang Nanxian for this report, but one (Gu Zhongxiu) does not include such an account, nor does Liu Xingnan's day-by-day account of the assembly's decisions. I rather doubt that the delegates ever made such a decision. On the other hand, one of Huang Xing's aides reports that the revolutionaries in Wuhan (a different group from the delegates) all approved of a proposal, brought by an emissary from Wang Jingwei, for Yuan as president. (Li Shucheng, "Xinhai qianhou Huang Keqiang xiansheng de geming huodong" [The revolutionary activities of Huang Xing before and after 1911], in *Xinhai geming huiyilu*, vol. l: 191.)

35. See, for example, *Minlibao*, November 30, 1911, December 3 and 6, 1911.

36. Luo Gang, *Zhonghua minguo Guofu shilu*, vol. 2: 1573, dates this decision to December 5; *Minlibao*, December 5, 1911; Gu Zhongxiu, *Zhonghua minguo kaiguo*, 48, and Zhang Kaiyuan and Lin Zengping, *Xinhai geming shi*, vol. 3: 292–93, seem correct in giving December 4, as the date. Liu Xingnan's precise daily record ("Xinhai gesheng daibiao huiyi rizhi," 248) gives December 3, but Liu's dating is often one day earlier than other accounts. See also Chun-tu Hsueh, *Huang Hsing and the Chinese Revolution* (Stanford: Stanford University Press, 1961), 121–25.

37. Ju Zheng, "Xinhai zhaji," 527–28. Ju Zheng dates the meeting on December 6, but this is after the *Minlibao* account, and Ju's dates are quite consistently unreliable.

38. Esherick, *Reform and Revolution*, 227–28.

39. Liu Xingnan, "Xinhai gesheng daibiao," 248. Note the theatrical metaphor for the action of the new assembly. Ju Zheng ("Xinhai zhaji," 527–28) likened it to a "children's game"—a term (*erxi* 兒戲) that in Chinese also includes a theatrical metaphor. Young-tsu Wong (*Search for Modern Nationalism*, 89–90) notes Zhang Binglin's strong disapproval of this move.

40. *Minlibao*, lead editorial by [Ma] Junwu, November 15, 1911.

41. Ibid.; lead editorial by [Xu] Xue'er, December 3, 1911. On the Shanghai-Wuchang rift, see also the *Times* of London, December 13, 1911.

42. Zhang Kaiyuan and Lin Zengping (*Xinhai geming shi*, vol. 3: 293–94) provide data to support this interpretation, but needlessly and unconvincingly downplay the TMH leaders' role. One contemporary account does highlight the military governors' role (Ping Yi, "Linshi zhengfu chengli ji," 6). Significantly, however, a participant in these events ascribes this motivation to Li Yuanhong. Wang Youlan, "Ying Zhongshan xiansheng xuanju zongtong fuzongtong qinli ji" [A record of my personal experiences in welcoming Dr. Sun Yat-sen to the election of president and vice-president], in *Sun Zhongshan shengping shiye zhuiyi lu* [Recollections of the accomplishments of Sun Yat-sen's life] (Beijing, Renmin chubanshe, 1986), 778. The idea of leaving the presidency to Yuan was not confined to any particular regional group.

43. Liu Xingnan, "Xinhai gesheng daibiao," 243, 247–49.

44. Ibid., 247. The Hankou group apparently learned of the move from the Western press.

45. Yi Guoqian et al., *Li Fuzongtong (Yuanhong) zhengshu*, vol. 1: 21–22; Gu Zhongxiu, *Zhonghua minguo kaiguo shi*, 48.

46. *Minlibao*, December 5, 6, and 7, 1911.

47. Liu Xingnan, "Xinhai gesheng daibiao," 246–47, 249–50.

48. Ibid., 249–50. The intended victim was Lin Changmin from Fujian. Behind the plot were Lin Sen and Chen Qimei, acting through Green Gang toughs.

49. Gu Zhongxiu, *Zhonghua minguo kaiguo shi*, 48–49. Gu was himself one of the accused representatives from the north. Gu misstates the dates here by one month, but the presumably correct dates can be found in Luo Jialun, ed., *Geming wenxian*, vol. 1: 8; cf. Wang Youlan, "Ying Zhongshan," 778; Li Shoukong, *Minchu zhi guohui* [The parliament of the early republic] (Taibei, 1964), 7–10; Liu Xingnan, "Xinhai gesheng daibiao," 249–51 (with dates one day earlier than the others).

50. Two participants, Wang Youlan, ("Ying Zhongshan," 779) and Gu Zhongxiu (*Zhonghua minguo kaiguo shi*, 49), suggest precisely this logic; cf. Hsüeh Chun-tu, *Huang Hsing*, 125.

51. Hu Hanmin autobiography, in Wang Gengxiong, *Sun Zhongshan shishi xianglu*, 57; cf. Luo Gang, *Zhonghua minguo Guofu shilu*, vol. 2: 1598–602.

52. See note 29.

53. Wang Gengxiong, *Sun Zhongshan shishi xianglu*, 60.

54. *Minlibao*, December 26, 1911; Wang Gengxiong, *Sun Zhongshan shishi xianglu*, 61–63, includes the press accounts and a concession police report; Luo Gang, *Zhonghua minguo Guofu shilu*, vol. 2: 1606–10.

55. Wang Gengxiong, *Sun Zhongshan shishi xianglu*, 64–65.

56. *Minlibao*, December 28 and 29, 1911; Liu Xingnan, "Xinhai gesheng daibiao," 251; Luo Gang, *Zhonghua minguo Guofu shilu*, vol. 2: 1615; Wang Gengxiong, *Sun Zhongshan shishi xianglu*, 68.

57. Zhang Tianjue and Hu Hanmin, in Wang Gengxiong, *Sun Zhongshan shishi xianglu*, 66–67; Luo Gang, *Zhonghua minguo Guofu shilu*, vol. 2: 1612–14.

58. Hu Hanmin, in Wang Gengxiong, *Sun Zhongshan shishi xianglu*, 67.

59. I can offer no definitive answer to this puzzle. I am inclined to believe that Wang, in his retrospective recollections, was wrong by a day about the dates. (Elsewhere in his recollections, his dates do conflict with other sources.) Liu Xingnan ("Xinhai gesheng daibiao," 251) dates the selection of Wang and the other delegates to visit Sun as December 24. If the delegates left Nanjing on the 25th, and arrived in Shanghai on the 26th, they would still have been concerned about the generalissimo problem and may have been unaware of the assembly's decision on the 26th to elect a president. It is, of course, possible that Wang mistakes the post to be offered to Sun, but given his recollection of an exchange in which Sun rejects the idea of a generalissimo, that seems unlikely.

60. Wang Youlan, "Ying Zhongshan," 779.

61. Ibid., 780

62. Hu Hanmin, in Wang Gengxiong, *Sun Zhongshan shishi xianglu*, 67–68; Luo Gang, *Zhonghua minguo Guofu shilu*, vol. 2: 1612. Hu Hanmin actually places this

meeting on December 27 and 28; but I follow Zhang Kaiyuan and Lin Zengping (*Xinhai geming shi*, vol. 3: 301n) in placing it on the 26th.

63. Zhang Tianjue, in Wang Gengxiong, *Sun Zhongshan shishi xianglu*, 73.

64. In addition to the sources in notes 61 and 62, see Ju Zheng, "Xinhai zhaji," 529.

65. Gu Zhongxiu, *Zhonghua minguo kaiguo shi*, 51–53, 59–60; Liu Xingnan, "Xinhai gesheng daibiao," 255, also 248–49.

66. Liu Xingnan, "Xinhai gesheng daibiao," 252.

67. *Minlibao*, December 30, 1911; Gu Zhongxiu, *Zhonghua minguo kaiguo shi*, 49–50; Wang Gengxiong, *Sun Zhongshan shishi xianglu*, 75–76.

68. Gu Zhongxiu, *Zhonghua minguo kaiguo shi*, 51–54. Note also press criticisms of the original charter in *Minlibao*, December 11, 23, and 24, 1911.

69. *Minlibao*, December 31, 1911.

70. *New York Tunes*, December 30, 1911.

71. Gu Zhongxiu, *Zhonghua minguo kaiguo shi*, 45–46, 60; *Minlibao*, December 30 and 31, 1911.

72. Ju Zheng, "Xinhai zhaji," 530.

73. Wang Youlan, "Ying Zhongshan," 780.

74. Wu Tiecheng, in *Zhonghua Minguo kaiguo wushinian wenxian*, series 2, vol. 2, 68; Liu Xingnan, "Xinhai gesheng daibiao," 253.

75. *Minlibao*, January 4, 1912; Wu Tiecheng in *Zhonghua minguo kaiguo wushinian wenxian*, series 2, vol. 2: 68–69.

76. *Minlibao*, January 4, 1912; Gu Zhongxiu, *Zhonghua Minguo kaiguo shi*, 56–59.

77. See Joseph W. Esherick and Jeffrey N. Wasserstrom, "Acting out Democracy: Political Theater in Modern China," *Journal of Asian Studies* 49, no. 4 (November 1990): 849, 851–53, and chapter 11 in this volume.

Chapter Six

Reconsidering 1911

Twenty years after the previous chapter was originally written, the centennial of the 1911 Revolution provided a fresh opportunity to reconsider China's first revolution. This time, the occasion coincided with the Arab Spring and the unexpected fall of Hosni Mubarak in Egypt. The chapter here was first delivered in Chinese in Wuhan, the city where the revolution began, and the English version was published in a Chinese-edited journal. The careful reader will detect that it was written with a Chinese audience in mind. The opening paragraph concludes with a reference to "farewell to revolution," the title of a banned book by two exiled Chinese intellectuals, and an idea much criticized in the PRC media.* The mention of the Arab Spring was a transparent suggestion that even the seemingly stable Chinese Communist regime might be susceptible to sudden change. Finally, the essay directly confronted a theme I kept hearing in private conversations in China: that the country would have been better off if the Manchus had never been overthrown.

A foundational framework of American scholarship on East Asia has been the notion that Japan successfully modernized by adapting and reforming its imperial institutions while China traveled the problematic path of revolutionary change.† A key moment in this narrative is the late Qing, when China replicated many of the Japanese reforms in its own New Policies.‡ I had long questioned the official Chinese narrative that the reforms were merely the last gasp of a dying dynasty, and recent Chinese scholarship has looked much

---

* Li Zehou (李澤厚) and Liu Zaifu (劉再復), *Gaobie geming* (告別革命) (Hong Kong: Cosmos Books, 1996). A web search for this title will produce a wealth of critical articles from the PRC.

† This is the framework of the textbook (then in mimeographed form) that introduced me to the field: John King Fairbank, Edwin O. Reischauer, and Albert M. Craig, *East Asia, the Modern Transformation* (Boston: Houghton Mifflin, 1965).

‡ Douglas Robertson Reynolds, *China, 1898–1912: The Xinzheng Revolution and Japan* (Cambridge, MA: Council on East Asian Studies, Harvard University: 1993).

more favorably on the accomplishments of the late Qing.* The first decade of the twentieth century was marked by the competition between anti-Manchu revolutionaries and constitutional reformers. The question thus arises: Why were the reforms suddenly abandoned in favor of revolution in 1911? Here my answer is that, in the spring of 1911, the new Manchu Regent undermined the democratizing thrust of the reforms in favor of a new autocracy of Manchu princes. In part, this answer built on American scholarship that paid much greater attention to ethnicity than did Chinese scholarship in the People's Republic; in part, it alluded indirectly to growing autocratic tendencies in contemporary Chinese politics.

Most importantly, I wished to question the notion of inevitability that envelops so much historiography, especially in China, where it is one of the few remaining relics of Marxism. The official historiography of modern China moves inexorably from the Republican Revolution against the empire, to the National Revolution reuniting the country after a decade of warlordism, and finally the Communist Revolution of Mao Zedong. What this essay argues is that unexpected contingencies can radically redirect the course of history. The fall of the Qing was by no means a foregone conclusion; indeed, the Qing reforms were working quite well until the death of the Empress Dowager brought a reactionary clique of Manchu princes to power. In this sense, this essay is a harbinger of my efforts to wrestle with the issue of contingency in history—a theme that would dominate much of my later work.

RECONSIDERING 1911: LESSONS OF A SUDDEN REVOLUTION†

In this centennial year, it is fitting to reconsider the meaning and significance of the 1911 Revolution. We can start by looking both forward and backward from the year 1911. Looking forward from 1911, we see the beginning of the long series of revolutions that dominated the history of twentieth-century China.[1] Because the 1911 Revolution resulted in internal divisions, warlordism, and further imperialist encroachments (especially by Japan), by the May Fourth era many Chinese intellectuals concluded that the revolution had failed because it had not been thorough enough.[2] There ensued the successive revolutions that have punctuated modern Chinese history: the National Revolution of the Guomintang (Kuomintang), the Communist Revolution,

---

* Much of the scholarship from the centennial conferences on 1911 was translated and published in Joseph W. Esherick and C. X. George Wei, eds., *China: How the Empire Fell* (New York: Routledge, 2014).

† Originally published as "Reconsidering 1911: Lessons of a 'Sudden Revolution,'" *Journal of Modern Chinese History* 6, no. 1 (2012): 1–14. Republished with permission.

and finally the Cultural Revolution. Each sought to overcome the disappointments of the previous revolution by making it more thoroughgoing, more comprehensive, and more penetrating into the lives of individual Chinese. It was only with the Cultural Revolution that the Chinese leadership and the Chinese people decided that this final revolution to touch people's souls was surely thorough enough, and China bid farewell to revolution and pursued a policy of reform.

Looking backward from 1911, most have stressed the revolution's accomplishment in ending 2,000 years of imperial rule. Here I would like to concentrate on the significance of the end to the impressive 270-year rule of the Qing dynasty. In 1911, the Qing was condemned as weak, corrupt, and incompetent. Viewed from the present, however, the achievements of China's Manchu rulers look much more impressive. In China, the massive Qing History Project and abroad the scholarship of the New Qing History have given us a new appreciation of the achievements of the Qing. Especially under the three extraordinary early Qing emperors, Kangxi, Yongzheng, and Qianlong, China enjoyed unprecedented peace and prosperity. The population doubled in these years, and had almost tripled by the mid-nineteenth century, aided in part by an efficient system of granaries and national attention to crop yields and famine relief.[3] The imperial government ran a budget surplus through much of the eighteenth century, despite fixing taxes at an extraordinarily low rate (by international standards).[4] The provinces that have become such a fundamental feature of modern Chinese governance were essentially a Qing creation.[5] Finally, it was under the Manchus that China established its present borders, successfully incorporating Mongolia, Tibet, and the Muslim regions of Xinjiang into the empire.[6]

Much of the nineteenth century was, of course, marked by a series of humiliating defeats at the hands of Western and Japanese imperialism. But the New Policy (*xinzheng* 新政) reforms following the Boxer fiasco and the occupation of the capital by the International Expeditionary Force showed that the Qing state was not without imagination, vitality, and the capacity to reform itself. As the much-vaunted examination system proved incapable of fostering the sort of talent required by the new age of imperial conquest and commercial competition (*shangzhan* 商戰), it was abolished in favor of a new school system closely modelled on the successful educational reforms of Japan. The army that had proved so ineffective in protecting the country was retrained or replaced by the New Army with modern Western arms and drill; and police forces were organized to better preserve domestic order—all, once again, with significant advice from Japan. Industry was promoted, initially through the officially supervised and merchant managed (*guandu shangban* 官督商辦) enterprises and later with private enterprise encouraged by the new chambers of commerce; mineral rights were protected in the Rights Recovery Movement; railways were built with both Chinese and foreign capital; and, as a result of all this, China experienced in its coastal cities the first burst of a small-scale industrial revolution.[7]

Nor were these reforms restricted to growing the economy and increasing the power of the state. The Qing court also began tentative steps to open the political system to broader participation by the educated elite. The old proscriptions on public discourse were eliminated, and, in response, a vibrant press arose with an almost uniformly progressive and reformist tint.[8] Most importantly, after Japan's victory in the Russo–Japanese War—a contest that was interpreted as a victory of constitutionalism over autocracy—the Qing embarked on an ambitious program of constitutional reforms that began with missions to study models of constitutional monarchy abroad, and ended with the election of provincial assemblies (Ziyiju 咨議局) and the organization of the National Assembly (Zizhengyuan 資政院) in Beijing. Though it has long been fashionable to follow the revolutionary rhetoric that characterized these reforms as phony constitutionalism or the last gasp of a dying dynasty, most scholars now recognize that the New Policy reforms were real, they truly did transform China, and in many ways, they laid the foundations for the modern Chinese state.[9] We should not take for granted that they were destined to fail.

The most fundamental question that the serious historian faces is "Why?" If, as I have suggested, 1911 started China on its tumultuous path of revolution, we must ask why this revolution occurred. If, furthermore, the Qing was as successful and the New Policy reforms as effective as I have argued, how did the 1911 Revolution succeed in overthrowing Manchu rule and establishing the Republic of China? I first addressed these questions thirty-five years ago in *Reform and Revolution in China*, and in many respects my views are unchanged. I continue to believe that Sun Yat-sen and the Tongmenghui were minor factors in causing the revolution. Sun Yat-sen was of course abroad at the time, and feuding with the other revolutionary leaders.[10] There is no question that revolutionaries within the Hubei army sparked the Wuchang Uprising, but those revolutionaries had minimal connections to the Tongmenghui leadership.[11] More importantly, the spark provided by their mutiny would not have developed into the full-scale prairie fire of revolution if the relatively weak and isolated revolutionary parties had not quickly attracted support from other important actors—in this case New Army officers like Li Yuanhong and constitutionalist provincial assembly leaders like Tang Hualong.* It was New Army and constitutionalist support that caused the revolution to

---

* Tang Hualong (湯化龍, 1874–1918) held the *jinshi* degree, studied law in Japan, and was elected president of the Hubei Provincial Assembly. He joined the revolution in 1911 and was assassinated in Canada in 1918.

spread beyond Hubei, so that within two months, ten provinces had declared their independence of the Qing and the Manchu dynasty's fate was sealed.

To understand why this happened, it is important to distinguish between two fundamentally different types of revolution. Some revolutionary struggles are long and protracted, as was the case with the Chinese Communist Revolution (and also the Nationalist Revolution) or the Vietnamese revolution. In these cases, a well-organized and disciplined revolutionary party with its own army fought for years against a number of foes, domestic and foreign, before it achieved victory. There was no clear revolutionary moment when the old regime collapsed. It was, instead, conquered by sustained military conflict. Compare this to the French Revolution of 1789, or to Russia in 1917, or indeed to Egypt and Tunisia in 2011—where the fall of the old regime was quite sudden and the revolutionary coalition was composed of a variety of different elements rather than a single-party army. In this latter type of sudden revolution, the revolutionary moment (or revolutionary milieu) is critical. At some point, confidence in the old regime becomes so fragile and the confluence of opposition forces so powerful that the country reaches a tipping point and the old structures of state power crumble and fall.[12] In China, this happened in the autumn of 1911.

In *Reform and Revolution in China*, I noted that prior to 1911, the membership of the revolutionary organizations in Hubei was very small. Despite years of organizing, the largest Hubei revolutionary organizations in 1910 listed only some 240 members; but by the fall of 1911, numerous reports put the number of revolutionaries (many in the army) between 3,000 and 5,000.[13] Clearly something fundamental happened during the course of 1911 to create a revolutionary situation in Hubei. I pointed to a number of factors that seemed important to me. There was a general economic recession, set off by Shanghai bank failures in 1910 and exacerbated by flooding along the Yangzi in 1911. The stalled economy affected government revenues, and soldiers in Hubei were often unpaid, with predictable effects on their morale. The New Policy reforms required new taxes, always unpopular, and reforms were slow to produce visible results, leading to widespread discontent and such violent outbreaks as the Changsha rice riot of 1910. Inflation in copper cash prices was pronounced and unpopular. Then in the spring of 1911 came railway nationalization and financing from foreign loans, and the notorious Princes' Cabinet (Huangzu neige 皇族內閣) along with the flood of negative reaction that ensued. My earlier research focused on Hunan and Hubei, but the rapid, successive provincial declarations of independence following the Wuchang Uprising indicate that the crisis of confidence in the Qing court affected most of the country. To understand why, research on the 1911 Revolution needs a different model. Past research has focused too much on Sun Yat-sen and the series of small uprisings that his revolutionary parties sparked, trying to make the 1911 Revolution fit the model of protracted revolution that the Nationalist and Communist parties would later follow to victory. The 1911 Revolution was of a different type; it was a sudden revolution, and it requires a different explanatory framework.

One factor that I surely underestimated in *Reform and Revolution* was anti-Manchu sentiment, which I called "a new panacea . . . the only issue [that] could unite all the different strains of discontent."[14] While I would not dispute that conclusion, it still pays insufficient attention to the sources, functions, and significance of anti-Manchuism. Edward Rhoads' prize-winning book *Manchus and Han* has called important attention to the role of Manchu rule and ethnic privilege in the period leading up to the revolution.[15] Together with scholarship by the New Qing History school, Rhoads's work forces us to reconsider the nature of Manchu rule. The books of Pamela Crossley, Mark Elliott, Evelyn Rawski, and Michael Chang stress the efforts of Qing rulers to maintain a distinct Manchu identity and distinguish themselves from the Han majority through membership in the banner system and the legal privileges and financial stipends that came with it, separate residence in Manchu garrisons (sometimes called Manchu apartheid), the promotion of Manchu language and the preservation of the martial skills of horseback riding and archery, seasonal hunting, summer residence beyond the Great Wall, imperial touring with its impressive martial displays, distinct styles of dress, the prohibition of foot binding among Manchu women, and of intermarriage between Manchus and Han.[16]

All of this fine scholarship has added much to our understanding of Qing rule, but most of it focuses on the seventeenth and eighteenth century. As is well known, by the end of the Qing, Manchus were overwhelmingly speaking Chinese; their military skills had decayed and they no longer rode and shot arrows from horseback; the emperors stopped hunting at the summer retreat in Chengde or going on imperial tours; and in this respect most of the markers of ethnic identity had disappeared. Indeed, progressive Manchus in the overseas journal *Great Unity* (Datongbao 大同報) argued that with the same language, customs, and religion, Manchus and Han were already one people (*minzu* 民族).[17] It is therefore something of a puzzle to explain the rise of racist anti-Manchu sentiment, and, in the end, what would be called racial revolution (*zhongzu geming* 種族革命), at precisely the point when ethnic differences were disappearing.

This is the problem that Rhoads addressed in his book, and much of his answer consists of arguing that at the end of the Qing, the Manchus were not so much a distinct ethnicity as an occupational caste.[18] It was the political privilege represented by Manchu posts (*Manque* 滿缺), the balancing of

Manchu and Han officials at the top of the metropolitan bureaucracy, and the continued Manchu domination of the Grand Council that most rankled Han elites at the end of the dynasty. The entire issue of anti-Manchu sentiment is difficult for historians to assess. On the one hand, until the last years of the dynasty, ethnicity was a forbidden topic in the official documents that form the most important records upon which historians rely.[19] One of the functions of Qianlong's vast *Four Treasuries* (*Siku quanshu* 四庫全書) project was to purge the Chinese literary tradition of disparaging ethnic references to the Manchus.[20] On the other hand, revolutionaries were so active in promoting anti-Manchu sentiment in the last decade of the dynasty that it is difficult to determine how much they were gaining support from preexisting resentment of the Manchus and how much they were, through their propaganda, giving an ethnic focus to a general disenchantment with the ruling dynasty. That is, to what degree were the revolutionaries *creating* anti-Manchu sentiment as much as *appealing to* it?

Both the example of the Taiping Rebellion and the widespread influence of such secret societies as the Triads (Sandian hui 三點會, or Tiandi hui 天地會) in south China suggest that anti-Manchu sentiment was more common there than in the north—and this is of course consistent with the southern concentration of the revolutionary provinces of 1911.[21] More importantly, I am convinced that the disaster brought about by the court's support for the Boxer Uprising provoked a fundamental shift in elite opinion. The most prominent supporters of the Boxers at court were Manchus—Gangyi* and Prince Duan,† in particular—and Gangyi was particularly hated for his alleged statement that he would rather yield power to foreigners than to Han household slaves.[22] In 1900, the provincial officials in Zhili, Shanxi (where Yuxian‡ was sent after protecting the Boxers in Shandong), Inner Mongolia and the Northeast—the areas where the Boxers were most active and Christian and foreign casualties greatest—were all Manchus. In contrast, Han officials dominated in the south where they negotiated with the foreign powers to preserve order in the southeast. Following the occupation of the capital by the International Expeditionary Force, the flight of the court, and the harsh terms of the Boxer Protocol, many Chinese officials felt that this disaster had been brought on by the pernicious influence of Manchu rule. Zhang Zhidong§ had no hesitation in

---

* Gangyi (剛毅, 1837–1900), Manchu bannerman, grand councillor and trusted adviser of the Empress Dowager, was fiercely anti-foreign and a strong supporter of the Boxer Uprising.

† Prince Duan (端王, Zaiyi 載漪, 1856–1922), Manchu prince, in charge of the Zongli Yamen managing foreign affairs, and a supporter of the Boxer Uprising.

‡ Yuxian (毓賢, 1842–1901), bannerman, governor of Shandong where the Boxers rose, and of Shanxi when foreign missionaries were killed. Executed by imperial order in 1901.

§ Zhang Zhidong (張之洞, 1837–1909), *jinshi*, late Qing statesman and long-serving governor general in Wuchang where he promoted industrial and military reform, was famous for promoting "Chinese learning for the foundation, Western learning for utility."

revealing these thoughts to the British consul in Hankow who reported that "He hates the Manchus as do all the Chinese officials I have met because of their hanging on to and eating up China and the absurd way in which they are promoted irrespective of their ability or fitness."[23]

The rise of the revolutionary movement and its publications abroad, in Hong Kong, and in the treaty ports brought anti-Manchu sentiment into the open. The famous accounts of Manchu atrocities during their conquest of China—"Ten Days in Yangzhou" (Yangzhou shiriji 揚州十日記), "Account of the Jiading Massacre" (Jiading tucheng jilüe 嘉定屠城紀略)—long banned in China, were recovered from Japanese libraries and widely reprinted. Such anti-Manchu pamphlets as Zou Rong's *Revolutionary Army* (Gemingjun 革命軍) became some of the most widely read tracts among radical young students. And, of course, the Tongmenghui made the crimes of the Manchus the heart of its revolutionary appeal. Edward Rhoads has ably summarized the revolutionary indictment of the Manchus: their barbarian origins, the atrocities of the conquest, their imposition of the queue and barbarian clothes, their privileged yet cloistered life in the Manchu garrisons, their domination of the central government and privileged access to office, and the hostility toward the Han expressed by such notorious reactionaries as Gangyi.[24]

The New Policy moves toward constitutional government were in part an effort to respond to this challenge to Manchu legitimacy, and to involve Han elites more effectively in the governance of the empire. Manchu officials such as Duanfang* focused particular attention on this problem, proposing in one unusually comprehensive memorial the end of Manchu legal privilege, the reform of marriage rituals to promote intermarriage of Manchus and Han, the abolition of Manchu posts in the bureaucracy, the reform of Manchu naming practices to adopt surnames comparable to Han, the abolition of foot-binding among Han, the elimination of separate ethnic banners in the capital guards, and the abolition of banner garrisons in the provinces with a termination package to assist bannermen to enter civilian life.[25] Progressive Manchus studying in Japan and supported by such reformers as Yang Du† published a journal, *Great Unity*, devoted to eliminating all distinctions between Manchus and Han.[26]

The hope of the late Qing constitutionalist reformers was that the election of provincial and national assemblies, their gradual transformation from advisory bodies to legislative assemblies, and finally the selection of a responsible

---

* Duanfang (端方, 1861–1911), Manchu bannerman (though perhaps of Han ancestry), served as governor general in Nanjing and was a major Manchu advocate of reform. He was killed by troops under his command during the 1911 Revolution.

† Yang Du (楊度, 1875–1931), from Hunan, studied politics and law in Japan and promoted cautious reform in the late Qing. In 1916, he attracted notoriety as a supporter of Yuan Shikai's monarchical project, then ended his career as an underground communist.

cabinet of officials selected by and from the parliament could gradually transfer power to the people under principles of electoral democracy and majority rule in which the Han would inevitably dominate by virtue of their numbers. To be sure, in order to make this transition palatable to the Empress Dowager Cixi* and the Qing court, the reforms were modeled on the German and Japanese versions of constitutional monarchy in which the emperor retained ultimate power, especially over military and security affairs. There was, in this model, the important notion that by passing administrative power to officials responsible to an elected parliament, the court could be protected from political controversy—and of course from responsibility for political failures.[27] In this way, constitutionalism was always proposed as a way to protect Manchu rule. Of course, the only way that the court could be fully protected was if it became a fully symbolic monarchy on the English model, what Liang Qichao would later call a republic with a nominal monarch (*xujun gonghe* 虛君共和), but this was not openly broached during the constitutional debates.

From 1906 through 1910, there was a good deal of optimism about the pace of constitutional reforms. The preparations for local self-government and the elections to provincial assemblies went smoothly enough, and despite some complaints about lack of enthusiasm for electoral politics, the results of the provincial assembly elections were particularly pleasing. Although the electorate was basically limited to members of the gentry (holders of examination degrees), the membership of the provincial assemblies and especially their leadership was impressive, with half of the presidents and vice presidents of the assemblies holding the *jinshi* degree. Many had training in Japan, and they were of an age (average: forty-six) that was old enough to have some experience in the world but still young enough to be vigorous leaders of reform. The quality of the provincial assembly leadership, especially when compared to the relatively mediocre provincial officials of the Qing's last years, led Liang Qichao to revise his views on the time needed to prepare for constitutional government. While Liang had initially agreed with the court's judgment (and Japanese experience) that fifteen to twenty years would be necessary to prepare the Chinese electorate for constitutional rule, he later decided that this calculation held China up to inappropriate international standards for electoral politics. If, he now declared, one judged the quality of the provincial assemblies by Chinese standards, then it was clear that the assemblymen were more qualified than the imperial officials, and it made sense to move immediately to summon a parliament and organize a responsible cabinet.[28]

---

* Empress Dowager Cixi (慈禧太后, 1835–1908), concubine of the Xianfeng emperor (1851–1861) and mother of the Tongzhi emperor (1862–1874), Cixi dominated the Qing court for the forty-seven-year reigns of her son and her nephew, the Guangxu (光緒) emperor (1875–1908).

Though the success of the constitutional reforms was by no means assured, a critical change came with the November 1908 death of the Empress Dowager and the Guangxu emperor (the latter now presumed to have died at the hands of Cixi's agents) and the ensuing regency of the young (twenty-six years old in 1909) and inexperienced Zaifeng.* Edward Rhoads' fine research has called attention to the centralizing and pro-Manchu policies of Zaifeng and their critical role in alienating key Han power-holders.[29] What does seem clear is that by 1911, Zaifeng had succeeded in antagonizing virtually every important constituency except for a small group of relatives and Manchu princes.

The consistent thread in Zaifeng's policy was his effort to centralize power in the court and restore Manchu control over the military. To this end Zhang Zhidong's long tenure in Huguang was brought to an end when he was summoned to the Grand Council in Beijing. Yuan Shikai was dismissed, removing the late empire's most capable reformer. This opened the way for Manchu control over the military and was welcomed by Kang–Liang supporters who still resented Yuan's role in the 1898 coup against Guangxu (Liang Qichao in his letters of this period refers to Yuan as graveyard bones (*zhonggu* 冢骨).[30] Yuan himself played a role in facilitating the ouster of Cen Chunxuan.† Duanfang was overly aggressive in pressing the regent to end Manchu privilege, and he too was dismissed.[31] As a result of all this clique struggle and bureaucratic turmoil, Zaifeng succeeded in centralizing power at court—but at the expense of removing the most able officials and replacing them with relatively mediocre and often Manchu (or Han bannermen) governors general.

While Zaifeng was relatively decisive in removing powerful Han officials, he was hopelessly timid in carrying out reforms to end Manchu privilege. He backtracked on Cixi's edict to disband the Manchu garrisons and vacillated in reforming the Manchu dress code and abolishing the queue. Most disastrously, when the time finally came in the spring of 1911 to replace the Grand Council with a cabinet of ministers, Zaifeng appointed nine Manchus and four Han—with the notoriously corrupt and much despised Prince Qing‡ as chief minister. The unprecedented concentration of power in this infamous Princes' Cabinet becomes particularly clear when we realize that with one brief exception in the Jiaqing period, Prince Gong's§ elevation to the Grand

---

* Zaifeng (載灃, 1883–1951) was the father of the last Qing emperor, Puyi (溥儀), and regent during his brief reign.

† Cen Chunxuan (岑春煊, 1861–1933) was a late Qing official of the Zhuang nationality from Guangxi, famous as a foe of corruption.

‡ Prince Qing (慶親王, 1838–1917) was a leading late Qing official and grand councilor, responsible for foreign affairs and thus held responsible for some of the most humiliating treaties forced on China.

§ Prince Gong (恭親王, 1833–1898) was the son of the Daoguang emperor and half-brother of Xianfeng. In the 1850 to the 1870s, he was a powerful and respected court official, responsible for foreign affairs, until sidelined after 1884 for China's defeat in the Sino-French War.

Council in 1853 was the first appointment of an imperial prince (*qinwang* 親王) to the Grand Council.³² The Prince's Cabinet, with seven members of the imperial family (including two of the regent's brothers) was a remarkable and disastrous step backward toward concentration of power in the imperial family and the final blow to all hopes that constitutionalism could produce a gradual transfer of power to the Han majority.³³

By the spring of 1911, Zaifeng had isolated himself from any possible source of support in the late Qing political system. Zhang Zhidong was dead. Yuan Shikai, Cen Chunxuan, and Duanfang had been dismissed. The nationalization of the railroads and the agreement to build them with foreign loans outraged patriotic partisans in Guangdong, Hunan, and Hubei and propelled Sichuan into the arms of the Railway Protection Movement and its leaders in the provincial assembly. The rejection of the provincial assemblies' petition movement for a national parliament had already led many constitutionalists to accept the necessity of revolution, in a process that has been well described by Zhang Pengyuan.³⁴ I would like here to emphasize the notable change of tone in National Assembly debates over impeachment of the Grand Council in December 1910, all of which were fully reported in the press. After the assembly passed a motion to impeach the Grand Council, it memorialized the court, taking care to respect and protect imperial authority:

> A monarchy is founded on the inviolability of its sacred ruler. When officials offer proposals, the ruler gets credit for successes and officials are blamed for failures. Recently countries in the East and West have ministers who assume responsibility and this is clearly specified in a constitution. In this way citizens (*guomin*) can direct the course of the government but cannot blame the court for its intent.³⁵

The wording was very much in the spirit of previous appeals for constitutional government: a constitution would protect the court from responsibility for unpopular political decisions. When, however, Zaifeng rejected this appeal in an edict issued directly from the court and not through the Grand Council, the tone of the assembly shifted abruptly, and now for the first time came direct attacks on the regent. In the words of one assembly member: "The recent vermillion edict was issued directly by the Regent himself. It leaves us no room to maneuver. . . . Now the legislature and the court stand in direct opposition. How is this any different from autocracy?"³⁶ For all these reasons, it seems to me that by the spring of 1911, revolution had become inevitable. China had reached its tipping point.³⁷

But what form would the revolution take? What would its consequences be? Revolution is always facilitated by a clear enemy, with an identifiable villain as the focus of attack. For the American Revolution it was King George

III; for the French Revolution, Louis XVI; in Russia, Czar Nicholas II; in Egypt, Hosni Mubarak. In China, the frustration of public aspirations was now clearly attributed to Zaifeng's court and its pro-Manchu policies. Now the anti-Manchu appeals of the revolutionary parties achieved wide support, and as noted above, the revolutionary parties in Hubei mushroomed in size. In the words of Zhang Jian, "In an instant, the ideas of political revolution were transformed into a mania for racial revolution."[38] When the Wuchang Uprising broke out, its appeal was unmistakably anti-Manchu Han nationalism. The song of the revolutionary army rang out: "Restore the Han (*xing-Han* 興漢), Restore the great Han! Eliminate the Manchus (*mie-Man* 滅滿)! Eliminate the bandit Manchus!"[39]

The flag of the new revolutionary government featured eighteen stars for the eighteen Han-majority provinces of China proper. Perhaps most importantly of all, when the president of the provincial assembly, Tang Hualong, joined the revolutionary government and issued an appeal to other provinces to join—an appeal that was quickly answered and guaranteed the success of the revolution—he focused on the court's narrow protection of Manchu interests and expressed the aspirations of the revolution in the language of Han Nationalism:

> The Qing court is without principle and has brought its own demise.... [The emperor] Puyi is a mere child; the Regent is ignorant and incompetent. Our survival depends on financial and military power, but in these areas [the court] has excluded all Han and granted all power to imperial princes. Pulun and Zaitao, mere children playing games, now control the army and navy ministries; the rapacious Zaize controls the Treasury, intent on constraining the Han and forcibly imposing autocratic rule. Our hopes for reform have been dashed. Our great land is nearing disaster. How can we allow ourselves, the descendants of the Yellow Emperor, to perish along with this land?[40]

Anti-Manchuism was unquestionably a banner around which all could rally. It could encompass the young revolutionaries, disillusioned constitutionalists like Tang Hualong, and probably a substantial portion of the south Chinese population for whom the anti-Qing Ming restoration ideals of secret societies had always had a certain forbidden appeal. At the very least, the Manchus had done little in recent memory to attract dedicated supporters. On the contrary, Zaifeng and his close relatives had done everything possible to alienate such support as his ancestors had earned. But revolution is not only about toppling an old regime, and 1911 would soon demonstrate that destruction is much easier than reconstruction. It is a truism in the comparative study of revolutions since the French Revolution of 1789 that no sooner do the diverse forces that have rallied against the old order succeed in bringing it down than they start quarreling among themselves. China after 1911 would quickly revert to that pattern.

With the elimination of the common enemy, the Manchus, divisions quickly arose within the revolutionary camp. Key constitutionalist allies like Tang Hualong, who as a *jinshi* and provincial assembly president did so much to lend credibility to the initial revolutionary coup, was quickly sidelined by the Hubei revolutionary camp and forced out of the province. In Wuchang the revolutionaries soon turned to squabbling among themselves, with power struggles degenerating into political assassinations from which Li Yuanhong and former New Army officers emerged as the main beneficiaries.[41] After its liberation, Shanghai became a major center of revolutionary activity, but also of endless factional struggle of which the most famous incident was probably Chen Qimei dispatching Chiang Kai-shek to arrange the assassination of the Guangfuhui (光復會) leader Tao Chengzhang.* The Constitutionalists were certainly the most politically legitimate and socially acceptable adherents of the revolution, but they were viewed with suspicion by the revolutionaries, and divided among themselves between more radical and moderate factions (with the powerful Zhang Jian the most famous of the moderates). Zhang Jian had visited and made his peace with Yuan Shikai in the spring of 1911, but the Kang–Liang ideological leadership of the reformist camp could never forgive Yuan for his role in 1898.

In many important ways that deserve further study, Zhang Jian emerged as the arbiter of the revolution. He had met with Yuan Shikai in the spring, was in Wuchang conferring with Ruicheng† on an industrial project when the revolution broke out, then hurried back to Shanghai to announce his opposition to it. As had always been the case in the constitutionalist camp, his concern was that revolutionary violence would provoke foreign intervention on the model of the Boxer incident, bringing about the breakup of China. But the Wuchang revolutionaries' solicitousness toward foreign interests and the Great Powers' declaration of neutrality in China's civil war soon removed that threat. Once it became clear that one could have a revolution without foreign intervention, Zhang Jian began to tilt toward support of a republic.[42]

Another consistent concern of Zhang Jian's was the fate of China's borderlands. The rhetoric of Han restoration and racial revolution that prevailed in Wuhan had alarmed the Manchus' Mongol allies in particular.[43] The constitutional group felt that "Some in the revolutionary camp favor abandoning the borderlands and seeking the independence of China Proper."[44] In Beijing, Mongol princes were resisting abdication by the Qing emperor over just

---

* Tao Chengzhang (陶成章, 1878–1912) of Zhejiang joined the Tongmenghui while studying in Japan but became a rival of Sun Yat-sen, and was assassinated in 1912.

† Ruicheng (瑞澂) was the Manchu governor-general in Wuchang at the time of the 1911 Revolution, fleeing the city and living in retirement in Shanghai.

this issue.[45] It seems likely that the influence of Zhang Jian and his allies in Jiangsu and Zhejiang was critical in turning the rhetoric of revolution away from racial revolution and toward a republic of five peoples (*wuzu gonghe*) and once this was accomplished, Zhang Jian came to support the revolutionary government and even assisted in arranging crucial support for Sun Yat-sen's provisional government in Nanjing,[46] despite his negative impression of Sun Yat-sen, of whom he had written in his diary after their first meeting: "he has no sense of practical limits."[47]

By way of conclusion, let me offer a few thoughts on how this reconsideration differs from my interpretation of the 1911 Revolution in *Reform and Revolution*. In that book, the central argument was that the revolution was "politically progressive . . . [but] socially regressive."[48] The socially regressive part of this formula was more original (and more controversial) and it pointed to the role of the urban reformist elite in the revolution and their enhanced local power in its wake. My reconsideration today still focuses on this group of constitutionalist gentry, though today I have used Zhang Jian as a key example rather than Tan Yankai or Tang Hualong. I would also give more credit today to the politically progressive side of their contribution in leading the transition to a republican form of government which, however flawed, had provisions through the press, the courts, and legislative bodies for public participation in the political process. I would further note that by focusing on the unity of the five races the constitutionalists were instrumental in keeping the border regions of the Qing Empire together, supplanting the focus on the Han provinces of China Proper that prevailed among the revolutionaries in Wuchang with their eighteen-star flag.

My emphasis here, following Edward Rhoads, on the disastrous policy failures of Zaifeng and my argument that China reached its revolutionary tipping point only after the spring of 1911 also leads me to ask whether different policies might have saved the Qing. This is a potentially useful thought experiment. I noted at the outset that 1911 launched China on a revolutionary course that lasted until the disasters of the Cultural Revolution convinced China's leaders that reform and opening was a more promising road to prosperity and national revival. This was, in a sense, the same position held by people like Liang Qichao in the last years of the Qing. Revolution, Liang warned, would lead only to domestic turmoil and likely foreign intervention, and to some degree he was right. But was continued rule by a Manchu dynasty a viable alternative to revolution? Late in 1911, Liang Qichao tried to rescue constitutional monarchy with his vision of a republic with a nominal emperor, in which all Manchu privilege and the banner system would be abolished, and Manchus would adopt Chinese customs and surnames. Liang pointed out that in Europe, the constitutional monarchs of Greece and Norway were foreigners in those lands.[49] The example that occurs to me is Queen Victoria in Great

Britain—as great a symbol of British civilization as any, and yet she was of the House of Hanover, with both mother and father from German noble families.[50] Since the Manchus had already largely Sinified, they could just as easily have become Chinese as Victoria had become British. But as we have seen, Zaifeng and his Manchu allies at court were unwilling, in the final years of the Qing, to abandon the trappings and privileges associated with a distinct Manchu identity. This suggests that the point that Edward Rhoads and the New Qing History scholars have been making is correct: Manchu ethnicity mattered, and we need to take greater account of it in our scholarship.

There is one final point to be made. At the very last moment, when everything else was lost following the Wuchang Uprising, the Qing court did agree in its Nineteen Fundamental Principles (Zhongda xintiao shijiu tiao 重大信條十九條) to a symbolic emperor basically on the English model.[51] But it was too late. The revolutionaries were already empowered in the south and they would never accept continued Manchu rule. The lesson here is clear. The relationship between reform and revolution is complex and not easily predicted. Reform is often advanced as an alternative to revolution, as a weak or unpopular regime attempts to revive its fortunes. But as Alexis de Tocqueville taught us long ago, reform is just as likely to lead to revolution as to prevent it.[52] That was surely the case in China in 1911, when the products of the reforms—the students in the new schools and those returning from Japan, the members of the New Army, and the constitutionalists in the provincial assemblies—all turned against the dynasty and brought it down. Much of the difference between success and failure in political reform lies in the degree of commitment and leadership at the top. From 1901 through 1909, the court and key provincial leaders like Yuan Shikai and Zhang Zhidong led an aggressive program of reform. But under Zaifeng the court pulled back and its moves became reactive rather than preemptive—responding only to pressures from the press and the provincial assemblies and making only partial concessions. Their dithering on such issues as the queue and disbanding the banners were hopelessly incompetent, and their final retreat into the protection of Manchu supremacy in the Princes' Cabinet sealed their fate. At that point, the dynasty was lost and the 1911 Revolution became inevitable. Reform, if it is to succeed, must be proactive. The Qing court in the end lost the courage for decisive action.

NOTES

1. Mary Wright's seminal volume on the 1911 Revolution was entitled *China in Revolution: The First Phase, 1900–1913* (New Haven, CT: Yale University Press, 1968).

2. Luo Zhitian, *Jindai dushuren de sixiang shijie yu zhixue quxiang* [The intellectual world and scholastic orientation of modern scholars] (Beijing: Peking University Press, 2009), 9, 104–41.

3. Ping-ti Ho, *Studies on the Population of China* (Cambridge, MA: Harvard University Press, 1959); Pierre-Etienne Will, *Bureaucracy and Famine in Eighteenth-Century China*, trans. Elborg Forster (Stanford: Stanford University Press, 1990); Pierre-Etienne Will, R. Bin Wong, and James Lee, *Nourish the People: The State Civilian Granary System in China, 1650–1850* (Ann Arbor, MI: University of Michigan Center for Chinese Studies, 1991).

4. Li Huaiyin, "Fiscal Cycles and the Low-Equilibrium Trap under the Qing" (paper presented at the Association for Asian Studies annual meeting, Honolulu, Hawaii, 2011).

5. R. Kent Guy, *Qing Governors and their Provinces: The Evolution of Territorial Administration in China, 1644–1796* (Seattle: University of Washington Press, 2010).

6. Peter C. Perdue, *China Marches West: The Qing Conquest of Central Eurasia* (Cambridge, MA: Belknap Press, 2005).

7. Recent Chinese scholarship on the New Policies period will be cited in the notes below, so I will only mention one general work in English, stressing the Japanese connection: Douglas R. Reynolds, *China: 1898–1912—The Xinzheng Revolution and Japan* (Cambridge, MA: Harvard University Council on East Asian Studies, 1993).

8. Joan Judge, *Print and Politics: "Shibao" and the Culture of Reform in Late Qing China* (Stanford: Stanford University Press, 1996); Barbara Mittler, *A Newspaper for China?: Power, Identity and Change in Shanghai's News Media, 1872–1912* (Cambridge, MA: Harvard University Asia Center, 2004); Tang Haijiang, *Qingmo zhenglun baokan yu minzhong dongyuan: yizhong zhengzhi wenhua de shijiao* [Late Qing political journals and popular mobilization: A political culture perspective] (Beijing: Tsinghua University Press, 2007).

9. Xu Shuang, *Jiu wangchao yu xin zhidu: Qingmo lixian gaige jishi (1901–1911)* [Old dynasty and new system: A history of constitutional reform in the late Ch'ing (1901–1911)] (Beijing: Falü chubanshe, 2009).

10. Kit Siong Liew, *Struggle for Democracy: Sung Chiao-jen and the 1911 Chinese Revolution* (Berkeley: University of California Press, 1971); Chün-tu Hsueh, *Huang Xing and the Chinese Revolution* (Stanford: Stanford University Press, 1961). Recently I was struck by a letter of Liang Qichao, written shortly after the Wuchang Uprising on October 29, 1911, in which he says: "Sun [Yat-sen] and Huang [Xing] have long been at odds. Huang is courageous and committed to action, while Sun is crafty and a dreamer. Huang's group despises him. Last year they at one point decided to remove Sun." See Ding Wenjiang and Zhao Fengtian, *Liang Rengong xiansheng nianpu changbian (chugao)* [Chronological biography of Liang Qichao (draft)] (Beijing: Zhonghua shuju, 2010), 287.

11. The best recent Chinese scholarship seems to support this view. See Feng Tianyu and Zhang Duqin, *Xinhai shouyi shi* [A history of the 1911 uprising] (Wuhan: Hubei renmin chubanshe, 2011), 198–212.

12. Malcolm Gladwell, *The Tipping Point: How Little Things Can Make a Big Difference* (New York: Back Bay Books, 2002).

13. Joseph W. Esherick, *Reform and Revolution in China: The 1911 Revolution in Hunan and Hubei* (Berkeley: University of California Press, 1976), 171.

14. Ibid., 168.

15. Edward J. M. Rhoads, *Manchus and Han: Ethnic Relations and Political Power in Late Qing and Early Republican China, 1861–1928* (Seattle: University of Washington Press, 2000).

16. The most important and representative books of the New Qing History are Mark C. Elliott, *The Manchu Way: The Eight Banners and Ethnic Identity in Late Imperial China* (Stanford: Stanford University Press, 2001); Evelyn S. Rawski, *The Last Emperors: A Social History of Qing Imperial Institutions* (Berkeley: University of California Press, 1998); Pamela Kyle Crossley, *A Translucent Mirror: History and Identity in Qing Imperial Ideology* (Berkeley: University of California, 1999); and Michael G. Chang, *A Court on Horseback: Imperial Touring and the Construction of Ethno–Dynastic Hegemony in Qing China, 1680–1785* (Cambridge, MA: Harvard University Press, 2005).

17. One of the clearest statements of this position is in Wu Zesheng, "*Man-Han wenti*" [The Manchu–Han problem], *Datong bao*, no. 1 (June 25, 1907) (Taipei reprint edition, 1985), 57–106.

18. Rhoads, *Manchus and Han*, 290–91.

19. Elliott, *Manchu Way*, xv. Much of Elliott's argument is that ethnic discourse *does* exist in the Manchu documents, which makes them so essential to the New Qing History (xv, 169).

20. R. Kent Guy, *The Emperor's Four Treasuries: Scholars and the State in the Late Ch'ien-lung Era* (Cambridge, MA: Harvard University Council on East Asian Studies, 1987), 157–200.

21. The best new work on the Triads is Barend J. ter Haar, *Ritual and Mythology of the Chinese Triads: Creating an Identity* (Leiden: Brill, 1998). See esp. 23–25, 324–64, 400–402.

22. Liang Qichao is the source of this alleged statement by Gangyi, cited in Rhoads, *Manchus and Han*, 18.

23. Everard Fraser, December 1900, cited in Rhoads, *Manchus and Han*, 75.

24. Rhoads, *Manchus and Han*, 12–18.

25. Duanfang memorial (July 31, 1907), in Gugong bowuyuan Ming-Qing dang'anbu, ed., *Qingmo choubei lixian dang'an shiliao* [Historical materials on late Qing constitutional preparations], (Beijing: Zhonghua shuju, 1979), vol. 2, 915–18.

26. See note 17.

27. Xu Shuang, *Jiu wangchao yu xin zhidu*, 77–81.

28. Zhang Pengyuan, *Lixianpai yu xinhai geming* [The constitutionalists and the 1911 Revolution], third edition (Changchun: Jilin chubanshe, 2007), 16–39. Zhang's path-breaking study of the constitutionalist movement and the 1911 Revolution, first published in 1969, remains an indispensable study of the topic. See also Xu Shuang, *Jiu wangchao yu xin zhidu*, 140–41.

29. Rhoads, *Manchus and Han*, 121–72. The complexity of court politics in this period, the paucity of reliable documentation, and the problematic quality of various *yeshi* (野史) accounts make it difficult to discern exactly how political decision-making went so terribly wrong in 1910–1911. Having done no research on this myself, I find it difficult to understand the intersecting and competing networks of Manchu princes, Yuan Shikai's supporters, conservatives around Qu Hongji, corruption-fighting Cen Chunxuan with his links to Liang Qichao and the constitutionalists abroad, Manchu reformers like Duanfang with their own complex networks, and senior established figures like Prince Qing and Zhang Zhidong. There seem to me important issues to be understood here, and new Chinese research may be exploring these important questions.

30. Ding and Zhao, *Liang Rengong nianpu*, 290.

31. Zhang Hailin, *Duanfang yu Qingmo xinzheng* [Duangfang and the late Qing New Policy reforms] (Nanjing: Nanjing University Press, 2007), 484–504.

32. Jin Chengyi, *Qingchao diwei zhizheng shishi kao* [Studies of the evidence on Qing imperial succession struggles] (Beijing: Zhonghua shuju, 2010), 229–30.

33. Rhoads, *Manchus and Han,* 131–72; Xu Shuang, *Jiu wangchao yu xin zhidu*, 167–70.

34. Zhang Pengyuan, *Lixianpai yu xinhai geming*, 84–95.

35. *Guofeng bao*, vol. 1: 32, 89–92, cited in Zhang Pengyuan, *Lixianpai yu xinhai geming*, 77.

36. Yi Zongkui speech, cited in Zhang Pengyuan, *Lixianpai yu xinhai geming*, 79.

37. Gladwell, *Tipping Point.* There are specific parts of Gladwell's insightful analysis that may be particularly appropriate to the Chinese situation in 1911, especially his stress on the importance of three types of people—connectors, mavens (information specialists), and salesmen (charismatic persuaders)—and on the importance of context.

38. Zhang Jian, "Dai Lufu Sun Baoqi Sufu Cheng Dequan zouqing gaizu neige xuanbu lixian shu" [Memorial written on behalf of Shandong governor Sun Baoqi and Jiangsu governor Cheng Dequan requesting a reorganization of the cabinet and proclamation of constitutional government], October 1911, in *Zhang Jian quanji* [Complete works of Zhang Jian], vol. 1 (Nanjing: Jiangsu guji chubanshe, 1994), 176.

39. *Minlibao*, October 25, 1911.

40. Cited in Zhang Pengyuan, *Lixianpai yu xinhai geming*, 115.

41. Zhang Pengyuan, *Lixianpai yu xinhai geming*, 114–20; Esherick, *Reform and Revolution*, 221–33.

42. Zhang Pengyuan, *Lixianpai yu xinhai geming*, 169–86; *Zhang Jian quanji*, vol. 1, 163–216.

43. Henrietta Harrison, *The Making of the Republican Citizen: Political Ceremonies and Symbols in China, 1911–1929* (Oxford: Oxford University Press, 2000), 16–22. For an interesting recent Chinese web posting on the impact of revolutionary ideology on the frontiers, see Caoyuan de erlang [Son of the Grasslands] Quexuejun, "Xinhai geming shiqi de shibasheng jianguo sixiang ji qi houguo" [The idea of establishing a nation of eighteen provinces at the time of the 1911 Revolution and its consequences], http://bbs.tiexue.net/post2_4225367_1.html

(accessed January 6, 2012). I have also explored this issue in "How the Qing became China," chapter 4 above.

44. Sheng Xianjue letter to Liang Qichao, in Ding and Zhao, *Liang Rengong nianpu*, 297.

45. Rhoads, *Manchus and Han*, 217.

46. Zhang Pengyuan, *Lixianpai yu xinhai geming*, 182–83.

47. "Zhang Jian riji" [Zhang Jian diary], February 2, 1912, in *Zhang Jian quanji*, vol. 6, 662.

48. Esherick, *Reform and Revolution*, 8.

49. Liang Qichao, "Xin zhongguo jianshe wenti" [The problem of constructing a new China], cited in Ding and Zhao, *Liang Rengong nianpu*, 294.

50. For a simple introduction, see Antonia Fraser, ed., *The House of Hanover and Saxe-Coburg-Gotha*, part of the series *A Royal History of England* (Berkeley: University of California Press, 2000).

51. Xu Shuang, *Jiu wangchao yu xin zhidu*, 170–72.

52. Alexis de Tocqueville, *The Old Regime and the French Revolution*, trans. Gerald Bevan (New York: Penguin, 2008 [from 1865 edition]).

Part IV

REVOLUTION

Chapter Seven

War and Revolution

When I was trained as a Chinese historian, the conventional narrative held that the victory of Mao's Chinese Communist Party resulted from the flaws of Chiang Kai-shek's Nationalist regime. The first half of twentieth-century China's history was a story of failure. When the Free Press published a series of textbooks on Chinese history, the volume on republican China (1911–1949) was entitled *China in Disintegration*.[*] The one bright spot in this grim picture was the Nanjing decade (1927–1937) when Chiang's Nationalist Party restored China to a new level of unity and progress. Still, John K. Fairbank's popular volume on *The United States and China* taught us that the "most poignant feature of the Nanking period . . . [was] the superficiality of China's modernization."[†] Lloyd Eastman, the leading American expert on Nationalist rule, identified "one dominant theme of the period, the failure of revolution."[‡]

After the mid-1980s, this verdict began to change. On the one hand, Chiang Kai-shek's son, Chiang Ching-kuo (Jiang Jingguo), initiated a process of political democratization on top of Taiwan's already significant economic achievements. Suddenly the Nationalist Party did not seem quite so moribund. On the other hand, the PRC opened its archives to research, and a number of studies began to reassess the negative verdicts on the Nanjing era. In 1997, the *China Quarterly* published a special issue on "Reappraising Republican China." However, as this essay notes, most of these studies were limited to the Nanjing decade, lending strength to the new verdict that the Nationalists

---

[*] James E. Sheridan, *China in Disintegration: The Republican Era in Chinese History, 1912–1949* (New York: The Free Press, 1975).
[†] John King Fairbank, *The United States and China*, third edition (Cambridge, MA: Harvard University Press, 1971), 219.
[‡] Lloyd E. Eastman, *The Abortive Revolution: China under Nationalist Rule, 1927–1937* (Cambridge, MA: Harvard University Council on East Asian Studies, 1990), xiii. Other titles referenced in the endnotes of this chapter.

were doing quite well in until 1937, and only the war with Japan set Chiang Kai-shek's regime on the road to decline and ultimate defeat.

There is no question that the War of Resistance (1937–1945) opened the door to a spectacular increase in the size and strength of the Chinese Communist Party and its Eighth Route and New Fourth armies. This meant that the CCP was much better positioned to challenge Nationalist rule in the Civil War that broke out after the war against Japan. It does not follow, however, that the war weakened the Nationalists. The key focus of this essay is the impact of the war itself, and the extent to which the Civil War was experienced as a continuation of the wartime era, forming a single "long 1940s" from 1937 to 1949. The social changes that accompanied World War II have been much studied in other countries, but less so in China. This essay seeks to examine the impact of the war in laying the groundwork for the People's Republic of China.

While there were socio-political changes in the Communist areas that had an enduring impact—especially the growth of the party apparatus and the growing importance of class labels—there were also important, and certainly less studied, changes in the Nationalist areas. The state's role in the economy was vastly expanded; mass education was promoted with a stress on technical competence; gender norms changed as more women gained employment; clothing styles were transformed as the military-style Sun Yat-sen jacket replaced the long gown of students and intellectuals; and artistic styles moved from Western expressionism to more traditional Chinese styles and woodblocks. When Chiang Kai-shek returned to Nanjing at the end of the war with Japan, he was welcomed as the nation's wartime hero. One of the least expected events of modern Chinese history was the rapid collapse of his regime in the years that followed. This essay argues that one explanation of this event lies in the ways in which the wartime measures of the Nationalist Party prepared the population for Communist rule—as a less corrupt and self-serving executor of the Nationalists' wartime agenda.

RETHINKING THE RISE OF COMMUNIST CHINA*

A central narrative of modern Chinese history treats Japan's aggression and China's War of Resistance (1937–1945) as decisive for the triumph of the Chinese Communist Party and the founding of the People's Republic of China. As Steven Levine put it, "If not for the Sino-Japanese War, it is doubtful whether the Chinese Communist Party would ever have come to power."[1] This verdict builds on the seminal work of Chalmers Johnson, whose *Peasant*

---

* This essay was adapted from "War and Revolution: Chinese Society During the 1940s," *Twentieth-Century China* 27, no. 1 (November 2001): 1–37. Reprinted with permission.

Nationalism and Communist Power juxtaposed the failure of the CCP's Jiangxi Soviet to the dramatic growth of the Communist guerrilla movement during the war against Japan. Mao Zedong himself acknowledged the revolution's debt to Japan when he famously (perhaps facetiously) thanked a Japanese prime minister for his country's contribution to the Communist cause.[2] The rapid collapse of the Nationalist regime during the Civil War of 1946–1949 makes this conclusion inescapable. After all, at the outset of the war with Japan, the Red Army was reduced to roughly 20,000 troops in the poor and barren area around Yan'an plus scattered guerrilla forces in the south. By the end of the war, the Communists had a million men under arms and controlled much of the countryside in North China. Clearly the war was decisive in this massive growth of the Communist forces, turning the Red Army into an existential threat to the Nationalist regime. But to say that the war weakened the Nationalists and saved the Communists begs the question of how and why the war strengthened one while weakening the other, and it assumes that the wartime growth of Communist movement was sufficient to explain its swift victory in the Civil War.

For years our image of the collapse of Chiang Kai-shek's Nationalist regime was colored by the accounts of such wartime witnesses as Theodore White, Graham Peck, and John Fairbank. Fairbank's 1967 introduction to Peck's *Two Kinds of Time* describes it as an "insider's book" on the "death throes of the old Chinese society."[3] The final war-torn years of the Guomindang were the last act in a long process of China's social and political decay. Theodore White and Annalee Jacoby painted a similarly bleak picture of corruption, cynicism, and collapsing morale under "the feudal-minded men who control the Guomindang."[4] Lloyd Eastman's *Seeds of Destruction* lent academic weight to the contemporary accounts. His final verdict on wartime and postwar China endorsed the same "disintegration theory" that informed James Sheridan's *China in Disintegration*.[5] In this view, the Nationalist era was simply the final doomed attempt to shore up the old regime before it was swept away in a great wave of revolutionary change.

In recent years, however, the history of republican China has experienced a pronounced revival, rescuing it from the theme of disintegration and the verdict of failure. Significantly, this trend extends to Chinese scholarship, where new work has discomfited the CCP leadership with its "republican fever" (*minguore* 民國熱).[6] While Chinese scholarship has mainly celebrated the intellectual achievements of republican China, Anglophone studies have documented significant growth in industry, finance, and transportation; military modernization; urban renewal, policing, and public spaces; and major achievements in higher education under the Nanjing regime. Unfortunately, most of the key works have focused on the Nanjing Decade (1927–1937) and stopped short of the anti-Japanese war, with scholarly studies ending with the outbreak of the War of Resistance in 1937.[7] These studies provide critical evidence for the vitality and achievements of the Nanjing regime, especially in its Lower Yangzi heartland. To a large degree, this 1927–1937 focus reflects the new availability of archival sources in Nanjing and Shanghai, and has succeeded in rescuing republican China from the verdict of progressive disintegration and decay. The 1937 terminus of the new republican history, however, leaves us in an unenviable position: studies of Nationalist politics and society end in 1937, while analyses of the Communist Revolution focus on the wartime period or the PRC after 1949. The prewar modernist narrative is broken by the outbreak of war, while a new revolutionary narrative begins in the Communist areas. In a sense, the Johnson thesis that the war decided the question of who would rule China has relegated republican history after 1937 to historical oblivion and protected the Nationalists' reputation for nation-building from close scrutiny of its record during the war.

There have been important exceptions to the 1937 terminus—especially in studies of students and workers, who were active and important in social protests of the late 1940s. These studies have exposed important fault lines in the Guomindang regime.[8] In addition, recent years have seen a body of solid scholarship on wartime and postwar diplomatic and military history. Much of this work has sought to correct contemporary observers' negative assessments of Chiang Kai-shek's military leadership, defend Chiang's defensive strategy against Japan, and stress the limited nature of Allied assistance to China.[9] Odd Arne Westadt has written a comprehensive and careful new history of the Civil War, stressing the strategic decisions of both sides in what was, after all, largely a military conflict, and disputing the conventional wisdom by arguing that the outcome "was in no way predetermined in 1945."[10]

If the war against Japan did not ensure a Communist victory, the Civil War scholarship suggests a critical turning point during the 1947 military campaigns in the Northeast (Manchuria). Since the Soviet Union's Red Army had occupied Manchuria in the final days of World War II, these campaigns raised the question of the amount and consequences of the support the Communist armies received from the Soviet Union. Lin Biao commanded the Communist armies, and his skillful use of artillery reflected training he had received in the Soviet Union, and field guns that probably came from there as well. This has lent support to the old Cold War notion that Russian assistance (or the withholding of American aid) was critical to the Chinese Communist victory.[11] In the end, however, Great Power intervention was hardly decisive. The Nationalist armies had complete superiority in weaponry, with all the tanks, total control of the air, and superior equipment and logistics as a result of Allied aid during World War II. In 1945 alone, the Nationalists received four times the Allied aid of the previous three years, including the training and equipping of thirty-nine divisions—and most of these troops and equipment were never used against Japan, only on the Communists.[12] A close study of the Manchurian campaigns concludes: "the United States did give Chiang's regime over $1 billion worth of military aid between 1945 and 1949—far more than the Soviet Union gave to the Chinese Communists."[13] The Communist victory in the Civil War may have been military, but it was not decided by superior weaponry or external aid.

After the decisive campaigns in Manchuria, the collapse of the Nationalist regime was rapid. Though major clashes followed, especially the massive Huai-Hai battle involving millions of troops, most of these confrontations were decided by the defection of Nationalist armies. When the final stage came as the Communists occupied Beijing, Shanghai, and other major cities, the Nationalist armies either surrendered or melted away. They had simply lost the will to fight.[14] This is not to say that the Chinese population warmly welcomed the Communist victory. When the People's Liberation Army marched into the cities of China, they were generally met with cautious crowds.[15] But it is necessary to probe the reasons for and historical import of the Guomindang's postwar collapse. After all, the Civil War was not just won by the Communists; it was lost by the KMT. Most importantly, we must acknowledge certain fundamental socioeconomic and cultural changes that took hold in Nationalist China during the war, continued through the postwar years, and laid the foundation for broad popular acceptance of the new society that would emerge after 1949.

COMMUNIST BASES: AN ALTERNATIVE MODEL

In proposing a new way to understand the process of war and revolution, I am not suggesting that we discard the old paradigm, only that we revise and augment it. In particular, we must note that, unlike any other Allied Power, China endured a domestic political competition coterminous with the war against fascism.[16] During the War of Resistance, the Communists' Eighth Route Army and New Fourth Army established a number of reasonably secure base areas where they enacted policies that promoted an alternative model for Chinese politics and society. Young people flocked to Yan'an where most found an alternative universe of sacrifice, commitment, and optimism about China's future. In the early war years, the Communist Party promoted a moderate policy of alliance with patriotic intellectuals, "enlightened gentry," "progressive" landlords, and rich peasants to carry out rent and interest reduction, progressive taxation, and political mobilization through rural elections, all of which increased the burden on the old elite and gradually undermined its political domination of the countryside.[17] After 1942, the rectification movement in Yan'an was followed by an "anti-traitor" movement that ruthlessly targeted class enemies. Through these campaigns, party members were schooled in the techniques of political struggle, the party's enemies were clearly on the defensive, and party control in the base areas was securely established.[18] It is important to recognize that American observers of the Dixie Mission and Chinese and foreign journalists and intellectuals who visited Yan'an in the late war years all arrived *after* the rectification campaigns had silenced dissident voices and firmly united the party around Mao's line. Their generally positive accounts—many of which circulated widely in China—should be read in that light.[19] This meant that as China emerged from the war, its population was confronted with two alternative futures.

The shift from the cross-class United Front policies of the early war years to the more class-conscious policies of the mid-1940s was accelerated by the Civil War and had lasting impact on the PRC. In the Civil War, class lines were drawn hard and fast, and landlords became the enemy. Now the object was to mobilize the party's class base among the rural poor, to give poor peasants land rights as a stake in the revolution, providing an incentive for them to resist the return to power of the Guomindang and the old elite.[20] Land reform, which went through several stages of radical advance, correction, and moderate consolidation, dominated the agenda of social change in the Communist areas. There was, however, one central defining theme: it promoted class consciousness with unprecedented thoroughness and defined class status with labels that would last for generations and shape lives for decades.

In terms of social structure, the most important result of this process was the elimination of the economic base of the rural elite; but just as important was the socio-cultural effect of land reform, for it taught peasants the importance of the new class labels. The final meetings to establish the class status of each household in a village were hotly contested affairs, for peasants quickly recognized that however incomprehensible the official criteria for "rich peasant" status might be, that label was one to be avoided at all cost, and, if possible, one sought to join the favored ranks of the "poor peasants."[21] Peasants may not have realized it at the time, but as the system of class labels evolved in the 1950s and 1960s, class background would be inherited by one's children, recorded on household registers and identity cards, and have enormous influence on all aspects of life. Those with "bad" class backgrounds would become targets of periodic political campaigns, and their children's chances for education, a good marriage, or social advance would be greatly reduced. On the other hand, those with "good" class backgrounds would be sought out for educational opportunities or positions in the party. This politically constructed notion of "class," unknown to most peasants a few years before, became one of the most important aspects of their new identity in the PRC.[22]

Land reform and civil war were supported by a massive increase in the party apparatus. The party called upon local cadres to "boldly recruit hired farmhands, tenants, poor peasants, and activists into the party, to double and triple party membership."[23] Nationally, they succeeded. At the time of the Seventh Party Congress in the spring of 1945, party membership was 1,211,128. Two years later, it was 2,759,456; and on the eve of the founding of the PRC in 1949, 4,488,080.[24] In the four years of the Civil War, party membership increased almost four-fold. This rapid growth went hand in hand with the geographical extension of the party apparatus, providing cadres for the newly incorporated regions, which in turn offered fertile recruiting grounds for new members. The larger party membership permitted the intensification of party authority in its old bases, as young activists with some education were recruited and used as secretarial aides (*wenshu*) to village-level cadres.[25]

In the Communist bases, the enlarged party apparatus mobilized the population to support the Civil War: grain was requisitioned, porters and stretcher-bearers gave logistical support for the army, women were mobilized to knit socks and make shoes for soldiers, and young men were conscripted to fight. Mass organizations were created to involve peasants, youth, and women in the revolutionary movement. Through this process, a new society was being created, increasingly politicized, much more organized, much more closely linked to the state apparatus. The rectification campaign had unified the party, but also made it more autocratic, and cadres could be arbitrary or even self-serving; but by and large they worked hard for little material reward. Corruption in the new regime was usually petty, and while the power of party cadres could be substantial, their economic status was scarcely superior to the general population. Non-communists who visited these areas were impressed by the austere living conditions of the Communist cadres, their efficient work style, candid self-criticism meetings, and above all by their confident commitment to the revolutionary struggle.[26]

"DILEMMAS OF VICTORY"

For the other Allied Powers, World War II ended in glorious victory as the nation was saved and the national cause affirmed. This was the "good war," and it affirmed the justice of the Allied cause and the governments that had fought against fascism. China was not completely outside this world: there, too, victory was celebrated, and Chiang Kai-shek was welcomed back to Nanjing with great parades honoring his leadership.[27] But the celebrations proved short-lived as hostilities quickly resumed, the country moved from war to civil war, and the social divisions of the era were exacerbated.

Every account of the Civil War stresses the process whereby the Guomindang dashed the hopes and squandered the opportunity presented by the Allies' victory over Japan.[28] One sees the theme again and again in the press and in films of the postwar period: the great expectations that accompanied the celebration of Victory (*Shengli* 勝利), and the dashing of those hopes in the corruption, poverty and despair that followed. Paul Pickowicz has analyzed postwar films under the theme "Victory as Defeat," and their popularity leaves no doubt that these movies resonated with Chinese urban audiences.[29] Residents of the Japanese-occupied coastal cities who had eagerly awaited the return of Chinese rule were quickly put off by carpetbagging officials who seemed interested only in enriching themselves off confiscated Japanese property and enjoying the night life of bars and dance halls. The theme of disenchantment with the returning Guomindang runs through accounts of rural areas and small towns as well. In many parts of the north, the Guomindang temporarily replaced local communist regimes only to lose peasant support by reversing rent reduction, welcoming back hated collaborators, and applying discriminatory exchange rates for the border region currencies held by residents.[30] From a small county in Hubei came a typical story of a new young magistrate, welcomed after the war as he arrived in "cheap, government-allotted clothing of coarse quality," only to be removed after amassing 100 ounces of gold in a single month of corrupt rule.[31] The initial enthusiasm that greeted the Guomindang's recovery of occupied China should give pause to retrospective convictions of the Nationalist regime's inevitable collapse. At the very least, we should recognize that few Chinese at the time realized how quickly the old order would fall. Among longer-term effects, we should acknowledge that the last years of the Guomindang regime etched an indelible impression on a generation of Chinese, leaving a deep fear of runaway inflation and an enduring record of extravagant political corruption.

In January 1948, President Chiang Kai-shek offered a scathing indictment of his own party and regime:

> To tell the truth, never, in China or abroad, has there been a revolutionary party as decrepit and degenerate (*tuitang he fubai* 頹唐和腐敗) as we [the Guomindang] are today; nor has there been one as lacking in spirit, in discipline, and even more in standards of right and wrong as we are today. This kind of party should long ago have been destroyed and swept away![32]

Censorship prevented ordinary citizens from publishing such blunt condemnations of the Nationalist Party, but the press was certainly full of reports of a regime and social order in collapse.

The last years of the Guomindang established the contemporary Chinese standard for political corruption. Suzanne Pepper summarizes press reports of the time describing "a bureaucracy permeated with corruption. . . . Essentially money and favors greased the wheels that made the KMT political system move, ensuring that it moved less effectively."[33] In the immediate postwar period, the press regularly reported bribery to gain rights to Japanese property or to secure Guomindang testimony that one's collaboration with the enemy was secretly in the service of the government; and these became standard tropes for the rich degenerates who served as the anti-heroes of Civil War movies.[34] Chiang Kai-shek railed repeatedly against such abuses, but to no avail. People were left with the impression that the postwar Guomindang served only those with money or powerful connections.

Runaway inflation was the other great cancer consuming the legitimacy of the regime. The Shanghai wholesale price index showed the trend. With the immediate postwar month of September 1945 taken as 100, the index increased to 1,475 one year later, 12,534 in September 1947, then after the disastrous failure of the Gold Yuan reforms, climbed to 1,368,049 in August 1948—a 13,000-fold increase in just three years.[35] Shops closed to protect their inventories; funds were diverted from productive investment to the hoarding of gold, silver, and scarce commodities, or to the safety of Hong Kong and foreign bank accounts. Industry slowed, workers were laid off, and with the cities' population swollen by refugees fleeing the Civil War battlefields, unemployment soared.[36] With other economies, including Japan's, shifting more quickly and efficiently to a peacetime economy, Chinese exports lagged far behind imports, draining off valuable foreign exchange.[37]

Because industrial workers' wages were pegged to the price index, labor unrest in the immediate postwar months was not as widespread as might be expected. Soon, however, as economic slowdown reduced industrial employment, lay-offs became the focus of a growing number of strikes.[38] But industrial workers were not the only source of social unrest. In Shanghai, an attempt to crack down on hawkers produced a riot in which dance halls, cinemas, and automobiles—the symbols of affluent pleasure-seeking—became the focus of mass destruction.[39] In 1948, it was time for cabaret hostesses to riot, trashing the offices of the Social Affairs Bureau that sought to ban their activities.[40] Across the country, as the *China Weekly Review* reported, there was "an upsurge of social unrest in all branches of the variegated Chinese society," including "rice riots, counter-riots by dealers, disputes . . . demonstrations, strikes of all kind, and even the closure for a period of the stock exchange because brokers turned down a government revision of the bourse regulations."[41] Of course, not all frustration was expressed collectively. The press was also littered with reports of suicides, often of the newly impoverished middle class who were unable to support their families.[42]

No symbol of social unrest so preoccupied the press as the postwar student movement. Almost every day, the leading newspapers carried on their front pages news of a student strike or demonstration, faculty petition, or the arrest and beating of students in some Chinese city. Few would question Doak Barnett's 1948 assessment of "an increasing alienation of students from the Central Government and a definite shift to the Left."[43] Though political demands for an end to the Civil War and a cessation of American aid to the Guomindang dominated the most famous student demonstrations, and though underground Communist influence was certainly important, there is no question that both widespread student participation and broad public support for their protests derived in large measure from the economic hardships of students brought on by inflation and a stagnant economy. Students were the future of the nation, and most were saying quite clearly that their future did not lie with the current regime.[44]

Riots, strikes, demonstrations, protests, and petitions all testify to the public mood of discontent. Especially on issues like inflation and the Civil War, students and the independent press were eager to blame the government. But when one looks at the popular and much discussed movies of this period, one immediately senses a broader social critique. The villains are consistent, clear, and starkly portrayed: they dress in Western suits and wear leather shoes, live in large, elaborately furnished Western apartments with many servants, have their own cars and chauffeurs, rarely seem to work, but are constantly engaged in drinking, dancing, romancing, and visiting night clubs or cocktail parties. They are rich—but their wealth is inevitably ill-gotten, the result of collaborating with the Japanese or some special "opportunity" gained through powerful connections—and money makes them frivolous, selfish, corrupt and cruel. The reform-era slogan "To get rich is glorious" would never have gained credence in this era. On the contrary, in one of the memorable lines at the end of the film *Spring Dreams of Heaven*, the long-suffering mother cries out "The good suffer, the evil prosper! What kind of times are these?"[45] One cannot dismiss these movies as the product of leftist film-makers. *Spring Dreams* was in fact produced by a government-run studio, and it played to enthusiastic urban audiences. The Guomindang elite had lost its commitment to sacrifice for the nation, and young people especially were anxious to look for alternative leaders.

This picture of a bankrupt social order in the Guomindang areas and a radically new society in the Communist bases is very much the conventional wisdom. It suggests that the logical result of the Civil War was the replacement of the old society with the Communists' revolutionary alternative. This conventional view is not wrong, for with the military victory of the People's Liberation Army the old order did come to an end, and the essential elements of the Communist order in the base areas were extended to the entire nation. But this view is incomplete, for the Civil War era witnessed important continuities to the wartime Nationalist order, and there were important ways in which social and institutional changes initiated by the Guomindang may in fact have facilitated the acceptance of the Communists' PRC regime.

SEEDS OF THE NEW SOCIETY GERMINATE IN THE OLD

The most interesting and important changes of the long 1940s were those that grew out of the war with Japan, for they illustrate the fact that the War of Resistance, as much as the Communist Revolution, reshaped Chinese society. In many ways, the war prepared the way for the Communist Revolution, not only by strengthening the Communist Party and its armies, but by introducing a new social and cultural order that primed the population to accept the Communist regime. In a sense, the Nationalists had already introduced enough elements of the New China so that the Communists could be welcomed as a less corrupt and self-serving group to replace the failing Guomindang and preside over the birth of New China.

Throughout the world, one of the consequences of World War II mobilization was an expansion of state authority. This change was most notable in the economy, where planning, rationing, price controls, and industrial conversion were commonplace. But it was also evident in other areas: in culture and the media, in the mobilization of civilians, and in education.[46] In China, the growth of the state and the extension of its functions in social engineering, nation-building, and the promotion of economic growth were trends that began with the New Policies of the late Qing and accelerated after the Guomindang came to power in 1927. But the war brought new urgency to these efforts and helped create the political consensus that allowed their implementation to an unprecedented degree. For all its corruption and failings, the Guomindang state's institutional reach was far more pervasive (in its areas of control) in 1946–1947 than that of any earlier Chinese regime.

As William Kirby has noted, economic planning and nationalized industry were an important legacy of Guomindang rule. Though the Guomindang traced the origins of this policy to Sun Yat-sen's 1922 *Shiye jihua* (事業計劃; English title: *The International Development of China*), concrete moves toward a planned economy only date to the founding of the National Resources Commission (NRC), organized in the 1930s to prepare the national economy for resistance to Japanese aggression. The 1937 outbreak of war with Japan and the forced relocation of industry to the interior greatly expanded the scale of the NRC and brought it much closer to its goal of "state-run, import-substituting, military-related, heavy industrial development."[47] From a prewar total of 23 industrial and mining enterprises, it expanded to 103 enterprises with 160,000 workers by 1944. Even more significantly, 70 percent of the total paid-up capital in Free China industries belonged to state-run concerns. The end of the war did nothing to reverse this trend. On the contrary, the nationalization of Japanese-owned firms expanded the state's reach from the war-related heavy industrial sector to light industry, especially textiles. By 1947, the NRC's industrial empire (including joint ventures with the provinces) employed over 500,000 workers and accounted for 67.3 percent of China's industrial capital.[48] In Tianjin, seven of the nine postwar textile mills were government-run enterprises confiscated from the Japanese, and Doak Barnett echoed a common complaint that "The omnipresence of the Central Government in the economy has made things extremely difficult for private enterprise since the end of the war."[49]

The Guomindang shift toward state capitalism meant more than state domination of the industrial economy. It also transformed the nature of working life within the large state-owned enterprises. Company administration was bureaucratized; a wartime "Work Emulation Campaign" (*gongzuo jingsai yundong* 工作競賽運動) sought to provide ideological incentives to replace the capitalist profit-motive; and the larger enterprises provided a wide range of welfare benefits including housing, dining halls, schools, hospitals, consumer cooperatives, and even company cemeteries. The large state enterprises of the Nationalist era prefigured the self-contained life of the work unit (*danwei* 單位) of the PRC.[50]

The new state-dominated industrial economy also implied a new role for workers. Much of the power of the prewar labor movement had been predicated on appeals to the workers' nationalist sentiment in their struggles with foreign enterprises in the treaty-ports' industrial economy.[51] Even workers employed by private Chinese enterprises could appeal for state protection of their interests against abusive employers. Now most workers were employees of the Chinese state. On the one hand this meant a loss of leverage in industrial disputes, with state and capital now joined against labor; but, on the other hand, it made workers direct participants in the national project. In the short run, workers seem to have gained from this new status: unlike the middle class, their wages were pegged to the price index, working conditions improved, and their government-sponsored unions enjoyed significant leverage.[52] In the longer run, their lives and working conditions would be increasingly subject to direct state control.[53]

The wartime expansion of state authority was also pronounced in the field of education. In 1938, CC-Clique leader Chen Lifu was appointed minister of education. The Pittsburgh-educated mining engineer and enthusiastic promoter of Confucian values immediately embarked on a thorough-going reform of China's educational system to ensure that it supported the state's wartime agenda. The result was arguably one of the most significant legacies of Guomindang rule. The first objective was total statist control. The Ministry of Education would set curriculum, prepare textbooks, administer national exams for admission to public higher education *and* for the issuance of college degrees, and take control of all public universities including university budgets, required curriculum, and the appointment of professors. The rationale was the establishment of uniform standards, but the effect was to create the institutional infrastructure for a Guomindang educational orthodoxy. The Ministry of Education then set about reforming the content of the curriculum at all levels. There were required courses in physical education, military training, and Sun Yat-sen's Three People's Principles. Chen Lifu wrote an *Outline for Ethical Teaching* (*Xunyu gangyao* 訓育綱要) to be followed at all school levels, in which the Confucian virtues were reinterpreted "to argue for self-discipline and service to the nation."[54] In policies reminiscent of Xi Jinping's China, there was a rigorous effort to "sinify" the curriculum, ridding it of Western texts and models, making it more appropriate to China's nation-building project. Chen aimed to eliminate the Anglophone higher education of the prewar years, so tellingly described in Yeh Wen-hsin's *Alienated Academy*.[55] In Chen's view, these foreign influences had turned China's colleges into "cultural foreign concessions," which a sovereign China could no longer tolerate.[56] In higher education, liberal arts were subordinated to more practical disciplines, especially engineering, but also agriculture and geology. Ministry of Education statistics show that 55.8 percent of college students studied liberal arts and law in 1932, as against 28.1 percent in science, engineering, medicine, and agriculture. By 1939, these ratios had almost been reversed: 31.3 percent in arts and law, 51.0 percent in science and technical disciplines.[57] Science courses put less emphasis on theory and more on practical application. The national crisis created by Japan's invasion provided both the need and the rationale for a transformation of Chinese education to serve the Guomindang's nation-building project, and many of the effects of that transformation were replicated in the early PRC and have proven exceptionally enduring.[58]

The success of these reforms depended on a firm foundation in primary and secondary education. The precision of government statistics on the extension of education should be treated with some skepticism, but the available data and scattered local reports provide solid evidence that the war brought remarkable progress in spreading mass education. Normal school enrollments increased more rapidly than any other area of higher education—a good measure of the government's commitment to train teachers.[59] By 1946, the Ministry of Education could claim 23,813,705 students in primary schools, which is consistent with Chen Lifu's claim that 70 percent of the 34 million school-age children in the Guomindang areas had received some education.[60] Middle school enrollments increased at an even more rapid rate (and the statistics are perhaps slightly more reliable). Against a prewar (1936) figure of 627,246 students in middle, normal, and vocational schools there were 1,001,734 in the much-reduced areas under Guomindang control in 1942–1943. By the fall of 1945, this figure had increased to 1,566,392. Because of the shifting areas covered by National Government figures, provincial statistics from the interior provide an even clearer measure of the progress made. The number of Sichuan middle schools increased from 273 to 773 (183 percent) between 1936 and 1946, and students from 63,494 to 266,301 (319 percent); in Guizhou, middle schools increased from 39 to 158 (305 percent) and students from 8,769 to 37,224 (324 percent).[61] By the end of the war, most Chinese youngsters were provided basic literacy and numeracy, through textbooks that embodied the Guomindang's distinctive blend of Confucian virtues and national consciousness.

The final link in the complex of education reforms was the system of national examinations for admission to higher education, and a system of subsidies for students who gained admission. The subsidies were the brainchild of Chen Lifu, and a deliberate attempt to keep poorer students from going to the Communist areas. As John Israel has observed, they soon came to be regarded "as a right rather than a privilege" and the postwar inadequacy of the subsidies became a focal point for student protests. Still, it would appear that competitive exams and student subsidies—together with the wider availability of secondary education—began to open up China's universities to more than the narrow urban elite whose offspring had filled prewar campuses.[62] On the other hand, just as government credentialing of professors provided a lever that the government could use for political purposes, so did government subsidies create a system in which students were dependent on state support.[63]

Radio and cinema, the new media of the mid-twentieth century, were another key area where state control expanded during and after the war. Technology limited the state's media ambitions during the war, but in the postwar period the Guomindang regained control of the coastal cities equipped with the modern infrastructure to support their initiatives. Recognizing the considerable power that radio had shown in wartime propaganda, the Guomindang in 1946 established the Chinese Broadcasting Administration as its national propaganda organ, and issued stringent regulations on private stations which liberals saw heralding "an almost state-controlled industry." While large cities like Shanghai still had a variety of radio stations, in the interior, the government's voice was dominant.[64] In the movie industry, the National Government lacked the studio facilities for significant initiatives during the war. After the war, however, they quickly took over the Japanese studios that had the best equipment available in China and reorganized them into China's first state-owned film studies, preparing the way for the state-run studios of the PRC.[65]

The war increased the reach of the Chinese state in one final way that was both symbolically and practically important: it eliminated the foreign-administered concessions in the treaty ports. When Japan took over the foreign concessions in Shanghai and Tianjin in 1941, it unified administration in those cities for the first time in modern history.[66] In the postwar period, both of these cities (along with Beijing, Nanjing, Canton, Shenyang, and Chongqing) became Special Municipalities under the direct administration of the National Government. Wartime treaties had abolished extraterritoriality, and now China regained sovereignty over its most important ports and industrial centers. No longer would treaty ports be colonial outposts of Euro-American privilege, or places of refuge for China's political dissidents.[67] In Shanghai, the end of divided sovereignty reduced the need for gangs to enforce agreements across jurisdictional boundaries, and Du Yuesheng* and the Green Gang never returned to their prewar prominence.[68] During Jiang Jingguo's† coercive effort to enforce the Gold Yuan reforms of 1948, the state demonstrated the lengths to which it would go to control China's largest city and economic center.[69] Unfortunately, the net effect of such policies was that both political dissidents and valuable capital fled to the security of the last colonial outpost on China's coast: Hong Kong.[70] Postwar Shanghai looked like a very different city from the treaty port society described in the flood of Shanghai studies on the prewar era. The "Shanghai modern" so eloquently described by Leo Lee for the earlier period had become a corrupt oasis of gambling, opium, and dancing by the remnants of a failing elite.[71]

As this brief review shows, the war with Japan significantly expanded the reach and functions of the Chinese state, and there was no significant retreat in the Civil War period. Its domination of the modern economy gave postwar China—at least in the industrial, mining, and banking sectors—an

---

* Du Yuesheng (杜月笙, 1888–1951) was the Green Gang leader in Shanghai, who combined opium dealing with major philanthropy and vigorously supported Chiang Kai-shek's anti-Communist campaigns.

† Jiang Jingguo (Chiang Ching-kuo 蔣經國, 1910–1988) was the son of Chiang Kai-shek, educated in the Soviet Union and married to a Russian woman. He returned to China in 1937, gained his father's trust during the war, and governed Shanghai with an iron fist during the Civil War. He was President of the Republic of China on Taiwan from 1978–1988, cautiously guiding it on the path to democracy.

economy in which the market operated to a degree, but the state controlled the "commanding heights." Improvements in transportation, media and education greatly increased the influence of the National Government. With the elimination of extraterritoriality and foreign concessions, the Guomindang rid China of the most visible and hated symbols of imperialist privilege. As an outgrowth of the war with Japan, an institutional infrastructure was created that would prove well suited to the CCP's authoritarian impulses.

A NATION IS BORN

On the eve of the war with Japan, when activists of the December 9 student movement went into the countryside to spread their patriotic message, they were greeted by impassive peasants, to whom "'China' is an abstraction."[72] Japanese troops occupying North China in the summer of 1937 were astonished at the Chinese toleration of their invasion, "as if the Chinese did not feel they had a nation worth fighting for."[73] The brutality of Japan's aggression quickly changed this reaction, but this was more than the peasantry "spontaneously" mobilizing in reaction to Japan's invasion, as Chalmers Johnson argued.[74] The effect of patriotic propaganda and the extension of mass education in both Nationalist and Communist areas also played an important role: in unprecedented numbers, young people were taught about China's glorious past, promising future, and the need to defend the nation against foreign invaders. It is a telling fact that when the Communists launched their land reform campaign in the postwar period, they gained popular support by focusing their initial attacks on Japanese collaborators—linking their new program of class revolution to a Nationalist agenda that was now locally experienced and widely accepted.[75]

Among young people in urban centers, patriotic commitment was even more important. The war uprooted millions from their coastal enclaves to travel far into the interior to escape the invaders. In the process, people from across the country, speaking a babel of dialects, with different clothes and customs and dietary traditions, learned that they all belonged to one nation—to one imagined community. For many young students, this great migration to China's interior provided their first experience in the countryside and their first real opportunity to interact with commoners. Their patriotic retreat gave them a new understanding of the nation they hoped to defend.[76] Many of these young people joined drama groups that performed patriotic street theatre in towns and rural markets, spreading an explicitly nationalist message to a wide audience.[77] Needless to say, the millions of young men conscripted into the army also received a new introduction to their national mission.

The great migration that brought millions to the interior was part of a larger process that transformed the economic geography of the country. On the eve of the war, National Government statistics showed that of 3,935 registered factories in China, only 17 percent were located in the interior. (Thirty-one percent were in Shanghai, 52 percent in the other coastal provinces.)[78] After war broke out in 1937, hundreds of coastal factories were disassembled and moved to the unoccupied areas of the interior.[79] Many more were founded during the war. In 1943, the Ministry of Economic Affairs reported 3,758 factories with 241,662 workers in the interior, only 590 of which were in existence in 1937.[80] By June of 1944, this figure had risen to 4,346 factories, of which 1,228 were in Chongqing, 729 in other parts of Sichuan, 825 in Hunan, 338 in Guangxi, and 267 in Shaanxi.[81] None of these areas had seen any significant modern industry before the war, so this wartime development brought a major change in the economic geography of the country.

In the postwar period, some of the relocated industries returned to Shanghai and the coastal areas, but there was by no means a complete deindustrialization of the interior. Though asserting that "Sichuan again became a backwater," Doak Barnett reported from the province in the summer of 1948 that "the war had left a mark that could not be completely erased. . . . [S]ome industries stayed on, particularly around Chongqing, and formed a nucleus of arsenals, coal mines, flour mills, and cotton and wool factories that looked as if it might be permanent."[82] A similar, if less dramatic, transformation had taken place in such cities as Xi'an, Lanzhou, and Baoji in the Northwest, and Kunming, Liuzhou, Guiyang, and Guilin in the southeast. Communications among these cities improved dramatically during the war, which saw the first efforts at railway construction in the southwest and a substantial improvement of roads connecting the major cities.[83] All of this development of industry and transport in the interior (together with the earlier noted expansion of education) would continue and accelerate under the Five-Year Plans of the PRC.[84]

The transformation of China's interior during the wartime and postwar period has been little studied—in part because it has been obscured by the larger narrative of Guomindang political and military collapse. But there is substantial evidence that social and economic change was significant in the 1940s. Yunnan is an obvious example. Its capital, Kunming, became the wartime refuge to which North China's elite universities fled to establish Southwest United University (Lianda), the end of both the Burma Road and the Hump airlift over which military supplies were brought from India, and a major base for American soldiers and airmen. The combined influence of coastal intellectuals and American servicemen transformed life in Yunnan. Forty-nine factories were established in the province in two years; 60,000 coastal refugees joined Kunming's prewar population of 143,000; Kunming's first cinema opened in 1939; banks, restaurants, and bookstores proliferated; and by the end of the war, a foreign resident would note the well-lit streets, record players blaring, streams of automobiles, trucks and jeeps, and "throngs of young men in European clothes."[85]

Less obvious but even more striking is distant Qinghai. Doak Barnett visited the province in 1948 and proclaimed Governor Ma Bufang's regime "one of the most efficient in China, and one of the most energetic. While most of the rest of China is bogged down, almost inevitably, by civil war, Qinghai is attempting to carry out small-scale, but nevertheless ambitious, development and reconstruction schemes on its own initiative." Barnett was most impressed by Ma's reforestation, horse-breeding and fly-swatting campaigns; but he also noted an industrialization program (state-run, of course) that had begun during the war, advances in education and medical care, irrigation projects, and a new sewage system for Xining.[86] Another postwar report noted the new movie theater, motor roads, and the uniforms and food subsidies provided to all students in both state and private schools.[87]

Qinghai was perhaps extraordinary, but there is good reason to believe that as the eastern section of the country was wracked by war, the western provinces experienced significant development of industry, communications infrastructure, education, and health care. It is also clear that social norms were significantly affected by the influx of students, intellectuals, functionaries, technicians, and skilled workers from the coast. Most of these wartime refugees returned to the eastern cities at the end of the war, but some stayed and the social impact of their eight-year sojourn would prove indelible. Though in some respects, the effect of cosmopolitan cultural influences from the coast may have been liberating, in political terms there was nothing liberal about the modernizing regimes of the interior. Ma Bufang in Qinghai was every bit as authoritarian as Guomindang administrators elsewhere.[88] The press was more subject to local official control, so that even in Yunnan, a wartime bastion of political dissent, the postwar journalistic world spoke with a single voice.[89] The economy was more developed, the population more diverse and (with improved transport) more mobile, but the state was more powerful and intrusive as well—all perfectly standard indications that the Chinese interior was being transformed by the prevailing patterns of the new order.

SOCIAL MOVEMENTS AND CULTURE: EVOLVING PRACTICES OF A NEW ORDER

One of the lessons of modern history is that expanding state power need not imply a reduction in social activism. The old notion that authoritarian governments produce passive citizens is no longer tenable. Political power is not a zero-sum game. Rather, it is clear that even as the resources and functions of the modern state expanded and intrusions into previously private zones increased, ordinary people found new ways to express their agency, organizing in social or occupational groups, engaging in social movements, expressing their identities and values through innovative or traditionally sanctioned social practices. These truths were as evident in the 1940s as the early twentieth century, when state-building went hand in hand with the emergence of civil society—leaving historians to argue over which trend was primary.[90]

The social movement that dominated press reports and captured public imagination in the Civil War era was the endless tide of student strikes, demonstrations, and petitions. Such student activism was nothing new in modern China. Indeed, as Jeffrey Wasserstrom and others have shown, the basic rituals of student demonstrations had been set by the May Fourth Movement of 1919 and adapted and improved in periodic waves of activism ever since.[91] What distinguished the student movement of the 1940s was the degree to which students moved beyond the level of commitment and activism of their elders. In prewar student movements, there had always been a core of progressive faculty and intellectuals who provided important support, protection, and guidance to the student movement. But as John Israel has observed of the student movement in Kunming at the end of the war, a "generation gap" appeared when the majority of Lianda's senior faculty signed a petition demanding Soviet withdrawal from Manchuria while "most students refused to be diverted by anti-Soviet appeals.... For the first time since the beginning of the war, student and faculty political views sharply diverged, a phenomenon that would persist into the Communist era."[92]

In the Civil War years, this "generation gap" became an explicit topic of discussion, notably in the youth page of the *Dagongbao*. A persistent theme was the notion that the May Fourth generation of liberal leaders (one senses that Peking University President Hu Shi* was the unspoken target) had become the conservative establishment, which was portrayed as selfishly protecting its own position. Students were ready to go beyond that, to overcome selfishness, to unite with the masses, to commit themselves to a new, progressive, democratic China representing all the common people.[93] In this rhetoric and social practice, the students were clearly headed down a road that would prepare them for a future role as critics of their liberal professors, who in the 1950s and 1960s would be identified as reactionary bourgeois elements.

---

* Hu Shi (胡適, 1891–1962), an American-trained philosopher and literary theorist, returned to China as a professor at Peking University where he was a major advocate for liberal values during the May Fourth Movement of 1919. He served as ambassador to the United States during the war, was chancellor of Peking University from 1946 to 1948, and ended his career as president of Academia Sinica in Taiwan.

Workers were another group active in protests of this period. In some respects, this is a bit surprising, for several reports indicate that workers' wages were higher than before the war. In the fall of 1948, Doak Barnett wrote from Shanghai that "Working conditions have improved considerably by comparison with before the war," with higher real wages, shorter hours (but still almost ten hours per day), the virtual elimination of child labor, and the reduced role of contract hiring for skilled workers.[94] The Guomindang consciously sought to co-opt labor support and lure workers away from Communist sympathies. To this end, they encouraged their own unions which increased from 295, with 227,949 members in 1945, to 453 unions, with 527,499 members in early 1947.[95] But as unemployment grew and wages began to fall behind runaway inflation, even these "yellow unions" could provide a vehicle to assert worker interests.[96] In addition (as noted earlier) industrial workers were now largely employees in state enterprises. By the end of the decade, workers would be quite accustomed to social action within the confines of state enterprises and state-affiliated unions, and well-prepared to claim a privileged position in the newly proclaimed proletarian dictatorship.

Studies of rural society and peasant social action in the Guomindang areas have often stressed the absence of the kind of class struggles that erupted in the Communist-led land reform campaign.[97] But we should not conclude from this that the Guomindang's rural hinterland witnessed no social change—or that the changes were not comparable in important respects to those taking place in the base areas. Land reform is a case in point. The appeal of the Communist program, with its claim to be carrying out Sun Yat-sen's "land to the tiller" policy, finally forced the Guomindang, after the war, to initiate a land reform program of its own. It would not effectively implement the program until the government fled to Taiwan in 1949; but the government did finally move to take up land reform, and public support for the policy was widespread in the press and many government circles.[98] John Melby noted that "nothing in this country has the remotest possibility of popular appeal which does not call for agrarian reform," and cited the example of a newly formed South Seas Basketball Association for Agrarian Reform.[99] All this talk did little to alleviate the distress of peasants in the Guomindang areas, but it did mean that when the Communists arrived to carry out their own land reform program, much of the ideological groundwork had been prepared.

Of more concrete relevance to the peasantry were the changes the Guomindang introduced into rural administration. In 1939, the Guomindang initiated a New County System (*xinxianzhi* 新縣制) to reform local administration. A recent study by Wang Qisheng shows that this wartime reform vastly expanded the rural apparatus: the 12 million subcounty officials made the

Chinese bureaucracy seventy-four times larger than that of the Qing empire. Local officials as petty as *baozhang* (保長) were salaried, though their quality was low and most seemed attracted by their exemption from conscription. At the township (*xiangzhen* 鄉鎮) level, there were elected assemblies.[100] Doak Barnett observed the local apparatus in postwar Sichuan. It involved a village-level *baojia* (保甲) organization and above it a *xiang* office, all elected subcounty institutions after 1939. The *bao* (with about 150 households) had a head and an elected assembly and was mostly responsible for tax collection and conscription. Most accounts of the rural *baojia* heads are decidedly unflattering. Eastman calls them "notorious for their corruption."[101] But Barnett's account suggests that many rural functionaries were relatively ordinary, often young, and usually literate peasants chosen to do the dirty work of the state. One would not expect the people responsible for tax collection and conscription (especially at a time when the state's demand for men and money seemed insatiable) to be very popular, but Graham Peck reports that peasants often selected tough *baozhang* precisely for their ability to deal with rapacious officials.[102] Above all, one is impressed by the similarity between their functions and those of rural cadres in the Communist areas.[103] The Communist Party structure certainly gave it more effective tools to discipline its rural apparatus, making corruption and abuse of power less common (while by no means absent) in the Communist areas. The Guomindang expanded the size of its party apparatus during the war, with a six-fold increase in its membership, but never succeeded in instilling the discipline expected of a Leninist party.[104] This wartime intensification of the Guomindang rural apparatus meant that when the Communists arrived to take over the Guomindang areas—and for most of the country it was simply a matter of military takeover—the peasantry was already prepared for an intrusive rural apparatus, and quite possibly saw the communist cadres as a better and more disciplined version of the *baojia* heads so widely established during the war.

Women—young, educated women and female workers in particular—played a significant role in the Chinese Revolution.[105] In the Communist areas, there was a major effort to enlist women in the revolutionary struggle. Programs to promote voluntary marriage and divorce were effective enough to arouse male fears, but gender issues were inevitably subordinated to the politics of class struggle. In the Guomindang rural areas, other than some advance in women's education, there is little evidence of significant change. It is in urban society that interesting issues arise, for there is substantial evidence that women's position in urban society was undergoing important changes in the Nationalist era—and that the war accelerated those changes. One of the most striking (and still much understudied) indicators of social change is the gender ratio of urban populations.

Urban gender ratios in late imperial China are extremely difficult to estimate. There seem to have been extra males (especially in the young adult age cohort) in cities with a large commercial population requiring poor unskilled laborers and young apprentices. Major imbalances in gender ratios can be documented from the late nineteenth century and appear to be associated with China's modern transformation.[106] For example, the International Settlement in Shanghai had a gender ratio of 290:100 in 1870; and the French Concession recorded 217:100 in 1910.[107] In Beijing in 1917, the greatest concentration of men (often more than 75 percent of the population) was in the commercial and artisanal districts in the southern section of the city.[108] By the time we have fairly reliable police-based population records in the Nationalist era, most major Chinese cities displayed a significant gender imbalance, but the imbalances decreased markedly in the 1940s. We have relatively good statistics for nine cities: Shanghai, Beiping, Nanjing, Tianjin, Qingdao, Wuchang, Zhenjiang, Chongqing, and Xi'an. Not accounting for population differences, the average prewar (1934–1936) gender balance in these cities was 151 males per 100 females. By the end of the war (1943–1945), the average had fallen to 140, and by 1948, to 132, which was not so far from the 1953 census figure of 125 for the major cities: Beijing, Shanghai, and Tianjin.[109]

It is possible that some of the reduction of the gender imbalance was the product of more efficient counting of women as the registration system developed. But the trend is so widespread and consistent that there seems little doubt that a significant change in the social composition of urban populations was coming about. It is also clear that, although the trend began well before the war and Civil War, the war accelerated the changes. We need to understand how this process took place. In most cities, the total urban population did not decline during the war and Civil War, so the change was not simply the result of males being drawn off to serve in the army. How much of the change resulted from more single women moving from the countryside to take up urban employment (many replacing men drafted into the army or relocated to the interior), and how much resulted from the poor bachelors who dominated the lower levels of the working class being able to bring wives from their villages to settle in the cities? We know that the wartime cities relied on a significant number of young males to work the docks, carry water, pull rickshaws, police the streets, guard gates, and run errands for the rich. Were these young men now able to marry and raise families? Whatever the process, urban China was certainly moving steadily toward the gender balance and nuclear families that would prevail under the PRC.

During the war, many women served as teachers, nurses, and propaganda and clerical workers. As more men were called to the front, they also moved into industrial jobs.[110] But when postwar unemployment replaced the wartime demand for their skills and labor, women were often the first to lose their jobs, and patriarchal appeals for women to return to their proper role in child-rearing and domestic chores justified the shift. The change was not uncontested. Even before the war, Olga Lang's surveys had found female factory workers unusually independent in their attitudes and more likely to resist patriarchal control.[111] In the postwar era, there was a lively debate in the women's press over women's proper role in modern society. A substantial group of vocal feminists defended the rights of "career women" and the notion that society should provide institutional support (especially child care) for women to pursue both rewarding careers and a fulfilling family life.[112] The postwar debate over the cult of domesticity reminds us that the war fundamentally changed social institutions in ways that would prove irreversible. The war offered women meaningful public roles in service to the nation—and from that time forward, any return to traditional notions of domesticity became impossible. In growing numbers, women would demand the right to work—and in the PRC they would work.

There were symbolically important changes in social customs. The long gowns favored by students, intellectuals, and many professional men in the early twentieth century would virtually disappear with the war. Photographs of the May Fourth demonstrations, and of most other prewar student demonstrations, are dominated by young men in long blue or gray gowns. These were largely gone by the postwar era. During the war, the popular outfit—worn by many women as well as men—was the high-collared Sun Yat-sen jacket and cotton pants (both padded in winter), variations of which served as army and student uniforms and ordinary daily dress. In Kunming, clothing and hair styles for both men and women were permanently changed, from the bobbed hair and slit skirts of young women to the leather shoes and Sun Yat-sen jackets of men; and in a blatant transgression of past norms, young men and women so attired could be seen walking together on the streets, or sharing intimacies in restaurants or parks.[113] In postwar films, the gown does not reappear except on gangsters and evil accountants; the "good guys" usually appear in the Sun Yat-sen jacket, the villains in fancy Western suits. The "Mao jackets" of the PRC were in many ways a continuation of the simple, pragmatic (and unisex) fashions established during the War of Resistance.

In high culture, as well, the war had a fundamentally transformative impact. Before the war, the art academies of the lower Yangzi and Canton fostered experimentation and lively debate in which Western schools of Impressionism, Post-Impressionism, Cubism, Surrealism, Expressionism, and Futurism were important influences. But with the war, in Michael Sullivan's words, "Paris was forgotten, and modernism lost its momentum."[114] As artists fled to the interior, they lost access to foreign-made oil paint, stiff brushes, and linen canvass. Most shifted to the traditional media of ink and watercolor or to woodblock prints. Propaganda posters and wall paintings on patriotic themes dominated their subject matter in the early years of the war—but these gave way to grimmer, critical drawings, woodblocks, and cartoons of social criticism as time went on. The minority peoples of the West provided the only source for happier images, and the artistic depiction of national minorities assumed a new importance in the national fine arts repertoire. Chen Lifu dispatched teams of artists to copy the Buddhist frescoes in the caves of Dunhuang, thus preserving and popularizing that medieval style. In Chongqing, in 1940, the All-China Arts Association was formed, and the National Government's minister of information urged its members "to weave their art more closely into the lives of the people"[115]—a theme we usually associate with Mao Zedong's address to the Yan'an Forum on Literature and Art. In the world of painting, Xu Beihong's (徐悲鴻) academic realism eclipsed the modernism of the prewar period, and he moved easily from his wartime job directing the National Art Research Institute under the Guomindang to heading the Central Academy of Fine Arts in Beijing under the PRC. The great watershed in Chinese fine arts came in 1937, not 1949.[116]

In the values propagated by the postwar media we again see a distinct shift from the prewar era, and important continuities to the PRC. I have already mentioned the vilification of the rich, so readily apparent in postwar films. It is important to stress that this was not simply the product of left-wing cinematographers. When Jiang Jingguo sought to tame Shanghai to his own revolutionary vision, his target was also the rich: "Their wealth and their foreign-style homes are built on the skeletons of the people. How is their conduct any different from that of armed robbers? . . . [A]utomobiles, refrigerators, perfumes, and nylon hosiery imported from abroad [for the wealthy classes] are like the cells that thrive parasitically on this impoverished nation, or like opium that destroys the national economy, because using foreign currency to obtain high-class luxuries is a suicidal policy for the nation."[117] In the movies, the dialectical opposite of the evil rich were the virtuous poor, who bonded together to help each other in crises—loaning money, taking care of orphaned children, even arranging marriages for a shy couple in one comedy.[118] In the collective solidarity of the poor one found virtue and strength.

In the press, these values came to be expressed, by 1948, in the evils of "selfishness" and the virtues of identifying with the masses. In some of these pieces, the appeal for fundamental self-criticism was quite radical—and reminiscent of what many Chinese would be forced to endure under the PRC. One student who inquired solicitously of the living conditions of a pedicab driver was subjected to piercing criticism: "This is just like our intellectuals! We seem to be sympathetic to the people, but the true feeling is enjoying the fact that we are so progressive!"[119] Youths were admonished to subordinate themselves heart and soul to the group, and to unite with the masses. Even such slogans as "Serve the people"—later so clearly identified with Maoist propaganda—can be heard in the movies of the era.[120]

CONCLUDING THOUGHTS

This brief look at Chinese society during the War of Resistance and Civil War should remind us that, by the end of the decade, the old order was completely discredited and its collapse inevitable. Jack Belden's caustic assessment of the Guomindang in its final years was not wide of the mark: "an indigestible mixture of YMCA secretaries, Shanghai gangsters, ambitious sycophants, disillusioned visionaries, party thugs, tired revolutionaries, wistful liberals, palace eunuchs, feudal clowns, corrupt bureaucrats, Confucian mystics and sick psychopaths."[121] For many years, Western historians and political scientists of China were trained by men who had witnessed China in that era—John Fairbank and Doak Barnett being the most prominent—and the corruption of the Guomindang order and the inevitability of revolutionary change were a foregone conclusion. Now a new generation of scholars, many disillusioned by the excesses and failures of Mao's China and impressed by the achievements of the Republic of China on Taiwan, is reappraising republican history and arriving at a much more positive *pingjia* (評價, evaluation). But too often this new scholarship stops in 1937 and fails to come to grips with the meaning of the wartime and postwar period.

During the 1940s, the basic structures of the PRC order were being forged in the rapidly expanding Communist base areas. The party grew at breakneck speed, but displayed a remarkable ability to discipline and control its basic-level cadres, even as those cadres were engaged in Herculean efforts to mobilize resources for civil war, and transform society through land reform. The land reform process was both brutal and thorough. It involved transforming exceedingly complex property, employment and personal relations into simple class formulas around which peasants could be mobilized to active participation. In this the party generally succeeded, and in the process gave peasants a stake in the revolution that many were willing to fight to protect. But it also etched indelible class lines that would have long-term consequences for the entire social fabric.

In 1949–1950, the institutions and structures of this new order were spread across China. We must ask ourselves how that process was accomplished so easily—for the greater part of the country, and almost all of the major urban areas, were still in Guomindang hands just a year before the October 1949 founding of the PRC. Despite the rapidity with which most of China came under Communist rule, and despite years of Guomindang propaganda against the Red menace, the new regime was accepted with remarkable ease and strikingly little active resistance. The explanation for this puzzle, I believe, is to be found not just in popular disillusionment with the Guomindang and the acceptance of the CCP as the only possible alternative. Another part of the answer lies in the fact that the War of Resistance brought fundamental changes to Nationalist as well as Communist areas. The economy was planned and industry nationalized; the interior was developed; improved transport served national integration; education was expanded, centralized, and given new practical and nationalistic content; modern media were developed and put under more direct state control; art and popular culture moved away from the cosmopolitan styles of the treaty ports towards an austere pragmatism and politically engaged realism; the state penetrated further into rural society; students and workers were organized and mobilized; and new egalitarian and nationalistic values were promoted. The War of Resistance brought fundamental social, economic and cultural change to China, and those changes were critical factors in preparing the population for Communist rule.

If this conclusion is correct, if the 1940s brought social changes that were greater and more important than we had previously imagined, there is still the question of how, exactly, this dynamic came about. To what extent do we attribute these changes to the exigencies of the war itself? How much did they derive from that increase in state power, popular mobilization, and national consciousness seen in all countries involved in the new twentieth-century style of total war? Alternatively, how much did these changes derive from that "Confucian fascism" that Frederic Wakeman has described in the Nanjing decade,[122] or the state socialism so evident in William Kirby's study of the economy? To the extent that the Guomindang's wartime accomplishments were prefigured (but not achieved) in plans from the earlier period, what happened during the war that allowed the GMD to carry them out? Past scholarship may have focused so much on the roots of the Nationalists' failures that we have neglected to account for their successes. Finally, we need to consider the extent to which many of the populist efforts of the wartime Guomindang were inspired by the need to compete with the rapidly expanding CCP. Many of Chen Lifu's educational reforms certainly had such a motivation. To the extent that this logic applied elsewhere, it would mean that the continuity between the wartime era and the early PRC was in part the product of the Guomindang modeling itself on the CCP in order to compete for popular support.

It has become a truism of recent scholarship on twentieth-century China that we need to think across the 1949 divide. This essay has attempted to suggest one way to address that problem, by recognizing the social changes of the long 1940s as a harbinger of the early years of the PRC. But we still need to understand the precise historical dynamic that created those changes of the 1940s. For that, further research is necessary, and it will only come when studies of republican China move beyond that newly recognized *terminus ad quem* in 1937 and seriously confront the significance of the wartime and Civil War periods.

NOTES

1. Steven Levine, "Introduction" to James C. Hsiung and Steven I. Levine, *China's Bitter Victory: The War with Japan, 1937–1945* (Armonk, NY: M. E. Sharpe, 1992), xvii.

2. Hans van de Ven, *China at War: Triumph and Tragedy in the Emergence of the New China* (Cambridge, MA: Harvard University Press, 2018), 134; Li Zhisui and Anne F. Thurston, *The Private Life of Chairman Mao: The Memoirs of Mao's Personal Physician*, first edition (New York: Random House, 1994), 568.

3. John K. Fairbank, "Introduction" to Graham Peck, *Two Kinds of Time* (Boston: Houghton-Mifflin, 1967), 1.

4. Theodore White and Annalee Jacoby, *Thunder out of China* (New York: William Sloan Associates, 1946), citation from 310.

5. Lloyd E. Eastman, *Seeds of Destruction: Nationalist China in War and Revolution, 1937–1949* (Stanford, CA: Stanford University Press, 1984), 216; James Sheridan, *China in Disintegration: The Republican Era in Chinese History* (New York: Free Press, 1975).

6. Du Xiaoning, "Chubanye de 'Minguore" xianxiang fansi" [On the phenomenon of "Republican Fever" in the publishing world], *Qianyan* 2013, no. 5: 179–80.

7. Thomas G. Rawski, *Economic Growth in Prewar China* (Berkeley: University of California Press, 1989); Wen-hsin Yeh, *The Alienated Academy: Culture and Politics in Republican China, 1919–1937* (Cambridge, MA: Harvard University Press, 1990); Christian Henriot, *Shanghai, 1927–1937: Municipal Power, Locality, and Modernization*, translated by Noel Castelino (Berkeley: University of California Press, 1993); Frederic Wakeman Jr., *Policing Shanghai 1927–1937* (Berkeley: University of California Press, 1995); Bryna Goodman, *Native Place, City, and Nation: Regional Networks and Identities in Shanghai: 1853–1937* (Berkeley: University of California Press, 1995); Brian G. Martin, *The Shanghai Green Gang: Politics and Organized Crime, 1919–1937* (Berkeley: University of California Press, 1996); Lynda S. Bell, *One Industry, Two Chinas: Silk Filatures and Peasant-Family Production in Wuxi County, 1865–1937* (Stanford, CA: Stanford University Press, 1999); Kristin Stapleton, *Civilizing Chengdu: Chinese Urban Reform, 1895–1937* (Cambridge, MA: Harvard University Asia Center, 2000); Hans J. van de Ven, *War and Nationalism in China, 1925–1945* (London: RoutledgeCurzon, 2003). For an overview, see "Reappraising Republican China," special issue of *China Quarterly* 150 (June 1997).

8. Gail Hershatter, *The Workers of Tianjin, 1900–1949* (Stanford, CA: Stanford University Press, 1986); Emily Honig, *Sisters and Strangers: Women in the Shanghai Cotton Mills, 1911–1949* (Stanford, CA: Stanford University Press, 1986); Elizabeth J. Perry, *Shanghai on Strike: The Politics of Chinese Labor* (Stanford, CA: Stanford University Press, 1993); Jeffrey N. Wasserstrom, *Student Protests in Twentieth-Century China: The View from Shanghai* (Stanford, CA: Stanford University Press, 1991).

9. Mark R. Peattie, Edward J. Drea, and Hans J. Van de Ven, eds., *The Battle for China: Essays on the Military History of the Sino-Japanese War of 1937–1945* (Stanford, CA: Stanford University Press, 2011); Hans J. Van de Ven, *War and Nationalism*; Rana Mitter, *Forgotten Ally: China's World War II, 1937–1945* (Boston, MA: Houghton Mifflin Harcourt, 2013); Jay Taylor, *The Generalissimo: Chiang Kai-Shek and the Struggle for Modern China* (Cambridge, MA: Harvard University Press, 2009).

10. Odd Arne Westad, *Decisive Encounters: The Chinese Civil War, 1946–1950* (Stanford, CA: Stanford University Press, 2003), 7.

11. Chiang Kai-shek, *Soviet Russia in China: A Summing-up at Seventy* (New York: Farrar, Straus and Cudahy, 1957); John Pomfret, *The Beautiful Country and the Middle Kingdom: America and China, 1776 to the Present* (New York: Henry Holt and Company, 2016); van de Ven, *China at War*.

12. Zhang Baijia, "Foreign Military Aid," in Peattie, Drea, and van de Ven, *Battle for China*, 302–3.

13. Harold M. Tanner, *Where Chiang Kai-Shek Lost China: The Liao-Shen Campaign, 1948* (Bloomington: Indiana University Press, 2015), 277. See a similar judgement in Tang Tsou, *America's Failure in China, 1941–1950* (Chicago: University of Chicago Press, 1963), 482–83.

14. Westad, *Decisive Encounters*, 197–211, 221–55; van de Ven, *China at War*, 251–55.

15. James Gao, *The Communist Takeover of Hangzhou: The Transformation of City and Cadres, 1949–1954* (Honolulu: University of Hawai'i Press, 2004), 69–74; Derk Bodde, *Peking Diary: A Year of Revolution* (New York: Schuman, 1950).

16. van de Ven, *China at War*, 1.

17. Suzanne Pepper, *Civil War in China: The Political Struggle, 1945–1949* (Berkeley: University of California Press, 1978), 246–77; Odoric Y.K. Wou, *Mobilizing the Masses: Building Revolution in Henan* (Stanford, CA: Stanford University Press, 1994), 254–314; Yung-fa Chen, *Making Revolution: The Communist Movement in Eastern and Central China, 1937–1945* (Berkeley: University of California Press, 1986), esp. 121–258.

18. Lyman Van Slyke, "The Chinese Communist movement during the Sino-Japanese War, 1937–1945," in *The Cambridge History of China*, vol. 13: *Republican China 1912–1949*, Part II, eds. John K. Fairbank and Albert Feuerwerker, (Cambridge: Cambridge University Press, 1986), 687–712; Chen Yongfa, *Yan'an de yinying* [Yan'an's shadow] (Taibei: Academia Sinica, Institute of Modern History, 1990), 35–94; Joseph W. Esherick, "Revolution in a Feudal Fortress: Yangjiagou, Mizhi County, Shaanxi, 1937–1948," *Modern China* 24, no. 4 (October 1998): 352–62.

19. Kenneth E. Shewmaker, *Americans and Chinese Communists, 1927–1945: A Persuading Encounter* (Ithaca: Cornell University Press, 1971); Joseph Esherick, ed., *Lost Chance in China: The World War II Despatches of John S. Service* (New York: Random House, 1974).

20. Pepper, *Civil War*, 290–91.

21. William Hinton, *Fanshen: A Documentary of Revolution in a Chinese Village* (New York: Vintage, 1966), 434–41. The most important contribution of Hinton's classic study is his detailed account of the difficult process of teaching and promoting class consciousness in the countryside. For a recent study, see Brian De Mare, *Land Wars: The Story of China's Agrarian Revolution* (Stanford, CA: Stanford University Press, 2019), 72–99.

22. See Edward Friedman, Paul G. Pickowicz, and Mark Selden, with Kay Ann Johnson, *Chinese Village, Socialist State* (New Haven, CT: Yale University Press, 1991), 101–4, on the "castelike" social system that resulted from land reform. On the vocabulary and political functions of "class" in the PRC, see Richard Kurt Kraus, *Class Conflict and Chinese Socialism* (New York: Columbia University Press, 1981); on the enduring salience of class status in the Maoist period, William Parish and Martin King Whyte, *Village and Family in Contemporary China* (Chicago: University of Chicago Press, 1978), 98–100, 110–12, 179–80; Martin King Whyte and William Parish, *Urban Life in Contemporary China* (Chicago: University of Chicago Press, 1984), 45–54, 126–30.

23. May 28, 1946 directive of the Central China bureau, cited in Odoric Wou, *Mobilizing the Masses*, 343.

24. Hong Yung Lee, *From Revolutionary Cadres to Party Technocrats in Socialist China* (Berkeley: University of California Press, 1991), 16.

25. Joseph W. Esherick, "Deconstructing the Construction of the Party-State: Gulin County in the Shaan-Gan-Ning Border Region," *China Quarterly* 140 (December 1994): 1070–71. Included as chapter 9 in this volume.

26. For examples from the Chinese press, see Pepper, *Civil War*, 201–7. The classic eye-witness accounts of Hinton. *Fanshen*, and the Crooks (David and Isabel Crook), *Revolution in a Chinese Village: Ten Mile Inn* (London: Routledge and Paul, 1968), are equally compelling in this regard, even if discounted substantially for the authors' obvious political sympathies.

27. Diana Lary, *China's Civil War: A Social History, 1945–1949* (Cambridge: Cambridge University Press, 2015), 39.

28. Pepper, *Civil War*, 8–9; John F. Melby, *The Mandate of Heaven: A Record of a Civil War, China 1945–1949* (Garden City, NY: 1971), 55, 60–62.

29. Paul G. Pickowicz, "Victory as Defeat: Postwar Visualizations of China's War of Resistance," in Wen-hsin Yeh, *Becoming China: Passages to Modernity and Beyond, 1900–1950* (Berkeley: University of California, 2000). The best examples of such films are "Eight Thousand Li of Clouds and Moon" [*Baqianli lu yun he yue* 八千里路雲和月] directed by Shi Dongshan (1947); and the second part of Cai Chusheng's "A Spring River Flows East" [*Yijiang chunshui xiangdong liu* 一江春水向東流], entitled "At Dawn" [*Tianliang qianhou* 天亮前後], also from 1947. Of the former, one reviewer wrote that "you will recognize almost everyone on the screen"

(Theodore Herman, "Portrait of a Nation on the Way," *CWR* 105, no. 4 [March 22, 1947]: 98–99).

30. Jack Belden, *China Shakes the World* (New York: Monthly Review Press, 1970), 221ff.; *Wenhuibao,* September 30, 1946, in US Consulate-General, Shanghai, *China Press Review* (hereafter cited as *CPR*) 164: 6.

31. *China Weekly Review* (hereafter cited as *CWR*) 104, no. 4 (December 28, 1946): 119.

32. Cited in Eastman, *Seeds of Destruction*, 203.

33. Pepper, *Civil War*, 147.

34. Pepper, *Civil War*, 16–28. For the film images, see especially Tang Xiaodan's *Spring Dreams of Heaven* [*Tiantang chunmeng*], and the second part of *A Spring River Flows East.*

35. Eastman, *Seeds of Destruction*, 174.

36. Eastman, *Seeds of Destruction*, 175–76; Pepper, *Civil War*, 118–22. *Zhongguo shibao*, November 14, 1946, reported 1,353,000 people (a third of the population) unemployed in Shanghai (*CPR*, 200: 10).

37. *Wenhuibao,* September 9, 1946, reported that Chinese exports had fallen from a prewar level of 88 percent of the value of imports to 13 percent (*CPR* 176: 10). The *Economic Weekly* 3, no. 11 (September 12, 1946) reported January to June imports to Shanghai running at ten times the value of exports (*CPR* 182: 9–10).

38. Perry, *Shanghai on Strike*,118–20, 209–11; Hershatter, *Workers of Tianjin*, 230–32; Pepper, *Civil War*, 99–100, 107–12.

39. Pepper, *Civil War*, 137; *CWR* 104, no. 1 (December 7, 1946): 7–8; *Dagongbao*, December 2, 1946 (*CPR* 214: 1–2).

40. *CWR* 108, no. 11 (February 14, 1948), 313; Gail Hershatter, *Dangerous Pleasures: Prostitution and Modernity in Twentieth-Century China* (Berkeley: University of California Press, 1997), 300–303.

41. John Perkins, "Current Labor Problems," *CWR* 105, no. 3, May 24, 1947, 354.

42. See, for example, *Dagongbao*, April 8, 1948, where three separate suicides are reported including a Nankai school doctor unable to support his family, whose suicide by drowning was followed by his pregnant wife's failed attempt to poison herself.

43. A. Doak Barnett, *China on the Eve of Communist Takeover* (New York: Praeger, 1963), 47.

44. On the student movement, see Wasserstrom, *Student Protests*, 240–76; Pepper, *Civil War*, 42–94; on Communists in the movement, Joseph K. S. Yick, *Making Urban Revolution in China: The CCP-GMD Struggle for Beiping-Tianjin, 1945–1949* (Armonk, NY: M. E. Sharpe, 1995), 80–136. For a contemporary account of the economic background, see Henry Lee, "Behind the Demonstrations of Nanking's Students," *CWR* 106, no. 1, June 7, 1947, 16.

45. See also Paul Pickowicz's discussion of this film in "Melodramatic Representation and the 'May Fourth' Tradition of Chinese Cinema," , in Ellen Widmer and David Der-wei Wang, eds. *From May Fourth to June Fourth: Fiction and Film in Twentieth-Century China*, 308–11 (Cambridge, MA: Harvard University Press, 1993).

46. Richard Polenberg, *War and Society: The United States, 1941–1945* (New York: J. B. Lippencott, 1972); John Morton Blum, *V Was for Victory: Politics and*

American Culture During World War II (New York: Harcourt Brace Jovanovich, 1976); Geoffrey T. Mills and Hugh Rockwell, eds., *The Sinews of War: Essays on the Economic History of World War II* (Ames: University of Iowa Press, 1993); Michael A. Bernstein, *A Perilous Progress: Economists and Public Policy in Twentieth-century America* (Princeton: Princeton University Press, 2000), chap. 3.

47. William C. Kirby, "The Chinese Wartime Economy," in Hsiung and Levine, eds. *China's Bitter Victory*, 189.

48. William C. Kirby, "Continuity and Change in Modern China: Economic Planning in the Mainland and on Taiwan, 1943–1958," *Australian Journal of Chinese Affairs* 24 (July 1990): 125–32.

49. Barnett, *China on the Eve*, 56–57, quote from 57.

50. Morris L Bian, *The Making of the State Enterprise System in Modern China: The Dynamics of Institutional Change* (Cambridge, MA: Harvard University Press, 2005); see also Wen-hsin Yeh, "Republican Origins of the Danwei: The Case of Shanghai's Bank of China," in Xiaobo Lü and Elizabeth J. Perry, *Danwei—the Changing Chinese Workplace in Historical and Comparative Perspective* (Armonk, NY: M. E. Sharpe, 1997): 60–88.

51. Perry, *Shanghai on Strike*, 62–63, 112; Jean Chesneaux, *The Chinese Labor Movement, 1919–1927*, trans. H. M. Wright (Stanford, CA: Stanford University Press, 1968), esp. 43–47, 274–77, 290–91; S. Bernard Thomas, *Labor and the Chinese Revolution: Class Strategies and Contradictions of Chinese Communism, 1928–1948* (Ann Arbor: University of Michigan Center for Chinese Studies, 1983), 30–31, 43–50.

52. Barnett, *China on the Eve*, 78–80.

53. James Gao, *Communist Takeover*, 76–92.

54. Ch'en Li-fu, *The Storm Clouds Clear Over China: The Memoir of Ch'en Li-fu, 1900–1993*, eds. Sidney H. Chang and Ramon H. Myers (Stanford, CA: Hoover Institution Press, 1993), 157.

55. Wen-hsin Yeh, *Alienated Academy*, 10–22.

56. Chen Li-fu, cited in Ou Tsuin-Chen, "Education in Wartime China," in Paul K. T. Sih, *Nationalist China During the Sino-Japanese War, 1937–1945* (Hicksville, NY: Exposition Press, 1977), 107.

57. *Zhongguo jiaoyu nianjian, 1948* [Chinese education yearbook] (Nanjing: 1948), 1402, 1412. In later years of the war and civil war, these trends reversed somewhat—but the primacy of science and engineering was never threatened.

58. Chen Li-fu, *The Storm Clouds Clear Over China?* 147–70; John Israel, *Lianda: A Chinese University in War and Revolution* (Stanford, CA: Stanford University Press, 1998), 98–114, 195, 197; *China Handbook*, 231–42. In one of the symbolic moments in the postwar transformation of higher education, Nankai University, North China's premier private institution, was made a national university by order of the Ministry of Education on April 9, 1946 (Liang Jisheng, *Zhang Boling jiaoyu sixiang yanjiu* [Studies in the educational thought of Zhang Boling] [Shenyang: Liaoning Educational Press, 1994], 334–37).

59. *Zhongguo jiaoyu nianjian* (1948), 1402, 1412.

60. Ch'en Li-fu, *The Storm Clouds Clear Over China*,159; see a similar claim for 1942 in *China Handbook*, 244, which also counts 266,926 primary schools in March 1944. Primary student statistics from *Zhongguo jiaoyu nianjian* (1948), 1455. For local accounts, see Barnett, *China on the Eve*, 148–49 on Sichuan, 186 on Qinghai.

61. *Zhongguo jiaoyu nianjian* (1948), 1428, 1441–44.

62. Israel, *Lianda*, 304–6; Ch'en Li-fu, *The Storm Clouds Clear Over China*,168–69; Barnett, *China on the Eve*, 49.

63. Pepper, *Civil War*, 68; *Dagongbao*, October 26, 1946 (*CPR* 186: 1).

64. "Broadcasting in China," *CWR* editorial 104, no. 12 (February 22, 1947): 313–14; also Bill Conine, "China Broadcasting," *CWR* 107, no. 3 (September 20, 1947): 82–83.

65. Pickowicz, "Victory as Defeat."

66. The French Concession in Shanghai remained nominally under Vichy French control until 1944, when the Nanjing puppet government assumed direct rule.

67. Wasserstrom, *Student Protests*, 145; Barnett, *China on the* Eve, 31–32, 52.

68. Perry, *Shanghai on Strike*, 122, 126.

69. Eastman, *Seeds*, 180–93.

70. Barnett, *China on the Eve*, 83–95; *Xinwen bao*, October 23, 1946 (*CPR* 173: 10); *Dongnan ribao* (Shanghai), October 18, 1946 (*CPR* 179: 9).

71. Leo Ou-fan Lee, *Shanghai Modern: The Flowering of a New Urban Culture in China, 1930–1945* (Cambridge, MA: Harvard University Press: 1999); Robert Bickers, *Out of China: How the Chinese Ended the Era of Western Domination* (London: Penguin Books, 2018), 174–210, 248–49.

72. Hubert Freyn, *Prelude to War: The Chinese Student Rebellion of 1935–1936* (Shanghai: China Journal Pub. Co., 1939): 48. (Freyn was an Austrian exchange scholar who accompanied the students into the countryside.)

73. Dick Wilson, *When Tigers Fight: The Story of the Sino-Japanese War, 1937–1945* (New York; Viking Press, 1982), 4.

74. Chalmers Johnson, *Peasant Nationalism*, esp. ix, 2, and 49. For a critique of the Johnson thesis, see Kathleen Hartford, "Repression and Communist Success: The Case of Jin-Cha-Ji, 1938–1943," in *Single Sparks: China's Rural Revolutions,* eds. Kathleen Hartford and Steven M. Goldstein (Armonk, NY: M. E. Sharpe, 1990), 92–127.

75. Hinton, *Fanshen*; Isabel and David Crook, *Revolution in a Chinese Village*; Friedman, Pickowicz, and Selden, *Chinese Village, Socialist State*; Pepper, *Civil War*.

76. Liu Lu, "A whole nation walking: the "great retreat" in the War of Resistance, 1937–1945" (PhD diss., University of California San Diego, 2002); John Israel, *Lianda*, 57; Lin Yutang, *Between Tears and Laughter* (Garden City, NY: Blue Ribbon Books, 1945), 214–18.

77. Chang-tai Hung, *War and Popular Culture: Resistance in Modern China, 1937–1945* (Berkeley: University of California Press, 1994).

78. Albert Feuerwerker, "Economic trends, 1912–1949," in *The Cambridge History of China*, vol. 12: *Republican China, 1912–1949*, Part I (Cambridge: Cambridge University Press, 1983), 43.

79. Statistics are clearly problematic here. Feuerwerker, "Economic Trends," 45, cites one source listing 448 factories; Lloyd E. Eastman ("Nationalist China during the Sino-Japanese War, 1937–1945," *The Cambridge History of China*, vol. 13: *Republican China, 1912–1949*, Part II [Cambridge: Cambridge University Press, 1986], 562) records 639 private factories of which three-fourths ultimately resumed production.

80. Cited in Feuerwerker, "Economic Trends," 45.

81. Ministry of Economic Affairs figures in *China Handbook, 1937–1944* (Chongqing: Chinese Ministry of Information, 1944), 276.

82. Barnett, *China on the Eve*, 107.

83. *China Handbook, 1937–1944*, 146–52; Barnett, *China on the Eve*, 104. Despite its negative tone, B. P. Shoyer's "In the Kuomintang Backyard," *CWR* 108, no. 2 (December 13, 1947), 48–49, reflects the substantial improvement of communications in Central China. On wartime road-building in Guizhou, see Christian Hess, "From Mountain Paths to Motor Roads: Politics, Economics and Road-Building in Guizhou, 1926–1949," University of California San Diego seminar paper, spring 2000.

84. For an example of the continuation of this trend in the Third Front campaign of the PRC, see Judd C. Kinzley, "Crisis and the Development of China's Southwestern Periphery: The Transformation of Panzhihua, 1936–1969," *Modern China* 38, no. 5 (2012): 559–84.

85. Robert Payne, *Chinese Diaries, 1941–1946* (New York: Weybright and Talley, 1970), 189–91; Eastman, *Seeds*, 17–18

86. Barnett, *China on the Eve*, 185–87.

87. Ruth Ingram, "Incredible Chinghai," *CWR* 108, no. 3 (December 27, 1947), 119. It is perhaps worth noting that Qinghai has some of the best-preserved republican archives in China, and if some adventuresome scholar could gain access, a study of this province in the republican era would certainly be quite significant and rewarding (Ye Wa and Joseph W. Esherick, *Chinese Archives: An Introductory Guide* [Berkeley: University of California Institute of East Asian Studies, 1996], 230–33.)

88. Barnett, *China on the Eve*, 187, observes that Ma Bufang's "stern authoritarianism" left "little room for personal freedom."

89. Helen P. F. Shih, "No Liberal, Independent Papers in Yunnan," *CWR* 106, no. 11 (August 16, 1947), 318–19.

90. Mary Rankin, *Elite Activism and Political Transformation in China: Zhejiang Province, 1865–1911* (Stanford, CA: Stanford University Press, 1988); R. Keith Schoppa, *Chinese Elites and Political Change: Zhejiang Province in the Early Twentieth Century* (Cambridge, MA: Harvard University Press, 1982); David Strand, *Rickshaw Beijing: City People and Politics in the 1920s* (Berkeley: University of California Press, 1989); William Rowe, "The Public Sphere in Modern China," *Modern China* 16, no. 3 (July 1990): 309–29; Frederic Wakeman, "The Civil society and Public Sphere Debate," *Modern China* 19, no. 2 (April 1993): 108–38 and other essays in this issue.

91. Wasserstrom, *Student Protests*.

92. Israel, *Lianda*, 375.

93. For examples see Wang Feng (pseud.?) "*Liangdai zhi jian*" [Between Two Generations], *Dagongbao*, July 4, 1947; and a series of article on the theme "going beyond May 4" (*kuaguo wusi*), *Dagongbao*, May 4, 1948.

94. Barnett, *China on the* Eve, 79; cf. Pepper, *Civil War*, 100–101.

95. Perry, *Shanghai on Strike*, 121.

96. Pepper, *Civil War*, 95–118. On the role of "yellow unions," see Perry, *Shanghai on Strike*, 88–108.

97. Lucien Bianco, "Peasant Movements," in *The Cambridge History of China*, vol. 13: *Republican China, 1912–1949*, Part II (Cambridge: Cambridge University Press, 1986), 301–5, 326–28; Eastman, *Seeds*, 84–85, 88.

98. Eastman, *Seeds*, 82–84; Pepper, *Civil War*, 207–8, 230–31. See *Dagongbao*, August 30, 1946 (*CPR* 167: 9–11) for a sample of press opinion. *CWR* 105, no. 7 (April 12, 1947): 171–83 printed the Land Law promulgated by the National Government in April 1946.

99. Melby, *Mandate of Heaven*, 38.

100. Wang Qisheng, *Geming yu fangeming: shehui wenhua shiyexia de minguo zhengzhi* [Revolution and counter-revolution: Socio-cultural perspectives on republican politics] (Beijing: Shehui kexue chubanshe, 2010), 403–38, also Hsi-sheng Ch'i, *Nationalist China at War: Military Defeats and Political Collapse, 1937–1945* (Ann Arbor: University of Michigan Press, 1982), 132–40.

101. Eastman, *Seeds*, 65. See also Duncan Lee, "Pao Chief Omnipotent to Honan's Ignorant, Oppressed Peasantry," *CWR* 104, no. 7 (January 18, 1947): 197.

102. Peck, *Two Kinds of Time*, 315.

103. Barnett, *China on the* Eve, 114–23.

104. Wang Qisheng, "Zhanshi Guomindang dangyuan yu jiceng dang zuzhi" [Wartime Guomindang party members and base-level party organization], *Kang-Ri zhanzheng yanjiu* 2003, no. 4.

105. Gail Hershatter, *Women and China's Revolutions* (Lantham. MD: Rowman & Littlefield, 2019), 189–218.

106. Systematic data on pre-twentieth century urban populations are virtually nonexistent, as cities in a county or prefecture were not distinguished from their rural hinterlands. In addition, separate counting of men and women seems only to have begun during the Ming dynasty, then quickly succumbed to a serious undercounting of women. See Yang Zihui, ed., *Zhongguo lidai renkou tongji ziliao yanjiu* [Studies in statistical materials on China's population history] (Beijing: China Reform Publishing House, 1996), 988–99; Linda Cooke Johnson, *Shanghai: From Market Town to Treaty Port, 1074–1858* (Stanford, CA: Stanford University Press, 1995), 51–52. There are scattered Qing gender-specific data that provide clues to urban population. For example, Shanghai County population data for the nineteenth century were probably substantially from the urban area, and they indicate only a slight gender imbalance: 105 males per 100 females in 1810, 111:100 in 1864 and 110:100 in 1881 (Johnson, *Shanghai*, 120; Yang Zihui, 1192). Gilbert Rozman, who associates gender imbalance with female infanticide, hypothesizes that an "unusually low [male:female] sex ratio" was characteristic of urban areas in the Qing (*Population and Marketing Settlements in Ch'ing China* [Cambridge: Cambridge University Press, 1982], 62). G. William

Skinner, by contrast, argues from data on late nineteenth-century Canton and early republican Beijing that in late imperial cities, "The sex ratio was sharply skewed because of the high proportion of sojourners who had left their families behind in their native places and the large number of unmarried apprentices" ("Urban Social Structure in Ch'ing China" in *The City in Late Imperial China*, G. William Skinner, ed. [Stanford, CA: Stanford University Press, 1977], 533).

107. Hershatter, *Dangerous Pleasures*, 423n45. By the 1930s, these figures were closer to those in the Chinese city (see table 1): 156:100 in the International Settlement in 1935, 155:100 in the French Concession in 1936 (ibid.).

108. Sydney D. Gamble, *Peking: A Social Survey* (New York: George H. Doran, 1921), 99–101, 412. Gamble calls these "industrial districts," but that seems misleading as the "industry" here was largely handicraft and closely related to commercial shops.

109. *Tongji yuebao* 25 (September–October 1938), 32 (June 1937), 35 (September–October 1938), 121–22 (September–October 1947), 125–26 (January–February 1948), 133–34 (September–October 1948]; PRC data for Shanghai, Beijing and Tianjin from Yang Zihui, ed., *Zhongguo lidai renkou*, 1565.

110. Lü Fangshang, "Kangzhan shiqi Zhongguo de fuyun gongzuo" [Women's movement work in wartime China], Li Youning, Zhang Yufa, *Zhongguo funüshi lunwen ji* [Essays on Chinese women's history], vol. 1 (Taibei: Taiwan Shangwu Yinshuguan, 1981), 404–5. Figures in Luo Suwen, *Nüxing yu jindai Zhongguo shehui* [Females in modern Chinese society] (Shanghai: Shanghai People's Press, 1996), 288–89, suggest that women as a percentage of industrial workers in Shanghai increased from 43.1 percent in the 1930s to 57.2 percent in 1946.

111. Olga Lang, *Chinese Family and Society* (New Haven, CT: Yale University Press, 1946), 102–9, 203–10, 260–67.

112. Liu Lu, "*Xingui yuan*: Controversy over Domesticity in Postwar China (1945–1949)," in *Modern Chinese Literature and Culture* (2001).

113. John Israel, *Lianda*, 80–87.

114. Michael Sullivan, *Art and Artists of Twentieth-Century China* (Berkeley: University of California Press, 1996), 90.

115. Cited in ibid., 96.

116. Ibid., 90–125; Julia F. Andrews and Kuiyi Shen, eds., *A Century in Crisis: Modernity and Tradition in the Art of Twentieth-Century China* (New York: Guggenheim Museum, 1998), 6, 146, 173–79, 228. I am indebted to Joan Cohen for suggesting art as another area where the war's impact was crucial.

117. Cited in Eastman, *Seeds*, 182.

118. "*Jietou xiangwei*" [On the streets and alleys], 1947.

119. Li Wenni, "Bie lao xiangzhe ziji, xinxiang ziji" [Don't always think of yourself and enjoy yourself], *Dagongbao*, April 20, 1948.

120. In Shi Dongshan's "Eight thousand Li of Clouds and Moon," where he has one of the villains express the view that "serving the people is stupid."

121. Belden, *China Shakes the World*, 438.

122. Frederic Wakeman Jr. "A Revisionist View of the Nanjing Decade: Confucian Fascism," in *China Quarterly* 150 (June 1997): 395–432.

Chapter Eight

Rethinking the Communist Revolution

Modern Chinese history has long been dominated by the Chinese Communist Revolution. Though revolution dominated the narrative of twentieth-century China, from the Republican Revolution of 1911 to the National Revolution of the 1920s, it was the revolution that brought the Chinese Communist Party to power in 1949 that truly remade China, transforming political, economic, social, and cultural life in such fundamental ways that it has been an enduring focus of scholarly inquiry. What accounts for China's revolutionary path? How did the Communists come to power? What mix of economic, social, and political factors led to this result; and to what extent were domestic or international factors involved?

Though I had never done research on the Communist Revolution, it had long been a staple in my teaching on modern China, and that effort kept me abreast of the secondary literature. In addition, in 1974, I had edited a volume of John S. Service's diplomatic reports from China. Jack Service was a former foreign service officer, a victim of the McCarthy era, who had known, observed, and interviewed Mao Zedong and other Communist leaders as a member of the Dixie Mission to Yan'an in 1944–1945. Jack worked at Berkeley's Center for Chinese Studies when I was a graduate student, and those contacts led to a long friendship and my editing of his reports from China.[*] With this background, I embarked in 1988 on a year of archival research and field work on the revolution in northern Shaanxi, a project that has lasted for thirty years and only now has finally produced a monograph: *Accidental Holy Land: The Chinese Revolution in Northwest China*.[†]

---

[*] Jack S. Service, *Lost Chance in China: The World War II Despatches of John S. Service* (New York: Random House, 1974).

[†] Joseph W. Esherick, *Accidental Holy Land: The Chinese Revolution in Northwest China* (Berkeley: University of California Press, 2022).

This essay originated in a UCLA conference organized by Philip Huang on "Rethinking the Chinese Revolution" and represented an early effort to understand the Chinese Revolution. As will be clear, there is a good deal of rethinking here, especially for someone who began with a sympathetic view of the Chinese Revolution and a commitment to the notion, ultimately derived from my Harvard years under Fairbank, that the origins of the Chinese Revolution were distinctly Chinese.* The next essay in this collection presents some specific findings from my research in Shaanxi, but is also concerned with more general questions, especially the relationship between the party and the peasantry, and the different functions of diverse levels of party organization.

This essay argues for treating the Chinese Revolution as part of a larger revolutionary process, neither a liberation from the past nor the end point of a teleological journey. In this process, the Nationalist Party of Chiang Kai-shek was as much precursor as enemy of Mao's revolution; and for all China's later conflicts with the Soviet Union, Stalinist models, texts, and even orders conveyed through the Communist International were important in shaping revolutionary practice. Finally, this essay suggests ways to think about issues of structure and agency in history. Objective conditions, both domestic socioeconomic and political structures and international relations, limited the range of choices that historical actors made; but there remained enough contingency in history for such subjective factors as revolutionary commitment and strategic policy decisions to be decisive.

TEN THESES ON THE CHINESE REVOLUTION[†]

> The function of the historian is neither to love the past nor to emancipate himself from the past, but to master and understand it as the key to the understanding of the present.
>
> —E. H. Carr

The twentieth century has been the century of revolution. Although the revolutionary model began with the eighteenth-century revolutions of North

---

[*] For a classic statement, see John K. Fairbank, *China: The People's Middle Kingdom and the USA* (Cambridge, MA: Harvard University Press, 1967).

[†] Originally published as "Ten Theses on the Chinese Revolution," *Modern China* 21, no. 1 (January 1995): 45–76. Some footnotes have been added to bring the references up to date. In addition to the participants in the UCLA Symposium on "Rethinking the Chinese Revolution," I thank the many friends and colleagues who offered suggestions and criticisms on earlier drafts of this essay. I am especially indebted to my colleagues at UCSD—Chalmers Johnson, Dorothy Ko, Barry Naughton, and Paul Pickowicz. Steven Averill, Elizabeth Perry, Mark Selden, Lyman Van Slyke, Alexander Woodside, and Ernest Young also offered telling and useful critiques. This revised chapter will not fully satisfy any of these critics, and I remain fully responsible for the shortcomings that remain.

America and France, the nineteenth century (except in Latin America) was an era of failed revolution, and it was only in the twentieth century that revolution swept the world—most notably in the revolutions of Mexico, Russia, Yugoslavia, China, Korea, Vietnam, and Cuba, but also in the national revolutions of Algeria, the Middle East, Indonesia, and much of Africa. Some would even subsume the radical changes brought by the Nazi and fascist movements of Germany and Italy within the definition of "revolution."[1] Revolutions have reshaped the global environment and reordered the structures of daily life.[2]

An enormous, useful, and insightful literature analyzes both the general phenomenon of revolution and the variety of specific national revolutionary movements. That literature provides an essential foundation for understanding the world in which we live. But as we enter the twenty-first century, we face a world in which, one after the other, revolutionary regimes are falling and revolutionary changes are being reversed. Gone are the revolutionary regimes of Russia, Yugoslavia, and Eastern Europe. Mexico is slowly dismantling the structures created by its revolution. Cuba waits only for Castro's death. China struggles to replace state socialism with a market economy while maintaining Communist Party dictatorship and the transparent fiction of revolutionary ideology. To all present appearances, the revolutionary era as we know it ended with the twentieth century. In this context, the narrative of revolutionary progress (and of progress through revolution) is no longer compelling. The revolutionized populations no longer accept its legitimacy. It is time to rethink revolution.

As Berenson's essay in *Modern China* indicates, revolutions elsewhere—even the French Revolution, which inspired so many of our revolutionary models—are also undergoing radical re-evaluation.[3] My task in this essay is to suggest and provoke a rethinking of the Chinese Revolution, of the historical process that brought to power a revolutionary party that radically reshaped the Chinese polity, economy, and society. In the Chinese case, a rethinking is not only called for by world historical events, it is also facilitated by a wealth of new scholarship, an explosion of new materials on party history and the beginnings of access to archives and field work in the People's Republic of China (PRC). The ideas that follow have been inspired by this new scholarship and by my own archival and oral history research on the revolution in the Shaan-Gan-Ning border region. Although much of the argument here is derivative and even commonplace, the form I have chosen—ten theses—is designed to provoke debate. I subscribe to these theses with varying degrees of conviction. Some are old friends with whom I would be reluctant to part. Others are newer formulations, designed to fill out the logical structure and decimal integrity of this essay. All can be read as an autocritique of my own past thinking and writing on modern China. As a whole, I am striving for a reassessment of the revolution that acknowledges both the failings and the contingency of the revolution without reverting to the shibboleths of anti-Communist scholarship whose purpose is to deny all legitimacy to revolutionary change, and for an interpretation that recognizes the revolution's importance, but not necessarily its centrality, in China's modern history.

I. Guomindang rule was as much the precursor of the Chinese Revolution as its political enemy.

Journalistic writing on China during the 1930s and 1940s by authors such as Edgar Snow, Theodore White and Annalee Jacoby, or Jack Belden and much of the scholarship of the 1950s and 1960s were shaped by the political context of life-and-death struggle between the Guomindang and the Chinese Communist Party (CCP).[4] In that competition, each of the actors tended to paint its rival as a dialectical opposite. Much of the picture of the Guomindang era, even by judicious liberal scholars such as John Fairbank and Lloyd Eastman was colored by the persuasive discourse of the Guomindang's leftist and progressive critics.[5] The Guomindang was seen to be trapped in a conservative political culture, defending the forces of tradition, suppressing progressive intellectuals, and abandoning workers and peasants to their miserable fates. Its leaders were inspired by both fascism and Confucianism and opposed the democratic forces in China.

The problem with this picture is not that it is hostile to the Guomindang; the historian is not obliged to sympathize with the object of his or her scholarship. The problem is its failure to take due account of important continuities between the Guomindang and the CCP. William Kirby's work on the National Resources Commission is an important example of continuity in economic planning in the pre- and post-1949 period.[6] One aspect of Prasenjit Duara's work is its focus on state building under the Guomindang and the unprecedented attacks on the "cultural nexus" of traditional values and religion.[7] But there are many more examples that could be raised: the structures of Leninism in the Nationalist Party, the attempts at mass organization especially among youth,[8] the establishment of a party-army, the use of censorship to control culture and the press, the establishment of a national system of education and significant advances (especially during the war) in using this system to mold a modern citizenry, and the appeal to science against "superstition" and to "Chinese national characteristics" against foreign efforts to impose Western standards on Chinese politics and society.

The CCP did not only rise to power as the dialectical opposite of the Guomindang. There were important points of unity in the dialectic—areas where the Guomindang paved the way for the Communists, where the latter built on the foundations laid by the former. Many activists joined both parties during the 1920s. Memories and friendships from that first Guomindang-CCP collaboration were never erased at the local level. Millions of Chinese rallied to the CCP during the war against Japan in part because the Communists seemed the proper heirs of the revolutionary anti-imperialism of Sun Zhongshan's (Sun Yat-sen's) party during the 1920s, and seemed better to embody the nationalist rhetoric of Guomindang propaganda and public school textbooks than did the Guomindang itself.

Corollary: 1949 was a watershed, not an unbridgeable chasm.

A corollary to Thesis I is the need to break the 1949 barrier. Already the best scholars of modern China are doing this: Philip Huang on rural China, Elizabeth Perry on Shanghai strikes, Jeffrey Wasserstrom on student protests, Friedman, Pickowicz, and Selden in their *Chinese Village, Socialist State*.[9] Fortunately, the time is past when historians worked on China before 1949 and political scientists and sociologists worked on the period since, neither attending the others' conferences or reading enough of the others' books. But we need to go further.

If we are really to understand the ways in which the PRC built on Guomindang foundations, we need to study specific continuities in models, discourse, and personnel. We need to understand both the magnitude of the social changes attempted in the PRC and the limits of Mao's achievements in creating a wholly new socialist China. Topics in economics, popular culture, demography, gender relations, and political culture need to be studied across the 1949 barrier. The example of French historiography is instructive. When one turns to these areas of French history, the French Revolution looms a good deal less large; amid the significant political changes, there were important continuities in the daily lives of individual Frenchmen.

II. The revolution was not a Liberation but (for most) was the replacement of one form of domination with another.

In rethinking the Chinese Revolution, we must rethink the analytical baggage that comes with the term *revolution*. As a historical metaphor, the term revolution has, since the French Revolution, been associated with liberty.[10] Most Marxist historiography (which has been so important in shaping our understanding of revolutionary processes) has taken France as the original model for revolution and seen revolution as bringing *liberation* from the oppressive constraints of the old regime.[11] The Chinese Communists themselves build on this implied meaning by calling their revolution a Liberation.* Much of our own scholarship has accepted this conceptualization, as we studied Chinese struggles for liberation from imperialist domination, peasants' and workers' struggles for freedom from landlords' exactions or employers' exploitation, and women's struggles to escape the bondage of patriarchy.

While we should not deny that the revolution was fueled by the efforts of millions of Chinese actors to escape some form of oppression, we should also realize that there was probably an even greater number of Chinese who experienced the revolution as the replacement of one form of domination with another. Most Chinese did not experience the success of the revolution and the coming to power of the CCP as some form of personal liberation. It was a new world, in many respects, and for most it was a better world. But the PRC ushered in a better world in part because the CCP brought order and discipline to their environment, and this was probably as important to many as was any sense of liberation.

In the countryside, peasants demanded above all that the new regime be fair *(gongdao* 公道), and the party made tremendous efforts in rectification campaigns to ensure that cadres not be guilty of favoritism, that they take the lead in making sacrifices, that they lead simple lives free of corruption, and that they ensure that the burdens of revolutionary struggle were borne equitably.[12] Thus peasants were highly approving of party efforts to force idlers and paupers (*erliuzi* 二流子) into productive work.[13] When we consider that there was little to distinguish the Communist pauper policy from the poor houses of eighteenth-century England, it is difficult to see this as any sort of liberation of the poor. But the measures were welcomed because they were perceived as a discipline that was fair—idlers would have to work for an honest living like everyone else.

The importance of this principle is self-evident. Given the tight PRC controls over employment, residence, education, culture, political activity, and even biological reproduction, if one views the revolution as liberation, then one must view the postrevolutionary regime as a betrayal. Yet, few Chinese see it that way, and I would suggest that such a "betrayal" theory is ill-founded. It makes far more sense to recognize that the revolution was not so much a process of liberation as a process wherein a new structure of domination was created to do battle with, to defeat, and to replace another structure of domination. In this process, the Communists certainly empowered new actors and mobilized new social constituencies. They also broke down old structures of domination—eliminating, expelling, humiliating, and intimidating old elites.

---

* When this essay was first published, it was common to speak of the PRC era as *jiefanghou* (解放后, after Liberation). With the rise of a new nationalist narrative of revolution, this term has been replaced by *jianguohou* (建国后, after the nation's founding) with the bizarre implication that China was not a country (*guo* 国) before 1949.

But those who escaped the domination of these old elites were not just liberated; they were also implicated in a revolutionary process, indebted to a revolutionary party, and subordinated to a new revolutionary regime.

III. Despite Mao's "Sinification of Marxism," the Soviet model of Lenin and Stalin exerted a powerful influence on the Chinese Revolution.

Since the 1950s, it has been a staple of anti-Communist propaganda to portray the Chinese Revolution as the product of a Moscow-directed conspiracy.[14] In reaction to such propaganda and right-wing scholarship, the liberal and progressive conventional wisdom has been to stress the nationalism of the revolution and Mao Zedong's "Sinification of Marxism."[15] There is no questioning Mao's creative adaptations of Marxist thought, the original development of a rural revolutionary model, the struggles of Mao and his cohorts against the "28 Bolsheviks" who adhered more closely to the Comintern's line, the importance of nationalism in the revolutionary movement, or the political independence of the CCP—an independence that ultimately produced the Sino-Soviet split of the 1960s. These aspects of the conventional wisdom are beyond dispute.

Nonetheless, recent scholarship suggests that Soviet influence on the CCP was greater than once thought. The role of Comintern agents in founding the party and guiding its early members out of their intellectual study societies and into revolutionary work in combination with the reorganized Guomindang is now well known and noncontroversial.[16] I would only revise the conventional wisdom by suggesting that, despite Stalin's mistakes in 1927, the net effect of Comintern advice was positive. Only the prodding of Comintern agents forced Chinese Communist intellectuals out of their Marxist study groups and into the work of organizing workers and peasants. Only the protective shield of its Guomindang ally allowed the CCP to grow from between 100 and 250 members in June 1923 to more than 57,000 in April 1927.[17] Especially in the interior, many Communists made important personal and political connections to local Guomindang leaders—contacts that would be revived to excellent effect during the war against Japan.[18] Whereas the White Terror of 1927 decimated the Communist Party, it also stained forever the Guomindang's reputation in progressive intellectual circles. The CCP's dramatic wartime revival would not have been possible without the stature it had acquired during the National Revolution of the 1920s.

Less well appreciated than the Comintern's role during the 1920s—and certainly obscured in official party histories—is Soviet influence during the War of Resistance. The conventional history of this period stresses Mao's struggle with Wang Ming as the triumph of the home-grown Communist over the Soviet stooge. Little mentioned are the important roles of others who returned on the same plane with Wang Ming: Chen Yun and Kang Sheng. Kang Sheng's role in the rectification movement of the 1940s suggests that, as security chief, although he may have substituted Mao's injunction to "cure the sickness and save the patient" for a bloody Soviet-style purge, he was nonetheless quite adept at Stalinist political struggle. Later, Ren Bishi brought the Soviet system of ranks and privilege to the supply system that supported cadres in Yan'an.[19]

My point is not to suggest that Yan'an became a little Moscow. It is merely to urge a reassessment of the Soviet influence on Chinese Communist practice during this period. We must not forget that Mao's first act on assuming leadership of the Long March at Zunyi was to dispatch Pan Hannian and Chen Yun to report to Moscow,[20] that Mao's key contribution to the first session of the critical Senior Cadres' Meetings of 1942–1943 was to rehearse (in a three-day speech) Stalin's twelve conditions for achieving Bolshevism,[21] that many of the key documents for study in the rectification movement were Stalinist tracts,[22] and that China is one of the few Communist states that defended Stalin's legacy after Khrushchev's secret speech of 1956. If we achieve a better appreciation of Soviet and Stalinist influences on CCP revolutionary practice, the systematic importation of the Soviet model during the 1950s looks much more logical. The degree to which so much of China's political, military, scientific, educational, and cultural apparatus continues to this day to follow the Soviet model becomes a good deal more understandable.

It should be possible to acknowledge Soviet influence without succumbing to silly Cold War arguments that the CCP was a tool of Moscow. There is no question that Mao, reacting against leftist mistakes made by Moscow-trained leaders in the Jiangxi Soviet, fought, in Yan'an, against the Internationalists' uncritical importation of "foreign models" from the Soviet Union. The evidence would seem to support Mao's claim that, during the Civil War period, the CCP led the revolution to victory by acting contrary to Stalin's will. *Politically*, the CCP has certainly been an autonomous actor at least since 1935. But that political independence is not inconsistent with the notion that Mao and other CCP leaders would find the experience of the Soviet Union highly instructive, even essential, in their own search for a Chinese road to socialism.[23]

For the critical Yan'an period, I would suggest two important sources of Soviet influence. First, following the return of Wang Ming in 1937, Mao Zedong prepared himself for theoretical struggle with the Internationalists by engaging in the most intensive period of Marxist study in his life, and the texts studied were largely translations of standard Stalinist tracts on philosophy, political economy, and Bolshevik history.[24] Mao certainly did not absorb these texts uncritically, and the writings that emerged from this period of study managed to imbue Soviet Marxism with a distinct Chinese style. But there were certain products of this experience—a phrasing of problems in terms of "two-line struggle," an almost paranoid attitude toward the threat of Trotskyism, a concern for the leading role of cadres and the related commitment to seeing that cadres' thought and behavior be correct—that became enduring features of party life.

Second, there is the role, mentioned earlier, of key returnees from the Soviet Union who rather quickly signaled their adherence to Mao in his struggles with Wang Ming. Kang Sheng in the security apparatus, Ren Bishi in organizational matters, and Chen Yun in party rectification and economic policy were all returned students from Stalin's Russia, and all played critical roles during the 1940s and after. They were most important in the areas of economic policy, party organization, and rectification, and it is here that Soviet models were most important.

IV. The triumph of the CCP was the product of a series of contingent events.

In the summer of 1989, a retired cadre—aging, blind, and bitterly critical of recent corruption in the party—sat on a *kang* in his cave in Yan'an and talked about his experiences in the Chinese Revolution. At one point, he stated flatly, "Without the Xi'an Incident, the Shaanbei revolution could not have survived to the War of Resistance."[25] The comment struck me because my own research was also suggesting that before the war, the Communist foothold in northern Shaanxi was very fragile indeed. In 1936, the Red Army totaled some 20,000 men and controlled only a few county seats. They were surrounded in a desolate corner of Northwest China by more than 300,000 Guomindang and Northeast Army forces.[26] It seemed reasonable to accept this participant's judgment that, without the Communists' spring 1936 truce with the Northeast Army and that army's December kidnapping of Chiang Kai-shek (Jiang Jieshi), the Guomindang might have tightened the noose and eliminated the Red Army.

The Xi'an Incident may indeed have saved the Red Army and been one of those critical turning points in Chinese history.[27] But it was only the most striking of many points where the contingency of history was demonstrated. Obviously, the Long March is replete with instances in which the party and the Red Army were almost eliminated, saved only by a combination of extraordinary determination, incompetent adversaries, and plain old luck. In 1947, Hu Zongnan's pincer movement to trap Mao and the party Center in northern Shaanxi between forces advancing from north and south failed when the southern force was delayed one day. In this case, even had Hu Zongnan's trap succeeded in catching Mao, the party had ample forces elsewhere to survive for some time; but it is abundantly clear that without Mao, the Chinese Revolution would have taken a very different course. (Indeed, Mao came so close to embodying the revolution that one could argue that his death marked the end of the revolutionary era.)

If the contingency of the revolution is evident in these turning points of the national struggle, it is also evident in a vast number of smaller events and struggles chronicled in local studies of the revolutionary process. My research on the revolution in northern Shaanxi shows how local defections in reaction to the ultra-left *sufan* (肅反) campaign of 1935 virtually wiped out the Soviet base on the Shaanxi-Gansu border until the arrival of the Central Red Army overturned the verdicts and reversed the process.[28] Similarly, essays by Gregor Benton, David Paulson, Kathleen Hartford, and Steven Levine in the volume *Single Sparks* stress the precarious nature of the revolutionary struggle in Jiangxi, Shandong, Hebei, and the Northeast, respectively—and how close the party came to failure in each of these cases.[29]

My point is not to reduce the revolution to a series of historical accidents. It is simply to counsel against excessive determinism. We should be suspicious of suggestions that China's economic, political, or agrarian crisis predetermined China's revolutionary history. I suspect that, to some degree, broad theoretical approaches to the Chinese Revolution commit what David Hackett Fischer has called "the *fallacy of identity*"—the "assumption that a cause must somehow resemble its effect" and, in particular, that "big effects [such as a revolution] must have big causes."[30] It is intellectually unsatisfying to conclude that a momentous social and political transformation like the Chinese Revolution was simply the product of a series of contingent events—that, indeed, if things had happened just a little bit differently, it might not have occurred at all. This is the fundamental attraction of the grand theories of Barrington Moore or Theda Skocpol. I would not advocate the abandonment of these powerful and thought-provoking models, but we should not give them an overly deterministic reading. Our search for the causes of the Chinese Revolution must acknowledge that however much socioeconomic structures formed the preconditions for revolution, the revolution itself was an extended historical process in which a series of contingent events interacted over time and space to constrain and ultimately determine the revolutionary outcome.

V. The revolution was produced by a conjuncture of domestic and global historical processes among which the worldwide depression and Japanese imperialism were particularly important.

Returning to the Xi'an Incident, I would argue that although we should recognize it as an important demonstration of the contingency of China's revolutionary history, we should not follow Guomindang apologists such as Ramon Myers and Thomas Metzger to suggest that the incident, and the war and revolution that they see deriving from it, were only accidents of history.[31] While recognizing the pivotal role of the Xi'an Incident, we should understand it as the product of a rising tide of anti-Japanese agitation among students and military men throughout the 1930s. Zhang Xueliang did not just act because the Japanese had invaded his Manchurian homeland. He was moved to action by public (and especially student) resistance to continued concessions to Japan's creeping imperialism in North China, including critical student demonstrations in Xi'an on the eve of the kidnapping.[32]

Parkes Coble's fine book on the politics of the 1930s focuses on the Japanese challenge as Chiang Kai-shek's Achilles' heel. From the time of the Manchurian Incident, Chiang's halfhearted and ineffective efforts to forestall Japanese aggression left the Nanjing government open to constant criticism from the Reorganizationists in Guangzhou, the Guangxi Clique in the southwest, and students and intellectuals everywhere. Despite Guomindang censorship, a public opinion calling for an end to civil war and unified resistance to Japan slowly gathered force. When that public opinion began to infect the Northeast and Northwest Army troops sent to suppress the Communists in northern Shaanxi, their officers entered into a series of contacts with the Communists resulting in local and regional accommodations between the two sides. With this, the groundwork was laid for the Xi'an Incident and subsequent moves toward a united front against Japan.[33]

Should we then proceed along a reductionist course and say that Japanese militarism caused the Chinese Revolution by its insatiable demands for power and resources in North China? That is obviously a question for Japanese historians to answer, but my own view is that Japanese imperialism during the 1930s cannot be understood apart from the Great Depression and the worldwide crisis of capitalism. The closing of Western markets to Japanese goods made Japan all the more intent on pressing a colonialist policy in its East Asian sphere of influence. Depression-caused distress in the Japanese countryside gave both cause and pretext for the military to seek new areas to colonize and develop as a Japanese-dominated East Asian co-prosperity sphere.

This was the global political-economic context for the Chinese Revolution, and it interacted with national and local politics in China to produce the revolutionary conjuncture. At a minimum, a satisfactory explanation of the Chinese Revolution will have to include (a) the Chinese state's military weakness in peripheral areas that gave the Communists their initial room to maneuver, (b) an agrarian regime that allowed the party to gain a measure of popular acquiescence and support on the basis of class (anti-landlord) and tax-resistance (anti-state) appeals, (c) rising nationalist sentiment (especially in urban areas) to which the Communists successfully appealed in united front declarations and which the Nationalists antagonized by pursuing the civil war, and (d) a world economic crisis that both weakened the Chinese state and economy and helped impel Japanese imperialism in Northeast and Northern China.

VI. The larger structures of China's state and society did not make revolution inevitable, but they imposed significant constraints on the agents of revolution and counterrevolution.

Recognizing the contingency of the Chinese Revolution does not require us to ignore the larger socioeconomic structures that constrained the agents of revolution and counterrevolution. These structures have formed the focus of some of the most fruitful comparative scholarship on revolution, especially the work of Barrington Moore but including that of Theda Skocpol, Eric Wolf, Joel Migdal, and Jeffrey Paige.[34] Comparative analysis certainly suggests that China's largely agrarian but highly commercialized economy, its relatively weak and dependent bourgeoisie, and its centralized bureaucratic political system were related to its modern revolutionary experience. But how are we to describe that relationship without violating our thesis on the contingency of the revolution?

The problem is both enormous and highly contentious, but I would venture the following. The apparent strength of the late imperial state (prior to the nineteenth century) lay in the absence of powerful rivals, either domestic or foreign. The Chinese landed elite, lacking judicial or military functions and weakened economically by the practice of partible inheritance, was a much smaller threat to central authority than were any of the European aristocracies or the daimyo of Japan. Internationally, the late imperial state was not seriously threatened prior to the arrival of the West. Precisely because it had no rivals, the Chinese imperial state was quite weak by world standards. It commanded an extraordinarily small portion of national revenues: the land tax, which was the basis of state finances, took only 5 to 6 percent of the harvest against some 30 to 40 percent in Japan.[35]

Low tax rates meant that, in comparative terms, the state's burden on the peasantry was quite light. In addition, the practice of partible inheritance restrained land concentration so that most peasants were guaranteed access to at least a small plot of land. These barriers to complete pauperization, plus the access to wage or petty trade incomes afforded by China's highly commercialized rural economy and the efficient safety net provided by the centralized Qing state's famine relief measures lay behind China's enormous population increase during the late imperial period.[36]

These characteristics of China's political economy meant that during the modern era, China confronted the West and Japan with a weak state and an enormous population. The modern Chinese state was never able to control anything like the Meiji state's hefty proportion of the agricultural product, in part because population had now grown to an extent that even marginal tax increases were seen by peasants as subsistence threats and provoked violent resistance. In consequence, the weak and impoverished Chinese state was humiliated repeatedly by the foreign powers, and the massive indemnities of the Sino-Japanese War and the Boxer Protocol meant that just as China roused itself to a major state-building effort with the late Qing reforms, it was further drained of potential revenues.

During the twentieth century, the Chinese economy showed significant signs of real growth. Although one might quarrel with some details, Thomas Rawski's argument for an extremely respectable 8.1 percent growth rate in industrial production seems entirely plausible. His arguments for 1.4 to 1.7 percent annual growth in the agricultural sector are far more controversial,[37] but there is no denying that some growth in per capita earnings was taking place.[38] But there are two problems.

First, as Rawski acknowledges, virtually all of the recorded growth was taking place along the coast and in core areas. There is little evidence that real economic growth was occurring in the peripheries, and Kenneth Pomeranz has argued that the modernization process actually hurt the neglected hinterland.[39] This meant that the peripheries still harbored a depressed peasantry left out of the modernization process. It was, of course, precisely in these peripheries that the Chinese Revolution took root.

Second, even in the coastal and core areas, the modernization process was not progressing fast enough to allow Chinese state-making and military self-strengthening to keep pace with Japan. The modern sector of the economy furnished new sources of revenue for the republican state, but China was always playing catch-up to its primary rival and threat. In all its modern interactions with Japan, China came out on the losing end. In 1915, in part because many of its modern enterprises had gone heavily into debt to Japanese banks, China was forced to agree to Japan's Twenty-One Demands. In 1917, warlord governments turned to Japan for the Nishihara Loans and, in exchange, acquiesced to Japan taking over Germany's sphere of influence in Shandong. Finally, during the 1930s, as Japan's designs on China became openly imperialist, Chiang Kai-shek was compelled to retreat, trading space for time, hoping in vain that political unification and defense-related economic construction could be completed before Japan launched a full-scale invasion.

In short, the key byproduct of China's social structure and political economy was a weak Chinese state. Unable to protect the Chinese nation during an age of imperialism, the late Qing and republican states were constantly criticized and challenged by nationalist rivals in the urban classes and civil and military elites. Unable to penetrate or bring the benefits of modernization to peripheral and "backward" areas of the country, the state left a vast hinterland where the Communists were able to organize those left out of the fragile modernization process.

VII. The determination, sacrifice, and commitment of individual Communist revolutionaries—the subjective element of the revolutionary dialectic—were both essential to the revolution's success and critical in shaping its nature.

The revolution was not easily made. One of the greatest weaknesses of determinist theories of revolution is their underestimation of the effort made by revolutionaries. The success of the revolution required dedicated revolutionaries and much sacrifice. Time and again, the Communist Party suffered catastrophic defeats: in Chiang Kai-shek's White Terror of 1927; after the suicidal attacks on urban centers under the Li Lisan line in 1930; during 1933–1934 when, one after the other, the Red Soviets fell to Guomindang extermination campaigns; during 1941–1942 when Japanese counterattacks following the Hundred Regiments offensive reduced Communist forces and territory by roughly one half. Yet, brought to the brink of disaster, the Communists regrouped, retreated to safer havens, revised their strategies, and fought on. Any satisfactory interpretation of the revolution must acknowledge and explain the personal commitment and determination that led thousands of young men and women, often scattered in small groups across the map of China, to fight on against overwhelming odds.

The Long March is a tale filled with close calls and remarkable sacrifice. In the end, less than 4,000 of the 86,000 who started out arrived in Shaanxi with Mao.[40] Every river crossing was a potential disaster, and some—like the famous crossing of the Luding Bridge over the Dadu River—have been mythologized as acts of supreme revolutionary courage. China's revolutionary history is replete with such tales of heroism, large and small, and every local struggle saw comparable evidence of revolutionary commitment. Gregor Benton's rich study of those left behind when the Long Marchers departed the south is filled with examples of incredible determination and faith in the revolutionary cause, even as every rearguard unit was suffering losses of about 90 percent of its forces.[41]

The period from 1927 to 1937 is critical in this regard because these years of civil war were certainly the most trying for the party. In North China on the eve of the war, there remained at best a few thousand Communist Party members—scattered in isolated party cells and many in jail. These men (and a few women) had survived years of political persecution as underground party members, and many of their comrades had been arrested and executed or had died in prison. Those who lacked the commitment to carry on—and there were many—dropped out or defected to the Guomindang. But a dedicated few struggled on. Then, with rising anti-Japanese nationalism in 1936, and especially after the Xi'an Incident, Communists were quietly released from jail and returned to their homes where they formed the core of the Communist resistance during the war.[42] The rapid growth of the North China base areas during the early years of the war relied on the critical role of these local cadres. Their survival to play this role is testimony to a remarkable revolutionary dedication.

This revolutionary commitment helps to explain more than the success of the revolution; it also helps explain the *nature* of the revolution. The Long March did more than preserve the Red Army; it also changed forever the lives of the survivors. Remembering the lives lost, they fought on to ensure that their comrades had not died in vain. As the march itself (or other great watersheds of party history) passed from history to legend, the survivors became ever more committed to protecting that myth and their part in it—to ensuring that their contribution would be one chapter in a glorious tale of revolutionary triumph. They knew that should their revolution fail, should the Japanese or the Guomindang succeed in reversing the tide of history (and, struggling against great odds, *they* understood the contingency of revolution), they would lose not only their lives but everything that gave their lives meaning.[43]

At the same time, we must recognize that no one began with an intense commitment to Communist revolution. Even the senior party leaders were only slowly transformed from radical friends to Communist Party cadres.[44] Among ordinary peasants, the initial commitment to revolutionary struggle was quite tentative. One peasant informant told me that he joined the Red Army in 1935 because it was the fad (*shimao* 時髦). Others joined because they were hungry and the army fed them.[45] But once in the ranks, the very process of revolutionary participation increased commitment. Meetings and propaganda taught party discipline and party spirit; struggle sessions and rectification movements rooted out personal weaknesses and competing loyalties. The longer one survived, the higher one rose in the party and the greater one's commitment grew. In time, a fad became a cause, and the revolution became a way of life.

Those who made the revolution a way of life naturally sought comrades with a like-minded faith in the justice and certain victory of their cause. They were suspicious of those who wavered or showed signs of skepticism, cynicism, or doubt because these people might give up the struggle, defect to the enemy, or break under torture, revealing the identity and location of their comrades and endangering an entire local revolutionary base. This dynamic of revolutionary struggle helps to explain why Communist revolutionaries so frequently—even while fighting for their lives as small guerrilla bands in isolated mountain bases—turned on their comrades in bloody and destructive purges.[46] The revolutionary survivors were the winners of these inner-party struggles and, as their revolution became increasingly successful during the 1940s, they became convinced of the correctness of their methods. Purging the hesitant and cautious became integral to party life. The inevitable result was a pattern of party conflict that automatically favored the left—with well-known and often disastrous consequences in the PRC.[47]

VIII. The CCP was a social construct of considerable internal complexity, not an organizational weapon of obedient apparatchiks commanded by the Party Center.

Few questions have provoked more contentious debate than the role of Communist Party organization in the revolutionary dynamic. Those stressing the role of organization have usually discounted social factors as a basis for revolution.[48] The organizational strengths of the party are deemed sufficient to explain Communist victory even in the absence of popular support. Drawing on early Cold War scholarship such as Philip Selznick's *The Organizational Weapon*,[49] organizational interpretations have often been associated with a conservative anti-Communist political stance that challenges the legitimacy of Communist rule.[50]

Despite this political stance, some of the best scholarship on the revolution has demonstrated the essential role of the Communist Party and its military forces in mobilizing the peasantry for revolution and resistance to Japan.[51] Virtually all close studies of the revolution have come to the conclusion that popular support for the revolution was always the product of painstaking efforts by party members to demonstrate the benefits of tax relief, rent reduction, defense against the Japanese, political participation in elections, land reform, production campaigns, mutual aid, cooperatives, and so forth. The party's own attention to party building and organizational questions is obvious in internal documents from this period. (Indeed, recent scholarship's stress on organizational factors in part reflects the concerns of the inner-party documents on which much of this research is based.) A recognition of the key role of party organization need not be read as either hostility to the revolution or an alternative to popular support, but as evidence that support for the revolution depended on the new party-state's ability to penetrate village society and mobilize the populace for its program.

There are, however, two analytical traps waiting to snare those who rely too much on organizational explanations. First is the danger of fetishizing organization. My own research on the northern Shaanxi revolution during the 1930s suggests that significant success came only when the CCP's Shaanxi provincial organization was destroyed following the arrest and defection of its party secretary in 1933. The destruction of the provincial party apparatus freed the guerrilla forces under Liu Zhidan from higher party directives that they avoid "flightism" and "opportunism" and engage in suicidal attacks on major urban centers. Released from the discipline of a party organization following an adventurist line, Liu Zhidan built a significant guerrilla base on the Shaanxi-Gansu border. Then, in 1935, new representatives from the Center arrived, arrested Liu and his officers, executed a number of his followers, and nearly destroyed the base until stopped by the arrival of Mao and the Central Army. As this case illustrates, disciplined party organization could be a recipe for disaster, not a guarantee of victory.[52]

Second, there is the danger of reifying the party. Because reference to "the Party" is a convenient stylistic shorthand and because party documents constantly stress the role of the party in the revolution, we stand in constant danger of writing and thinking about the party acting as some unified, disciplined historical agent. But we know that, in fact, this was not the case. Recent work on the origins of the CCP by Hans van de Ven has demonstrated that the party did not come into being full-blown with the First Congress in 1921. A gradual process turned local cells of friends into a national organization of comrades. Patterns of association among intellectuals, schoolmates, and fellow provincials were slowly transformed through experience and struggle into the new habitus of a Leninist party. According to van de Ven, a true Communist Party worthy of the name did not come into being until 1927.[53]

If we turn from the founding of the CCP to the collapse of communist parties in the former Soviet Union and Eastern Europe, we see that in every case but that of Romania, communist party leaders made key decisions not to resist with force the dismantling of the party-state. Thus, at the end of their historical paths as well, communist parties prove to be anything but monolithic machines. They are composed of a variety of historical actors with important identities beside their roles as party members. These people are not all mindless apparatchiks in a communist machine. They are also members of society—with families and social connections, personal lives and aspirations, and national, regional, and ethnic identities.

Party discipline at the height of communist power was no doubt more effective than it was at a party's founding or during its last days. Nonetheless, that discipline was never perfect. Even in the most secure bases such as Shaan-Gan-Ning, the rural party included an enormous number of peasants with marginal literacy, little education, and no knowledge whatsoever of Marxist-Leninist theory. These peasant communists' consciousness and behavior had little in common with the thinking and activities of the urban intellectuals of the Party Center who wrote the key documents that inform our thinking of what "the Party" represented. Rural cadres were deeply enmeshed in a variety of local networks from which they could never be completely separated. Between rural cadres and the Party Center were county party members who partook imperfectly of both worlds—but whom the Party Center periodically recalled to work conferences in efforts to bind them ever more closely to the Party Center's way of thinking.

The CCP, at all its levels, was a historical product, a cultural construction, an association of human beings. Its successes were not just the successes of organization and discipline. They were also the successes of a complex interaction among central and base area strategists, county executives and enforcers, and village activists. Out of that interaction, new social roles were constructed. Rural cadres began as young village activists who placed a value on work and struggle over face and harmony. And then gradually, as their own actions tied their interests and identities ever more closely to the new regime, they were themselves transformed into leaders "not afraid to offend" their fellow villagers and eager to complete the tasks assigned by their party-state superiors. This certainly made them effective agents of state-directed social change. But the party-state of which they were agents was itself a multilayered social construct—full of new public rituals and confidential bureaucratic routines. To understand the workings of that party-state, we must deconstruct it, not reify it. We need a historical anthropology of the Chinese party-state that can chart the evolution of its customs and habits, its discourse and rhetoric, its methods of cooptation and patterns of domination.[54]

IX. *Revolution is a process.*

Between the extremes of a deterministic view of the revolution as the inevitable product of the political-economic structures of Chinese society and the analytically defeatist view of the revolution as a historical accident, we need to conceive of the revolution as an evolving historical process in which each stage built on the political consequences, the institutional creations, the evolving habits, and the collective memories of what went before. We need a processual model of the Chinese Revolution, similar to George Lefebvre's conception of the French Revolution as a series of revolutions that followed from and built on one another.[55] I would tentatively propose the following sketch of such a processual model.

When the 1911 Revolution left China without a strong central government or any elite consensus about what a legitimate government might look like, the way was left open for the Guomindang to reorganize and revitalize itself as a claimant to national leadership. During the 1920s, with the advice and assistance of the Soviet Union, the reorganized Guomindang established some of the fundamental contours of twentieth-century Chinese politics: Leninist party organization, a party-army with political officers binding the military to the party's political agenda; party-directed mass organizations of students, workers, and peasants with nationalist and social reformist agendas; political rituals involving public celebrations of obedience to the national leader and the creation of a new citizenry, and a revolutionary discourse that stigmatized opponents as counterrevolutionary agents of imperialism and feudal reaction.[56]

Among students and intellectuals, the Guomindang's nationalist and social reformist agenda attracted growing support, especially after the May 30 Movement of 1925. But in part because the foreign and conservative Chinese press stressed the role of Russian aid and Bolshevik advisers in the movement, the Guomindang's Chinese Communist allies shared in the support garnered by the National Revolution. In consequence, when Chiang Kai-shek purged the Communists in 1927, although his short-term success was complete, he created the impression among many that he had betrayed the revolutionary legacy of Sun Yat-sen. The Communists were able to claim that they were the true heirs to the revolutionary tradition of the 1920s.

Driven from the cities and forced into the hinterland in 1927, the revolution first required military forces. These were usually, in the first instance, defectors from the Guomindang armies—or, more accurately, men who saw the Guomindang betraying the revolution in 1927 (or, later, in their failure to resist to Japan)—who resumed some prior contact or affiliation with leftist forces. Second, civil adherents to the revolution worked through established elite networks to establish the basis for revolutionary action. Third, bandits, secret society members, and a variety of discontented individuals were recruited to join the initial Red Army units and form small but powerful guerrilla bands in isolated peripheral areas.[57]

These initial guerrilla bands represented a miniscule portion of the rural population. At this stage, there was nothing resembling mass mobilization. However, by selective and "just" violence against hated state agents and cruel landlord and militia elites, they managed to eliminate or neutralize their political opponents. Once this was done, they could spread propaganda, recruit more broadly into the party, organize mass organizations, and eventually abolish the old tax regime and carry out land reform or (during the War of Resistance) rent and interest reduction and progressive tax reform.

As successful as these efforts were, they could not have succeeded without the war with Japan. Economic development and Guomindang state-building efforts were proceeding well enough along the coast and in economic core areas so that the Nationalists were able to contain the Communist appeal to peripheral zones. As Japanese aggression intensified following their 1931 occupation of the Northeast, Chiang Kai-shek and the Nanjing government lost political support in urban areas, but there was no urban opposition strong or cohesive enough to pose an alternative. Once full-scale war with Japan broke out in 1937, however, the rapid retreat of Guomindang officials and regular army units from North China left rural elites and former warlord forces to contend with the Communists (and Japanese) on their own.

In this situation, a number of factors favored the Communists. Many local Communists had contacts going back to the 1920s to establish their local credibility. Most of these had superior nationalist credentials to Guomindang rivals who had defended Chiang's attempts to appease the Japanese aggressors. Years in the political wilderness made these Communist leaders more capable of accepting the hardships of partisan warfare, and both their egalitarian ideology and their years of struggle led them to enforce a severely spartan lifestyle on all full-time political cadres and military officers. In the context of war with Japan, the new Communist party-state built support for a program of shared sacrifice in which the burden of progressive taxation and rent and interest reduction fell heavily on the elite. But in large measure because the regime's leaders could demonstrate that they were not benefiting materially from these new burdens, their demands were regarded as fair (*gongdao*) by the rural population—and fairness was all that was required.

These factors allowed the CCP to establish a number of reasonably stable bases in North and Central China. But midway through the war, their victory was by no means assured. The New Fourth Army Incident of January 1941 effectively brought the united front with the Guomindang to an end. The economic blockade of Shaan-Gan-Ning was resumed, and the Guomindang subsidy for the Communist armies ended. At roughly the same time, Japanese mopping-up campaigns severely tested the other Communist bases. Faced with these challenges, the party-state was forced to increase significantly its demands on the rural population, but it also undertook a serious rectification of its own work.[58]

The rectification campaign of 1942 to 1944 was one of the most important turning points in China's revolutionary history. To the extent that the party was transformed into an effective organizational weapon, this is when it was done. Three aspects of this movement strike me as essential. First, the initial campaign in Yan'an unified the revolutionary leadership around Mao. The

Internationalist group around Wang Ming was finally eliminated as a force in the party. Equally important, dissenting voices among the intellectuals were both cowed into submission by the vehemence of the attack on Wang Shiwei* and won over to a new and deeper commitment by a process of criticism and self-criticism that ended by excusing their sins and welcoming them into the beleaguered revolutionary community.[59]

With the revolutionary leadership in Yan'an thus solidified, the campaign was spread to other areas of Shaan-Gan-Ning and to other base areas. In the Shaan-Gan-Ning hinterland, anti-traitor work took center stage. Intellectuals and the wealthier elements in rural society were subjected to intense examination. Large numbers were accused of traitorous activities—often for having voiced some discontent with the new regime. These people were treated harshly, although not executed, as Mao's injunction to "cure the illness and save the patient" was followed—in deliberate contrast to Stalinist purge practices. Nonetheless, the party made its power and will clear enough so that discordant voices were silenced.

The third and final stage of rectification was to raise political consciousness and improve discipline among rural cadres. Most of these had been hurriedly recruited during times of mass mobilization—often in the more leftist phases of the revolution. Largely poor and middle peasants of marginal literacy, their knowledge of either Marxist theory or Leninist discipline was minimal. Once the party apparatus had been unified and disciplined down to the county level, that apparatus could be brought to bear on the rural party. Petty corruption was rooted out, and less competent or activist cadres were reformed or replaced. The end result was a party organization reaching right down to the village level that could effectively carry out a series of important mobilization campaigns during the late war years: for increased agricultural and handicraft production, cooperatives, mutual aid teams, elections, and conscription. The foundations of the new party-state had been laid.

The final test was to come during the Civil War years, 1947–1948. Here, military advantage lay with the Guomindang, and the Communists no longer had the benefit of fighting a national enemy. By this time, the party leadership had been effectively unified and rank-and-file cadres had committed themselves to the revolutionary regime. Their past victimization of class and political enemies meant that any return of the old regime would leave them in great personal danger. Faced with an enemy that often had the option of fleeing to the cities or deserting, these communist cadres had a clear edge in

---

* Wang Shiwei (王實味, 1906–1947) was a journalist and literary scholar who first joined the CCP in 1926, studied in Moscow, then went to Yan'an during the war. His criticisms of the party in 1942 were widely publicized, earning the ire of Mao and the Party leadership. He was criticized as a "Trotskyite," expelled, and finally executed in 1947.

political dedication. As for the ordinary peasantry, the poorest certainly benefited from the land reform carried out at this time. Middle peasants benefited politically from the new regime, with a larger voice in village affairs. Convinced in sufficient numbers that a return of the Guomindang would bring back the bad old days of arbitrary taxes and abusive officials, they too tended to side with the revolution.

The basic features of this processual overview of the revolution are not so different from the conventional wisdom. But the emphases and formulations support certain essential points. First, initial support for the Communist Party came from a small group of intellectuals and rural revolutionaries whose commitment to the revolutionary cause was steeled in years of bitter combat. Second, the experience of the wartime base areas allowed these Communist cadres to create a party-state whose influence permeated village life as never before. Third, the wartime and Civil War demands of the new party-state were unprecedented in their extent, but they were tolerated because progressive taxes targeted those with the ability to pay and state cadres were able to demonstrate that they were not using their authority for personal enrichment. Fourth, land reform policies established guarantees that each peasant family would have sufficient land to guarantee a basic subsistence whereas the encouragement of handicrafts, cooperatives, and market exchange promised the revival of commercial activity.

The advantage of this formulation is, first, that it highlights the state-building activities of the Chinese Revolution. When we observe that, including officials, clerks, and runners, the Qing state probably had about 750,000 functionaries, or one for every 600 people, whereas the PRC had 5.3 million cadres in 1952 and 29 million cadres in 1988, or one for every 35 citizens,[60] it is clear that state-building was a central facet of the Chinese Revolution. Second, a critical appeal of the new party-state was the selfless dedication of its cadres. Once the party's monopoly of power (together with the spread of a market economy) made corruption and abuse of privilege commonplace during the 1980s, the revolutionary era was over and the revolution's own legitimacy was called into question. Finally, nothing in the revolutionary process suggested popular support for an economic program that went beyond small peasant farming, private and (voluntary) cooperative ownership, and free market activity.

Seen in this way, it becomes easier to understand both the pervasive influence of the Chinese state and the current enthusiasm for market reforms. And if we understand the political demands behind the Chinese Revolution to be for fairness and order (far more than democracy or liberation), it becomes easier to understand both the crisis of 1989 and the current resilience of the authoritarian state in China.

X. *The history of modern China is not a teleology of revolution.*

Having devoted nine theses to analyzing the origins and nature of the Chinese Revolution, it is necessary to conclude by observing that one of the most pernicious characteristics of the historiography of modern China is an excessive focus on revolution. Modern Chinese history has been dominated and distorted by a teleology of revolution.[61] All history is seen as leading up to 1949 (or, for a time, to a broader revolutionary process culminating in the Cultural Revolution). The central problem of intellectual history was the rise of Marxism.[62] Economic history analyzed the weakness of Chinese capitalism.[63] Rural society and peasant uprisings were studied to understand the roots of peasant revolution.[64] The 1911 Revolution was seen as the "first phase" of a revolutionary process leading up to 1949.[65] The May Fourth Movement was the start of a process leading to the founding of the CCP.[66]

This historiographic tradition is perfectly understandable. The history of the past is written in the present.[67] We seek answers about the past to questions formed in the present. For some time, that present has been one in which the CCP sat securely in control of a Leninist party-state and a fundamentally Stalinist economy. In ideology and organization, in political economy and cultural norms, the new revolutionary China was a radical break with the past. This was one of the great revolutions of world history,[68] and the task of the historian was to explain the historical foundations of the remarkable political and social transformation wrought by the PRC.

Since the 1990s, this sort of history is clearly outdated. The year 1949 was not the end of history. Indeed, within a few years, the era of revolutionary socialism may appear as much a transitional period as the republican era. Our study of the revolution must pay as much attention to the antecedents of China's post-socialist present as to those contradictions that produced the revolution itself.[69]

In the realm of politics, scholars have been impressed by the Chinese Communists' success in political mobilization. Supported by substantial contemporary evidence of popular support for the Communists during the 1940s, historians have seen that mass base as a key factor in the CCP's triumph over the Guomindang.[70] It would be excessively presentist to abandon inquiry into popular support for the CCP. On the other hand, it would be excessively naive to deny that much popular mobilization in contemporary China has been distinctly coercive. Amid its appeals to "new democracy," the party was building a structure that concentrated power (and increasing degrees of privilege) in the Party Center. The critical political process in modern China was state-building. Founded on popular support gained through the revolutionary process, consolidated by the organizational efficacy of the Leninist party-state, inspired by nationalist pride in a new China, and supported by new technologies of violence, communications, surveillance, and medicine (especially birth control), the contemporary Chinese state has brought unprecedented discipline and control over the lives of Chinese people.

In economic history, it will not do to see China's prerevolutionary economy as hopelessly trapped in a process of agricultural involution broken only by socialism and collective agriculture.[71] Although the recent boom in China's economy is more industrial than agricultural, and although agricultural advances under the new quasi-private farming have been made on a foundation in infrastructure and modern inputs built under socialism, the fact remains that small peasant farming has been quite successful during recent years and that, in the larger economy, foreign investments and private and small collective enterprises have been spectacularly successful. In this context, it is clearly dated for historians to focus on China's economic failures or the retarded development of capitalism. We need to recognize the substantial vitality of China's prerevolutionary economic structures—a vitality that is now able to flourish under a regime that provides national sovereignty, peace, a degree of political stability, basic technical education, and broad tolerance for market activity.

At the same time, we need to recognize an enduring contradiction between a dynamic coastal economy and a disadvantaged interior. It is no accident that China's current economic boom is concentrated in the coastal provinces of the south and east—long the most commercialized parts of China and the most tied to foreign trade—or that overseas Chinese are integral to the growing economic integration of "Greater China" and all of East Asia.[72] The Guomindang-Communist conflict was in part the struggle between the modernized, overseas-connected coastal zones and the depressed and forgotten rural interior. The gap between coastal prosperity and interior poverty helped feed the revolution, was checked by the planned economy of the early PRC, and is now regaining salience with the return of the market economy.[73]

In the past, it has always been the powerful unifying forces of state power and official culture that have held such regional disparities and tensions in check. The state is now surely stronger than any prerevolutionary government. In the realm of culture, however, the penetration of the market economy is weakening the state's ability to subordinate cultural practices to its centralizing purposes. The cultural history of urban China is increasingly characterized by a merging of styles and combining of resources of Greater China. In film, music, and dance, in clothing and material culture, Hong Kong, Taiwan, and coastal China are increasingly drawing together—a cultural blending tied to their economic integration.* But the relevance and appeal of these cultural products to the rural interior is questionable.

---

* It goes without saying that in Xi Jinping's China, many of these trends have been reversed.

Finally, it is likely that historians looking back from the next century will be impressed by the alteration and degradation of China's physical environment brought about by the twentieth century's tripling of China's already huge population combined with the prolonged and now very rapid growth of industrial production. Vaclav Smil has detailed the serious problems of air and water pollution, soil erosion, water depletion, and deforestation in contemporary China.[74] China's cities become increasingly crowded, plagued by congestion and air pollution, and burdened by an unchecked influx of "mobile population."

In all of these changes—political, economic, cultural, demographic, and environmental—the Chinese Revolution has played a crucial role in the transformative process. But in the end, these historical processes are larger than the revolution, and it will be necessary to subordinate the history of the revolution to these larger patterns of change. Only then can we escape the teleology of revolution and gain an understanding of China's past that provides a better key to understanding its present.

NOTES

1. David Schoenbaum, *Hitler's Social Revolution: Class and Status in Nazi Germany, 1933–1939* (Garden City, NY: Doubleday, 1966).

2. Hannah Arendt, *On Revolution* (New York: Viking, 1963).

3. Edward Berenson, "A Permanent Revolution: The Historiography of 1789," *Modern China* 21, no. 1 (January 1995): 77–104.

4. Edgar Snow, *Red Star Over China* (New York: Grove, 1961); Theodore White and Annalee Jacoby, *Thunder out of China* (New York: William Sloane Associates, 1946); Jack Belden, *China Shakes the World* (New York: Harper, 1949).

5. John King Fairbank, *The United States and China*, fourth edition (Cambridge, MA: Harvard University Press, 1983); Lloyd Eastman, *The Abortive Revolution: China under Nationalist Rule, 1927–1937* (Cambridge, MA: Harvard University Press, 1974) and *Seeds of Destruction: Nationalist China in War and Revolution, 1937–1949* (Stanford, CA: Stanford University Press, 1984).

6. William C. Kirby, *Germany and Republican China* (Stanford, CA: Stanford University Press, 1984), chap. 4.

7. Prasenjit Duara, *Culture, Power, and the State: Rural North China, 1900–1942* (Stanford, CA: Stanford University Press, 1988); Rebecca Nedostup, *Superstitious Regimes: Religion and the Politics of Chinese Modernity* (Cambridge, MA: Harvard University Press, 2009).

8. Jeffrey N. Wasserstrom, *Student Protest in Twentieth-Century China: The View from Shanghai* (Stanford, CA: Stanford University Press, 1991).

9. Philip C. C. Huang, *The Peasant Economy and Social Change in North China* (Stanford, CA: Stanford University Press, 1985) and *The Peasant Family and Rural*

Development in the Yangzi Delta, 1350–1988 (Stanford, CA: Stanford University Press, 1990); Elizabeth J. Perry, *Shanghai on Strike: The Politics of Chinese Labor* (Stanford, CA: Stanford University Press, 1993); Wasserstrom, *Student Protest*; Edward Friedman, Paul G. Pickowicz, and Mark Selden, with Kay Ann Johnson, *Chinese Village, Socialist State* (New Haven, CT: Yale University Press, 1991).

10. Arendt, *On Revolution*, 25.

11. François Furet, *Interpreting the French Revolution*, trans. Elborg Forster (Cambridge: Cambridge University Press, 1981), 81–89.

12. Mark Selden, *The Yenan Way in Revolutionary China* (Cambridge, MA: Harvard University Press, 1971), chaps. 5–6; Chen Yung-fa, *Making Revolution: The Communist Movement in Eastern and Central China, 1937–1945* (Berkeley: University of California Press, 1986), chap. 6; Richard Madsen, *Morality and Power in a Chinese Village* (Berkeley: University of California Press, 1984), chap. 3; Joseph W. Esherick, "Deconstructing the Construction of the Party-State: Gulin County in the Shaan-Gan-Ning Border Region," *China Quarterly* 140 (and next chapter).

13. Harrison Forman, *Report from Red China* (New York: Wittlesey House, 1945), 70; Pauline Keating, *Two Revolutions: Village Reconstruction and Cooperativization in North Shaanxi, 1934–1945* (Stanford, CA: Stanford University Press, 1997), 120–21; Janet Y. Chen, *Guilty of Indigence: The Urban Poor in China, 1900–1953* (Princeton, NJ: Princeton University Press, 2012) while largely devoted to Guomindang treatment of the poor, also mentions (176–77) these policies in the Communist border region.

14. Chiang Kai-shek, *Soviet Russia in China: A Summing-up at Seventy*, trans. Wang Chung-hui (New York: Farrar, Straus & Cudahy, 1957).

15. Stuart Schram, *The Political Thought of Mao Tse-tung* (New York: Praeger, 1969); Benjamin I. Schwartz, "The Legend of the 'Legend of Maoism,'" *China Quarterly* 2 (April–June 1960): 35–42.

16. See, especially, Tony Saich, *The Origins of the First United Front in China: the Role of Sneevliet (alias Maring)* (Leiden: Brill, 1991); Tony Saich and Benjamin Yang, eds. *The Rise to Power of the Chinese Communist Party: Documents and Analysis* (Armonk, NY: M. E. Sharpe, 1996); and Yoshihiro Ishikawa, *The Formation of the Chinese Communist Party*, trans. Joshua A. Fogel (New York: Columbia University Press, 2013).

17. Hans J. van de Ven, *From Friend to Comrade: The Founding of the CCP, 1920–1927* (Berkeley: University of California Press, 1991), 194.

18. Odoric Y. K. Wou, *Mobilizing the Masses*, 209, 289, 337.

19. Chen Yung-fa, *Making Revolution*; "The Yenan Way reconsidered," paper presented to the annual meeting of the Association for Asian Studies, March 1993, Los Angeles.

20. Harrison E. Salisbury, *The Long March: The Untold Story* (New York: McGraw Hill, 1985), 134–35.

21. P. J. Seybolt, "Terror and Conformity: Counterespionage Campaigns, Rectification and Mass Movements, 1942–1943," *Modern China* 12, no. 1 (1986): 53.

22. Boyd Compton, *Mao's China: Party Reform Documents, 1942–1944* (Seattle: University of Washington Press, 1966), x–xi, xxxix–xlvi.

23. Sergei N. Goncharov, John W. Lewis, and Xue Litai, *Uncertain Partners: Stalin, Mao and the Korean War* (Stanford, CA: Stanford University Press, 1993).

24. Joshua A. Fogel, *Ai Ssi-ch'i's Contribution to the Development of Chinese Marxism* (Cambridge, MA: Harvard University Council on East Asian Studies, 1987), 61–71; Stuart Schram, *The Thought of Mao Tse-tung* (Cambridge: Cambridge University Press, 1989), 61–65.

25. Author's Shaanbei interview, June 1989.

26. Otto Braun, *A Comintern Agent in China, 1932–1939*, trans. Jeanne Moore (Stanford, CA: Stanford University Press, 1982), 149.

27. Tien-wei Wu, *The Sian Incident: A Pivotal Point in Modern Chinese History* (Ann Arbor: University of Michigan Center for Chinese Studies, 1976); "New Materials on the Sian Incident: A Bibliographic Essay," *Modern China* 10, no. 1 (1984): 115–41.

28. Joseph W. Esherick, *Accidental Holy Land: The Communist Revolution in Northwest China* (Oakland: University of California Press, 2022).

29. Kathleen Hartford and Steven M. Goldstein, eds. *Single Sparks: China's Rural Revolutions* (Armonk, NY: M. E. Sharpe, 1989), 28–31, 124, 155.

30. David Hackett Fischer, *Historians' Fallacies: Toward a Logic of Historical Thought* (New York: Harper & Row, 1970): 177.

31. R. H. Myers and T. A. Metzger, "Sinological Shadows: The State of Modern China Studies in the US," *Australian Journal of Chinese Affairs* 4 (1980): . One should recall E. H. Carr's observation that it is history's losers who stress the role of accident in history: "It is amusing to note that the Greeks, after their conquest by the Romans, also indulged in the game of historical 'might-have-beens'—the favorite consolation of the defeated" (Edward Hallett Carr, *What Is History?* [New York: Vintage, 1961], 130).

32. Tien-wei Wu, *Sian Incident*, and "New Materials on the Sian Incident."

33. Parkes Coble, *Facing Japan: Chinese Politics and Japanese Imperialism, 1931–1937* (Cambridge, MA: Harvard University Press, 1991).

34. Barrington Moore Jr., *Social Origins of Dictatorship and Democracy: Lord and Peasant in the Making of the Modern World* (Boston: Beacon, 1966); Theda Skocpol, *States and Social Revolutions: A Comparative Analysis of France, Russia, and China* (Cambridge, MA: Harvard University Press, 1979); Joel S. Migdal, *Peasants, Politics and Revolution: Pressures toward Political and Social Change in the Third World* (Princeton, NJ: Princeton University Press, 1974); Jeffery M. Paige, *Agrarian Revolution: Social Movements and Export Agriculture in the Underdeveloped World* (New York: Free Press, 1975); Eric R. Wolf, *Peasant Wars of the Twentieth Century* (New York: Harper & Row, 1969).

35. Wang Yeh-chien, *Land Taxation in Imperial China, 1750–1911* (Cambridge, MA: Harvard University Press, 1973), 131.

36. Pierre-Etienne Will, *Bureaucracy and Famine in Eighteenth-Century China*, trans. Elborg Forster (Stanford, CA: Stanford University Press, 1990).

37. Huang, *Peasant Family*, 137–39; R. Bin Wong, "Chinese Economic History and Development: A Note on the Myers Huang Exchange," *Journal of Asian Studies* 51, no. 3 (1992): 600–612; *Republican China*, November 1992.

38. Thomas Rawski, *Economic Growth in Prewar China* (Berkeley: University of California Press, 1989).

39. Kenneth Pomeranz, *The Making of a Hinterland: State, Society and Economy in Inland North China, 1853–1937* (Berkeley: University of California Press, 1993).

40. Salisbury, *Long March*, 2.

41. Gregor Benton, *Mountain Fires: The Red Army's Three-Year War in South China, 1934–1938* (Berkeley: University of California Press, 1992).

42. Lyman Van Slyke, "The Chinese Communist Movement," 631.

43. The commitment of party survivors to the revolutionary myth has filled the speeches of elders such as Wang Zhen: "The leadership of the Communist Party is not granted by heaven, but by the countless revolutionary martyrs who, wave after wave, shed blood and sacrificed themselves for half a century" (quoted in Orville Schell, *Discos and Democracy: China in the Throes of Reform* [New York: Pantheon, 1988], 235). It was certainly no accident that when the fate of the revolution was called into question during the spring of 1989, it was to elders like Wang Zhen that Deng Xiaoping first appealed for guidance and support.

44. Van de Ven, *From Friend to Comrade*.

45. Joseph W. Esherick, "The Chinese Communist Revolution from the Bottom Up: Shaan-Gan-Ning," paper presented at the annual meeting of the American Historical Association, December, San Francisco, 1989.

46. Benton, *Mountain Fires*, 172, 198–99, 237–39, 283, 354–56.

47. Li Rui, *Lushan huiyi shilu* [True record of the Lushan Plenum] (Taibei: Xinrui, 1994; mainland edition 1988) provides a vivid example.

48. Roy Hofheinz Jr., *The Broken Wave: The Chinese Communist Peasant Movement, 1922–1928* (Cambridge, MA: Harvard University Press, 1977); Steven I. Levine, *The Anvil of Victory: The Communist Revolution in Manchuria, 1945–1948* (New York: Columbia University Press, 1987).

49. Philip Selznick, *The Organizational Weapon: A Study of Bolshevik Strategy and Tactics* (New York: McGraw-Hill, 1952).

50. Hartford and Goldstein, *Single Sparks*, 9–18.

51. Chen Yung-fa, *Making Revolution*; Tetsuya Kataoka, *Resistance and Revolution in China: The Communists and the Second United Front* (Berkeley: University of California Press, 1974).

52. For a full elaboration, see Esherick, *Accidental Holy Land*.

53. Van de Ven, *Friend to Comrade*, 199–201.

54. More on this in chapter 9: "Deconstructing the Party-State."

55. George Lefebvre, *The Coming of the French Revolution*, trans. R. R. Palmer, (New York: Vintage, 1957; French edition, 1939).

56. Wasserstrom, *Student Protest*; Michael Tsang-Woon Tsin, *Nation, Governance and Modernity in China: Canton, 1900–1927* (Stanford, CA: Sanford University Press, 1999); Henrietta Harrison, *The Making of the Republican Citizen: Political Ceremonies and Symbols in China, 1911–1929* (Oxford : Oxford University Press, 2000) and *China, Inventing the Nation* (London : New York: Oxford University Press, 2001).

57. Stephen C. Averill, "Party, Society and Local Elite in the Jiangxi Communist Movement," *Journal of Asian Studies* 46, no. 2 (1987): 279–303; and Averill, "Social Elites and Communist Revolution in the Jiangxi Hill Country," in Joseph W. Esherick and Mary Backus Rankin, eds. *Chinese Local Elites and Patterns of Dominance* (Berkeley: University of California Press, 1990): 283–84; Esherick, *Accidental Holy Land*.

58. Selden, *Yenan Way*; Peter Schran, *Guerrilla Economy: The Development of the Shensi-Kansu-Ninghsia Border Region, 1937–1945* (Albany: SUNY Press, 1976).

59. Gao Hua, *How the Red Sun Rose: The Origin and Development of the Yan'an Rectification Movement, 1930–1945*, trans. Stacey Mosher and Guo Jian (Hong Kong: Chinese University of Hong Kong Press, 2019); David E. Apter and Tony Saich, *Revolutionary Discourse in Mao's Republic* (Cambridge, MA: Harvard University Press, 1994); Chen Yongfa, *Yan'an de yinying* [Yan'an's shadow] (Taibei: Academia Sinica Jindaishi yanjiusuo, 1990).

60. Hong Yung Lee, *From Revolutionary Cadres to Party Technocrats in Socialist China* (Berkeley: University of California Press, 1991), 207–9.

61. For an extended critique of the "revolution paradigm" in modern Chinese history, see Myers and Metzger, "Sinological Shadows." Needless to say, I do not agree with much of this article, which is a defense of Taiwan as the worthy product of modern Chinese history and an appeal for support from the new Reagan administration. But we should not allow the political bias of the authors to blind us to an important argument they are making.

62. Joseph R. Levenson, *Confucian China and Its Modern Fate*, 3 vols. (Berkeley: University of California Press, 1958–1965); Benjamin I. Schwartz, *Chinese Communism and the Rise of Mao* (Cambridge, MA: Harvard University Press, 1951); Maurice Meisner, *Li Ta-chao and the Origins of Chinese Marxism* (Cambridge, MA: Harvard University Press, 1967).

63. Albert Feuerwerker, *China's Early Industrialization: Sheng Hsuan-huai (1844–1916) and Mandarin Enterprise* (Cambridge, MA: Harvard University Press, 1958).

64. Huang, *Peasant Economy*; Perry, *Rebels and Revolutionaries*; Esherick, *Origins of the Boxer Uprising*.

65. Mary C. Wright, ed., *China in Revolution: The First Phase, 1900–1913* (New Haven, CT: Yale University Press, 1968); Joseph W. Esherick, *Reform and Revolution in China: The 1911 Revolution in Hunan and Hubei* (Berkeley: University of California Press, 1976).

66. Tse-tsung Chow, *The May Fourth Movement: Intellectual Revolution in Modern China* (Cambridge, MA: Harvard University Press, 1960).

67. Carr, *What is History?* 29.

68. Moore, *Social Origins*; Skocpol, *States and Social Revolutions*; Jack A Goldstone, *Revolution and Rebellion in the Early Modern World* (Berkeley: University of California Press, 1991).

69. The following sections are inspired by the comments of Alexander Woodside on an earlier draft of this essay.

70. Johnson, *Peasant Nationalism*; Selden, *Yenan Way*.

71. Huang, *Peasant Economy*, 179–84.

72. Takeshi Hamashita, "The Tribute Trade System and Modern Asia," *Memoirs of Toyo Bunko* 46 (1988): 7–25.

73. Nicholas Lardy, *Economic Growth and Distribution in China* (Cambridge: Cambridge University Press, 1978).

74. Vaclav Smil, *The Bad Earth: Environmental Degradation in China* (Armonk, NY: M. E. Sharpe, 1984); *China's Environmental Crisis: An Inquiry into the Limits of National Development* (Armonk, NY: M. E. Sharpe, 1993); Elizabeth C. Economy, *The River Runs Black: The Environmental Challenge to China's Future* (Ithaca, NY: Cornell University Press, 2011).

Chapter Nine

Deconstructing the Party-State

China was in many respects the classic example of peasant revolution, and the model for future revolutions in Vietnam, Cambodia, and even Cuba. In his brilliant and influential comparative study of revolution, Barrington Moore wrote that "In China . . . the peasant provided the dynamite that finally exploded the old order."[*] Given that the Communist Party and its armies were composed primarily of peasants, this was certainly true. But as Moore also observed, "the peasants needed outside leadership before they could turn actively against the existing social structure."[†] That leadership would come from the Communist Party, and a large body of Chinese and Western scholarship points to the crucial role of the party in mobilizing the peasantry for revolution. These two dimensions of the Chinese Revolution reflect a dilemma that has plagued all studies of the revolution: how exactly does one understand the relationship between the peasantry and the Communist Party?

Numerous detailed studies of the process whereby the Chinese Communists built their revolutionary bases reveal that there was no single template for rural mobilization.[‡] China was a country of such diversity that

---

[*] Barrington Moore Jr., *Social Origins of Dictatorship and Democracy: Lord and Peasant in the Making of the Modern World* (Boston: Beacon Press, 1967), 227.

[†] Ibid., 222.

[‡] In addition to the works cited in this and the former chapter, see especially David S. G. Goodman, *Social and Political Change in Revolutionary China: The Taihang Base Area in the War of Resistance to Japan, 1937–1945* (Lanham, MD: Rowman & Littlefield, 2000); Elizabeth J. Perry, *Anyuan: Mining China's Revolutionary Tradition* (Berkeley: University of California Press, 2012); Stephen C. Averill, *Revolution in the Highlands: China's Jinggangshan Base Area* (Lanham, MD: Rowman & Littlefield, 2006) and in Chinese, Huang Daoxuan, *Zhangli yu xianjie: Zhongyang suqu de geming, 1933–1934* [Power and limits: Revolution in the Central Soviet, 1933–1934] (Beijing: Shehui kexue chubanshe, 2011).

the process differed from place to place. For this reason, it was clear that only a series of detailed local case studies would be able to establish patterns that illuminated the peasant-party interaction. This chapter is one such case study that came from my year of archival and field work in Shaanxi, 1988–1989.

The focus of this chapter is Gulin county (固臨縣), the subject of a detailed 1941 survey by the party's Northwest Bureau. The county no longer exists: it was created to encompass Communist-controlled areas of neighboring Yichuan (宜川) and Ganquan (甘泉) during the War of Resistance to Japan. My field work in Gulin took place in June and July 1989, immediately after the massacre in Beijing. The Committee on Scholarly Communication with the People's Republic of China, which funded my research, had ordered all Americans to evacuate the country; but after the situation quieted down, I flew to Yan'an and claimed that I had not received the message. As it happened, the local authorities were quite happy to welcome any foreigner who had not fled the country, and this trip yielded unusual access to local archives and informants. This access proved invaluable to my research as in later years, especially after Xi Jinping (whose father had been active in the Shaanxi revolution) came to power, archival access in Shaanxi essentially came to an end.

Oral history and archival records made clear that the new Communist party-state was far larger, and more successfully penetrated rural society than any previous Chinese state. But this did not mean that the party acted as some unified historical agent. Party operatives differed at the village, county, regional, and, ultimately, national level and we needed to understand how those different levels cohered. It was clear, for example, that most rural cadres were recruited during the most radical periods of the revolution, from rural activists with minimal education. Only through persistent rectification campaigns was the rural party disciplined, with some staying at the village level, some advancing to the district (*qu* 區), and some to the county. Different skills and temperaments were required at each level, but the whole organization had to operate in disciplined response to higher party authorities. How this worked was not entirely clear, but I was convinced that we needed to get beyond the reified image of a unitary party, and to understand the party as an evolving social construct of substantial internal diversity.* In the end this essay suggests that an anthropological approach to the party is most likely to yield fruitful conclusions.

---

* To stress the fact that the CCP was not a unitary agent, this essay deliberately used the lower case to refer to the party.

DECONSTRUCTING THE PARTY-STATE*

It used to be a truism that twentieth-century China witnessed one of the great peasant revolutions of world history. The Chinese Communist Party built a popular base in the countryside, and eventually a massive army of peasant soldiers surrounded the cities and drove the urban-based Guomindang from the mainland. In the comparative literature, the Chinese Revolution was classified as a peasant revolution, and a number of important studies sought to explain the social origins of that phenomenon.[1]

More recent scholarship, reacting against the conflation of peasant revolution and Communist seizure of state power, has tended to dichotomize party and peasant. One of the finest, most detailed studies of the revolution, Chen Yung-fa's *Making Revolution*, repeatedly differentiates "the Party and peasants," stressing, for example, how they "differ sharply in values, aspirations, and visions."[2] To Steven Levine, "the Communists were an *urban nucleus* sojourning in the countryside" and the Chinese revolution was "the triumph of revolutionary organization."[3] A similar tendency is visible in the theoretical literature, where exchange theory conceives party and peasants engaging in an exchange of material benefits for political support.[4] In a somewhat different mode, Theda Skocpol stresses the critical and autonomous role of the Chinese Communist Party because, "uniquely in China [and unlike France and Russia], the peasantry could not make its own revolution."[5]

This renewed stress on the role of the party in revolutionary mobilization is an important corrective. No longer tenable is Chalmers Johnson's notion of "peasant mobilization . . . *initiated* by the Japanese invasion," a peasant mobilization of which "the Communists were the beneficiaries and not the main source."[6] Nor is it possible to accept Mark Selden's vision of a revolution wherein "the peasantry emerged from the [wartime] resistance at the center of the movement for China's revolutionary transformation."[7] These earlier works clearly gave too much autonomous agency to the Chinese peasantry. The new generation of scholarship, relying heavily on internal party documents, was able to demonstrate the indispensable role of the Chinese Communist Party (CCP) in mobilizing the peasantry for revolutionary action.

Yet this return to an organizational theory of revolution is itself fraught with problems.[8] Most importantly, any theory that dichotomizes party and peasant cannot account for the fact that the vast majority of party members in the 1930s and 1940s were peasants, and most rural cadres in the revolutionary base areas were peasants engaged in agriculture. In the rural localities where

---

* Originally published as "Deconstructing the Construction of the Party-State: Gulin County in the Shaan-Gan-Ning Border Region," *China Quarterly*, no. 140 (December 1994): 1052–79. Reprinted with permission.

the revolution was won, it is not at all clear where to draw the line between party and peasant. I suggest that this problem may be overcome by thinking less in terms of the party mobilizing the peasant and more about the *process* whereby a new structure of revolutionary power (the party-state) was constituted, by avoiding reifying "the Party" as though it were some monolithic entity, and instead analyzing the internal composition of the party-state and the complex relations among its different levels.

This chapter attempts to describe the linked historical processes of revolution and state-building in a single county in the Shaan-Gan-Ning Border Region. The county, Gulin, was chosen because, in the autumn of 1941, a team from the Northwest Bureau of the Chinese Communist Party conducted a survey of party work there. The Northwest Bureau's *Gulin diaocha* (固臨調查) serves as the central reference for this study. Materials from provincial and local archives in Shaanxi provide data on the period before and after 1941. Further information comes from field work in 1989 when peasant memories of the early revolutionary period were recorded. The 1941 survey, archival materials, and oral histories all represent new, previously inaccessible sources for the history of Shaan-Gan-Ning.[9] The study of a single county cannot resolve the larger theoretical questions of the Chinese Revolution, but this essay is an attempt to analyze the revolutionary process in a way that avoids reifying "the Party" and restores some sense of agency to peasants and local cadres.

THE SETTING: BACKGROUND AND ENVIRONMENT

Gulin lies in an area of rolling, loess hills and arid, treeless plateaus at the southeast corner of the wartime Shaan-Gan-Ning (SGN) Border Region. It was created by the border region government in 1937 out of portions of Yichuan and Ganquan counties, and much of it was contested with the Guomindang, which remained in control of Yichuan's county seat (see map 9.1). Like most of this part of northern Shaanxi, Gulin's economy was totally dominated by agriculture and sheep-herding. In 1949, the population of neighboring Yanchang was counted as 97.3 percent rural.[10] Even today, official commentators are frustrated by the inhabitants' conservative agrarianism.

> Yanchang has historically relied on agriculture for its livelihood and neglected industry and commerce. The methods of cultivation are careless; the people are too lazy to study new skills or seek skilled crafts. The dull peasants are content with their lot, sowing broadly and reaping a meagre harvest, trusting Heaven for a good crop. For generations these bad habits have been passed on until they have become a superstition (*mi* 迷), and nobody thinks them strange.[11]

Map 9.1. The Shaan-Gan-Ning Border Region.

The few shopkeepers and artisans in the area were almost exclusively immigrants from Henan and Shanxi.[12]

With scant rainfall and a growing season shortened by cold weather, northern Shaanxi has always been a sparsely populated peripheral zone. In the 1870s, the western and southern portions of the future border region were devastated by the Moslem rebellion, and they remained sparsely populated in the 1930s.[13] Population density was only fifteen people per square kilometer when the revolution came in 1935, less than one-tenth the figure for counties in the Wei River valley around Xi'an. Even this reflected a significant flow of immigrants in the preceding decade, as Yanchang's population had increased from 12,863 in 1923 to 21,863 in 1935.[14] Most came from the Suide-Mizhi area of Shaanxi and from Henan, Shandong, and Shanxi. Some were driven by famine (especially in 1928–1929), others were attracted to the profits that could be made growing opium in the isolated gullies and high plateaus of Shaanbei.[15] About two-thirds of the households grew the poppy in the early 1930s.[16] With land plentiful (note the large per capita holdings in table 9.1, below) and yields low, landlordism was rare. In Yanchang, landlords controlled only 2.34 percent of the farmland.[17] Draft animals were a more important resource, as donkeys were essential for carrying grain and straw from distant fields and water to hillside villages. Indeed, it was not unusual for poor peasants to give up their own land in order to sharecrop for a landlord—drawn by access to the landlords' seed, animals, and cave dwellings.[18]

In the pre-revolutionary period, all of northern Shaanxi (Shaanbei) was isolated from the Wei River center of provincial power, and Gulin was also far from Shaanbei's political and military center in Yulin. Even local power centers were distant: the Yichuan county seat almost 100 kilometers to the south and Ganquan about the same distance south-west. Rural administration was left in the hands of district (*qu*) headmen known as *gongzheng* (公正). The *gongzheng* commanded small militia detachments and collected taxes—from which they skimmed a comfortable profit. But all of Gulin had only a few of these militia detachments with about ten men each, and no regular army forces.[19]

Isolated and weakly defended, the area was plagued by bandits. Some were small groups of three to five nighttime outlaws who robbed with covered or painted faces—men disdained by law-abiding peasants as "poor people who don't want to work yet want to eat well."[20] More threatening were the "soldier-bandits" based in the Huanglong Mountains to the south.[21] The water in these thickly forested mountains contains chemicals that produce birth defects and chronic illness, especially affecting women and small children, so the area has long been void of regular settlements.[22] From the 1920s, however, large bands of defeated or deserting soldiers went into hiding there, sending out raiding parties to kidnap wealthy peasants or merchants for ransom. The largest bands numbered more than one thousand men, and many were later recruited into the Communist revolution.[23]

The most important peasant grievance was tax-collection. The regular land tax was fairly light, but the *gongzheng* and his militia would come as frequently as once a month to collect additional levies (*tanpai* 攤派). In 1934, the demands were too much for peasants around Linzhen, the largest town in the area. Several hundred assembled to drive off the assistant magistrate stationed there. In this case, the district functionaries and militia were secretly in league with the protesters—an alliance of local residents against the outside power of the magistrate. When the county sent its own militia to arrest the *gongzheng*, he was rescued by the local inhabitants and the county militia sent packing. The affair was finally settled with a 20 percent reduction of the taxes.[24] The net effect of this incident was to leave government power significantly weakened on the eve of the Communist incursion.

1935: "NAOHONG"

Early Communist mobilization in northern Shaanxi was characterized by a distinction between the movement in the northeast part of the province along the Wuding River, and in the area south and west of Yan'an. In the northeast, rural party organizations of peasants and young intellectuals were considerably more developed, while in the west and south the party relied heavily upon guerrilla bands recruited from former soldiers and bandits.[25] Indeed, in December 1932, when a party delegation found 765 party members in Shaanbei, it reported only eighty members in the five southern and western counties of Yan'an, Yanchang, Yanchuan, Bao'an, and Ansai. Furthermore, party superiors had lost contact with these eighty, many of whom were also under the cloud of poor class backgrounds.[26] Even local party historians admit that from late 1933 to the spring of 1935 party organization in the Yanchang-Gulin area was "in a state of paralysis."[27]

Revolution came to Gulin from the outside. In May 1935, Liu Zhidan, the guerrilla leader and hero of the Northern Shaanxi revolutionary movement, brought a large force from the west. After a series of successful battles with local militia, the guerrillas took Yanchang city—the first county seat to fall to the Communist forces. A number of soviet governments were established under a variety of names prior to the formal establishment of Gulin county in January 1937. Many of the soldier-bandits from the Huanglong mountains were recruited into the Red Army, including a contingent led by Hei Zhide (黑志德). Hei had received a middle school education in Xi'an, where his father had been a brigade commander in the forces of Northwest warlord Yang Hucheng. The father had resigned in disgust in 1928 and been arrested and killed in a tax protest in the following year. After this, Hei Zhide led the life of a soldier-bandit, sometimes in the mountains, sometimes brought into the local military establishment. In 1935, he re-emerged as chairman of the local revolutionary committee, and the Gulin county government was established in his family home.[28]

Once the Communist forces had established basic military control of the area, political cadres organized peasants into mass organizations of poor peasants and agricultural laborers, and Red Guard security forces (*chiweidui* 赤衛隊). From these organizations, activists were recruited into the party. Under a policy of open registration, virtually any willing poor or middle peasant was accepted.[29] Those who joined the party or Red Army were promised the best land in land reform.[30] Despite these enticements, there was no rush by masses of ordinary peasants to rally to the revolutionary cause. In fact, interviews with old revolutionaries suggest that the young men who joined up usually had special personal reasons for doing so: recent loss of a father, unhappiness in an adopted family, or difficulty in relations with a new stepmother.[31]

At this early stage of the revolutionary struggle, commitments to one side or the other were by no means firm. In the autumn of 1936, a leading county cadre forced the head of the local soviet to defect with a small guerrilla force of twelve men.[32] To deter others from thoughts of defecting, the Red Army was willing to take extreme measures. One veteran recalled an incident in which a group of thirteen planned to desert but were caught and taken to an execution ground. There the leader was bayonetted to death, another was beheaded and the remainder, presumably chastened by this example, were led off to a term of hard labor for the army.[33] Defections of this sort indicate that even among local party leaders, ideological commitment to the revolution was still quite weak. Indeed, the image of the party at this time had little to do with Marxism-Leninism. Above all, it represented secrecy, omniscience and power. Nobody knew who the party was; but the party knew all, and the party was *lihai* (厲害, tough). Peasants understood, for example, that they must say nothing of a Red Army unit which had passed through their village. If anyone spoke of a guerrilla unit's size or whereabouts, the party would know, and one could be killed. The danger was greatest if one spoke standing on the ground—for the party's underground organization would hear. One could, however, gain a measure of security by standing on a rock or stool while speaking.[34]

In autumn and winter 1935, the Communists began carrying out land reform. This was the most important social movement of the period remembered colloquially as the "Red Ruckus" (*naohong* 鬧紅). The first targets were the old regime's widely hated rural functionaries and tax-collectors, the *gongzheng*. In the Linzhen area, the last four incumbents in that post were all classified "gentry bosses" (*haoshen* 豪紳) and killed.[35] A common slogan of the day was "Haul out the gentry bosses and kill the landlords." The Red Guards executed these policies at the village level, and as one informant put it: "The Red Guards were very powerful. Whoever raised any nonsense was dragged out and shot."[36] If any local actors were empowered in this first stage of revolution, it was certainly these tough young men.

The process of determining class status was carried out in a distinctly ad hoc manner. There was hardly time to study and follow the complex land reform regulations, and some cadres found it easier to designate as a rich peasant anyone with an upper primary education (that is, more than three years of schooling).[37] Once class status had been determined, land, caves, and animals were redistributed from the wealthier to the poorer classes. Unfortunately, there was simply not enough landlord and rich peasant land to satisfy the land hunger of the poor.

Table 9.1. Landholding Patterns in Yanchang

	Before land reform mu	After land reform mu
Landlord area	12,635 (2%)	4,953 (1%)
per capita	226	88
Rich peasants	15,605 (3%)	8,904 (2%)
per capita	181	104
Middle peasants	353,202 (65%)	291,563 (54%)
per capita	119	98
Poor peasants	146,767 (27%)	216,599 (40%)
per capita	58	86
Agricultural laborers	11,771 (2%)	17,664 (3%)
per capita	52	78
Total	539,980	539,683

Source: *Yanchang xianzhi* (1988 draft) 1:1 (*tudi gaige*).

Table 9.1, showing landholdings before and after land reform, indicates what happened. The effects were obviously dramatic. The rough equality of per capita holdings indicates that this was a true leveling experience. But of roughly 75,000 *mu* gained by poor peasants and agricultural laborers, only about 14,000 came from landlords and rich peasants; the rest, despite all the regulations protecting the rights of middle peasants, came from that stratum, which lost over 60,000 *mu*.[38]

THE NEW RURAL SOCIETY

The land revolution ushered in a new society in Gulin. Families held roughly equal amounts of land and the debts of the poor were cancelled. Wealthier households fell to the status of middle peasants, and some of the poorer families rose to the same status, though their places at the bottom of the economic hierarchy were soon taken by new immigrants. With the redistribution of farm animals, most families now had access to draft animals and donkeys, but the redistribution of sheep produced herds too small to be economical. As a result, many peasants sold or slaughtered and ate their sheep, decreasing the total herd and the valuable fertilizer it produced.[39]

Immediately after the land revolution, taxes were abolished and the new regime was able to function almost entirely on confiscations from the wealthy. Once the war with Japan broke out, the National Government subsidy to the border region allowed taxes to be kept low, and these early years of freedom from the hated tax-collector were critical in gaining popular acceptance for the new regime. With the end of the Guomindang subsidy in 1940, however, taxes and the burdens of salt-transport, stretcher-bearing, corvée labor and unpaid labor on the fields of soldiers, workers, and full-time cadres began to weigh more heavily on the peasantry. Nevertheless, in 1941, the team from the Northwest Bureau was able to demonstrate that taxes were still lighter than before the revolution. Despite lower taxes and major efforts to increase production and bring new land under cultivation, peasant living standards fell. The reason was simple: they had lost the substantial income that they used to earn from now prohibited opium production.[40]

The social changes in rural society are more difficult to gauge. Though county and higher-level cadres expressed dismay at the slow pace of change, a fairly good example of gradual change can be found in gender relations and the position of women. The changes are significant because the Northwest Bureau repeatedly inquired into "women's work" and was generally dissatisfied with what it found: in the party, the few women who joined became inactive after they had children. In the schools, girls were a tiny minority or absent altogether. Literacy classes for women were formed and were often well subscribed—but officials were disappointed that few women were learning many characters. At key village meetings, there were often no women in attendance.[41]

Nevertheless, a few bold women were beginning to challenge the old order, and their example was felt. The new marriage law (in effect, a divorce law) allowed some women to sue for divorce, or actively to resist abuse at home.[42] That real changes were occurring is evident in the fact that some of the strongest complaints against the new regime came from men upset by the new divorce law: "If women are just lightly struck, or feelings are bad for a time, they immediately demand divorce and the government grants it. As a result, poor people can't get a wife even if their family line depends upon it. But the "old ladies" of the rich do not demand divorce."[43]

Wartime mobilization was also affecting gender relations in the villages of Shaanbei. There was a significant departure of young men to work in the new revolutionary government, serve in the army or evade conscription by fleeing to the nearby Guomindang zone. In one area, although two-thirds (twenty-two of thirty-three) of the new immigrants between 1934 and 1941 were male, 88 percent (thirty-five of forty) of the departures were male.[44] Figures for neighboring Yanchang reflect the effect of such departures on sex ratios in the county (see table 9.2).

With many young husbands drawn away for army and government service, women's lives were inevitably affected. Beginning in the later years of the war and increasing dramatically during the Civil War, women were mobilized in production campaigns—especially to knit socks and make shoes for the army. This introduced women to unprecedented roles outside the domestic sphere. Public involvement plus the absence of their husbands

Table 9.2. Sex Ratios in Yanchang

Year	male/female 100
1935	124.9
1938	135.4
1946	115.8
1948[a]	103.4

Source: Yanchang xianzhi (1988 draft), renkouzhi.

[a] 1948 figure from [Yanchang magistrate] Wang Zhiguo, "Wei cheng bennian nongyeshui buzhi zhengshou baogao" (Report on preparations for collection of this year's agricultural taxes) (December 1, 1948) (Yanchang archives).

also left them more vulnerable to (or perhaps, for some, more able to accept) the sexual advances of one newly empowered group in the countryside: the party cadres.

Cadres' abuse of power for sexual gratification is usually treated as a "feudal" habit left over from the old patriarchal society. It is notable, however, that in Shaanbei the practice was called "playing guerrilla" (*da youji* 打游擊), suggesting a more recent origin of such sexual transgressions. A report on a particularly bad district complained that one *xiang* (鄉) party secretary "does not attend to work, and 'plays guerrilla' with the people's women, as a result of which he makes a very negative impression on the people of the township." Efforts to discipline him in a district (*qu*) meeting were complicated by the fact that the district secretary was also "playing guerrilla." When a work team tried to mend the latter's ways he replied that if he could just once play guerrilla with that girl in the south village, he would die without any regrets. If his superiors were dissatisfied with his work, they could reassign him: "I really don't want to work in this damn district anyway."[45]

One should also note an unexpected social consequence of wartime mobilization: a decline in the number of literate villagers. In one hamlet with a rather good record on education (as it had had a small private school [*sishu* 私塾] since the late Qing), there were seventeen literate peasants in thirty-three households in 1934, but only five remained in 1941. The reason was simple: the others had been recruited to join the revolution.[46] Facts like this suggest that the greatest social changes in Shaanbei derived from the construction of the new party-state and the implications it had for rural life. Women gained some degree of leverage against oppressive family situations, but they were also more vulnerable to sexual advances from cadres and labor demands from the party-state. Families had sons drawn away for state service (to become *gongjia ren* 公家人) or had members mobilized locally for public purposes.

THE NEW REGIME

The growth of the party-state structure in Shaan-Gan-Ning represented a fundamental change for the region. In the prewar border region territory, there were 20,000 people "divorced from production." This number increased six-fold to a maximum of 130,000 in civil, military, and educational institutions during the war.[47] Much of this increase came from the influx of personnel associated with the Red Army and the Party Center in Yan'an, and the substantial number of intellectuals and students who trekked up to the "revolutionary holy land." But this totaled only about 30,000 people,[48] and far more important for the peasant population was the enormous increase of rural cadres in the much denser Communist system of local control. In two villages surveyed by the Northwest Bureau, where the old regime had one *lianbao* (聯保) head, one *gongzheng* and three militia members, the new regime had fifty-three people working in cadre and mass organization positions—a tenfold increase of the state apparatus.[49] A 1941 report listed 268 cadres in the county, a further major increase over the old regime.[50]

The key innovations of the new system were a larger party and state office at the district (*qu*) level, and the addition of a township (*xiang*) level of administration between district and village. The critical *xiang* level allowed a much more efficient penetration of rural society. But the new party-state by no means felt secure in its rural base, and in the early years of the border region it fought hard to preserve its monopoly of power in the countryside. The fact that most of Gulin was carved out of Yichuan county meant that along the edge of the border region there was regular competition with Yichuan's Guomindang magistrates trying to assert the authority of their rural administration or re-establish a *baojia* (保甲) system.[51] As map 9.1 shows, between 1938 and 1940, the border region abandoned a number of isolated (and probably disease-threatened) villages in Yichuan.

The party's response to competing political forces was to prevent rivals from spreading their complaints (*guaihua* 怪話)—the standard term for dissident opinion. People who complained publicly were "disciplined," usually through "anti-traitor" work. In 1939, 7,212 individuals were registered in 1,012 anti-traitor groups in Gulin, and these became a valuable resource for mobilizing pressure against anti-party voices.[52] Much of this organization probably existed largely on paper, and there is no evidence that anti-traitor activity was carried out with the same violence employed during the 1935 land reform. However, an essential dynamic of village politics was that having once employed extreme violence against political opponents, it was not necessary to repeat the executions to achieve the same effect. People knew what this new revolutionary party was capable of. Once a significant network was established to carry out anti-traitor work (a network which certainly included many of the same youths who formed the earlier Red Guards), few peasants were likely to press their luck just to make a political point.

It proved easier, however, to prohibit organized political opposition than to transform the rural branches of the new party-state into obedient agents of higher authority. Most rural cadres had been recruited in great haste in 1935. Largely illiterate or barely literate, they had no knowledge of Marxist theory and no experience with the organizational discipline of a Leninist party. They were attracted by the excitement of guerrilla life, or the promise of land and relief from oppressive tax-collection, and their appreciation of the larger goals of the Communist Party was questionable at best. It comes as no surprise that a major focus of higher-level reports from this early period was the effort to discipline the rural party.

An instructive example of higher authorities' problems was the influence within the party of the Gelaohui (哥老會, Elder Brothers Society)—a secret society with considerable influence in many parts of Northern Shaanxi.[53] In 1936, Mao Zedong made a famous appeal for a united front with the Gelaohui in the national struggle against Japan.[54] But three years later, party authorities were greatly troubled by the continuing influence of the Gelaohui *within* rural party organizations. The problem was particularly severe in nearby Yanchuan where in one district there were 115 members of the Gelaohui, 64 of whom were also party members, 35 having joined the Gelaohui *after* joining the party. In one pair of villages all but two of the 34 party members were also in the Gelaohui, and under the influence of a local bandit leader. Two other township heads were apparently not involved with the Gelaohui, but still, the report said, they "completely rely on the methods of the old society and use every method to resist higher authority."[55] The party had obviously succeeded in recruiting a substantial base in the countryside, but there was no guaranteeing that its new recruits would prove completely loyal and obedient to the Party Center.

The Northwest Bureau's *Gulin Survey* revealed the inability of the party to discipline its own members. There were several members who gambled or smoked opium and failed to attend meetings—but were still kept in the party. For one branch, the team noted four criteria for a good party member: attendance at meetings, payment of dues, model behavior in mobilization and fairness in work. These were fairly minimal expectations, but one member failed on all four counts and the branch still refused to expel him. Challenged to discipline its members, the branch's response was "There's no way.... You cannot just openly punish party members."[56] While higher party authorities felt that retaining such members damaged the party's reputation, local cadres believed that expelling the miscreants would produce an even more damaging loss of face in the community.

In general, higher party authorities were concerned about two types of problem. One was improper personal behavior: sexual peccadillos, opium-smoking, gambling, and so on. The fact that few were seriously disciplined for adultery or opium problems suggests that on these matters, superiors were willing to be tolerant. Contemporary documents reveal a much greater concern for organizational virtues. They wanted people who could get the job done. One rural cadre nicely reflected the new priorities of the instrumental regime: "In the past, if you had no face [*mianzi* 面子], you couldn't handle affairs. Now in the border region, if you just have some ability [*benshi* 本事] you can do things."[57]

But party authorities were not finding it easy to get rural cadres to carry out the myriad tasks put before them: collecting grain taxes, selling public bonds, organizing salt transport and stretcher-bearers, fulfilling conscription quotas, organizing cultivation of the fields of army members, workers and full-time cadres, enrolling the young in school, reclaiming new land, increasing irrigated acreage, reforesting hillsides, raising more sheep and draught animals, promoting cotton cultivation, prohibiting opium cultivation and consumption, enforcing the new marriage law, and so forth.[58] One possible cadre response to these multiple demands was to file false reports and try to evade detection.[59] Far more common was the practice of ignoring any directive that did not include a clear quota and a deadline. In the words of one rural cadre, "If we cannot do something, we just do not report. That's the way work is in the countryside. You don't dare be short at all in grain and public bonds. But these other things are just official routines. The people up above know perfectly well that they can't be carried out."[60] Documents in the archives confirm these practices. While grain targets were taken seriously and fulfilled, the same was not true of plans to increase animal husbandry, irrigated acreage or cotton cultivation.[61]

Within the party, ordinary members accepted the practice of looking to higher levels for direction. As one local cadre put it, "a party member's work is 'whatever is assigned from above.'"[62] Nevertheless, party meetings reflected a clear understanding of higher levels' priorities: "At these two meetings we discussed how party members should do propaganda work to explain [grain and salt delivery burdens], collect the opinions of the masses, not trail behind the masses, etc., etc. But in fact, we did little of that. If you can meet your quotas, nobody will review those aspects of your work."[63]

In general, higher authorities had two strategies for disciplining lower levels of the party-state apparatus. The first was direct oversight. If a meeting was to accomplish anything, a representative from some higher level of the party would have to preside.[64] This was the short-term solution, and its equivalent for major movements was a work team sent from above. But for a longer-term solution, the party's clear hope lay with the process of political study. The belief was that political study would produce a higher level of political consciousness and that in turn would enhance political commitment.

Again and again, the Northwest Bureau's *Gulin Survey* expressed frustration with the level of political education among rural party cadres. In 1941, one of the key documents for study was the charter of the border region, but few rural (or even county!) cadres could remember its basic principles.[65] The fundamental idea of the United Front was still not grasped. At one meeting, when people were asked how Guomindang die-hards should be handled, they all immediately responded "kill them!"—only to be told that the correct answer was "educate them."[66] It is clear from the survey's detailed accounts of study meetings that most local cadres saw little purpose in this sort of study. They arrived late for the meetings, slept, complained of headaches, left early, and generally treated political study as a most unwelcome imposition. But for higher levels, such study was crucial if the party was to act as a unified Leninist machine.

RECTIFICATION

In order to make political study work in local units, it was necessary to raise the stakes. In essence, the higher party authorities decided that disciplining lower levels of party and government administration required the same methods that local cadres had used to silence dissent in the general population. It was necessary to politicize the struggle into a campaign against "traitors," and this was the primary focus of Rectification once it spread beyond Yan'an in 1943–1944.

I have unfortunately been unable to locate any archival sources on the Rectification Movement in Gulin. However, sources on the campaign elsewhere in the SGN Border Region make the pattern reasonably clear. In the initial Yan'an struggles in 1942–1943, criticism of the "subjectivism" and "dogmatism" of the Internationalist group under Wang Ming was quickly superseded by the attack on Wang Shiwei and a general criticism of the "liberal" failings of bourgeois intellectuals. Then, in July 1943, Kang Sheng launched a campaign to "save backsliders" (*qiangjiu shizuzhe* 搶救失足者) which soon developed into a campaign to identify "traitors" throughout the border region. The campaign unfolded in the context of a general mobilization to defend the border region against a Guomindang attack which appeared imminent when, in June and July, Nationalist troops were moved from the Yellow River front to the southern border of SGN. In this tense atmosphere, "secret agents" (*tewu* 特務) were discovered throughout the border region, spreading rumors, corrupting women and youths, and organizing assassination teams to ambush cadres on mountain trails.[67]

In most documented cases, the leading targets of this campaign were young intellectual cadres from outside the border region, who were the most likely to have had some contact with "enemy" (Guomindang) agents before coming to Yan'an. But the campaign had the undeniable effect of turning any grumbling against the party, the border region government or one's superiors, or the spreading of "rumors" about unpopular border region policies into a serious political crime. The logic was simple: since the Japanese and Guomindang also spread stories critical of the border region, any grumbling or rumor-mongering could be evidence that one was working for the enemy. In addition, what had previously been seen as purely personal failings were widely publicized as political crimes, as the Guomindang was said to use money and women to lure weak-willed cadres into their schemes.[68]

Evidence from several localities indicates that this campaign was taken up with great energy in counties throughout the border region in 1943–1944.[69] Cadres were subjected to unprecedented scrutiny, forced to write complete autobiographies and self-examinations for their dossiers, and sometimes subjected to pressure both from activist-mobilized masses below and higher-level work teams above. Intense pressure brought a wave of false confessions, usually followed by lenient forgiveness. But the net effect in the localities was to raise the level of cadre activism and political consciousness, to stress the importance of resolute "party spirit" (*dangxing* 黨性), and once again to silence any opposition to the new party-state.[70]

PASSING THE TEST

On March 13, 1947, after the wartime United Front gave way to Civil War, the Guomindang launched a major attack against the SGN Border Region. A large force set out from Yichuan and passed through Linzhen on its way north and west to Yan'an. Though the main army pressed on to attack Yan'an and the Communist forces under Peng Dehuai, Linzhen and the main lines of communication in Gulin remained under the loose control of the Guomindang. Few peasants went over to the enemy: only 169 out of 3,898 people in one district of the Linzhen area. Following orders prepared in November 1946, grain was hidden in dispersed locations, wells filled, grindstones and cooking utensils buried, and the people with their movable property fled to the hills. There they survived for a full year on grain stored from the good 1946 harvest.[71]

All accounts agree that in the areas still under Communist control, the burdens on the peasantry were heavier than ever. Yanchang's public grain quota in December 1946 was 4,710 *dan* (石). Then in March 1947, the county was required to furnish 12,351 *dan* in public grain plus an additional 11,000 *dan* for the army—a total of 23,351 or roughly five times the previous year's quota.[72] Grain requisitions were based not just on the year's harvest, but on stored grain—and those with any surplus usually lost it all. Some who could not pay had family members tied up and taken away as hostages until they sold tools or other belongings to ransom them back.[73]

Even worse were the demands on peasant labor and animals for transport and stretcher-bearing teams. In 1946, the regime required 1,311 animals (usually donkeys) from Yanchang. In 1947, the number rose to 10,376 for a total of 206,490 days. No stretcher-bearers had been required in 1946, but 16,989 were mobilized in 1947 for a total of 239,283 days (an average of two weeks per man).[74] In one district, it was calculated that the total cost in grain and lost work came to 45 percent of the harvest.[75]

Conscription demands were extraordinarily heavy, as most able-bodied men were called to duty. At the end of the War of Resistance, this same district had fifty-two men in the eighteen to thirty-five age bracket. Of these, thirty were conscripted into the army and nine into government work, a drain of 75 percent of the young adult males. It was estimated that in Gulin county 60 percent of the households had at least one member in the army or working for the government.[76] Another village reported its difficulty in filling a conscription quota of nine men. In the end, it could supply only seven, one of whom was under age, one over age, and one wounded earlier in 1947 and still slightly crippled.[77]

Women's labor was mobilized to make shoes and socks for the army, and here too the demands were intense. One set of figures from Yanchang reports 12,000 pairs of shoes or socks in 1947, 845,022 in 1948 and a scarcely believable (from a population of about 10,000 women) 2,535,022 in 1949.[78] In the winter of 1947, the pressure was so heavy that women were given a quota and materials one day and required to deliver the next. Many worked all night to fill their quota—others simply surrendered their husbands' shoes.[79]

The point here is not just to stress the extraordinary burdens borne by the peasants of Shaanbei. It is to demonstrate the remarkable efficacy of the party-state in mobilizing the population to do battle against a militarily superior foe. Quite clearly, by 1947, the new regime had fashioned a system that could effectively transmit and execute orders right down to the village level—even orders that villagers must have found extraordinarily harsh and onerous.[80]

Even more remarkable was the party's success in the land registration movement following the expulsion of the Guomindang. The purpose of the movement was to establish an accurate survey of cultivated land for tax purposes. Obviously, the government's interest was in uncovering previously unreported or under-reported land, which in sparsely populated zones could be 2.5 times the reported area.[81] Not surprisingly, *xiang* cadres "played the leading role in concealing land." But by 1949, party work teams were able to get others to inform on those who concealed land, or to persuade cadres in intense private meetings to take the lead in correctly reporting their land for the public good.[82] Thus less than fifteen years after these cadres had joined the revolution for the personal benefits of land and lower taxes, they found themselves part of an organization that could force them to act in ways that were clearly contrary to their own and their communities' immediate economic interest.

In the critical Civil War battles of 1947–1948, the Communists proved their political superiority over the Guomindang. On the eve of the founding of the PRC, the CCP demonstrated the enormous strides it had made in disciplining its organization. An examination of the local apparatus of the new party-state—its recruitment and composition, its strengths and weaknesses—will help to explain how it did this.

DECONSTRUCTING THE PARTY

In the wake of their victories in northern Shaanxi and on the eve of national triumph in the Civil War, the Communists prepared the groundwork for the next stage of state-building and socialist construction. In Shaanbei (and other base areas), these preparations included a party rectification movement, and data were collected on all cadres. In Yanchang (which after 1948 included most of wartime Gulin), the local archives contain a large number of cadre registration forms from this period. They provide an unusually detailed look at the party-state apparatus at the local level.[83]

In some respects, the data on these forms indicate a significant uniformity. Most notably, every one of the surveyed cadres was male: the local party-state was definitely a male preserve. At all levels of the local hierarchy, men in the thirty-one to forty age bracket were the largest group, representing about 40 percent of the total. However, younger people were prominent in two roles: *qu* cadres, where 53 percent were thirty and younger; and *xiang* aides (*wenshu* 文書) where 69 percent were thirty and younger. The leading village cadres (*xiangzhang* and *xiang* party secretaries) were generally older: 86 percent over thirty, and 38 percent over forty. At the county level, only 25 percent were over forty, and at the *qu* level, only 8 percent.

Tables 9.3 and 9.4 tabulate the dates when cadres joined the party, and when they began working for the revolution—either in the army or in administrative positions. What is most striking about these figures is the overwhelming predominance of people who joined at the first stage of the "Red Ruckus" in 1934–1936.[84] Some 44 percent of the party members joined

Deconstructing the Party-State 277

Table 9.3. Yanchang Cadres: Year Cadres Joined the CCP

	Xiang wenshu	Xiang heads & secretaries	Qu cadres	County cadres	Total	Percentage
1927	–	1	–	1	2	
1928	–	–	–	–	–	
1929	–	–	–	–	–	
1930	–	–	–	–	–	
1931	–	–	–	–	–	46
1932	–	1	–	–	1	
1933	–	–	–	–	–	
1934	–	–	–	2	2	
1935	1	29	12	23	65	44
1936	–	5	–	4	9	
1937	1	5	2	4	12	
1938	–	3	2	1	6	
1939	–	1	–	–	1	
1940	2	1	2	–	5	21
1941	–	1	1	1	3	
1942	–	1	1	4	6	
1943	1	–	–	3	4	
1944	–	–	–	–	–	
1945	3	4	1	1	9	
1946	–	2	–	4	6	
1947	1	4	2	2	9	20
1948	10	4	6	6	26	
1949	2	2	1	–	5	33
1950	–	1	–	1	2	
Totals	21	65	30	57	173	

Source: "Ganbu dengji biao" from Yanchang archives: YC x-x-43-1, YC x-x-43-2, YC x-x-43-4 (all November 23, 1948); YC x-x-60-2 (July 5, 1949); YC x-x-60-3 (January 1951); YC x-x-60-5 (April 24, 1949); YC x-x-60-6 (December 16, 1949); YC x-x-60-8 (n.d).

in those three years, and 41 percent began work then. If the younger group of township aides (*xiang wenshu*) is excluded, the percentage of party members from these years rises to fully 50 percent; and 46 percent began work in 1934–1936. The other major period of party recruitment was during the Civil War in 1947–1948, accounting for 20 percent of the party members, especially a substantial group of younger township aides. The years 1947 to 1949 also saw a significant expansion of the rural apparatus (especially with the addition of township aides), and 26 percent began working for the revolution in these years.

In part, these patterns represent the party's eagerness to expand its mass base rapidly in times of intense "class struggle." As shown above, the party took virtually any poor or middle peasant willing to join in 1935–1936, then became somewhat more selective during the war years. The Civil War period was another time of major party-building activity. Nevertheless, the wartime decline in recruitment was not entirely the product of the party's self-restraint. It also resulted from the fact that remarkably few people were willing to join, especially after the burdens of the new regime increased in the early 1940s. The Northwest Bureau survey reported that one Gulin district had planned

Table 9.4. Yanchang Cadres: Year Cadres Joined the Revolution[a]

	Xiang wenshu	Xiang heads & secretaries	Qu cadres	County cadres	Total	Percentage
1927	–	–	–	–	–	
1928	–	–	–	–	–	
1929	–	–	–	–	–	
1930	–	–	–	–	–	
1931	–	–	–	–	–	
1932	–	–	–	–	–	
1933	–	–	–	–	–	
1934	–	–	–	1	1	
1935	2	15	10	38	65	41
1936	–	3	2	8	13	
1937	1	7	1	1	10	
1938	–	2	1	4	7	
1939	–	1	1	2	4	
1940	1	–	2	3	6	25
1941	–	1	–	1	2	
1942	–	1	–	–	1	
1943	1	3	1	4	9	
1944	1	3	2	3	9	
1945	1	3	–	3	7	
1946	1	1	6	2	10	
1947	3	6	5	1	15	35
1948	5	8	3	–	16	
1949	12	2	4	1	19	
1950	–	1	–	–	1	
Totals	28	57	38	72	195	

Source: Same as table 9.3.

a On the forms, this is the date of *ruwu*: "joined the ranks." This term is not defined, but it clearly means more than "joined the army," the usual use of this term. In filing out the form, some glossed the entry as "began work." It evidently refers to the year one joined the army or began work as a cadre. The larger total than table 9.3 reflects the presence of some cadres who had not joined the party.

to recruit twenty new members in a two-month period in 1941, but only one signed up.[85]

The party was most successful in recruiting new cadres in periods of intense (and violent) political struggle and leftist activism. It made it fairly easy to join in these times, and it targeted young male village activists. Some 65 percent of the sample were twenty-five or younger when they joined the revolution, and 81 percent were thirty or younger.[86] This meant that local party and state organizations were dominated by young men recruited during the more leftist stages of the revolution—and more comfortable with the methods employed in these periods.[87] It also meant that local cadres were often implicated in the variety of violent acts carried out in these radical stages, and thus particularly dedicated to ensuring that their class enemies not be allowed to make a comeback. The extraordinary mobilization of personnel and resources in the Civil War period required a dedicated rural party apparatus—and these men were certainly determined to see the revolutionary regime survive.

Table 9.4 on the year in which cadres joined the revolution suggests another pattern: rewards to seniority, and to early commitment to the revolution. At the *xiang* level, 32 percent of the *xiang* heads and secretaries began work in 1934–1936, and an identical percentage at the *qu* level. But at the county level, fully 65 percent of the cadres began work during this period. County work was dominated by cadres from the land revolution period, and it was very difficult for someone who joined the revolution later to rise to the county level.

There was another way in which county cadres differed from rural cadres at both the district and township levels. While one might have expected the higher levels of literacy required for work at the county level to have disadvantaged those from the poorer classes, in fact the opposite was the case. Poor peasants and workers represent 55 percent of county cadres, against 29 percent at the *qu* and 35 percent at the *xiang* level. The rural organization depended much more heavily on the middle peasant stratum, which represented 61 percent of *xiang* cadres and 71 percent at the *qu* level. Thus the real power in rural organization—the county apparatus which sent the work teams and directed the work of the districts and villages—was dominated by cadres of "good" class background recruited during the more leftist phases of the revolution. If these Yanchang data are typical, on the eve of the PRC, the party organization in the old base areas had a "class structure" in which upper classes and urban intellectuals dominated the central and provincial levels, poor peasants predominated in the county apparatus, and middle peasants in the countryside.

Table 9.5. Yanchang Cadres: Class Background

	Xiang wenshu	Xiang heads & secretaries	Qu cadres	County cadres
Landlord	–	–	–	1 (1%)
Rich peasant	–	1 (1%)	–	1 (1%)
New rich peasant	2 (7%)	1 (1%)	–	–
Middle peasant	20 (67%)	45 (59%)	27 (71%)	30 (42%)
Poor peasant	8 (27%)	28 (37%)	11 (29%)	37 (51%)
Agricultural laborer	–	1 (1%)	–	–
Worker	–	–	–	3 (4%)
Totals	30	76	38	72

Source: Same as table 9.3.

The middle peasant domination of rural administration is not altogether surprising. These posts consumed much time away from the fields, and it was not unusual for peasants with some economic cushion to take them up. The surprising finding is the poor peasant strength at the county level. Most similar data on the class background of base area personnel are on the elected assemblies, where "enlightened gentry" were often encouraged to run at the county level. In these assemblies, Chen Yung-fa has argued that "the higher the administrative level, the greater the percentage of landlords and rich peasants."[88] But these assemblies may not reflect the class distribution in the more important party and government posts. It may also be that during the wartime United Front, county cadres of "bad" class background were more acceptable than during the Civil War. Archival evidence suggests that in a secure base area like SGN, county governments were often more radical than their base area superiors,[89] and this may reflect both the class background and the land-revolution recruitment of county cadres.

Even more intriguing than the background of local cadres is the information in these forms on "strengths" and "weaknesses" (*youdian* 優點 and *quedian* 缺點) of each cadre—a series of conventional phrases describing the individual's political virtues and shortcomings. The following is an example of a particularly full entry on one district head (*quzhang*):

> *Strengths:* Activist in work. Goes down to the countryside and returns on schedule. Can take responsibility. When a directive or order comes, he can make arrangements right away. When reporting to higher levels, can carefully prepare materials. Unites (*tuanjie* 團結), amiable (*heqi* 和氣). Good reputation (*weixin hao* 威信好). Relatively good at study. *Weaknesses:* Pays too much attention to his family problems. Does not want to leave this area. Doesn't watch his tongue. Likes to complain—but hasn't done so in [his own] 4th district. Concerned about face. Rarely criticizes others (*ti yijian* 提意見).[90]

Table 9.6. Yanchang Cadres: Strength and Weaknesses

Xiang wenshu		Xiang heads & secretaries		Qu cadres		County cadres	
Strengths							
activist	15	activist	36	tuanjie	19	activist[a]	21
good study	8	experienced	22	chiku	13	responsible	20
tuanjie	7	chiku	15	wenhe	10	Strong organization/ party sense	13
chiku	7	tuanjie	13	experienced	8	tuanjie	10
laoshi	4	follows orders/ completes tasks	11	good study	8	chiku	10
not afraid to offend	4	good thinking	9	responsible	6	progressive thinking	9
careful	3	careful	8	activist	6	experienced	7
experienced	3	good study	7	considers problems	4	careful	6
good character	3	capable	7	not afraid of mafan	4	good study	6
		not afraid to offend	5			wenhe	6
		laoshi	5			special expertise	5
		fair (gongdao)					
Weaknesses							
no independence	11	afraid of study	27	afraid of study	19	afraid of study	18
jiating guannian	10	lacks experience	21	jiating guannian	11	no independence	8
lacks experience	9	jiating guannian	17	thinking not progressive	9	violent temper	5
afraid of study	8	afraid to offend	10	lacks experience	7	doesn't offer opinions	5
not careful	7	thinking not progressive	9	violated rules	7	not careful	5
thinking not progressive	4	no effort to improve	8	no independence	5	strong willed	4
timid	4	strong willed	8			lacks experience	4
lazy	3	sloppy work	7				
procrastinates	3						
not responsible	3						
commandist	3						

Source: Same as table 9.3.

[a] Among county cadres, the usual phrase was "actively responsible" (jiji fuze). Where this combination occurs, I have counted it as both "activist" and "responsible," but this no doubt inflates the importance of "activism" at the country level—at least as the term is usually understood.

Table 9.6 sets out the most frequently mentioned strengths and weaknesses for *xiang* aides (*wenshu*), *xiang* heads and secretaries, district (*qu*) cadres and county cadres. There are real problems in interpreting these data and the "texts" from which they derive. To what extent do these forms accurately reflect the characteristics of rural cadres? To what extent do they merely reflect the values and biases of the higher-level cadres who filled out the forms? Were most rural cadres really "afraid of study" (*pa xuexi* 怕學習)? Or did they just pay less attention to party documents and study materials than the county cadres wished? Did *xiang* cadres really lack experience? Or was this just a politically harmless "weakness" that sympathetic superiors could use to fill the blank on the form? All of these are serious problems that should not be belittled. Nevertheless, the considerable variation in the particular strengths and weaknesses of the cadres suggests that these forms did reflect some real differences among the individuals, and are thus a useful indicator of the characteristics of rural cadres. Even if the forms are regarded as largely reflecting higher authorities' vision of what the party should represent, these same authorities were appointing lower-level cadres, and so the end result should tend to be a local party-state with the characteristics described.

The lists of strengths and weaknesses contain a number of common elements that appear at all levels of the apparatus. Common strengths were the ability to endure difficulties without complaint—to *chiku* (吃苦)—and the ability to get along with others—to *tuanjie,* a category which was often phrased "to get along with other *cadres.*" The most common weakness was in political study, followed (among rural cadres) by an excessive concern for one's family: "*jiating guannian nonghou*" (家庭觀念濃厚) or ". . . *zhong*" (. . . 重). These reflected important notions of what made a good cadre: someone who was willing to suffer on behalf of the revolution, willing to study the party orthodoxy and overcome "backward" thinking, one who would not be distracted from party tasks by concern over whether his family had enough labor to cultivate its fields.

The most interesting findings from these forms are the differences in the strengths and weaknesses observed at *xiang*, district and county levels. At the *xiang* level, the party wanted activists. It was the *xiang* cadres who had to deal directly with peasants. Here they needed energy and commitment. It was important that these cadres were not afraid of offending others (*bu pa reren* 不怕熱人), and the party could tolerate the often associated weakness of being strong-willed (*gexing qiang* 個性強) or commandist. What mattered was that they followed orders and got the job done.

At the district level, activism was much less common. Here the key virtue was the ability to get along with others (*tuanjie*)—which, as already noted, usually meant the ability to get along with other *cadres.* These cadres were team players with a keener sense of the organization and the collective. One does not find cadres criticized for being "strong-willed." On the contrary, they were often praised for being "mildmannered" (*wenhe* 溫和)—a virtue that did not exist at the *xiang* level.

At the county level, organizational concerns dominate. The most common strength was "actively responsible" (*jiji fuze* 積極負責), which I have coded under both activist and responsible, but it is clear that administrative responsibility was the chief concern. These are followed by strong organizational or party sense (*zuzhi guannian* 組織觀念 or *dangxing*) and the ability to unite with other cadres. Conversely, at the county level, an excessive concern for one's family was not tolerated. Finally, only at the county level are there comments on cadres' specific functional expertise (legal, economic, educational).

If there are surprises at the county level, the greatest is the rather frequent reference to violent temper and to strong-willed cadres. These failings do not appear at all at the *qu* level. In normal circumstances, county cadres were the supreme local authorities, only irregularly supervised by higher levels. They could afford to resort to coercive measures, and more forceful and arbitrary work styles had a place in the county apparatus. In addition, as noted above, county cadres were most likely to be poor peasants recruited during the land revolution. Perhaps here especially one was likely to find those "old cadres" described by Gao Gang "who subjectively think themselves loyal to the revolution, but who lack the mass viewpoint and do not pay attention to workstyle, who lack the spirit of seeking truth from facts and thus frequently adopt the simple methods of coercive command."[91]

TOWARDS AN ANTHROPOLOGY OF "THE PARTY"

These glimpses of the rural party-state in one small area of northern Shaanxi suggest that there was a tremendous degree of human diversity within the various levels of the Chinese Communist Party. The continuing problems that the new party-state had in disciplining its rural apparatus remind us that party members were more than just cogs in the great party machine. Indeed, I would suggest that many of the metaphors used to describe Communist parties—"machine," "apparatus," "organizational weapon"—suggest an inappropriately mechanistic model of how the Chinese Communist Party operated.

It is necessary to get beyond interpretations that see "the Party" acting as a single and unified agent in the historical process. Access to archives and party history publications have made available a tremendous wealth of internal party documents and reports. These new materials have permitted the sort of research presented in this study, but they have the danger of seducing researchers to accept the party's (especially higher party authorities') view of itself as a disciplined, unified Leninist party involved in the task of making revolution. By focusing on what the party was doing and trying to do, internal party documents can lead to exaggeration of its role. There is a risk of reifying it when (often for simple stylistic convenience) "the Party" is spoken of as doing one thing or another.

Recent work on the origins of the Chinese Communist Party by Hans van de Ven and Arif Dirlik has demonstrated that it did not come into being full-blown with the First Congress in 1921.[92] There was a gradual process of small local cells of friends being turned into a national organization of comrades. Patterns of association among intellectuals, schoolmates and fellow provincials were slowly transformed through experience and struggle into new habits and a new discourse appropriate to a Leninist Party. According to van de Ven, a true Communist Party worthy of the name did not come into being until 1927.

Turning from the founding of the Chinese Communist Party to consideration of the collapse of Communist parties in the former Soviet Union and Eastern Europe, I would suggest that at the end of their historical paths as well, Communist parties are anything but monolithic machines. They are composed of a variety of historical actors, most of whom have important identities affecting their behavior beside their roles as party members. These people are not all mindless apparatchiks in a Communist machine. They are also members of society, with families and social connections, with personal lives and aspirations, with different social backgrounds and educational training, with national and perhaps ethnic or regional identities.

If Communist parties inter-penetrate with society at the beginning and end of their histories, the same is true in the middle as well. The Gulin party-state may have been striving for autonomy from society—but it was an impossible struggle. It was impossible in part because rural cadres in particular were deeply enmeshed in a variety of local networks from which they could never be completely separated. And, perhaps even more importantly, the relationship between different levels of the party was not and could not be one of simple mechanical obedience to the Party Center. As Lin Boqu, chairman of the SGN Border Region, said in 1945, "the border region government does not understand conditions at lower levels; and there are things that the county does not understand about the districts and townships."[93] The party, at all its levels, was an historical product, a cultural construction, an association of human beings. Its successes were not just the successes of organization and discipline, they were also those of a complex interaction among village activists, district facilitators, county enforcers and central and regional strategists.

Out of that interaction, new social roles were constructed. The rural cadres were neither asocial apparatchiks nor a revived Red gentry. The great majority joined the party as teenagers or in their early twenties, young men drawn into the heat of revolution at its most radical phases. Gradually, as their own often violent actions tied their interests and identities ever more closely to the new regime, they were themselves transformed into leaders "not afraid to offend" their fellow villagers and able to complete the tasks assigned by their party-state superiors. Those who stayed at the lowest level as *xiang* cadres tended to be older, often with family responsibilities and burdens, but able to work alone and not afraid to use their new authority. Another younger group, more willing and able to leave their villages, with social skills and organizational abilities more appropriate to group work, rose to the district or county level. The massive expansion of the party-state provided major opportunities for upward mobility for those willing to cast their lot with the revolutionary regime.

The county cadres were the critical middlemen between the Party Center and the villages. Usually locally recruited, they had social ties and natural affiliations with the local society, political ties and organizational affiliations with the Center. Through political study and rectification campaigns, the central party-state sought to bind them to its agenda. Slowly, they mastered the public rituals of endless meetings and political campaigns, and the confidential mysteries of inner-party directives and bureaucratic routines.

Such was the process of revolutionary state-building. To understand the construction of the party-state, it must be deconstructed, not reified. An anthropology of the Chinese party-state is required—an historical anthropology which can chart the recruitment and socialization of its agents, the invention and propagation of its rituals, the development and implementation of its methods of social co-optation and patterns of political domination.

NOTES

1. Most notably, Barrington Moore, *Social Origins of Dictatorship and Democracy: Lord and Peasant in the Making of the Modern World* (Boston: Beacon Press, 1966), and Eric Wolf, *Peasant Wars of the Twentieth Century* (New York: Harper & Row, 1969).

2. Yung-fa Chen, *Making Revolution: The Communist Revolution in Eastern and Central China, 1937–1945* (Berkeley: University of California Press, 1986), 162.

3. Steven I. Levine, *Anvil of Victory: The Communist Revolution in Manchuria, 1945–1948* (New York: Columbia University Press, 1987), 13, 243. Levine's organizational explanation of the Chinese Revolution is presaged in Tetsuya Kataoka, *Resistance and Revolution in China: The Communists and the Second United Front*

(Berkeley: University of California Press, 1974) and Roy Hofheinz Jr., *The Broken Wave: The Chinese Communist Peasant Movement, 1922–1928* (Cambridge, MA: Harvard University Press, 1977), which argues that "the Communist party . . . was a device to impose solutions on and extract power from the countryside" (303).

4. See especially Jeffrey Race, "Toward an exchange theory of revolution," in *Peasant Rebellion and Communist Revolution in Asia*, ed. John W. Lewis (Stanford, CA: Stanford University Press: 1974), and Joel S. Migdal, *Peasants, Politics, and Revolution: Pressures toward Political and Social Change in the Third World* (Princeton, NJ: Princeton University Press, 1974). With respect to China, see Levine, *Anvil of Victory*.

5. Theda Skocpol, *States and Social Revolutions: A Comparative Analysis of France, Russia, and China* (Cambridge: Cambridge University Press, 1979), 279.

6. Chalmers A. Johnson, *Peasant Nationalism and Communist Power: The Emergence of Revolutionary China, 1937–1945* (Stanford, CA: Stanford University Press: 1962), 49. For correctives to Johnson's path-breaking study, see, in addition to Chen Yung-fa and Kataoka, the essays in Kathleen Hartford and Steven M. Goldstein, eds. *Single Sparks: China's Rural Revolutions* (Armonk, NY: M. E. Sharpe, 1989).

7. Mark Selden, *The Yenan Way in Revolutionary China* (Cambridge, MA: Harvard University Press, 1971), 278.

8. It should be noted that Johnson's early work (*Peasant Revolution*, 11–12, 72) presented cogent reasons for rejecting "organizational weapon" explanations of Communist revolution.

9. It goes without saying that, in this chapter, I am reviewing much of the ground explored in Mark Selden's seminal study of *The Yenan Way*. Although new sources provide a different perspective on this history, *The Yenan Way* could be cited for comparative data and insight on every page of this essay. I have not done so only because endless notes of confirmation and dissent seem unnecessary and petty for Selden's path-breaking work.

10. *Yanchang xianzhi* (1988 draft), *renkouzhi*. Gulin was renamed in 1948 and abolished in 1949, its territory incorporated into Yanchang and Yan'an counties. Surviving Gulin documents are held in the Yanchang County Archives, and Yanchang records are often cited here to illustrate the Gulin case.

11. *Yanchang xianzhi* (1988 draft), *shehuizhi*, 43.

12. *Yanchang xianzhi* (1988 draft), *xiangzhen qiyezhi*.

13. Zhonggong xibei zhongyangju xuanchuanbu, *Gulin diaocha* [*Gulin Survey*] ([Yan'an?]: April 1942), 98–99; Pauline Keating, *Two Revolutions: Village Reconstruction and Cooperativisation in North Shaanxi, 1934–1945* (Stanford, CA: Stanford University Press), 22–25.

14. *Yanchang xianzhi* (1988), *renkouzhi*; *Tongji cailiao yuekan* 2, no. 5 (1937.11): 2–11. Judging from the population densities of 1964 and 1982, the areas of eastern Yanchang which included the former Gulin county probably had even lower population densities than the 15/km^2 indicated here.

15. "Shaanbei daibiao baogao" [Report of the Shaanbei representative], no. 1 (December 10, 1932) in *Shaanxi dangshi tongxun* (hereafter *SXDSTX*) 1985, no. 13: 17; *Gulin diaocha*, 2–3, 98–99; Gulin interviews, no. 16.

16. *Yanchang xianzhi* (1988 draft) *shehuizhi.*
17. *Yanchang xianzhi* (1988 draft), *tudigaige*, 1.
18. Gulin interviews, nos. 1, 3.
19. Gulin interviews, nos. 9, 10, 18.
20. Gulin interviews, nos. 1, 10.
21. This term is borrowed from Phil Billingsley, *Bandits in Republican China* (Stanford, CA: Stanford University Press, 1988).
22. See the discussion and maps of environmental illness in Shaanxi shifan daxue dilixi, ed., *Shaanxi sheng Yan'an diqu dili zhi* [A geography of Yan'an prefecture in Shaanxi] (Xi'an: Shaanxi People's Press, 1983), 196–210. The severity of the problem is indicated by mortality rates of 31 percent within two years suffered by migrants into forested areas of Ganquan under policies sponsored by the SGN Border Region ("Shaan-Gan-Ning bianqu diquan wenti") [Property rights in the Shaan-Gan-Ning Border Region], October 1946, in *Shaan-Gan-Ning bianqu zhengfu wenjian xuanbian* [Selected documents of the Shaan-Gan-Ning Border Region government] (hereafter *WJXB*) (Beijing: Archives Press, 1991), vol. 10: 294.
23. Gulin interviews, nos. 8 (whose mother-in-law was kidnapped) and 17 (who was himself kidnapped).
24. *Gulin diaocha*, 101; Gulin interviews, nos. 15, 18.
25. I have explored this issue in more detail in "The Chinese Communist Revolution from the Bottom Up," paper presented to the 1989 meeting of the American Historical Association. See also Keating, *Two Revolutions*, 39–41; Edgar Snow, *Red Star Over China* (New York: Grove Press, 1961), 221–22. For an early but still useful overview of the revolutionary movement in Shaanbei, see Mark Selden, "The Guerrilla Movement in Northwest China: The Origins of the Shensi-Kansu-Ninghsia Border Region," *The China Quarterly* 28 (December 1966): 63–81, and 29 (March 1967): 61–81.
26. "Shaanbei daibiao baogao," no. 2 (December 13, 1932), in *SXDSTX* 1985, no. 13: 24–25. "Shaanbei tewei gongzuo baogao" (October 20, 1933), ibid. 38–42, lists no branches or members from this area.
27. Yanchang Party History Office, "Yanchang xian dangshi dashiji" [A chronology of Yanchang party history] (discussion draft, 1986), 13. The *Gulin diaocha* (23, 183) reveals this pattern at the village level: of fourteen party members in one administrative village, none had joined before 1935.
28. "Yanchang xian dangshi dashiji"; Yanchang county briefing (June 20, 1989); Gulin interviews, nos. 2, 17.
29. Wang Hua in *SXDSTX* 1985, no. 12 (September 15, 1985), 18–21.
30. "Luohechuan ershiwu wei hongjun zhanshi, jiceng ganbu he qunzhong de huiyi diaocha" [A survey of the recollections of 25 Red Army soldiers, local cadres and masses from the Luo River valley] (May 15, 1959) in *SXDSTX* 1985, no. 12: 30. Gulin interviews, no. 8.
31. Gulin interviews, nos. 1, 5, 8.
32. "Yanchang xian dangshi dashiji," 5.
33. Gulin interviews, no. 4.
34. Gulin interviews, no. l; cf. Chen Yung-fa, *Making Revolution*, 299, 300, 302.

35. Gulin interviews, no. 10. A former yamen secretary similarly reported deep hatred of the local functionaries: "Why did the people hang officials from the trees and let them die during the Red period of the revolution? Because they really hated them to their very bones!" (*Gulin diaocha*, 99).

36. Gulin interviews, no. 19. Another elderly peasant (no. 15), when asked why a particular bankrupt, opium-addicted landlord had been killed, replied "1935 was like that. If somebody said something against you, you were taken out and shot. No investigation was done."

37. Gulin interviews, no. 19.

38. *Yanchang xianzhi* (1988 draft) vol. 1: 1 *tudi gaige*. Comparable figures for smaller areas are found in *Gulin diaocha*, 17, 30, 106, which also includes references (29) to redistribution of middle peasant land. Party historians speak of a correct land reform in the area just west of Gulin, followed by a radical and incorrect "land investigation movement" often blamed on the Twenty-fifth Army of Xu Haidong arriving from the Eyuwan Soviet. (See, for example, Zhang Wenhua's recollections in *SXDSTX* 1985, no. 12: 16–17.) However, no peasants that I interviewed spoke of such a two-stage movement. They recalled a quite uniformly leftist line.

39. *Gulin diaocha*, 2–3, 7–8, 18–19, 29, 31.

40. Ibid., 2–3, 19–20, 35, 112–15, 205.

41. Ibid., 24, 48–50, 86–90, 113, 133; Feng Junde, "Gulin xian si'er [1942] nian gongzuo zongjie baogao" [Summary report of work in Gulin in 1942] (January 30, 1943), Shaanxi Provincial Archives (hereafter SA) 2-1-216; Gulin xian zhengfu (Zhao Jianguo), "Cheng wei yi zhi liuyue shengchan dongyuan kangzhan dongyuan tongyi zhanxian xingzheng quyu renkou tudi ganbu deng gongzuo baogao" [Report on mobilization for production and the War of Resistance, the United Front, administrative subdivisions, population, land, cadres and other work between January and June] (June 27, 1939), SA 2-1-141-11. Western scholars have also been disappointed by the CCP's more conservative record on women's issues in the Yan'an period: see Kay Ann Johnson, *Women, Family and Peasant Revolution in China* (Chicago: University of Chicago Press, 1983), 63–83; Delia Davin, *Woman-Work: Women and the Party in Revolutionary China* (Oxford: Clarendon Press, 1976), 32–52.

42. *Gulin diaocha*, 118–19.

43. Feng Junde, "Gulin xian si'er [1942] nian gongzuo zongjie baogao," (January 30, 1943), SA 2-1-216.

44. *Gulin diaocha*, 26. The distribution of the departees is probably typical: nineteen to the army, ten to government work, five fleeing conscription, and one divorced.

45. Li Jingrui report (October 21 [*sic* in catalogue, but from context probably December 21, 1939]), SA 2-1-292-15.

46. *Gulin diaocha*, 116.

47. Feng Zhengming, "Qiantan Kang Ri zhanzheng shiqi Shaan-Gan-Ning bianqu cong ban zigei zizu xiang quan zigei zizu de zhuanbian" [A brief discussion of the Shaan-Gan-Ning Border Region's transition from semi-self-sufficiency to self-sufficiency during the Anti-Japanese War of Resistance] *SXDSTX* 1985, no. 10: 16.

48. Chen Yongfa, *Yan'an de yinying* [Yan'an's shadow] (Taipei: Academia Sinica, 1990), 92.

49. *Gulin diaocha*, 35.

50. "Gulin xian zhengfu gongzuo baogao (sanshiyi nian yiyue zhi jiuyue)" [Work report of the Gulin county government (January to September 1942)] (October 18, 1941 [*sic*: 1942?]), SA 2-1-215-1.

51. A number of documents in the SGN archives reflect this competition. For examples, see Zhao Jianguo, "Gulin xian dui tongyi zhanxian gongzuo baogao" [Gulin county report on united front work] (February 4, 1939), SA 2-1-274-27; "Cheng wei yi zhi liuyue shengchan" (June 27, 1939), SA 2-1-141-1; Tan Shengbin to SGN government (May 11, [1939]), SA 2-1-293-3.

52. "Cheng wei yi zhi liuyue shengchan," SA 2-1-141-11; Liu Jingrui report, SA 2-1-292- 15.

53. Gary Jacobson, *Brotherhood and Society: The Shaanxi Gelaohui, 1867–1912* (PhD diss., University of Michigan, 1993).

54. See Stuart Schram, "Mao Tse-tung and Secret Societies," *The China Quarterly* 27 (September 1966).

55. Liu Jingrui report, SA 2-1-292-15; Liu Jingrui and Chang Deyi report (November 10, 1939), SA 2-1-292-16. For a report on the Gelaohui in Gulin, see June 27, 1939 report cited above (SA 2-1-141-11).

56. *Gulin diaocha*,131; see also 43, 120, 185.

57. Ibid., 187. I would suggest that in fact, this shift began even before the revolution. My reading of the work of Prasenjit Duara is that the shift he sees from old village elites with "face" to the new style entrepreneurial broker in fact reflects this same shift from a concern for status and "face" to a concern for ability to get the job done—especially in relation to the new state (*Culture, Power, and the State: Rural North China, 1900–1942* [Stanford, CA: Stanford University Press, 1988], 217-43; "Elites and the Structures of Authority in the Villages of North China, 1900–1949," in *Chinese Local Elites and Patterns of Dominance*, ed. Joseph W. Esherick and Mary Backus Rankin [Berkeley: University of California Press, 1990], 261–81.

58. This list of tasks can be found in almost any of the routine reports from county magistrates in the Shaan-Gan-Ning archives.

59. "Gulin xianzhengfu gongzuo baogao (sanshiyi nian yiyue zhijiuyue)," SA 2-1-215-1.

60. *Gulin diaocha*, 126. The people up above *did* understand. As Gao Gang put it: "We must remember that among lower-level cadres and common folks, there are few who can read. They are busy with production during the day, and at night they need to sleep. If they are given too many tasks, what are they to do besides go through the motions of conforming?" (Speech to Northwest Bureau on work style problems, January 9, 1945, *WJXB*, vol. 9: 344.)

61. Gulin xian zhengfu, "Cheng wei yiyue zhi liuyue," SA 2-1-141-11.

62. *Gulin diaocha*, 122. Odoric Y. K. Wou, *Mobilizing the Masses: Building Revolution in Henan* (Stanford, CA: Stanford University Press, 1994), 135–37, presents an interesting analysis of patriarchal authority relations within the party.

63. *Gulin diaocha*, 121.

64. Ibid., 43, 65, 134.

65. Ibid., 81–82, 144, 149, 186.

66. Ibid., 189.

67. The best discussion of Rectification in SGN, including both its Yan'an and rural phases, is Chen Yongfa, *Yan'an de yinying* (Taipei: Academia Sinica, 1990). (More recently: Gao Hua, *How the Red Sun Rose: The Origins and Development of the Yan'an Rectification Movement, 1930–1945*, trans. Stacey Mosher and Guo Jian [Hong Kong: Chinese University of Hong Kong Press, 2019].) For accounts of the campaign against secret agents, see, *inter alia, Jiefang ribao*, July 29, August 31, September 15, 21, 22, October 1, 2, December 27, 1943.

68. The most dramatic plots were uncovered at Matian, in the Jin-Cha-Ji Border Region (*Jiefang ribao*, August 31, 1943), and in Suide in SGN (ibid. September 15, 22, October 1, 2, 1943; Chen Yongfa, *Yan'an de yinying*, 111–14.

69. I have treated this stage of the revolution in Mizhi county, based upon interview and archival sources, in "Revolution in a Feudal Fortress: Yangjiagou, Mizhi County, Shaanxi, 1937–1948," *Modern China* 24, no. 4 (October 1998): 339–77.

70. For a wonderful colloquial account of the effect this had on one rural cadre, see Shao Yunshan, "Wo zai zhengfeng xuexi zhong" [My experiences in rectification study], *Jiefang ribao*, November 16, 1943.

71. Gulin interviews, no. 11; *WJXB*, vol. 11: 135–37.

72. "Yanchang renmin zhiyuan jiefang zhanzheng" [The people of Yanchang support the war of liberation] (Yanchang archives).

73. Gulin interviews, no. 6 (a village head in 1947).

74. *Yanchang xianzhi* (1988 draft) *junshizhi*.

75. "Gulin xian Qingyuan qu Baihu xiang dianxing diaocha" [A survey of typical cases in Baihu township of Qingyuan district in Gulin county], Yanchange Archives x-5–24-x [1948] (hereafter cited as YC).

76. Ibid.

77. "Gulin xian Gengluo qu Baofa xiang Xiabanshi cun 1946 zhi 1948 nian bingyuan qingkuang diaocha" [A survey of conscription campaigns in Xiabanshi village of Baofa township, Gengluo district, Gulin county from 1946 to 1948], YC.

78. "Shaan-Gan-Ning bianqu minbingjianshe youguan qingkuang tongji biao" [Statistics on militia organizing in the Shaan-Gan-Ning Border Region] (n.d.), YC.

79. "Gulin xian Zhangjia xiang 1947 nian zhiqian gongzuo qingkuang" [Support for the front lines in 1947 in Zhangjia township of Gulin county], YC.

80. See "Linzhen qu zhengfu quannian gongzuo baogao" [Annual work report of the Linzhen district government] (6th day of the 12th lunar month, 1947), YC x-5–24-x, for examples of stretcher teams and conscripts fleeing back to their villages.

81. "Shaan-Gan-Ning bianqu diquan wenti," 284–85.

82. Yanchang county government, "Liangge qu de tudi gongzuo baogao" [Report on land work in two districts] (November 20, 1949), YC x-x-2–1.

83. Unless otherwise noted, all the discussion below is based on these forms, called *ganbu dengji biao* (干部登记表, cadre registration forms). Available to me were registers with the following archive numbers: YC x-x-43–1, YC x-x-43–2 and YC x-x-43–4 (all November 23, 1948); YC x-x-60–2 (July 5, 1949); YC x-x-60–3 (January 1951); YC x-x-60–5 (April 24, 1949); YC x-x-60–6 (December 16, 1949); YC x-x-60–8 (n.d.).

84. *Gulin diaocha* (183) reveals the same pattern: of twenty-five party members in one township, nineteen (76 percent) joined in 1935–1936 (sixteen in 1935 alone).

85. *Gulin diaocha*, 153.

86. For this calculation, "joined the revolution" means either joined the party or "entered the ranks," whichever occurred first. Note also that "age" on these forms is probably recorded in *sui* (岁), so biological age is roughly one year less.

87. Edward Friedman, Paul Pickowicz, and Mark Selden conclude in their study of the revolution in Central Hebei that the party "rooted its state power in the cultural expressions of tough, parochial young males" (*Chinese Village, Socialist State* [Berkeley: University of California Press, 1991], xiv).

88. Yung-fa Chen, *Making Revolution*, 250. See also Mark Selden on "councillors" elected in SGN (*Yenan Way*, 133).

89. For examples, see *WJXB*, vol. 9: 102–5 on property seizure in Gulin; vol. 9: 306–11 on land policy in 1945; vol. 10: 291–92 on land policy in 1946.

90. From YC x-x-60–0 (December 16, 1949).

91. Gao Gang speech on work style, February 5, 1945, in *WJXB*, vol. 9: 345.

92. Hans J. van de Ven, *From Friend to Comrade: The Founding of the Chinese Communist Party, 1920–1927* (Berkeley: University of California Press, 1991); Arif Dirlik, *The Origins of Chinese Communism* (New York: Oxford University Press, 1989).

93. Lin Boqu speech on work style problems, June–July, 1945, *WJXB*, vol. 9: 353.

Part V

CONTEMPORARY CHINA

Chapter Ten

On "The Restoration of Capitalism"

It was once common to take seriously the role of Marxist ideology in guiding the development of contemporary China. In part, this was because there was little else to study. China was closed to academic research by independent observers. The main source of information was the state-controlled press, and its publications were subject to strict ideological guidance. It remained possible, however, for astute scholars to penetrate these sources for pathbreaking insights into Chinese politics. The titles, however, revealed the special focus on ideology of these early works: Franz Schurmann's *Ideology and Organization in Communist China*, Benjamin Schwartz's *Communism and China: Ideology in Flux*, and Stuart Schram's *The Political Thought of Mao Tse-tung*.* In China today, ideology has become little more than a justification for continued Communist Party rule; but in Mao's China, there is reason to believe that Marxist-Leninist theory really mattered, that it actually played a role in the inner-party debates that determined policy-formation.

The Great Proletarian Cultural Revolution was, of course, the apotheosis of Mao Zedong's revolutionary agenda. In the PRC's official propaganda of the time, the Cultural Revolution was waged against the threat of "capitalist restoration." Most Western analysts paid scant attention to such rhetoric, concentrating on Mao's resentment of the party establishment and its attempt to rescue the country from the disastrous results of his Great Leap Forward, which had resulted in widespread famine and the death of perhaps thirty million peasants. I, however, had been trained in an era when ideology mattered. More importantly, I had grown increasingly interested in Marxist theory and

---

* Franz Schurman, *Ideology and Organization in Communist China* (Berkeley: University of California Press, 1966); Benjamin I. Schwartz, *Communism and China: Ideology in Flux* (Cambridge, MA: Harvard University Press, 1974); Stuart R Schram, *The Political Thought of Mao Tse-Tung* (New York: Praeger, 1969).

read deeply in it to try to understand where Mao's ideas came from. In 1978, while studying in Japan, I joined a group of left-leaning American China scholars who gathered every few weeks to read Marx, starting with *Capital* and working through the *Grundrisse* and other works of the early Marx. On my return to the University of Oregon, I joined May Day, a Marxist study group led by the sociologist Al Szymanski, where a good deal of Lenin and Stalin was added to my reading.

When this article was written, China had just emerged from the Great Proletarian Cultural Revolution, which Mao had launched to rescue China from the "restoration of capitalism." Today, most works on the Cultural Revolution treat capitalist restoration as a convenient excuse for Mao to attack his rivals in the party.* While this may be an overly Mao-centered analysis of recent Chinese history, the preeminent importance of the Chairman seems to me undeniable, and that means we need to understand his thinking. One side-effect of the Cultural Revolution was the illicit publication of a number of Mao's secret writings. The most important item for this article was Mao's notes on a Soviet text on political economy that he read in 1960–1961. There is no question that Mao was thinking seriously about the question of "capitalist restoration" at that time, and it seems to me important to understand how his use of this concept related to other works in the Marxist-Leninist canon.

This essay is included here largely to acknowledge the overtly Marxist stage of my early career. Perhaps the most important data point in the essay is its publication date: January 1979. In the fall of that year, I made my first trip to China to conduct research on the Boxer Uprising. During a year living in China, I found little evidence that Marxism had any real impact on the dynamics of Chinese society, and read again some forty years later, much of this essay seems remarkable naïve. My discussion here is basically sympathetic to Mao. Now I believe that Mao's preoccupation with class struggle led him dangerously astray. He was clearly mistaken in treating Peng Dehuai's criticism of the Great Leap Forward as an example of class struggle within the party. He was equally misled in following Lenin and Stalin to believe that the rich peasant economy could be the economic base for a restoration of capitalism. Nonetheless, Mao's obsession with issues of class was fundamental to his revolutionary and ruling strategy. To understand it, we must take its Marxist-Leninist roots seriously.

In China today, schools of Marxism are more concerned with "Xi Jinping Thought on Socialism with Chinese Characteristics for the New Era" than any serious engagement with Marxist theory. I doubt, however, that the same should be said of the Mao era. Steven Kotkin's exhaustive biography of Stalin

---

* See, for example, Roderick MacFarquahar and Michael Schoenhals, *Mao's Last Revolution* (Cambridge, MA: Harvard University Press, 2006), 12–13.

argues that Stalin's reign was crucially shaped by the dictator's deep commitment to Marxist-Leninist theory.[*] I am inclined to think the same was true under Mao. Of particular note from the perspective of contemporary China is Mao's repeatedly expressed concern for the children of cadres: "They lack life experiences and social experience, but they put on airs and have great feelings of superiority." Since China is now ruled precisely by these Red princelings, who dominate an economy that surely looks a lot like state capitalism, this is a reminder that some aspects of Mao's analyses may deserve a second look.

TAKING MARXISM (TOO) SERIOUSLY: THE "RESTORATION OF CAPITALISM" IN MAO AND MARXIST THEORY[†]

Since 1962, Mao Zedong and other Chinese Communist theorists have written a great deal about the "Restoration of Capitalism"—in Yugoslavia, in the Soviet Union, and (potentially) in China itself. They have perceived a "privileged stratum" and "new bourgeois elements" emerging in socialist society, worming their way into the Communist Party and usurping control of the state. Mao has insisted that only continued class struggle under the dictatorship of the proletariat can overcome these threats and guarantee continued development to higher stages of socialist and eventually communist society. Western scholars have tended to take the concept of capitalist restoration with a grain of salt—as either rhetorical excess, or (as one recent book terms it) a "seemingly obsessive preoccupation" of Chairman Mao.[1] There have unquestionably been times—particularly during the Cultural Revolution—when the labelling of any deviation as a "capitalist road" robbed the concept of real analytical utility. Nevertheless, I believe that in its origins and essence, the concept is significant and meaningful enough to deserve serious attention.

The history of recent political struggles in China should convince us that behind a rhetorical epithet lies a real political difference. In the case of the "restoration of capitalism," the political differences are obviously of considerable significance, for they involve the very definition of socialism. The definition of socialism implied by Mao's theory of capitalist restoration is evidently more complex than that of earlier Marxist orthodoxy. Most obviously, since, in the Soviet Union, the means of production are demonstrably owned by the state, and the state is demonstrably controlled by the Communist Party, the party of the proletariat, the normal Marxist (or perhaps "vulgar

---

[*] Stephen Kotkin, *Stalin* (New York: Penguin Press, 2014).
[†] Originally published as "On the 'Restoration of Capitalism:' Mao and Marxist Theory," *Modern China* 5, no. 1 (1979): 41–77. I would like to thank Lowell Dittmer, Jack Gurley, Mark Selden, and John Starr for their helpful and incisive criticisms of the initial draft of this essay. I am much indebted to their expertise.

Marxist") criteria for the existence of socialism have been met. If the Chinese insist that the USSR is not socialist but in fact capitalist, or even "fascist," then they are operating with a somewhat more restrictive definition of socialism, which it would behove us to understand.

Because of the conflict between the Chinese view[2] and earlier Marxist orthodoxy, this problem also affords an opportunity to explore the relationship between Mao's thought and Marxist theory. I embark on such an exploration with some trepidation, for in doing so one inevitably courts the danger of a kind of Talmudic scholasticism that seeks isolated passages in Marxist scripture as a source or justification for particular Maoist dictums. In this case, however, the exercise seems justified since it is known that precisely when Mao was developing his ideas on the restoration of capitalism, he was himself studying Marxist political economy and recommending Marxist classics for study by high party cadres.[3] It does seem, then, that if we are properly to understand "where Mao is coming from," we are going to have to understand him not only in the context of Chinese history, but also in the broader context of Marxist theory.

I shall begin this chapter with a brief examination of some relevant aspects of Marx's thought, and then pass on to Lenin's explicit treatment of the danger of capitalist restoration in the Soviet Union. The first section of the essay will conclude with a glance at theoretical and polemical debates about the restoration of capitalism and related subjects by the competing factions of the Bolshevik party in the 1920s. Having demonstrated, hopefully, that the concept of "capitalist restoration" had a substantial history before Mao started writing about it, I shall trace in the second part the development of Mao's ideas on the subject from about 1956 through 1964. Finally, I shall try to analyze the salient aspects of Mao's theory and note in passing some interesting convergences between Mao's theories and contemporary Marxist theory in the West.

MARXIST AND LENINIST SOURCES FOR THE CONCEPT

Marx, of course, was enough of a materialist to avoid a lot of speculation about the nature of a socialist society that did not yet exist. He took as his task the critique of the capitalist society that did exist and left only a few scattered comments indicating his vision of life under socialism. He was certainly under no illusions that a socialist revolution would bring immediate utopia. He realized that initially communists would have to deal with a society "just as it *emerges* from capitalist society; which is thus in every respect, economically, morally and intellectually, still stamped with the birth marks of the old society from whose womb it emerges."[4] In order to combat the remnants of bourgeois culture and society, the state, during the transition from capitalism to communism "can be nothing but *the revolutionary dictatorship of the proletariat*."[5]

At his dialectical best, Marx makes it clear that socialism is not to be understood in terms of static definitions of social and economic organization but as a *process* of continuous struggle and development toward a classless communist society. Though he is not always so anti-teleological, at one point Marx writes that communism "is not as such the goal of human development," but only a *"real* phase, necessary for the next period of historical development, in the emancipation and recovery of mankind."[6] Communism is thus but part of a continuing dialectic of human development. There is certainly no questioning the stress on process in what is perhaps Marx's most famous definition of "revolutionary socialism":

> This socialism is the declaration of the permanence of the revolution, the class dictatorship of the revolution, the class dictatorship of the proletariat as the inevitable transit point to the abolition of class differences generally, to the abolition of all the productive relations on which they rest, to the abolition of all the social relations that correspond to those relations of production, to the revolutionizing of all the ideas that result from these social connections.[7]

There would seem to be little doubt that Marx conceived socialism as a process of continuing class struggle, radical social change, and cultural revolution ("the revolutionizing of ideas") on the road to communist society. We need only question whether he regarded the outcome of this struggle to be at all contingent, whether his theory allowed the possibility that revolutionary socialism might be overturned and capitalism restored. This inevitably leads us into an area of some speculation, but I do not believe that Marx's determinism ruled out such temporary reversals. In *Capital*, he often mentions instances of social retrogression: Roman "plebian debtors" being ruined and "displaced by slaves," a reversion from a non-slave (perhaps feudal, perhaps even proto-capitalist) to a slave society;[8] or the emancipation of Italian serfs being followed by "a movement in the reverse direction" in which proletarians were forced back to a feudal countryside of *petite culture* with Northern Italy's fifteenth-century loss of commercial supremacy.[9] He describes the entire course of the French Revolution of 1848 after February as a "state of retrogressive motion."[10] Certainly given Marx's extreme skepticism of the possible success of a proletarian revolution within the bounds of one or several nation-states,[11] I would think that the "restoration of capitalism" in post-revolutionary Russia or China was a possibility totally consistent with the thrust of his analysis.

With Lenin, there is no need to speculate. His post-revolutionary writings show that he regarded the restoration of capitalism as a real possibility and a genuine threat. Like Mao in the early 1960s, Lenin saw the economic basis for capitalist restoration in free markets and the individual peasant economy.

> Take the economic front, and ask whether capitalism can be restored economically in Russia. We have combated the Sukharevka black market. . . . The old Sukharevka market in Sukharevskaya Square has been closed down, an act that presented no difficulty. The sinister thing is the "Sukharevka" that resides in the heart and behavior of every petty proprietor. . . . That "Sukharevka" is the basis of capitalism. While it exists, the capitalists may return to Russia and may grow stronger than we are. . . . While we live in a small-peasant country, there is a firmer economic basis for capitalism in Russia than for communism.[12]

Beyond these dangers of an economic undermining of the revolution, Lenin was also, in his last speeches and writings, increasingly concerned about the threat from the state bureaucracy. To understand the full significance of Lenin's views here, we must go back to his debates with Bukharin and the "left Communists" on the subject of state capitalism. In 1918, the "left Communists" attacked the restoration of capitalistic production relations and management techniques in the factories on grounds that "the introduction of labor discipline in connection with the restoration of capitalist management in industry . . . [would] diminish the class initiative, activity and organization of the proletariat. It threatens to enslave the working class."[13] Bukharin, who regarded state capitalism as the "New Leviathan" of the modern age, saw in these new measures of the Soviet state a threat to the very essence of socialism.[14]

In "'Left Wing' Childishness and the Petty Bourgeois Mentality" (the relevant portion of which he remained committed to and reproduced unchanged three years later in "The Tax in Kind"), Lenin defended state capitalism as the proper road to socialism. The real enemy, Lenin argued, was the "petty bourgeoisie plus private capitalism" and it was necessary to form an alliance with state capitalism to combat these two.[15] (We shall see later how Mao significantly reversed the terms of this alliance.) Lenin makes his case with characteristic bluntness:

> To make things even clearer, let us first of all take the most concrete example of state capitalism. Everybody knows what that example is. It is Germany. Here we have "the last word" in modern large-scale capitalist engineering and planned organization, *subordinated to Junker-bourgeois imperialism.* Cross out the words in italics, and in place of the militarist, Junker, bourgeois, imperialist *state* put *also a state*, but of a different social type, of a different class content—a *Soviet* state, that is, a proletarian state, and you have the *sum total* of the conditions necessary for socialism.[16]

It followed inevitably from this theory that proletarian control of the state was of the utmost importance, for only the form of the state distinguished the Bolshevik regime from state capitalism. Lenin was, consequently, extremely disturbed by indications that the massive state bureaucracy was *not* clearly under proletarian control, was filled with petty bourgeois officials carried over from the old tsarist administration, and was not necessarily so different from the bourgeois state. At the Eleventh Congress of the Russian Communist Party (Bolshevik), he referred to the contemporary equivalent of modern convergence theorists who see modernization forcing capitalism and socialism into increasingly similar molds. In 1922, the spokesman for this view was the emigré Ustrayalov in Prague who had written "the Bolsheviks . . . will arrive at the ordinary bourgeois state, and we must support them."[17] Said Lenin: "We must say frankly that the things Ustrayalov speaks about are possible. History knows all sorts of metamorphoses."[18] What most disturbed Lenin were indications that the state was growing increasingly autonomous of proletarian control: "If we take Moscow and its 4,700 Communists in responsible positions, if we take that huge bureaucratic machine, that gigantic heap, we must ask: who is directing whom?"[19] Or, as he put it elsewhere: "*Often:* this apparatus does not belong to us, we belong to it!"[20]

With these extremely critical remarks on the state bureaucracy late in life, Lenin left a highly ambiguous legacy. Within the Party, Lenin had always been an unequivocal defender of centralism, discipline, and even bureaucracy. In his 1904 polemic, "One Step Forward, Two Steps Back," he answered the appeals of Axelrod and Martov for more democracy with this analysis:

> Bureaucracy *versus* democracy is in fact centralism *versus* autonomism, it is the organizational principle of Revolutionary Social-Democracy as opposed to the organizational principle of opportunist Social Democracy. The latter strives to proceed from the bottom upward and, therefore, wherever possible and as far as possible, upholds autonomism and "democracy," carried (by the overzealous) to the point of anarchism. The former strives to proceed from the top downward and upholds an extension of the rights and powers of the centre in relation to the parts.[21]

After the revolution, however, Lenin was a persistent critic of bureaucracy— though more so in the state than in the Party. As we have seen, he believed that only firm proletarian control of the state distinguished the Bolshevik regime from state capitalism and protected Russia from the restoration of capitalism. He was intensely disturbed by tendencies toward bureaucratic autonomy, and the measures he proposed were precisely designed to make the apparatus more responsive to the masses. The similarity to policies that are often treated as Maoist innovations is notable. At one point, noting that the "the evils of bureaucracy are concentrated at the centre," he recommends "downgrading" high-ranking cadres to local work—similar to what the Chinese would later call *xiafang* (下放).[22] Elsewhere he calls for the equivalent of an "open-door rectification" of the Party, relying on the "fine intuition" of the non-Party workers to distinguish honest Communists from corrupt cadres.[23]

Above all, Lenin advocated continuing class struggle under the dictatorship of the proletariat as the only overall defence against backsliding into capitalism. In one of his most notable statements, he projects an image remarkably similar to that which Mao would later see:

> The proletariat does not cease class struggle after it has captured political power, but continues it until classes are abolished. . . . Clearly in order to abolish classes completely, it is not enough to overthrow the exploiters, the landowners, and capitalists, not enough to abolish *their* rights of ownership; it is necessary also to abolish *all* private ownership of the means of production, it is necessary to abolish the distinction between town and country, as well as the distinction between manual workers and brain workers. This requires a very long period of time.[24]

It is clear that the restoration of capitalism and related issues were almost as central to the debates in the Soviet Union in the 1920s as they were in China in the 1960s. But one must not uncritically equate the two debates. Often similar terms are used with quite different meanings. For example, Lenin placed great stress in his last writings on the need for a "cultural revolution," but what he meant was the need to spread basic literacy and "real bourgeois culture" among peasants and proletarian cadres.[25] In his last article, he scorned those who were "dilating at too great length and too flippantly on 'proletarian' culture."[26] Lenin and others after him paid great attention to a "new bourgeoisie," but unlike the Chinese use of the same term to refer to elements in the party and state apparatus, the Bolshevik term referred to the "Nepmen"—entrepreneurs operating under the New Economic Policy (NEP) of restricted capitalism in the 1920s.

In general, it is probably accurate to say that the Bolshevik leaders who came closest to Mao's subsequent analysis of the degeneration of Russian socialism were those who influenced him least. I have in mind Trotsky and especially Bukharin, who as pariahs of the international communist movement by the 1930s, were not an acceptable source of inspiration for Mao. I think it unlikely that Mao ever read their works with a sympathetic eye. If direct intellectual influence is doubtful, the similarity of views is all the more remarkable. It suggests that similar problems of building socialism, seen through a shared Marxist mode of analysis, led very different men to conclusions that were often quite similar.

Between 1924 and 1927, the Trotskyite Left Opposition within the Bolshevik Party repeatedly warned that the New Economic Policy could lead to a restoration of capitalism. According to their analysis—remarkably similar to the analysis of Mao and others during China's post-Great Leap "NEP"—free trade threatened to polarize the peasantry, lead to the emergence of kulak power in the villages, and a spread of capitalist relations that would ultimately affect the cities as well.[27] On the political level, though the Trotskyites did not introduce a class analysis into their critique of Stalinist bureaucracy, there were occasional references to, in Rakovsky's words, "social, if not economic, differentiation" ("automobiles, housing, regular holidays, etc.") setting the apparatchiki apart from the working masses.[28]

But the most striking parallels to Mao are found in Bukharin's warnings of the dangers of a new ruling class emerging in Soviet society, for Bukharin seems to have been one ranking Bolshevik who was willing to add a class analysis to the Leninist attacks on bureaucracy. As summarized in Stephen Cohen's important biography, Bukharin saw that in contrast to the bourgeoisie, which had been able to nurture its intellectual foundations and administrative elites in the womb of feudal society, the proletariat at the time of the Bolshevik Revolution remained culturally oppressed. Thus, Bukharin argued, the leaders of the proletariat were necessarily drawn "*from a hostile class . . . from the bourgeois intelligentsia.*"[29] If this group were then assimilated into the prevailing administrative elite—much of which had been carried over wholesale from the tsarist bureaucracy[30]—there was the danger that the two would coalesce into a privileged and "monopolistic caste" and turn into "*the embryo of a new ruling class.*"[31]

It is important to be aware of these ideas of Burkharin and the Trotskyites, for they remind us that Mao's notion of the restoration of capitalism" was not just the paranoia of an aging revolutionary, but a reaction to concrete conditions—many of which had also existed in Russia in the 1920s. But it is highly doubtful that Mao's thinking was directly influenced by the writings of Burkharin or the Trotskyites. If anything, he owes the greatest debt (after Lenin) to the target of Trotsky's and Bukharin's criticism: Stalin. What Stalin and his supporters did, in effect, was to combine the Trotskyite criticism of NEP to a variant of the Bukharinite criticism of a new class in the administration. This two-fold attack was then turned against Bukharin and the "Right." In 1929, as Stalin geared up for collectivization and a major push to industrialize, the cautious gradualism of the "Right" and its continuing defence of NEP policies toward the peasantry were attacked in class terms: as conservatism and lack of zeal for socialist construction on the part of the "bourgeois intelligentsia" in the state and Party administration.[32] Stalin would later characterize the dangers posed by this opposition to collectivization in the following terms:

> The restoration of the kulaks is bound to lead to the creation of a kulak power and to the liquidation of Soviet power—hence, it is bound to lead to the formation of a bourgeois government. And the formation of a bourgeois government is bound to lead in its turn to the restoration of the landlords and capitalists, to the restoration of capitalism.[33]

In this categorically stated form, Stalin's prognosis lacked real plausibility. But that should not blind us to the link that *did* exist between the cautious policies of NEP and the relatively privileged position of "bourgeois" administrators in the state apparatus. In any case, this passage illustrates as well as any that many of the elements of the Chinese theory of capitalist restoration of the 1960s were also current in Russia in the 1920s.

THE EVOLUTION OF MAO'S THEORY

In order truly to understand the source of Mao's ideas on the restoration of capitalism, it is not enough, of course, to demonstrate their foreshadowing in Marx's dialectical notion of socialism as a *process* leading to the elimination of all classes, or in Lenin and his Bolshevik successors' explicit discussions of the restoration of capitalism. It is true that many of the writings we have quoted were later cited by Mao and others—especially in the polemics with the Soviet Union. But the citation of texts does not prove the origins of theory. In this case, while reading Marx, Lenin, Stalin, and Soviet writings on political economy obviously helped Mao to develop his ideas on the restoration of capitalism, it is clear that his theory was developed above all through the practice of making revolution and building socialism in China.

I would trace the origins of Mao's ideas on the subject to his first steps, in 1955–1956, to chart an independent road to socialism. Concern over the potential effect of applying the Soviet model of development to China was an important impetus to his own independent theorizing. Unquestionably, the most important early writing on the subject was his April 1956 speech on the "Ten Great Relationships," whose intricate dialectical arguments called into serious question the Soviet model's stress on heavy industry, military investment, and a tightly centralized political and economic system.[34] Mao underlined the significance of this speech two years later: "The Ten Great Relationships constitute basic viewpoint, which is comparison to the Soviet Union." He was ready, as he put it, to "vie with the teacher."[35]

A central element in his comparison to the Soviet Union would emerge in 1957 in a renewed stress on class struggle. The Eighth Congress of the Chinese Communist Party (CCP) in September 1956, seemingly dominated by Liu Shaoqi and Deng Xiaoping, had stated that the class struggle between the proletariat and the bourgeoisie was "basically resolved" with the nationalization of most industry and the collectivization of agriculture, and the principal contradiction in China was between the advanced social system and the backward productive forces. The outburst of rightist criticism of the CCP and socialism during the Hundred Flowers Movement convinced Mao that this judgment was in error, and that "the two roads—bourgeois and proletarian, socialist and capitalist—are the main contradiction of the transition period."[36] One year later he was willing to admit openly that there were some who would prefer to take the capitalist road: "In a socialist society there is a minority, such as landlords, rich peasants, rightists. They wish to return to capitalism (*huidao ziben zhuyi* 回到资本主义) and advocate capitalism."[37] Mao stressed the need for class struggle to deal with such elements, but was careful to distinguish his methods from Stalin's. "Take class struggle for example: we adopt Lenin's method, not Stalin's. In discussing 'The Economic Problems of Socialism,' Stalin said that after the revolution, reform is peaceful reform from the top down. Stalin did not carry out class struggle from the bottom up."[38]

In 1959, at the Lushan Plenum, Mao began to analyze disputes within the Party in class terms. The "wavering" and lack of resolution of Peng Dehuai et al. in the face of difficulties during the Great Leap Forward were now interpreted as reflecting the pessimism and "coolness" of the bourgeoisie.[39] One month after the conference he would write that "The struggle that appeared at Lushan was a class struggle. It was a continuation of the life and death struggle of the past ten years of socialist revolution between two great opposing classes, the bourgeoisie and the proletariat." Lushan, then, was a clear demonstration of the dictum that "struggle within the Party reflects the class struggle in society."[40]

While Mao was learning through practice the correctness of Lenin's predictions of protracted class struggle under socialism, another stream of thought was growing that would later merge with his broader theory. This was the resurgence of his long-held concern for the problem of bureaucratism (*guanliao zhuyi* 官僚主义). Much of the object of the Hundred Flowers Campaign was of course to correct this abuse. At that time Mao displayed the depth of his feelings on the subject by suggesting that strikes be allowed against bureaucratism, even though no right to strike was guaranteed by the constitution.[41] He spoke often against the "official styles and official airs" (*guanfeng guanqi* 官风官气)[42] of cadres who take the attitude that "I have authority over you."[43] At this time his criticisms were still largely directed at poor work style, but by highlighting the issue of authority and officials' refusal to put themselves on the level of workers, he was dealing with elements that would later contribute to a new conception of class and the capitalist road.

As the practice of the Chinese Revolution was forcing Mao to rethink some assumptions about building socialism, he seems also to have been guided by Lenin's famous dictum: "Without revolutionary theory there can be no revolutionary movement."[44] Beginning in 1957 and intensifying in 1958, Mao made a number of references to the need to study Marxist theory. His first concern was that Marx be read critically. "We must respect the classics, but not have blind faith (*mixin* 迷信) in them."[45] The term he used here, *mixin*, is often translated "superstition," and it is that sort of uncritically reverential attitude that Mao warned against. Later he would scorn foreign critics of the Great Leap Forward who cited a Marxist text like a "sutra."[46] According to Mao, Marxism, studied improperly, can even be harmful: "Unless you have a conquering spirit it is very dangerous to study Marxism Leninism."[47]

The logic of Mao's position was soon made clear. First feudalism propagandized Chinese to obey Confucius, then imperialism propagandized them to obey foreigners. Consequently Chinese "fear Marx," another foreigner, and lack the self-confidence to study and amend him on the basis of Chinese practice. In particular, Mao seemed to be bothered by the belief of some Chinese, including high-ranking cadres, that the foreigners to China's north, who were beginning by 1958 to be publicly critical of Mao's independent ideas on building socialism, had a naturally superior claim to Marxist orthodoxy. He was quite explicit, therefore, on the need to develop theory on the basis of China's own revolutionary practice: "What we have done surpasses Marx. . . . Our practice surpasses Marx. Through practice, new principles are produced. Marx never succeeded in making revolution; we succeeded. The practice of this revolution, reflected in the form of consciousness, becomes theory."[48]

The particular "superstitious" understanding of Marxism that Mao seemed most concerned with at this time was Stalinism. Though the CCP has often publicly defended Stalin against criticism by the Soviet Union, and though Mao (as mentioned earlier) clearly sympathized with Stalin's arguments on such subjects as the need for collectivization, he maintained a considerable ambivalence toward the late Soviet leader. His speeches were peppered with juxtapositions of positive comments on Lenin and negative comments on Stalin. He particularly recommended Lenin's writings of 1919 to 1921, many of which we have treated above.[49] In one such passage, after describing Lenin's success in mobilizing the masses, his attacks on bureaucracy and his practice of personally visiting factories, Mao concluded philosophically: "Lenin's dialectics, Stalin's partial metaphysics, today's dialectics. This is also the negation of the negation."[50]

From 1958, Mao became particularly concerned with problems of political economy. At the Zhengzhou Conference in November, Mao offered a detailed criticism of Stalin's "Economic Problems of Socialism in the Soviet Union."[51] At the Sixth Plenum of the Eighth Central Committee in December, he reinforced an earlier recommendation that in addition to Stalin's pamphlet, all higher cadres should study the Soviet *Textbook on Political Economy* and a compilation entitled *Marx, Engels, Lenin and Stalin on Communist Society*.[52] But Mao did not immediately follow his own advice, for at the Lushan Conference of July 1959, he admitted that he still had not read the textbook himself.[53]

Mao's year to study came in 1960. The absorbing enthusiasm and confusion of the Great Leap years and the trials of the Lushan splits were behind him. But the problems of the Great Leap had also left Mao somewhat on the defensive within high party circles. Occasions like this had often, during Mao's long revolutionary career, moved him to undertake more intensive theoretical study. He seems to have made few speeches or public appearances in 1960. Though his extensive notes on the Soviet political economy text are variously dated 1960 or 1961–1962, on internal evidence I would accept the earlier date.[54] This was also a year in which the Party Center was preoccupied with relations with the Soviet Union—with the Bucharest Conference in June, the withdrawal of Soviet technicians in August, and the Moscow Conference in November.[55] It would seem that the combination of Mao's lessened responsibilities for day-to-day affairs, having stepped down as Chief of State and retired to the "second line," and the need to systematize China's theoretical position in relation to the Soviet Union as well as his own position in relation to critics within the Party, allowed and impelled Mao to put together the ideas that in the 1960s would emerge as a theory of capitalist restoration. It is largely in his "reading notes" on the Soviet textbook that we will discover, below, the origins of his ideas on the restoration of capitalism.

It seems that by the early 1960s the one missing ingredient of a fully developed theory of capitalist restoration was an analysis of the peasant economy. We have seen that in the writings of Lenin, it was the "small producer economy" of the peasantry, and in Trotsky and Stalin the re-emergence of "kulak power," that were regarded as the social base for the restoration of capitalism. In the course of 1961–1962, Mao perceived that the retreat from the Great Leap Forward carried with it dangers very similar to those that the Bolshevik Left had seen in the NEP. With the weakening of the collective economy and the opening of rural free markets, class divisions were beginning to sharpen together with the spread of corruption among many rural cadres. At the Ninth Plenum of the Eighth Central Committee Mao warned against the "restoration of the landlords"—the first reference I have seen to the specific term "restoration" (*fubi* 复辟).[56] By January 1962, he speaks of all the "reactionary classes" seeking "restoration," of the emergence of "new bourgeois elements" in a socialist society, and of Yugoslavia whose example showed that "a proletarian dictatorship can be transformed into a bourgeois dictatorship, transformed into a reactionary fascist dictatorship."[57] Finally, after a much briefer treatment of the subject at the Beidaihe Central Work Conference in August,[58] the full theory emerges—albeit still in somewhat sketchy form—at the Tenth Plenum of the Eighth Central Committee in September 1962:

> We can now affirm that classes exist in socialist countries and class struggle assuredly exists. Lenin once said: after the victory of the revolution, the overthrown classes of a country—because of the existence of the bourgeoisie internationally, and the existence of the petty bourgeoisie and remnants of the bourgeoisie internally, which continually generate a bourgeoisie—because of this, the overthrown bourgeoisie will continue to exist for a long time and will even want a restoration. The European bourgeois revolutions, as in England and France, all passed through several reversals (*fanfu* 反复). After feudalism was overthrown, it had several restorations, passed through several reversals. This sort of reversal can also appear in a socialist country, as in the transformation of Yugoslavia which is now revisionist. From a workers' and peasants' country it has changed into a country ruled by reactionary nationalist elements.[59]

THE COMPLETED THEORY

By the fall of 1962, the basic outlines of Mao's theory of the restoration of capitalism had been drawn. Many of the details remained to be worked out and would be worked out especially in the course of the polemics between the CCP and the CPSU. Our task is now to examine the different aspects of the Chinese theory. I would not pretend that the following analysis exhausts *all* aspects, and some topics I will pass over lightly. But I believe that this catalogue of sources and aspects of capitalist restoration covers the heart of Mao's theory.

Abandonment of class struggle. Lenin made quite clear that class struggle under the dictatorship of the proletariat was socialism's most essential defence against capitalist restoration. The Chinese have also placed the issue of class struggle at the center of their theory. They have viewed the denial of class struggle as symptomatic of bourgeois ideology that rationalizes the rule of one class by claiming that the formal equality of bourgeois democracy eliminates class distinctions and causes the state to represent all the people. Thus when, in 1961, the Twenty-Second Congress of the CPSU asserted that the dictatorship of the proletariat had been replaced by the "state of the whole people," the Chinese found this to be clear evidence that Khrushchev was leading Russia toward the restoration of capitalism.[60] But Mao and the Chinese have always traced the source of this error back to the 1930s and Stalin:

> As Stalin departed from Marxist-Leninist dialectics in his understanding of the laws of class struggle in socialist society, he prematurely declared after agriculture was basically collectivized that there were "no longer antagonistic classes" in the Soviet Union and that it was "free of class conflicts," one-sidedly stressing the internal homogeneity of socialist society and overlooking its contradictions.[61]

"Spontaneous capitalist tendencies" of the peasantry. Among the critical internal contradictions of socialist society were those associated with the peasant economy. Lenin and the early Bolsheviks always identified the primary threat of capitalist restoration with the spontaneous capitalist tendencies of the "small-producer economy." This was also an important part of the Chinese theory, and for some—notably Liu Shaoqi, who *also* warned against the restoration of capitalism—it was the *most* important part of the theory.[62] The Socialist Education Movement of 1962–1965 was designed to root out "spontaneous capitalist tendencies" in the countryside, especially the sharpening of class divisions that ensued from the post-Great Leap weakening of collective institutions, and the related problem of corruption among local cadres.[63] If there was an important feature that distinguished Mao's theoretical ideas on the subject, it would probably be that he seems to have consistently argued that the "small-producer economy" would be ended not just by collectivization, but only when collective ownership advanced to ownership by the whole people.[64] This, of course, helps explain the repeated stress in recent "Learn from Dazhai" campaigns on progressively raising the level of accounting from the team to the brigade to the commune as steps toward ownership by the whole people.

Theory of productive forces. All advances toward higher levels of collective ownership obviously entail changes in the relations of production, which are, in turn, linked to the development of productive forces. The nature of this link has been a matter of considerable disagreement. Since the debates over agricultural collectivization in 1955, Mao had been a persistent critic of what has come to be labelled the "theory of productive forces." In essence, that theory holds that changes in the relations of production (e.g., collectivization of agriculture or socialization of industry) depend on the development of the productive forces (on the level of industrialization, mechanization, and the like). Mao's 1960 "reading notes" repeatedly criticize the Soviet text on political economy for upholding this theory. "The history of every revolution proves that a full development of the productive forces is not necessary for the transformation of backward production relations."[65] This is a judgment the historical accuracy of which is difficult to contradict. It was important to Mao in two respects.

First, Mao perceived that the contrary argument of the Soviet textbook supported cautious and conservative policies toward the collectivization of agriculture in other underdeveloped socialist countries. He repeatedly cited the negative example of Eastern European countries which lost much of their revolutionary momentum by failing to "strike when the iron is hot" and collectivize soon after liberation and land reform.[66] Those countries' decision to wait until a higher level of industrialization permitted agricultural mechanization and large-scale farming meant the preservation of an individual peasant economy. This, of course, provided an economic base for the restoration of capitalism. Equally importantly, by delaying the forward progress of revolutionary transformation, it forestalled or even denied socialism as a continuous process of struggle toward an eventual communist society.

Second, Mao held that the tendency to stress productive forces and mechanization led to a dangerous neglect of people's consciousness:

> The textbook often insists on the function of machines in socialist transformation. But if you don't raise the consciousness of peasants, don't transform people's thinking, but only rely on machines, how will that work? In the struggle between the two roads, the issue of using socialist ideas to transform people and train people is a major problem in our country.[67]

Material incentives. The Cultural Revolution attacks on material incentives have made them a well-known aspect of the "capitalist road" that needs relatively little treatment here. Mao obviously felt that excessive reliance on material incentives would lead to inadequate attention to political consciousness and collective interest as possible motivating forces.[68] He saw such policies to be "fostering individualism."[69] But he also regarded them as an undialectical stress on one side of a classic Marxist policy:

> From each according to his abilities [in Chinese, literally: each exhausts his abilities], to each according to his work." The first half of the sentence says one should exert one's greatest effort to produce. Why do they want to divide the two parts of the sentence and always one-sidedly talk of [the latter half:] material incentives? If you propagandize material incentives in this way, capitalism becomes invincible.[70]

In addition, Mao found the stress on material incentives and the distribution of consumer goods as determining factors in socialist society to be a serious reversal of Marxist economics. He pointed out that while bourgeois economics treats consumer demand, mediated by the market, as the decisive governor of the economy, Marxist economics stresses the relations of production as the determining factor. By "making absolute" the satisfaction of individual material interest, Mao argued, the Soviet text had succumbed to bourgeois economics.[71]

"Bourgeois right." One of the most important Chinese theoretical discussions of capitalist restoration, Yao Wenyuan's* 1975 article, "On the Social Basis of the Lin Biao Anti-Party Clique," placed great stress on the question of "bourgeois right" (*zichan jieji faquan* 资产阶级法权). This was a notion that Marx had discussed in his *Critique of the Gotha Program*, a discussion that Lenin followed up in *State and Revolution*. It referred to the survival in socialist society of such remnants of capitalist society as the sale of commodities in a market, and the payment of wages for labor—wages that would be equal for equal amounts of work, but would produce *inequalities* because of the *unequal* distribution of skills and capacities in the work force.[72] Yao identified "bourgeois right" and the inequities rising from it as the economic foundation of "new bourgeois elements" that arise in socialist society.[73] In essence he argued that the skilled workers, technicians, managers, and higher cadres who are favored by the prevailing wage scale can become "new bourgeois elements" if they attempt to protect their privileged position and even expand it by legal and illegal means.

Yao's argument is an extremely important one. Though it is more explicit than anything we have of Mao's writings and is now most decidedly out of favor in China,[74] I believe it is generally consistent with much of Mao's thinking. It does, however, tend to stress only one side of Mao's dialectical legacy, which argued that while "bourgeois right" had to be restricted, it remained a necessary element of the socialist economy. On a number of occasions, especially in 1958 when many were calling for the institution of a free supply system under the communes, Mao defended the commodity system and explicitly denied that it would lead to capitalism. "We must destroy a portion of bourgeois right. But commodity production, commodity exchange we still must maintain."[75] His argument for this was the same practical argument that Lenin had given for the NEP: the peasants demand equal exchange for their agricultural produce and view the commodity system as the only guarantee of that.[76]

The aspect of "bourgeois right" that Mao did oppose and urge the gradual limitation of was the wage system and the system of grade levels that went with it.

---

   * Yao Wenyuan (姚文元, 1931–2005) was a leftwing literary critic in Shanghai whose attack on a play by Beijing's deputy mayor set off the Cultural Revolution. He became a member of the "Gang of Four" and was arrested and imprisoned after the Cultural Revolution.

Bourgeois right must be destroyed, destroyed every day, such as stressing qualifications or grade levels and not stressing the benefits of the supply system. . . . In 1953 we changed the supply system to a wage system. This method was basically correct. We had to compromise. But there were defects. On grade levels we also compromised. . . . The grade level system is a father-son relationship, a cat-mouse relationship.[77]

The last sentence here is particularly intriguing, for it seems to imply that what Mao found most obnoxious was not the *economic* inequality, but the distinctions in status and authority that the grade level system implied.

The 1975 debates on "bourgeois right" revealed another aspect of Mao's concern. He was quoted as saying "We now practice the commodity system. Our wage system is also unequal: there is the eight-grade wage scale, etc. These can only be restricted under the dictatorship of the proletariat. Therefore, were the likes of Lin Biao to take power, it would be very easy to establish a capitalist system."[78] The implication of this statement, I believe, is that the survival of "bourgeois right" in the economic system makes control of the state crucial in determining whether a country will follow a socialist or capitalist road. (We shall return to this point below). Even after the means of production have been substantially socialized, there remain enough remnants of the bourgeois economy to enable "new bourgeois elements," should they seize state power, easily to transform the entire social system back to capitalism.

The concept of class—relations of production and superstructure. One of the most difficult problems for any theory of capitalist restoration has been the definition of "class." Obviously if there is to be a restoration of the bourgeoisie, there must somewhere be a bourgeois class. But if the means of production are no longer privately owned, one can no longer define the bourgeoisie as the segment of society that owns the means of production. Most analysts who have addressed this problem have noted Mao's tendency to define class in terms of consciousness, as a derivative of his greater attention to the political and ideological superstructure of society.[79] There is excellent justification for this point of view, not only in the practice of the Chinese revolution, but also in theoretical statements by Mao and the Chinese press. The Chinese have stated that "class is not only an economic concept; it is a political concept. Class struggle manifests itself in different forms—political, economic and ideological."[80] Mao himself begins his critique of Stalin's "Economic Problems of Socialism in the Soviet Union" by noting that "Stalin talks only about relations of production and does not talk about the superstructure."[81]

While recognizing this distinctly Maoist sensitivity to the importance of the superstructure, we should not assume that he is inattentive to relations of production nor should we assume that his notion of class and of capitalist restoration is divorced from any consideration of the relations of production. Part of the problem simply derives from an inconsistency on Mao's part in defining the line between the realm of production relations and the realm of superstructure. Immediately following the above quoted criticism of Stalin's neglect of the superstructure, Mao continues: "He doesn't talk about the relationship between superstructure and economic base. In China cadres participate in labor, workers participate in management, cadres are sent down for tempering and we have destroyed the old system of regulations [in factory management]. All these pertain to the superstructure, to the state of consciousness."[82] Elsewhere, Mao follows Stalin in analyzing production relations in terms of three aspects: ownership, "mutual relations between people," and distribution. He pays particular attention to the middle category, and under that category discusses the "two participations," the reform of regulations, the equal treatment of cadres, technicians, and workers—precisely the policies earlier discussed as part of the superstructure.[83]

Clearly in both of these analyses, Mao is concerned with the same problem—with the problem of "mutual relations between people" and the institutional and authoritative context in which they take place. He is above all concerned with *systems*, at one point stating, "The basic issue is systems: systems determine which direction a country will go."[84] What are most important are those systems that mediate relations of authority between people. The function of the "two participations" and the other institutional reforms in factory management is to eliminate the sense of alienation and social distance that authority relations are likely to produce. In the absence of such reforms, cadres are likely to exercise their authority in an arrogant and commandist fashion that would be no different from that of bourgeois factory owners or managers. In one passage, which admittedly deals more with *consciousness* of class than with the definition of class itself, Mao writes: "In our experience, if cadres do not discard their airs, do not become one with the workers, the workers often do not regard the factory as their own, but as the cadres'."[85]

By the time Mao's theory of capitalist restoration is fully developed, these ambiguities have largely been resolved by defining the origins of classes substantially in terms of *power*. And it is in this sense that I would interpret the statement that "class is not only an economic concept; it is a political concept." It points not so much to the realm of ideology as to the realm of power and authority—to the "bourgeois power holders" so much under attack in the Cultural Revolution. This is important because instead of leading to the superstructure, it leads us back to the relations of production, and control over the means of production. The case is stated most clearly in the crucial article "On Khrushchev's Phoney Communism."

[The members of the Soviet privileged stratum] are abusing their powers over the means of production and of livelihood for the private benefit of their small clique.

The members of this privileged stratum appropriate the fruits of the Soviet people's labour and pocket incomes that are dozens or even a hundred times those of the average Soviet worker and peasant. They not only secure high incomes in the form of high salaries, high awards, high royalties and a great variety of personal subsidies, but also use their privileged position to appropriate public property by graft and bribery. Completely divorced from the working people of the Soviet Union, they live the parasitical and decadent life of the bourgeoisie.[86]

Obviously what Mao has done is to make the critical leap from talking about class in terms of *ownership* of the means of production, to talking about *control* of the means of production. And in this he is totally in keeping with some of the most important thinking of Western and (the unity of opposites?) Yugoslav Marxist theory. The trend in that theory is to recognize that ownership is only one particular form of authority over the disposition of property;[87] that "class relations are relations of power;"[88] and that even in such works as *Capital*, Marx was as concerned with politics as he was with economics.[89]

"New bourgeois elements." The foregoing discussion has attempted to show how Mao arrived at a notion of capitalist restoration through a consideration of the relations of production. But that is not the only analytical road that he traveled. He came to a very similar conclusion from a discussion of the emergence of new "strata" in socialist society. One of his earliest discussions of this problem comes in disputing the Soviet textbook's assertion that "the transition to communism will be accomplished without going through a social revolution." Mao retorts: "Although a socialist society has abolished classes, in the process of its development, it may have certain problems with 'vested interest groups' (*jide liyi jituan* 既得利益集团). They are content with the existing system, and do not wish to change this system."[90] He raises the example of production team leaders who may resist the assumption of their powers by brigades, communes, or other higher levels of ownership or accounting.[91] Mao here seems to be making exactly the argument that Franz Schurmann has ascribed to him: "Property is interest—defined space buttressed by power, wealth and prestige. . . . [In China] the 'capitalist-roaders' were the elements within the Chinese state that had developed new bureaucratic and political interests, new property, and in that sense had become 'capitalist.'"[92]

But Mao goes one step further, and it is a step that makes the characterization of this stratum that he describes as a class all the more justified. In the following passage, Mao begins by quoting and then accepting with qualifications an idea from the Soviet textbook that he will later reject utterly.

> "Under socialism, there are no classes striving to maintain outdated economic relations." This interpretation is correct. However, there are still conservative strata in socialist society, still something like "vested interest groups." Divisions between mental and manual labor, between town and city, between workers and peasants still exist. Although these are non-antagonistic contradictions, it is only through struggle that contradictions can be resolved.
>
> The children of cadres cause great concern. They lack life experiences and social experience, but they put on airs and have great feelings of superiority. We must teach them not to rely on their parents, or on revolutionary martyrs, but to rely completely on themselves.[93]

The immediate shift from a discussion of "vested interest groups" to a discussion of the children of cadres is extremely important. On the one hand, the latter comments are reminiscent of Mao's January 1965 comments to Edgar Snow, where he pessimistically refers to the possibility that the youth of China might "negate the revolution."[94] On the other hand, in his comments to Snow, Mao seems concerned with youth's lack of steeling in war, revolution, and the hardships of the old society and with a consequent ideological flabbiness to which the Cultural Revolution responded. In his comment on the Soviet text, Mao is concerned that the sons and daughters of cadres might inherit the status and privileges of their parents. Obviously, to the extent that this happened, a "vested interest group"—by perpetuating itself over several generations—would transform itself into a class. The problem would thus be more than ideological; it would be a structural problem of the whole society.

Mao's comments on the children of cadres are so frequent and his willingness to discuss the problem in class terms so marked, that it is clear that this represented an important part of his total conception. One final quote should illustrate his willingness to contemplate dangerous similarities between the new China and the old:

> The intelligent often come from those of low positions, the despised, the oppressed and the young. Socialist society is no different. According to the rules of the old society, the oppressed had a low cultural level but were smarter; the oppressors had a high cultural level but were more stupid. The high salaried stratum also presents dangers: their culture and knowledge are greater, but compared to the low salaried stratum, they are more stupid. The children of our cadres are not as good as non-cadre children.[95]

Around 1960, when these comments were written, Mao's terminology had not reached its final form. What are here called "vested interest groups" and a "high salaried stratum" would later often be described as a "privileged stratum" or "degenerate elements" (*tuihua bianzhi fenzi* 蜕化变质分子)[96]—a term remarkably reminiscent of the Trotskyite Left's complaints about the "degeneration" of leadership under Stalin.[97] It was probably only in 1964–1965 that Mao decided to group all of these into the category of "new bourgeoisie," as in his comment on corrupt cadres under attack in the Socialist Education Movement: "As for the minority of evil and vicious ones, they must wear the cap of 'new bourgeois elements.'"[98]

Were we to combine, in summary form, Mao's analyses of the relations of production under socialism and the emergence of new bourgeois elements, I believe an argument along these lines would emerge. If cadres and/or technicians acquire unmediated authority over the means of production, they will use that authority to protect their own political and bureaucratic interests, and with their higher salaries, powerful connections, access to better urban schools, and other privileges, will be able to guarantee for their children superior opportunities to obtain favored political or economic positions. When this happens, a new bourgeois class will have emerged. Not only will it control the means of production, but it will be able to pass that control on to future generations of new bourgeois elements.

The state. Since political power and formal control of much of the means of production—especially industrial production—are concentrated in the Party and state apparatus, a consideration of the emergence of new bourgeois power holders led naturally to a concern for the nature of the state. Like Lenin, Mao paid considerable attention to the problem of the state under socialism. Not only did he share Lenin's intense distaste for bureaucracy, but he also realized that only firm proletarian control of the state distinguished socialism from state capitalism. It has been noted that one of the innovations of Mao's article "On the Correct Handling of Contradictions Among the People" is its frank facing of the contradictions between the state and the people, or as expressed there, between the leaders and the led. Mao himself was well aware of this divergence from earlier Soviet theory, which he regarded as having abandoned dialectics: "The Soviet Union stresses unity and does not talk about contradictions, especially the contradictions between the leaders and the led."[99] Later he would remark on the Soviet textbook, "This book mentions the state, but it does not research it. This is one of the shortcomings of the book."[100] Again he notes that in discussing the various rights enjoyed by workers, the text "did not talk about the right to control the state, to control various enterprises, to control culture and education. In fact these are the workers' greatest rights under socialism, their most basic rights."[101]

The danger, of course, is that if the contradiction between the state and the people is not constantly recognized and if the workers are not constantly reminded of their right to control the state as the only correct resolution of the contradiction, the state may achieve a degree of autonomy, may become alienated from the people and even exploit the people. Mao was not at all averse to treating the state as similar to a class. In criticizing excessive collections from the peasantry, and in the context of repeated criticisms of Stalin, he writes "If we collect 70 percent for the state, that's just like the landlords."[102]

It is in this context too that I think we must understand Mao's criticisms of "independent kingdoms:" they were the epitome of the autonomous state. "The [Party] Committees of the finance and economic ministries never make reports. They don't ask for directives before the fact; they don't report after the fact. Independent kingdoms. At 4:40 they force you to sign your name. They don't link up with the Center above; they don't link up with the masses below."[103] Once divorced from society—divorced from proletarian control— the autonomous state becomes both vulnerable to bourgeois infiltration and likely to breed new bourgeois elements. Should these new bourgeois elements manage to entrench themselves in the state, then the proletariat will have lost state power and, given the survivals of "bourgeois right" in the economic base, the restoration of capitalism will be easily accomplished. Ultimately, the Chinese would analyze this process with a notion of "peaceful evolution." Here is their explanation of the process in Yugoslavia:

> The degeneration of the state power in Yugoslavia occurred not through the overthrow of the original state power by violence and the establishment of new state power, but through "peaceful evolution." In appearance, the same people remain in power, but in essence these people no longer represent the interests of the workers, peasants and working people but those of imperialism and the old and new bourgeoisie in Yugoslavia.[104]

There are significant difficulties with this notion of "peaceful evolution" in terms of Marxist-Leninist theory. The Leninist theory of the state insists that it cannot be peacefully transformed, it must be smashed. The Chinese have resolutely held to this view and criticized the arguments of the Soviet Union and the Euro-Communists that a "peaceful transition" from capitalism to socialism is possible. It is unclear why a "peaceful evolution" in the other direction should be possible. To take the example of the Soviet Union, the official Chinese position is that under Stalin the workers controlled the state—including its critical instruments of violence, the army and the police. How, then, did Khrushchev and his "new bourgeois elements" usurp control of the state without provoking the violent reaction of the working class?

I have never seen a truly satisfactory resolution of this contradiction, which means that the *process* whereby capitalism is restored is probably the weakest part of Mao's theory. The closest the Chinese come to addressing the problem is in this statement: "The whole history of the dictatorship of the proletariat tells us that peaceful transition from capitalism to socialism is impossible. However, there is already the Yugoslav precedent for the 'peaceful evolution' of socialism back to capitalism. Now Khrushchev's revisionism is leading the Soviet Union along this road."[105] In a sense what this says is: "It happened. Don't tell me the theory says it can't happen!" It is similar to one of Mao's general criticisms of the Soviet textbook: the text proceeds from general principles instead of investigating history and proceeding inductively.[106] I am relatively certain that if Mao were convinced that his ideas on capitalist restoration violated Lenin's theory of the state, he would simply have replied that Lenin's theory would have to adjust to the knowledge gained in the practice of building socialism since Lenin's death.

But there is one additional answer to the question that can be suggested. For all Mao's need to defend Stalin in order to prevent attacks on the "cult of personality" from going too far in China in 1956–1957, and in order to criticize the truly revisionist policy of Stalin's successors in international relations, Mao's analyses of the origins of the erroneous *internal* policies of the Soviet Union almost invariably went back to Stalin himself. Thus in the intra-Party documents we have been relying on in this essay, Mao is far more critical of Stalin than the CCP usually is in public. In essence, what this suggests is that in Mao's eyes, the bureaucratic perversions of the Soviet state that Lenin so mercilessly criticized in the last years of his life were never eliminated under Stalin. Thus, a firm mass-based proletarian state power was never established in the Soviet Union. If a proletarian state power was never established, then there was no need to smash the state to accomplish a restoration of state capitalism. Because of Stalin's failures in dialectics—his denial of class struggle, his ignoring of the contradictions between leaders and led—and because of further revisionist policies of his successors, capitalism could be restored through the "peaceful evolution" of the existing, substantially autonomous, state power.

Dare I press further? I shall. We have seen that Mao's criticisms of Stalin often took the form of unfavorable comparisons to Lenin. But we should not assume that Mao regarded the course of the Bolshevik Revolution during Lenin's lifetime as beyond reproach. In one interesting comparison of the early course of the Chinese and Russian revolutions, Mao explicitly criticizes the policy under war communism of requisitioning from the peasantry.[107] He also notes Lenin's justification of the alliance with state capitalism in order to combat the bourgeoisie and the petty bourgeoisie. China's own revolution had taken exactly the opposite strategy: the proletariat and the peasantry allying with the petty bourgeoisie and the national bourgeoisie to oppose landlords, comprador capital, and bureaucratic (state) capitalism. Though Mao attributes these different policies to different historical conditions rather than to any error of Lenin's, he leaves no doubt that he considers China's course superior.[108] Having based his revolution on the peasantry—the petty bourgeoisie of the countryside—Mao rarely shows anything comparable to Lenin's considerable antipathy toward the petty bourgeoisie. In fact, he criticized Marx for fearing the petty bourgeoisie excessively and overemphasizing its shortcomings.[109] To the extent that the Bolshevik's alliance with state capitalism and the revolution's reliance on state power were products of this fear of the petty bourgeoisie, I believe that Mao found it an unfortunate policy.

Finally, if we compare Lenin's above-quoted posing of the problem of democratic centralism as "bureaucracy *versus* democracy" to Mao's own analysis that "Without democracy, it is impossible to have correct centralism,"[110] I think it fair to say that in some instances Mao would have found even Lenin weak in dialectics. In effect, I believe the unspoken implication of Mao's theory is that from the beginning the Soviet Union was insufficiently wary of the dangers of state capitalism and bureaucracy in the party. This insufficiently wary attitude, plus the particular historical circumstances of the Bolshevik revolution, and the weakness in dialectics in the Party under Stalin, allowed a new class to emerge in the Party and state bureaucracy. That class in turn spawned a leadership that guided the Soviet Union not to socialism but to state capitalism. Mao remained convinced to his death that China could tread a different path. But his theory of capitalist restoration points to the numerous sources of political and political economic degeneration that are harbored within any socialist state. Mao's successors now face the challenging task of avoiding those pitfalls while building a prosperous, modern socialist society.

NOTES

1. Baum, Richard, *Prelude to Revolution: Mao, the Party and the Peasant Question, 1962–1966* (New York: Columbia University Press. 1975), 1.

2. Throughout this chapter, I often refer to "the Chinese view" or "the Chinese theory." I do not mean to imply by this rather nebulous expression that all Chinese held a uniform view on the subject of capitalist restoration. Rather, the purpose of this formulation is to contrast theoretical treatments of the problem in China to those in the Soviet Union or the West. I use the term in particular to refer to formulations that have appeared, without personal attribution, in such official Party publications as *Renmin Ribao* and *Hongqi*. While I would hesitate to assert that such publication makes these views either official or unanimously accepted CCP positions, it does, I believe, allow me to ascribe such opinions to a group much broader than Mao and his immediate supporters. Thus, when I speak of "the Chinese theory" instead of "Mao's

theory" it is often to stress that the views in question were supported even by Mao's opponents within the Party.

3. Mao Zedong, "Xiang gaogan tuijian de jingdian zhuzuo" [Classical works recommended to high cadres], in *Mao Zedong sixiang wansui* (n.p. [Red Guard collection], 1967), 256.

4. Karl Marx, *Critique of the Gotha Programme* (Beijing: Foreign Languages Press, 1972; original 1875), 15.

5. Ibid., 28.

6. Karl Marx, "Economic and Philosophical Manuscripts" (1844) in *Early Writings* (New York: Vintage), 358, emphasis in the original. Note, however, Stojanovic's balancing of such passages with more teleological notions of communist society in Marx's writings: Svetozar Stojanovic, *Between Ideals and Reality: A Critique of Socialism and Its Future* (New York: Oxford University Press., 1973), 22–28.

7. Karl Marx, *The Class Struggles in France (1848–1850)* (New York: International Publishers, 1972; original 1850), 26.

8. Karl Marx, *Capital*, vol. 1: *A Critical Analysis of Capitalist Production* (Moscow: Foreign Languages Publishing House, 1961; original 1877), 135.

9. Ibid., 716.

10. Karl Marx, *The Eighteenth Brumaire of Louis Bonaparte* (New York: International Publishers, 1963; original 1852), 43.

11. Marx, *Class Struggles in France*, 42.

12. V. I. Lenin, "Communism and Electrification" (Speech at the Eighth Congress of Soviets), December 22, 1920, in *The Lenin Anthology*, ed. R. C. Tucker (New York: W. W. Norton, 1975), 494.

13. Charles Bettelheim, *Class Struggle in the USSR, First Period: 1917–1923* (New York: Monthly Review Press 1976), 375.

14. Stephen F. Cohen, *Bukharin and the Bolshevik Revolution: A Political Biography, 1888–1938* (New York: Vintage, 1975), 69–78.

15. Lenin, "'Left-Wing' Childishness and the Petty Bourgeois Mentality," May 1918, in *Collected Works* (Moscow: Progress Publishers, 1965), vol. 27, 336.

16. Ibid., 339.

17. Cited in Lenin, "Political Report of the Central Committee [at the Eleventh Congress] of the R.C.P. (B.)," March 27, 1922, *Collected Works*, vol. 33 (1966), 286.

18. Ibid., 287.

19. Ibid., 288

20. Lenin, "Outline of Speech at the Tenth All-Russia Congress of Soviets," December 1922, *Collected Works*, vol. 36 (1966), 589.

21. Lenin, "One Step Forward, Two Steps Back," May 1904, *Collected Works*, vol. 7 (1965), 396–67.

22. Lenin, "The Tax in Kind," April 21, 1921, in *Collected Works*, vol. 32 (1965), 355–57.

23. Lenin, "Purging the Party," September 20, 1921, in *Collected Works*, vol. 33 (1966), 40.

24. Lenin, "A Great Beginning: On the Heroism of Workers in the Rear," July 1919, in Tucker, *The Lenin Anthology*, 478–79.

25. Lenin, "On Co-operation," January 6, 1923, *Collected Works*, vol. 33 (1966), 474–75.

26. Lenin, "Better Fewer, but Better," March 2, 1923, in *Collected Works*, vol. 33 (1966), 487.

27. Cohen, *Bukharin*, 189.

28. Edward Hallett Carr, *Foundations of a Planned Economy, 1926–1929* (New York: Macmillan, 1971), vol. 2: 433.

29. Cohen, *Bukharin*, 142.

30. Edward Hallett Carr, *Socialism in One Country, 1924–1926* (New York: Macmillan, 1959). vol. 1, 113–19.

31. Cohen, *Bukharin,* 143.

32. Carr, *Foundations*, 307–11.

33. J. V. Stalin, "Speech delivered at the First All-Union Congress of Collective-Farm Shock Brigaders," February 19, 1933, in *Works* (Moscow: Foreign Languages Publishing House, 1955), vol. 13, 248.

34. Mao Zedong, "Shi da guanxi" [Ten great relationships], April 25, 1956, *Mao Zedong xuanji*. (Beijing: Renmin chubanshe, 1977), vol. 5, 267–88. An earlier version of this fundamentally important speech appears in *Wansui* (1969), 40–59, and is translated in Stuart Schram, *Chairman Mao Talks to the People* (New York: Pantheon, 1974), 61–83. Schram compares the two texts in "Chairman Hua edits Mao's literary heritage: 'On the 10 Great Relationships,'" *China Quarterly* 69 (March 1977): 126–35.

35. Mao Zedong, "Zai badaerci huiyi shang de jianghua: diyici jianghua" [Speeches at the second session of the Eighth Congress: first speech], May 8, 1958, in *Wansui* (1969), 222.

36. Mao Zedong, "Zai bajie sanzhong quanhui shang de jianghua" [Speech at the third plenum of the Eighth Central Committee], October 7, 1957, in *Wansui* (1969), 123.

37. Mao Zedong, "Guanyu 'Shehui zhuyi jingji wenti' yishu dejianghua" [Speech on [Stalin's] "Economic Problems of Socialism [in the Soviet Union]"], mid-November 1958, *Wansui* (1969), 249.

38. Mao Zedong, "Zai badaerci huiyi shang de jianghua: dierci jianghua" [Speeches at the second session of the Eighth Congress: second speech], May 17, 1958, in *Wansui* (1969), 205.

39. Mao Zedong, "Zai Lushan huiyi shang de jianghua" [Speech at the Lushan plenum], July 23, 1959, in *Wansui* (1969), 299.

40. Mao Zedong, "Jiguanqiang he pojipao de laili ji qita" [On the origins of machine guns and artillery, and other matters], August 16, 1959, *Wansui* (1969), 308.

41. Mao Zedong, "Zai zuigao guowu huiyi shang de jieshuyu" [Concluding remarks at the supreme state conference], March 2, 1957, *Wansui* (1969), 93–95.

42. Mao Zedong, "Zai Hankou huiyi shang de jianghua" [Speech at the Hankou conference], April 6, 1958, in *Wansui* (1969), 156.

43. Mao Zedong, "Zai badaerci huiyi shang de jianghua: disanci jianghua" [Speeches at the second session of the Eighth Congress: third speech], May 20, 1958, in *Wansui* (1969), 210.

44. Lenin, "What Is to Be Done? Burning Questions of Our Movement," March 1902, in Tucker, *The Lenin Anthology*, 19.

45. Mao Zedong, "Zai Chengdu huiyi shang de jianghua: sanyue ershierri de jianghua" [Speeches at the Chengdu conference: Speech of March 22 (1958)], in *Wansui* (1969),174.

46. Mao Zedong, "Guanyu sange wenjian de anyu" [Note on three documents], July 29, 1959, in *Wansui* (1967), 76.

47. Schram, *Chairman Mao Talks*, 115. This passage appears in Mao's March 22 speech at Chengdu, in *Wansui* (1969), 172–80, but I have cited Schram because his translation seems quite apt. The troublesome phrase which he translates as "conquering spirit" is *shi ru pozhu de fengge* (势如破竹的风格) literally: "spirit whose power [makes things as easy] as splitting bamboo."

48. Mao Zedong, "Zai badaerci huiyi shang," May 8, 1958, in *Wansui* (1969), 187.

49. Mao Zedong, "Dui 'Makesi zhuyizhe yingdang ruhe zhengque de duidai geming qunzhong yundong" [A critique of the article "How should Marxists correctly treat the revolutionary mass movement?"], August 15, 1959, in *Wansui* (1967), 89; "Zai Hankou huiyi," April 6, 1958, in *Wansui* (1969), 183.

50. Mao Zedong, "Zai badaerci huiyi," May 8, 1958, in *Wansui* (1969), 195.

51. Mao Zedong, "Guanyu 'Shehui zhuyi jingji wenti'" in *Wansui* (1969), 247–51. *Wansui* (1967), 156–66, contains a detailed set of notes by Mao on the text by Stalin. It is dated November 1959, but I would guess that these are Mao's 1958 notes for the Zhengzhou speech. The Zhengzhou text in the 1969 volume is explicitly identified as only notes by a member of the audience.

52. Mao Zedong, "Zai bajie liuzhong quanhui shang de jianghua" [Speech at the sixth plenum of the Eighth Central Committee], December 19, 1958, in *Wansui* (1969), 262.

53. Mao Zedong, "Zai Lushan huiyi," in *Wansui* (1969), 298.

54. The two texts, "Sulian 'Zhengzhi jingjixue' dushu biji" [Reading notes on the Soviet text, "Political Economy"], in *Wansui* (1967), 167–247 and (1969), 319–99, are virtually identical. The 1967 text gives 1960 as a date, the 1969 text gives 1961–1962. However in an appendix at the end of the notes, Mao refers to the "great experiment" of "these two years." That could only mean the Great Leap Forward of 1958–1959, and would seem to require us to accept 1960 as the date the notes were first made—which would not, of course, rule out the possibility that Mao made later revisions in 1961–1962.

55. Mao Zedong, "Zai bajie shizhong quanhui shang de jianghua" [Speech at the tenth plenum of the Eighth Central Committee], in *Wansui* (1969), 432.

56. Mao Zedong, "Zai bajie jiuzhong quanhui shang de jianghua" [Speech at the ninth plenum of the Eighth Central Committee], January 18, 1961, in *Wansui* (1967), 258–59.

57. Mao Zedong, "Zai kuoda de zhongyang gongzuo huiyi shang de jianghua" [Speech at an enlarged central work conference], January 30, 1962, in *Wansui* (1969), 407, 420.

58. Mao Zedong, "Zai Beidaihe zhongyang gongzuo huiyi shang de jianghua" [Speech at the Beidaihe central work conference], August 9, 1962, in *Wansui* (1969), 423.

59. Mao Zedong, "Zai bajie shizhong quanhui" in *Wansui* (1969), 431. The passage from Lenin that Mao is apparently paraphrasing appears in "'Left-Wing' Communism—An Infantile Disorder." It reads: "The dictatorship of the proletariat means a most determined and ruthless war waged by the new class against a *more powerful* enemy, the bourgeoisie, whose resistance is increased *tenfold* by their overthrow (even if only in a single country), and whose power lies not only in the strength of international capital, the strength and durability of their international connections, but also in the *force of habit,* in the strength of *small-scale production.* Unfortunately, small-scale production *engenders* capitalism and the bourgeoisie continuously, daily, hourly, spontaneously, and on a mass scale. All these reasons make the dictatorship of the proletariat necessary, and victory over the bourgeoisie is impossible without a long, stubborn, and desperate life-and-death struggle which calls for tenacity, discipline, and a single and inflexible will" (Tucker, *Lenin Anthology*, 552–53).

60. Renmin ribao and Hongqi Editorial Departments "On Krushchev's phoney communism and its historical lessons for the world," *Peking Review* 29 (July 17, 1964): 16–18. This article, "On Khrushchev's Phoney Communism and Its Historical Lessons for the World," is unquestionably the fullest statement of the Chinese position on the restoration of capitalism. It is the ninth and last of the CCP's comments on the July 14, 1963 "Open Letter" of the CPSU. If I were to guess which of the Chinese replies were drafted by Mao, this would certainly head the list—partly because both content and style seem closest to Mao's other writings, partly because *Hongqi* never printed it, though its editorial department was supposedly its co-author!

61. Ibid., 11.

62. Lowell Dittmer, *Liu Shao-ch'i and the Chinese Cultural Revolution: The Politics of Mass Criticism* (Berkeley: University of California Press, 1974), 58.

63. Richard Baum and Frederick Teiwes, *Ssu-ch'ing: The Socialist Education Movement of 1962–1966* (Berkeley: Center for Chinese Studies, 1968); Baum, *Prelude to Revolution.*

64. Mao Zedong, "Zai diyici Zhengzhou huiyi," in *Wansui* (1969), 247; Renmin ribao and Hongqi, "Khrushchev's Phoney Communist," 9.

65. Mao Zedong, "Sulian 'Zhengzhi jingjixue,'" in *Wansui* (1969), 334.

66. Ibid., 332, 346, 370.

67. Ibid., 337.

68. Ibid., 361–62.

69. Ibid., 357.

70. Ibid., 358.

71. Ibid., 357.

72. Marx, *Critique of Gotha*, 14–18; Lenin, *State and Revolution*, in Tucker, 375–78.

73. Yao Wenyuan, *On the Social Basis of the Lin Piao Anti-Party Clique* (Beijing: Foreign Languages Press, 1975), 5–9.

74. Xu Dixin, "Zichan jieji faquan shi chansheng zichan jieji de jingji jichu ma?" [Is bourgeois right the economic base for generating a bourgeois class?] *Guangming ribao*, June 13, 1977.

75. Mao Zedong, "Guanyu shehui zhuyi jingji wenti," 249. See also "Dui Sidalin," 162–63.

76. Mao Zedong, "Dui Sidalin," 160–62.

77. Mao Zedong, "Guanyu shehui zhuyi jingji wenti," 250; "Dui 'Da A. B. Saningna he B. F. Wenshener liangtongzhi' dejiduan piyu" [Several criticisms of "A reply to comrades A. B. Sanina and B. F. Vinshire"] in *Wansui* (1967), 122. For a particularly radical statement by Mao (which seems to be the same as that which appears in a slightly garbled version in Dittmer, *Liu Shaoch'i*, 193) see *Wansui* (1967), 248. This contains a great deal of atavistic yearning for the simplicity and sacrifice of the Yan'an era.

78. Zhang Chunqiao, "Lun dui zichan jieji de quanmian zhuanzheng" [On all-round dictatorship against the bourgeoisie], *Hongqi*, 1975, no. 4.

79. Richard C. Kraus, "Class conflict and the vocabulary of social analysis in China," *China Quarterly* 69 (March 1977): 54–74; John Bryan Starr, "Theoretical treatments of embourgeoisement in post-Liberation China," presented at the 1977 Annual Meeting of the American Political Science Association, and "Conceptual foundations of Mao Tse-tung's theory of continuous revolution," *Asian Survey* 11 (June 1971): 610–28.

80. John Bryan Starr, *Ideology and Culture: An Introduction to the Dialectic of Contemporary Chinese Politics* (New York: Harper & Row, 1973), 128.

81. Mao Zedong, "Guanyu shehui zhuyi jingji wenti," 248; "Dui Sidalin," 156.

82. Mao Zedong, "Guanyu shehui zhuyi jingji wenti," 248.

83. Mao Zedong, "Zai Hankou huiyi,"183; "Sulian 'Zhengzhi jingjixue,'" 347–48, 385–86.

84. Mao Zedong, "Sulian 'Zhengzhi jingjixue,'" 380.

85. Ibid., 364. Later in this passage, Mao goes on to argue that a natural reaction to this problem is to turn to material incentives to motivate workers, with all the negative implications implied by that. Mao's analysis is quite similar to Bettelheim's *Cultural Revolution and Industrial Organization in China* (New York: Monthly Review Press, 1974), 22–24.

86. Renmin ribao and Hongqi, "On Khrushchev's Phoney Socialism," 15.

87. Ralf Dahrendorf, *Class and Class Conflict in Industrial Society* (Stanford, CA: Stanford University Press, 1959; Bettelheim, *Class Struggle in the USSR*; Svetovar Stojanovic, *Between Ideals and Reality: A Critique of Socialism and Its Future* (New York: Oxford University Press, 1973).

88. Nicos Poulantzas, *Political Power and Social Class* (London: New Left Books, 1973), 99.

89. Louis Althusser and Etienne Balibar, *Reading Capital* (London: New Left Books, 1970).

90. Mao Zedong, "Sulian 'Zhengzhi jingjixue,'" 343–44.

91. Ibid., 343

92. Franz Schurmann, *The Logic of World Power: An Inquiry into the Origins, Currents and Contradictions of World Politics* (New York: Pantheon, 1974), 137.

93. Mao Zedong, "Sulian 'Zhengzhi jingjixue,'" 351; cf. "He Wang Hairong tongzhi de tanhua" [A talk with comrade Wang Hairong], June 24, 1964, in *Wansui* (1969), 531.

94. Edgar Snow, *The Long Revolution* (New York: Vintage, 1973), 221.

95. Mao Zedong, "Sulian 'Zhengzhi jingjixue,'" 306.

96. Mao Zedong, "Zai kuoda de zhongyang gongzuo huiyi shang de jianghua" [Speech at an enlarged central work conference], January 30, 1962, in *Wansui* (1969), 420.

97. Carr, *Foundations*, 428.

98. Mao Zedong, "Zhongyang gongzuo zuotanhui jiyao" [Excerpts from a central work symposium], December 20, 1964, in *Wansui* (1969), 584.

99. Mao Zedong, "Zai Zhengzhou huiyi," in *Wansui* (1969), 165.

100. Mao Zedong, "Sulian 'Zhengzhi jingjixue,'" 360.

101. Ibid., 360.

102. Mao Zedong, "Dui Xin, Luo, Xu, Xin sige diwei zuotanshi de tanhua" [Talk with the Xin, Luo, Xu, and Xin local committees], February 21, 1959, in *Wansui* (1967), 5.

103. Mao Zedong, "Zai Beidaihe," in *Wansui* (1969), 429.

104. Renmin ribao and Hongqi, "Is Yugoslavia a socialist country?" *Peking Review* 39 (September 27, 1963): 24.

105. Renmin ribao and Hongqi, "On Khrushchev's phoney communism," 7.

106. Mao Zedong, "Sulian 'Zhengzhi jingjixue,'" 383.

107. Ibid., 393.

108. Ibid., 393–94.

109. Mao Zedong, "Zhongyang gongzuo zuotanhui," 595.

110. Mao Zedong, "Zai kuoda gongzuo huiyi," 403.

Chapter Eleven

Political Theater in Modern China
Joseph W. Esherick and Jeffrey Wasserstrom

China's revolutionary era ended with the death of Mao Zedong in 1976. His demise was soon followed by the arrest of his wife and the other members of the so-called Gang of Four, including two, Zhang Chunqiao and Yao Wenyuan, who were deeply involved in developing the "restoration of capitalism" arguments examined in the previous chapter. Mao's death was followed by the rise of Deng Xiaoping and his policies of Reform and Opening (*gaige kaifang* 改革开放). Under Deng, China entered a new era of export-oriented economic growth, which was further fueled by China's accession to the World Trade Organization (WTO) in 2001. Gradually, the socialist planned economy gave way to a market economy, and China's gross domestic product (GDP) grew at an unprecedent double-digit rate year after year. Now, after more than forty years, a resurgent China has emerged as the United States' primary rival for dominance in the Asian region and, to some degree, on the world stage.

With China's emergence as a world power in the twenty-first century and a model for self-confident and often aggressive authoritarian rule, it is easy to forget that China's rise was not always a smooth one. Under Mao, the utopian experiment of the Great Leap Forward produced a disastrous famine that left perhaps thirty million or more dead. The Great Leap was followed by the Great Proletarian Cultural Revolution, which brought higher education to a halt and decimated the intellectual class. Those disasters could of course be blamed on Mao's erratic leadership, but the years of Reform and Opening were not without setbacks as well. Most prominent among these was the wave of protests that swept the country in 1989 and resulted in the bloody suppression of the Beijing "democracy movement" on June 4, 1989. One common feature links these three events—the Great Leap Forward, Cultural Revolution, and the 1989 protest movement. All are taboo subjects in China today:

banned from the history books, prohibited as topics of research, and scrubbed from the internet. A whole generation of young Chinese has grown up with no knowledge of these episodes of China's recent past. This fact makes it especially important for foreign scholars to continue research on these forbidden topics of Chinese history.

This final essay, co-authored with Jeffrey Wasserstrom, was written soon after the 1989 protest movement. I was in China at the time, witnessed the events in Xi'an first-hand, and wrote about them for a volume on the protests beyond Beijing.* In writing that essay, I was struck by the number of theatrical metaphors I was using (street theatre, new actors, official script, left the scene) and later turned from metaphor to analysis for a lecture at the University of Michigan, which in turn led to this collaboration with Jeffrey Wasserstrom for an analysis of ritual and theater in China past and present. Here our interest in protest repertoires and the inspiration of recent anthropological literature is evident, and we examined the way in which the Confucian-inspired ritualized governance of imperial China was transformed into the more public, more speech-oriented, and more theatrical modes of twentieth-century Chinese politics. At the core of this analysis is the historic and cultural link between ritual and theatre, and the difference between the more rigidly proscribed norms of ritual, and theater's greater room for creative agency.

Needless to say, the literature on the events of 1989 has grown exponentially since this essay was written in the immediate aftermath of the massacre. Most importantly, leaked internal documents, memoirs, and unofficial sources have given us much greater insight into the secret deliberations of the party-state. Many of these publications have been the subject of considerable controversy, but we certainly know much more about the decision to violently suppress the movement than we did in 1990.† What is clear and generally acknowledged, is that the years 1989 and 1990 saw a major divergence in the evolution of Communist systems. The Soviet bloc states of Eastern Europe collapsed and a troubled evolution toward democracy emerged, while the Soviet Union dissolved into its constituent republics. The dissolution of the

---

* "Xi'an Spring," *Australian Journal of Chinese Affairs* 24 (July 1990): 209–36. Reprinted in Jonathan Unger, ed., *The Pro-Democracy Protests in China: Reports from the Provinces* (Armonk, NY: M. E. Sharpe, 1991)

† In addition to early publications cited below, see especially Andrew Nathan and Perry Link, eds., *The Tiananmen Papers: the Chinese Leadership's Decision to use Force Against its own People—In Their Own Words*, comp. by Zhang Liang (New York: Public Affairs, 2001) and a critique by Alfred Chan and rejoinder from Nathan in *China Quarterly* 177 (March 2004); Craig J. Calhoun, *Neither Gods nor Emperors: Students and the Struggle for Democracy in China* (Berkeley: University of California Press, 1994); Timothy Brook, *Quelling the People: The Military Suppression of the Beijing Democracy Movement* (New York: Oxford University Press, 1992); and Jeremy Brown, *June Fourth: The Tiananmen Protests and Beijing Massacre of 1989* (Cambridge: Cambridge University Press, 2021).

Soviet Union became a major focus of study for the Chinese leadership and a lesson from which the CCP was determined to learn. The party-state authoritarianism of China today is in many ways a reaction to the events of 1989, but this chapter suggests ways in which the different trajectories of China and Eastern Europe are the result of different social meanings of the role of ritual and theater in the different societies.

ACTING OUT DEMOCRACY: POLITICAL THEATER IN MODERN CHINA[*]

JOSEPH W. ESHERICK AND JEFFREY N. WASSERSTROM

For two and a half months in the spring of 1989, China's student actors dominated the world stage of modern telecommunications. Their massive demonstrations, the hunger strike during Gorbachev's visit, and the dramatic appearance of the Goddess of Democracy captured the attention of an audience that spanned the globe. As we write in mid-1990, the movement and its bloody suppression have already produced an enormous body of literature—from eyewitness accounts by journalists and special issues of scholarly journals, to pictorial histories and documentary collections, and most recently, textbook chapters and analytical works—tracing the development of China's crisis.[1] Despite a flood of material too massive to review in the present context, we still lack a convincing interpretive framework that places the events within the context of China's modern political evolution, and also provides a way to compare China's experience to that of Eastern Europe. Such an interpretation should help us to understand why massive public demonstrations

---

[*] Originally published as "Acting Out Democracy: Political Theater in Modern China," co-authored with Jeffrey Wasserstrom, *Journal of Asian Studies* 49, no. 4 (November 1990): 835–65. As befits an essay that continually crosses disciplinary lines between history and anthropology, this chapter is based upon the our firsthand observation as well as upon written and pictorial sources. Joseph Esherick was in Xi'an, Jinan, and Northern Shaanxi during the spring and summer of 1989, and Jeffrey Wasserstrom was in Shanghai in December 1986. Where no additional citation is given, information on these times and places came from personal observation or discussions with participants. For additional detail, see Esherick "Xi'an Spring" and Jeffrey Wasserstrom, *Student Protests in Twentieth-Century China: The View from Shanghai* (Stanford, CA: Stanford University Press, 1991), Epilogue.

We would like to thank the following for sharing thoughts, criticisms, recollections, and/or unpublished papers: Jeffrey Cody, Dru Gladney, James Hevia, David Jordan, Barry Naughton, Michel Oksenberg, Elizabeth Perry, Frank Pieke, Henry Rosemont Jr., Clark Sorensen, Frederic Wakeman Jr., and two anonymous readers. Audiences at the University of Michigan, University of Washington, University of California, San Diego, and the University of Oregon provided helpful comments on an earlier version of this chapter. Grants from the Committee on Scholarly Communication with the PRC and Fulbright-Hayes supported our research in China, and a grant from the University of Kentucky helped make the writing of this chapter possible

spurred an evolution toward democratic governance in Eastern Europe, but in China led only to the massacre of June 3 and 4 and the present era of political repression.

None of the most frequently mentioned characterizations of the movement seem truly adequate. The Chinese leadership, for example, has portrayed both the 1989 movement and its predecessor in 1986–1987 as manifestations of "bourgeois liberalism," or acts of *luan* (乱, chaos) reminiscent of the Red Guards in the Cultural Revolution, or some combination of the two.[2] But if the 1989 protests were the result of "bourgeois" contamination, why was the most prominent anthem of the student demonstrators "The Internationale," and why did protesters carry pictures of Mao Zedong and Zhou Enlai?[3]

Official characterizations of recent protests as acts of *luan* and Red Guardism are even more deeply flawed. Protesters unquestionably committed disorderly acts in both 1986 and 1989, and there were certainly continuities between the 1960s and the 1980s in student tactics (e.g., the use of wall posters and the insistence upon free train passage to Beijing) in part because some young teachers advising the students were former Red Guards. Yet most foreign observers were impressed by the discipline and orderliness of the students.[4] The prominent role of march monitors, the security forces that maintained order in Tiananmen Square, the student "arrest" of youths for defacing a portrait of Mao—these activities hardly suggest an atmosphere of *luan*. The complete lack of either anti-Western rhetoric or devotional loyalty to any living CCP leader by the students of the late eighties makes all analogies with the Red Guards extremely tenuous.[5]

The analyses offered by Western social scientists, foreign journalists and Chinese dissidents, though considerably more persuasive than the official CCP line, are also problematic. Many, especially the professional Pekingologists of political science, stress the role that power struggles between Li Peng and Zhao Ziyang[*] played in shaping the 1989 events.[6] There is no doubt that internal divisions paralyzed the party leadership in April and May, preventing an effective response to the demonstrators. But at the start of the movement, one of the protesters' most common abusive rhymes in Beijing and Tianjin was "*Ziyang, Ziyang, xinge buliang*" (紫阳，紫阳，性格不良，Zhao Ziyang, Zhao Ziyang, you are not a good man);[7] and as late as May 19 (long after the Voice of America and BBC broadcasts had been focusing on the Li-Zhao conflict) the protesters' posters and slogans in Xi'an still had two central targets: Deng Xiaoping and Zhao Ziyang. Corruption in Zhao's immediate family made him so unpopular that it is impossible to see him

---

[*] Li Peng (李鹏, 1928–2019) was Premier from 1987 to 1998 and an anti-protest hard-liner in 1989. Zhao Ziyang (赵紫阳, 1919–2005) was general secretary of the Communist Party in 1989, somewhat sympathetic of the demonstrators' aims, and dismissed as a result.

successfully manipulating the movement for his own ends. Indeed, like Hu Yaobang* before him, Zhao Ziyang became a hero only after (and to a large degree because) he was ousted from power by the alliance of hard-liners and party elders around Deng.

The Western press and Chinese dissidents abroad usually characterize the events of China's spring as a "democracy movement." There is no question that "*minzhu*" was frequently invoked in the protesters' banners and slogans, but it would be hasty to associate *minzhu* (民主, literally: "rule of the people") with any conventional Western notion of democracy. Consider, for example, Wuerkaixi's words in the televised dialogue with Li Peng on May 18. Early in the meeting, Wuerkaixi† explained what it would take to get students to leave Tiananmen Square: "If one fasting classmate refuses to leave the square, the other thousands of fasting students on the square will not leave." He was explicit about the principle behind this decision: "On the square, it is not a matter of the minority obeying the majority, but of 99.9 percent obeying 0.1 percent."[8] This may have been good politics—and Wuerkaixi certainly made powerful theater—but it was not democracy.

The hunger-striking students in Tiananmen Square adopted a position designed to preserve their unity and enhance their leverage with the government. But in elevating the principle of unity above that of majority rule, they were acting within the tradition of popular rule (*minzhu*) thinking in modern China. When Sun Yat-sen assumed the presidency of the Republic of China in January 1912, his message to the revolutionary paper *Minlibao* was a simple slogan (in English): "'Unity' is our watchword"—not "democracy" or "republicanism," but "unity."[9] Closer to the present, the dissident magazine *Enlightenment* wrote in 1979 of the miraculous effects that the "fire" of democracy would have on the Chinese people:

> The fire will enable people completely to shake off brutality and hatred, and there will be no quarrel among them. They will share the same views and principles and have identical ideals. In lofty and harmonious unity they will produce, live, think, pioneer, and explore together. With these dynamic forces they will enrich their social life and cultivate their big earth.[10]

While Western democratic notions are normally linked to pluralism and the free competition of divergent ideas, *minzhu* in China is here linked to a vision in which people will "share the same views" and have "identical ideals." It is

---

* Hu Yaobang (胡耀邦, 1915–1989) was General Secretary of the CCP from 1982 to 1987, when he was ousted after the student demonstrations in 1987. His death in April 1989 sparked the demonstrations in that spring.
† Wuerkaixi (吾尔开希, Örkesh Dölet, 1968–), a Uighur from Xinjiang, was a student at Beijing Normal University, and a prominent hunger striker during the protests.

thus difficult to analyze the events of China's 1989 spring as a "democratic movement" in the pluralist sense of the term.[11]

Nor do the words and deeds of the protesters of either 1986–1987 or 1989 fit easily with more radical Western ideas of direct or participatory democracy. In many cases the students seem to have read the *min* in *minzhu* in a limited sense to refer not to the populace at large but mainly or exclusively to the educated elite of which they were a part. This elitist reading of *minzhu* was clear in the wall posters that appeared in Shanghai in December 1986, many of which took their lead from the speeches Fang Lizhi* gave at the city's Tongji University earlier that year. The main theme in these posters, as in Fang's lectures and writings, was not that the CCP should be more responsive to the ideas of China's masses, but rather that it should allow the intelligentsia a greater voice in national affairs.[12] This elitist strain carried over into student tactics in 1986: at one point, when Shanghai workers came out to support their protesting "younger brothers," the students told them just to go home.

The situation in 1989 was somewhat different, since at times the students actively sought (and received) the support of non-intelligentsia groups. Nonetheless, some educated youths continued to see democratic reforms in elitist terms. For example, two foreign observers found Fujian students "horrified at the suggestion that truly popular elections would have to include peasants, who would certainly outvote educated people like themselves."[13] Other reports highlight student distrust of the *laobaixing* (老百姓) or untutored masses (a distrust symbolized by groups of students who roped themselves off from bystanders during some marches), and the intelligentsia's lack of concern for the needs of workers and peasants.[14] Western critics and Chinese dissidents alike have taken leaders of the movement to task for behaving in nondemocratic and elitist ways, both at the time of the occupation of Tiananmen Square and during the formation of new protest leagues in exile.[15]

The preceding comments do not mean that there was nothing "democratic" about the movement. Clearly, there was a great deal about the protests—the calls for freedom of speech, the demands for more popular input into the way China is governed—that Westerners associate with the term "democracy." We do not wish to imply that Chinese are somehow incapable of understanding or acting upon Western concepts of democracy. Nor do we wish to imply that a Chinese movement must meet a stringent set of contemporary Western standards before it can earn the accolade "Democracy Movement." After all, as Donald Price has observed, we consider many Western states to have been "democratic" long before they reached the stage of universal suffrage.[16] The

---

* Fang Lizhi (方励之, 1936–2012) was an astrophysicist, former vice-president of the University of Science and Technology, whose ideas inspired the protests of 1986–1987 and again in 1989. After June 4, he fled to the US Embassy to avoid arrest and later emigrated to the United States.

point we do wish to stress is simply that, given the various contours of meaning the term *minzhu* had in 1989, labeling the protests a "Democracy Movement" does not take us very far in our effort to make sense of the movement. In some cases, in fact, it obfuscates more than it clarifies.

CHINA'S SPRING AS POLITICAL THEATER

It would seem that a more productive way to understand the events of April through June, 1989, is to view them as an exercise in political theater. Scholars as diverse as E. P. Thompson and Clifford Geertz, working on political systems as dissimilar as eighteenth-century England and nineteenth-century Bali, have demonstrated the value of interpreting politics in theatrical terms, that is, as symbol-laden performances whose efficacy lies largely in their power to move specific audiences.[17] This approach would seem ideally suited for analysis of the Chinese protests of 1989. As essentially nonviolent demonstrations that posed no direct economic or physical threat to China's rulers, the power of the protests derived almost exclusively from their potency as performances which could symbolically undermine the regime's legitimacy and move members of larger and economically more vital classes to take sympathetic action.

A number of the more insightful analysts of the Chinese protests of 1989 have already highlighted the importance of symbolism and role playing. Frank Pieke analyzes the "ritualized" quality of the protest actions and the significance of audience participation in the Chinese marches.[18] Perry Link has compared the petitioning at Tiananmen Square to "morally charged Beijing opera."[19] In a related vein, Dru Gladney and Lucien Pye have interpreted the symbolic implications of a variety of student actions and texts, and David Strand uses theatrical metaphors to capture the mood and explain the impact of student demonstrations in Beijing since 1919.[20] Our goal is to expand on these themes and to place the events of 1989 in a larger historical and theoretical context. In particular, it seems important to examine the relationship between political theater and ritual—a more tightly prescribed form of cultural performance which was so vital to the governance of imperial China.

What, then, was the political theater of 1989? First of all, it was street theater: untitled, improvisational, with constantly changing casts. Though fluid in form, it nevertheless followed what Charles Tilly calls a historically established "repertoire" of collective action.[21] This means that, even when improvising, protesters worked from familiar "scripts" which gave a common sense of how to behave during a given action, where and when to march, how to express their demands, and so forth. Some of these scripts originated in the distant past, emerging out of traditions of remonstrance and petition stretching back for millennia. More were derived (consciously and unconsciously) from the steady stream of student-led mass movements that had taken place since 1919. Thus, for example, when youths paraded from school to school in 1989, carrying banners emblazoned with the name of their alma maters, and called on students at other institutions to join their fight to *jiuguo* (救国, save the nation), they were following closely in the footsteps of the May Fourth Movement's participants and other republican-era protesters.[22]

State rituals and official ceremonies supplied other potential scripts.[23] The April 22 funeral march in memory of Hu Yaobang was a classic example of students usurping a state ritual, improvising upon an official script to make it serve subversive ends. Chinese funerals—especially those of wealthy and/or politically important figures—have always been key moments for public ritual.[24] As newspaper accounts of early twentieth-century funeral processions show, these ceremonies were an important opportunity for elite families to display their status, with musicians and hired mourners joining family and friends carefully ordered by age, gender, and social status in a symbolic representation of the proper social order.[25] In the PRC, memorial services for important political leaders are a critical political moment, and the composition of funeral committees is carefully scrutinized for clues to changing political alignments.[26] Here is political ritual with all the liminality that Victor Turner's conception requires: transition between two preferably stable political states, and thus highly dangerous.[27]

The particular danger in the case of political funerals arises from the possibility that unauthorized people will usurp the ritual and rewrite the script into political theater of their own. The most famous previous example of this was, in fact, not quite a funeral, but the Qingming remembrance that followed soon after the death of Zhou Enlai in 1976.[28] It produced the first "Tiananmen Incident" in which thousands of Beijing residents used the opportunity to pay their respects to Zhou and, in the process, level a variety of direct and indirect attacks on the Gang of Four. Critical to the nature of such ceremonies is the authorities' inability to prohibit them: they are politically required rituals of respect for revolutionary heroes. But when students usurp the ritual, they can turn it into political theater. Thus the funeral march becomes a demonstration. Though they march behind memorial wreaths to the deceased and carry their official school banners, they also chant slogans and hoist signs with their own political messages.

Marches of this sort inevitably lead to the central square of the city. That square normally faces the seat of government authority, which is also likely to be the venue for an official memorial service. At this point, the demonstration becomes a petition movement. The most dramatic was the petition of

1989 presented by three students kneeling on the steps of the Great Hall of the People. The symbolism of this petition was important, for it demanded an explanation of the background to Hu Yaobang's resignation as General Secretary of the Party in 1987. This demand focused on the fact that the party leaders who were orchestrating the official ceremonies inside the Great Hall were precisely the men who had removed Hu Yaobang from power. Thus the street theater unmasked the hypocrisy of the official ritual, and revealed the students on the streets to be the true heirs of the legacy of Hu Yaobang. In the end, the officially required ritual, once captured by the student actors, became the mechanism for attacking the authorities.[29]

Once the public stage has been captured, the street actors are all the more free to write their own script. In Beijing, they proved extraordinarily creative. They successfully upstaged two more state rituals: on the seventieth anniversary of the May Fourth Movement, the party's formal commemorations paled before the students' protest marches; and in mid-May, the welcoming rally students held for Gorbachev—complete with signs bearing slogans in Russian and Chinese—stole the thunder from the official ceremonies of the summit. One reason for the success of these protests, and for the relative weakness of the official rituals they mocked, came from their respective settings. Throughout much of May, students were in full control of Beijing's symbolic center, Tiananmen Square. The government was forced to hold its gatherings in less public and/or less powerful venues—the Great Hall of the People for May Fourth, the airport to welcome Gorbachev.

The group hunger strike launched in Beijing in mid-May, which was replicated in several other cities within days, was another stroke of creative genius. Although dissident officials in imperial times occasionally refused food to show their displeasure with a ruler, and at least one republican-era labor dispute involved a hunger strike, this kind of group fast was not a central element in the Chinese student protest repertoire until the influential one performed in Hunan in 1980.[30] Its use in 1989, by students who compared their strike to those of dissidents in other nations, showed how internationalized models for dissent had become.[31] This hunger strike proved a potent piece of political theater and earned the protesters enormous public sympathy.

The placement of the Goddess of Democracy in Tiananmen Square—directly between two sacred symbols of the Communist regime, a giant portrait of Mao and the Monument to the People's Heroes—was another powerful piece of theater. Though Western journalists often treated this twenty-eight foot icon as a simple copy of the Statue of Liberty, and the Chinese government insisted that this was so, the goddess was in reality a more complex symbol combining Western and Chinese motifs, some employed reverently, others ironically.[32] Some features of the goddess did resemble the

Statue of Liberty—an exact replica of which *was* carried through Shanghai in mid-May,[33] but others called to mind traditional Bodhisattva, and even the socialist-realist sculptures of revolutionary heroes found in Tiananmen Square. It was also, as Dru Gladney notes, reminiscent of the giant statues of Mao that were carried through the square during some National Day parades of the sixties.[34] A potent pastiche of imported and native symbolism, the goddess appeared in the square just as the movement was flagging, bringing new crowds of supporters and onlookers to the area.

Street theater of this sort is also dangerous because it is impossible to control the cast. As noted above, students tried at times to keep the *laobaixing* at arm's length, but this was not always possible, and in many cases organizers anxious to swell the number of protesters encouraged bystanders from all walks of life to join the crowd. Inevitably, this attracted members of the floating population of youths who had been in and out of trouble with the state apparatus. Mistreated by public security men in the past, many bore grudges they were anxious to settle. It appears that these young men were responsible for some of the violence that broke out as early as April 22 in Xi'an and Changsha, and on June 3 in Beijing.

Once one recognizes the movement as an instance of political theater, it becomes tempting to rate the performances. One of the best acts was put on by Wuer Kaixi in the May 18 dialogue with Li Peng. The costuming was important: he appeared in his hospital pajamas. So, too, was the timing: he upstaged the Premier by interrupting him at the very start. And props: later in the session, he dramatically pulled out an oxygen tube inserted into his nose in order to make a point. Especially for the young people in the nationwide television audience, it was an extraordinarily powerful performance.

For older viewers, perhaps the most riveting act was performed on May 20 when the CCTV news announcer Xue Fei read the official martial law announcement. Again, costuming was important: he wore all black, the suit apparently borrowed for the occasion. He read the announcement from beginning to end without lifting his eyes from the page, in a perfect imitation of the tone reserved for funeral eulogies. Xue Fei's performance was witnessed, understood, and remembered by television viewers throughout the country.

In any performance, the audience is critical. In street theater, audience participation always becomes part of the drama, and this was certainly true in Beijing and other cities in 1989.[35] First, citizens lined the parade route to applaud the student demonstrators. Then there were banners announcing support, and stands set up to provide food and drink. By the end, the nonstudent crowds had been fully drawn into the act, as the citizens of Beijing came out in force to block the army's entrance to the city after the declaration of martial law. Television provided a powerful new dimension to the movement's audience appeal. Most obviously, with the world press gathered for the Gorbachev visit, the demonstrators gained a global audience. That audience certainly helped dissuade the regime from an early use of force against its critics, but the domestic television audience was at least as important. Through it, by mid-May, Chinese across the country directly witnessed the scale of the massive demonstrations in Beijing, and that knowledge emboldened young people to launch their own protest marches in cities across China. Furthermore, the Beijing demonstrators were keenly aware of the power of this new medium as they showed through their demand for a live broadcast of their dialogue with the government. As a political mode, theater is only as powerful as the audience that it can move; and this theater certainly inspired and energized hundreds of millions of people in China and across the world.

As ritual and theater, the actions of demonstrators naturally call forth certain responses from the authorities, and the efficacy of official performance is substantially dependent on how well they play these roles. The party leadership's failure to acknowledge in any way the petition of the students kneeling on the steps of the Great Hall was a major violation of ritual, and it significantly increased public anger against official arrogance.[36] This is important because ritually correct responses to earlier student petitions—such as those submitted in 1918 (the year before May Fourth) and 1931 (when Japan invaded Manchuria) by youths angered by the Chinese authorities' handling of relations with Japan—had helped to defuse potentially volatile situations.[37]

The refusal to acknowledge the student petition in April was but the first of a series of unskillful official performances. When Li Peng was forced to join the televised dialogue with the student leaders, he was clearly unsuited for the role and very uncomfortable in it—and, predictably, he played it very badly. Later, the visit of Li, Zhao Ziyang and other party leaders to the hospitalized hunger strikers was a ritually required act of compassion, this one performed more adroitly. The loyalist rallies the party organized in the Beijing suburbs during the week before the massacre were remarkable, but far less effective, acts of official theater: participants told Western journalists that officials had instructed them to take part, and televised coverage of the events showed a mixture of bored, unhappy, and embarrassed faces.[38] Even the tanks of June 4 were a kind of theater. One does not choose tanks for their efficacy in crowd control—this was a performance designed to show irresistible power. It was a bad act, but the videotapes were skillfully edited and played over and over for the domestic television audience.

For official theater, however, nothing was more important than the ritual *biaotai* (表态) that followed the movement's suppression. These public statements of position (and here the only permissible position was one in favor of the regime) began with provincial leaders, regional military commands, and functional ministries of the national government. Rebroadcast on national television and reported in the press, they announced the speed with which the constituent parts of the state apparatus fell in behind the new party leadership. These *biaotai* of party and military elites were followed by similar performances in schools, factories, research institutes, and administrative bodies across the nation as virtually every urban citizen was required to account for his or her actions since April and publicly announce solidarity with the new hard-line policies. *Biaotai* is a special form of performance (*biaoyan* 表演). The participants were clearly *acting*—most were not sincere—and everyone knew it. They recited memorized scripts, with key phrases lifted from articles and editorials in *People's Daily*. Because few believed the words they were uttering, most of these *biaotai* were poorly performed and bad theater. But the regime's unremittent insistence on these *biaotai* performances testifies to the importance of such theater in the Chinese political system.

It should be noted that politically sensitive members of the Chinese public recognize the practices described above as a form of theater. In their view, politics is a performance; and public political acts are often interpreted in that way. Thus, for example, a typical reaction to Li Peng's speech announcing martial law was to evaluate it as a performance, and the reviews were uniformly bad: words were mispronounced, the tone was too shrill, etc. As one Beijing intellectual put it: "He should have been wearing a patch of white above his nose"—the standard makeup of the buffoon in Beijing opera. Similarly, protesters at times represented Li as the clown or villain in propaganda skits based on traditional theatrical forms. One Beijing street performance (described for us by Henry Rosemont, Jr.) combined comic cross talk with operatic motifs to portray the attempts of a courtesan (representing Li Peng) to flatter, appease, and thereby gain the protection of an old man (representing Deng Xiaoping).

Metaphors from the world of theater are so much a part of the language of politics in modern China (as elsewhere) that protesters and observers continually adopted theatrical terms of speech. When protesters attacked Li Peng and Deng Xiaoping, their slogans included "Li Peng *xiatai* (下台)!" (Li Peng, get off the stage) and "Xiaoping, Xiaoping, *kuaixie xiatai* (快些下台)!" (Deng Xiaoping, Deng Xiaoping, hurry off the stage).[39] Whenever previously little-known actors assume a major political role, there is discussion of who their *houtai* (后台, backstage managers) might be. And after the Tiananmen incident, there was significant debate as to whether or not it should be termed a "tragedy."[40] But the sense in which the Chinese people see all this as performance was most powerfully suggested by a wise old peasant from northern Shaanxi who, when asked the difference between Mao Zedong and Deng Xiaoping, simply laughed and said, "They were just singing opposing operas (*chang duitai xi*, 唱对台戏)!"

RITUAL AND THEATER

Our discussion to this point has used two terms to describe public political performances: "ritual" and "political theater." These terms refer to two distinct genres of action, though the line demarking the two is not always clear, since many acts involve both ritualistic and theatrical elements.[41] Before exploring the gray area where ritual and theater overlap, we must distinguish the two ideal types, because the differing degrees to which a polity depends upon and leaves legitimate space for one or the other genre have profound implications for the nature of politics in that system. Thus the ritual-infused politics of imperial China was qualitatively different from China's twentieth-century politics with its distinctive political theater.

There are almost as many definitions of ritual as there are anthropologists. Defined most loosely, the term includes virtually any "rule-governed" or "communicative" activity, in which case everything from strictly ordered coronations to highly improvisational demonstrations would qualify as political rituals.[42] We will use the term in a narrower sense here. Borrowing heavily from Clifford Geertz, we will define rituals as traditionally prescribed cultural performances that serve as models *of* and models *for* what people believe.[43]

Such a definition conforms well with the Confucian sense of "*li* (禮)," a term that is frequently translated as "ritual." *Li* serves to support and reinforce the status quo, bringing order to a community by reaffirming the distinctions between and bonds connecting its individual members.[44] Taking our lead from Confucius and his followers, we will highlight this system-maintenance function of ritual, a function also stressed by Durkheim and his followers.[45]

We must also, however, take account of critics of the functionalist approach to ritual, which in the words of one writer treats ritual acts as "a sort of all-purpose social glue."[46] Again building upon the work of Geertz, we will highlight the symbolic nature of rituals as acts with hidden meanings that need to be decoded.[47] And following Victor Turner, we will stress the processual and dynamic nature of rituals. According to Turner, while rituals serve to confirm existing hierarchical relations, these relationships are frequently suspended or temporarily overturned during the ritual *process*.[48] This creates a volatile and potentially dangerous situation: there is always the chance (as with Hu Yaobang's funeral) that people will capitalize upon the instability or liminality of the process and subvert it to other ends.

To put Turner's point another way, there is always the chance that people will turn a ritual performance into an act of political theater. Central to the notion of ritual is the idea that only careful adherence to a traditionally prescribed format will ensure the efficacy of the performance.[49] With any departure from a traditional script, a ritual ceases to be ritual. Ritual thus gives relatively limited play to the creative powers of scriptwriters or actors, and as soon as participants break away from traditional structures their actions become theatrical. Theater, by nature, is more liberated from the rigid constraints of tradition, and provides autonomous space for the creativity of playwrights, directors, and actors. This gives theater a critical power never possessed by ritual: it can expose the follies of tradition (or the follies of abandoning tradition), mock social elites, or reveal the pain and suffering of everyday life.[50]

Although he is talking about *aesthetic* theater (the formal dramas of the stage), Turner makes additional distinctions between theater and ritual that are relevant to our more metaphorical use of the term.[51] One such distinction, particularly important in the Chinese context, has to do with role playing and the audience. Role playing is central to all ritual; and Chinese ritual is particularly concerned to fix each individual in his or her proper social role. Participation is by invitation only, and each participant has a specified role. Rituals separate people into superior and inferior, elder and younger, male and female. According to the *Liji* (禮記, *Classic of Ritual*), "without [rituals] ... there would be no means of distinguishing the positions of ruler and subject, superior and inferior, old and young." But paired with this role for ritual is the role that Confucians give to music: music unites. Thus the *Liji* notes that *li* "make for difference and distinction," but "music makes for common union."[52] It does so because it creates an undifferentiated audience, and that is what theater does as well. As a leading dramatic theorist writes, "Theater comes into existence when a separation occurs between audience and performers."[53] The homogeneity of the audience should not be overstressed, because different members of the audience might identify with different characters or respond to different themes. But in general, the relatively undifferentiated audience in theater (as opposed to the carefully stratified *participants* in ritual) enjoy a shared experience and may be drawn toward a common identity. At the very least, the audience, in its anonymity, is freed to interpret the drama and identify with particular roles as it wishes. This is quite different from ritual, which, by involving all the "audience," forces each participant into a prescribed role and a particular place in the socio-political structure.

Theater, then, is cultural performance before a mass audience. *Political theater* is theater which expresses beliefs about the proper distribution and disposition of power and other scarce resources. Unlike political rituals, which in our limited definition always perform a hegemonic function of confirming power relations, political theater often challenges or subverts the authority (in E. P. Thompson's phrase, "twists the tail") of ruling elites.[54]

While political theater can be (and often is) counter-hegemonic, it is by no means always so. Groups within the ruling elite can use political theater to defend their position against attacks from below or to maximize their power vis-à-vis other elite groups. The rowdy London street parades by eighteenth-century supporters of the new Hanoverian regime, which were staged to offset Jacobin mockeries of George I; the gatherings held by American political parties to show support for presidential candidates, or the parades for national holidays; and the patriotic mass rally German students organized for Bismarck in 1895 to honor the Iron Chancellor's eightieth birthday—these are but a few examples of political theater that upheld rather than challenged the hegemony of ruling institutions or elites.[55]

Having distinguished ritual and theater, we must now note what the two forms have in common. Perhaps the most fundamental similarity is that both ritual and theater are performed for social effect. Language and symbols are used not primarily to convey truths, but to produce effects—on the participants, the audience, the gods. This is "pragmatic speech," whose function is to *move*, not to inform. Linguistically, one sees this most clearly in what J. L. Austin has called the "performative utterances" of ritual. In a marriage ceremony, the "I do" is not a report on one's mental act of acceptance; the words *in themselves* complete the act.[56] As such, it is not meaningful to debate the truth value of such utterances: all that counts is that uttering the words have the prescribed effect of completing the marriage ceremony. Similarly, in the Chinese ritual discourse codified in such texts as the *Yili*,[57] it would be quite inappropriate to take literally the polite refusal of a gift, or the confession of unworthiness when offered a position. These polite phrases are not spoken to express one's true intentions, and a literal reading of the words could cause a major breach of etiquette. It is the *symbolic effect* of the words, in the context of the total verbal and nonverbal *performance*, that counts: the words and actions convey a posture of humility, of thanks, and of respect for the other party in the social transaction.[58]

These simple points are important in interpreting events in China, for we will understand the protesters' actions better if we focus on their symbolic meanings and intended effects than if we scrutinize their words in search of some coherent political program. The slogans, big-character posters, pamphlets, open letters, and speeches of the protesters were replete with emotive statements of commitment and dissent. They were proclamations of personal positions, moral statements of resolve. They announced the role one was committed to play in the emerging political drama, but they rarely analyzed the failings of the Chinese political system or proposed a concrete program for political change. But this was natural, for theirs was a performance designed to impress and move an audience, not a lecture designed to inform. To say this is certainly not to suggest that the movement was *merely* play-acting.

In the post-Reagan era, there are grave risks in writing of politics as performance. One can easily be misunderstood as suggesting that it is all fakery: artificial props, carefully staged events, all medium and no substantive message. That is not our intent. Our point is rather that it makes a good deal more sense to analyze performed acts and utterances not for their truth value, but for their symbolic meaning. For example, on April 21 and again on April 27, many students at Beijing universities wrote out last testaments (*yiyan* 遗言, or *yishu* 遗书). They proclaimed their willingness to die for democracy, freedom, the motherland; they said good-bye to their parents and begged their forgiveness and understanding.[59] It makes little sense to ask whether these students really knew what "freedom" and "democracy" meant, and still less sense to ask whether they were truly prepared to die. These last testaments were powerful public statements of great symbolic meaning. They revealed a fundamental alienation from the regime and a willingness to make great (perhaps the ultimate) sacrifice for an alternative political future.

Ritual and theater have more in common than symbolic action. There is also a great deal of borrowing of scripts between ritual and theatrical performances, in part because the roots of the two cultural forms are so closely intertwined. Most aesthetic theater grew directly out of ritual performance: Greek tragedy from the dithyramb sung around the altar of Dionysus, medieval European "passion plays" from the Catholic mass, acrobatics and magic acts from shamanistic practices.[60] The earliest forms of Chinese drama likewise had their roots in sacrificial rites.[61] The bond between Chinese opera and ritual performance is evident in everything from the use of "Mulian" plays in conjunction with funeral rites to the tradition of staging theatrical performances to entertain the gods.[62]

Political theater also borrows heavily from ritual scripts, though often inverting the meaning of those scripts. In sixteenth-century France, religious rioters mocked their opponents' most sacred rites in acts of political theater: Protestant paraders would force a priest to burn his vestments; Catholics would parody Protestant prayers by transposing the words "Devil" and "God."[63] The decisions of American anti-war protesters to hold demonstrations on Veterans' or Memorial Day are another example of Western protesters transforming a ritual occasion into a theatrical one.[64]

The transmission of texts between ritual and political theater is by no means unidirectional: some ritual performances have their roots in what Turner calls "social dramas." This is not surprising, since one function of rituals is to heal wounds between groups by symbolically reenacting social conflicts (ranging from wars and feuds to shouting matches and bitterly contested elections) and then concluding with a symbolic reintegration of the community.[65] Thus some political rituals simultaneously commemorate and deradicalize subversive acts of political theater. Recent work on the French Revolution by Mona Ozouf and others suggests that the Jacobins and others were interested in creating new festivals precisely in order to "represent radical aspirations, while at the same time curbing them."[66] As Lynn Hunt argues, French festivals of the decade after 1789, combining symbolic reenactments of attacks on the ancien régime with ritualized pledges of loyalty to the new order, both "recognized" and "partially defused" the revolutionary potential of the populace.[67]

The mutual borrowing of scripts between political theater and ritual gives the relationship between the two forms what one theorist calls a "braided" quality: the two strands continually overlap and reemerge, alternately taking precedence over each other.[68] One of the best illustrations of this relationship has direct relevance to the events of 1989: the transformations of the May Fourth Movement from theater to ritual and back. When students took to the streets in 1919 to protest imperialist threats from abroad and warlord corruption at home, they established the classic script for student political theater. Subsequently, both the Guomindang (GMD) and the CCP have tried to use the political theater of the May Fourth Movement as the basis for new rituals of conciliation. Though the two parties commemorated May Fourth differently, both sought to turn the May Fourth anniversary into a safe revolutionary festival.[69] The script begins with a replay of the conflict of 1919, usually through speeches praising the actions of former student protesters. The ritual then moves into a healing phase, in which official speakers emphasize that there is no longer a division between the nation's rulers and its youth, since the present regime is carrying on in the May Fourth tradition. These speakers claim that the duty of contemporary students is to prove their patriotism by working hard to help the party build a new China, rather than by protesting, and the members of the audience (often students) show their acceptance of this interpretation by clapping, shouting loyalist slogans, and singing party songs.

These official attempts to "recognize" and "defuse" the revolutionary potential of students have never been wholly successful, as educated youths have repeatedly managed to transform May Fourth rituals back into May Fourth theater.[70] They have done this by emphasizing the reenactment aspect of the official ritual, while denying the reconciliatory phase. In 1947 under the Guomindang, some Shanghai students chose to engage in anti-GMD propaganda rather than attend official commemoration activities. But the most dramatic case of subversion occurred in 1989, when Beijing students upstaged the Communist Party's festival to literally retrace the steps of their predecessors of seventy years before. What made this piece of street theater so subversive was its implication (clearly spelled out in banners and slogans) that the ideals of the May Fourth Movement (which the CCP claimed to represent) remained unfulfilled and needed to be fought for again on the streets.

Despite these symbolic links between ritual and theater, it remains important to distinguish the two forms and to note when one or the other predominates within a specific political system. It is particularly important for our purposes, because the impact of street theater is in part determined by the degree to which political theater is seen to have a legitimate connection to governance. To illustrate this point, we must briefly review the roles of ritual and theater in Chinese politics, past and present.

POLITICAL RITUAL IN IMPERIAL CHINA

Few cultures have given ritual as crucial a role in governance as did China. Confucius had argued that "If [a ruler] could for one day 'himself submit to ritual,' everyone under Heaven would respond to his goodness."[71] As Confucianism emerged as a distinct school of thought in ancient China, this notion of rule through ritual became central to its teaching. In the imperial era, the administrative weakness of the state and the comparatively small size of its formal bureaucracy combined with the Confucian disdain for rule by regulation and coercive punishment to make ritual indispensable for the maintenance of social order.[72] Confucian ritual was primarily a secular ritual; but for Confucius, as Herbert Fingarette has put it, the secular was sacred.[73] Elaborate ceremonies governed all social relationships and guaranteed that human society would operate in harmony with the cosmic order. A central concern of political philosophers was defining, categorizing, and describing the correct practice of ritual (*li*) associated with relationships between Heaven, the emperor, officials, and members of the populace at large.

Imperial ritual, the highest genre of *li*, was overwhelmingly confined to the palace and the special temples for imperial sacrifices near the capital. Within the walls of the Forbidden City, the rituals were extraordinarily elaborate (one can recall the opening scene of the movie, "The Last Emperor"). The places, costumes, gestures, and words of the participants were all carefully choreographed to display the ordered hierarchy of the court and bureaucracy, and the emperor's unique role connecting human society to the greater cosmos. But high walls and imperial guards excluded the general public from any participation, and the carefully prescribed roles of the participants excluded all possibility of political theater.[74]

The most notable exceptions to the pattern of imperial confinement were the hunts and southern tours of the Kangxi and Qianlong emperors of the Qing. The emperors were greeted by vast crowds as forerunners assembled all officials, as well as local gentry and commoners, to kneel and greet the imperial arrival and departure. But the emperor traveled in an enclosed sedan chair or barge, before which the people were to prostrate themselves, so that even on tour, the pattern of imperial seclusion was not entirely abandoned. The Kangxi emperor occasionally used his tours and hunts to meet ordinary peasants and inquire of their crops and especially of any oppression by local officials.[75] But the extraordinary nature of these contacts is suggested in a Jesuit account according to which the peasants "were all eager to see his Majesty, who instead of concealing himself gave everyone the liberty of coming near him."[76] Such Jesuit sources are important because the official record is silent on contacts of this sort between the Emperor and the people—a fact that itself suggests the ritually problematic nature of such contact.[77]

Official ritual tended to imitate the imperial. Officials were, to paraphrase Alexander Woodside, "spiritual micro-monarchs."[78] They replicated the imperial sacrifice to the Altar of Soil and Grain and led worship at the Confucian temple. Day-to-day official ritual was largely confined to the tribunal, or to the private ritual of visits with local notables or other bureaucrats. Officials on tour were preceded by criers and banners ordering silence and reverence, and the public bowed before them. The arrival and departure of officials did at least provide the ritual (at these liminal moments) of a procession, which allowed the public an opportunity to express its regret over the departure of a popular official (or opposition to the arrival of an unpopular one).[79] But, in general, *participatory* political rituals, of the sort most easily transformed into political theater, were absent from the official vision of how politics should operate. Instead, there were rigidly stratified hierarchic forms in which the ritual leader (emperor, official, or kin group patriarch) confronted a mute audience which in many cases (because prostrate) never even *saw* the ceremonial head.[80]

The contrast to European royal and civic ritual is striking. From the fourteenth century, the royal entry to a city was one of the most important forms of ritual procession. But on entering a city, the monarch would be met (confronted?) by the city's armed militia, handed the keys to the city (an act of fealty, but also a gesture to a guest), and welcomed with street pageants symbolically portraying the virtues which the citizenry expected of its ruler.[81] In some German cities jealous of their civic autonomy, the burghers' welcome of their prince or bishop could turn into an armed show of force in which townsmen confronted their sovereign as a rival.[82] But everywhere these ceremonies provided an opportunity for the corporate bodies of urban life (universities, guilds, *parlements* or Senates, clergy, militia, lawyers, merchants and tradesmen) to organize and publicly announce their place in the public order. As a consequence, even monarchical rituals "tended to describe the essence of national kingship in such a way as to exalt civic virtues and encourage the preservation of urban liberties."[83] All the more was this true of civic rituals on such feast days as Corpus Christi, where the autonomous strength of the corporate groups that made up European civil society was regularly given ritual legitimacy and public display.[84]

One notable feature of Chinese political rituals is the general absence of any public speaking. There were, of course, the *xiangyue* (鄉約), the public lectures on the Sacred Edict. But all accounts agree that this form quickly atrophied in the Qing, and never caught on in Chinese culture.[85] China lacked the rhetorical tradition of Greek and Roman forums or of many illiterate societies. Confucius was suspicious of men with "clever words,"[86] and Confucian bureaucrats preferred the authority of the brush. Even in the academies, Qing evidential scholars reacted against the lecturing styles of the Song Neo-Confucians, preferring the more solitary scholarship of textual criticism.[87] Religious ritual provided no rhetorical models: China lacked a congregational religion with weekly sermons. Consequently, in the limited civil society of guilds and *huiguan* that grew up in late imperial China, there were neither the ecclesiastic nor the Roman republican models for public meetings and speeches that one finds in merchants' and artisans' guilds in Europe.

The one legitimate political activity that provided an opening for political theater was the right to petition officials for redress of grievances. In ancient China, a "complaint drum" (*dengwen gu* 登聞鼓) was supposedly placed before a ruler's palace to summon attendants to hear a grievance. The drum continued in use in imperial times, and the Qing placed it just southwest of Tiananmen. Nonetheless, the Qing code was interpreted in such a way as to discourage strongly such direct appeals to Beijing, and most petitions were presented to local authorities.[88] Naturally, the right to petition led frequently to a political theater of mass demonstrations, which might develop into riots or even rebellions.[89] A late nineteenth-century account of such a petition movement evokes images of modern protest repertoires:

> I once saw a procession of country people visit the yamens of the city mandarins. . . . Shops were shut and perfect stillness reigned as twenty thousand strong, they wended their way through the streets, with banners flying, each at the head of a company and each inscribed with the name of the temple where that company held its meetings. "What is the meaning of this demonstration?" I inquired. "We are going to reduce the taxes," was the laconic answer.[90]

Such mass petition movements were surely unusual, but the script was well enough known to be replicated when necessary. Furthermore, a significant feature of the Chinese case was the replication of the bureaucratic hierarchy in the world of the gods. Consequently, gods were also petitioned—and far more frequently than officials. Thus religious ritual could serve, in Emily Ahern's words, as a "learning game," teaching ordinary Chinese "how to analyze (and so manipulate) the political system that governed them."[91]

Petitions provided one small avenue of public access into the otherwise closed realm of legitimate politics in imperial China. But the state dealt harshly with any attempt to use petitions for more than personal grievances. They were not to be an excuse for public debate on matters of policy. As Confucius said, "He who holds no rank in a state does not discuss its politics."[92] Even as China began the slow process of reform in the wake of the Opium War, movement toward a public politics outside the state was exceptionally slow. When Lin Zexu, in disgrace after the outbreak of the Opium War, revealed his support for the acquisition of ships and guns in a letter to a friend, he closed by urging, "I only beg that you keep [these ideas] confidential. By all means, please do not tell other persons."[93] Even the famous reform essays of Feng Guifen, written around 1860, were not published until they were brought to the attention of the emperor in 1898.[94] But after the Sino-Japanese War, and especially in the course of the twentieth century, Chinese politics changed fundamentally, and central to that change was the emergence of a new space for, and new kinds of, political theater.

POLITICAL THEATER IN TWENTIETH-CENTURY CHINA

In the final years of the Qing dynasty, the New Policy reforms ushered in a new era of Chinese politics. First there were the new schools, which brought together a politically engaged student class in urban centers across China. Soon these students were organizing protests against foreign-financed railways, for boycotts of American goods because of US restrictions on Chinese immigration, and for broad movements for political reform. They wrote big-character posters, spoke from street corners, and staged mass demonstrations, including costumed characters to dramatize their concerns.[95] Some of these demonstrations built upon classic ritual forms—as in a 1906 funeral procession by Changsha students to bury the ashes of two revolutionaries who had committed suicide.[96] As Mary Rankin and William Rowe have shown, an increasingly assertive civil society grew out of earlier networks of gentry activists, local managers, merchant guilds, and charitable organizations.[97] Chambers of Commerce and Educational Associations aggressively sought to set agendas for local political affairs. As constitutional reforms began in 1909–1910, China had its first experience with electoral politics. Provincial Assemblies elected in 1909 provided the basis for political parties, as like-minded individuals came together in a variety of reformist associations. But reformers also relied upon established political forms to press their views—most notably the petitions presented to the court in favor of rapid transition to full constitutional government. The new local, provincial, and national assemblies became forums for speechmaking. Political rhetoric became important to the political process; and especially among students and dissident intellectuals abroad, some (like Wang Jingwei) established their political reputations as eloquent public speakers.

Chambers of Commerce and the Provincial Assemblies were two of the most prominent institutions in this new civil society. It is significant that all of the Provincial Assemblies and many of the Chambers of Commerce were located in new, specially constructed buildings. The architecture of these structures symbolized the break with the past. Chinese-style walled compounds and enclosed courtyards were generally eschewed. Instead, the chambers and assemblies were located in large Western-style buildings of brick or stone, opening directly onto the streets and including spacious auditoria (*huitang* 會堂) for a modern politics of meetings. The new schools also built auditoria, especially in the republican period, and the function of the new architecture was explicitly acknowledged. One commentator on the auditorium at Qinghua University in Beijing noted that since the art of public speaking was so undeveloped in China, the school's new auditorium "may well be regarded as the Forum Romanum where budding Ciceros will deliver their orations."[98] Sports stadiums attached to missionary schools, another imported form of architecture, also provided venues for the new politics.[99]

This politics of public meetings, speeches, and demonstrations was so new to China that its forms and models had to be borrowed from other types of performance. Foreign models were one natural source, especially since so many speakers and protesters had either studied abroad or been trained in missionary schools in China (where preachers' sermons provided regular reminders of the power of oratory). A *North China Herald* account of a 1903 meeting to condemn Russian imperialism notes that one of the first things that happened was that "a set of rules, translated from the English [*Robert's Rules of Order?*], for the governance of public speakers and meetings were . . . read, printed copies of which were also distributed to the audience."[100] Two years later, in an article on the anti-American boycott of 1905, the same Shanghai newspaper noted that Americans should at least be heartened by the fact that the movement was being carried out in a "characteristically American manner," complete with public assemblies and the election of delegates to representative bodies.[101] Many of the most ardent protesters in 1905 had been trained by American missionaries, and these missionaries' conferences and assemblies may well have served as influential "object lessons" in governance for radical Chinese youths. It is no mere coincidence that one of the most effective public speakers at Shanghai boycott meetings was Ma Xiangpo, an educator and former priest who had studied under those most skillful of rhetoricians: the Jesuits.[102]

Alongside foreign models for oratory and rallies, activists in the new politics also borrowed metaphors and techniques from Chinese theater. When the first public organizing went on in the late nineteenth and early twentieth centuries, before the new architecture was in place, the most common meeting places were guild halls (*huiguan* 會館) and temples, which were equipped with stages for operatic performances. There politicians mounted platforms (stages: *tai* 台) to address the audience. Meetings began with a *kaimushi* (開幕式), a curtain-raising. Speechmaking was a kind of performance: *yanjiang* (演講) or *yanshuo* (演説).

Given the influence of imported political models and theatrical venues and metaphors, it should come as no surprise that both operas and *xinju* 新劇, new theater) plays—dramatic performances that mixed Chinese and Western dramatic genres—became "important vehicles of propaganda" for revolutionaries.[103] Shanghai's Chunliu She (Spring Willow Society) performed *xinju* works with names such as "Blood of Patriotism" that "advocated revolution and satirized and laid bare the corruption of the ruling government." The troupe's founder, Wang Zhongsheng, was executed for his activities in 1911—a sign that the Manchus understood the persuasive power of theatrics.[104]

The new republic inaugurated in 1912 brought forth a political theater appropriate to China's new democratic forms. We see this in magazines and photo albums about this period.[105] Politicians array themselves at railway stations or in front of meeting halls for ceremonial photographs. Naturally, they mount stages to deliver speeches. They parade into cities in open limousines, with flag-waving crowds lining the streets. Now, for the first time, political leaders are brought face to face with the people: gone is the bowing and the taboo on visual contact. The people see, hear, evaluate, and react to the politicians of the early republic. The purpose, of course, is to make the new politics public and *open*. Indeed, the term for holding a meeting symbolizes this new politics: *kaihui* (開會), to open an assembly.

The Guomindang's experiments with patriotic mass mobilization were the most conscious efforts to use political theater to foster political commitment and legitimacy for the new regime. Their most dramatic efforts would begin with an incident that threatened China's national sovereignty. Guomindang leaders at national and local levels would sponsor mass rallies against the aggressor, usually Japan. Yellow trade unions, pro-GMD youth groups, and other loyalist organizations would mobilize people to attend these rallies, at which official speakers would praise the GMD as the nation's leading patriotic and revolutionary force, and the crowd would be encouraged to mix cries of "Long Live the Republic" and "Long Live the Nationalist Party" with slogans criticizing the foreign foe. Later, local party branches or government bureaus might arrange for petitioners or carefully screened representatives of "legitimate" groups to travel to Nanjing to present their views to top GMD figures, or urge civic groups to launch patriotic fundraising drives.[106]

Whatever the specific techniques, the intent was the same: to mobilize popular outrage to reinforce rather than subvert the status quo. Sometimes, as during the New Life Movement, this mobilization merged with attempts to foster Jiang Jieshi's personality cult. Even when not directly associated with cultic practices, GMD mass mobilization drives always relied heavily on ritual forms—bows to party and national flags, recitations of Sun's last will at the start of meetings, orchestrated visits to the National Father's tomb by petitioners who visited the capital.

Most of these drives left a great deal of room for more spontaneous political theater. As such, they might have served as the basis for a new form of politics, in which mass expressions of popular opinion, albeit carefully stage-managed, would play a role in determining and legitimizing public policy. But these new forms of public performance never seemed to catch on in China. The foreign rhetorical models were alien, and the analogy to theater linked politics to an occupation viewed as morally suspect in China.[107]

Concretely, political theater encountered two problems. First, China's rulers never developed a mechanism to connect this new open politics of speeches and meetings to the "real" politics of governing. As studies by Andrew Nathan and Lloyd Eastman have shown, the governance of China remained a matter of factional alliances and patronage networks, of personal connections and secret deals.[108] Electoral politics, the most common Western form connecting political theater to the business of governing, never appealed to the Chinese. Liang Qichao observed it in the United States and found it fraught with fraud, ignorance, and corruption.[109] When Yuan Shikai disbanded the elective assemblies in 1914, there was minimal protest from the disenfranchised citizenry.[110] In the years after 1927, the Guomindang tried sporadically to reimplement electoral politics. But campaigns at the local level were so fraught with corruption that they convinced neither foreign observers nor the Chinese electorate that casting votes had any real impact on governance.[111]

Secondly, experiments at mass mobilization were consistently undermined by the tendency of patriotic popular movements to get out of hand and end up as attacks on those in power. Thus the Nationalist era witnessed periodic swings between official encouragement and violent repression of popular mobilization, the complex dynamics of which are explicated in recent works by Christian Henriot and Wang Ke-wen.[112] The first major swing took place in the spring of 1928, when party leaders first supported, then suppressed popular outrage over the Jinan Incident;[113] one of the last important swings came in the spring of 1946, when party leaders encouraged urbanites to attend rallies against "Soviet Imperialism" in February, then quickly, as the United States replaced the USSR as the target of popular patriotic indignation, began to argue that all mass gatherings were subversive acts.[114]

When officials failed to turn the mass movements into controlled performances, they turned to a set of repressive tactics that observers of the 1989 events will find all too familiar. The regime would declare all collective gatherings illegal, close newspapers (except for foreign ones protected by extraterritoriality) that printed favorable accounts of popular protests, arrest activists, and, if necessary, use violence against those who continued to take to the streets. This kind of repression reflected a continuation of the traditional dichotomy of *li* (ritual) and *fa* (法, law or coercive control).[115] Though imperial rulers called such collective action "heterodox," and the GMD branded it "counter-revolutionary," both regimes ultimately saw force as the only response left when ritual or "ritualized" political theater failed.

The Guomindang's failure to make either elections or mass mobilization an integral part of governance meant that the open politics of political theater became increasingly associated with repertoires of protest. The traditional forms for mass petitions provided, for protest movements, a well-established Chinese repertoire that was lacking for hegemonic political theater. May Fourth established the republican model for petition-based mass action: students from the leading universities marched to the central square, Tiananmen, and attempted to present their petitions—in 1919, calling for the rejections of the terms of the Versailles Treaty that would cede German rights in Shandong to Japan rather than returning them to China. Further demonstrations followed in Beijing in the early 1920s, but the May 30 Movement was the next episode of truly national significance. These were, in the words of Mao Zedong, the years in which "the Chinese proletariat and the Chinese Communist Party mounted the political stage."[116] A new wave of student activism followed the Japanese invasion of Manchuria, culminating in the December 9 Movement of 1935.

These dates—May 4, May 30, December 9—were watersheds in the history of republican China. They form the markers for conventional periodization, the topics of classroom lectures. They also became anniversaries calling forth celebratory rituals modelled on the original events. Most importantly, they defined the repertoires for a new political street theater. Students always played a leading role, marching from their campuses behind banners proclaiming their school affiliations. They shouted slogans, waved flags, cheered onlookers, petitioned the authorities, and clashed with police. On their campuses they wrote big-character posters; outside they set up platforms to speak to the citizenry. Although the authorities criticized them for neglecting their studies, suppressed their illegal marches and condemned their disruption of law and order, the press broadcast news of their activities throughout the country, and the power of theater was undeniable. From the December 9th Movement of 1935, and increasingly in the late 1940s, the Communists recognized the power of this theater and its capacity to delegitimize Guomindang rule, and they worked diligently behind the scenes to encourage further demonstrations.

After 1949, the Communist Party sought to ritualize this theater: to incorporate and domesticate its repertoires into campaigns. The party was well aware of the danger of uncontrolled political theater: many of its key leaders had risen to prominence through student and worker demonstrations. They understood the power of independent student unions, which were called, under the Guomindang as in 1989, *xuesheng zizhihui* (学生自治会), student self-government societies.[117] Accordingly, the Communists banned all autonomous associations. But they did not wish to abandon the theater—only to monopolize the capacity to organize it, to succeed here (as elsewhere) where the Guomindang had failed. Thus it became one of the important functions of work units and the party-sponsored mass organizations (of youth, women, workers, peasants, etc.) to mobilize constituencies for mass demonstrations.

The result was the "campaign style" of Maoist policies—a style that prevailed until the late 1970s.[118] In the ritualized demonstrations that accompanied every major campaign and marked key dates on the revolutionary calendar, people would march forth behind their unit's or mass organization's banners, with lots of red flags, drums, and cymbals, and head for the central square. In the nation's capital, national minorities would join in native costume while the party leaders looked down from the elevated platform of Tiananmen itself. The same ritual would be repeated in cities across the country, with local leaders on their own elevated reviewing stands.

During the Cultural Revolution, Mao loosened the controls on these political rituals, and the students quickly devised their own innovative repertoires of street theater. "Ghosts and monsters" were paraded through cities in dunce caps; offending teachers and cadres were put on stage in the "airplane position;" books were burned, art destroyed. But Cultural Revolution street theater quickly degenerated into something too disorderly even for Mao, as rival Red Guard gangs fought physical battles in schools, factories, and on the streets.

By the late '60s, this revived theater had to be suppressed; and by 1980, the party revised the constitution to prohibit all big-character posters, leaflets, and demonstrations. In fact, under Deng Xiaoping, the party tried to abandon both the campaign ritual of the pre-Cultural Revolution period and the political theater of the "ten years of chaos," and rule purely by administrative routine. But the 1976 Tiananmen demonstrations in honor of Zhou Enlai and against the Gang of Four, the Democracy Wall movement of 1978–1979, the Hunan protests of 1980, the student demonstrations in Beijing in 1985 and in Shanghai and other cities in 1986–1987, and finally China's spring of 1989 proved that political theater could not be totally suppressed. Some public rituals are always necessary, and in those rituals there is always the danger that students or other actors will usurp the stage and turn the official ritual into their own political theater.[119]

INTERPRETING THE POLITICAL THEATER

As performance, the truth-value of the words and actions in this political theater is not terribly important. But that does not imply that this theater is meaningless—only that we have to pay more attention to its symbolism than to the literal meaning of its utterances. Let us consider the symbolism of 1989. The first function of political theater is quite simply to be heard, to gain attention. Initially, the audience is a dual one: the general population (both urban residents who directly witness the demonstration and those who can be reached through the media) and the authorities. But the authorities are the real audience; the value of the people is largely instrumental. The more support the demonstrators can gain from the citizenry—the larger the applauding crowds lining the demonstration route, the more concrete contributions of food and drink, the more symbolic aid in the form of banners or citizens' support groups, the greater the monetary contributions from citizens and small business—the more leverage the demonstrators will gain with the authorities.

That the authorities are the real audience is demonstrated by the petition format. But a petition also acknowledges the fundamental legitimacy of the government to which one appeals. Later, the petition is replaced by the appeal for dialogue—also a demand to be heard. But underlying this demand—even more clearly in dialogue than in petition—is a claim to entrance into the polity.[120] Groups previously excluded from the political process seek through demonstration, petition, and dialogue to be taken seriously by the authorities as participants in the political decision-making process. Even some of the violence of the demonstrations, the rock-throwing and arson, can be interpreted as efforts to gain attention, to be heard—efforts by those less skilful with and less trusting of words than intellectuals and university students.

The *public* nature of political theater is its second most important characteristic. Open to all, street theater invites all citizens to join. Once Tiananmen

Square was occupied, the students often debated strategy and made decisions in public, there for all to see. They demanded a live broadcast of their dialogue with government leaders. Symbolically, such theater stands in direct contrast to the secrecy of the party-state. Significantly, the model for such demonstrations in China, the May Fourth demonstration of 1919, protested against the secret diplomacy that had preceded the Versailles conference. Street theater invariably symbolizes a call to open up the political process, and the very secrecy (and lack of accountability) of the party-state naturally calls forth this sort of dialectical opposite.

Thirdly, student strikes and, even more dramatically, the hunger strike, present images of selflessness—a key value in contemporary China, with models from Norman Bethune to Lei Feng. These acts were extraordinarily effective. The most common praise of the student movement was that their motives were entirely patriotic—for love of country (*aiguo* 爱国). They sought nothing for themselves—unlike workers who might strike for higher pay. These students asked nothing, accepted not even food, and wished only the good of the nation. Their acts of self-denial stood in obvious contrast to the self-serving and corrupt leadership they attacked. No privilege of the party leadership was more visible than the enormous banquets they consumed at public expense. Now here were students refusing to eat anything at all.

Finally, the last testaments that the students wrote out, plus the hunger strike and related gestures, located the students symbolically within a rich tradition of political martyrs. These activities, as Dru Gladney has noted, linked the students to Qu Yuan, the loyal minister of the third century BCE who showed his willingness to "die for the affairs of the nation" by committing suicide after his ruler refused to heed his advice.[121] Such actions also recalled earlier generations of student martyrs, from Chen Dong (a Song Dynasty protester executed for his criticisms of government corruption, who served as a model for some May Fourth protesters), to Yao Hongye and Chen Tianhua (two frustrated Hunanese activists who committed suicide in 1906), and the hundreds of youthful demonstrators killed by foreign and native authorities during the republican era.[122] When students at Tiananmen Square swore collective oaths to sacrifice their lives—the last and most prophetic of which was taken on June 3rd—they were reenacting a scene from the May Fourth Movement.[123] Similarly, when Chai Ling bit her finger and wrote out a protest slogan with her own blood, she stepped into a role that student protesters of 1915 and 1919 had played.[124] With all this theater, the students appealed to a tradition of principled dissent and revolutionary action that the party itself had legitimized and mythologized in the attempt to claim it as its own.

If we are to understand the enormous appeal of the student demonstrations in Beijing and across China, we must begin by appreciating these symbolic meanings of their protest. The slogans—attacking the corruption of official profiteers (*guandao* 官倒), calling for a freer press, mocking China's highest leaders, advocating a never-defined "freedom" and "democracy"—were certainly important. But they gained their power because the very repertoire of the movement symbolized a demand for a voice in government, for a more open political process, for an end to leadership by a self-serving elite.

A COMPARATIVE PERSPECTIVE

The 1989 demonstrations in China were clearly part of a larger, worldwide crisis of state-socialist systems. In Eastern Europe, Communist Parties have been toppled from power, one after the other. In the Soviet Union, the Party is in the process of renouncing its monopoly on power, and various ethnic groups—led by Lithuania, but including all the Baltic states and the peoples of the Caucasus region—have been moving steadily toward some form of greater autonomy from Moscow. Increasingly, China (along with North Korea, Vietnam, and Cuba) is looking like the last refuge of socialism. As a current Chinese joke has it—playing on the official cant that "Only socialism can save China"—now "Only China can save socialism."

In each of the European transitions, street demonstrations played a critical role. This was, of course, most obvious in the dramatic events of East Germany and Czechoslovakia. There, utterly peaceful political transformations—a "velvet revolution," to use the Czech phrase—were brought about by unarmed civilians protesting in the streets. Since exactly the same sort of political theater brought forth troops and tanks and unprecedented bloodshed in China, it is necessary to try to explain the contrasting result.

Clearly, part of the answer lies in factors quite beyond the scope of this essay. The Communist Party of China (like the parties of Vietnam, Cuba, and, to a lesser degree, Korea) made its own revolution. Each of these countries thus differs from the state-socialist regimes of Eastern Europe, which were, in varying degrees, all brought into being and propped up by the Soviets' Red Army. Consequently, when Gorbachev made it clear that the Brezhnev Doctrine was dead and the Soviet Union would no longer come to the rescue of unpopular East European regimes, those regimes fell very quickly.

In addition, China and the remaining state-socialist regimes are all poor Third World countries. They have large, impoverished, and still poorly educated rural populations. At least in China, there is unquestionably substantial peasant discontent over a variety of issues—the payment for grain requisitions in IOUs and scrip instead of money, and the failure to deliver promised supplies of chemical fertilizer. But, in general, peasants displayed little sympathy for the demands of the student demonstrators. Only the attack on corruption struck a responsive chord. When the crackdown came, rural residents tended to believe the government contention that the peasant soldiers of the People's Liberation Army would not fire on unarmed civilians unless there was a genuine threat to law and order. In short, China's huge peasant population remained largely preoccupied with its own material interests, and it viewed those interests as dependent on continued political stability. Consequently, China's peasantry provided a reservoir of support for the hard-liners in Beijing that was missing in any East European regime.[125]

More germane to our discussion, however, is the role played by the institutions of civil society in Eastern Europe.[126] These long-neglected institutions proved to have sufficient life to structure the opposition movement and sustain it to victory. The most obvious example is the Catholic Church in Poland.[127] As a gathering place and refuge for dissidents in the Solidarity movement, the Catholic opposition (with a Polish Pope) was fundamental to the breakthrough in Poland—which was, after all, the first domino to fall. Hungary was the next country to make serious moves in the direction of pluralism, and here the old democratic parties played a crucial role. In Czechoslovakia, the dissident groups among the intellectuals were clearly better organized than anyone previously believed. In East Germany, the Evangelical (Lutheran) Church helped to shelter dissident intellectuals and a small independent peace movement. Bulgaria witnessed a nascent environmental movement, which played a critical role. In Lithuania, there was again the Catholic Church, plus the role of national movements and linguistic solidarity.

Virtually all of the institutions of civil society in Europe are imbued, to one degree or another, with aspects of democratic culture. We sometimes forget, as we focus on the hierarchic structures and stately rituals of the Catholic Church, that the Pope is elected, and councils of bishops and other more local institutions have often operated on democratic principles. On a more mundane level, artisan guilds would, on their feast days, constitute themselves as a "republic" to manage their affairs and discipline their members.[128] When, therefore, civil society has been allowed to prosper, it has brought with it, in the West, a discourse and a culture imbued with electoral forms and at least a minimal tolerance of dissent.

In Eastern Europe, such institutions of civil society played a critical role of translating the symbolic meaning of street theater into systematic programs for political change. When the party-states of Eastern Europe were forced to sit down to negotiate with the street protesters, there were people with organizational experience and programmatic ideas who could manage the delicate transition to democracy. The glamour-seeking media has hardly focused on this process, sometimes leaving the impression that dramatic demonstrations led to government collapse and a natural evolution to electoral forms. But that is hardly a plausible scenario, and when the full story is told we will surely find a critical role of the institutions of civil society in presiding over that perilous political process.

It is not enough, however, to focus on institutions alone. The small and vulnerable groups of dissident intellectuals and workers in Eastern Europe could certainly not match the organizational might of the party-state in these countries. But if there is one thing that the rapid collapse of communist parties in Eastern Europe and Russia has taught us, it is that social scientists have misled us into accepting an excessively reified notion of what "institutions" are. We have been led to think of the party-state almost as a physical structure, of unshakable size and weight and power. Now we are in a position to focus on the fact that such "structures" are, in fact, made up of *people* who are bound together by certain rules and habits, interests and aspirations, rituals and shared identities. The people who make up these institutions are not mindless parts of a party "machine," acting always and unfailingly in the interest of that machine. (Gorbachev and his supporters in the Soviet Union obviously cannot be understood if we identify them only as leaders and servants of the Communist Party machine.)

Once we escape an excessively institutional approach to politics in state-socialist systems, we are in a better position to appreciate the impact of the culture of civil society, the *habitus* that reemerged from the collective memory to give life to the East European movements of dissent.[129] One participant/observer of the Polish experience has noted "the explosion of national memory . . . the massive turnout for anniversary celebrations" that followed the first Solidarity struggles of 1980–1981.[130] In small rituals and mass celebrations, the *habitus* of democratic governance was revived from a culture rich in civic rituals and the theater of popular rule.

As we noted above, China's imperial state allowed minimal development of civil society. The late Qing and the republican era witnessed a brief flowering of civil society, but its roots were not deep. In addition, as David Strand has shown, this new civil society found it difficult to escape the old politics of personal networks, and the leaders of the new civic institutions tended to look for patrons within the state system.[131] The *habitus* of autonomous association was still weakly developed. In addition, civil society in China never provided an adequate foundation for pluralist politics. To a large degree, it revealed this weakness in its rhetoric. The Chinese press (both a component and a mouthpiece of China's nascent civil society) tended to speak of the "people" as an undifferentiated whole—usually standing against an opposing symbolic category, "officials"—that is, the state.[132] Thus, when Chinese began to speak of "rule by the people" (*minzhu*), the "people" were a unified mass.

The separate "republics" of civil society were not sufficiently legitimized to bring, with the idea of democracy, the pluralism bred in the corporate roots of European civil society.

Under the PRC, the budding sprouts of republican civil society were cut off altogether. The rhetoric of the undifferentiated people was usurped by the state to establish a "people's democratic dictatorship." Dissidents were safely excluded as "enemies of the people." Pluralism existed neither in the organization of society nor in the rhetoric of politics. Both the party-state and its opponents appealed to the virtue of "unity." But only the party existed as a functioning political organization. The tragic result of this combination of circumstances is that the Chinese Communist Party can justly claim that there is no political force outside the party capable of ruling China. Many of the hunger-strikers conceded this point in May 1989, and they probably reflected the consensus of most protesters. In the wake of June 4, the party's claim to legitimacy rests on little more than this fact: there is no alternative to the CCP. The *reason* there is no alternative is simple enough: the party will not permit one to exist. To preserve their fragile legitimacy, the party leaders must rigorously suppress any hint of pluralism: no autonomous student or workers' unions, no publications which might provide an alternative voice, no civil society. Then they can present the Chinese people with a bleak choice: either continued Communist rule or chaos.

Without a civil society, only street theater remains as a mode of political expression. No Chinese regime has ever been able to suppress it altogether. The smooth functioning of Chinese politics requires public rituals to celebrate the ideals of the revolution and the party-state which emerged from it. In time, students will again find an opportunity to usurp those rituals to perform their own political theater. Then the question will again arise: can they (and the state) find a mechanism to link this theater to the complex task of governing 1.1 billion Chinese?

NOTES

1. By journalists: Donald Morrison, ed., *Massacre in Beijing: China's Struggle for Democracy* (New York: Warner Books, 1989), Zhao Qiang, Ge Jing, and Siyuan, *Xueran de fengcai* [Bloody scenes] (Hong Kong: Haiyan, 1989); special issues: *Australian Journal of Chinese Affairs*, nos. 23, 24; *The Fletcher Forum of World Affairs* 14, no. 4; pictorial histories: Peter Turnley and David Turnley, *Beijing Spring* (New York: Stewart, Tabori and Chang, 1989); documentary collections: Han Minzhu, ed., *Cries for Democracy: Writing and Speeches from the 1989 Chinese Democracy Movement* (Princeton, NJ: Princeton University Press, 1990), Wu Mouren et al., eds., *Bajiu Zhongguo minyun jishi* [English title: "Daily Reports on the Movement for

Democracy in China"] (New York: privately published, 1989); textbook chapters: Jonathan D. Spence, *The Search for Modern China* (New York: Norton. 1990), chap. 26; analytical works: Lee Feigon, *China Rising: The Meaning of Tiananmen* (Chicago: Ivan Dee, 1990) and Andrew J. Nathan, *China's Crisis: Dilemmas of Reform and Prospects for Democracy* (New York: Columbia University Press, 1990).

2. Han Minzhu, *Cries for Democracy*, 83–103; "Quarterly Chronicle and Documentation," *China Quarterly* 119 (1989): 672; and on 1986–1987, *China News Analysis* 1328 (February 1, 1987): 8; *Renmin ribao*, December 25, 1986.

3. Leo Orleans, "Dissidents Lack Strong New Leader," *Washington Post*, May 24, 1989; San *Francisco Chronicle*, May 19, 1989.

4. Keith Forster, "Impressions of the Popular Protest in Hangzhou, April/June 1989," and Josephine Fox, "The Movement for Democracy and Its Consequences in Tianjin," *Australian Journal of Chinese Affairs* 23 (1990); Frank Pieke, "Observations during the People's Movement in Beijing, Spring 1989," paper presented at the International Institute of Social History, Amsterdam, July 7, 1989, cited with author's permission.

5. Although the official rhetoric had some effect in alienating support for the students in 1986, such Cultural Revolution imagery was much less effective in 1989, in part because the students confronted the official line head on. They demanded that the leadership apologize for labeling the movement a form of *dongluan* (动乱, turmoil)—a term that had become a code word for the Cultural Revolution (CQ Chronicle 1989: 677; Yi Mu and Mark V. Thompson, *Crisis at Tiananmen: Reform and Reality in Modern China* [San Francisco: China Books, 1989], 28). For a contrast between Red Guard uses of Mao pictures and those of 1989 students, see Orleans, "Dissidents." The Mao honored in 1989 was the selfless hero of the pre-1949 years and the early days of the PRC, not the demigod of the Cultural Revolution. As one worker from Hubei put it: "At least Mao was honest. . . . He even sent his son to the Korean War. Nowadays, the leaders send their sons to America" (*San Francisco Chronicle*, May 19, 1989: A24).

6. Feigon, *China Rising*; Lowell Dittmer, "China in 1989: The Crisis of Incomplete Reform," *Asian Survey* 30, no. 1 (January 1990): 25–41; Gerrit W. Gong, "Tiananmen: Causes and Consequences," *Washington Quarterly* 13, no. 1 (Winter 1990): 79–95.

7. Fox, "Movement for Democracy,"139.

8. Zhao Qiang et al., *Xueran de fengcai*, 204.

9. *Sun Zhongshan xiansheng hauce* [Dr. Sun Yat-sen: A photo album] (Beijing and Hong Kong: 1986), plate 199.

10. Cited in Andrew J. Nathan, *Chinese Democracy* (New York: Knopf, 1985), 6.

11. Although Nathan's *Chinese Democracy* is replete with useful examples of the sort just cited, Nathan seems blind to this issue, and concludes with a quite unsupported discussion of "the West's—and the Chinese democrats'—identification of democracy with pluralism" (*Chinese Democracy*, 227). The stress that Chinese dissidents continued to place on a non-competitive unity in 1989 is clear from one of the students' earliest demands: that the Chinese leadership affirm the virtues of "democracy, freedom, magnanimity and *harmony*" (*China Quarterly Chronicle* 1989: 668 [emphasis added]).

12. Richard Kraus, "The Lament of Astrophysicist Fang Lizhi," in *Marxism and the Chinese Experience*, eds. Arif Dirlik and Maurice Meisner (Armonk, NY: M. E. Sharpe, 1989).

13. Mary S. Erbaugh and Richard C. Kraus, "The 1989 Democracy Movement in Fujian and Its Consequences," *Australian Journal of Chinese Affairs* 23 (January 1990): 153.

14. Forster, "Impressions in Hangzhou," 98; Anita Chan and Jonathan Unger, "China After Tiananmen: It's a Whole New Class Struggle," *The Nation*, January 22, 1990, 79–81.

15. Note this May 1989 exchange between a youth, barred from boarding a bus where Wuer Kaixi was resting, and a student security guard. "'What kind of democracy is this?' [the youth] fumed. 'What kind of freedom? You are just like the country's leaders.' Responded the guard: 'You are right. But you are harming our unity. Don't say such things.'" *Newsweek*, (May 29, 1989), 21; cf. Sarah Lubman, "The Myth of Tiananmen Square: The Students Talked Democracy but They Didn't Practice It," *Washington Post*, July 30, 1989. Criticisms of the new exile leagues appear in Yuen Ying Chan and Peter Kwong, "Trashing the Hopes of Tiananmen," *The Nation* (April 23, 1990), and Chan and Unger, "China after Tiananmen." Henry Rosemont Jr. ("China: The Mourning After," *Z Magazine* [March 1990], 85–96) notes the influence that the "new authoritarianism" has had in Chinese dissident circles.

16. Donald Price, Comments at a roundtable at the annual meeting of the American Historical Association, San Francisco, 1989.

17. E. P. Thompson, "Patrician Society, Plebian Culture," *Journal of Social History* 7, no. 4 (1974): 382–405; and "Eighteenth-Century English Society: Class Struggle Without Class?" *Social History* 3, no. 2 (1978): 71–133; Clifford Geertz, *Negara: The Theatre State in Nineteenth-Century Bali* (Princeton: Princeton University Press, 1980.

18. Frank Pieke, "Observations during the People's Movement," and "A Ritualized Rebellion: Beijing, Spring 1989." Unpublished paper (1990) cited with author's permission.

19. Perry Link, cited in David Strand, "'Civil Society' and 'Public Sphere' in Modern China: *A* Perspective on Popular Movements in Beijing, 1919–1989," *Duke Working Papers in Asian/ Pacific Studies* 1990: 30–31.

20. Dru Gladney, "Bodily Positions and Social Dispositions: Sexuality, Nationality and Tiananmen," paper presented at the Institute for Advanced Study, Princeton, April 26, 1990, cited with the author's permission; Dru Gladney and Lucien Pye, "Tiananmen and Chinese Political Culture: The Escalation of Confrontation from Moralizing to Revenge," *Asian Survey* 30, no. 4 (April 1990): 331–47; Strand, "'Civil Society' and 'Public Sphere.'"

21. Charles Tilly, *From Mobilization to Revolution* (Reading, MA: Addison-Wesley, 1978).

22. Strand, "'Civil Society' and 'Public Sphere;'" Jeffrey Wasserstrom, "Student Protest and the Chinese Tradition," in *The Chinese People's Movement: Perspectives on Spring 1989*, ed. Tony Saich (Armonk, NY: M. E. Sharpe, 1990).

23. Cf. Charles Tilly, *The Contentious French* (Cambridge, MA: Harvard University Press, 1986), 116–17,

24. Pye, "Tiananmen," 333–37.

25. *North China Herald* (hereafter *NCH*), November 19, 1902: 1076–77; November 24, 1917: 467–68.

26. James Watson and Evelyn Rawski, eds., *Death Ritual in Late Imperial and Modern China* (Berkeley: University of California Press, 1988).

27. Victor Turner, *The Ritual Process: Structure and Anti-Structure* (Ithaca, NY: Cornell University Press, 1969).

28. Yan Jiaqi and Gao Gao, "*Wenhua dageming" shinianshi* [A ten-year history of the "Cultural Revolution"] (Tianjin: Tianjin renmin chubanshe,1986): 586–640.

29. This pattern is hardly unique to China. Compare this account of a demonstration by tens of thousands of youths on November 17, 1989, in Prague. It was one of the key events leading to the fall of the Communist government in Czechoslovakia. "The memorial for Jan Opletal, the student killed by the Nazis, was sponsored by the official student organization but was transformed into a demonstration for freedom, political change and the dismissal of the Communist Party leader, Milos Jakes" (*New York Times*, November 18, 1989).

30. James Watson, "The Renegotiation of Chinese Cultural Identity in the Post-Mao Era: An Anthropological Perspective," paper presented at the Four Anniversaries China Conference, Annapolis, MD, September 1989; Pye, "Tiananmen," 341–42; Elizabeth Perry, personal communication; Yi and Thompson, *Crisis at Tiananmen*, 42–44.

31. Yi and Thompson, *Crisis at Tiananmen*, 172; *Newsweek,* May 29, 1989, 21.

32. Yi and Thompson, *Crisis at Tiananmen*, 72; Han Minzhu, *Cries for Democracy*, 342–48.

33. *New York Times Magazine,* June 4, 1989, 28.

34. Gladney, "Bodily Positions"; *China Reconstructs*, December 1966, 3; *Beijing Review*, October 3, 1969, 7.

35. Frank Niming, [pseudonym], "Learning How to Protest," in Saich, *The Chinese People's Movement*, 82–104; Pieke, "Observations during the People's Movement."

36. Among the students, there was significant criticism of the kneeling petitioners' servile posture, but it appears that by adopting this traditional ritual, the petitioners gained substantial sympathy from the general populace. (See *Lianhebao* Editorial Department, *Tiananmen yijiubajiu* (Tiananmen 1989) (Taibei: Lianjing chuban shiye gongsi, 1989), 60–61.

37. *NCH*, June 8, 1918, 571–72; *Minguo ribao,* June 1 and 2, 1918; John Israel, *Student Nationalism in China, 1927–1937* (Stanford, CA: Stanford University Press, 1966), 60–61 and passim.

38. *San Francisco Chronicle*, June 1, 1989, A21–25.

39. Wu Mouren, *Bajiu Zhongguo minyun*, 262, 267.

40. Michel Oksenberg provoked our thinking on this point. It became clear during Nixon's November 1989 visit to China that Chinese and Western connotations of the term "tragedy" were quite different. Western notions, derived from Greek drama, link "tragedy" to unalterable fate and to some "tragic flaw" in the victim of the tragedy.

Thus, from a Western perspective, calling the events of June 3–4 a "tragedy" tends to objectify them, and even to remove responsibility for the bloodshed from the hands of the Chinese leadership. In this sense, "tragedy" was an attempt to soften the implications of the term "massacre," and it is perhaps significant that years earlier, Nixon had no difficulty in terming the student deaths at Kent State a "tragedy." (Kirkpatrick Sale, *SDS* [New York: Random House, 1973], 638). But Chinese "tragedy" is closer to our sense of "melodrama" and implies a clear villain—which the Chinese leadership correctly understood to be themselves.

41. Richard Schechner, "From Ritual to Theater and Back," in Richard Schechner and Mady Schuman, eds., *Ritual, Play, and Performance* (New York: Seabury Press, 1976), 196–222.

42. Stephen Lukes, "Political Ritual and Social Integration," *Sociology* 9, no. 2 (1975): 289–308; Jeffrey Wasserstrom, *Student Protests in Twentieth-Century China: The View from Shanghai* (Stanford, CA: Stanford University Press, 1991), 277–293.

43. Clifford Geertz, *The Interpretation of Cultures* (New York: Basic Books, 1973), 87–125.

44. Benjamin I. Schwartz, *The World of Thought in Ancient China* (Cambridge, MA: Harvard University Press, 1985), 67–68 and passim.

45. Emile Durkheim, *The Elementary Forms of the Religious Life*, trans. J. W. Swain (London: Allen and Unwin, 1915).

46. Robin Horton, cited in Victor Turner, *From Ritual to Theatre* (New York: Performing Arts Journal Press, 1982), 82.

47. Geertz, *Interpretation of Cultures*; "Blurred Genres: The Refiguration of Social Thought," *American Scholar* (spring 1980).

48. Victor Turner, *Ritual Process*; *Ritual to Theater*; and "Social Dramas and Ritual Metaphors," in Schechner and Schuman, *Ritual, Play and Performance*, 97–122.

49. If, for example, a priest at mass were just to pour wine into a chalice, dump wafers into a bowl, and pass them around without the proper words and gestures, transubstantiation would not occur and the communicants would not partake in the body and blood of Christ. Schechner uses the believed efficaciousness of rituals as the main criterion for differentiating them from theatrical performances in his essay, "From Ritual to Theater and Back."

50. Turner, *Ritual to Theatre*, 52–55; Jean-Christophe Agnew, *Worlds Apart: The Market and the Theater in Anglo-American Thought, 1550–1750* (Cambridge: Cambridge University Press, 1986), 103–12.

51. Turner, *From Ritual to Theatre*. Here, Geertz is less helpful. Although he has written at length about the "theater state" of Bali, his language (he writes of "the ritual extravaganzas of the theater state" [*Negara*, 102]) both fails to distinguish between ritual and theater and tends to treat theater as a mass ritual to which all responded with the same uniform belief.

52. *Liji*, chapter 1, 27: 63 and 28: 97–99; in Fung You-lan, *A History of Chinese Philosophy*, trans. Derk Bodde (Princeton: Princeton University Press, 1952), vol. 1: 339, 343.

53. Schechner, "Ritual to Theater," 211.

54. Thompson ("Patrician Society" and "Eighteenth-Century English Society: Class Struggle Without Class?" *Social History* 3, no. 2 [1978]: 71–133) analyzes the "countertheater" of "threat and sedition" through which English commoners challenged the gentry's "theater of hegemony." While these insightful articles forcefully illustrate the subversive potential of theater, we have avoided Thompson's "theater/countertheater" terminology because the term "theater of hegemony" blurs the important distinction between regularly repeated "rituals" (such as coronations) and other kinds of improvised, theatrical displays of force or majesty that support the status quo.

55. Nicholas Rogers, "Popular Protest in Early Hanoverian London," *Past and Present* 79 (1978.): 70–100; Susan G. Davis, *Parades and Power: Street Theatre in Nineteenth-Century Philadelphia* (Philadelphia, PA: Temple University Press, 1986); Konrad Jarausch, *Students, Society, and Politics in Imperial Germany* (Princeton, NJ: Princeton University Press,1982), 3–6.

56. J. L. Austin, "Performative Utterances," in *Philosophical Papers*, third edition (London: Oxford University Press, 1979), 233–52.

57. John Steele, trans. *The I-li* (London: 1917).

58. In divination rituals which mimic these social transactions, an undesirable result may come from choosing the wrong polite words. Therefore, according to one informant, "You keep throwing the blocks until a yes comes up, each time slightly changing what you say. This is because you might have made a mistake in giving your address, or you might not have been polite (*kheq-khi* [*keqi*]) enough in speaking to the god." (Emily Martin Ahern, *Chinese Ritual and Politics* [Cambridge: Cambridge University Press, 1981], 32).

59. Lianhebao, *Tiananmen yijiubajiu*, 69–71; Han Minzhu, *Cries for Democracy*, 126–27; Pye, "Tiananmen," 341.

60. James Burdick, *Theater* (New York: Newsweek Books, 1974), 7–41; E. T. Kirby, "The Shamanistic Origins of Popular Entertainments," in Schechner and Schuman, *Ritual, Play and Performance*.

61. Colin Mackerras, *The Chinese Theatre in Modern Times* (Amherst: University of Massachusetts Press, 1975), 13.

62. Susan Naquin, "Funerals in North China," in *Death Ritual in Late Imperial and Modern China*, ed. James Watson and Evelyn Rawski (Berkeley: University of California Press, 1988), 60; Joseph W. Esherick, *The Origins of the Boxer Uprising* (Berkeley: University of California Press,1987), 67–68. Mulian plays deal with the search of the Buddha's disciple, Mulian, through various hells to find his mother and release her from suffering.

63. Natalie Davis, *Society and Culture in Early Modern France* (Stanford, CA: Stanford University Press, 1975), 152–88.

64. Stephen Lukes, "Political Ritual and Social Integration," *Sociology* 9, no. 2 (1975): 294, 299.

65. Schechner, "From Ritual to Theater,"196–202; Turner, *From Ritual to Theater*, 68–87.

66. Mona Ozouf, *Festivals and the French Revolution,* trans. Alan Sheridan (Cambridge, MA: Harvard University Press, 1988).

67. Lynn Hunt, *Politics, Culture, and Class in the French Revolution* (Berkeley: University of California Press,1984), 60, 99.

68. Schechner, "From Ritual to Theater and Back," 211.

69. Vera Schwarcz, *The Chinese Enlightenment* (Berkeley: University of California Press, 1986), 240–82.

70. Jeffrey Wasserstrom, "Revolutionary Anniversaries in Guomindang and Communist China," Paper presented at the annual meeting of Asian Studies on the Pacific Coast, Stanford, California (1990).

71. *Lunyu* 12: 1, as trans. in Arthur Waley, *The Analects of Confucius* (New York: Vintage, n.d), 162.

72. Charles Hucker, *The Traditional Chinese State in Ming Times* (Tucson: University of Arizona Press, 1961), 67–68; Susan Naquin and Evelyn Rawski, *Chinese Society in the Eighteenth Century* (New Haven: Yale University Press. 1987); Angela Zito, *Of Body and Brush: Grand Sacrifice as Text/Performance in Eighteenth-Century China* (Chicago: University of Chicago Press, 1997).

73. Herbert Fingarette, *Confucius—the Secular as Sacred* (New York: Harper Torchbooks, 1972).

74. Zito, *Of Body and Brush*; Gugong bowuguan yuan [Palace Museum], *Zijincheng dihou shenghuo* (Lives of the emperors and empresses in the Forbidden City) (Beijing: China Travel and Tourism Press, 1983).

75. Jonathan D. Spence, *Ts'ao Yin and the K'ang-hsi Emperor, Bondservant and Master* (New Haven: Yale University Press, 1966), 125–36.

76. Jean Baptiste Duhalde, *The General History of China*, trans. Richard Brooks (London: J. Watts, 1736), 349.

77. Spence, *Ts'ao Yin*, 131.

78. Alexander Woodside, "Emperors and the Chinese Political System," paper presented at the Four Anniversaries China Conference, Annapolis, Maryland, September 1989.

79. Hsiao Kung-ch'üan, *Rural China: Imperial Control in the Late 19th Century* (Seattle: University of Washington Press, 1967), 449–50.

80. Especially when compared to Chinese theater audiences, the silence of ritual "audiences" is notable. In this regard, the "profound silence" that Jesuit observers recorded in the vast crowds greeting the Kangxi emperor suggests that his imperial tours were closer to ritual than theatrical performances (Spence, *Ts'ao Yin*, 136).

81. Roy Strong, *Art and Power: Renaissance Festivals, 1450–1650* (Berkeley: University of California Press, 1984), 7–11.

82. Thomas A. Brady Jr., "Rites of Autonomy, Rites of Dependence: South German Civic Culture in the Age of Renaissance and Reformation," in Steven Ozment, ed., *Religion and Culture in the Renaissance and Reformation* (Kirksville, Mo.: Sixteenth-Century Journal Publishers, 1989).

83. Lawrence M. Bryant, *The King and the City in the Parisian Royal Entry Ceremony: Politics, Ritual, and Art in the Renaissance* (Geneve: Librairie Droz S.A., 1986), 22.

84. Edward Muir, *Civic Ritual in Renaissance Venice* (Princeton: Princeton University Press, 1981); David M. Bergeron, *English Civic Pageantry, 1558–1642* (Columbia: University of South Carolina Press, 1971).

85. Hsiao Kung-ch'üan, *Rural China*, 194–201; Victor Mair, "Language and Ideology in the Written Popularizations of the Sacred Edicts," in *Popular Culture*, eds. David Johnson et al.

86. *Lunyu* 1: 3, as trans. in Wing-Tsit Chan, *A Sourcebook of Chinese Philosophy* (Princeton, NJ: Princeton University Press, 1985), 325–59.

87. Benjamin Elman, *From Philosophy to Philology: Intellectual and Social Aspects of Change in Late Imperial China* (Cambridge, MA: Harvard University Press, 1984), 48.

88. Derk Bodde and Clarence Morris, *Law in Imperial China* (Philadelphia: University of Pennsylvania Press, 1973), 464–66.

89. Elizabeth Perry, "Tax Revolt in Late Qing China," *Late Imperial China* 6, no. 1 (June 1985): 83–112.

90. William Martin, *A Cycle of Cathay* (New York: F. H. Revell, 1900), 91–92, cited in Hsiao Kung-ch'üan, *Rural China*, 434.

91. Ahern, *Chinese Ritual and Politics*, 92.

92. *Lunyu* 8: 14, as trans. in Waley, *Analects*, 135.

93. Lin Zexu, cited in eds. Teng Ssu-yu and John K. Fairbank, *China's Response to the West; A Documentary Survey, 1839–1923* (Cambridge, MA: Harvard University Press, 1979), 28.

94. Ibid., 50.

95. Edward M. Rhoads, *China's Republican Revolution: The Case of Kwangtung, 1895–1913* (Cambridge, MA: Harvard University Press, 1975), 86, 95–96.

96. Joseph W. Esherick, *Reform and Revolution in China: The 1911 Revolution in Hunan and Hubei* (Berkeley: University of California Press, 1977), 56; cf. Rhoads, *China's Republican Revolution*, 88.

97. Mary B. Rankin, *Elite Activism and Political Transformation in China: Zhejiang Province, 1865–1911* (Stanford, CA: Stanford University Press, 1986) and William T. Rowe, "The Public Sphere in Modern China," *Modern China* 16, no. 3 (1990): 309–29.

98. Chao Hsueh-hai, cited in Jeffrey Cody, "Architectural Fusion in the Design of Fudan University and 'Lilong' Housing," paper presented at the annual meeting of the Association for Asian Studies, Chicago, April 1990.

99. Zhou Yuehua, ed. *Anecdotes of Old Shanghai* (Shanghai: Shanghai Cultural Publishing House, 1985), 154–56.

100. *NCH*, May 7, 1903, 885.

101. *NCH*, August 11, 1905, 322.

102. Ruth Hayhoe, "Towards the Forging of a Chinese University Ethos: Zhendan and Fudan, 1903–1919," *China Quarterly* 94 (1983): 323–41; British Foreign Office records 228/2155.

103. Mackerras, *Chinese Theatre*, 48;

104. Zhou Yuehua, *Anecdotes*, 32; Mackerras, *Chinese Theatre*, 49.

105. *Sun Zhongshan xiansheng huace*; *Guomin geming huashi* [An illustrated history of the national revolution] (Taibei: 1965).

106. Wasserstrom, *Student Protests*, chapters 6, 7, 8.

107. Mackerras, *Chinese Theatre*, 78–79, 95–96.

108. Andrew Nathan, *Peking Politics, 1918–1923: Factionalism and the Failure of Constitutionalism* (Berkeley: University of California Press, 1976); and Lloyd Eastman, *The Abortive Revolution* (Cambridge, MA: Harvard University Press, 1974).

109. Chang Hao, *Liang Ch'i-ch'ao and Intellectual Transition in China, 1890–1907* (Cambridge, Mass.: Harvard University Press, 1971), 239.

110. Ernest P. Young, *The Presidency of Yuan Shih-k'ai: Liberalism and Dictatorship in Early Republican China* (Ann Arbor: University of Michigan Press, 1977), 148–55.

111. *China Weekly Review,* issues of March-April 1946; *Shanghai Evening Post*, April 30, 1946, 8.

112. Christian Henriot, *Shanghai, 1927–1937: Municipal Power, Locality and Modernization* (Berkeley: University of California Press, 1993); and Wang Ke-wen, "The Kuomintang in Transition: Ideology and Factionalism in the 'National Revolution,' 1924–1932" (PhD diss., Stanford University, 1985).

113. Israel, *Student Nationalism*,10–46; Patrick Cavendish, "The 'New China' of the Kuomintang," in *Modern China's Search for a Political Form*, ed. Jack Gray (London: Oxford University Press, 1969).

114. Wasserstrom, *Student Protests*, 270–76.

115. Schwartz, *World of Thought*, 102–4, 321–49.

116. Mao Zedong, "Xin minzhu zhuyi lun" [On New Democracy], in *Mao Zedong xuanji* [Collected works of Mao Zedong] (Beijing: People's Publishing House, 1952), vol. 2: 690.

117. Israel, *Student Nationalism*, 24.

118. Charles P. Cell, *Revolution at Work: Mobilization Campaigns in China* (New York: Academic Press, 1977).

119. In addition to examples given earlier, the student protests of both 1985 and 1986–1987 began on anniversary dates, September 18 and December 9, for official commemorations.

120. Cf. Tilly, *Mobilization to Revolution*.

121. Gladney, "Bodily Positions and Social Disposition."

122. Thomas Lee, *Government Education and Examinations in Sung China* (New York: St. Martin's Press, 1985), 190–92; Zhongguo shehui kexueyuan, *Wusi aiguo yundong* [The patriotic May Fourth Movement] (Beijing: Zhongguo shehui kexueyuan, 1979), vol. 1: 473.

123. *Shen Bao*, May 27, 1919, 10; on 1989: Yi and Thompson, *Crisis at Tiananmen*, 266.

124. Shanghai Municipal Police Files, reel 65, I.D. 6691.

125. David Zweig, "Peasants and Politics," *World Policy Journal* (Fall 1989): 633–45.

126. Vladimir Tismaneanu, "Eastern Europe: The Story the Media Missed," *The Bulletin of the Atomic Scientists* 46, no. 2 (March 1990): 17–21.

127. Pawel Machcewicz, "The Solidarity Revolution," *Polish Perspectives* 32, no. 4 (1989): 14–25.

128. Robert Darnton, *The Great Cat Massacre and Other Episodes in French Cultural History* (New York: Vintage, 1985), 85–89.

129. Pierre Bourdieu, *Outline of a Theory of Practice*, trans. Richard Nice (Cambridge: Cambridge University Press, 1977), 72–87.

130. Machcewicz, "Solidarity Revolution," 19.

131. Strand, *Rickshaw Beijing*, 98–120; Strand, "'Civil Society' and 'Public Sphere.'"

132. Rankin, *Elite Activism*, 166.

Afterword

History Lessons

For centuries, scholars have drawn lessons from the history of China. The results have not been encouraging. Hegel found only a timeless empire; and Marx's "Oriental despotism" led to much the same conclusion. When Western diplomats and merchants arrived in the nineteenth century, they saw China as a proud, conservative, and backward-looking society. A century later, modern scholars discovered a model of peasant revolution, soon to be eclipsed by those preaching the threat of a new totalitarianism. Pundits endlessly promoted lessons from China's past, from Henry Kissinger's "Singularity of China" to explain (or justify) China's autocratic government to Graham Allison's warning that China's economic rise and challenge to American global supremacy threatened war and a repeat of the Thucydides trap.[1] Everywhere we were reminded of Santayana's warning that "Those who do not learn history are doomed to repeat it," or at least Mark Twain's amended version that "History does not repeat itself, but it does rhyme."[2]

Serious historians are more doubtful that history offers clear lessons for the present and future. Michael Oakeshott proposed a radical break between the scholar's "historical past" and the "practical past" of myths, legends, and ideological pronouncements that nations and their political elites use to justify current policies. The former is an academic attempt to reconstruct, from the best surviving evidence, an account of what actually happened in a past that is now dead and gone; while the latter is the use of history for present-day purposes.[3] I began my career as a member of the Committee of Concerned Asian Scholars, convinced that while historical research must be rigorously honest to its sources, it could also inform a concerned citizen's contemporary commitments. In the context of the 1970s, that concern meant opposition to American involvement in Vietnam, and more broadly, a critical stance toward imperial and colonial interference in Asian affairs. Over time, I became more self-critical, more vigilant against letting political commitments guide my conclusions, and wary of ideologically driven scholarship. As postmodern theories blurred the line between history and fiction,[4] it often seemed that political correctness trumped a concern for rigorous scholarship, technical training, and a commitment to seeking the truth about the past.

As the essays in this collection indicate, I also became convinced that contingent circumstances played an important role in directing the course of watershed historical events. As I argued in "Reconsidering 1911," the late Qing progress toward constitutional monarchy was interrupted only when the Regent Zaifeng succeeded the Empress Dowager and concentrated power in a small group of Manchu princes, pushing the constitutionalist leaders to support the revolutionary coup in Wuchang. Again in "Ten Theses," I argued that "The triumph of the CCP was the product of a series of contingent events." My most recent monograph on the Communist movement in the area around Yan'an is entitled *Accidental Holy Land*, though I was at pains to explain that "accidental," while often translated as *ouran* (偶然) in Chinese and clearly used in opposition to "inevitable" (*biran* 必然), does not make history a matter of chance. Accidents have causes, and so did the Chinese revolution. The problem is simply that these causes involve multiple interacting circumstances not a confirmation of historical destiny. In *The Philosophy of History*, Hegel wrote that "Each period is involved in such peculiar circumstances, exhibits a condition of things so strictly idiosyncratic, that its conduct must be regulated by considerations connected with itself, and itself alone. Amid the pressure of great events, a general principle gives no help." I do not often agree with Hegel, and the implication of his argument would render this volume useless, for he concluded that "what experience and history teach is this—that peoples and governments never have learned anything from history."[5]

Despite my discomfort in agreeing with Hegel, the logic of his position seems unassailable. Hegel's history was concerned with the decisions of statesmen (always men, of course) who guided the progress of history. Each acted in "such peculiar circumstances" and under conditions "so strictly idiosyncratic," that the decisions they made were not determined by any general principles that we might learn from history. It seems to me that this is clear both for the decisions Zaifeng made in appointing the Prince's Cabinet in 1911, and for those of Chiang Kai-shek as he negotiated the united front with Communists in the wake of the Xi'an Incident. In the same vein, it seems to me that the actions of Mao Zedong during his twenty-seven-year rein in the People's Republic of China are not likely to tell us much about Xi Jinping's decisions in governing a far more developed, complex, and internationally connected China today. But the path-breaking importance of state leaders' decisions, and the unique circumstances in which those decisions are made does not mean that history tells us nothing about developments at the level on which most people live. This is the advantage of social history. Though the decisions of state leaders are made in unique and idiosyncratic circumstances, when scholars are concerned with broad socio-economic developments—demographic change, commercialization, the impact of industrialization, the rise of mass media and nationalism, the transformation of the family—where the accretion of large numbers of small changes produce general trends, the result should be a history from which we can learn a great deal.

From Manchu emperors to Chiang Kai-shek to Xi Jinping, Chinese rulers have claimed that the "particular characteristics" of China set it apart from global historical trends. It is certainly true that China is different from other nations, unique in many respects. That is true of any country: each is unique in its own way. It does not follow, however, that countries are immune from global historical trends. In the nineteenth century, the world was ruled by empires: British, French, Russian, German, Japanese, Chinese and others. All are now gone, and we have instead a world of nations, whose organizing body is appropriately called the United Nations. China's transition from empire to nation had its unique characteristics: it maintained (basically) its imperial borders. But the transformation from imperial to national statehood was a trend that spanned the globe. It took place in the context of a revolution against imperial and colonial forms of rule in which China participated. The rise of anti-imperialism and the assertion of national sovereignty and identity were both fundamental to China's modern transformation and to processes shared by people across the globe. On the social level, it is incontestable that despite all the rhetoric about the unique strength of the Chinese family, most Chinese today live in small nuclear families in urban apartment blocks that are utterly different from the rural lineages of their forefathers and have much more in common with nuclear families in other parts of the world.[6]

All this is to say that China is different, to be sure, but it is also part of a human drama that is open to comparative study. The task of the historian is to identify and analyze what is distinctive about China while making that difference legible to comparative scholars. We must study both the global trends of which China is a part, and the things that are particular to China. An obvious place to start is with revolution. China's twentieth century was dominated by revolution, and China has long been regarded as a classic case of peasant revolution. Barrington Moore presented a sophisticated and powerful argument that the weakness of the Chinese bourgeoisie and the rentier landlord class's failure to provide any vital social function left China particularly vulnerable to the threat of peasant revolution.[7] I doubt, however, that these structural features of Chinese society are sufficient to account for China's Communist revolution. I have argued, instead, that the victory of the Chinese revolution was far more contingent: from the Long March, to the Xi'an Incident, to the long war against Japan, there were many instances in which the Communist triumph was in doubt. What does seem clear, however, is that after the sudden and quite unexpected triumph of the 1911 Revolution, and then the disappointments of the warlord era that followed, Chinese political leaders, intellectuals, and military officers turned again and again to revolution for a solution to China's problems. We must always remember that Sun Yat-sen's Nationalist Party was revived in the 1920s to complete the revolutionary mission of 1911. Chiang Kai-shek, as Sun's successor and leader of the Nationalist Party, endlessly promoted Sun's dying testament that "The revolution is not finished, comrades must struggle on," while condemning the Communists as "counter-revolutionary." Intellectuals promoted the vernacular in a literary revolution, education was reorganized in an educational revolution; there were even calls for a Buddhist revolution or a poetic revolution. Only the Great Proletarian Cultural Revolution's effort to touch human souls convinced both the people and the nation's leaders that revolution was not the optimal solution to China's myriad problems. Yet all this commitment to revolution began with the quite accidental triumph of the 1911 Revolution.

Revolution became the process through which China would resist imperialist incursions and make the transition from empire to nation. As elsewhere, both nation-building and revolution involved a substantial increase in the size and functions of the state. During the May Fourth Movement, as young people and intellectuals promoted democracy and freedom as a liberation from the strictures of both capitalist and Confucian culture, anarchism had real appeal, even to future communists like Mao Zedong.[8] But it soon became clear that anarchist collectives could not produce the powerful political organization necessary to overthrow the old order, and radicals turned to Leninism, in both the Communist Party and in Sun Yat-sen's reorganized and Soviet-armed Nationalist Party. When the Nationalist-Communist united front fractured following the death of Sun Yat-sen, Chiang Kai-shek unified the country under a government of unprecedented strength. From 1927 to 1937, the Nanjing government recovered some concessions from the Great Powers, gained tariff autonomy, grew industry at a 10 percent annual rate, vastly extended the railway network, modernized the army, established an air force, expanded education at all levels, promoted urban reform, carried out extensive social surveys and built the foundations of a modern state with all the requisite functional agencies.

Then came the Japanese invasion of 1937 and the eight-year War of Resistance. As I have argued in the essay on "War and Revolution," the war with Japan was as important to China's transformation as the revolution itself. The war allowed the CCP to establish an independent regime in Yan'an and in base areas behind Japanese lines, achieving the kind of autonomy from the central government that the PRC so fears in Tibet, Xinjiang or Hong Kong today. More importantly, that independent regime had its own army, so Chiang Kai-shek called it a new warlordism. Today, of course, the Communists claim credit for defeating Japan, a fiction that is maintained by ignoring the US war in the Pacific and the impact of the atom bomb. As is widely recognized in foreign scholarship (and indeed by Chinese academic specialists), the bulk of the Chinese fighting against Japan was done by the Nationalist forces, while the Communists focused on guerrilla warfare in the hills.[9] Under both regimes, however, the battle against Japanese invasion fused with the national struggle against imperialism and the effort to end the "hundred years of national humiliation." The total war waged in China, as elsewhere during World War II, was accompanied by a massive cultural, educational and media propaganda campaign that fostered a much broader and deeper sense of national identity so that when, in the years after Mao, the appeal of Marxism-Leninism faded, the party could readily shift to the appeal of Chinese nationalism.

The war transformed China in ways that were critical to the revolutionary process. Education was expanded, nationalized, and focused, at higher levels, on such practical subjects as engineering. Women were recruited into the labor force as teachers, nurses, and factory workers. Clothing styles favored Sun Yat-sen jackets and military uniforms. In the arts, Western expressionism was replaced by traditional watercolor brushwork and bold nationalist propaganda in styles reminiscent of socialist realism. The Nationalist government built a rural organization to support conscription that prepared the way for the more intrusive Communist rural apparatus. The interior was transformed with new roads, public squares, and its first industrial factories. All of this was done in the name of sacrifice for the nation, but when the war was over and Nationalist officials seemed more interested in personal aggrandizement than service to the nation, the Chinese people—from students and intellectuals to common soldiers and patriotic officers—decided that the cadres of the Communist Party represented the wartime ideals of self-sacrifice for national liberation better than the corrupt officials of the Nationalist Party. The armies of the Nationalists collapsed, and the Communists emerged as rulers of China.

The new Communist regime was unquestionably harsh. Millions died in the course of land reform and campaigns against "counterrevolutionaries." Yet the new regime quickly brought the runaway inflation of the 1940s under control and stamped out the most visible forms of corruption. The Korean War was horribly costly in lives lost, but tight media control kept the worst news from the public, and by fighting the United States to a standstill the PRC gained further national legitimacy. In the 1950s, Soviet style industrialization was clumsy and inefficient, but the emphasis on heavy industry built the steel, cement, and electrical capacity necessary for industrial and transport infrastructure. Education was expanded and opened to more than a narrow elite, and rudimentary health care extended life expectancy by twenty years during the Mao era.[10]

It is far too simple to explain the disasters of the Great Leap Forward and the Cultural Revolution by the decisions of Mao Zedong alone, but it is equally gratuitous to ignore Mao's role. The rectification campaigns and the Seventh Congress of the 1940s elevated Mao to supreme leadership of the CCP, but the Yan'an years still saw a healthy debate within the top party leadership. Mao's dramatically successful leadership of the army and party during the Civil War made it ever more difficult to challenge his decisions after 1949; the norms of rectification were perverted; and Mao himself became increasingly autocratic in purging his adversaries, first during the Great Leap Forward and then in the Cultural Revolution.[11] The role of the supreme leader in Communist systems certainly enabled these disasters; but Mao's leftist convictions, the impatience that increased with age, and his suspicion that party colleagues had become rivals clearly made matters worse.

Following Mao's death in 1976, Deng Xiaoping rose to primacy and cautiously guided China on the road to "reform and opening." In China's Leninist system, the role of the supreme leader is decisive, and while Deng alone could not rescue China from the poverty and turmoil of the Mao years, he certainly pointed the country in a new direction. The dramatic expansion of the Chinese economy was unprecedented. By 2020, the per capita GDP of Chinese citizens had risen sixty-three-fold since 1976.[12] The country is now laced with high-speed rail lines; there are clean, modern, efficient airports in every Chinese city; supermarkets offer processed foods, fresh vegetables. and meat year around; cell phone service is readily available even in distant mountain villages; the city streets are safe at night and crime is low. Where people used to cram into small apartments with shared bathrooms and perhaps six square meters per person, cities now mushroom with towering modern apartment blocks with forty square meters per capita.[13] All of this spectacular economic growth has been accompanied by the continuing domination of autocratic governance, strict control of media, censorship of the internet behind the Great Firewall, and unimpeded control by the Chinese Communist Party. The rise of China has become a staple of pundits, a magnet for global investment, and a source of rising concern for security analysts. What, if anything, can history teach us about China today?

In some respects, China's economic growth is the least surprising aspect of China's rise. For centuries, Chinese businessmen dominated the markets of Southeast Asia. Max Weber and other early scholars notwithstanding, there is nothing in Chinese culture that inhibits commercial enterprise. The slow growth of the Chinese economy was largely the result of a weak state, and here the limitations imposed by foreign imperialism were certainly one factor. Once China had mastered the secrets of modern science, freed itself of foreign domination and the shackles of the socialist economy, the economy boomed. In addition, the inheritance of the socialist system in a literate, healthy, and disciplined labor force must be acknowledged, as well as the substantial advances in engineering under the socialist planned economy.[14]

We are still, however, left with the puzzle of how a Marxist-Leninist party devoted to the triumph of socialism (even an ersatz socialism "with Chinese characteristics"), presided over the remarkable growth of an advanced market economy. Here it is necessary to recall that for the critical support of the peasantry, the fundamental Communist promise was land reform: granting peasants ownership rights to the lands they tilled. This was, as Mao himself admitted, fundamentally a bourgeois democratic revolution.[15] The peasants' enthusiasm for collective agriculture was never great, and when China returned to small peasant agriculture in the 1980s, the productive energy of the peasantry drove the first stage of economic reform. In this sense, the market economy of the reform era was the logical outcome of what the Chinese revolution was all about.

It is also necessary to acknowledge that Leninism, especially in the Chinese context with the addition of Mao's "mass line," always sought to temper its authoritarianism with an attention to the wishes of the people.[16] The "masses," of course, were to be guided by the party to the correct policy choices, but when it was most successful, the party was anxious to respond to popular sentiment. In the wartime Shaan-Gan-Ning Border Region, for example, routine reports from the counties always included a critical section on popular "complaints" (*guaihua* 怪话).[17] In the growing literature on authoritarian resilience in China, there is good evidence that local cadres were often quite successful in representing the interests of their local communities within the authoritarian structures of state power. Most intriguing is the evidence that they were most effective when they acted in concert with a community consensus achieved through established lineage or village temple bonds.[18]

Many of these findings about the resilience and the responsiveness of the Chinese state appear within a body of literature that I have come to regard as "without" books: *Accountability without Democracy*, *Capitalism without Democracy*, *Mobilizing without the Masses*, and (citing the sub-title) *Participation without Democracy*.[19] By highlighting what China is "without," we presume that China was somehow deviating from the norm, and in this case, the norm clearly held that democracy is associated with capitalism, and accountability is accomplished through democracy. That China should have capitalist entrepreneurs without democracy, or that an authoritarian Communist state should be responsive to its people was an anomaly to be explained.[20] The Euro-American bias and the historical inaccuracy of such conclusions are clear. The first generation of democracies—Britain, France and the United States—were founded on capitalist economies, but the late-developing economies of Germany, Japan and the Soviet Union opted for authoritarianism, and many contemporary nations are making the same choice. Modernization theory to the contrary notwithstanding, there is no contradiction between authoritarianism and rapid economic growth.[21]

History is clearly an important factor in the Chinese case. After the initial hopes of the republic, aside from a few Western influenced intellectuals, most Chinese showed little interest in electoral democracy. Strengthening the nation in the struggle against imperialism was far more important.[22] During the war against Japan, the Communists held elections in villages, but only under strict party control, and largely to establish a legitimate foundation for their separatist regime.[23] There is no question that in the 1989 protests, in the context of growing inflation and public concern over official corruption, democracy held a certain appeal, but I and other regular visitors to China in the twenty-first century found that the appeal of multi-party democracy, even among intellectuals, disappeared as the Chinese economy took off while the United States and other Western democracies were mired in destructive inter-party quarrels and political paralysis. Now most Chinese (informed by selective state-controlled media to be sure) look at the United States and see a stagnant economy, a society wracked by crime, a spreading opioid addiction, fatalities from covid approaching a million, and a government incapable of generating a coherent, unified response. Most Chinese feel comfortable in the superiority of their own system.

To some observers, this only demonstrates the enduring Chinese preference for autocratic governance. I would propose that history suggests another lesson. In Part II on "A Diverse and Changing China," Mary Rankin and I have argued that the image of a unified and changeless China derived from an excessive focus on the relatively uniform structures of the empire. When we turn our attention to social life, we find a variety of regions and local ecologies, a land of fractious highlands and peaceful plains, varied crops and landholding systems, single-surname villages and multi-family communities, local dialects and differing customs, and of course substantial ethnic populations on China's frontiers. Not only was China's social life exceptionally diverse, it was constantly changing. In the late imperial period, new crops and silver were introduced from the New World, the economy was commercialized and markets developed, land-holding patterns changed and the small-peasant economy prevailed, merchants prospered and sought status in gentry lifestyles. With the arrival of the West and the growth of treaty ports came compradors to interact with foreign firms, newspapers, a nascent public sphere, and the wide range of social and political changes that ushered in the Republic of China. Then the republic witnessed the growth of universities and a relatively autonomous and critical intellectual class, a far stronger and more assertive military, and the Leninist parties that were to dominate political life.

There were aspects of this social diversity that help to explain the growth of the Communist revolution, especially the difference between the hilly peripheries where the Communists established their bases and the lowlands where the Guomindang military prevailed. What is most important, however, is the extent to which the stronger and more intrusive regime of the PRC set about erasing the historic social diversity. Revolutions strengthen states, and the party-state of the PRC created a far stronger government than China had ever seen. Initially, that state built upon preexisting social structures. Communes were formed on the boundaries of the old market towns. Production brigades utilized preexisting lineage structures. As noted above, village governments were most effective when they relied upon lineage or temple communities.

In the last few decades, however, the party-state seems to be in the process of divorcing itself from society. In part, this is the direct result of urbanization. Villages are being hollowed out, occupied by the very young and the very old, as working-age adults seek urban employment. Some distant mountain villages are simply disappearing, as the remaining population is moved to new well-ordered and better served settlements on the plains. In the cities, young couples establish their separate residence, breaking old lineage ties that were already weakened as the one-child policy eliminated siblings and cousins. With family and community ties weakened, the state now confronts a much more malleable population of atomized individuals, and by banning the institutions of civil society its control of the population is further enhanced. It is mainly on China's frontiers, especially in Tibet and Xinjiang, that ethnic populations with their own religions are able, to some extent, to resist the intrusive state. With the roll-out of the proposed Social Credit System, in which each individual as assigned a social credit score based on their individual social and economic behavior, a system served by a massive web of surveillance cameras and AI-informed facial recognition, the party-state seems poised to establish the ultimate Big Brother manipulation and control of the population without any interference by intervening social groups.

This, surely, is the dystopian conclusion one might draw from the recent efforts of Xi Jinping to instill a firm "party spirit" so that the party-state can control society.[24] The essays in this collection have argued, however, that the

CCP is not a monolithic entity, and as an organization with close to one hundred million members, there is significant internal diversity within the party. It is not to be expected that all members will mechanically follow central directives.[25] In addition, one clear lesson from past authoritarian systems is the difficulty posed by the problem of succession. Think only of the changes that followed the deaths of Stalin and Mao or (in non-Communist systems) the death of Franco in Spain or the fall of Peron in Argentina. Dictators most fear their political rivals, but this prevents them from cultivating successors. Deng Xiaoping saw this problem with Mao and so established a system of term limits and an orderly transfer of power, but Xi Jinping has eliminated term limits and thus commands a party in which none can compete or expect to succeed him. He has also asserted firm party control of the People's Liberation Army, to ensure that the military will protect the party-state and avoid the fate of the Soviet Union. This may guarantee stability during his lifetime, but it promises a future of political turmoil.[26] Stripped of any guiding norms beyond loyalty to the party's supreme leader, the CCP's social cohesion is likely to be fatally weakened.

The lessons of 1989 also suggest that sooner or later, social groups will find ways to resist the state. Despite the remarkable achievements of the Chinese economy, the future is not entirely rosy. The population is aging rapidly and the success of the one-child policy has reduced the youthful work force. North China faces severe water shortages, which climate change will certainly worsen. The new tech economy relies on imported chips which China may be unable to produce on its own, and "wolf warrior" diplomacy is causing China's international prestige to plummet. Foreign commentators have been predicting the collapse of China for decades, only to be proven wrong again and again.[27] There is no reason to doubt that China will find ways to combat these and other problems in the future. There is, however, plenty of reason to believe that Chinese society will continue to change and evolve in ways that the state will not be able to control.

The Chinese people have proved incredibly creative in finding ways to resist and mock the state. The internet and mobile apps may be tightly censored, but people find creative means to express dissident opinions. Intellectuals are surely not happy with the restraints on academic freedom and the right to publish their research. Young people resist cultural mandates and limits on personal expression. Lawyers trained to introduce the rule of law are not happy to be told that their first duty is to obey the party. If, however, I were to predict one area in which the Xi Jinping regime is most likely to encounter resistance, it would be in the area of women's rights and gender relations. In an era when women have led democratic governments from Britain to Germany to New Zealand, there has not been a single woman on the

PRC's ruling Politburo standing committee since the founding of the PRC.[28] The continuing ritual of introducing a new ruling group of middle-aged men in identical suits with the same dyed black hair is not sustainable in a nation that claims that women "hold up half of the sky." The outrage that surfaced in the case of the tennis star Peng Shuai, and the PRC's quick effort to censor all web discussion of the incident, reveal the party's sensitivity to the problem. Throughout China, women are claiming a place outside the traditional domestic sphere. In China's universities today, women often outnumber and outperform men, and their labor fuels the manufacturing economy. The number of capable, educated, and ambitious women is large, and they are not easily identified as a disaffected minority or special interest group. If there is one issue over which people are able to stand up to and even reform the powerful party-state, it may well be gender discrimination.

NOTES

1. Henry Kissinger, *On China* (New York: Penguin Books, 2012); Graham Allison, "The Thucydides Trap: Are the US and China Headed for War?" *The Atlantic*, September 24, 2015.

2. The original quote is "Those who cannot remember the past are condemned to repeat it" (Nicolas Clairmont, "Those Who Do Not Learn History Are Doomed to Repeat it. Really?" *Culture and Religion*, July 31, 2013).

3. Michael Oakeshott, *On History and other Essays* (Oxford: Basil Blackwell, 1983); see also Martyn P. Thompson, *Michael Oakeshott and the Cambridge School on the History of Political Thought* (London: Rutledge, 2019).

4. Hayden White, *Metahistory: The Historical Imagination in Nineteenth-century Europe* (Baltimore: Johns Hopkins University Press 1975).

5. G. W. F. Hegel, *The Philosophy of History*, trans. J. Sibree (Kitchener, Ontario: Batoche Books, 1900), 192–200.

6. I have explored this process in *Ancestral Leaves: A Family Journey Through Chinese History* (Berkeley: University of California Press, 2011).

7. Barrington Moore, Jr., *Social Origins of Dictatorship and Democracy: Lord and Peasant in the Making of the Modern World* (Boston: Beacon Press, 1966), 162–227.

8. Arif Dirlik, *The Origins of Chinese Communism* (New York: Oxford University Press, 1989); on Mao: Edgar Snow, *Red Star Over China* (New York, Grove Press, 1961), 151; on global anarchism in this period, Tim Harper, *Underground Asia: Global Revolutionaries and the Assault on Empire* (Cambridge, MA: Belknap Press, 2021), 85–94.

9. Rana Mitter, *Forgotten Ally: China's World War II, 1937–1945* (Boston: Houghton Mifflin Harcourt, 2013); Hans J. Van de Ven, *China at War: Triumph and Tragedy in the Emergence of the New China* (Cambridge, MA: Harvard University Press, 2018); Mark R. Peattie, Edward J. Drea, and Hans J. Van de Ven, eds., *The Battle*

for China: Essays on the Military History of the Sino-Japanese War of 1937–1945 (Stanford, CA: Stanford University Press, 2011).

10. https://www.macrotrends.net/countries/CHN/china/life-expectancy (accessed December 10, 2021).

11. Frederick C. Teiwes, *Politics and Purges in China: Rectification and the Decline of Party Norms, 1950–1965*, second edition (Armonk, NY: M.E. Sharpe, 1993) and *Politics at Mao's Court: Gao Gang and Party Factionalism in the Early 1950s* (Armonk, NY: M. E. Sharpe, 1990); Roderick MacFarquhar, *The Origins of the Cultural Revolution: The Coming of the Cataclysm, 1961–1966* (New York: Columbia University Press, 1999).

12. https://www.macrotrends.net/countries/CHN/china/gdp-per-capita (accessed December 9, 2021).

13. Hanming Fang, Quanlin Gu, Wei Xiong, and Li-an Zhou, "Demystifying the Chinese Housing Boom," *NBER Macroeconomics Annual* 30 (2015); "China GDP Per Capita 1960–2022," *macrotrends*, https://www.ceicdata.com/en/china/residential-area-per-capita/floor-area-of-residential-building-per-capita-urban (accessed January 5, 2022).

14. Barry J. Naughton, *The Chinese Economy: Adaptation and Growth*, second edition (Cambridge MA: MIT Press, 2018); Joel Andreas, *Rise of the Red Engineers: The Cultural Revolution and the Origins of China's New Class* (Stanford, CA: Stanford University Press, 2009) esp. chaps. 10–11.

15. Mao Zedong, "The Chinese Revolution and the Chinese Communist Party" (1937) translated in Stuart Schram, Nancy Hodes, and Lyman van Slyke, *Mao's Road to Power: Revolutionary Writings, 1912–1949*, vol. 7 (Armonk, NY: M. E. Sharpe, 2005), 302.

16. Dimitar D. Gueorguiev, *Retrofitting Leninism: Participation without Democracy* (Oxford, Oxford University Press, 2021), 1–40.

17. Joseph W. Esherick, *Accidental Holy Land: The Communist Revolution in Northwest China* (Berkeley: University of California Press, 2022), 188.

18. Lily L. Tsai, *Accountability without Democracy: Solidarity Groups and Public Goods Provision in Rural China* (Cambridge: Cambridge University Press, 2007); Daniel Koss, *Where the Party Rules: The Rank and File of China's Communist State* (Cambridge: Cambridge University Press, 2018).

19. In addition to the titles cited in notes 16 and 18, Kellee S. Tsai, *Capitalism without Democracy: The Private Sector in Contemporary China* (Ithaca, NY: Cornell University Press, 2007); Diana Fu, *Mobilizing without the Masses: Control and Contention in China* (Cambridge, Cambridge University Press, 2018).

20. Needless to say, I am not suggesting that the authors regard China as an anomaly. At best, their publishers have reasonably discerned that this use of "without" is a good way to sell books.

21. Kellee S. Tsai, *Capitalism without Democracy*, 14–23.

22. Andrew J. Nathan, *Chinese Democracy* (Berkeley: University of California Press, 1985; Edmund S.K. Fung, *In Search of Chinese Democracy: Civil Opposition in Nationalist China, 1929–1949* (Cambridge: Cambridge University Press, 2000).

23. Esherick, *Accidental Holy Land*, 170–71.

24. Xi Jinping, "Dangxing he renminxing conglai doushi yizhide" (February 19, 2016, published August 12, 2021), http://www.locpg.gov.cn/jsdt/20210–8/12/c_1211328645.htm (accessed January 3, 2022).

25. A recent insider exposé reveals the corruption that infects and limits the power of the party: Desmond Shum, *Red Roulette: An Insider's Story of Wealth, Power, Corruption and Vengence in Today's China* (New York; Scribner, 2021).

26. Jude Blanchette and Richard McGregor, "China's Looming Succession Crisis: What Will Happen when Xi is Gone?" *Foreign Affairs*, June 20, 2021.

27. The poster child for such predictions in Gordon C. Chang's *The Coming Collapse of China* (New York: Random House, 2001).

28. BBC News, "Reality Check: Does China's Communist Party have a Woman Problem," *BBC News*, October 25, 2017, https://www.bbc.com/news/world-asia-41652487 (accessed December 10, 2021).

ASIA/PACIFIC/PERSPECTIVES

Series Editor: Mark Selden

Crime, Punishment, and Policing in China
edited by Børge Bakken

Woman, Man, Bangkok: Love, Sex, and Popular Culture in Thailand
by Scot Barmé

Making the Foreign Serve China: Managing Foreigners in the People's Republic
by Anne-Marie Brady

Marketing Dictatorship: Propaganda and Thought Work in China
by Anne-Marie Brady

Collaborative Nationalism: The Politics of Friendship on China's Mongolian Frontier
by Uradyn E. Bulag

The Mongols at China's Edge: History and the Politics of National Unity
by Uradyn E. Bulag

Transforming Asian Socialism: China and Vietnam Compared
edited by Anita Chan, Benedict J. Tria Kerkvliet, and Jonathan Unger

Bound to Emancipate: Working Women and Urban Citizenship in Early Twentieth-Century China
by Angelina Chin

The Search for the Beautiful Woman: A Cultural History of Japanese and Chinese Beauty
by Cho Kyo, translated by Kyoko Iriye Selden

China's Great Proletarian Cultural Revolution: Master Narratives and Post-Mao Counternarratives
edited by Woei Lien Chong

North China at War: The Social Ecology of Revolution, 1937–1945
edited by Feng Chongyi and David S. G. Goodman

The People between the Rivers: The Rise and Fall of a Bronze Drum Culture, 200–750 CE
by Catherine Churchman

Prosperity's Predicament: Identity, Reform, and Resistance in Rural Wartime China
by Isabel Brown Crook and Christina Kelley Gilmartin with Yu Xiji, compiled and edited by Gail Hershatter and Emily Honig

Little Friends: Children's Film and Media Culture in China
by Stephanie Hemelryk Donald

China in Revolution: History Lessons
By Joseph Esherick

Beachheads: War, Peace, and Tourism in Postwar Okinawa
by Gerald Figal

Gender in Motion: Divisions of Labor and Cultural Change in Late Imperial and Modern China
edited by Bryna Goodman and Wendy Larson

Social and Political Change in Revolutionary China: The Taihang Base Area in the War of Resistance to Japan, 1937–1945
by David S. G. Goodman

Rice Wars in Colonial Vietnam: The Great Famine and the Viet Minh Road to Power
by Geoffrey C. Gunn

Islands of Discontent: Okinawan Responses to Japanese and American Power
edited by Laura Hein and Mark Selden

Masculinities in Chinese History
by Bret Hinsch

The Rise of Tea Culture in China: The Invention of the Individual
by Bret Hinsch

Women in Early Imperial China, Second Edition
by Bret Hinsch

Chinese Civil Justice, Past and Present
by Philip C. C. Huang

Local Democracy and Development: The Kerala People's Campaign for Decentralized Planning
by T. M. Thomas Isaac with Richard W. Franke

Hidden Treasures: Lives of First-Generation Korean Women in Japan
by Jackie J. Kim with Sonia Ryang

North Korea: Beyond Charismatic Politics
by Heonik Kwon and Byung-Ho Chung

A Century of Change in a Chinese Village: The Crisis of the Countryside
by Juren Lin, edited and translated by Linda Grove

Postwar Vietnam: Dynamics of a Transforming Society
edited by Hy V. Luong

From Silicon Valley to Shenzhen: Global Production and Work in the IT Industry
by Boy Lüthje, Stefanie Hürtgen, Peter Pawlicki, and Martina Sproll

Resistant Islands: Okinawa Confronts Japan and the United States, Second Edition
by Gavan McCormack and Satoko Oka Norimatsu

The Indonesian Presidency: The Shift from Personal toward Constitutional Rule
by Angus McIntyre

Nationalisms of Japan: Managing and Mystifying Identity
by Brian J. McVeigh

Poisoning the Pacific: The US Military's Secret Dumping of Plutonium, Chemical Weapons, and Agent Orange
by Jon Mitchell

The Korean War: A Hidden History
edited by Tessa Morris-Suzuki

To the Diamond Mountains: A Hundred-Year Journey through China and Korea
by Tessa Morris-Suzuki

To Hell and Back: The Last Train from Hiroshima
by Charles Pellegrino

From Underground to Independent: Alternative Film Culture in Contemporary China
edited by Paul G. Pickowicz and Yingjin Zhang

Wife or Worker? Asian Women and Migration
edited by Nicola Piper and Mina Roces

Social Movements in India: Poverty, Power, and Politics
edited by Raka Ray and Mary Fainsod Katzenstein

Pan-Asianism: A Documentary History, Volume 1, 1850–1920
edited by Sven Saaler and Christopher W. A. Szpilman

Pan-Asianism: A Documentary History, Volume 2, 1920–Present
edited by Sven Saaler and Christopher W. A. Szpilman

Biology and Revolution in Twentieth-Century China
by Laurence Schneider

Contentious Kwangju: The May 18th Uprising in Korea's Past and Present
edited by Gi-Wook Shin and Kyong Moon Hwang

Thought Reform and China's Dangerous Classes: Reeducation, Resistance, and the People
by Aminda M. Smith

When the Earth Roars: Lessons from the History of Earthquakes in Japan
by Gregory Smits

Subaltern China: Rural Migrants, Media, and Cultural Practices
by Wanning Sun

Japan's New Middle Class, Third Edition
by Ezra F. Vogel with a chapter by Suzanne Hall Vogel, foreword by William W. Kelly

The Japanese Family in Transition: From the Professional Housewife Ideal to the Dilemmas of Choice
by Suzanne Hall Vogel with Steven K. Vogel

The Korean War: An International History
by Wada Haruki

Longmen's Stone Buddhas and Cultural Heritage: When Antiquity Met Modernity in China
by Dong Wang

The United States and China: A History from the Eighteenth Century to the Present, Second Edition
by Dong Wang

The Inside Story of China's High-Tech Industry: Making Silicon Valley in Beijing
by Yu Zhou

Selected Bibliography

Adshead, S. A. M. *The Modernization of the Chinese Salt Administration.* Cambridge, MA: Harvard University Press, 1970.

Ahern, Emily, and Hill Gates, eds. *The Anthropology of Taiwanese Society.* Stanford, CA: Stanford University Press, 1981.

Allen, George C., and Audrey G. Donnithorne, *Western Enterprise in Far Eastern Economic Development: China and Japan.* New York: Macmillan, 1954.

Andreas, Joel. *Rise of the Red Engineers: The Cultural Revolution and the Origins of China's New Class.* Stanford, CA: Stanford University Press, 2009.

Andrews, Julia F., and Kuiyi Shen, eds. *A Century in Crisis: Modernity and Tradition in the Art of Twentieth-Century China.* New York: Guggenheim Museum, 1998.

Appleby, Joyce, Lynn Hunt, and Margaret Jacob. *Telling the Truth about History.* New York: Norton, 1994.

Apter, David E., and Tony Saich. *Revolutionary Discourse in Mao's Republic.* Cambridge, MA: Harvard University Press, 1994,

Arnold, Julean. *China: A Commercial and Industrial Handbook.* Washington: Government Printing Office, 1926.

Averill, Stephen C. "Party, Society and Local Elite in the Jiangxi Communist Movement." *Journal of Asian Studies* 46, no. 2 (1987): 279–303.

———. "Social Elites and Communist Revolution in the Jiangxi Hill Country." In *Chinese Local Elites and Patterns of Dominance*, edited by Joseph W. Esherick and Mary Backus Rankin, 283–84. Berkeley: University of California Press, 1990.

———. *Revolution in the Highlands: China's Jinggangshan Base Area.* Lanham, MD: Rowman & Littlefield Publishers, 2006.

Bailey, F. G. *Stratagems and Spoils: A Social Anthropology of Politics.* New York: Schoken Books, 1969.

Balazs, Etiènne. *Chinese Civilization and Bureaucracy,* trans. H. M. Wright. New Haven, CT: Yale University Press, 1964.

Barnett, A. Doak. *China on the Eve of Communist Takeover.* New York: Praeger, 1963.

Baum, Richard. *Prelude to Revolution: Mao, the Party and the Peasant Question, 1962–1966.* New York: Columbia University Press, 1975.
Baum, Richard, and Frederick Teiwes. *Ssu-ch'ing: The Socialist Education Movement of 1962–1966.* Berkeley: Center for Chinese Studies, 1968.
Beattie, Hilary. *Land and Lineage in China: A Study of T'ung-ch'eng County, Anhwei, in the Ming and Ch'ing Dynasties.* Cambridge: Cambridge University Press, 1979.
Belden, Jack. *China Shakes the World.* New York: Monthly Review Press, 1970.
Bell, Lynda S. *One Industry, Two Chinas: Silk Filatures and Peasant-Family Production in Wuxi County, 1865–1937.* Stanford, CA: Stanford University Press, 1999.
Benton, Gregor. *Mountain Fires: The Red Army's Three-Year War in South China, 1934–1938.* Berkeley: University of California Press, 1992.
Bernhardt, Kathryn. *Rents, Taxes, and Peasant Resistance: The Lower Yangzi Region, 1840–1950.* Stanford, CA: Stanford University Press, 1992.
Bettelheim, Charles. *Cultural Revolution and Industrial Organization in China.* New York: Monthly Review Press, 1974.
Bian, Morris L. *The Making of the State Enterprise System in Modern China: The Dynamics of Institutional Change.* Cambridge, MA: Harvard University Press, 2005.
Bianco, Lucien. "Peasant Movements." In *The Cambridge History of China*, vol. 13: *Republican China, 1912–1949*, Part I. Cambridge: Cambridge University Press, 1986.
Bickers, Robert. *Out of China: How the Chinese Ended the Era of Western Domination.* London: Penguin Books, 2018.
Bodde, Derk. *Peking Diary: A Year of Revolution.* New York: Schuman, 1950.
Bodde, Derk, and Clarence Morris. *Law in Imperial China.* Philadelphia: University of Pennsylvania Press, 1973.
Bourdieu, Pierre. *An Outline of a Theory of Practice*, trans. Richard Nice. Cambridge: Cambridge University Press, 1977.
Braun, Otto. *A Comintern Agent in China, 1932–1939.* trans. Jeanne Moore. Stanford, CA: Stanford University Press, 1982.
Brook, Timothy. *Quelling the People: The Military Suppression of the Beijing Democracy Movement.* New York: Oxford University Press, 1992.
Brown, Jeremy. *June Fourth: The Tiananmen Protests and Beijing Massacre of 1989.* Cambridge: Cambridge University Press, 2021.
Calhoun, Craig J. *Neither Gods nor Emperors: Students and the Struggle for Democracy in China.* Berkeley: University of California Press, 1994.
Cao Xueqin. *The Story of the Stone*, trans. David Hawkes. Baltimore: Penguin, 1974.
Carlson, Ellsworth C. *The Kaiping Mines. 1877–1912)*, second edition. Cambridge, MA: Harvard University Press, 1971.
Carlson, Evans Fordyce, ed. *The Chinese Army: Its Organization and Military Efficiency.* New York: Institute of Pacific Relations, 1940.
Cell, Charles P. *Revolution at Work: Mobilization Campaigns in China.* New York: Academic Press, 1977.
Ch'en Li-fu, *The Storm Clouds Clear Over China: The Memoir of Ch'en Li-fu, 1900–1993*, edited by Sidney H. Chang and Ramon H. Myers. Stanford, CA: Hoover Institution Press, 1993.

Ch'i, Hsi-sheng. *Nationalist China at War: Military Defeats and Political Collapse, 1937–1945.* Ann Arbor: University of Michigan Press, 1982.

Ch'ü, T'ung-tsu. *Local Government in China under the Ch'ing.* Stanford, CA: Stanford University Press, 1962.

Chang, Chung-li. *The Chinese Gentry: Studies on their Role in Nineteenth-Century Chinese Society.* Seattle: University of Washington Press, 1955.

Chang, Hsin-pao. *Commissioner Lin and the Opium War.* Cambridge, MA: Harvard University Press, 1964.

Chang, John K., "Industrial Development in China, 1912–1949." *Journal of Economic History* 27 (March 1967).

Chang, Michael G. *A Court on Horseback: Imperial Touring and the Construction of Ethno–Dynastic Hegemony in Qing China, 1680–1785.* Cambridge, MA: Harvard University Press, 2005.

Chen Han-seng, *Industrial Capital and Chinese Peasants.* Shanghai: Kelly and Walsh, 1939.

Chen Yongfa, *Yan'an de yinying* (Yan'an's Shadow). Taibei: Academia Sinica, Institute of Modern History, 1990.

Chen, Janet Y. *Guilty of Indigence: The Urban Poor in China, 1900–1953.* Princeton, NJ: Princeton University Press, 2012.

Chen, Yung-fa. *Making Revolution: The Communist Movement in Eastern and Central China, 1937–1945.* Berkeley: University of California Press, 1986.

Cheng, Yu-kwei. *Foreign Trade and Industrial Development of China: An Historical and Integrated Analysis through 1948.* Washington, DC: University Press of Washington, 1956.

Chesneaux, Jean. *The Chinese Labor Movement, 1919–1927*, trans. H. M. Wright. Stanford, CA: Stanford University Press, 1968.

Chia, Ning. "The Lifanyuan and the Inner Asian Rituals in the Early Qing (1644–1795)." *Late Imperial China* 14 (1993): 60–92.

Chiang Kai-shek. *Soviet Russia in China: A Summing-up at Seventy.* New York: Farrar, Straus and Cudahy, 1957.

China Weekly Review. Shanghai, 1923–1950.

Chow, Kai-Wing. *The Rise of Confucian Ritualism in Late Imperial China: Ethics, Classics, and Lineage Discourse.* Stanford, CA: Stanford University Press, 1994.

Chow, Yung-teh. *Social Mobility in China: Status Careers Among the Gentry in a Chinese Community.* New York: Atherton Press, 1966.

Coble, Parkes. *Facing Japan: Chinese Politics and Japanese Imperialism, 1931–1937.* Cambridge, MA: Harvard University Press, 1991.

Cole, James. "The Shaoxing Connection: A Vertical Administrative Clique in Late Qing China." *Modern China* 6 no. 3 (1980): 317–26.

Compton, Boyd. *Mao's China: Party Reform Documents, 1942–1944.* Seattle: University of Washington Press, 1966.

Cranmer-Byng, J. L. *An Embassy to China, being a Journal Kept by Lord Macartney during His Embassy to the Emperor Ch'ien-lung, 1793–1794.* London: Longmans, 1962.

Crook, David, and Isabel Crook. *Revolution in a Chinese Village: Ten Mile Inn*. London: Routledge and Paul, 1968.
Crossley, Pamela. "The Rulerships of China." *American Historical Review* 97, no. 5 (1992): 1468–83.
———. *A Translucent Mirror: History and Identity in Qing Imperial Ideology.* Berkeley: University of California Press, 1999.
———. *Orphan Warriors: Three Manchu Generations and the End of the Qing World*. Princeton: Princeton University Press, 1990.
Dai Yi. *Qianlong di jiqi shidai* (The Qianlong Emperor and his times). Beijing: Renmin daxue chubanshe, 1992.
Da-Qing tongli (Comprehensive Rituals of the Qing), in *Siku quanshu* (The Four Treasuries) vol. 655. Taipei: Commercial Press reprint, 1756.
Davin, Delia. *Woman-Work: Women and the Party in Revolutionary China.* Oxford: Clarendon Press, 1976.
De Mare, Brian. *Land Wars: The Story of China's Agrarian Revolution*. Stanford, CA: Stanford University Press, 2019.
Dennerline, Jerry. *The Chia-ting Loyalists: Confucian Leadership and Social Change in Seventeenth-Century China*. New Haven, CT: Yale University Press, 1981.
Di Cosmo, Nicola. "Qing Colonial Administration in Inner Asia." *International History Review* 20, no. 2 (June 1998): 287–309.
Dikötter, Frank. *The Discourse of Race in Modern China*. Stanford, CA: Stanford University Press, 1992.
Ding Wenjiang and Zhao Fengtian. *Liang Rengong xiansheng nianpu changbian (chugao)* (Complete chronological biography of Liang Qichao [draft]). Beijing: Zhonghua shuju, 2010.
Dirlik, Arif. *The Origins of Chinese Communism.* New York: Oxford University Press, 1989.
Dittmer, Lowell. "China in 1989: The Crisis of Incomplete Reform." *Asian Survey* 30, no. 1 (January 1990): 25–41.
———. *Liu Shao-ch'i and the Chinese Cultural Revolution: The Politics of Mass Criticism*. Berkeley: University of California Press, 1974.
——— and Samuel S. Kim. *China's Quest for National Identity*. Ithaca: Cornell University Press, 1993.
Dongfang zazhi (Shanghai), 1904–1948.
Duara, Prasenjit. *Culture, Power, and the State: Rural North China, 1900–1942*. Stanford, CA: Stanford University Press, 1988.
———. *Rescuing History from the Nation: Questioning Narratives of Modern China* Chicago: University of Chicago, 1995.
Durand, P-H (Dai Tingjie). "Jianting ze ming—Majia'erni shihua zaitan" (Listening to it, it becomes clear: a new look at the Macartney mission), YSSL, preface, 89–150.
Eastman, Lloyd E. *The Abortive Revolution: China under Nationalist Rule, 1927–1937*. Cambridge, MA: Harvard University Press, 1974.
———. "Nationalist China during the Sino-Japanese War, 1937–1945," *The Cambridge History of China*, vol. 13: *Republican China, 1912–1949, Part II*. Cambridge: Cambridge University Press, 1986.

———. *Seeds of Destruction: Nationalist China in War and Revolution, 1937–1949*. Stanford, CA: Stanford University Press, 1984.

Ebrey, Patricia and James Watson. *Kinship Organization in Late Imperial China, 1000–1940*. Berkeley: University of California Press, 1986.

Eisenstadt, S. N. and L. Roniger. *Patrons, Clients, and Friends: Interpersonal Relations and the Structure of Trust in Society*. Cambridge: Cambridge University Press, 1984.

Elliott, Mark C. The Manchu Way: The Eight Banners and Ethnic Identity in Late Imperial China. Stanford, CA: Stanford University Press, 2001.

Elman, Benjamin. *From Philosophy to Philology: Intellectual and Social Aspects of Change in Late Imperial China*. Cambridge, MA: Harvard Council on East Asian Studies, 1984.

Elvin, Mark. *The Pattern of the Chinese Past*. Stanford, CA: Stanford University Press, 1973.

Esherick, Joseph W. *Accidental Holy Land: The Communist Revolution in Northwest China*. University of California Press, 2022.

———. "Number Games: A Note on Land Distribution in Prerevolutionary China." *Modern China* 7, no. 4 (1981).

———. *The Origins of the Boxer Uprising*. Berkeley: University of California Press, 1987.

———. *Reform and Revolution in China: The 1911 Revolution in Hunan and Hubei*. Berkeley: University of California Press, 1976.

———. "Revolution in a Feudal Fortress: Yangjiagou, Mizhi County, Shaanxi, 1937–1948." *Modern China* 24, no. 4 (October 1998): 352–62.

———. "Xi'an Spring." *Australian Journal of Chinese Affairs* 24 (July 1990): 209–36.

Fairbank, John King, ed., *The Chinese World Order: Traditional China's Foreign Relations*. Cambridge, MA: Harvard University Press, 1968.

———. *The United States and China*, third edition. Cambridge, MA: Harvard University Press, 1971.

Fairbank, John King, and Kwang-ching Liu, eds. *The Cambridge History of China*, vol. 11, *The Late Ch'ing, 1800–1911*, Part II. Cambridge: Cambridge University Press, 1980.

Fairbank, John King, and S. Y. Teng, "On the Ch'ing Tributary System." *Harvard Journal of Asiatic Studies* 6 (1941): 135–246.

Fairbank, John King, Edwin O. Reischauer and Albert M. Craig, *East Asia: The Modern Transformation*. Boston: Houghton Mifflin, 1965.

Farquhar, David M. "Emperor as Boddhisattva in the Governance of the Ch'ing Empire." *Harvard Journal of Asiatic Studies* 37 (1978): 5–34

Faure, David. *The Structure of Chinese Rural Society: Lineage and Village in the Eastern New Territories, Hong Kong*. Oxford: Oxford University Press, 1986.

Fei, Hsiao-tung. *China's Gentry: Essays on Rural-Urban Relations*, edited by Robert Park Redfield. Chicago: University of Chicago Press, 1953.

Fei, Hsiao-tung, and Chang Tse-i. *Earthbound China: A Study of Rural Economy in Yunnan*. Chicago: University of Chicago Press, 1945.

Feigon, Lee. *China Rising: The Meaning of Tiananmen.* Chicago: Ivan Dee, 1990.

Feng Tianyu and Zhang Duqin. *Xinhai shouyi ji* (History of the 1911 Wuchang Uprising). Wuhan: Hubei renmin chubanshe, 2011.

Feuerwerker, Albert. *China's Early Industrialization: Sheng Hsuan-huai (1844–1916) and Mandarin Enterprise.* Cambridge, MA: Harvard University Press, 1958.

———. "China's Nineteenth Century Industrialization: The Case of the Hanyehping Coal and Iron Company, Ltd." In *The Economic Development of China and Japan*, edited by C. D. Cowan. London: G. Allen and Unwin, 1964.

———. "Economic Trends in the Late Ch'ing Empire, 1870–1911." In *The Cambridge History of China*, vol. 11: *The Late Ch'ing, 1800–1911*, Part II, edited by John K. Fairbank and Kwang-ching Liu. Cambridge: Cambridge University Press, 1980).

———. "Economic Trends, 1912–1949." In *The Cambridge History of China*, vol. 12: *Republican China 1912–1949*, Part I, edited by John K. Fairbank. Cambridge: Cambridge University Press, 1983.

———. "Handicraft and Manufactured Cotton Textiles in China, 1871–1910." *Journal of Economic History* 30 (1970): 2.

Fewsmith, Joseph. *Party, State and Local Elite in Republican China: Merchant Organizations and Politics in Shanghai, 1870–1930.* Honolulu: University of Hawai'i Press, 1985.

Fletcher, Joseph. "Ch'ing Inner Asia c. 1800" (35–106) and "The Heyday of the Ch'ing Order in Mongolia, Sinkiang and Tibet" (351–406). In *Cambridge History of China*, vol. 10, Part I, edited by Denis Twitchett and John King Fairbank. London: Cambridge University Press, 1978.

Fogel, Joshua A. *Ai Ssi-ch'i's Contribution to the Development of Chinese Marxism.* Cambridge, MA: Harvard University Council on East Asian Studies, 1987.

Folsom, Kenneth E. *Friends, Guests, and Colleagues: The "Mu-fu" System in the Late Ch'ing Period.* Berkeley: University of California Press, 1968.

Forman, Harrison. *Report from Red China.* New York: Wittlesey House, 1945.

Freedman, Maurice. *Chinese Lineage and Society: Fukien and Kwangtung.* London: Anthone, 1966.

———. *Lineage Organization in Southeast China*, London: Anthone, 1958.

Freyn, Hubert. *Prelude to War: The Chinese Student Rebellion of 1935–1936.* Shanghai: China Journal Pub. Co., 1939.

Friedman, Edward, Paul G. Pickowicz, and Mark Selden, with Kay Ann Johnson, *Chinese Village, Socialist State.* New Haven, CT: Yale University Press, 1991.

Fu, Diana. *Mobilizing without the Masses: Control and Contention in China.* Cambridge, Cambridge University Press, 2018.

Fung, Edmund S. K. *The Military Dimension of the Chinese Revolution: The New Army and its Role in the 1911 Revolution.* Vancouver: University of British Columbia Press, 1980.

———. *In Search of Chinese Democracy: Civil Opposition in Nationalist China, 1929–1949.* Cambridge: Cambridge University Press, 2000.

Galbiatti, Fernando. *P'eng P'ai and the Hai-Lu-Feng Soviet.* Stanford, CA: Stanford University Press, 1985.

Gamble, Sydney D. *Peking: A Social Survey*. New York: George H. Doran, 1921.
Gao Hua. *How the Red Sun Rose: The Origin and Development of the Yan'an Rectification Movement, 1930–1945*, trans. Stacey Mosher and Guo Jian. Hong Kong: Chinese University of Hong Kong Press, 2019.
Gao, James. *The Communist Takeover of Hangzhou: The Transformation of City and Cadres, 1949–1954*. Honolulu: University of Hawai'i Press, 2004.
Geertz, Clifford. *The Interpretation of Cultures*. New York: Basic Books, 1973.
———. *Negara: The Theatre State in Nineteenth-Century Bali*. Princeton: Princeton University Press, 1980.
Goldstein, Melvyn C. *A History of Modern Tibet, 1913–1951*. Berkeley: University of California Press, 1989.
Goldstone, Jack A. *Revolution and Rebellion in the Early Modem World*. Berkeley: University of California Press, 1991.
Goncharov, Sergei N., John W. Lewis, and Xue Litai. *Uncertain Partners: Stalin, Mao and the Korean War*. Stanford, CA: Stanford University Press, 1993.
Goodman, Bryna. *Native Place, City, and Nation: Regional Networks and Identities in Shanghai: 1853–1937*. Berkeley: University of California Press, 1995.
Goodman, David S. G. *Social and Political Change in Revolutionary China: The Taihang Base Area in the War of Resistance to Japan, 1937–1945*. Lanham, MD: Rowman & Littlefield, 2000.
Gray, Jack, ed. *Modern China's Search for a Political Form*. London: Oxford University Press, 1969.
Grove, Linda. *A Chinese Economic Revolution: Rural Entrepreneurship in the Twentieth Century*. Lanham, MD: Rowman & Littlefield, 2006.
Grove, Linda, and Christian Daniels, eds. *State and Society in China: Japanese Perspectives on Ming-Qing Social and Economic History*. Tokyo: University of Tokyo Press, 1984.
Grove, Linda, and Joseph W. Esherick. "From Feudalism to Capitalism: Japanese Scholarship on the Transformation of Chinese Rural Society." *Modern China* 6, no. 4 (1980): 397–438.
Gu Zhongxiu. *Zhonghua minguo kaiguo shi* (The founding of the Republic of China) Taibei: Wenxing shudian, 1962 (original 1914).
Gueorguiev, Dimitar D. *Retrofitting Leninism: Participation without Democracy*. Oxford, Oxford University Press, 2021.
Gugong bowuyuan Ming-Qing dang'anbu, ed., *Qingmo choubei lixian dang'an shiliao* (Archival materials in the late Qing constitutional preparations). Beijing: Zhonghua shuju, 1979.
Guy, R. Kent. *Qing Governors and their Provinces: The Evolution of Territorial Administration in China, 1644–1796*. Seattle: University of Washington Press, 2010.
———. *The Emperor's Four Treasuries: Scholars and the State in the Late Ch'ien-lung Era*. Cambridge, MA: Harvard University Council on East Asian Studies, 1987.
Haar, Barend J. *Ritual and Mythology of the Chinese Triads: Creating an Identity*. Leiden: Brill, 1998.

Han Minzhu, ed. *Cries for Democracy: Writing and Speeches from the 1989 Chinese Democracy Movement.* Princeton, NJ: Princeton University Press, 1990.

Hao, Chang. *Liang Ch'i-ch'ao and Intellectual Transition in China, 1890–1907.* Cambridge, MA: Harvard University Press, 1971.

Hao, Yen-p'ing. *The Comprador in Nineteenth-Century China: Bridge Between East and West.* Cambridge, MA: Harvard University Press, 1970.

Harper, Tim. *Underground Asia: Global Revolutionaries and the Assault on Empire.* Cambridge, MA: Belknap Press, 2021.

Harrell, Stevan. *Ploughshare Village: Cultural and Context in Taiwan.* Seattle: University of Washington Press, 1986.

Harrison, Henrietta. *Inventing the Nation: China.* New York: Oxford University Press, 2001.

———. *The Making of the Republican Citizen: Political Ceremonies and Symbols in China, 1911–1929.* Oxford: Oxford University Press, 2000.

Hartford, Kathleen, and Steven M. Goldstein, eds. *Single Sparks: China's Rural Revolutions.* Armonk, NY: M. E. Sharpe, 1989.

Hayhoe, Ruth. "Towards the Forging of a Chinese University Ethos: Zhendan and Fudan, 1903–1919." *China Quarterly* 94 (1983): 323–41.

He Bingdi (Ping-ti Ho), *Zhongguo huiguan shilun* (Historical Survey of Landsmannshaften in China). Taibei: Xuesheng shuju, 1966.

Henriot, Christian. *Shanghai, 1927–1937: Municipal Power, Locality, and Modernization,* trans. Noel Castelino. Berkeley: University of California Press, 1993.

Hershatter, Gail. *Dangerous Pleasures: Prostitution and Modernity in Twentieth-Century China.* Berkeley: University of California Press, 1997.

———. *Women and China's Revolutions.* Lanham, MD: Rowman & Littlefield, 2019.

———. *The Workers of Tianjin, 1900–1949.* Stanford, CA: Stanford University Press, 1986.

Hevia, James L. *Cherishing Men from Afar: Qing Guest Ritual and the Macartney Embassy of 1793.* Durham, NC: Duke University Press, 1995.

Hinton, William. *Fanshen: A Documentary of Revolution in a Chinese Village.* New York: Vintage, 1966.

Ho, Dahpon. "The Men Who Would Not Be Amban and the One Who Would: Four Frontline Statesmen and Qing Tibet Policy, 1905–1911." *Modern China* 34, no. 2 (2008): 210–46.

Ho, Ping-ti. "The Salt Merchants of Yangchou." *Harvard Journal of Asiatic Studies* 17 (1954): 130–68.

———. *Studies on the Population of China.* Cambridge, MA: Harvard University Press, 1959.

———. *The Ladder of Success in Imperial China: Aspects of Social Mobility, 1368–1911.* New York: Columbia University Press, 1962.

———. "In Defense of Sinicization: A Rebuttal of Evelyn Rawski's 'Reenvisioning the Qing.'" *The Journal of Asian Studies* 57, no. 1. (February 1998): 123–55.

Hobsbawm, E. J. *Nations and Nationalism since 1780: Programme, Myth, Reality.* Cambridge: Cambridge University Press, 1990.

Hofheinz. Roy Jr. *The Broken Wave: The Chinese Communist Peasant Movement, 1922–1928.* Cambridge, MA: Harvard University Press, 1977.

Honig, Emily. *Sisters and Strangers: Women in the Shanghai Cotton Mills, 1911–1949.* Stanford, CA: Stanford University Press, 1986.

Hou, Chi-ming. *Foreign Investment and Economic Development in China: 1840–1937.* Cambridge, MA: Harvard University Press, 1965.

Hsiao, Kung-ch'üan. *Rural China: Imperial Control in the Nineteenth Century.* Seattle: University of Washington Press, 1960.

Hsieh, Winston. *Chinese, Historiography of the 1911 Revolution: A Critical Survey and Selected Bibliography.* Stanford, CA: Hoover Institution Press, 1975.

Hsiung, James C., and Steven I. Levine. *China's Bitter Victory: The War with Japan, 1937–1945.* Armonk, NY: M. E, Sharpe, 1992.

Hsueh, Chün-tu. *Huang Xing and the Chinese Revolution.* Stanford, CA: Stanford University Press, 1961.

Huang Daoxuan. *Zhangli yu xianjie: Zhongyang suqu de geming, 1933–1934* (Power and limits: revolution in the Central Soviet, 1933–1934). Beijing: Shehui kexue chubanshe, 2011.

Huang, Philip C. C. *The Peasant Economy and Social Change in North China.* Stanford, CA: Stanford University Press, 1985.

———. *The Peasant Family and Rural Development in the Yangzi Delta, 1350–1988.* Stanford, CA: Stanford University Press, 1990.

Hung, Chang-tai. *War and Popular Culture: Resistance in Modern China, 1937–1945.* Berkeley: University of California Press, 1994.

Hymes, Robert. *Statesmen and Gentlemen: The Elite of Fu-chou, Chiang-hsi, in Northern and Southern Sung.* Cambridge: Cambridge University Press, 1986.

International History Review 20, no. 2 (June 1998), special issue on Manchu colonialism.

Isett, Christopher M. "Village Regulation of Property and the Social Basis for the Transformation of Qing Manchuria." *Late Imperial China* 25, no. 1 (June 2004): 124–86.

Ishikawa, Yoshihiro. *The Formation of the Chinese Communist Party*, trans. Joshua A. Fogel. New York: Columbia University Press, 2013.

Israel, John. *Lianda: A Chinese University in War and Revolution.* Stanford, CA: Stanford University Press, 1998.

———. *Student Nationalism in China, 1927–1937.* Stanford, CA: Stanford University Press, 1966.

Jeuschert, Dorothea. "Legal Pluralism in the Qing Empire: Manchu Legislation for the Mongols." *International History Review* 20, no. 2 (June 1998): 310–24.

Johnson, Chalmers A. *Peasant Nationalism and Communist Power: The Emergence of Revolutionary China, 1937–1945.* Stanford, CA: Stanford University Press: 1962.

Johnson, David, Andrew Nathan, and Evelyn S. Rawski, *Popular Cultural in Late Imperial China.* Berkeley: University of California Press, 1985.

Johnson, Kay Ann. *Women, Family and Peasant Revolution in China.* Chicago: University of Chicago Press, 1983.

Johnson, Linda Cooke. *Shanghai: From Market Town to Treaty Port, 1074–1858*. Stanford, CA: Stanford University Press, 1995.

Ju Zheng, "Xinhai zhaji" (Notes on 1911), in *Ju Juesheng xiansheng quanji* (Complete works of Mr. Ju Zheng) Taibei: n.p., 1954.

Judge, Joan. *Print and Politics: "Shibao" and the Culture of Reform in Late Qing China*. Stanford, CA: Stanford University Press, 1996.

Kataoka, Tetsuya. *Resistance and Revolution in China: The Communists and the Second United Front*. Berkeley: University of California Press, 1974.

Keating, Pauline. *Two Revolutions: Village Reconstruction and Cooperativization in North Shaanxi, 1934–1945*. Stanford, CA: Stanford University Press, 1997.

Kinzley, Judd C. "Crisis and the Development of China's Southwestern Periphery: The Transformation of Panzhihua, 1936–1969." *Modern China* 38, no. 5 (2012): 559–84.

Kirby, William C. "Continuity and Change in Modern China: Economic Planning in the Mainland and on Taiwan, 1943–1958." *Australian Journal of Chinese Affairs* 24 (July 1990).

———. *Germany and Republican China*. Stanford, CA: Stanford University Press, 1984.

Koss, Daniel. *Where the Party Rules: The Rank and File of China's Communist State*. Cambridge: Cambridge University Press, 2018.

Kraus, Richard C. *Class Conflict and Chinese Socialism*. New York: Columbia University Press, 1981.

———. "Class Conflict and the Vocabulary of Social Analysis in China." *China Quarterly* 69 (March 1977): 54–74.

———. "The Lament of Astrophysicist Fang Lizhi." In *Marxism and the Chinese Experience*, edited by Arif Dirlik and Maurice Meisner. Armonk, NY: M. E. Sharpe, 1989.

Kuhn, Philip A. *Rebellion and its Enemies in Late Imperial China: Militarization and Social Structure, 1769–1864*. Cambridge, MA: Harvard University Press, 1970.

Laitinen, Kauko. *Chinese Nationalism in the Late Qing Dynasty: Zhang Binglin as an anti-Manchu Propagandist*. Copenhagen: Nordic Institute of Asian Studies, 1990.

Lamley, Harry J. "Hsieh-tou: The Pathology of Violence in Southeastern China." *Ch'ing-shih wen-t'i* 3, no. 7 (1977): 1–39.

Lang, Olga. *Chinese Family and Society*. New Haven, CT: Yale University Press, 1946.

Lardy, Nicholas. *Economic Growth and Distribution in China*. Cambridge: Cambridge University Press, 1978.

Lary, Diana. *China's Civil War: A Social History, 1945–1949*. Cambridge: Cambridge University Press, 2015.

Lattimore, Owen. *The Mongols of Manchuria*. New York: John Day, 1934.

Lee, Hong Yung. *From Revolutionary Cadres to Party Technocrats in Socialist China*. Berkeley: University of California Press, 1991.

Lee, Leo Ou-fan. *Shanghai Modern: The Flowering of a New Urban Culture in China, 1930–1945*. Cambridge, MA: Harvard University Press: 1999.

Lee, Robert H. G. *The Manchurian Frontier in Ch'ing History*. Cambridge, MA: Harvard University Press, 1970.
Lefebvre, George. *The Coming of the French Revolution*, trans. R. R. Palmer. New York: Vintage, 1957; French ed. 1939.
Legge, James. *The Chinese Classics*, second edition, vol. 1: *Confucian Analects, The Great Learning, and the Doctrine of the Mean*. Taipei reprint, n.d.
Lenin, V. I. *Collected Works*. 45 vols. Moscow: Progress Publishers, 1963–1970.
Levenson, Joseph R. *Confucian China and its Modern Fate*, 3 vols. Berkeley: University of California Press, 1958–1963.
———. *Liang Ch'i-ch'ao and the Mind of Modern China*. Cambridge, MA: Harvard University Press, 1959.
Levine, Steven I. *The Anvil of Victory: The Communist Revolution in Manchuria, 1945–1948*. New York: Columbia University Press, 1987.
Lewis, John W., ed., *Peasant Rebellion and Communist Revolution in Asia*. Stanford, CA: Stanford University Press: 1974.
Li Guoqi, ed. *Jindai Zhongguo sixiang renwu lun: Minzu zhuyi* (Essays on major figures in modern China and their thinking: nationalism), Taibei: Shibao wenhua chubanshe, 1982 (first edition 1970).
Li Rui. *Lushan huiyi shilu* (True Record of the Lushan Plenum). Taibei: Xinrui, 1994; mainland ed. 1988.
Li Shoukong. *Minchu zhi guohui* (The parliament of the early republic) Taibei: Zhongguo xueshu zhuzuo jiangzhu weiyuanhui, 1964.
Li Youning, Zhang Yufa. *Zhongguo funüshi lunwen ji* (Collected essays on Chinese women's history). Taibei: Taiwan Shangwu Yinshuguan, 1981.
Li Zhisui and Anne F. Thurston. *The Private Life of Chairman Mao: The Memoirs of Mao's Personal Physician*. New York: Random House, 1994.
Liang Qichao. *Liang Qichao quanji*. Beijing: Beijing chubanshe: 1999.
———. *Yinbingshi heji*. Shanghai: Zhonghua shuju, 1941.
Lieu, D. K. *The Silk Industry of China*. Shanghai: Kelly and Walsh, 1941.
Liew, K. S. *Struggle for Democracy: Sung Chiao-jen and the 1911 Chinese Revolution*. Berkeley: University of California Press, 1971.
Lin Yutang. *Between Tears and Laughter*. Garden City, NY: Blue Ribbon Books, 1945.
Lipmann, Jonathan N. *Familiar Strangers: A History of Muslims in Northwest China*. Seattle: University of Washington Press, 1997.
Liu Lu. "A Whole Nation Walking: The 'Great Retreat' in the War of Resistance, 1937–1945." PhD diss., University of California San Diego, 2002.
Liu Lu. "*Xingui yuan*: Controversy over Domesticity in Postwar China (1945–1949)." *Modern Chinese Literature and Culture* (2001).
Liu Ta-chung and Yeh Kung-chia. *The Economy of the Chinese Mainland: National Income and Economic Development, 1933–1959*. Princeton, NJ: Princeton University Press, 1965.
Liu, Kwang-ching, and Richard J. Smith, "The Military Challenge: The Northwest and the Coast." In *The Cambridge History of China*, vol. 11: *The Late Ch'ing*, Part

II, edited by John K. Fairbank and Kwang-ching Liu, 235–43. Cambridge: Cambridge University Press, 1980.

Lü, Xiaobo and Elizabeth J. Perry. *Danwei—The Changing Chinese Workplace in Historical and Comparative Perspective*. Armonk, NY: M. E. Sharpe, 1997.

Luo Gang, *Zhonghua minguo Guofu shilu* (The true record of the Father of the Republic of China). Taibei: Zhongzheng shuju, 1988.

Luo Jialun, ed. *Geming wenxian* (Documents of the revolution). Taibei: Zhongguo Guomindang dangshi shiliao, 1953.

Luo Jialun et al., *Guofu nianpu* (Chronological biography of the Father of the Republic), enlarged edition (Taibei: Zhongguo Guomindang zhongyang weiyuanhui, 1985.

Luo Suwen. *Nüxing yu jindai Zhongguo shehui* (Females in modern Chinese society). Shanghai: Shanghai People's Press, 1996.

Luo Zhitian. *Jindai dushuren de sixiang shijie yu zhixue quxiang* (The intellectual world and scholastic orientations of modern scholars). Beijing: Peking University Press, 2009.

Macauley, Melissa. *Social Power and Legal Culture: Litigation Masters in Late Imperial China*. Stanford, CA: Stanford University Press, 1998.

MacFarquhar, Roderick. *The Origins of the Cultural Revolution: The Coming of the Cataclysm, 1961–1966*. New York: Columbia University Press, 1999.

Mackerras, Colin. *The Chinese Theatre in Modern Times*. Amherst: University of Massachusetts Press, 1975.

Madsen, Richard. *Morality and Power in a Chinese Village*. Berkeley: University of California Press, 1984.

Mann, Susan (Susan Mann Jones). *Local Merchants and the Chinese Bureaucracy, 1750–1950*. Stanford, CA: Stanford University Press, 1987.

Mao Zedong. *Mao Zedong sixiang wansui* (Long live the Thought of Mao Zedong). n.p., 1967.

———. *Mao Zedong sixiang wansui* (Long live the Thought of Mao Zedong). n.p. 1969.

———. *Mao Zedong xuanji* (Selected Works of Mao Zedong), vol. 5. Beijing: Renmin chubanshe, 1977.

———. *Report from Xunwu*, trans. Roger R. Thompson. Stanford, CA: Stanford University Press, 1990.

Marks, Robert B. *Rural Revolution in South China: Peasants and the Making of History in Haifeng County, 1570–1930*. Madison: University of Wisconsin Press, 1984.

Marsh, Robert. *The Mandarins: The Circulation of Elites in China, 1600–1900*. Glencoe, IL: Free Press, 1961.

Martin, Brian G. *The Shanghai Green Gang: Politics and Organized Crime, 1919–1937*. Berkeley: University of California Press, 1996.

Marx, Karl. *Capital*, vol. 1: *A Critical Analysis of Capitalist Production*. Moscow: Foreign Languages Publishing House, 1961 (original 1877).

———. *Early Writings*. New York: Vintage, 1975.

———. *The Class Struggles in France (1848–1850)*. New York: International Publishers, 1972 (original 1850).
———. *The Communist Manifesto*. Chicago: Gateway Edition, 1954.
———. *The Eighteenth Brumaire of Louis Bonaparte*. New York: International Publishers, 1963 (original 1852).
McCord, Edward A. "Militia and Local Militarization in Late Qing and Early Republican China: The Case of Hunan." *Modern China* 14, no. 2 (1988): 156–97.
Meisner, Maurice. *Li Ta-chao and the Origins of Chinese Marxism*. Cambridge, MA: Harvard University Press, 1967.
Melby, John F. *The Mandate of Heaven: A Record of a Civil War, China 1945–1949*. Garden City, NY: Anchor Books, 1971.
Meskill, Johanna Menzel. *A Chinese Pioneer Family: The Lins of Wu-feng, Taiwan, 1729–1895*. Princeton, NJ: Princeton University Press, 1979.
Migdal, Joel S. *Peasants, Politics and Revolution: Pressures toward Political and Social Change in the Third World*. Princeton, NJ: Princeton University Press, 1974.
Millward, James A. *Beyond the Pass: Economy, Ethnicity, and Empire in Qing Central Asia, 1759–1864*. Stanford, CA: Stanford University Press, 1998.
Min Tu-ki. *National Polity and Local Power: The Transformation of Late Imperial China*, edited by Philip Kuhn and Timothy Brook. Cambridge, MA: Harvard Council on East Asian Studies, 1989.
Minlibao. Shanghai: 1910–1912.
Mitter, Rana. *Forgotten Ally: China's World War II, 1937–1945*. Boston: Houghton Mifflin Harcourt, 2013.
Mittler, Barbara. *A Newspaper for China?: Power, Identity and Change in Shanghai's News Media, 1872–1912*. Cambridge, MA: Harvard University Asia Center, 2004.
Moore, Barrington Jr. *Social Origins of Dictatorship and Democracy: Lord and Peasant in the Making of the Modern World*. Boston: Beacon, 1966.
Mori Masao. "Nihon no Min-Shin jidai shi kenkyū ni okeru kyūshinron ni tsuite" (Theories on local gentry in Japanese studies of the Ming-Qing period). *Rekishi hyōron*, 308, 312, 314. 1975–1976.
Morrison, Donald, ed. *Massacre in Beijing: China's Struggle for Democracy*. New York: Warner Books, 1989.
Murphey, Rhoads. *The Treaty Ports and China's Modernization: What Went Wrong?* Ann Arbor, MI: Center for Chinese Studies, 1970.
Myers, Ramon. *The Chinese Peasant Economy, Agricultural Development in Hopei and Shantung, 1890–1949*. Cambridge, MA: Harvard University Press, 1970.
Myers, Ramon, and T. A. Metzger. "Sinological Shadows: The State of Modern China Studies in the US." *Australian Journal of Chinese Affairs* 4 (1980).
Nakami Tatsuo, "A Protest against the Concept of the 'Middle Kingdom': The Mongols and the 1911 Revolution." In *The 1911 Revolution in China: Interpretive Essays*, edited by Etô Shinkichi and Harold Z. Schiffrin. Tokyo: University of Tokyo Press, 1984.
Naquin, Susan. *Shantung Rebellion: The Wang Lun Uprising of 1774*. New Haven, CT: Yale University Press, 1987.

Naquin, Susan, and Evelyn S. Rawski. *Chinese Society in the Eighteenth Century.* New Haven, CT: Yale University Press, 1987.

Nathan, Andrew J. *China's Crisis: Dilemmas of Reform and Prospects for Democracy.* New York: Columbia University Press, 1990.

———. *Chinese Democracy.* Berkeley: University of California Press, 1985.

Nathan, Andrew J., and Perry Link, eds., *The Tiananmen Papers: the Chinese Leadership's Decision to use Force Against its own People—In Their Own Words*, comp. by Zhang Liang. New York: Public Affairs, 2001.

Naughton, Barry J. *The Chinese Economy: Adaptation and Growth*, second edition. Cambridge MA: M.IT Press, 2018.

Nedostup, Rebecca. *Superstitious Regimes: Religion and the Politics of Chinese Modernity.* Cambridge, MA: Harvard University Press, 2009.

Niida Noboru et al., eds, *Chūgoku nōson kankō chōsa* (Survey of village customs in China). Tokyo: Iwanami Shoten, 1981.

Onon, Urgunge and Derrick Pritchatt, *Asia's First Modern Revolution: Mongolia Proclaims its Independence in 1911.* Leiden: E. J. Brill, 1998.

Overlach, T. W. *Foreign Financial Control in China.* New York: Macmillan, 1919.

Parish, William, and Martin King Whyte, *Village and Family in Contemporary China.* Chicago: University of Chicago Press, 1978.

Pasternak, Burton. "The Role of the Frontier in Chinese Lineage Development." *Journal of Asian Studies* 28, no. 3 (1968): 551–61.

Payne, Robert. *Chinese Diaries, 1941–1946.* New York: Weybright and Talley, 1970.

Peattie, Mark R., Edward J. Drea, and Hans J. Van de Ven, eds., *The Battle for China: Essays on the Military History of the Sino-Japanese War of 1937–1945.* Stanford, CA: Stanford University Press, 2011.

Peck, Graham. *Two Kinds of Time.* Boston: Houghton-Mifflin, 1967.

Perdue, Peter C. *China Marches West: The Qing Conquest of Central Eurasia.* Cambridge, MA: Belknap Press, 2005.

———. *Exhausting the Earth: State and Peasant in Hunan, 1500–1850.* Cambridge, MA: Harvard Council on East Asian Studies, 1987.

Perry, Elizabeth J. *Anyuan: Mining China's Revolutionary Tradition.* Berkeley: University of California Press, 2012.

———. *Rebels and Revolutionaries in North China, 1845–1945.* Stanford, CA: Stanford University Press, 1980.

———. *Shanghai on Strike: The Politics of Chinese Labor.* Stanford, CA: Stanford University Press, 1993.

Perry, Elizabeth J., and Lu, Xiaobo. *Danwei—The Changing Chinese Workplace in Historical and Comparative Perspective.* Armonk, NY: M. E. Sharpe, 1

Peyrefitte, Alain. *The Immobile Empire.* Jon Rothschild, trans. New York: Knopf, 1992.

Pickowicz, Paul G. "Victory as Defeat: Postwar Visualizations of China's War of Resistance." In *Becoming China: Passages to Modernity and Beyond, 1900–1950*, edited by Wen-hsin Yeh. Berkeley: University of California Press, 2000.

Pomeranz, Kenneth. *The Making of a Hinterland: State, Society and Economy in Inland North China, 1853–1937.* Berkeley: University of California Press, 1993.

Pomfret, John. *The Beautiful Country and the Middle Kingdom: America and China, 1776 to the Present*. New York: Henry Holt and Company, 2016.

Pritchard, Earl F. *The Crucial Years of Early Anglo-Chinese Relations, 1750–1800*. New York: Octagon, 1970 (original 1936).

———. "The Kowtow in the Macartney Embassy to China in 1793." *Far Eastern Quarterly* 2, no. 2 (February 1943): 163–203.

Pusey, James Reeve. *China and Charles Darwin*. Cambridge, MA: Harvard Council on East Asian Studies, 1983.

Rankin, Mary Backus. *Elite Activism and Political Transformation in China, Zhejiang Province, 1865–1911*. Stanford. CA: Stanford University Press, 1986.

———. "Rural-Urban Continuities: Leading Families of Two Chekiang Market Towns." *Ch'ing-shih wen-t'i* 3, no. 2 (1977): 67–104.

Rawski, Evelyn S. "Presidential address: Reenvisioning the Qing: The Significance of the Qing Period in Chinese History." *The Journal of Asian Studies* 55, no. 4 (Nov. 1996): 829–50.

———. *The Last Emperors: A Social History of Qing Imperial Institutions*. Berkeley: University of California Press, 1998.

Rawski, Thomas G. *Economic Growth in Prewar China*. Berkeley: University of California Press, 1989.

Reid, John Gilbert. *The Manchu Abdication and the Powers, 1908–1912: An Episode in Pre-War Diplomacy*. Berkeley: University of California Press, 1935.

Reinsch, Paul S. *An American Diplomat in China*. Garden City, NY: Doubleday, 1922.

Remer, C. F. *Foreign Investments in China*. New York: Macmillan, 1933.

Reynolds, Douglas R. *The Xinzheng Revolution and Japan*. Cambridge, MA: Harvard University Council on East Asian Studies, 1993.

Rhoads, Edward J. M. *Manchus and Han: Ethnic Relations and Political Power in Late Qing and Early Republican China, 1861–1928*. Seattle: University of Washington Press, 2000.

Rowe, William T. *Hankow: Conflict and Community in a Chinese City, 1796–1895*. Stanford, CA: Stanford University Press, 1989.

———. "The Public Sphere in Modern China." *Modern China* 16, no. 3 (1990): 309–29.

Rozman, Gilbert. *Population and Marketing Settlements in Ch'ing China*. Cambridge: Cambridge University Press, 1982.

———. *Urban Networks in Ch'ing China and Tokugawa Japan*. Princeton: Princeton University Press, 1973.

Saich, Tony. *The Origins of the First United Front in China: The Role of Sneevliet (alias Maring)*. Leiden: Brill, 1991.

Saich, Tony, and Benjamin Yang, eds. *The Rise to Power of the Chinese Communist Party: Documents and Analysis*. Armonk, NY: M. E. Sharpe, 1996.

Salisbury, Harrison E. *The Long March: The Untold Story*. New York: McGraw Hill, 1985.

Sang Bing. *Gengzi qinwang yu wan-Qing zhengju* (The 1901 loyalist movement and late Qing politics). Beijing: Peking University Press, 2004.

Sangren, P. Steven. "Traditional Chinese Corporations: Beyond Kinship." *Journal of Asian Studies* 43, no. 3 (1984): 391–415.

Schell, Orville. *Discos and Democracy: China in the Throes of Reform.* New York: Pantheon, 1988.

Schoppa, R. Keith. *Chinese Elites and Political Change: Zhejiang Province in the Early Twentieth Century.* Cambridge, MA: Harvard University Press, 1982.

———. *Xiang Lake—Nine Centuries of Chinese Life.* New Haven, CT: Yale University Press, 1989.

Schram, Stuart. *Chairman Mao Talks to the People.* New York: Pantheon, 1974.

———. *The Political Thought of Mao Tse-tung.* New York: Praeger, 1969.

———. *The Thought of Mao Tse-tung.* Cambridge: Cambridge University Press, 1989.

Schran, Peter. *Guerrilla Economy: The Development of the Shensi-Kansu-Ninghsia Border Region, 1937–1945.* Albany: SUNY Press, 1976.

Schrecker, John E. *Imperialism and Chinese Nationalism: Germany in Shantung.* Cambridge, MA: Harvard University Press, 1971.

Schurmann, Franz. *Ideology and Organization in Communist China.* Berkeley: University of California Press, 1966.

———. *The Logic of World Power: An Inquiry into the Origins, Currents and Contradictions of World Politics.* New York: Pantheon, 1974.

Schwarcz, Vera. *The Chinese Enlightenment.* Berkeley: University of California Press, 1986.

Schwartz, Benjamin I. "The legend of the 'legend of Maoism.'" *China Quarterly* 2 (April–June 1960): 35–42.

———. *Chinese Communism and the Rise of Mao.* Cambridge, MA: Harvard University Press, 1951.

———. *The World of Thought in Ancient China.* Cambridge, MA: Harvard University Press, 1985.

Selden, Mark. "The guerrilla movement in northwest China: the origins of the Shensi-Kansu-Ninghsia Border Region." *The China Quarterly*, no. 28 (December 1966), 63–81, and no. 29 (March 1967), 61–81.

———. *The Yenan Way in Revolutionary China.* Cambridge, MA: Harvard University Press, 1971.

Service, John S. *Lost Chance in China: The World War II Despatches of John S. Service*, edited by Joseph Esherick. New York: Random House, 1974.

Seybolt, Peter J. "Terror and conformity: Counterespionage campaigns, rectification and mass movements, 1942–1943." *Modern China* 12, no. 1 (1986).

Shakya, Tsering. *The Dragon in the Land of Snows: A History of Modern Tibet Since 1947.* New York: Columbia, 1999.

Shenbao (Shanghai), 1895–1944.

Sheridan, James E. *China in Disintegration.* New York: Free Press, 1975.

Shewmaker, Kenneth E. *Americans and Chinese Communists, 1927–1945: A Persuading Encounter.* Ithaca, NY: Cornell University Press, 1971.

Sih, Paul K. T. *Nationalist China During the Sino-Japanese War, 1937–1945.* Hicksville, NY: Exposition Press, 1977.

Skinner, G. William, ed. *The City in Late Imperial China*. Stanford, CA: Stanford University Press, 1977.

———. "Marketing and Social Structure in Rural China," Parts I and II, *Journal of Asian Studies* 24, no. 1 (1964) and 24, no. 2 (1965).

———. "Mobility Strategies in Late Imperial China." In *Regional Analysis,* vol 1: *Economic Systems*, edited by Carol A. Smith. New York: Academic Press, 1976.

Skocpol, Theda. *States and Social Revolutions: A Comparative Analysis of France, Russia, and China*. Cambridge, MA: Harvard University Press, 1979.

Smil, Vaclav. *China's Environmental Crisis: An Inquiry into the Limits of National Development*. Armonk, NY: M. E. Sharpe, 1993.

———. *The Bad Earth: Environmental Degradation in China*. Armonk, NY: M. E. Sharpe, 1984.

Smith, Joanna H. "Benevolent Societies: The Reshaping of Charity During the Late Ming and Early Ch'ing." *Journal of Asian Studies* 46, no. 2 (1987), 309–38.

Snow, Edgar. *Red Star Over China*. New York: Grove, 1961.

———. *The Long Revolution*. New York: Vintage, 1973.

Spence, Jonathan D. *Ts'ao Yin and the K'ang-hsi Emperor, Bondservant and Master.* New Haven, CT: Yale University Press, 1966.

Spence, Jonathan D., and John E. Wills, eds. *From Ming to Ch'ing: Conquest, Region and Continuity in Seventeenth-Century China*. New Haven, CT: Yale University Press, 1979.

Stalin, J. V. *Works*. Moscow: Foreign Languages Publishing House, 1955.

Stapleton, Kristin. *Civilizing Chengdu: Chinese Urban Reform, 1895–1937*. Cambridge, MA: Harvard University Asia Center, 2000.

Starr, John Bryan. "Conceptual Foundations of Mao Tse-tung's Theory of Continuous Revolution." *Asian Survey* 11 (June 1971): 610–28.

———. *Ideology and Culture: An Introduction to the Dialectic of Contemporary Chinese Politics.* New York: Harper & Row, 1973.

Stone, Lawrence, and Jeane Fawtier Stone. *An Open Elite? England, 1540–1880*. Oxford: Oxford University Press, 1986.

Strand, David. *Rickshaw Beijing: City People and Politics in the 1920s*. Berkeley: University of California Press, 1989.

Sullivan, Michael. *Art and Artists of Twentieth-Century China*. Berkeley: University of California Press, 1996.

Sun Zhongshan (Sun Yat-sen). *Sun Zhongshan quanji* (Complete works of Sun Yat-sen). Beijing: Zhonghua shuju, 1981.

———. *Sun Zhongshan xuanji* (Selected works of Sun Yat-sen) Beijing: Renmin chubanshe, 1956.

Tang Haijing. *Qingmo zhenglun baokan yu minzhong dongyuan: yizhong zhengzhi wenhua de shijiao* (The political press of the late Qing and mass mobilization: a political culture perspective). Beijing: Qinghua University Press, 2007.

Tang Zhijun, ed., *Zhang Taiyan zhenglun xuanji* (A selection of the political writings of Zhang Binglin) Beijing: Zhonghua shuju, 1977.

Tanner, Harold M. *Where Chiang Kai-Shek Lost China: The Liao-Shen Campaign 1948*. Bloomington: Indiana University Press, 2015.

Taylor, Jay. *The Generalissimo: Chiang Kai-Shek and the Struggle for Modern China.* Cambridge, MA: Harvard University Press, 2009.

Teiwes, Frederick C. *Politics and Purges in China: Rectification and the Decline of Party Norms, 1950–1965*, second edition. Armonk, NY: M. E. Sharpe, 1993.

———. *Politics at Mao's Court: Gao Gang and Party Factionalism in the Early 1950s.* Armonk, NY: M. E. Sharpe, 1990.

Teng, Ssu-yu, and John K. Fairbank, *China's Response to the West: A Documentary Survey, 1839–1923.* New York: Atheneum, 1971.

Thomas, S. Bernard. *Labor and the Chinese Revolution: Class Strategies and Contradictions of Chinese Communism, 1928–1948.* Ann Arbor, MI: Unniversity Michigan Center for Chinese Studies, 1983.

Thompson, E. P. "Eighteenth-Century English Society: Class Struggle Without Class?" *Social History* 3, no. 2 (1978): 71–133.

Tilly, Charles. *From Mobilization to Revolution.* Reading, MA: AddisonWesley, 1978.

Togasheff, Boris P. *China as a Tea Producer.* Shanghai: Commercial Press, 1926.

Tsai, Kellee S. *Capitalism without Democracy: The Private Sector in Contemporary China.* Ithaca, NY: Cornell University Press, 2007.

Tsai, Lily L. *Accountability without Democracy: Solidarity Groups and Public Goods Provision in Rural China.* Cambridge: Cambridge University Press, 2007.

Tsin, Michael Tsang-Woon. *Nation, Governance and Modernity in China: Canton, 1900–1927.* Stanford, CA: Sanford University Press, 1999.

Tsou Jung. *The Revolutionary Army: A Chinese Nationalist Tract of 1903*, trans. John Lust. The Hague: Mouton, 1968.

Tsou, Tang. *America's Failure in China, 1941–1950.* Chicago: University of Chicago Press, 1963.

Tucker, Robert C., ed. *The Lenin Anthology.* New York: W. W. Norton, 1975.

Turner, Victor. *From Ritual to Theatre.* New York: Performing Arts Journal Press, 1982.

———. *The Ritual Process: Structure and Anti-Structure.* Ithaca, NY: Cornell University Press, 1969.

Turnley, David, and Peter Turnley. *Beijing Spring.* New York: Stewart, Tabori and Chang, 1989.

Unger, Jonathan, ed. *Chinese Nationalism.* Armonk, NY: M. E. Sharpe, 1996.

United States Consulate-General, Shanghai. *China Press Review*, 1946–1949.

Van de Ven, Hans J. *China at War: Triumph and Tragedy in the Emergence of the New China.* Cambridge, MA: Harvard University Press, 2018.

———. *From Friend to Comrade: The Founding of the CCP, 1920–1927.* Berkeley: University of California Press, 1991.

———. *War and Nationalism in China, 1925–1945.* London: RoutledgeCurzon, 2003.

Van Slyke, Lyman. "The Chinese Communist Movement during the Sino-Japanese War, 1937–1945." In *The Cambridge History of China*, vol. 13: *Republican China 1912–1949*, Part II, edited by John K. Fairbank and Albert Feuerwerker, 609–722. Cambridge: Cambridge University Press, 1986.

Von Glahn, Richard. *The Country of Streams and Grottoes: Expansion, Settlement and Civilization of the Sichuan Frontier in Song Times.* Cambridge, MA: Harvard Council on East Asian Studies, 1987.

Wakeman, Frederic Jr. "The Civil Society and Public Sphere Debate." *Modern China* 19, no. 2 (1993): 108–38.

———. *The Fall of Imperial China.* New York: Free Press, 1975.

———. *The Great Enterprise: The Manchu Reconstruction of the Imperial Order in Seventeenth-Century China.* Berkeley: University of California Press, 1985.

———. *Policing Shanghai 1927–1937.* Berkeley: University of California Press, 1995.

———. "A Revisionist View of the Nanjing Decade: Confucian Fascism." *China Quarterly* 150 (June 1997): 395–432.

———. *Strangers at the Gate: Social Disorder in South China, 1839–1861.* Berkeley: University of California Press, 1966.

Wakeman, Frederic Jr., and Carolyn Grant. *Conflict and Control in Late Imperial China.* Berkeley: University of California Press, 1975.

Wang Ermin, "Zhongguo mingcheng shuyuan jiqi jindai quanshi" (On the origins of the term "Zhongguo" and its modern Chinese explication). In *Zhongguo jindai sixiang shilun* (Studies on Modern Chinese Thought), edited by Wang Ermin, 441–80. Taibei: Huashi chubanshe, 1977.

Wang Gengxiong. *Sun Zhongshan shishi xianglu, 1911–1913* (A detailed record of Sun Yat-sen's activities, 1911–1913). Tianjin: Tianjin renmin chubanshe, 1986.

Wang Ke-wen. "The Kuomintang in Transition: Ideology and Factionalism in the 'National Revolution,' 1924–1932." PhD diss., Stanford University, 1985.

Wang Qinyu, *Menggu wenti* (The Mongol problem). Shanghai: Commercial Press, 1931.

Wang Qisheng. *Geming yu fangeming: shehui wenhua shiyexia de minguo zhengzhi* (Revolution and counter-revolution: Sociocultural perspectives on republican politics). Beijing: Shehui kexue chubanshe, 2010.

———. "Zhanshi Guomindang dangyuan yu jiceng dang zuzhi" (Basic level organization of the wartime Guomindang). *Kang-Ri zhanzheng yanjiu*, 2003, no. 4.

Wang Yeh-chien. *Land Taxation in Imperial China, 1750–1911.* Cambridge, MA: Harvard University Press, 1973.

Wasserstrom, Jeffrey N. *Student Protests in Twentieth-Century China: The View from Shanghai.* Stanford, CA: Stanford University Press, 1991.

Watson, James. "Chinese Kinship Reconsidered: Anthropological Perspectives on Historical Research." *The China Quarterly* 92 (1982): 589–622.

——— ed. *Class and Social Stratification in Post-revolutionary China.* Cambridge: Cambridge University Press, 1984.

Watson, Rubie. *Inequality Among Brothers: Class and Kinship in South China.* Cambridge: Cambridge University Press, 1985.

Weber, Max. *The Religion of China: Confucianism and Taoism*, trans. Hans H. Gerth. Glencoe, IL: Free Press, 1951.

Wei Gang, [pseud.] *E-Meng jiaoshe shimo* (Full account of the negotiations with Russia and Mongolia) (1912), in Zuo Shunsheng, *Zhongguo jinbainian shi ziliao chupian* (Historical materials on the last one hundred years of Chinese history, vol. 1). Taipei: Taiwan Zhonghua shuju, 1966.

Wei Yuan, *Shengwuji* (Military history of the Qing dynasty). Taibei reprint, n.d. (original preface 1842).

Weller, Robert. *Unities and Diversities in Chinese Religion*. Seattle: University of Washington Press, 1987.

Westad, Odd Arne. *Decisive Encounters: The Chinese Civil War, 1946–1950*. Stanford, CA: Stanford University Press, 2003.

White, Theodore, and Analee Jacoby. *Thunder out of China*. New York: William Sloan Associates, 1946.

Whyte, Martin King, and William Parish. *Urban Life in Contemporary China*. Chicago: University of Chicago Press, 1984.

Widmer, Ellen, and David Der-wei Wang, eds. *From May Fourth to June Fourth: Fiction and Film in Twentieth-Century China*. Cambridge, MA: Harvard University Press, 1993

Wiens, Mi-Chu. "Lord and Peasant: The Sixteenth to Eighteenth Century." *Modern China* 6, no. 1 (1980).

Will, Pierre-Etienne. *Bureaucracy and Famine in Eighteenth-Century China*, trans. Elborg Forster. Stanford, CA: Stanford University Press, 1990.

Will, Pierre-Etienne, and R. Bin Wong, and James Lee. *Nourish the People: The State Civilian Granary System in China, 1650–1850*. Ann Arbor, MI: University of Michigan Center for Chinese Studies, 1991.

Wills, John E. Jr. *Embassies and Illusions: Dutch and Portuguese Envoys to K'anghsi, 1666–1687*. Cambridge, MA: Council on East Asian Studies, Harvard University, 1984.

Wilson, Dick. *When Tigers Fight: The Story of the Sino-Japanese War, 1937–1945*. New York; Viking Press, 1982.

Wolf, Eric R. *Peasant Wars of the Twentieth Century*. New York: Harper & Row, 1969.

Wou, Odoric Y. K. *Mobilizing the Masses: Building Revolution in Henan*. Stanford, CA: Stanford University Press, 1994.

Wright, Mary. *China in Revolution: The First Phase, 1900–1913*. New Haven, CT: Yale University Press, 1968.

Wu, Tien-wei. "New Materials on the Sian Incident: A Bibliographic Essay." *Modern China* 10, no. 1 (1984): 115–41.

———. *The Sian Incident: A Pivotal Point in Modem Chinese History*. Ann Arbor: University of Michigan Center for Chinese Studies, 1976.

Xiang, Lanxin. *The Origins of the Boxer War: A Multinational Study*. London: RoutledgeCurzon, 2003.

Xinhai geming ziliao huiji (Selected materials on the 1911 Revolution). Hong Kong: Cuncui xueshe, 1980.

Xu Shishen. *Guofu dangxuan linshi dazongtong shilu* (A true record of the Father of the Republic's election as provisional president) Taibei: Guoshi zongbianshe, 1967.

Xu Shuang. *Jiu wangchao yu xin zhidu: Qingmo lixian gaige* (Old monarchy. new system: the late Qing constitutional reforms). Beijing: Falǜ chubanshe, 2009.

Yan Jiaqi and Gao Gao. *"Wenhua dageming" shinianshi* (A ten-year history of the "Cultural Revolution"). Tianjin: Tianjin renmin chubanshe,1986.

Yang Zihui, ed. *Zhongguo lidai renkou tongji ziliao yanjiu* (Studies in statistical materials on China's population history). Beijing: China Reform Publishing House, 1996.

Yao Wenyuan. *On the Social Basis of the Lin Piao Anti-Party Clique.* Beijing: Foreign Languages Press, 1975.

Ye Xian'en. *Ming-Qing Huizhou nongcun shehui yu dianpuzhi* (Servile tenancy in the rural Huizhou). Hefei: Anhui renmin chubanshe 1983.

Yeh, Wen-hsin. *The Alienated Academy: Culture and Politics in Republican China, 1919–1937.* Cambridge, MA: Harvard University Press, 1990.

Yi Guoqian et al., eds. *Li Fuzongtong (Yuanhong) zhengshu* (The official writings of Vice-President Li Yuanhong) Shanghai: Gujin tushuju, 1915.

Yi Mu and Mark V. Thompson. *Crisis at Tiananmen: Reform and Reality in Modern China.* San Francisco: China Books, 1989.

Yick, Joseph K. S. *Making Urban Revolution in China: The CCP-GMD Struggle for Beiping-Tianjin, 1945–1949.* Armonk, NY, M. E. Sharpe, 1995.

Young, Ernest P. *The Presidency of Yuan Shih-k'ai: Liberalism and Dictatorship in Early Republican China.* Ann Arbor: University of Michigan Press, 1977.

YSSL. *Yingshi Majia'erni fanghua dang'an shiliao huibian* (Collection of Archival Materials on the Macartney Embassy to China). First Historical Archives (ed.) Beijing: Guoji wenhua chubanshe, 1996.

Zelin, Madeleine. *The Magistrate's Tael: Rationalizing Fiscal Reform in Eighteenth-Century Ch'ing China.* Berkeley: University of California Press, 1984.

Zhang Dengji, "'Zhongguo' gainian de neihan yu liubian xiaokao" (A short study of the meanings and evolution of the term 'Zhongguo'). *Zhongguo dalu yanjiu jiaoxue tongxun* 53 (November 2002): 17–20.

Zhang Hailin. *Duanfang yu Qingmo xinzheng* (Duanfang and the late Qing New Policies). Nanjing: Nanjing University Press, 2007.

Zhang Jian. *Zhang Jian quanji* (Collected works of Zhang Jian). Nanjing: Jiangsu guji chubanshe, 1994.

Zhang Kaiyuan and Lin Zengping. *Xinhai geming shi* (A history of the 1911 Revolution) Beijing, Zhonghua shuju, 1981.

Zhang Pengyuan. *Lixianpai yu xinhai geming* (Constitutionalists and the 1911 Revolution), third edition. Changchun: Jilin chubanshe, 2007.

Zhang Qixiong, *Wai-Meng zhuquan guishu jiaoshe, 1911–1916* (English title: Disputes and Negotiations over Outer Mongolia's National Identity, Unification or Independence and Sovereignty, 1911–1916: An Observation based on the Principle of the Chinese World Order) Taibei: Academia Sinica, 1995.

Zhang Taiyan (Zhang Binglin). *Zhang Taiyan quanji.* Shanghai: 1985.

Zhang Yong, "Cong 'shiba xing qi' dao 'wuse qi'—Xinhai geming shiqi cong Hanzu guojia dao wuzu gonghe guojia de jianguo moshi zhuanbian" (From the eighteen-star flag to the five-color flag: the change in the form of the state from a Han national state to a republic of the five races in the 1911 Revolution period), *Beijing daxue xuebao (zhexue shehui kexue ban)* 39, no. 2 (March 2000).

Zhang Yuxin, *Qingdai qianqi geminzu tongyi guannian de lishi tezheng* (The historical characteristics of early Qing concepts of unity of the various peoples), *Qingshi yanjiu* 2 (1996).

Zhanggu congbian (Collected Texts for Grasping Antiquity) (1928–1930) Beijing: Palace Museum.

Zhao Gang, "Reinventing China: Imperial Qing Ideology and the Formation of Modern Chinese National Identity in the Early Twentieth Century." *Modern China* 32, no. 1 (2006): 3–30.

Zhao Qiang, Ge Jing and Siyuan, *Xueran de fengcai* (Bloody Scenes). Hong Kong: Haiyan, 1989.

Zhonggong xibei zhongyangju xuanchuanbu. *Gulin diaocha (Gulin Survey)* [Yan'an?]: April 1942.

Zhongguo dier lishi dang'an guan, ed. *Zhonghua minguo shi dang'an ziliao huibian.* Nanjing: Jiangsu Renmin chubanshe, 1979.

Zhongguo shixuehui ed., *Xinhai geming* (1911 Revolution) (Shanghai: Shanghai renmin chubanshe, 1957.

Zhonghua minguo kaiguo wushinian wenxian (Documents on the fiftieth anniversary of the founding of the Republic of China). Taibei: Wenxian bianzuan weiyuanhui, 1961.

Zhu Yong. *Buyuan dakai de Zhongguo damen: 18 shiji de waijiao yu Zhongguo mingyun* (The Chinese Door That Was Unwilling to Open: Eighteenth Century Foreign Relations and China's Fate). Nanchang: Jiangxi Renmin chubanshe, 1989.

Zhuo Hongmou, *Menggu jian* (Mongol reference) Beijing: self-published, 1919.

Zito, Angela. *Of Body and Brush: Grand Sacrifice as Text/Performance in Eighteenth-Century China.* Chicago: University of Chicago Press, 1997.

Index

1911 Revolution, 18, 92, 111, 128, 313; Chinese nationalism and, 118–23; frontier and the revolution, 123–27; Mongolian and Tibetan reactions following, 126–27, 133; reconsidering 1911 lessons, 171–72, 172–85
1949 barrier, 233

Adams, John Quincy, 7
Ahern, Emily, 347
Alexrod, Pavel, 302
anti-traitor work, 198, 249, 270–71
Appleby, Joyce, 45
Arab Spring, 171
arenas, 62, 63; bureaucratic arenas, 66, 86; elite dominance in, 52, 60–61, 80, 87, 90, 92; intersecting arenas, 79, 96; networking in shared or higher arenas, 76–77, 81; overlapping arenas and locality, 72–73; resource limitations in local arenas, 69–70
art, 54, 215–16, 218, 373
Ataturk counter-factual, 128
Austin, J. L., 341
Averill, Stephen, 52, 69, 88, 89

Bailey, F. G., 82, 94, 95
Balazs, Eltiènne, 54, 57

banditry, 65, 71, 77, 88, 92, 247, 264, 265, 271
banks and banking, 6, 12–16, 86–89, 207–8, 241
baojia system, 213, 270
Barkan, Lenore, 82
Barnett, A. Doak, 202, 204, 209, 210, 212, 213, 217
Beattie, Hilary, 59
Belden, Jack, 5, 217, 232
Benton, Gregor, 238, 242
Berenson, Edward, 231
Bolsheviks, 128, 235–36, 299, 304, 308, 309; Bolshevik Revolution, 136, 301–3, 319; Guomindang, as advisers to, 247
border regions, 118, 125, 200, 267, 272; Kham border region, 127; of Qing Empire, 184; SGN Border Region, 231, 245–46, 248–49, 262–85, 375
Bourdieu, Pierre, 62
bourgeois right, concept of, 311–12, 317
Boxer Uprising, 13, 15, 83, 91, 119, 177, 183, 241, 296
Britain, 119, 135, 153, 376, 378; Dalai Lama seeking British aid, 126, 133; diplomatic efforts, 28–30, 33, 35–36, 39–41, 43; merchant trade with China, 85, 86; opium trade, 7–8;

411

Queen Victoria as symbol of, 184–85; in South China market, 13–14, 16, 17; Tibet, presence in, 124, 126, 133, 136
brokers, 58, 65, 79–80, 89, 94, 96
Brook, Timothy, 52, 75, 76
Bukharin, Nikolai, 300–301, 303–4
bureaucracy, 40, 52, 58, 65, 78, 87, 93, 96, 180, 304, 315; autocratic power of, 53–54; bureaucratic arenas, 66, 86; bureaucratism, 306; centralized bureaucratic rule, 113, 115–16, 240; Confucian bureaucracy, 344–46; county as lowest level of, 55; elites and, 56, 74, 77, 90, 94; examination degrees, role in, 61, 70, 73; Guomindang, bureaucracy under, 201, 204, 213; Lenin, distaste for, 300–303, 307, 317; Manchu posts in, 177, 178; Mao, analysis of, 316–19; Qing bureaucracy, 37, 89; social mobility channeled through, 56, 70

Cai Yuanpei, 155
capitalism, 4, 10, 19, 39, 239, 303, 375; restoration of, 295–320; state capitalism, 204, 297, 300–302, 317, 319; weakness of Chinese capitalism, 54–55, 251, 252
Cen Chunxuan, 180, 181
Chai Ling, 354
Chamberlayn, Edward, 86
Chang Chung-li (Zhang Zhongli), 56, 59
Changsha rice riot, 17, 175
Chen Dong, 354
Chen Jiongming, 157
Chen Lifu, 205–6, 216, 218
Chen Qimei, 149, 150, 155, 157–58, 183
Chen Tianhua, 354
Chen Yun, 236, 237
Chen Yung-fa, 261, 280
Cheng Dequan, 151–52
Chia, Ning, 30
Chiang Ching-kuo (Jiang Jingguo), 193, 207, 216

Chiang Kai-shek (Jiang Jieshi), 3, 88, 183, 197, 201, 237, 242, 248, 350, 371; celebration of leadership, 199–200; Communists, relations with, 247, 370; Japan, as battling, 194, 196, 239, 241; Nationalist party of, 193, 195, 230; on new wardlordism, 373; successor to Sun Yat-sen, 372
China Proper, 131–32, 135–36, 182–84; administrative apparatus of, 123, 124, 125; China Proper position, 129; eighteen provinces of, 117, 122, 128; Manchu rule of China proper, 116; Manchus, attempts to confine Han to, 115
China Quarterly (periodical), 193
China Weekly Review (CWR), 201
Chinese Communist Party (CCP), 6, 329, 352, 358; anthropology of, 283–85; bandits in, 247, 265, 271; base areas, 91, 157, 197–99, 203, 212, 217, 243–49, 259, 261, 270–71, 276, 279–80, 373, 377; cadre transgressions, 249, 269, 271–73, 274, 279–83, 302, 306, 308, 309, 314, 316, 352; CCP-Soviet relations, 307–8; Communist China, rethinking rise of, 193–94, 194–97; contingent events, CCP triumph as a series of, 237–38; deconstruction of, 261–62, 276–83; dilemmas of victory, 199–203; Guomindang-CCP collaboration, 232–33; internal diversity in, 260, 378; May Fourth Movement and, 343; Northwest Bureau, 260, 262, 268, 270–73, 278–79; power, coming to, 229, 234; rural mobilization, 259–60; Soviet model for, 235–37, 305
Ch'ü T'ung-tsu (Qu Tongzu), 56
Chunliu She (Spring Willow Society), 349
Civil War, 196, 200–203, 211–12, 236, 274–76; CCP class-conscious policies of, 198; Communist party

during, 197, 199, 242–43, 249, 276–83; economy, effect on, 207–8; gender issues during, 214, 268–69; "long 1940s" and, 194; public opinion calling for end to, 239

class, 53, 84, 113, 194, 208, 216, 217, 239, 266, 303, 371; cadres, class background of, 279, *280;* capitalist restoration, in theory of, 309, 313–14; class enemies, 198, 249, 279; class struggle, 213, 278, 296, 298–310, 313, 319; class-consciousness, 198–99, 314; classless communist society, 299, 315; elites as a class, 61, 74; gentry class, 56, 85, 86; intellectual class, 327, 377; late imperial elite, status and class of, 68–69, 76; lower classes, 83, 96, 265; Mao, class divisions under, 305, 308, 315–16, 319; middle class, 202, 204; proletariat and, 301, 303–4; ruling class of scholar-officials, 54, 57; superstructure and the concept of class, 313–14; urban class, 242, 279; working class, 214, 301, 318

clothing, 178, 200, 215; Chinese clothing styles, 113, 208, 252; Communist influence on clothing styles, 194, 215, 373; European clothes, 35, 210

Coble, Parkes, 239
Cohen, Stephen F., 303
collectivization, 304, 305, 307, 309–10
commercialization, 60, 63–64, 68–73, 77, 84–87, 92, 240, 252, 371, 376
Committee of Concerned Asian Scholars, 4, 26, 369
Committee on Scholarly Communication with the People's Republic of China, 260
commodity system, 312
Communist International (Comintern), 230, 235
Confucian tradition, 52, 55, 59, 64, 67, 69, 71, 218, 306, 328, 340, 347, 372; Confucian bureaucrats, 56, 346; Confucian order, 3, 81, 86; Confucian ritual, 339–40, 344; Confucian virtues, 205–6; elites and, 54, 72; Guomindang looking to, 217, 232; merchants in, 65, 85

conscription, 94, 213, 249, 268, 272, 275, 373

constitutionalism, 146, 179, 370; constitutionalist gentry, 147, 162, 184; Qing constitutionalist reformers, 155–56, 178, 181–85; revolution, constitutionalist support for, 147–49, 174–75

contingency, 172, 230, 232, 237–39, 240, 243

convergence theory, 301

corruption, 213, 237, 249, 250, 343, 349, 350, 376; 1989 protests against, 330–31, 354; Communist regime, as low in, 199, 373; of Guomindang order, 195, 200–201, 203, 217; local cadres, corruption among, 308–9; peasants and, 234, 355–56; political corruption, 19, 200–201; counter-revolutionaries, 53, 351, 372

Court for Frontier Dependencies, 116
Cranmer-Byng, J. L., 28
Critique of the Gotha Program (Marx), 311
Crossley, Pamela, 30, 116, 176
cultural hegemony, 52, 63, 80–84, 88, 96–97
Customs, Imperial Maritime, 6, 51

Dalai Lama, 115–18, 126–27, 133, 135
democracy, 156, 172, 179, 193, 232, 250, 319, 349, 372, 378; bourgeois democracy, 7, 19–20, 94, 309, 375; bureaucracy *vs.* democracy, 302, 319; capitalism without democracy, 376; Democracy Wall movement, 353; democratic legitimacy, difficulty in establishing, 161, 164; dictatorship, forsaking democracy for, 148–49;

Eastern European evolution toward, 328, 330, 356; Goddess of Democracy, 329, 335–36; habitus of democratic governance, 357; June 4 "democracy" movement, 327, 337, 358; *minzhu,* not conflating with, 331–32, 357–58; "new democracy," CCP appeals to, 251; student calls for, 211, 342, 355

Deng Xiaoping, 305, 327, 330–31, 338, 352–53, 374, 378

dictatorship of the proletariat, 298, 299, 302, 309, 312, 318

Dirlik, Arif, 284

diversity, 52, 120, 259, 377; CCP, internal diversity, 260, 283, 378; of local elites, 56, 59, 60, 61, 62, 63, 97

Dixie Mission, 198, 229

The Dream of the Red Chamber (novel), 82

Du Yuesheng, 207

Duan Qirui, 18

Duanfang (Manchu bannerman), 178, 180–81

Duara, Prasenjit, 52, 79, 95, 232

Durand, Pierre-Henri, 33, 40–41

Durkheim, 339

Eastern Europe, 113, 137, 231, 245, 284, 310, 328, 329–30, 355–57

Eastman, Lloyd, 193, 195, 213, 232, 350

elites, 82, 83, 113, 174, 177–78, 202, 207, 209, 240, 334, 355; brokerage, mediation, and, 78–80; Bukharin on the administrative elite, 303–4; commerce, changing role in, 84–87; dominance patterns of local elites, 53–60, 61; education, expanding beyond the elite, 206, 374; elite continuity, 53, 66, 67–68; fragmentation of the elite, 91–93; frontier elites, 66–67, 116, 117, 125, 131; functional elites, 88–90; gentry elite, 55–57, 60, 85, 86, 88, 91, 93; lineage organization, shaping, 74–76; local arenas, acting within, 61–63; local elite resources, 51–53, 69–72; local elite strategies, 51–53, 73–74; local elites and the state, 93–97; Lower Yangzi elite, 63–64, 65, 75, 88; military elites, 60, 87–88, 92, 242, 338; old elites, 53, 88, 89, 93, 94, 198, 234–35; as patrons, 77–78, 81; political elites, 54, 118, 369; political theater, ruling elite use of, 340–41; reformist elite, 147, 148; regional variation, 63–67; rural elites, 58, 64, 92, 198, 248; urban elites, 92, 184, 206. *See also* gentry; scholar-officials

Elliott, Mark, 30, 176

Elman, Benjamin, 25, 88

Empress Dowager, 172, 179, 180

Ershiyi shiji (periodical), 25–26

Esherick, Joseph W., 4, 26, 83, 92, 112, 174–76, 184, 229, 295–96, 328, 329–33

examination system, 67, 68, 73, 74, 77, 85, 88; abolition of, 58, 92, 119, 173; bureaucrats as degree-holders, 54, 61; Confucian values, reflecting, 52, 55, 72, 81; elite pursuit of, 59, 64; gentry as degree-holders, 52, 55–57, 62–63, 91–92, 179; imperial examinations, 82, 113, 116; national examinations, 205, 206; successful exam candidates, 63, 70, 75, 78

exchange theory of revolution, 261

extraterritoriality, 14, 15–16, 207–8, 351

Fairbank, John K., 232; on China's Response to the West, 51; at Harvard, 3–6, 111, 230; on imperialism, 25; on the opium trade, 7–8; on the tribute system, 28–29, 43; *The United States and China* (Fairbank), 193; as a wartime witness, 195, 217

Fang Lizhi, 332

Fanon, Franz, 14

Fei Hsiao-tung (Fei Xiaotong), 54–55
Feng Guifen, 347
feudalism, 3, 115, 133, 269, 300, 306, 308
feuds and feuding, 71, 174, 342
Feuerwerker, Albert, 10–11, 15, 111
finance, 15, 17, 19, 92, 154, 195, 317; banks and banking, 6, 12–16, 86–89, 207–8, 241; foreign interests and, 6, 12–15, 147, 175, 347; Qing financial affairs, 123, 136, 176, 182; state finances, 132, 240
Fingarette, Herbert, 344
Fischer, David Hackett, 238
frontier region, 124, 129, 376, 377; border screen, frontier areas as, 132, 136; frontier elites, 66–67, 116, 117, 125, 131; imperialism on the frontiers, 133–37; Qing administration, 111, 115; Republic of China maintaining Qing frontier, 122, 136

Gang of Four, 327, 334, 353
Gangyi, 177
Gao Gang, 283
Ge Jianxiong, 26
Geertz, Clifford, 333, 339
Gelaohui (Elder Brothers Society), 271
gender relations. *See* women
gentry, 18, 19, 54, 266, 285, 347; degree-holding gentry, 52, 53–7; "enlightened" gentry, 197, 280; gentry elite, 55–57, 60, 85, 86, 88, 91, 93; landholding gentry, 57, 58, 71; *shengyuan* as lower gentry, 56, 62, 83
George III, King, 25, 35–37, 40–41, 181–82
Gibbon, Edward, 43
Gladney, Dru, 333, 336, 354
gold, 13, 200, 201
Gold Yuan reforms, 201, 207
Gorbachev, Mikhail, 329, 335, 337, 355, 357

Great Depression, 17, 238–39
Great Leap Forward, 295–96, 306–8, 327, 374
Great Wall, 115, 124, 176
Greater China principle, 128–29, 252
guanxi (connections), 53, 76, 96
Gulin county, 270, 276, 284; Communist party organization in, 265; conscription compliance, 275, 278–79; environment of, 262–64; field research on, 260, 262; *Gulin Survey* of Northwest Bureau, 271, 273; new society of, 267–69; rectification movement in, 273–74
Guomindang (GMD), 88, 95, 196, 205, 213, 239, 275–76, 350, 377; anti-GMD propaganda, 250, 343; border region, attacks on, 273–75; collapse of, 195–97, 209; Confucian tradition, as looking to, 206; GMD-Communist conflict, 212, 237, 242–44, 251, 252; mass mobilization experiments, 349–50; political corruption, 200, 201; political theater, 349–52; precursor of Chinese Revolution, 232–33; reputation, loss of, 201, 235; state-building efforts of, 94, 203–4, 248; subsidies to border regions, 267–68; US aid to, 202; White Terror of 1927, 235, 242; Yuan Shikai efforts to eradicate, 6, 18

handicrafts industry, 6, 7, 10–11, 14, 19, 79, 84–85, 249, 250
Hanyeping Coal and Iron Company, 13
Hartford, Kathleen, 238
Harvard School of Chinese Studies, 4, 6–7, 19, 25–26
Hay, John, 136
He Xin, 149
Hei Zhide, 265
Heriots, Christian, 350
Hashes, 36, 41
Hevia, James L.; anomalies in glossary of, 31; *Cherishing Men from Afar,*

critiques of, 25–26; postmodern approach of, 27–30, 42–45; on Qing guest ritual, 32, 37–42; translations of Qing sources, 33–37
Ho Ping-ti (He Bingdi), 56, 59, 111
Hong Kong, 25, 147, 156, 178, 201, 207, 252, 373
Hoover, Herbert, 13
Hou, Chi-ming, 5
Hu Hanmin, 151, 157–58, 163
Hu Shi, 211
Hu Yaobang, 331, 334, 335, 339
Hu Ying, 161
Hu Zongnan, 237–38
Huang, Philip, 230, 233
Huang Xing, 152–54, 155–56, 157–59, 160, 162, 163
Hundred Flowers Movement, 305–6
Hunt, Lynn, 45, 343
Huters, Ted, 25
Hymes, Robert, 58

imitation effect, 14
imperialism, 233, 306, 343, 348, 351; apologetics of imperialism, 5–20, 26, 43; frontiers, imperialism on, 133–37; Harvard School on, 4, 6–7, 19, 25–26; liberation of China, 234; negative effects of, 4, 26, 51; in postcolonial theory, 25–27, 29–30, 42–45. *See also under* Japan
Israel, John, 211

Jacob, Margaret, 45
Jacoby, Annalee, 195, 232
Japan, 8–9, 14, 44, 91, 134, 157, 197, 202, 243, 274, 296, 372; anti-Manchu literature from, 178; Chinese students in, 154, 161, 163, 179, 185; economy, 15, 85, 376; Hundred Regiments offensive, counterattacks after, 242; imperialism of, 3, 5, 18, 19, 118, 122, 172, 173, 238–41, 371; Japanese scholarship, 52, 57, 58, 69; Japanese-owned property in China, 200–201; Manchurian region, interference in, 125, 129, 135, 136, 337, 351; mass rallies against, 349; military intervention in China, 25, 112, 119, 248, 261; modernization efforts, 96, 171, 241; in racial classification of Zou, 121; Russo-Japanese War, 124, 134, 174; Twenty-One Demands, 13, 241. *See also* War of Resistance
Javzandamba Khutagt (Bogd Khan), 126, 130, 132
Jinan Incident, 351
Jing Yaoyue, 163
jinshi degree, 56, 70, 82, 179, 183
Johnson, Chalmers, 194–95, 196, 208, 261
Jordan, John, 153
Ju Zheng, 150, 161
juren degree, 56, 70

Kahler, Miles, 111
Kang Sheng, 236, 237, 273
Khrushchev, Nikita, 236, 309, 314, 318
Kirby, William, 203, 218, 232
Knox, Philander, 136
Kotkin, Steven, 296–97
kowtow, 7, 28, 40, 41
Kuhn, Philip, 58, 60, 69, 72, 77, 87, 90, 92
Kuomintang (KMT) *See* Guomindang

land reform, 53, 199, 208, 212, 244, 247, 265, 310; peasants benefiting from, 217, 250, 375; in Red Ruckus period, 266–67; socio-cultural effect of, 198; violence during, 53, 270, 373
landlords, 68, 69, 80, 88, 197, 234, 247, 304, 319, 371; absentee landlords, 63, 64; in CCP administration, 280; class consciousness and, 84, 198; gentry landlordism, 57, 58, 71; landlordism, 3, 57, 64–65, 264; Mao on, 305, 308, 317; in North China

villages, 64, 78 opium traders as, 59; patronage of, 77–78; Red Ruckus as targeting, 266
Lanza, Fabio, 26
law of avoidance, 55
Lea, Homer, 151, 157
Lee, Leo, 207
Lefebvre, George, 246
Legge, James, 34
Lenin and Leninism, 246, 249, 266, 271, 273, 295, 306, 318, 373; on bourgeois right, 311–12; on bureaucracy, 317, 319; on capitalist restoration, 298, 300–305, 308, 309; CCP as a Leninist party, 213, 245, 247, 251, 273, 284, 374–75, 377; Chinese Revolution, influence on, 235–37, 296; Nationalist Party, Leninism of, 232, 372; Soviet model of, 235–37; Stalin and Leninist writings, 297, 307
Levenson, Joseph R., 27–28, 111
Levenson Prize, 27–28
Levine, Steven, 194, 238, 261
Li Hongzhang, 17–18, 153
Li Peng, 330–31, 336, 337, 338
Li Yuanhong, 147, 149, 151–58, 160–62, 174, 183
Liang Qichao, 119–21, 128, 149, 179, 180, 184, 350
liberation, 133, 183, 233–35, 310, 373
lifestyle, 62, 68, 86, 116, 248; of the elite, 67, 81–82, 83, 92; of the gentry, 78, 86, 377
Lin Biao, 196, 311, 312
Lin Boqu, 284
Lin Shuqing, 150
Lin Zexu, 347
lineage, 58, 59, 62, 64, 66, 71, 78, 119, 371, 375; lineage organization, shaping, 74–76; in Lower Yangzi region, 63; networks, in construction of, 76–77; non degree-holding lineages, 81; production brigades and, 377

Link, Perry, 333
Liu Shaoqi, 305, 309
Liu Zhidan, 245, 265
Long March, 236, 237, 242, 243, 372
Lower Yangzi region, 63–64, 65, 70, 71, 73, 75, 77, 88, 150, 196, 215
Luo Zhitian, 26

Ma Bufang, 210
Ma Xiangpo, 349
Macartney, George, 25, 30, 33, 43
Macartney Mission, 36, 42; Chinese scholarship on, 33, 43–44; distortion of record, 34–35; postmodern interpretation of, 27–28; Qianlong emperor, audience with, 28, 40–41; ritual, role in, 29–30, 31–32, 39–40, 43
Mackay Treaty (1902), 17
Manchuria, 12, 91, 123, 211; Japanese interference in, 119, 125, 129, 135, 239, 337; Northern Manchuria, 124, 127, 134, 136; *Zhongguo*, as part of, 117
Manchus, 14, 29, 58, 128, 129, 136, 349; 1911 Revolution against, 111, 118, 122–23, 123–27; anti-Manchuism, 77, 121, 127, 130, 178; bannermen, 123, 130 178, 180, 181; borders of the Manchu regime, 117, 137; Manchu identity, 30, 120; overthrow of, 118–19, 122, 132, 171; Qing dynasty, as ruling, 115–18
Mann, Susan, 90
Mao Zedong, 5, 69, 172, 195, 229–30, 233, 271, 301, 303, 330, 338, 351–52, 374; on capitalist restoration, 295–300, 304–8, 309–20; on children of cadres, 297, 315–16; on class struggle, 298, 302, 305–6, 308; Communist regime, as symbol of, 335–36; death of, 327; Great Leap Forward, 295–96, 306–8, 327, 374; imperialism, responding to, 3, 9, 20; Sinification of Marxism by, 235–37

Marsh, Robert, 56
Martov, Julius, 302
Marx and Marxism, 112, 172, 251, 266, 311, 314, 318–19, 369, 375; capitalist restoration theory and, 297–99, 299–304, 305; in Chinese policy formation, 295–97, 373; Harvard school, Marxist critique of, 4; Marxist theory, cadres' deficiencies in, 246, 271, 306–7; Marxist-Leninist dialectics, 304, 309; on revolution as liberation, 233–34; Sinification of, 235–37
May Fourth Movement, 51, 172, 211, 215, 251, 334, 337, 343–44, 351, 354, 372
McCord, Edward, 87
Melby, John, 212
Mencius, 53
Meskill, Johanna, 59, 82
Metzger, Thomas, 239
Middle Yangzi region, 65, 71, 75, 87
military, 16, 19, 53, 59, 74, 77, 94, 157, 163, 175, 179, 194, 195, 197, 203, 205, 240, 247, 248, 264, 265, 305, 372, 373; Chiang Kai-shek, military leadership of, 196; frontier, military presence on, 66, 72, 80, 117; Guomindang military efforts, 209, 213, 249, 377; Japanese militarism, 5, 44, 118, 196, 239, 244; Lhasa, military presence in, 126, 133; Manchu military, 116, 125, 176, 180; militarization of society, 84, 87; military degrees, weight in peripheral zones, 70–71; military elites, 56, 60, 62, 87–88, 92, 96, 118, 242, 338; military self-strengthening, 18, 241; modernization, 125, 137, 173; new associations, military leaders in, 129–30; party-state protection and, 270, 275, 306, 378; provisional military government, 149–51, 161–62; Qing military, 67, 115, 119, 124; regional militarization, 58, 61, 337; Russian military policy toward China, 133–34; Soviet model, Chinese military following, 236; urban reformist elite, military arms of, 147; Yuan Shikai, military leadership of, 132, 145, 148

Ming dynasty, 55, 57, 58, 63, 64, 65, 68, 69, 70, 71, 74, 75, 80, 84, 86, 90, 116
mining, 6, 11, 13, 207
Minlibao (periodical), 121, 130, 131–32, 152, 153, 155, 157, 158, 331
missionaries, 17, 35, 51, 54, 124, 348
Modern China (periodical), 26, 231
Mongols and Mongolia, 111–12, 115–17, 120–22, 173; Inner Mongolia, 123–26, 134–35, 177; Mongol princes, 130–31, 183–84; Mongolian independence, 127, 129; Mongols and Tibetans, negative view of, 128–29; Outer Mongolia, 113, 118, 125, 126, 136; small population of, 132–33
Moore, Barrington, 238, 240, 259, 371
Mubarak, Hosni, 171
Myers, Ramon, 6, 239

Nanjing Decade, 193–94, 195–96, 218
Nathan, Andrew, 350
National Resources Commission (NRC), 203–4, 232
nationalism, 6–7, 18, 113, 118–23, 137, 208, 235, 371–73; anti-Manchu, 121–23, 182–83; five races concept, 129–30, 131–33, 184
Nationalist Party. *See* Guomindang
networks, 16, 58, 73; for anti-traitor work, 270–71; construction of networks, 76–77; elite networks, 52, 65, 73, 80, 81, 88, 96–97, 247; gentry networks, 62, 63, 64, 347; patronage networks, 53, 78, 87, 350; politics of personal networks, 90, 91, 357; rural cadre enmeshment, 246, 284; vertical networks, 77, 83

New Economic Policy (NEP), 303–4, 308, 312
New Left, 27
New Life Movement, 350
North China Herald (periodical), 348

objective factors, 45, 230
opium, 7–8, 18, 19, 59, 93, 207, 216, 263–64, 268
Opium War, 3, 5, 7, 11, 34, 43, 51, 85, 347
Orientalism (Said), 28–29
Ozouf, Mona, 343

Pan Hannian, 236
party-state, 112, 244, 248–49, 251, 269, 275, 282, 329, 358, 379; anthropology of, 246, 283–85; cadres, selfless dedication of, 250; control of society via, 377–78; deconstruction of, 259–62, 276–83; of Eastern Europe, 245, 356–57; opposition to, silencing, 274; secrecy of, 328, 354; in Shaan-Gan-Ning, 270–72. *See also* Chinese Communist Party; Gulin county
patronage, 52, 53, 62, 73, 77–80, 81, 84, 87, 96, 116, 350
peaceful evolution, 317–19
Peck, Graham, 195, 213
Peck, James, 4
Peng Dehuai, 274, 296, 305–6
Peng Shuai, 379
People's Liberation Army, 117, 197, 203, 256, 378
Pepper, Suzanne, 201
Perry, Elizabeth J., 233
Peyrefitte, Alain, 28, 30, 31, 33, 40, 41
Pickowicz, Paul G., 200, 233
Pieke, Frank, 333
pingjia (evaluation), 5, 217
political theater, 358; 1989 protests as political theater, 329–33, 333–38, 355; in Eastern Europe, 356–57; interpreting political theater, 353–55; ritual and theater, 339–44; in twentieth-century China, 347–53
Positions (periodical), 37, 44
post-modern theory: Hevia, applying to Macartney mission, 27–42; in historical scholarship, 25–27, 370; politics and methodology of, 42–45
Price, Donald, 332
Pritchard, Earl, 28, 30, 41, 43
productive forces, theory of, 310–11
public sphere, 43–44, 90–93, 377
Pye, Lucien, 333

Qin dynasty, 113, 117
Qing dynasty, 6, 34, 55–58, 86, 111, 133–35, 346, 357; 1911 Revolution against, 118–23; China's frontiers, 112–15; collapse of, 17, 18, 119, 127, 137; gentry during, 56, 57; guest ritual in, 37–42; New Policy reforms, 89, 91, 119, 125–26, 171, 173–75, 178, 203, 347; postmodern analysis of, 25–45; Qianlong emperor, 25, 28, 31, 34–37, 39–42, 44, 117, 344–45; Qing bureaucracy, 37, 89; railways built under, 93, 119; ritual protocols, 31–32, 33, 37, 39, 40; ROC as successor state of, 112, 118, 136; rule of China proper and frontiers, 115–18, 123–27, 128–33, 133–37; tribute system of, 28–29, 36, 39, 43
Qu Yuan, 354

race, 120, 125, 128, 163; anti-Manchu racism, 121–23, 182–83; five races concept, 129–30, 131–33, 184; ROC, protection of Mongol race in, 127; Tibetans as part of Chinese race, 121
railways, 175, 209, 349, 372, 374; foreign-financed railways, 14, 18, 148, 174, 347; Qing, railways built under, 93, 119; Railway Protection Movement, 181; Russian railways, 12, 124, 134

Rakovsky, Christian G., 303
Rankin, Mary B., 52, 60, 90, 92, 347
rectification movement, 243, 249, 276; Lenin on, 302; rectification campaigns, 198, 199, 234, 248, 260, 285, 374; in SGN Border Region, 273–74; Soviet models for, 236, 237
Red Ruckus, 266, 276–77
reform and opening policy, 184, 327, 374
Reinsch, Paul S., 13
Ren Bishi, 236, 237
Republic of China (ROC), 127, 150, 153, 217, 232–33, 377; defining the Republic of China, 128–33; frontiers included in, 122; as successor state to Qing, 112, 136–37, 174; Sun Yat-sen as president, 26, 118, 129, 145–47, 151–54, 160, 331
Republican era, 51, 52, 82, 94, 127, 135–36, 251, 334, 335, 354, 357
revolution, 3, 122, 261, 270, 306–7; Cultural Revolution, 173, 184, 251, 295–96, 298, 311, 314–15, 327, 330, 352, 372, 374; French Revolution, 68, 175, 182–83, 231, 233, 246, 300, 343; National Revolution, 172, 229, 235, 247; peasant revolution, 251, 259, 261, 369, 371; racial revolution, 123, 130, 176, 182–84; revolution as process, 234–35, 238, 246–50; revolutionary models of the West, 230–31; revolutionary socialism, 299–300; Shaanxi revolutionary movement, 245, 260, 265; sudden revolution, 1911 as, 172–85. *See also* 1911 Revolution; Ten Theses on the Chinese Revolution
Revolutionary Alliance (Tongmenghui), 145, 147, 151, 159, 163; generalissimo, in conflict over, 154–56; *Minbao* as TMH journal, 152–53; provisional government, role in forming, 149–50; Shanghai leaders, 158; Sun Yat-sen, in election of, 162–63

Rhoads, Edward, 176, 178, 180, 184–85
ritual, 26, 122, 341; *Da-Qing tongli* on ritual, 37, 39, 40; guest ritual, 29, 32, 36, 37–42; imperial ritual, 30, 31, 149, 344; kowtow, 28, 40, 41; political ritual, 339–40, 344–47; political theater and, 339–44; Qing ritual protocols, 31–32, 33; state ritual, 33–35, 334, 335, 337–38. *See also* Macartney Mission
Rosemont, Henry, Jr., 338
Rowe, William, 27, 32, 52, 71, 75, 90, 347
Russo-Japanese War, 124, 174

Said, Edward, 28–29, 43
scholar-officials, 53–57, 67, 74
Schoppa, R. Keith, 52, 59–60, 92
Schrecker, John, 6
Schurmann, Franz, 295, 315
Selden, Mark, 233, 261
Selznick, Philip, 244
Service, Jack S., 229
Sha Yuanbing, 82
Shaan-Gan-Ning (SGN) Border Region, 231, 248, 262, 270, 284, 375; anti-traitor work, 249; peasants of the rural party, 245–46; rectification movement in, 273–74. *See also* Gulin county
Sheridan, James, 195
Shigeta Atsushi, 57
silk trade, 9–10, 85, 89
silver, 13, 57, 84, 201, 376
Sino-French War, 118
Sino-Japanese War. *See* War of Resistance
Sino-Russian Treaty, 134
Skinner, G. William, 60, 73
Skocpol, Theda, 238, 240, 261
Snow, Edgar, 5, 232, 315
social mobility, 56, 84, 88, 89
Society for the Progress of Citizens of the Five Races, 130
Solidarity movement, 356, 357

Index 421

Song dynasty, 84, 346, 354; Southern Song era, 58, 74
Song Jiaoren, 152, 155, 159
sovereignty, 15, 17, 19, 29–30, 36, 118, 124, 136, 205, 207, 252, 349, 371
Soviet models, 235–37, 305
Soviet Union, 196, 230, 235–37, 300–306, 317–19, 351, 357; aiding and advising Guomindang, 197, 247; capitalist restoration in, 297–98, 302–3; dissolution of, 111–12, 245, 284, 328–29, 355; textbook on political economy, 296, 307–8, 310–11, 315–18
Spring Dreams of Heaven (film), 202
Stalin and Stalinism, 236, 249, 251, 303–4, 308, 316, 318, 378; on class struggle, 305, 309; Maoist critiques of, 307, 313, 317; Marxist-Leninist theory, commitment to, 297; Stalinist models, 230, 235–37
Staunton, George, 41
steamship navigation, 12, 14, 16, 93
Strand, David, 52, 94, 333, 357
students, 237, 239, 270; in Civil War era, 202, 211; clothing styles, 194; hunger strikes, 329, 331, 335, 337, 354, 358; Japan, Chinese students in, 154, 161, 163, 179, 185; political theater and, 333–36, 342–43, 347; at Tiananmen protests, 329, 331–32
subjective factors, 230, 242
Sun Yat-sen, 6, 51, 194, 203, 205, 350; election of, 160–62; *guofu,* 146–49; inauguration of, 162–64; land to the tiller policy, 212; as president of China, 26, 118, 129, 145–46, 147, 151–54, 160, 331; return to China, 156–59; as a revolutionary, 119, 174, 233
Szymanski, Al, 296

Tahara Tennan, 161
Taiping Rebellion, 19, 58, 60, 64, 75, 77, 84, 177
Taiwan, 85, 113, 193, 217; frontier society of, 59, 64, 66, 82; Guomindang fleeing to, 212; Japan, as ceded to, 119, 124, 136
Tan Renfeng, 153, 160, 162
Tan Yankai, 152
Tang dynasty, 34, 117
Tang Erhe, 160
Tang Hualong, 174, 182–83, 184
Tang Shaoyi, 156
Tao Chengzhang, 183
tariffs, 3, 10, 17, 372
taxes: border regions, lower taxes in, 267–68; grain taxes, rural cadres collecting, 272; lower taxes, revolution promising, 276; progressive taxes of Civil War period, 250; protests to reduce taxes, 346; tax-collection, 17, 56, 58, 90, 213, 264, 266, 267, 271; tax-resistance, 239, 241, 247, 265
tea exports, 8, 9, 66
Ten Theses on the Chinese Revolution, 230–32; CCP, internal complexity of, 244–46; contingency in, 237–38; on Guomindang rule, 232–33; Japanese imperialism and world depression, 238–40; liberation or domination, 233–35; revolution as a process, 246–50; Soviet model, 235–37; state constraints on agents of revolution, 240–42; subjective element, 242–44; teleology of revolution, 251–53
Teng Ssu-yu, 28, 29
Thompson, E. P., 333, 340
Three People's Principles *(Sanmin zhuyi),* 145, 205
Tiananmen Square, 330–33, 333–38, 351, 353–54
Tibet, 120, 125, 129; British involvement in, 124, 126, 133, 136; Chinese administration of, 111, 117, 131–32, 173; Chinese race, as part of, 121; independence efforts, 118, 126–27, 128; revolutionary plans

for, 130; Tibetan Buddhism, 30, 112, 115, 116, 122; Tibetan government in exile, 118, 135
Tilly, Charles, 333
tizhi (fundamental rules), 32, 34, 35, 41
Tocqueville, Alexis de, 185
Tongmenghui (TMH). *See* Revolutionary Alliance
trade, foreign, 8–11, 12, 17, 19, 64, 79, 84–87, 252
translation, 26, 31–32, 32–37, 38
treaty ports, 3, 5, 7, 12–13, 16, 64, 85, 178, 204, 207, 218, 377
tribute system, 29, 33, 36, 38, 39, 40, 42, 43
Trotsky and Trotskyism, 237, 303, 304, 308, 316
truth value, 43, 341, 342, 353
truth-seeking, 26–27, 45, 283, 370;
Turner, Victor, 334, 339–40, 342

unequal treaties, 3, 16–17
Upper Yangzi region, 65
Ustrayalov, Nikolay Vasilyevich, 301

Van de Ven, Hans, 245, 284
Versailles Conference, 136–37, 354
vested-interest groups, 315–16

Wakeman, Frederic, Jr., 11, 33, 58, 111, 218
Wang Jingwei, 152, 154, 348
Wang Ke-wen, 350
Wang Ming, 235–36, 237, 249, 273
Wang Qisheng, 212–13
Wang Shiwei, 249, 273
Wang Youlan, 158–59
Wang Zhongsheng, 349
War of Resistance (1937-1945), 17, 196, 204, 235, 237, 247, 260, 267, 271; army conscription for, 275; CCP strength during, 194, 197, 233, 372–73; Chinese state expansion, 207, 208; Communist activity during war, 195, 376; peasant mobilization and, 244, 261; as reshaping China, 203, 205, 217–18, 347; Sun Yat-Sen as *Guofu* during, 145; unisex fashion, 215
warlords, 3, 71, 87, 92, 172, 248, 265, 343; Japan and, 241; new warlordism, 373; warlord era, 18, 88, 372
Washington, George, 148, 158
Wasserstrom, Jeffrey, 211, 328, 329–33
Watson, Rubie, 75
Weber, Max, 54, 374
Wei Yuan, 117
Westadt, Odd Arne, 196
White, Theodore, 195, 232
Wills, John, 29, 43
women, 164, 176, 213; Guomindang treatment of, 273–74; labor force, entering, 194, 373; wartime mobilization of, 199, 214–15, 268–69, 275; under Xi Jinping regime, 379–80
Woodside, Alexander, 345
workers, 83, 232, 302, 306, 315, 317, 332, 352; cadres, workers as part of, 279, 313–14; crop fields of, 268, 272; Eastern European workers, 308, 318, 357; factory and industrial workers, 5, 201, 209, 212, 215, 373; female workers, 213–15; mobilization of workers, 218, 235, 247
World Trade Organization (WTO), 327
World War I, 14, 113, 137
World War II, 9, 10, 194, 196–97, 199, 203, 373
Wu Tingfang, 150
Wuchang Uprising, 118, 127–28, 146, 149, 153, 182–83, 185, 370; Hubei revolutionaries as precipitating, 154, 174; provincial independence following, 175
Wuerkaixi, 331, 336

Xi Jinping, 27, 205, 260, 296, 370–71, 377–78

Xi'an Incident, 237–39, 243, 370, 372
Xinjiang, 111, 125, 373, 377; as Chinese Turkestan, 115, 116; Han colonization of, 122–23, 127, 133, 135; Ili River area, Russian threat to, 124, 134; Manchu incorporation into China, 115, 173; Muslims of the region, 112, 120
Xu Shaozhen, 158, 163
Xue Fei, 336

Yang Du, 178
Yang Hucheng, 265
Yao Hongye, 354
Yao Wenyuan, 311–12, 327
Yeh Wen-hsin, 205
Yellow Emperor, 31, 119, 123, 182
yellow-sect Buddhism, 126–27
Younghusband expedition, 124
Yuan Keding, 153–54
Yuan Shikai, 6, 18, 145, 156, 164, 183, 350; dismissal of, 180, 181; Mongolia and, 132, 134; presidency of, 131, 151, 153–54, 155, 159, 161; as a reformist, 118, 148, 180, 185
Yugoslavia, 111, 231, 297, 308, 317–18

Zaifeng, 180–82, 184, 185, 370
Zelin, Madeleine, 52, 65, 75
Zeng Guofan, 87
Zhang Binglin, 121–22, 128, 152, 155
Zhang Chunqiao, 327
Zhang Jian, 87, 148, 149, 155–56, 183–84
Zhang Longxi, 26
Zhang Pengyuan, 181
Zhang Xueliang, 239
Zhang Zhidong, 177, 180–81, 185
Zhang Zuolin, 18
Zhao Ziyang, 330–31, 337
Zhongguo (Middle Kingdom), 116–17, 120, 121–22, 128
Zhou Enlai, 330, 334, 353
Zhu Fuhuang, 153–54
Zhu Yong, 28, 33
Zou Rong, 121, 178

About the Author

Joseph W. Esherick received his BA from Harvard in 1964 and his PhD from Berkeley in 1971. His scholarship has focused on China's modern revolutions from the last years of the Qing dynasty to the social and political transformation of the twentieth century. His dissertation and first monograph, *Reform and Revolution in China: the 1911 Revolution in Hunan and Hubei*, explored the social background of China's republican revolution. His book *The Origins of the Boxer Uprising* won the John K. Fairbank Prize of the American Historical Association and the Joseph R. Levenson Prize of the Association for Asian Studies. *Ancestral Leaves* detailed the tumultuous history of nineteenth and twentieth-century China through the lives of successive generations of one family. His most recent monograph, *Accidental Holy Land*, analyzes the origins of the Communist revolution in northwest China. In edited volumes, Esherick has examined Chinese local elites, the transformation of Chinese cities, American policy toward China during World War II, the Cultural Revolution, the transition from empire to nation in comparative perspective, and the year 1943 in China. After forty years of teaching at the University of Oregon and the University of California at San Diego, Esherick retired in 2012 and now lives in Berkeley, California.